Spring and Hibernate

Spring and Hibernate

Santosh Kumar K
Java trainer and independent consultant
Ameerpet, Hyderabad

Tata McGraw-Hill Publishing Company Limited
NEW DELHI

McGraw-Hill Offices
New Delhi New York St Louis San Francisco Auckland Bogotá Caracas
Kuala Lumpur Lisbon London Madrid Mexico City Milan Montreal
San Juan Santiago Singapore Sydney Tokyo Toronto

Tata McGraw-Hill

Published by Tata McGraw-Hill Publishing Company Limited,
7 West Patel Nagar, New Delhi 110 008.

ISBN (13): 978-0-07-068011-1
ISBN (10): 0-07-068011-6

Managing Director: *Ajay Shukla*
Head—Professional and Healthcare: *Roystan La'Porte*
Publishing Manager—Professional: *R Chandra Sekhar*
Junior Sponsoring Editor (Computing): *Ritesh Ranjan*
Asst. Manager—Production: *Sohan Gaur*
Manager—Sales & Marketing: *S Girish*
Product Manager (Science, Technology and Computing): *Rekha Dhyani*
Controller—Production: *Rajender P Ghansela*
Asst. General Manager—Production: *B L Dogra*

Typeset at Script Makers, 19, A1-B, DDA Market, Paschim Vihar, New Delhi 110 063, and printed at Pashupati Printers Pvt. Ltd., 1/429/16, Friends Colony, Shahdara, Delhi 110 095

Cover Printer: SDR Printers

Cover Design: Kapil Gupta

RQZCRRLFRBBRA

The McGraw-Hill Companies

To

my father (Sri Koona Vijay Kumar),
mother (K Narmada)
and all my students

Preface

Since 2001 I have been training students in Java technologies, and certainly was among the pioneers to introduce a full-fledged training on Spring framework at Hyderabad. I realised that professionals, and students keen on upgrading their skill set weren't able to find time from their busy work schedule for a classroom learning on Spring and Hibernate. Most of them were either learning the subject outline or were discontinuing the course due to time constraints. Therefore, I was motivated to write this book.

Spring and Hibernate

Working with J2EE APIs for developing enterprise applications is hard enough even with good tools. J2EE platform supports various infrastructural concerns for implementing enterprise applications but it turns out to be heavyweight, hard to control and inconvenient during the development cycle. Spring provides a lightweight solution for building enterprise applications. It is a multi-tier, open-source lightweight application framework, addressing most infrastructural concerns of enterprise applications. It is mainly a technology dedicated to enabling us to build applications using POJOs (Plain Old Java Objects). Spring supports transparent ways of integrating AOP into our application, the declarative transaction management, remote access to our logic using RMI or web services, infrastructure for mailing and messaging, and high-level abstraction frameworks for persisting the data to database. Spring includes an MVC framework, a well-structured exception hierarchy including automatic mapping from proprietary exception hierarchies. Overall Spring is on one-stop-shop for all the enterprise applications. Figure P1 depicts the multi-tier enterprise application architecture with the most common tier/layers and the technologies used to implement the respective layer or tier.

Hibernate is one of the object/relational mapping (ORM) implementations with high performance and features like dual cache support, object oriented query language (HQL) support for querying objects, transaction support, etc. It helps in quick implementation of a reliable data access layer.

Multi-tier Enterprise Application Architecture

	User Interface (UI) Tier	Presentation Tier	Business Tier	Data Access / Integration Tier
Desktop Application	AWT and Swing API		**Java EE Technologies:** Java Bean, RMI, EJB, and JTA / JTS **Other Frameworks:** Hessian, Burlap and Spring Remoting	**Java EE Technologies:** JDBC, JMS, Java Mail API, & Webservices API **Other Frameworks:** Spring JDBC Framework, Spring JMS Framework, Hibernate, JPA, JDO, ibatis, toplink
Web Application	Web Browser	**Java EE Technologies:** Servlet, JSP, JSF, and JSTL **Other Frameworks:** Struts, WebWorks, Spring Web MVC, Velocity, Tapestry, Tiles, Free Marker, and Portal APIs		

P1: Common tiers/layers of multi-tier enterprise application architecture, and the various technologies (including Java Platform APIs and the frameworks from different vendors) used in implementig the respective tiers/layers

ORGANIZATION OF THE BOOK

Part 1 – Introduction

This part of the book introduces Spring Framework.

Chapter 1 (Introduction to Spring Framework): This chapter explains the general problems in the enterprise application development using J2EE framework. It explains how Spring Framework provides convenience in implementing Java enterprise applications. This chapter includes an overview of Spring Framework and its six modules namely Spring Core Container, Spring AOP, JDBC and DAO, ORM, JEE and Web modules.

Part II – Understanding Spring Framework Core Concepts

This part of the book explains the core concepts of Spring Framework which include IoC and AOP implementations using Spring Framework.

Chapter 2 (Inversion of Control (IoC) and Spring Core Container): This chapter explains the IoC (Inversion of Control) and the need of IoC in the application development. It provides a detailed understanding on how to use Spring core container to implement IoC. Here you will learn how to implement the first application using Spring Framework (its core container). This chapter explains concepts like XML bean configuration for different ways of initializations, injecting values using constructor and setter methods, etc.

Chapter 3 (Understanding Aspect Oriented Programming (AOP)): This chapter dwells on the problems with OOP and how AOP addresses the problems. It even explains how to use Spring AOP low-level API for implementing AOP in our system.

Chapter 4 (Working with Spring Pointcut and Advisors): This chapter explains how to use Spring low-level pointcut and Advisor API for implementing custom pointcuts.

Chapter 5 (Understanding Spring 2.0 AOP Support): This chapter provides the details on new support included for AOP in Spring 2.0, that is, the XML-Schema based approach and @AspectJ based approach of implementing AOP.

Part III – Implementing Data Access Layer

This part of the book explains all the concepts of Spring Framework that are essential for implementing data access layer of an enterprise application (Fig. P1), such as JDBC Abstraction Framework, Hibernate and transactions.

Chapter 6 (JDBC and DAO Module): This chapter covers the DAO design pattern, its short comings, and how these short comings are handled using Spring DAO service. It also explains the Spring JDBC abstraction framework, how to use the JdbcTemplate to perform the database read and update operations with SQL statements, calling stored procedures, using batch updates, etc. This chapter even explains the Spring JDBC frameworks RDBMS operational classes, which provide a more high-level OO approach to access and update the database.

Chapter 7 (Understanding Hibernate): This chapter discusses the ORM and its need. It explains the basics of Hibernate, which is one of the ORM implementations, and discusses the important elements of Hibernate architecture.

Chapter 8 (Understanding Persistent Classes Mapping): This chapter covers the Hibernate mapping configurations to map persistent classes solving the mismatch problems such as granularity, subtypes, and relationships.

Chapter 9 (Understanding Hibernate Query Language (HQL) and Criterion API): This chapter explains the Object Oriented Query Language supported by Hibernate, that is, HQL. It also explains the Criterion API, the new approach for querying the objects from the database using Hibernate.

Chapter 10 (Implementing Hibernate with Spring): This chapter explains how to use Hibernate with Spring Framework. It also covers the platform independent transaction management support provided by Spring Framework, which includes Spring programmatic and declarative transaction management support.

PART IV – IMPLEMENTING WEB TIER

This part of the book explains the concepts of Spring Web MVC Framework used for implementing the Web tier of the enterprise applications.

Chapter 11 (Getting Started with Spring Web MVC Framework): This chapter explains the prerequisites for understanding Spring Web MVC framework including MVC architecture, Model-1 and 2 architectures, front controller design pattern. It also covers the Spring Web MVC framework.

Chapter 12 (Understanding DispatcherServlet and Request Processing Workflow): This chapter covers the initialization and the request processing workflow of Spring Web MVC application in detail. This chapter is the most important for the developers involved in Web tier development using Spring Framework.

Chapter 13 (Describing Controllers and Validations): This chapter explains the Spring Web MVC framework's built-in utility controllers that provide convenience in implementing the controllers for various requirements. The most commonly used controllers under the Spring Web MVC framework:

- **AbstractCommandController** – provides infrastructure to implement controllers that implement form submission request.
- **SimpleFormController** – a subtype of AbstractCommandController that includes additional infrastructures for processing form submissions as identifying request for new form to present a new form, and identifying the form submission request to process the form request data.
- **AbstractWizardFormController** – provides infrastructure to handle multi-wizards request processing.
- **MultiActionController** – provides infrastructure to implement multiple actions into a single controller class.

All these controllers are explained in detail with simple independent examples to help you understand how to use the spring provided infrastructures to implement your requirements.

Chapter 14 (Describing ViewResolver and View): This chapter explains the ViewResolver and View infrastructural elements of Spring Web MVC Framework. It discusses how to use the view technologies like JSTL and velocity to generate tag-based (html-based) response. It also discusses how to render document based views like Excel spreadsheet and PDF using the Jakarta POI and iText API's, respectively.

Chapter 15 (Integrating Spring with Other Web Frameworks): This chapter covers how to integrate Spring with other Web Frameworks like Struts. It explains why Spring needs to integrate with other frameworks when we have an ideal option for implementing Web MVC applications using Spring Web MVC Framework, identifying that Struts application wants to integrate with Spring for its enterprise level declarative services like IoC, AOP, transaction etc. This discussion is followed through understanding the various approaches to integrate Spring with Struts framework.

PART V – UNDERSTANDING REMOTING WITH SPRING

This part of the book explains the various concepts of Spring Framework that are useful for implementing remoting.

Chapter 16 (Implementing Remoting with Spring): This chapter covers the Spring Framework's support for implementing distributed systems in Java using the existing Remoting technologies like RMI, Hessian and Burlap. It also explains Spring HTTP invoker service that is Spring's own Remoting solution.

Chapter 17 (Working with EJBs using Spring): This chapter explains how to use Spring support for accessing and implementing EJBs.

Chapter 18 (Implementing JMS using Spring): This chapter discusses how to use Spring JMS integration Framework that simplifies the use of JMS API for communicating with asynchronous messaging systems to send/receive asynchronous messages.

This book will help in self-learning and being adept in Spring Framework for developing Java enterprise applications. It is useful not only for the readers interested in self-updating but also for those who are familiar with the concepts and want in-depth knowledge.

Santosh Kumar K

Acknowledgements

I'd like to thank everyone at McGraw-Hill Education (India). In particular, I want to thank Ritesh Ranjan (Junior Sponsoring Editor: Computing) for giving me the opportunity to write this book.

I thank my brother (Sai Kumar), sister (Phani Sree) and my friend (Subash Chandra) for encouraging to take up this project.

I am thankful to my parents and friends for their understanding and support during the course of developing this book, especially to my sister, her husband and their daughter (Bhavika).

Some errors may have accidentally crept in this book despite my best efforts. Readers are therefore encouraged to point out the errors so that they are rectified in the next edition. Your valuable suggestions to improve the book are welcome at tosantoshk@gmail.com or santosh@santosh technologies.com.

Santosh Kumar K

Contents

Introduction to Spring Framework

1 CHAPTER

1.1 INTRODUCTION

This book explains various utilities provided by Spring Framework. Spring Framework is a lightweight open-source application framework that simplifies the enterprise application development in Java. As we are aware that the Java 2 Platform Enterprise Edition (J2EE), which incorporates the various component and service APIs, from its release has become a good choice for implementing enterprise-level business applications in Java. However, the use of J2EE standards for implementing enterprise applications still present challenges related to application testing because finding the root cause of the problem in a multi-tiered or clustered J2EE application is complex, time consuming, and more challenging. J2EE applications are even hard to unit test. In addition to the application testing J2EE applications are identified with few other problems. They are:

- Configuration of J2EE applications and application servers is a complicated and error-prone process that involves various members from development, infrastructure, and support teams.
- Getting to the root cause of performance problems in J2EE applications is a difficult process.
- Using most of the J2EE APIs in an enterprise application results in the inclusion of a boilerplate code such as JNDI lookup code, opening and closing JDBC connections and JDBC, naming exception handling, etc. This increases the development time and makes it difficult to debug and maintain the application.

To solve these problems in using the traditional approach of J2EE for implementing enterprise applications, and to simplify the development process many developers and companies including non-commercial organizations have started implementing frameworks, since the experience of the experts states that using frameworks for reducing the application complexity avoiding boilerplate codes is far better than using tools (Integrated Development Environments—IDEs) for code generation. However, most of the successful frameworks including Struts are designed to address infrastructural concerns of a single tier such as web presentation tier. Using multiple frameworks independently with different configuration documents in an enterprise application results in an increase in the complexity of the system and makes it difficult to implement, test, and maintain. In order to handle these situations Spring Framework aiming to reduce the complexity in implementing the enterprise application and offering to take all the benefits of J2EE is introduced.

This chapter provides an introduction of Spring Framework, its benefits and a brief discussion on the various modules that Spring Frameworks is divided into such as Aspect Oriented Programming (AOP) Module, Web Module, etc.

1.2 INTRODUCING SPRING FRAMEWORK

Spring is a multi-tier open-source lightweight application framework, addressing most infrastructure concerns of enterprise applications. It is mainly a technology dedicated to enable us to build applications using POJOs (Plain Old Java Objects).

That means Spring framework provides support in simplifying the development of every single tier in an enterprise application. For instance, starting from the presentation to the integration tier (or sometimes data access layer) implementation it has its role in simplifying our job. Even though spring framework includes support for all the tiers in enterprise application it is never forced to use Spring framework to develop the entire application. Spring Framework provides various existing frameworks to integrate with it or work with, that is, if we are interested in using the basic technologies or any existing frameworks for implementing any of the tiers along with using Spring framework for implementing other tiers then Spring framework has a support.

The other interesting part of Spring framework is that it is complete and is modular which allows us to incrementally adopt the framework into our project. Spring framework implements the IoC (Inversion of Control) principal which makes the dependency injection easy and flexible. The various modules of Spring Framework are designed following AOP (Aspect Oriented Programming) style programming to make the framework services easily applicable for application-specific services. Now, as we have got the general idea of Spring Framework and its importance let us discuss the important benefits of using Spring framework for developing enterprise applications.

1.3 BENEFITS OF SPRING FRAMEWORK

Described above is that Spring Framework addresses most of the infrastructure functionalities of the enterprise applications. This comes with a number of benefits such as

- Spring Framework addresses important areas that many other frameworks do not like. It includes support for managing business objects and exposing their services to the presentation tier components so that the web and desktop applications can access the same business objects.
- Spring is both complete and modular**.** This is because Spring Framework has a layered architecture, meaning that you can choose to use just about any part of it in isolation, yet its architecture is internally consistent. So you get maximum value from your learning curve. And this makes it easy to introduce Spring incrementally into existing projects. For example, you might choose to use Spring only to simplify the use of JDBC to access the data from a data store, or you might choose to use Spring only to manage all your business objects.
- Spring Framework provides perfect support for write code that is easy to test. Meaning, Spring Framework is the best framework for test-driven projects.
- Spring is an increasingly important integration technology; its role is recognized by several large vendors.
- Spring can eliminate the creation of singletons and factory classes seen on many projects.
- Spring can eliminate the need to use a variety of custom properties file formats, by handling configurations in a consistent way throughout the application.
- Spring can facilitate good programming practice by reducing the cost of programming to interfaces, rather than classes, almost to zero.

- The Spring Framework has taken the best practices that have been proven over the years in several applications and formalized as design patterns, and coded these patterns as first class objects that we as an architect and developer can take away and integrate into our applications.

Now, as we have discussed the benefits of Spring framework it is time to learn about the Spring framework architecture and its elements in detail so that we can use it for developing our projects and get the preceding discussed one or more benefits for our projects. Let us start with the Spring framework overview and then a short description on it explaining each of its elements briefly, followed by the various Spring framework services in detail with relevant examples in subsequent chapters.

1.4 SPRING FRAMEWORK OVERVIEW

As we have discussed in the preceding section Spring framework provides a number of services, it implements several commonly used best practices and makes these objects available to integrate with our project instead of coding these patterns every time (or as a part of our project). The various services provided by the Spring framework are well organized into seven modules as per Spring 1.x but in Spring 2.0 these are redefined to form six modules. Here we will refer to Spring 2.x modules. The Spring framework modules overview picture given by the Spring framework community is shown in Fig. 1.1.

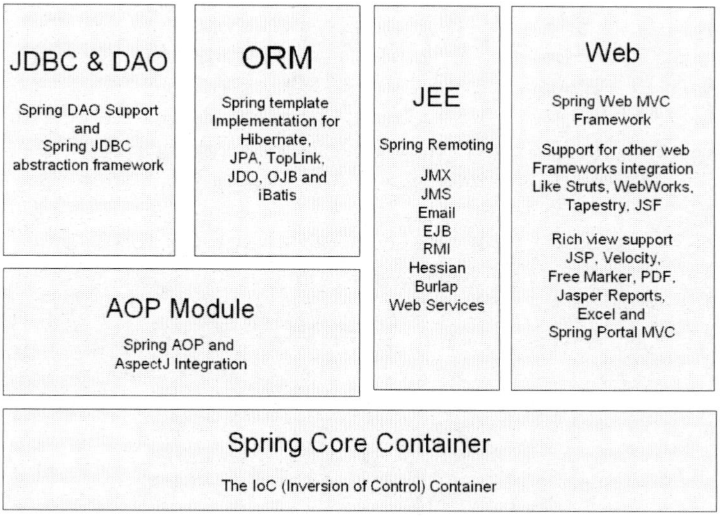

FIGURE 1.1 Spring framework overview

Figure 1.1 shows the big pitcher of Spring framework showing the proper arrangement of the various modules and their services in a single diagram. Now we will have a brief discussion on these six modules.

1.4.1 Spring Core Container

As shown in the overview diagram Spring Core Container is the basis for the complete Spring framework. The Spring core container provides an implementation for IoC supporting dependency injection. This provides a convenient environment to program the basic to enterprise applications avoiding the need of writing the factory classes and methods in most of the situations. This even avoids the need of programming the singletons.

1.4.2 AOP Module

Spring AOP Module provides an implementation of AOP (Aspect Oriented Programming). Spring AOP is a proxy-based framework implemented in java. Spring AOP is developed based on AOP Alliance API, which enables us to use the advices developed under Spring AOP to be used with other AOP implementations, meaning it allows us to migrate the components implemented using Spring AOP to some other AOP implementation or to integrate any existing AOP alliance complaint component to work with Spring AOP. Spring framework uses AOP for providing most of the infrastructure logic in Spring framework.

1.4.3 JDBC and DAO Module

The Spring framework support for DAO includes a consistent exception hierarchy and a convenient translation from data access API-specific exceptions to the Spring DAO exception hierarchy packaged into the org.springframework.dao package with DataAccessException as the base exception. Moreover, to perform this translation transparently, Spring framework includes templates for most of the generally used data access APIs like JDBC, Hibernate, JDO, JPA (Java Persistence API), iBatis, and Oracle Toplink. Spring framework also includes a set of abstract DAO classes that can be extended by our DAO implementations to simplify the DAO implementation in using the low-level data access APIs.

The Spring framework provides a solution for the various problems identified by using JDBC as low-level data access API for implementing DAO, by giving a thin, robust, and highly extensible JDBC abstraction framework. The JDBC abstraction framework provided under Spring framework as a value-added service takes care of all the low-level details like retrieving connection, preparing the statement object, executing the query, and releasing the database resources. While using the JDBC abstraction framework of Spring framework for data access the application developer needs to specify the SQL statement to execute and read the results. Since all the low-level logic have been written once and correctly into the abstraction layer provided by Spring JDBC framework this helps to eliminate the shortcomings found in using JDBC API to implement DAOs.

1.4.4 ORM Module

The Object/Relation Mapping (ORM) module of Spring Framework provides a high level abstraction for well-accepted object-relational mapping APIs such as Hibernate, JPA, JDO, OJB, and iBatis. The Spring ORM module is not replacing or a competitive for any of the existing ORMs, instead it is designed to reduce the complexity by avoiding the boilerplate code from the application in using the ORMs. For example, if we want to Hibernate we need to manage a single SessionFactory instance for the entire application, need to open a session for performing persistence operations and thereafter close the Hibernate Session properly to make sure that the resources are utilized by the application properly. While using Hibernate integrated with Spring as an application provider we never require to concentrate on these type of issues. In addition, it provides the exception translators that can convert the ORM-based exception to the Spring DAO exception hierarchy, which are unchecked exceptions and convenient to throw to the business process components. That means that the Spring ORM module allows us to use the existing proven ORMs in combination with all the other features such as simple declarative transaction management that the Spring Framework provides.

1.4.5 JEE (Java Enterprise Edition)

The JEE module of Spring Framework is build on the solid base provided by the core package. This provides a support for using the remoting services in a simplified manner. This supports to build POJOs and expose them as remote objects without worrying about the specific remoting technology given rules. Similarly, this simplifies the other Java enterprise edition services by allowing the services to dynamically combine with the business objects in AOP style.

1.4.6 Web Module

This module of Spring Framework includes all the support for developing robust and maintainable web application in a simplified approach. It even includes support for MVC-based web application development. This part of the support from Spring is titled as Spring Web MVC framework. The Spring Web MVC Framework is an open-source web application framework, which is a part of Spring Framework licensed under the terms of the Apache License, Version 2.0. Spring Web MVC is one of the efficient and high performance open source implementation of Model 2 based Model-View-Controller (MVC). Spring Web MVC framework provides utility classes to handle many of the most common tasks in Web application development.

Summary

In this chapter we have discussed what the general problems in the enterprise application development are and then discussed how Spring framework is beneficial in developing enterprise applications. Then we have studied the Spring framework overview and a brief description of the six modules that the Spring framework services are divided into—Spring Core Container, Spring AOP, JDBC and DAO, ORM, JEE, and Web. In the next chapter you will learn IoC, dependency injection, and Spring Core Container services.

Inversion of Control (IoC) and Spring Core Container

2

CHAPTER

Objectives

In this chapter we will cover:

- Inversion of control (IoC), its need and importance in application development
- Spring core container
- How to write a basic spring application
- Dependency injections and their configuration tags in the spring XML configuration file
- Bean configurations, ways of instantiating beans, the scopes of beans, and lifecycle callbacks

2.1 INVERSION OF CONTROL (IoC)

Inversion of Control is an architectural pattern describing an external entity (that is container) used to wire objects at creation time by injecting there dependencies, that is, connecting the objects so that they can work together in a system. In other words the IoC describes that a dependency injection needs to be done by an external entity instead of creating the dependencies by the component itself. Dependency Injection is a process of injecting (pushing) the dependencies into an object.

2.1.1 Why Dependency Injection (DI)?

In developing huge systems using the object oriented programming methodology, we generally divide the system into objects where each of the objects represents some functionality. In this case, the objects in the system use some other objects to complete the given request. The objects with which our object collaborates to provide the services are known as its dependencies. The traditional ways of obtaining the dependencies are by creating the dependencies or by pulling the dependencies using some factory classes and methods or from the naming registry. But these approaches result in some problems which are described below:

- The complexity of the application increases
- The development time-dependency increases
- The difficulty for unit testing increases

To solve the above stated problems we have to use a push model, that is, inject the dependent objects into our object instead of creating or pulling the dependent objects. The process of injecting (pushing) the dependencies into an object is known as dependency injection (DI). This gives some benefits as described below:

- The application development will become faster
- Dependency will be reduced
- DI provides a proper test environment for the application as it is much easier to isolate the code under test if we need not worry about the code necessary for instantiating and initializing lot of dependencies. Moreover, if we want to use test-model objects to validate whether our class is interacting correctly with its dependencies, we can inject the test-model objects into the class under test. If the class under test is creating or locating its own collaborators, it is hard to convince it to use test-model objects.

In this section we have discussed the importance of dependency injection and its benefits. We will discuss different types of dependency injections, how to use them, and the appropriate situations in which to use them in the next sections of this chapter. Before discussing this in detail we will discuss spring container and its configurations basics. The following sections explain the basics of spring container and its configurations.

2.2 SPRING CORE CONTAINER

Spring core container is the basis for the complete spring framework. It provides an implementation for IoC supporting dependency injection. This provides a convenient environment to program the basic to enterprise applications avoiding the need of writing the factory classes and methods in most of the situations. This even helps one to avoid the need of programming the singletons. The spring core container takes the configurations to understand the bean objects that it has to instantiate and manage the lifecycle. The one important feature of the spring core container is that it does not force the user to have any one format of configurations, as most of the frameworks which are designed to have XML–based or property file based configurations. Spring at present allows us to supply the configurations either as an XML format, properties file format, or programmatically using the spring beans API. But in most of the cases we use XML-based configurations since they are simple and easy to modify. The org.springframework.beans.factory. BeanFactory interface provides the basic end point for the spring core container towards the applications to access the core container services. The org.springframework.context. ApplicationContext interface is the subtype of BeanFactory that provides some added functionalities like message resource handling, event propagation, and application layer specific context. It provides support for infrastructure to enable enterprise-specific features like transactions, which we will discuss in the next chapters as we continue the discussion on enterprise services.

2.3 INITIALIZING SPRING CORE CONTAINER AND ACCESSING SPRING BEANS

The spring core container can be instantiated by creating an object of any one of the BeanFactory or ApplicationContext implementation classes supplying the spring beans configurations. The various implementations of BeanFactory are mainly differentiated based on the spring beans configuration format they understand and the way they locate the configurations. The following code snippet shows the sample code that instantiates the spring container using the Spring Beans XML configuration file as a configuration metadata.

Code Snippet

```
//Using BeanFactory to instantiate spring core container
BeanFactory beans = new XmlBeanFactory(
                        new FileSystemResources("mybeans.xml"));
```

In the preceding code snippet we are using XmlBeanFactory implementation for instantiating the spring container with 'mybeans.xml' file as a configuration file. We can even use ApplicationContext to instantiate the container; the following code snippet shows the sample code to instantiate spring

Code Snippet

```
//Using ApplicationContext to instantiate spring core container
ApplicationContext context=
  new ClassPathXmlApplicationContext("mybeans.xml");
```

In code snippet we are using ClassPathXmlApplicationContext implementation to instantiate the spring container with 'mybeans.xml' file as a configuration file, as the name describes the ClassPathXmlApplicationContext locates the XML configuration file in the classpath. Once after initializing the container we can use BeanFactory object methods to access the spring beans. The following table shows the most commonly used methods of BeanFactory and their descriptions.

TABLE 2.1 Methods of BeanFactory

Method	*Description*
boolean containsBean(String name)	Returns Boolean value describing whether this bean factory contains a bean definition with the given name. If available this returns 'true' otherwise it returns 'false'.
Object getBean(String name)	Returns an instance that is instantiated using the dean definition identified by the given name in this bean factory.
Object getBean(String name, Class requiredType)	This is the same as in the getBean(String) method but this method takes the expected type of the bean object. If the bean instance is not of the expected type then this method throws BeanNotOfRequiredTypeException.
Class getType(String name)	Returns the Class object representing the type of bean identified by the given name.
boolean isPrototype(String name)	Returns a Boolean value describing whether the bean with the given name in this bean factory is defined as prototype. If it is prototype (non-singleton) this returns 'true' otherwise it returns 'false'. How a bean is defined as prototype will be discussed in the next section under 'Bean Scopes'.
boolean isSingleton(String name)	Returns a Boolean value describing whether the bean with the given name in this bean factory is defined as singleton. If it is singleton it returns 'true' otherwise it returns 'false'.

We have learnt what a spring core container is and how it is instantiated. Now let us write an example to demonstrate the basic XML configuration and instantiate the spring core container. This is the very first example we are looking at in designing a simple bean class with getMessage() method that returns a 'hello' greeting to the application. The following listing shows the simple bean class that will be configured to be managed by the spring core container.

List 2.1: HelloService.java

```
package com.santosh.spring;

public class HelloService {

  String message;

  public HelloService() {
        message="Hello to Spring Framework (Default Message)";
  }

  public HelloService(String arg) {
        message=arg;
  }

  public String getMessage(){
         return message;
  }
}
```

As shown in List 2.1 the HelloService class is a simple plain java class with no spring API which makes the class to use out-of-the-box environment without any modifications. One of the most important features of the spring framework is that it does not force us to define the bean classes into a sub type of any spring class or interface. Now let us look at a simple XML configuration file to define this bean. List 2.2 shows the spring beans XML configuration file.

List 2.2: mybeans.xml

```
<beans xmlns="http://www.springframework.org/schema/beans"
xmlns:xsi="http://www.w3.org/2001/XMLSchema-instance"
xsi:schemaLocation="http://www.springframework.org/schema/beans
http://www.springframework.org/schema/beans/spring-beans-2.0.xsd">

  <bean id="helloService1" class="com.santosh.spring.HelloService"/>

  <bean id="helloService2" class="com.santosh.spring.HelloService">
        <constructor-arg>
              <value>
                Hello to Spring Framework from XML configuration file
              </value>
        </constructor-arg>
  </bean>
</beans>
```

As shown in List 2.2 the XML configuration file for this example. The <beans> tag is the root element of the Spring Beans XML configuration document. This encloses all the Spring Bean definitions. It supports some attributes to configure defaults (such as default-in it-method and default-destroy method) for the bean definition in this document. The <bean> tag defines a spring bean i.e. a POJO (Plain Old Java Object) to be initialized and managed by spring core container. The XML document of this example includes two bean definitions out of which one initializes the HelloService class using a no-argument constructor which is referred to with the name 'helloService1'. The other initializes the HelloService class using a one-argument constructor passing 'Hello to Spring Framework from XML configuration file' as a value where this definition is referred to with the name 'helloService2'. It is now time to test this configuration by instantiating the container and accessing the beans defined in the configurations. List 2.3 shows a test case.

List 2.3: HelloServiceTestCase.java

```
import org.springframework.beans.factory.*;
import org.springframework.beans.factory.xml.*;
import org.springframework.core.io.*;

import com.santosh.spring.HelloService;

public class HelloServiceTestCase {

  public static void main(String s[]) throws Exception {

        //Instantiate the Spring Core Container
        BeanFactory beans=new XmlBeanFactory(
                          new FileSystemResource("mybeans.xml"));

        //Get the HelloService object from the container
        //as per helloService1 bean definition
        HelloService helloService1=(HelloService)beans.getBean("helloService1");

        System.out.println("\n");
        System.out.println("Message from the helloService1 defined bean:");
        System.out.println("\t"+helloService1.getMessage());

        //Now, test logic to obtain the helloService2 definition
        HelloService helloService2=(HelloService) beans.getBean("helloService2");
        System.out.println("\n");
        System.out.println("Message from the helloService2 defined bean:");
        System.out.println("\t"+helloService2.getMessage());
  }//main
}//class
```

List 2.3 shows the class with a main method that instantiates the spring core container and accesses the bean defined in the spring beans XML configuration file shown in List 2.2. Now set the classpath, compile, and execute the application as shown in Fig. 2.1 in order to describe the example.

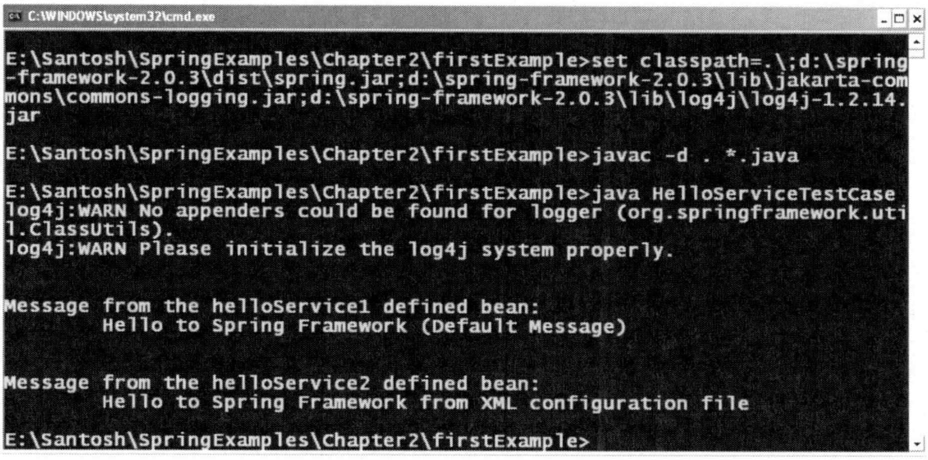

FIGURE 2.1 Output of HelloServiceTestCase

Figure 2.1 shows the output of the HelloServiceTestCase. When you execute the test case you will find some log4j warnings. We can either ignore or configure the log4j properties accordingly to avoid the warning messages. As we have completed with the basic example, now it is time to discuss the different types of injection processes and the other spring beans XML configurations in detail. We will begin by discussing the different types of injections and their configurations.

2.4 TYPES OF DEPENDENCY INJECTION

From the discussion in the preceding section, we have understood that the object requires some dependencies to complete the request process and the importance of injecting these dependencies into an object for various benefits. Now we will learn different types of dependency injection processes and their importance. We have two types of dependency injection options.

1. Constructor Injection.
2. Setter Method Injection.

These are explained in the next subsection.

2.4.1 Constructor Injection

The Constructor Injection method of dependency injection is the method of injecting the dependencies of an object through its constructor arguments. In this mechanism the dependencies are pushed into the object through the constructor arguments at the time of instantiating it. In the case when the object is instantiated by using some factory method then passing the dependencies as arguments to the factory method is also considered as constructor injection since the dependencies are injected at the time of constructing the object. The following code snippet shows the sample class that allows the injection of its dependencies as constructor arguments.

Code Snippet

```
package com.santosh.spring.dao;
import java.sql.*;
import javax.sql.*;

public class EmployeeDAODBImpl implements EmployeeDAO {

       private DataSource dataSource;
       public EmployeeDAODBImpl( DataSource ds) {
       dataSource=ds;
       }//cons

       public double getSal(int eno) {
       //use the dataSource to handle the request (i.e. set the salary into data base)
       }
       //rest of the code goes here
}
```

As shown in the preceding code snippet the EmployeeDAODBImpl is dependent on DataSource to complete its request which means that, to locate and connect to the database it has to represent it requires a javax.sql.DataSource object which is injected as a constructor argument. We want to learn how to configure the bean definition describing the usage of a constructor with arguments. The next section explains the spring beans XML configuration tags used to configure constructor arguments.

The <constructor-arg> element

The bean definition can describe to use a constructor with zero or more arguments to instantiate the bean. The <constructor-arg> element describes one argument of the constructor, which means that to specify a constructor with multiple arguments we need to use the <constructor-arg> element multiple times. The zero <constructor-arg> tags in bean definition describe the use of the no-argument constructor. The arguments specified in the bean definition correspond to either a specific index of the constructor argument list or are supposed to be matched generically by type. The <constructor-arg> element supports four attributes. Table 2.2 shows the attributes that the <constructor-arg> can have.

TABLE 2.2 Attributes of <constructor-arg> tag

Attribute	*Description*	*Occurrence*
index	This attribute takes the exact index in the constructor argument list. This is used to avoid ambiguities like in case of two arguments being of the same type.	optional
type	This attribute takes the type of this constructor argument. This is used to avoid ambiguities like in case of two single argument constructors that can both be converted from a String, for example, one 'int' and other 'double' types.	optional
value	A short-cut alternative to a child element 'value'. The child element <value> is explained in Table 2.3.	optional
ref	A short-cut alternative to a child element "ref bean=".	optional

The <constructor-arg> element supports to describe variety of types as argument, instead of only the direct basic values, The <constructor-arg> element supports various child elements each of which allows us to describe different types of values. The child elements of <constructor-arg> are described in Table 2.3.

TABLE 2.3 Child elements of <constructor-arg> tag

Element	*Description*
<value>*content*</value>	The <value> element describes the *content* in simple string representation which is converted into the argument type using the java beans PropertyEditors. Example: 1. *<constructor-arg type="int">* <value>10</value> *</constructor-arg>* The '10' content described by the <value> element is converted into 'int' type 2. *<constructor-arg type="java.util.Properties">* <value> name=abc password=xyz </value> </constructor-arg>

(Contd.)

	The content described by the <value> element in this case is converted into java.util.Properties type. Instead of the <value> child element we can use the 'value' attribute in <constructor-arg> or <property> elements. Using 'value' attribute is more recommended over the <value> child element.
<null>	The <null> element describes a Java null value. This is required because an empty <value> element will resolve to an empty String (that is, ""), which will not be resolved to a null value unless a special PropertyEditor is defined. This is an empty element, that is, it does not allow any content in its body part.
<ref>	The <ref> element describes a reference to another bean in this factory or an external factory, that is, the parent or included factory. This is an empty element and does not allow any content in its body part. But this element supports three attributes—*local, parent,* and *bean*. This element accepts any one of these three attributes. **The attribute *local*** is used to refer to another bean with its *id* in the same XML configuration file. These are checked by the DTD and are thus preferred for referring to beans within the same XML configuration file. **The attribute *parent*** is used to refer to another bean with its *id* in the parent or included XML configuration file. **The attribute *bean*** is used to refer to another bean with its name in the same XML configuration file.
<list>	The <list> element describes a java.util.List type. A list can contain multiple inner bean, ref, idref, value, null, another list, set, map, or props elements. The <list> can also map to an array type. The necessary conversion is automatically performed by the BeanFactory.
<set>	The <set> element describes a java.util.Set type. A set can contain multiple inner bean, ref, idref, value, null, another list, set, map, or props elements.
<map>	The <map> element describes a java.util.Map type. A map can contain zero or more <entry> elements, each of which describes one map entry. The map entry describes one key and value. The <entry> element takes one <key> element and either of inner bean, ref, idref, value, null, another list, set, map, or props elements. Example: <constructor-arg type="java.util.Map"> <map> <entry> <key><value>name</value></key> <value>Santosh</value> </entry> <entry> <key><value>address</value></key> <ref local="address"/> </entry> </map> </constructor-arg>
<props>	The <props> element describes a java.util.Properties type. A map can contain zero or more <prop> elements where each <prop> element describes one entry. The property entry describes one key and value. The <prop> element takes one key attribute and accepts text body content describing the value of the property entry.

(*Contd.*)

	Example: <constructor-arg type="java.util.Properties"> <props> <prop key="name"> Santosh</prop> <prop key="address">Hyderabad</prop> </props> </constructor-arg>
<bean>	The <bean> element describes a bean

Now that we have learnt about the <constructor-arg> element and its child elements it is time to look at some sample configurations to put more light on the preceding discussion. The following code snippet shows the bean definition for the EmployeeDAODBImpl class in the spring beans XML configuration file, which instructs the spring IoC core container to inject the DataSource object into EmployeeDAODBImpl while creating an object. You will learn more about this configuration and other elements in detail in some of the next sections of this chapter. The following code snippet is about partial bean definitions.

Code Snippet

```
<beans>
  <bean  id="empdao"  class="com.santosh.spring.dao.EmployeeDAODBImpl">
    <constructor-arg>
      <ref local="ds"/>
    </constructor-arg>
    </bean>
    <!–the other bean definitions goes here-->
</beans>
```

The configuration tags describe the spring container to inject the bean with an id 'ds' into the EmployeeDAODBImpl object as a constructor argument. The preceding code is describing a single argument constructor but we can even configure a bean definition to use multiple arguments the following code snippet shows a class with multiple construct arguments.

Code Snippet

```
public class MyClass {
  public MyClass(int id, String name){...}
  ...
}
```

To configure the bean definition for the bean class described in code snippet we use the constructor-arg for the element as shown.

Code Snippet

```
<bean id="myClass" class="com.santosh.spring.MyClass">
  <constructor-arg>
        <value>10</value>
  </constructor-arg>
```

(Contd.)

```
   <constructor-arg>
          <value>abc</value>
   </constructor-arg>
</bean>
```

In the scenario described just now we do not have any conflict. A bean is thus defined with two <constructor-arg> elements each describing one argument of the constructor. But when we have constructor overloading and conflict with their types we want to use index or/and type attributes of <constructor-arg> element as shown in the following code snippet.

Code Snippet

```
//Java Class
public class MyClass {
   public MyClass(int id, String name){...}
   public MyClass(String name, int id){...}
   ...
}

<!–bean definitions in xml configuration file -->
<!–this bean definition uses a constructor with int, String arguments -->
<bean id="myClass" class="com.santosh.spring.MyClass">
   <constructor-arg>
          <value>10</value>
   </constructor-arg>
   <constructor-arg>
          <value>abc</value>
   </constructor-arg>
</bean>

<!–this bean definition also uses a constructor with int, String arguments
'id' as 10, that is, first argument and 'name' as 100
-->
<bean id="myClass" class="com.santosh.spring.MyClass">
   <constructor-arg>
          <value>10</value>
   </constructor-arg>
   <constructor-arg>
          <value>100</value>
   </constructor-arg>
</bean>

<!–this bean definition uses a constructor with String, int arguments
'id' as 100 and 'name' as 10
-->
<bean id="myClass" class="com.santosh.spring.MyClass">
   <constructor-arg type="java.lang.String">
          <value>10</value>
```

(Contd.)

```
    </constructor-arg>
    <constructor-arg>
        <value>100</value>
    </constructor-arg>
</bean>

<!–this bean definition uses a constructor with int, String arguments
'id' as 100, that is first argument and 'name' as 10
-->
<bean id="myClass" class="com.santosh.spring.MyClass">
    <constructor-arg index="1" type="java.lang.String">
        <value>10</value>
    </constructor-arg>
    <constructor-arg index="0">
        <value>100</value>
    </constructor-arg>
</bean>
```

The preceding code snippet shows you the various configurations with <constructor-arg> element to describe our required constructor without ambiguity. Note that the constructor index starts from '0' and it is recommended to use index when describing multiple constructor arguments. Using this approach to inject many dependencies is not recommended. The constructor injection is generally used for injecting the dependencies that are minimum mandatory for the object to exist. We want that the object is not instantiated without confirming the dependencies.

2.4.2 Setter Method Injection

The Setter method Injection approach of dependency injection is the method of injecting the dependencies of an object by using the setter method. The setter method is more convenient to inject more number of dependencies since the large number of constructor arguments makes it awkward. In this case we require exposing our properties to the clients that make objects open to re-inject the dependencies at a later time in its life. The following code snippet shows the sample class that allows injecting its dependencies using the setter method of injection.

Code Snippet

```
package com.santosh.spring;

import com.santosh.spring.dao.EmployeeDAO;

public class EmployeeServicesImpl implements EmployeeServices {

    private EmployeeDAO employeeDAO;

    public void setEmployeeDAO(EmployeeDAO ed){
        employeeDAO=ed;
    }

    //rest of the code goes here

}//class
```

As shown in the above code snippet the EmployeeServicesImpl is dependent on EmployeeDAO. The EmployeeDAO object is used to perform persistence operations. Here the EmployeeDAO is injected as a setter method argument to EmployeeServicesImpl. Now, we want to learn how to configure bean definition and also describe how to perform setter method injection before making the bean available to the application. The following section explains the spring beans XML configuration tags that are used to configure properties.

The <property> element

The bean definition can describe the use of zero or more properties to inject before making the bean object available to the application. The <property> element is used to describe one-setter method of property which allows only one argument. That is, the <property> elements correspond to JavaBean setter methods exposed by the bean classes. Spring supports primitives and references to other beans in the same or related factories, lists, maps, and properties as property types. The <property> element supports three attributes as described in Table 2.4.

TABLE 2.4 Attributes of <property> tag

Attribute	*Description*	*Occurrence*
name	This attribute takes the name of the Java bean based property. That is, this follows Java bean conventions like a name of "uname" corresponds to setUname() as a setter method.	required
value	A short-cut alternative to a child element "value". The child element <value> is explained in Table 2.2.	optional
ref	A short-cut alternative to a child element "ref bean=".	optional

> **Note:** The child elements for the <property> element are same as of <constructor-arg> described in Table 2.3.

The following code snippet shows the sample configurations of setter method of injection.

Code Snippet

```
<bean id="employeeServices" class="com.santosh.spring.EmployeeServices">
   <property name="employeeDAO">
   <ref local="empdao"/>
   </property>
</bean>
```

This specifies to set a reference of a spring bean object named 'empdao' to the property 'employeeDAO' of EmployeeServices. That means this results to invoke setEmployeeDAO(Employee DAO) method of EmployeeServices object.

2.5 USING THE PROPERTY NAMESPACE

Spring 2.0 provides support to enhance the configuration information by combining implementation classes with the standard XML schema syntax. That means we can add our own tags with our own namespaces, as per our requirement and convenience. Using this feature Spring Framework implemented number of extension namespaces providing important extra functionality to the XML configuration such as Property Namespace, JMS Namespace, Transaction Namespace and AOP Namespace. In this section we will discuss about the Property Namespace, we will learn about the other namespaces in the later chapters.

The Property Namespace provides a convenience to simplify the configuration document. This eliminates the need of using <property> tag for specifying the property injection. To use the property namespace we need to import the following namespace:

```
xmlns:p="http://www.springframework.org/schema/p"
```

Importing this namespace in the <beans> tag allows us to use the property namespace with prefix 'p' throughout the definition. Note that this namespace does not have a schema definition for validation, because the attributes that are used within this namespace are the names of the properties for the bean that it is to apply for.

We use the property name as an attribute name, with a prefix 'p:' to specify the value for the property, for example:

```
<bean id="mybean" class="com.santosh.spring.MyBean" p:message="Hello"/>
```

This specifies to set a String value 'Hello' to the property 'message' of MyBean. However if we want to specify reference to another bean as a value to a property, we need to append '-ref' to the property name, for example:

```
<bean id="mybean1" class="com.santosh.spring.MyBean1"/>
<bean id="mybean2" class="com.santosh.spring.MyBean2"
      p:myBean-ref="mybean1"/>
```

This specifies to set a reference of a spring bean object named 'mybean1' to the property 'myBean' of MyBean2. That means this results to invoke setMyBean(MyBean1) method of MyBean2 object. Note that the property namespace is applicable only for configuring properties not for constructor arguments.

To configure collections as independent bean definitions and then inject them into the target bean we can use the util namespace. To use util namespace we need to import the following namespace:

```
xmlns:util="http://www.springframework.org/schema/util"
```

Apart from importing the above shown namespace, we need to include the "http://www.springframework.org/schema/util/spring-util-2.0.xsd" schema definition for validating. The following code snippet shows the example for configuring a list

Code Snippet

```
<bean id="mybean" class="com.santosh.spring.MyBean" p:myProp-ref="mylist"/>

<util:list id="mylist">
<value>item1</value>
<value>item2</value>
</util:list>
```

This configuration tells Spring container to create a List object with two String objects. And inject the List object reference into MyBean object i.e. by setting the List object reference to the property named 'myProp'. Similarly we can use <util:set> and <util:map> for configuring Set and Map objects respectively.

Now that we have learnt about the two types of dependency injection processes and the spring beans xml configuration tags to configure each of them, to make the discussion more clear. Let us look at an example showing the usage of the elements discussed in this and the preceding sections.

2.5.1 Dependency Injection Example

In this section we will design an example to demonstrate the constructor and setter method injection. To do this we will implement an increment salary business use-case of an employee management application. Figure 2.2 shows such a design.

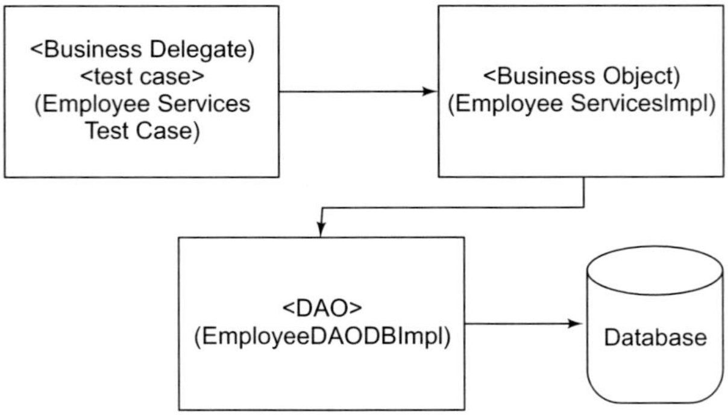

FIGURE 2.2 Class diagram for the example

As shown in Fig. 2.2 EmployeeServicesImpl is a business object that encapsulates employee related business services. In this example we consider only one service increment salary. The Employee DAODBImpl is a DAO that uses JDBC as a low level data access API to communicate with the database to access employee details. Finally we have the EmployeeServicesTestCase that can test the business object. We know that it is ever a good practice to use the principal of Program to an Interface (P2I). Thus all the objects are described with an interface. List 2.4 shows a simple business object interface that represents the services related to the employee.

List 2.4: EmployeeServices.java

```
package com.santosh.spring;

public interface EmployeeServices {

  public boolean incrementSalary(int empno, double amt);

}//class
```

List 2.5 shows the EmployeeServicesImpl class, while implementation of the EmployeeServices interface was already shown in List 2.3.

List 2.5: EmployeeServicesImpl.java

```
package com.santosh.spring;
import com.santosh.spring.dao.EmployeeDAO;
public class EmployeeServicesImpl implements EmployeeServices {
  public void setEmployeeDAO(EmployeeDAO ed){
        employeeDAO=ed;
  }
  public boolean incrementSalary(int empno, double amt) {
        //some business operations to calculate the salary
        //sample code
        double sal=employeeDAO.getSal(empno);
        sal+=amt;
        employeeDAO.setSal(empno, sal);
        System.out.println(sal);
        return true;
  }//incrementSal
  private EmployeeDAO employeeDAO;
}//class
```

List 2.6 shows the EmployeeDAO interface with a minimum set of methods, which can be further enhanced as per the requirement.

List 2.6: EmployeeDAO.java

```
package com.santosh.spring.dao;
public interface EmployeeDAO {
  //Methods that can represent the employee details
  //for example
  double getSal(int eno);
  void setSal(int eno, double sal);
}//intf
```

List 2.7 shows the EmployeeDAODBImpl class.

List 2.7: EmployeeDAODBImpl.java

```
package com.santosh.spring.dao;
import java.sql.*;
import javax.sql.*;
public class EmployeeDAODBImpl implements EmployeeDAO {
  public EmployeeDAODBImpl( DataSource ds) {
        dataSource=ds;
  }//cons
  public double getSal(int eno) {
        Connection con=null;
        try {
              con=dataSource.getConnection();
              PreparedStatement ps= con.prepareStatement(
```

```
                                        "select sal from emp where empno=?");
                ps.setInt(1,eno);
                ResultSet rs=ps.executeQuery();
                if (rs.next())
                        return rs.getDouble(1);
                throw new RuntimeException( "Employee Not Found");
        }//try
        catch(RuntimeException e){throw e;}
        catch(Exception e){
                //log the exception message
                e.printStackTrace();
                throw new RuntimeException();
        }//catch
        finally{
                try{con.close();}catch(Exception e){}
        }//finally
}//getSal

public void setSal(int empno, double sal) {
        Connection con=null;
        try {
                con=dataSource.getConnection();
                PreparedStatement ps= con.prepareStatement(
                                        "update emp set sal=? where empno=?");
                ps.setDouble(1,sal);
                ps.setInt(2,empno);
                int count=ps.executeUpdate();
                if (count==1 || count==Statement.SUCCESS_NO_INFO)
                        return;
        }//try
        catch(Exception e){
                //log the exception message
                e.printStackTrace();
        }//catch
        finally{
                try{con.close();}catch(Exception e){}
        }//finally
        throw new RuntimeException();
        }//setSal

        private DataSource dataSource;
}//class
```

Now it is time to configure these beans into spring beans XML configuration file with the respective datasource configuration. List 2.8 shows the spring beans XML configuration file.

List 2.8: mybeans.xml

```
<beans xmlns="http://www.springframework.org/schema/beans"
xmlns:xsi="http://www.w3.org/2001/XMLSchema-instance"
```

```
xsi:schemaLocation="http://www.springframework.org/schema/beans
http://www.springframework.org/schema/beans/spring-beans-2.0.xsd">
     <bean id="employeeServices"
                         class="com.santosh.spring.EmployeeServicesImpl">
          <property name="employeeDAO">
                    <ref local="empdao"/>
          </property>
     </bean>
     <bean id="empdao" class="com.santosh.spring.dao.EmployeeDAODBImpl">
          <constructor-arg>
               <ref local="ds"/>
          </constructor-arg>
     </bean>
     <bean id="ds" class="org.apache.commons.dbcp.BasicDataSource">
          <property name="driverClassName">
               <value>oracle.jdbc.driver.OracleDriver</value>
          </property>
          <property name="url">
               <value>jdbc:oracle:thin:@localhost:1521:sandb</value>
          </property>
          <property name="username">
  <value>scott</value>
  </property>
  <property name="password">
  <value>tiger</value>
  </property>
  </bean>
</beans>
```

We have completed the business use case implementation and xml configurations and now we want to test the configuration. List 2.9 shows the test case for testing the EmployeeServices.

List 2.9: EmployeeServicesTestCase.java

```
//A Test Case to test the EmployeeDAODBImpl incrementSalary business logic
import org.springframework.beans.factory.*;
import org.springframework.beans.factory.xml.*;
import org.springframework.core.io.*;
import com.santosh.spring.EmployeeServices;
public class EmployeeServicesTestCase {
  public static void main(String s[]) throws Exception {
       BeanFactory beans=new XmlBeanFactory(
                              new FileSystemResource("mybeans.xml"));
       EmployeeServices es= (EmployeeServices)
                              beans.getBean("employeeServices");
       es.incrementSalary(Integer.parseInt(s[0]), 1000);
  }//main
}//class
```

After writing all the files under lists 2.4 to 2.9 it is time to compile and execute the example to find the service in action. Figure 2.3 shows the compilation and execution statements along with the output of this example.

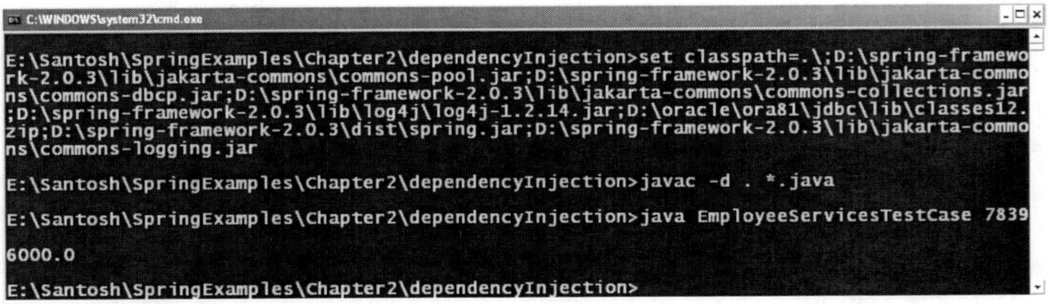

FIGURE 2.3 Output of EmployeeServicesTestCase

Figure 2.3 shows the classpath that is required to compile and execute the example, and the output of the execution. To explain further, the salary of the employee with employee number 7839 was 5000 and now it is incremented by 1000, the same being printed on to the output console. With this example we will end the discussion of the different types of injection processes and their configurations. We will use these configuration tags throughout in this book to configure bean properties and types. The next section explains the different ways of configuring beans for instantiation.

2.6 CONFIGURING BEANS

The spring core container supports the bean configurations for different types of instantiations. This is one of the important advantages of Spring framework allowing us to configure any existing java class to be instantiated and managed by the spring container. Spring even supports the configuration of a static inner class for instantiation. We have already seen earlier that the bean definition is configured using <bean> element in case of XML-based configurations. The three types of instantiations that spring supports are:

1. Using constructor.
2. Static factory method.
3. Non-static factory method.

Let us describe the three configurations.

2.6.1 Instantiating Bean using Constructor

When defining a bean to be created using its constructor we need to only specify the bean class into the <bean> elements class attribute. One of the most important features of the spring framework is that it does not force us to define the bean classes into a sub type of any spring class or interface or even code in a specific style. That is, spring allows all normal classes to be configured, discussed earlier in this chapter under the section 'Constructor Injection' about the configurations of defining a bean with no argument constructor and multiple arguments of constructor. The following code snippet shows some sample bean definitions for this approach.

Code Snippet

```
<!–instantiating bean with no argument constructor -->
<bean id="mybean1" class="MyBeanClass1"/>

<!–instantiating bean with one String argument constructor -->
<bean id="mybean2" class="MyBeanClass2">
  <constructor-arg type="java.lang.String">
        <value>Hello</value>
  </constructor-arg>
</bean>

<!–instantiating bean with two argument constructor -->
<bean id="mybean3" class="MyBeanClass3">
  <constructor-arg index="1">
        <value>Hello</value>
  </constructor-arg>
  <constructor-arg index="0">
        <ref local="mybean"/>
  </constructor-arg>
</bean>
```

The preceding code snippet shows how to configure a bean definition to be instantiated using constructors. But in some cases we want beans to be instantiated by using some existing static or non-static factory methods, Spring allows us to configure these requirements. The following two subsections describes such configurations.

2.6.2 Instantiating Bean using Static Factory Method

When defining a bean to be created using the static factory method of a class we need to specify the bean class that contains the static factory method. This can be done by using the <bean> elements class attribute. The factory method name can be specified by using the factory-method attribute. The advantage with the spring container configuration is that the factory class being configured does not need to be defined as a subtype of any specific interfaces or class. Even the factory method does not need to follow any specific rule, including any related to the number and types of arguments. The following code snippet shows the bean definition that is instantiated using static factory method.

Code Snippet

```
<bean id="myBean" class="com.santosh.spring.MyFactoryBean"
                  factory-method="getInstance"/>
```

The preceding code snippet shows the bean definition that describes the spring container to instantiate the bean using the no-argument getInstance() static method of com.santosh.spring. MyFactoryBean class. In this case we have used a no-argument static method to instantiate a bean but some times we would also want to use an argument method to instantiate the bean. For example, there could be an instance when we would want to configure a bean definition to get the JDBC connection using DriverManager class's getConnection() method which takes some arguments. The following code snippet shows how to use static factory method with arguments to instantiate bean.

Code Snippet

```
<bean id="con" class="java.sql.DriverManager" factory-method="getConnection">
  <constructor-arg>
        <value>jdbc:oracle:thin:@localhost:1521:sandb</value>
  </constructor-arg>
  <constructor-arg>
        <value>scott</value>
  </constructor-arg>
  <constructor-arg>
        <value>tiger</value>
  </constructor-arg>
</bean>
```

As per the bean definition shown in the preceding code snippet the static getConnection() method with three String arguments of DriverManager class is used to instantiate the bean, which results in java.sql.Connection type of object. If required we can even set properties for the object after it is instantiated. Like if we want to set the auto commit mode using setAutoCommit() method of Connection then the <property> element under the bean tag can be used as explained earlier. The following code snippet shows this configuration.

Code Snippet

```
<bean id="con" class="java.sql.DriverManager" factory-method="getConnection">
  <constructor-arg>
        <value>jdbc:oracle:thin:@localhost:1521:sandb</value>
  </constructor-arg>
  <constructor-arg>
        <value>scott</value>
  </constructor-arg>
  <constructor-arg>
        <value>tiger</value>
  </constructor-arg>

  <property name="autoCommit">
        <value type="boolean">false</value>
  </property>
</bean>
```

In this subsection you have learnt how to configure a bean definition to instantiate by using the static factory method. The next section explains how to configure a bean definition by using the non-static factory method for instantiation of bean.

2.6.3 Instantiating Bean using Non-static Factory Method

When defining a bean to be created using the non-static factory method we need to specify the bean id or name of the other bean that contains the non-static factory method. This can be done by using the class attribute of bean element. The factory method name can be specified by using the factory-method attribute. Note that in this case we should not use the class attribute of the <bean> element. The advantage with the spring container configuration is that the factory method does not need to follow any specific rules, including any related to the number or types of arguments. The following code snippet shows the bean definition that is instantiated using the non-static factory method.

Code Snippet

```
<bean id="myBean1" class="com.santosh.spring.MyFactoryBean"/>
<bean id="myBean2" factory-bean="myBean1" factory-method="getInstance"/>
```

The preceding code snippet shows the bean definition that describes the spring container to instantiate the bean with id 'myBean2' using the no-argument getInstance() non-static method of com.santosh. spring.MyFactoryBean class. In this case we have used a no-argument method but we are allowed to configure the bean definition to use a method with arguments also similar to the static factory method description described in the preceding section. With this we have completed the discussion on the different types of configurations of bean definitions to instantiate bean by spring framework. As we know the different types of bean definition configurations it is now time to learn bean scopes and life cycle.

2.7 BEAN SCOPES AND LIFECYCLE

We know that the beans configured in the spring beans XML configuration file are instantiated and managed by the spring core container. And one of the other great things of spring frameworks customization support is the configuration that it allows to specify the scope for each particular bean definition as per the requirement. The spring framework from its 2.0 version supports five built-in scopes but it supports to define custom scopes also, which we may generally require. The five bean scopes that are built-in from spring 2.0 are singleton, prototype, request, session, and global session. The spring 1.x supports only the first two scopes, even when using spring framework 2.x also the other three scopes are available only when using a web aware spring ApplicationContext like XmlWebApplicationContext to initialize the container. We use *scope* attribute of <bean> tag to specify the bean scope. In case of using Spring 1.x as mentioned above we are available with only two scopes singleton and prototype, which is described using *singleton* attribute of bean tag, if it is set to true then the bean is singleton scoped otherwise prototype. Table 2.5 describes these five scopes.

TABLE 2.5 Bean Scopes

Scope	*Description*
singleton	This is the default scope taken by the container for the bean definition which is not described with scope attribute. A bean definition configured with this scope is instantiated only once per container instance. And all the requests for this bean or references created for this bean in the context will be given with the single object reference.
prototype	A bean definition configured with this scope (that is, prototype—non-singleton) is instantiated every time it is requested for or referenced.
request	This scope is applicable only when using a web aware spring ApplicationContext. A bean definition configured with this scope is instantiated for each HTTP request.
session	This scope is also applicable only when using a web aware spring ApplicationContext. A bean definition configured with this scope is instantiated for each HTTP session. That is, the bean scoped with a session is shared between all the session's requests.

(Contd.)

global session	This scope is also applicable only when using a web aware spring ApplicationContext. A bean definition configured with this scope is the same as session scope described above; in fact, configuring this scope in a standard servlet-based web application makes the container use session scope, since this scope has significance only in portal-based web applications. Beans defined as the global session scope are scoped to the lifetime of the global portlet Session. According to the portlet specification the notion of a global Session is shared amongst the various portlets that make up a single portlet web application.

Apart from specifying the scopes as described in Table 2.5. Spring framework provides a supports bean to listen for its lifecycle events performed by the container. The spring frameworks support two important lifecycle operations— initialization and destruction. Spring framework includes two marker interfaces, InitializingBean and DisposableBean for this purpose. The following sub-sections explains these two lifecycle notifications and their configurations.

2.7.1 Initialization

To listen for the initialization lifecycle event the bean can implement org.springframework.beans. factory. InitializingBean interface. This interface declares only one method afterPropertiesSet(). This method signature is shown in the following snippet.

Code Snippet

```
public void afterPropertiesSet() throws Exception
```

The afterPropertiesSet() method allows bean to perform system-specific initializations, as the name itself implies that this method is invoked by the container immediately after the bean is instantiated and set with all the necessary properties. The following code snippet shows the bean that implements this interface to listen for the initialization event.

Code Snippet

```
package com.santosh.spring;
import org.springframework.beans.factory.*;
public class TestBean implements InitializingBean {
  public TestBean(){
        //invoked before the bean properties are set
        //can perform initializations, but bean properties are not available
  }
  public void afterPropertiesSet() throws Exception{
        //invoked after the bean properties are set successfully
        //can perform initializations even using the bean properties
  }
  //rest of the code goes here
}
```

The preceding code shows the bean class that wants to customize the initialization process by adding some system specific initializations for the bean. To do this, the bean is defined as subtype of InitializingBean and implement afterPropertiesSet() method. Using this approach makes the bean class bind to the spring API and thus is discouraged. Even a spring framework does not recommend the use of this approach. The use of InitializationBean interface can be avoided by defining the initialization method in the bean XML configuration file using the init-method attribute of <bean> element as shown in the following code snippet.

Code Snippet

```
<bean id="mybean" class="com.santosh.spring.TestBean"
                  init-method="initialize"/>
```

The TestBean class for this configuration

```
package com.santosh.spring;
import org.springframework.beans.factory.*;
public class TestBean {
  public TestBean(){
        //invoked before the bean properties are set
        //can perform initializations, but bean properties are not available
  }
  public void initialize() throws Exception{
        //invoked after the bean properties are set successfully
        //can perform initializations even using the bean properties
  }
  //rest of the code goes here
}
```

Apart from this configuration spring allows us to configure the default initialization method for all the beans configured in an XML configuration file. The following snippet shows the configuration defining the default init method.

Code Snippet

```
<beans default-init-method="initialize">
  <bean id="mybean1" class="MyBean1"/>
  <bean id="mybean2" class="MyBean2"/>
  <bean id="mybean3" class="MyBean3" init-method="init"/>
</beans>
```

As shown in the preceding snippet, using the default-init-method informs the spring container to find the 'initialize' method in the bean classes. If the bean class has such a method then it will be invoked immediately after the bean is instantiated and set with all the necessary properties. Moreover, if we want we can override the configuration for the necessary beans using the init-method attribute of the respective beans.

2.7.2 Destruction

To listen for the destruction lifecycle event the bean can implement the org.springframework.beans.factory.DisposableBean interface. This interface declares only one method destroy(). The method signature of this method is shown in the following code snippet.

```
public void destroy() throws Exception
```

The destroy() method allows bean to perform system specific finalizations. This method is invoked by the container just before it decides to put the bean out of service. The following code snippet shows the bean that implements this interface to listen for the destruction event.

Code Snippet

```
package com.santosh.spring;
import org.springframework.beans.factory.*;
public class TestBean implements DisposableBean {
  public void destroy() throws Exception{
        //invoked just before the bean is put out of service
        //can perform finalizations
  }
  //rest of the code goes here
}
```

As shown in the preceding code the bean class that wants to customize the destruction process by adding some system specific finalizations for the bean has to be defined as subtype of DisposableBean and implement destroy() method. Using this approach makes the bean class bind to the spring API and thus is discouraged. Even spring framework does not recommend the usage of this approach. The use of DisposableBean interface can be avoided by defining the destroy method in the bean XML configuration file using the destroy-method attribute of <bean> element as shown in the following code snippet.

Code Snippet

```
<bean id="mybean" class="com.santosh.spring.TestBean"
                  destroy-method="close"/>
```

The TestBean class for this configuration

```
package com.santosh.spring;
import org.springframework.beans.factory.*;
public class TestBean {
  public void close() throws Exception{
        //invoked just before the bean is put out of service
        //can perform finalizations
  }
  //rest of the code goes here
}
```

Apart from this configuration spring allows us to configure the default destruction method for all the beans configured in an XML configuration file. The following snippet shows the configuration defining the default-destroy method.

Code Snippet

```
<beans default-destroy-method="close">
  <bean id="mybean1" class="MyBean1"/>
  <bean id="mybean2" class="MyBean2"/>
  <bean id="mybean3" class="MyBean3" destroy-method="destroy"/>
</beans>
```

As shown in the preceding snippet using the default-destroy method informs the spring container how to find the 'close' method in the bean classes. If the bean class has such a method then it will be invoked just before the bean is put out of service. Moreover, if we want we can override the configuration for the necessary beans using the default-destroy method attribute of the respective beans.

2.8 METHOD INJECTION

In the earlier sections we learnt the constructor and setter method injection in which the dependencies are pushed into the object. This approach is suitable when a singleton object has to be injected into another singleton object, or a non-singleton object has to be injected into a non-singleton object. However using this push model causes problem when the bean instance and its collaborators life cycle are different. For example, consider injecting a non-singleton collaborator (say BusinessObject2) into a singleton instance (say BusinessObject1) using the setter method injection as shown below:

```
<bean id="businessObject1" class="com.santosh.spring.BusinessObject1"
scope="singleton">
 <property name="businessObject2" ref="businessObject2"/>
</bean>

<bean id="businessObject2" class="com.santosh.spring.BusinessObject2"
scope="prototype"/>
```

This creates businessObject1 bean only once and at the time of craetion, a new instance of businessObject2 is created and injected. It means all the clients accessing the BusinessObject1 will be serviced by a single BusinessObject2. If we want a separate instance of BusinessObject2 with BusinessObject1, still making the BusinessObject1 singleton. For example we want a separate instance of BusinessObject2 whenever a method myService1() is called on BusinessObject1. Here dependency injection is not applicable. Instead we need to pull the dependencies as required. One of the options is that we can obtain the BeanFactory object representing the container and request for the dependency each time it is needed. This approach is not recommended since it makes the bean depend on the Spring API. Method Injection of Spring Framework provides a better solution for this problem. Spring Framework provides a Lookup method injection option for Method Injection. The following section explains how to use lookup method injection.

2.8.1 Lookup Method Injection

In lookup method injection container creates a dynamic proxy for the container managed bean, implementing the specified lookup methods. Spring uses CGLIB API for preparing a dynamic proxy subclass for the bean. Thus the bean class should have a no-argument constructor and cannot be final. The bean class can be an abstract or non-abstract class and contains a method to be injected with the following signature.s

```
<public|protected> [abstract] <return-type> someMethodName(no-arguments);
```

As described above the method to be injected can be public or protected, the return type should describe the object that we want to obtain (i.e. the dependency object type) and strictly the method should be defined with no-arguments. Moreover, the method can be abstract or non-abstract. If the method is abstract, the dynamically generated subclass implements the method otherwise it overrides the concrete method. For example

```
package com.santosh.spring;

public abstract class BusinessObject1 {

   public void myService1(){
      ...
      BusinessObject2 bo2=getBusinessObject2();
      ...
   }
   public abstract BusinessObject2 getBusinessObject2();
}
```

Now to configure the getBusinessObject2() method in the Spring beans XML configuration file describing the container to implement getBusinessObject2() method for BusinessObject1 class, we use <lookup-method> tag as shown below:

```
<bean id="businessObject1" class="com.santosh.spring.BusinessObject1"
scope="singleton">
 <lookup-method name="businessObject2" bean="businessObject2"/>
</bean>

<bean id="businessObject2" class="com.santosh.spring.BusinessObject2"
scope="prototype"/>
```

The name attribute of <lookup-method> tag specifies the method name to override and the bean attribute specifies the bean id whose object has to be returned by this method.

Summary

In this chapter you have learnt Inversion of Control (IoC) and its need in application development. Later, we discussed spring core container which included the discussion of how to initialize the container, configure the beans that can be managed by the container, and access those which were initialized by the container. Then we discussed how to write a basic spring application and execute it as a standalone application testing the basic spring beans XML configurations. Thereafter we spoke about the different types of dependency injections and their configuration tags in spring XML configuration file. The last section of this chapter explained the bean configurations which included the different ways of instantiating beans, their scope, and lifecycle callbacks. All these configurations include most of the basics of spring framework which are used further in this book while understanding the other modules. The next chapter focuses on the AOP methodology and describes in detail the Spring AOP module with relevant examples.

Understanding Aspect Oriented Programming (AOP)

3 CHAPTER

Objectives

In this chapter, we will cover:

- Problem with OOP in developing enterprise applications
- Aspect oriented programming (AOP) methodology
- Program AOP-based applications by using Spring AOP implementation with the low-level Spring 1.2 basic approach.

3.1 INTRODUCTION

We are aware that nowadays the most widely used methodology for developing enterprise applications is object oriented programming (OOP). The OOP methodology was introduced in the 1960s to reduce the complexity of the software and improve its quality. This achieved by modularization and reusability. This allows developers to view the software as a collection of objects that interact with each other, allowing easy solving of critical problems and developing reusable units of software.

According to the OOP methodology we are allowed to separate the functionality of the system to develop in parts (units) which are termed as concerns (developed as objects), integrating them to a single system simplifying the application development. The major problem with OOP is its static approach of integrating the objects to build a system. Figure 3.1 explains the approach used by OOP to build the system.

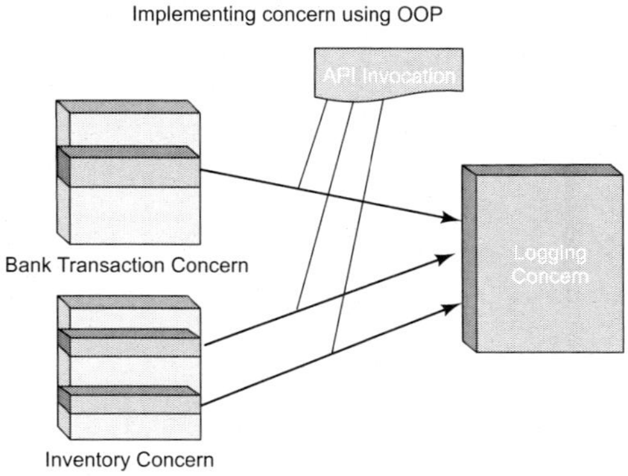

FIGURE 3.1 Implementing concern using OOP

As shown in Fig. 3.1, the system is divided into three concerns, namely bank transaction, inventory, and logging. The bank transaction and inventory concerns performs their specific functionalities as defined by the system but they have to depend on some other concerns for secondary requirements like logging functionality as shown in Fig. 3.1. To access the logging functionality we need to use the logging concern API while coding the bank transaction and inventory concerns. This is known as the static approach of integrating the concerns. This way of accessing the concerns that serve some secondary common functionality known as system-wide concerns or crosscutting concerns like logging, security, transaction, etc., increases development time dependency and the system's complexity. AOP is the programming methodology introduced to solve this problem.

3.2 INTRODUCING ASPECT ORIENTED PROGRAMMING (AOP)

Aspect oriented programming (AOP) is a programming methodology that allows the developers to build the core concerns (that is, primary functionality of the system) without making them aware of secondary requirements by introducing aspects that encapsulate all the secondary requirements logic and the point of execution where they have to be applied. The AOP methodology allows developers to implement the individual concerns in a loosely coupled fashion and weave them to build the final system.

Before we continue further about AOP and its usage we need to learn its terminology.

3.2.1 TERMINOLOGY

Concern: Concern is a term that refers to a part of the system divided on the basis of the functionality. Concerns are of two types—core and crosscutting. The concerns representing single and specific functionality for primary requirements are known as core concerns. The concerns representing functionalities for secondary requirements are referred to as crosscutting concerns or system-wide concerns. For example, logging, security, etc.

Joinpoint: This is a term used to refer to a point in the execution flow of a system, like method invocation, field access, etc.

Advice: This is an object which includes API invocations to the system wide concerns representing the action to perform at a joinpoint specified by a pointcut.

Pointcut: Pointcut is a construct that selects the joinpoints specifying where an advice is to be applied.

Aspect: The combination of advice and a pointcut is referred to as aspect.

Weaving: Weaving is a process that combines the individual concerns into a single system. Weaving can be done at different stages such as compilation, class loading, etc.

Weaver: Weaver is the actual processor that performs the weaving.

Now, as we have learnt the basics of the AOP methodology it is time to learn an AOP language to develop a system using the AOP methodology. Currently, most of the AOP languages are defined by some extensions for the existing OOP languages like Java, C++, etc. Some of the AOP languages are AspectJ, AspectC++, Spring AOP, etc. Like other languages, AOP languages also consist of two parts—language specification and language implementation. Language specification includes language constructs and grammar rules. Language implementation is responsible for verifying the code written by using the language specification and converting it into executable code. We will first discuss Spring AOP and then AspectJ style.

3.3 SPRING AOP

The Spring AOP is one of the key modules of Spring framework which includes support for developing AOP-based applications in Java. Spring AOP is a proxy-based framework implemented purely in Java. That means Spring AOP builds dynamic proxies to intercept the requests to the target object methods, which allows it to invoke interceptors that are relevant to that particular method call. Spring framework by default uses Java Standard editions dynamic proxies to build AOP proxies and it can also use CGLIB proxies since the Java Standard editions dynamic proxy API includes a support for proxy interface (or multiple interfaces). But sometimes we want to proxy classes instead of interfaces, which are supported by CGLIB dynamic proxy API.

Spring AOP is developed based on AOP Alliance API, which enables us to use the advices developed under spring AOP to be used with other AOP implementations. It is important to note that Spring AOP supports only method and not field interceptions.

Apart from allowing us to develop the concerns following the AOP style the Spring framework itself uses AOP to provide most of the infrastructure logics as declarative services. To provide declarative transaction service spring includes a TransactionInterceptor which is an AOP MethodInterceptor implementation.

The Spring AOP module includes Spring AOP low-level API for developing AOP-based applications which is the only support up to Spring 1.2. Spring 2.0 includes an additional support of AOP in the form of schema-based approach and @AspectJ annotation approach for defining aspects apart from the low-level AOP support provided in Spring 1.2. These two new approaches are simpler to program or configure and provide a high-level approach for creating aspects compared to the Spring 1.2 approach. However, even after the release of the Spring 2.0 high-level AOP support, it is even important to learn the Spring 1.2 style of creating aspects for two reasons—it gives a better basic idea of AOP programming based on OOP knowledge and there are still a number of projects that use Spring 1.2 and hence need to know the Spring 1.2 style of AOP application development. Note that Spring 2.0 continues support for the low-level approach defined in Spring 1.2. In this chapter you will learn all three approaches, the Spring 1.2 style low-level API, Schema based and @AspectJ annotation based for programming Spring AOP applications. As described the Spring 1.2 style of creating aspects gives a better basic idea of AOP programming. Let us start by learning how to build Spring 1.2 style aspects starting with the Schema based followed by the @AspectJ based approach.

3.4 SPRING ADVICE API

Advice is an object that includes API invocations to systemwide concerns representing the action to perform at a joinpoint specified by a pointcut. The different types of advices that Spring AOP framework supports are:

- **Before advice:** The advice that executes before the joinpoint.
- **After returning advice:** The advice that executes after the joinpoint execution completes with normal termination.

- **Throws advice:** The advice that executes after the joinpoint execution if it completes with abnormal termination.
- **Around advice:** The advice that can surround the joinpoint providing the advice before and after executing the joinpoint even controlling the joinpoint invocation.

Now, let us discuss these advices in detail with some practical examples, first starting with the before advice.

3.4.1 Before Advice

The before advice is the advice that executes before the joinpoint. That means this type of advice allows us to intercept the request and apply the advice before the execution of joinpoint (before the requested method invocation on target object). This advice has to be a subtype of *org.springframework.aop.MethodBeforeAdvice* interface. The *org.springframework.aop.MethodBeforeAdvice* interface has only one method with the following signature

public void before(Method m, Object args[], Object target) throws Throwable

The before() method can encapsulate the custom code that has to execute before the joinpoint executes. In general this code contains API invocations to the crosscutting concerns. After this method terminates normal (that is, without throwing an exception) the proxy continues the further execution of the interceptor chain and target method. Figure 3.2 shows a sample sequence diagram explaining the operations when before advice and joinpoint execution terminates normally. Moreover, if this advice decides to discontinue the joinpoint execution then it can throw some exception. But if the before advice throws an exception, apart from terminating the further execution of the interceptor chain, the client is throw with exception, not a normal termination. Figure 3.3 shows a sample sequence diagram explaining the operations when before advice execution terminates abnormally by throwing exception.

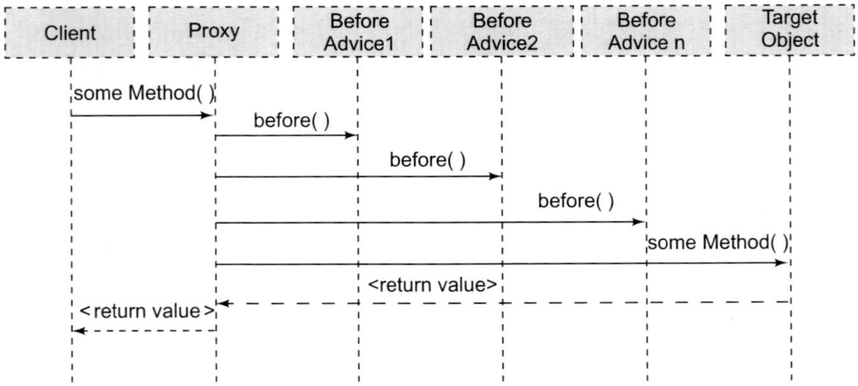

FIGURE 3.2 Sequence diagram describing the operations when before advice and joinpoint execution terminates normally, that is, without throwing exception

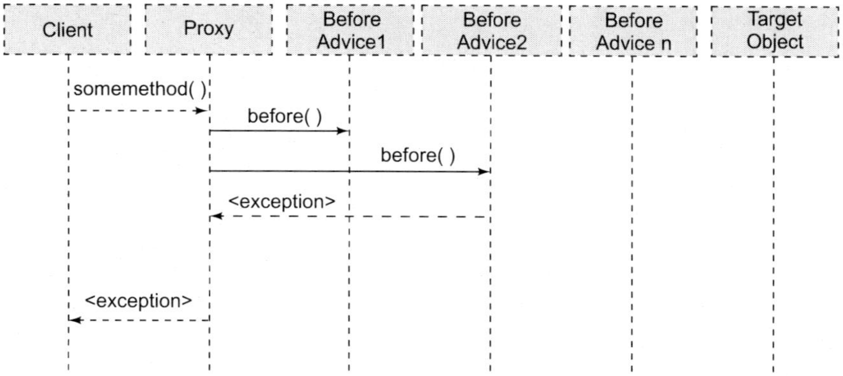

FIGURE 3.3 Sequence diagram describing the operations when before advice execution terminates abnormally, that is, throwing exception

As shown in Fig. 3.3, in the case where before advice throws an exception then an exception is thrown to the client without continuing further the interceptor's execution and the target object method. As described in code snippet ??the before() method's throws clause is defined with throws Throwable, which allows it to throw any type of exception including error, but the target method (implemented by proxy) may not be designed allowing to throw Throwable types. Thus proxy takes the responsibility to convert the exception thrown by the advice as shown in Fig. 3.4.

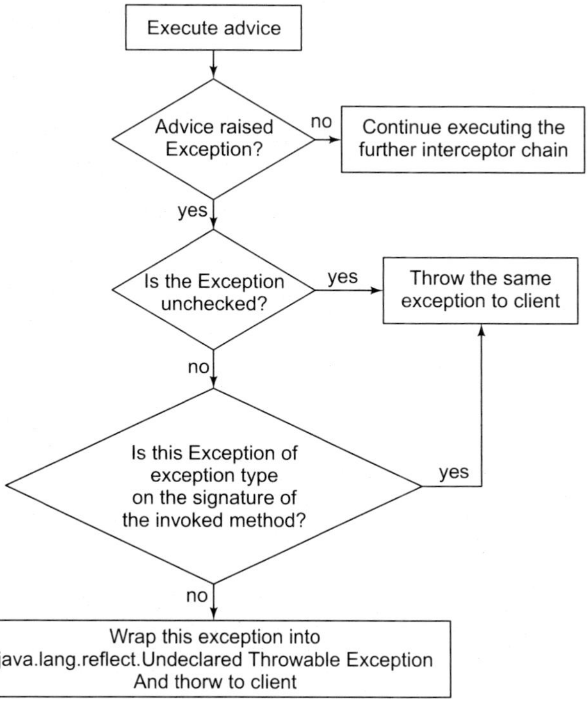

FIGURE 3.4 Flow diagram describing the exception handling done by proxy when advice throws an exception

As shown in Fig. 3.4 when advice throws an exception to proxy then it checks whether the exception thrown is of type unchecked exception (that is, java.lang.RuntimeException or its subtypes) or the exception type on the signature of the invoked method. If it is so then the same exception is thrown to the client. If not then the exception is wrapped in an unchecked exception *java.lang.reflect.Undeclared ThrowableException* and thrown to the client. As we have learnt about the before advice we will look at one sample program to throw more light on this topic.

3.4.1.1 Working with before advice

In this section we will develop an example to demonstrate how to write an advice that has to be applied before the joinpoint execution, and how to configure it according to the spring 1.2 low-level approach. In this example we will implement the well known simple account services withdraw and deposit which requires some secondary logics like logging, security, etc.

List 3.1 shows the AccountServices interface that declares withdraw and deposit methods to access the services.

List 3.1: AccountServices.java

```
package com.santosh.spring;
/**
 * @author Santosh
 */
public interface AccountServices {
   boolean deposit(int accno, double amt) throws MyException;
   boolean withdraw(int accno, double amt)throws MyException;
}
```

List 3.2 shows the implementation of AccountServices interface shown in the preceding section. The implementation includes simple test logic.

List 3.2: AccountServicesImpl.java

```
package com.santosh.spring;
/**
 * @author Santosh
 */
public class AccountServicesImpl implements AccountServices {

   public AccountServicesImpl(){}
   public AccountServicesImpl(AccountDAO ad){
      accountDAO=ad;
   }
   public boolean withdraw(int accno, double amt) throws MyException{
      System.out.println("In withdraw method");
      //A simple withdraw test logic
      double bal=accountDAO.getBalance(accno);
      bal-=amt;
```

```
      if (bal>=1000){
        accountDAO.setBalance(accno,bal);
        return true;
      }
      return false;
   }
   public boolean deposit(int accno, double amt) throws MyException{
      //A simple deposit test logic
      System.out.println("In deposit method");
      double bal=accountDAO.getBalance(accno);
      bal+=amt;
      accountDAO.setBalance(accno,bal);
      return true;
   }
   private AccountDAO accountDAO;
}
```

List 3.3 shows MyException user-defined application level exception that describes the abnormal condition raised in withdraw and deposit methods.

List 3.3: MyException.java

```
package com.santosh.spring;
/**
 * @author Santosh
 */
public class MyException extends Exception {
   public MyException(){}
   public MyException(String message){
      super(message);
   }
}
```

List 3.4 shows the AccountDAO interface that declares simple methods for getting and setting the balance.

List 3.4: AccountDAO.java

```
package com.santosh.spring;
/**
 * @author Santosh
 */
public interface AccountDAO {
   void setBalance(int accno, double amt)throws MyException;
   double getBalance(int accno)throws MyException;
}
```

List 3.5 shows the AccountDAO interface implementation class. This class is the dummy implementation of AccountDAO and is implemented for testing the AccountServices. We will learn how to implement the full version of the DAO while discussing the JDBC module.

List 3.5: AccountDAOTestImpl.java

```
package com.santosh.spring;
/**
 * @author Santosh
 */
public class AccountDAOTestImpl implements AccountDAO {
  public void setBalance(int accno, double amt)throws MyException{

  }
  public double getBalance(int accno)throws MyException{
    return 5000;
  }
}
```

List 3.6 shows the LoggingAdvice (a before advice) that implements the logging concern.

List 3.6: LoggingAdvice.java

```
package com.santosh.spring;
import org.springframework.aop.*;
import java.lang.reflect.*;
import org.apache.log4j.*;
/**
 * @author Santosh
 */
public class LoggingAdvice implements MethodBeforeAdvice {
  public void before (Method m, Object[] args, Object target) {

    System.out.println("Logging Advice applied for : "+ m.getName());
    Logger logger=Logger.getLogger(target.getClass());
    logger.info("Method: "+m.getName()+
                " invoked with "+args.length+" arguments");
  }//before
}//class
```

List 3.7 shows the log4j properties to print the log messages to the mylog.html file using HTML layout.

List 3.7: log4j.properties

```
log4j.rootLogger= info, myapp

#log4j.appender.myapp=org.apache.log4j.ConsoleAppender

log4j.appender.myapp=org.apache.log4j.FileAppender
log4j.appender.myapp.file=mylog.html
log4j.appender.myapp.layout=org.apache.log4j.HTMLLayout
log4j.appender.myapp.append=false
```

List 3.8 shows the spring beans XML configuration file that defines a proxy to wrap Account ServicesImpl object.

List 3.8: mybeans.xml

```
<!DOCTYPE beans PUBLIC '-//SPRING//BEAN DTD//EN' 'http://www.springframework.org/
dtd/spring-beans.dtd'>

<beans>
  <bean id="accdao"
              class="com.santosh.spring.AccountDAOTestImpl"/>
  <bean id="accservices"
              class="com.santosh.spring.AccountServicesImpl">
    <constructor-arg>
      <ref local="accdao"/>
    </constructor-arg>
  </bean>
  <bean id="logging" class="com.santosh.spring.LoggingAdvice"/>

  <bean id="accountServices"
    class="org.springframework.aop.framework.ProxyFactoryBean">
    <property name="targetName">
      <value>accservices</value>
    </property>
    <property name="proxyInterfaces">
      <list>
        <value>com.santosh.spring.AccountServices</value>
      </list>
    </property>
    <property name="interceptorNames">
      <list>
        <value>logging</value>
      </list>
    </property>
  </bean>
</beans>
```

Now it is time to implement a test case to make the preceding configuration work. List 3.9 shows the test case to demonstrate the configuration.

List 3.9: AccountServicesTestCase.java

```
import org.springframework.beans.factory.*;
import org.springframework.beans.factory.xml.*;
import org.springframework.core.io.*;

import com.santosh.spring.AccountServices;
/**
 * @author Santosh
 */
public class AccountServicesTestCase {
  public static void main(String s[]) throws Exception {

    BeanFactory beans=new XmlBeanFactory(
                  new FileSystemResource("mybeans.xml"));

    AccountServices as=(AccountServices)
                    beans.getBean("accountServices");

    System.out.println(as.withdraw(1,1000));
    System.out.println("\n");
    System.out.println(as.deposit(1,2000));
  }//main
}//class
```

After writing all the files of this example as described from List 3.1 through 3.9 it is time to compile and execute the example for it to work. To compile and execute this example, first set the classpath to spring.jar, log4j jar, and commons-logging.jar as shown in Fig. 3.5. The same can also be set in system environment variables.

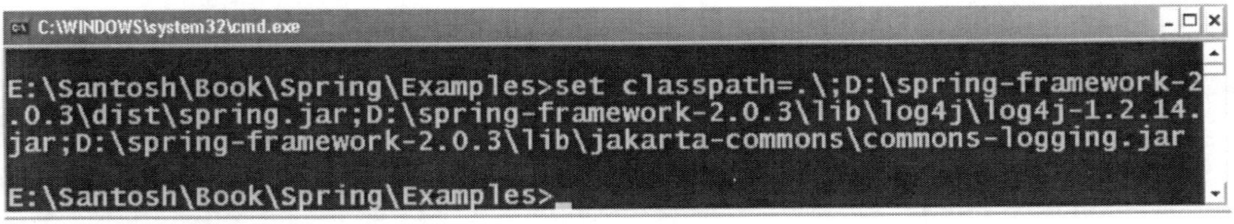

FIGURE 3.5 Setting Classpath for running the example

Now, if you compile the java files using the command javac –d . *.java, you will find the files as shown in Fig. 3.6.

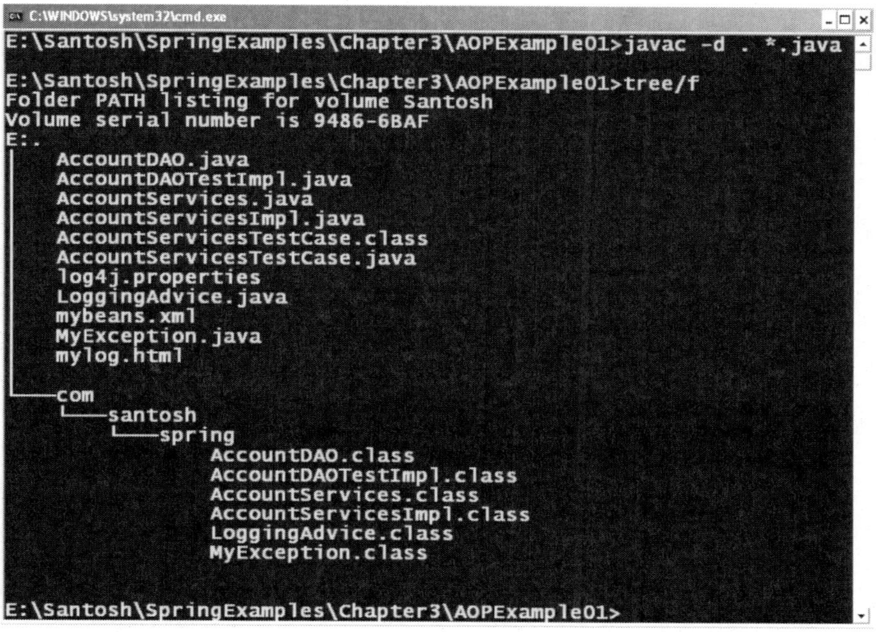

FIGURE 3.6 Tree structure showing the files of this example

Upon execution of the AccountServicesTestCase, the log file (mylog.html) will be generated and the output as shown in Fig. 3.7 will be presented. The log file content is as shown in Fig. 3.8.

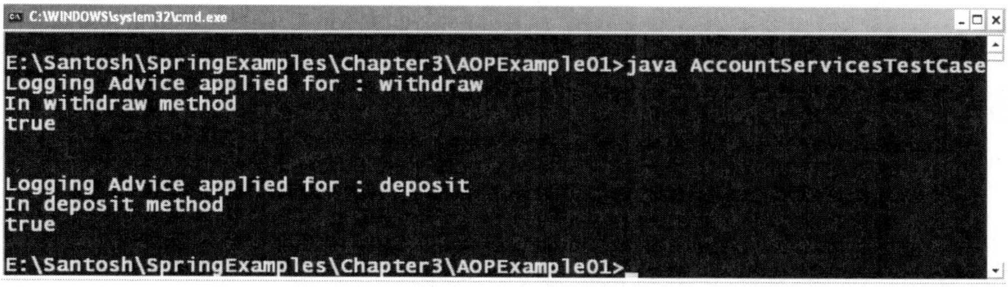

FIGURE 3.7 Output of AccountServicesTestCase

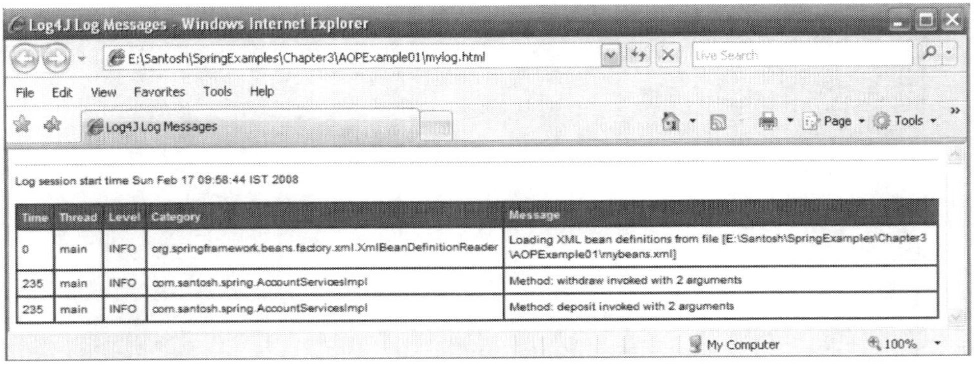

FIGURE 3.8 Log file, mylog.html

The following sequence diagram helps to understand the example's execution flow.

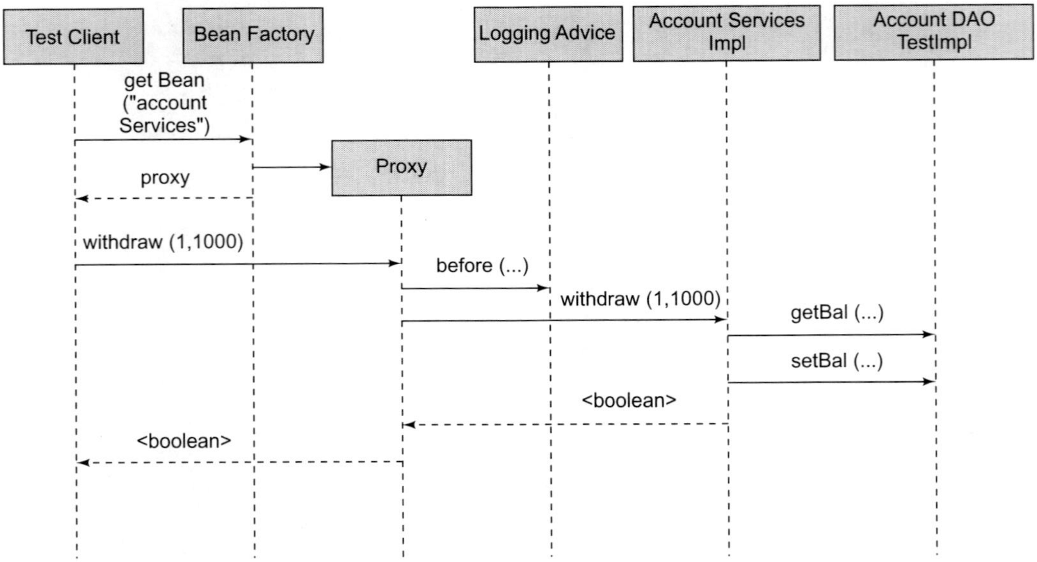

FIGURE 3.9 Sequence diagram.

As shown in Fig. 3.9 the Spring container dynamically creates a proxy object through the ProxyFactoryBean, where the dynamically built proxy class implements all the interfaces given under the proxyInterfaces list (in this example only one interface *com.santosh.spring.AccountServices*). All the methods are implemented to invoke the configured interceptors (advices) and the method on the given target object.

Note that in this example, we have designed an interface *com.santosh.spring.AccountServices* for target object type but in all the cases we may not have an interface as it is not mandatory to design. It is not mandatory to design an object implementing interface to proxy the object, Spring allows to proxy object without an interface. To configure the ProxyFactoryBean without proxy interfaces just avoid **proxyInterfaces** property in the ProxyFactoryBean bean definition and set the CGLIB jar file into classpath. If ProxyFactoryBean is configured without proxyInterfaces then the proxy that it builds dynamically will be a subtype of the target object type. In the preceding example if you remove the <property name="proxyInterfaces"> element from mybeans.xml then the proxy build will be extending *com.santosh.spring.AccountServicesImpl* class instead of implementing *com.santosh.spring.AccountServices* interface. Thus in AccountServicesTestCase we can cast the object type reference obtained from getBean() method of BeanFactory into *com.santosh.spring.AccountServicesImpl* instead of *com.santosh.spring.AccountServices*.

> **Note:** In Spring 2.0 if we do not configure proxyInterfaces property, then ProxyFactoryBean builds the proxy class, implementing all the interfaces implemented by the target object class. In case the target object does not implement an interface then it extends the target object class. Make sure that in this case, the target object class has a no-argument constructor where even the CGLIB jar file is set into classpath.

3.4.2 After Returning Advice

The after returning advice is the advice that executes after the joinpoints invocation completes with normal termination. This advice has to be a subtype of *org.springframework.aop.AfterReturningAdvice* interface. The *org.springframework.aop.AfterReturningAdvice* interface has only one method with the following signature.

Code Snippet

```
public void afterReturning(Object return_value, Method m, Object args[], Object
target) throws Throwable
```

The afterReturning() method can encapsulate the custom code that has to execute after the joinpoint execution completes successfully, in general this code contains API invocations to the cross-cutting concerns. As it can be observed from the method signature of the afterReturning() method this advice is available with the return value. After this method terminates normal (that is, without throwing an exception) the proxy continues the further execution of the interceptor chain. Figure 3.10 shows a sample sequence diagram explaining the operations when the after returning advice execution terminates normally. Moreover, if this advice decides to discontinue the interceptor's execution and not return the value to the client then it can throw some exception. Figure 3.11 shows a sample sequence diagram explaining the operations when the after returning advice execution terminates abnormally by throwing exception.

> **Note:** The after returning advice can access the return value of the invoked method on a target object but it cannot change the return value.

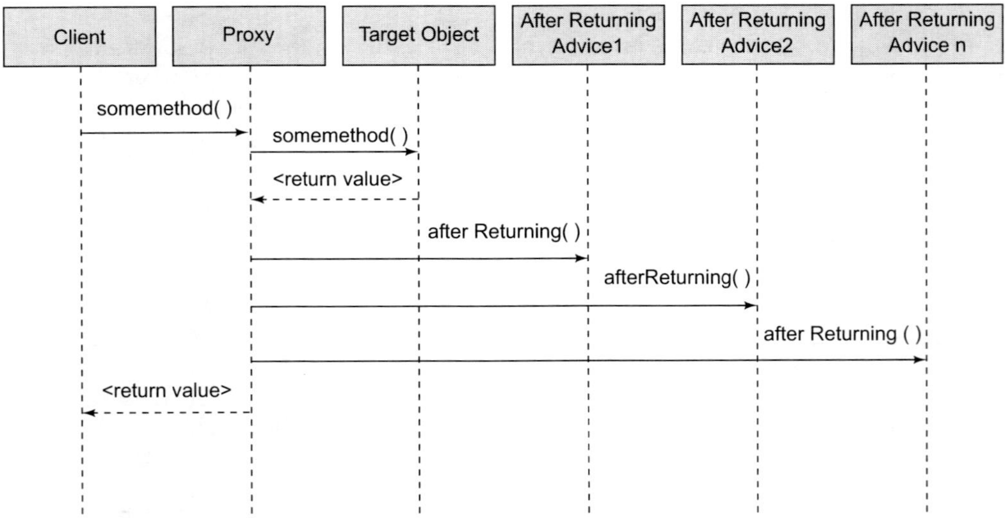

FIGURE 3.10 Sequence diagram for after returning advice.

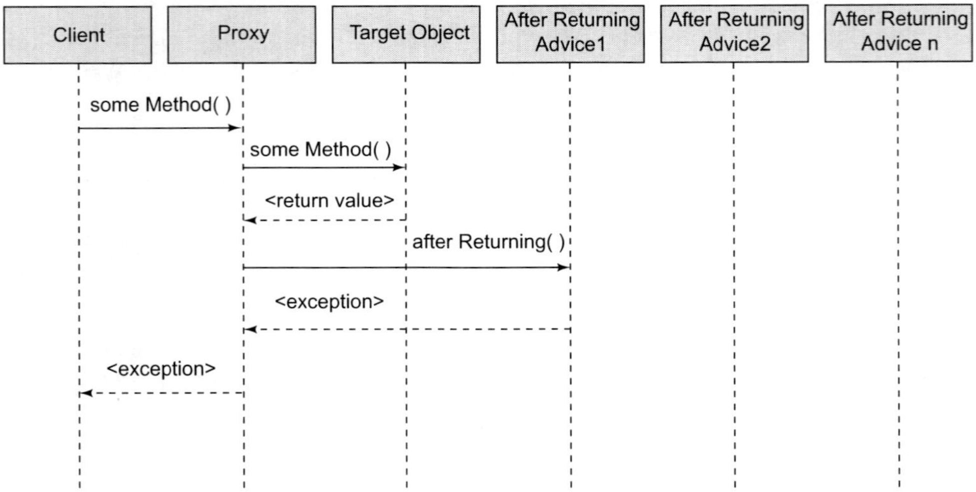

FIGURE 3.11 Sequence diagram for after returning advice when advice throws an exception

As shown in Fig. 3.11, in a case where the after returning advice throws an exception then an exception is thrown to the client without continuing further the interceptor's execution. As described in code snippet ?the afterReturning() method's throws clause is defined with throws Throwable, which allows it to throw any type of exception including error which is the same as in the case of before() of before advice. But as discussed, the target method (implemented by proxy) may not be designed in a way that would allow the throwing of Throwable types. Thus proxy takes the responsibility of converting the exception thrown by the advice as shown in Fig. 3.4. That is, if the exception thrown is of type java.lang.RuntimeException or the exception type on the signature of the invoked method then the same exception is thrown to the client. If not, then the exception is wrapped in an unchecked exception java.lang.reflect.UndeclaredThrowableException and thrown to the client.

3.4.3 Working with After Returning Advice

In this section we will design a simple example that demonstrates how to develop and configure after returning advice. The following list shows a simple plain java class named MyBusinessObject with one method businessService1() encapsulating a simple test logic returning three different possible string values for different inputs.

List 3.10: MyBusinessObject.java

```
package com.santosh.spring;

public class MyBusinessObject {

   public String businessService1(int id) throws MyException {
         System.out.println("In businessService1");

         /* Simple test logic to test the proxy behavior
         with respective to exception handling */

         if (id==0){
               System.out.println(" returning Test1...");
               return "Test1";
         }
         else if (id==1){
                 System.out.println(" returning Test2...");
                 return "Test2";
         }
         else {
           System.out.println(" returning Hello...");
           return "Hello from businessService1";
         }
    }
}
```

Now, List 3.11 shows the after returning advice implementation.

List 3.11: MyAfterReturningAdvice.java

```
package com.santosh.spring;

import org.springframework.aop.*;
import java.lang.reflect.*;
```

```
public class MyAfterReturningAdvice implements AfterReturningAdvice {

        public void afterReturning (
                        Object return_value, Method m,
                        Object[] args, Object target) throws Throwable {

            System.out.println("In MyAfterReturningAdvice for : "+ m.getName());
            System.out.println("Accessing return value...");
            if (return_value.equals("Test1")) {
                  System.out.println("Return value found Test1");
                  System.out.println("advice throwing MyException....");
                  throw new MyException("MyException from After Returning Advice");
            }
            if (return_value.equals("Test2")) {
                  System.out.println("Return value found Test1");
                  System.out.println("advice throwing Exception....");
                  throw new Exception("Exception from After Returning Advice");
            }
            System.out.println("Return value found "+return_value);
            System.out.println("advice ending without throwing exception....");

        }
}//class
```

After writing the business object and the advice now it is time to configure the proxy. List 3.12 shows the spring XML configuration file for this example.

List 3.12: mybeans.xml

```
<beans xmlns="http://www.springframework.org/schema/beans"
xmlns:xsi="http://www.w3.org/2001/XMLSchema-instance"
xsi:schemaLocation="http://www.springframework.org/schema/beans
http://www.springframework.org/schema/beans/spring-beans-2.0.xsd">

        <bean id="myser" class="com.santosh.spring.MyBusinessObject"/>
        <bean id="afterReturning"
              class="com.santosh.spring.MyAfterReturningAdvice"/>

        <bean id="myServices"
        class="org.springframework.aop.framework.ProxyFactoryBean">
            <property name="targetName" value="myser"/>
            <property name="interceptorNames">
                <list>
                      <value>afterReturning</value>
                </list>
            </property>
        </bean>
</beans>
```

To test this configuration for its workability we want to write a simple test case. List 3.13 shows the MyBusinessObjectTestCase.

List 3.13: MyBusinessObjectTestCase.java

```
import org.springframework.beans.factory.*;
import org.springframework.beans.factory.xml.*;
import org.springframework.core.io.*;

import com.santosh.spring.MyBusinessObject;
import com.santosh.spring.MyException;

public class MyBusinessObjectTestCase {

  public static void main(String s[]) throws Exception {

    BeanFactory beans=new XmlBeanFactory( new FileSystemResource("mybeans.xml"));

    MyBusinessObject bo=(MyBusinessObject) beans.getBean("myServices");

    System.out.println("Testing Normal flow...");

        System.out.println(bo.businessService1(2));
        System.out.println("\n");

        try{
        System.out.println("Testing flow when MyException is thrown by advice...");
              System.out.println(bo.businessService1(0));
        }
        catch(MyException e){
              System.out.println(e);
        }

        System.out.println("\n");
        try{
          System.out.println("Testing flow when Exception is thrown by advice...");

            System.out.println(bo.businessService1(1));
        }
        catch(Exception e){
              System.out.println(e);
        }
    }//main
}//class
```

After writing all the files related to this example from List 3.10 to 3.13 and 3.3 for MyException it is time to compile and execute an example. After compiling the java files using javac, you will find the files as shown in Fig. 3.12.

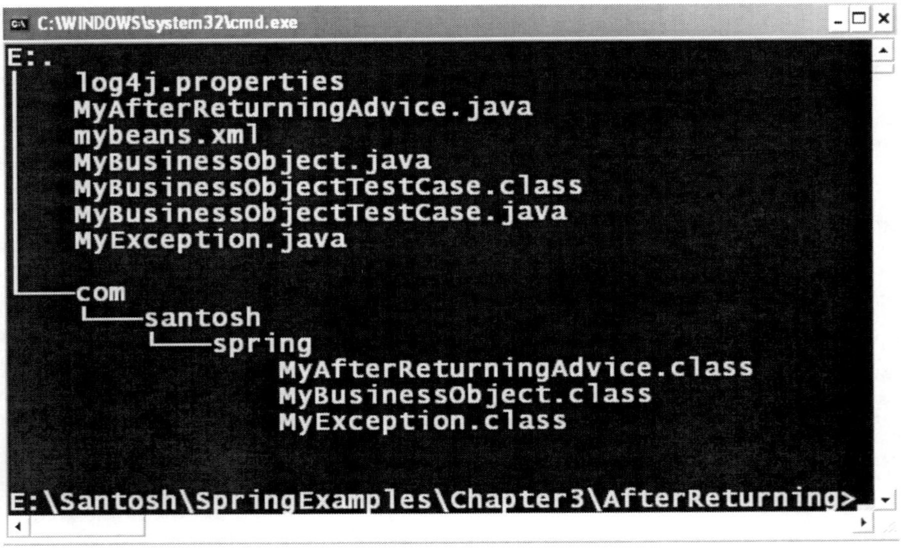

FIGURE 3.12 Tree structure showing the files of AfterReturning example

Now, execute the MyBusinessObjectTestCase to find the sample in action. Note that to execute this example we need to set CGLIB jar file into classpath in addition to the jar files configured to run the first example in this chapter.

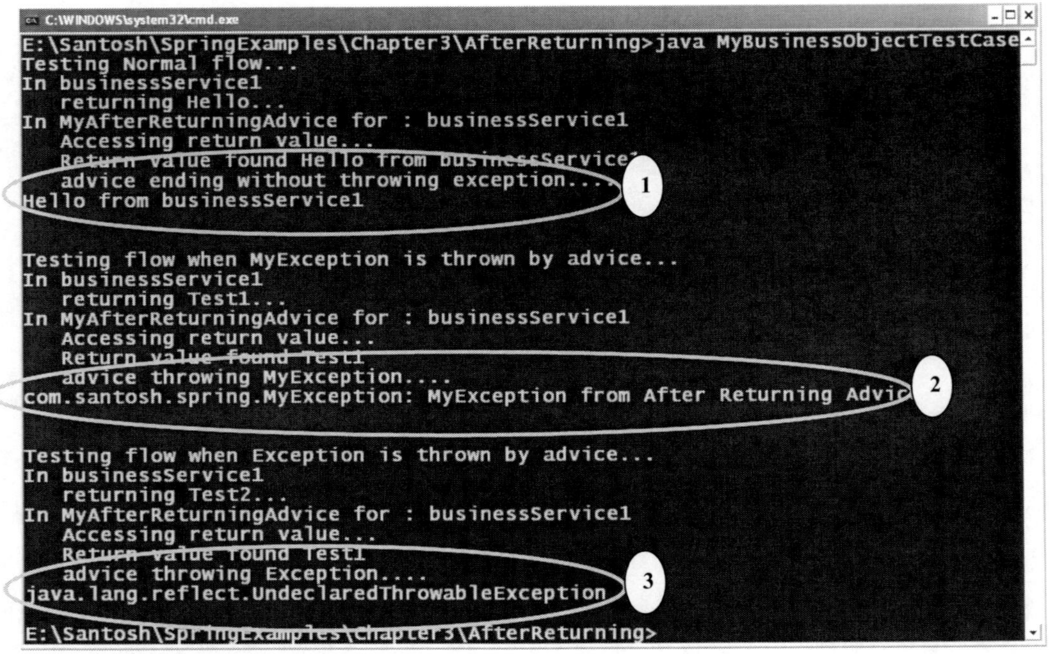

FIGURE 3.13 Output of MyBusinessObjectTestCase

Figure 3.13 shows the output of the MyBusinessObjectTestCase execution. The following points can be observed from the output.

1. When the afterReturning() method of MyAfterReturningAdvice is ended without throwing any exception then the client was returned with the value that has resulted by the businessService1() method of MyBusinessObject. You can find this output within circle **1** in Fig. 3.13.
2. When the afterReturning() method of MyAfterReturningAdvice is throwing MyException, which is in the exception type on the signature of the businessService1() method, the proxy method has thrown the same exception to the client. You can find this output within circle **2** in Fig. 3.13.
3. When the afterReturning() method of MyAfterReturningAdvice is throwing exception which is not in the exception type on the signature of the businessService1() method. It is not an unchecked exception even, thus as per our discussion the proxy wraps this exception in UndeclaredThrowableException and throws to the client. You can find this output within circle **3** in Fig. 3.13.

3.4.4 Throws Advice

The throws advice is the advice that executes after the joinpoints invocation completes with an abnormal termination (that is, if the method invoked throws any exception). This advice has to be a subtype of *org.springframework.aop.ThrowsAdvice* interface. The *org.springframework.aop.Throws Advice* interface is a marker interface and does not declare any methods. This type of advice should implement one or more methods with the following method signatures.

```
public void afterThrowing(Method m, Object args[], Object target, <any sub type of Throwable> t)
throws Throwable

public void afterThrowing(<any sub type of Throwable> t) throws Throwable
```

The afterThrowing() method can encapsulate the exception handling logic like in an instance when an SQLException is thrown we want to prepare a relevant message and send an email to the administrator. This advice allows us to separate exception handling from the business and presentation logics or in simple primary logics.

As described earlier, the ThrowsAdvice is a marker interface and has no method declarations. This is done to allow us to write the exception handling logic (advice) in a fine grained mode. The following Code snippet ? shows the samples of afterThrowing method signatures.

Code Snippet

```
public void afterThrowing(SQLException se) throws Throwable{
        ...
        //Logic that handles the SQLException
}
public void afterThrowing(MyException me) throws Throwable{
        ...
        //Logic that handles the MyException
```

```
}
public void afterThrowing(Method m, Object args[], Object target, IOException e)
throws Throwable{
       '...
       //Logic that handles the IOException with the Method, its arguments and the
target object
}
```

As per the methods shown in code snippet if the invoked method on target object throws SQLException then proxy invokes afterThrowing() method with SQLException argument, if the target method throws MyException then it invokes afterThrowing() method with MyException argument, and if target method throws IOException it invokes the four argument method with IOException as the fourth argument. In order to demonstrate this we are allowed to have afterThrowing() method with single and four arguments. We have defined the afterThrowing() method with four arguments for IOException. We can also use a single argument.

> **Note:** If afterThrowing method is overloaded for the same exception type then the afterThrowing method with single argument is invoked instead of the four arguments method. Example: if our advice has two methods as shown in code snippet then for SQLException proxy invokes the first method (that is, with a single argument).

Code Snippet

```
public void afterThrowing(SQLException se) throws Throwable{
...
//Logic that handles the SQLException
}
public void afterThrowing(Method m, Object args[], Object target, SQLException e)
throws Throwable{
...
//Logic that handles the SQLException with the Method, its arguments and the target
object
}
```

Figure 3.14 shows the sequence diagram for throws advice, as shown in the sequence diagram. When the target object throws an exception then the appropriate afterThrowing() method is invoked on the configured throws advice. And after the throws advice handles the exception, the same exception is then thrown to the client. It is important to remember the following two points while working with throws advice.

- The throws advice can listen for the exceptions thrown by the method invoked on the target object but not the exceptions thrown by the advices configured for the target object.
- The throws advice can handle the exception but it cannot stop the exception throwing to the client. But it can change the exception being thrown to the client, as if afterThrowing() method throws an exception then proxy performs the operations as described in Fig. 3.3.

Now, it is time to look at one example to throw more light on this topic.

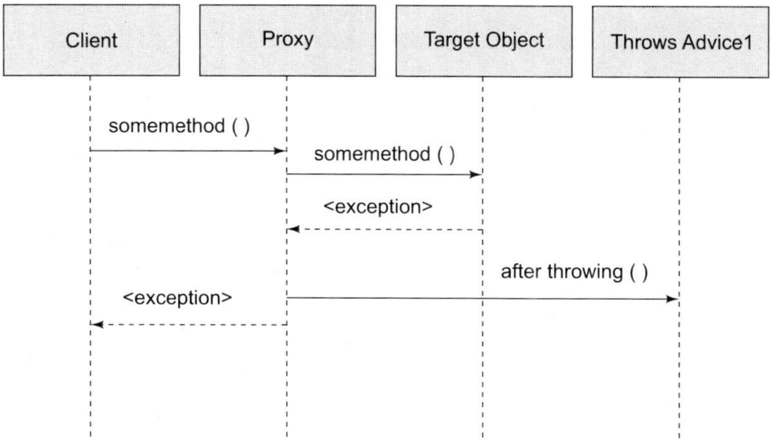

FIGURE 3.14 Sequence diagram for throws advice.

3.4.4.1 Working with throws advice

In this section we will design a simple example that demonstrates how to develop and configure throws advice. List 3.14 shows a simple plain java class named MyBusinessObject with one method businessService2() encapsulating a simple test logic throwing either MyException1 or MyException2 exceptions for different inputs.

List 3.14: MyBusinessObject.java

```
package com.santosh.spring;

public class MyBusinessObject {

      public void businessService2(int id) throws MyException1, MyException2 {
            System.out.println("In businessService2");

            if (id==0){
                  System.out.println(" throwing MyException1...");
                  throw new MyException1("MyException1 from MyBusinessObject");
            }
            else if (id==1){
                    System.out.println(" throwing MyException2...");
                    throw new MyException2("MyException2 from MyBusinessObject");
            }
            System.out.println(" ending without throwing any exception...");
      }
}
```

List 3.15 shows MyException1 which is a subtype of java.lang.Exception.

List 3.15: MyException1.java

```
package com.santosh.spring;

public class MyException1 extends Exception {
     public MyException1(){}
     public MyException1(String message){
          super(message);
     }
}
```

List 3.16 shows MyException2 which is a subtype of java.lang.Exception.

List 3.16: MyException2.java

```
package com.santosh.spring;

public class MyException2 extends Exception {
       public MyException2(){}
       public MyException2(String message){
              super(message);
       }
}
```

List 3.17 shows the throws advice implementation for this example. This advice is designed with two method—one to handle MyException1 and its subtypes exceptions and the other to handle MyException2 and its subtypes exceptions.

List 3.17: MyThrowsAdvice.java

```
package com.santosh.spring;

import org.springframework.aop.*;
import java.lang.reflect.*;

public class MyThrowsAdvice implements ThrowsAdvice {

       public void afterThrowing (MyException1 me) throws Throwable {
            //Exception handling logic as per our system requirement
            //Test Logic
            System.out.println("In afterThrowing(MyException1)");
       }
       public void afterThrowing (MyException2 me) throws Throwable {

            //Exception handling logic as per our system requirement
            //Test Logic
            System.out.println("In afterThrowing(MyException2)");
       }
}//class
```

Now let us configure the proxy for MyBusinessObject with one advice that is MyThrowsAdvice. List 3.18 shows the spring XML configureation file for this example.

List 3.18: mybeans.xml

```
<beans xmlns="http://www.springframework.org/schema/beans"
xmlns:xsi="http://www.w3.org/2001/XMLSchema-instance"
xsi:schemaLocation="http://www.springframework.org/schema/beans
http://www.springframework.org/schema/beans/spring-beans-2.0.xsd">

    <bean id="myser" class="com.santosh.spring.MyBusinessObject"/>
    <bean id="exceptionHandler"
                    class="com.santosh.spring.MyThrowsAdvice"/>

    <bean id="myServices"
    class="org.springframework.aop.framework.ProxyFactoryBean">
          <property name="targetName" value="myser"/>
          <property name="interceptorNames">
              <list>
                  <value>exceptionHandler</value>
              </list>
        </property>
    </bean>
</beans>
```

To get this configuration to work we want to write a simple test case for MyBusinessObject. List 3.19 shows the MyBusinessObjectTestCase.

List 3.19: MyBusinessObjectTestCase.java

```
import org.springframework.beans.factory.*;
import org.springframework.beans.factory.xml.*;
import org.springframework.core.io.*;

import com.santosh.spring.MyBusinessObject;
import com.santosh.spring.MyException1;
import com.santosh.spring.MyException2;

public class MyBusinessObjectTestCase {

public static void main(String s[]) throws Exception {

BeanFactory beans=new XmlBeanFactory( new FileSystemResource("mybeans.xml"));

MyBusinessObject bo=(MyBusinessObject) beans.getBean("myServices");
```

```
        try{
                System.out.println("\nTesting flow when MyException1 is thrown by
businessService2 ()...");
                bo.businessService2(0);
        }
        catch(MyException1 e){
                System.out.println(e);
        }

        System.out.println("\n");

    try{
                System.out.println("Testing flow when MyException2 is thrown by
businessService2 ()...");
              bo.businessService2(1);
    }
    catch(MyException2 e){
          System.out.println(e);
    }
    System.out.println("\n");
    System.out.println("Testing flow when there no exception thrown by
businessService2()...");
    bo.businessService2(2);
  }//main
}//class
```

After writing all the files under this example as shown under Lists 3.14 through 3.19, by compiling the files it will find the files as shown in Fig. 3.15.

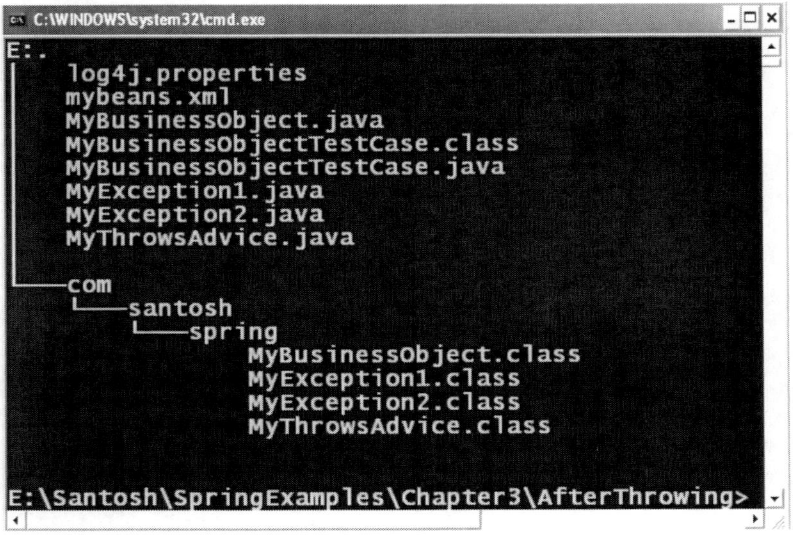

FIGURE 3.15 Tree structure showing the files of AfterThrowing example

Note that the log4j.properties file used here does not have any important significance in this example. You can use the log4j.properties file shown under List 3.7 or simply configure log4j to turn off the logger.

Now, execute the MyBusinessObjectTestCase to see the sample in action. Figure 3.16 shows the output of the test case execution.

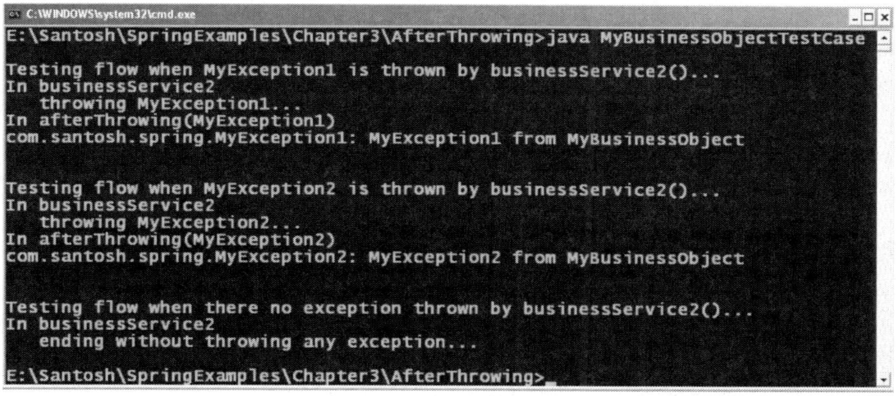

FIGURE 3.16 Output of MyBusinessObjectTestCase

The following points can be identified from the output shown in the preceding figure.

- When the businessService2() method has thrown MyException1 then the throws advice is applied by invoking the afterThrowing(MyException1) method.
- When the businessService2() method has thrown MyException2 then the throws advice is applied by invoking the afterThrowing(MyException2) method.
- When the businessService2() method has ended without throwing any exception then the throws advice is not applied.

3.4.5 Around Advice

The around advice is the advice that surrounds the joinpoint allowing us to perform operations before and after the execution of joinpoint. This is very useful if we want to share the state before and after the joinpoint execution in a thread-safe manner like starting the transaction before joinpoint execution and ending it after the joinpoint execution. The spring around advice is compliant with AOP Alliance that provides interpretability with other AOP Alliance compliant AOP implementations. This advice has to be a subtype of *org.aopalliance.intercept.MethodInterceptor* interface. The *org.aopalliance.intercept.MethodInterceptor* interface has only one method with the following signature.

```
public Object invoke(org.aopalliance.intercept.MethodInvocation) throws Throwable
```

The *org.aopalliance.intercept.MethodInvocation* allows us to get the details of the invoked method of the target object, method arguments, and Joinpoint. The MethodInvocation interface extends invocation, which is a subtype of joinpoint, the class diagram of which is shown in Fig. 3.17.

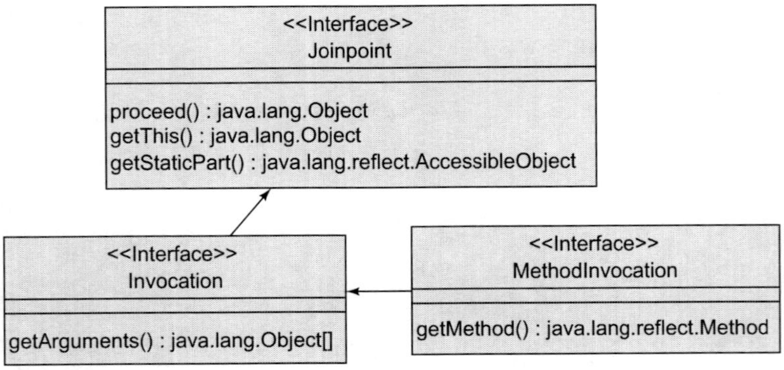

FIGURE 3.17 Class diagram of JoinPoint

The *invoke()* method implemented in around advice can call the *proceed()* method on the given MethodInvocation object. The code that has to execute before the joinpoint execution has to be written before calling *proceed ()* method and the code to execute after the joinpoint execution has to be written after the *proceed()* method invocation. In case, if we want to stop the proceeding of the interceptor chain then avoid *proceed()* method invocation.

Code Snippet

```
import org.aopalliance.intercept.*;
public class TransactionAdvice implements MethodInterceptor {

  public Object invoke(MethodInvocation mi) throws Throwable {
    //do all the pre preprocessing, like starting the TX
    System.out.println("In invoke, before executing method");
    Object o=mi.proceed();
    //do all the post processing, like end the TX
    System.out.println("In invoke, after the method execution");
    return o;
  }//invoke
}//class
```

The around advice allows us to implement before, after returning, and after throwing advices in a single method with some added features that are not supported with the respective individual advices discussed in the preceding sections. The around advice can provide the advice with additional support alternative to the individual advice types as described here.

1. The around advice allows us to apply the advice before the joinpoint execution, and at this point it allows us to decide to return (normal termination) to the client without delegating the request to the further interceptor chain and method on target object, which is not allowed with before advice. This can be done by returning the invoke() method without calling proceed().
2. The around advice allows us to apply the advice after the successful execution of the joinpoint, and at this point it allows us to change the return value, which is not allowed with after returning advice.

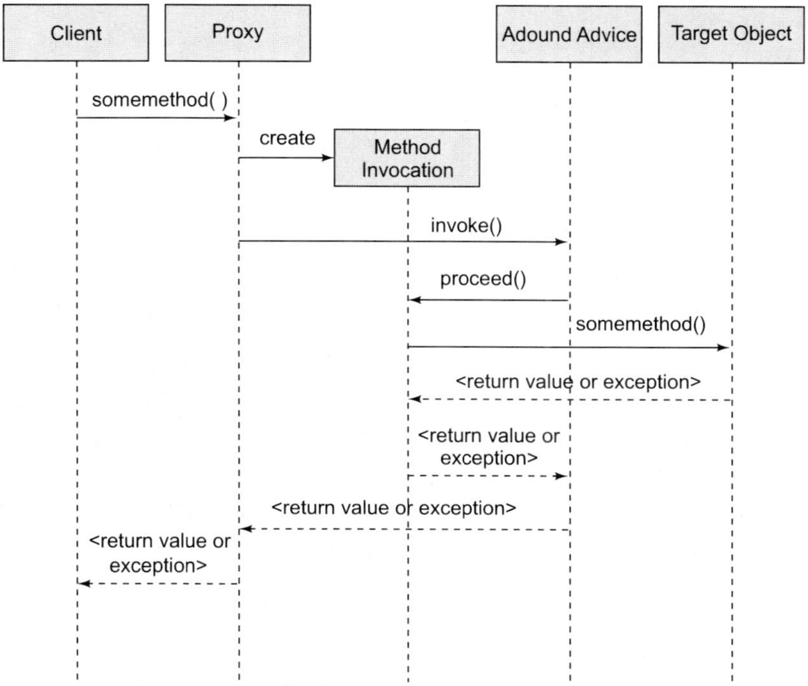

FIGURE 3.18 Sequence diagram for around advice

3. The throws advice allows us to apply the advice after the execution of the joinpoint if it throws an exception, and at this point it allows us to return some value to the client instead of throwing an exception, which is not allowed with throws advice. This can be done by enclosing the proceed() method invocation into a try-catch block and handling the exception in the catch block.

3.4.5.1 Working with around advice

In this section we will design a simple example that demonstrates how to develop and configure around advice. List 3.20 shows a simple plain java class named MyBusinessObject with one method businessService3() encapsulating a simple test logic throwing either MyException1 or MyException2 exceptions, or return a simple string for different inputs.

List 3.20: MyBusinessObject.java

```
package com.santosh.spring;

public class MyBusinessObject {

      public String businessService3(int id) throws MyException1, MyException2 {
          System.out.println("In businessService3");
```

```
            if (id==0){
                  System.out.println(" throwing MyException1...");
                  throw new MyException1("MyException1 from MyBusinessObject");
            }
            else if (id==1){
                System.out.println(" throwing MyException2...");
                throw new MyException2("MyException2 from MyBusinessObject");
            }
            else if (id==2){
                    System.out.println(" returning Test1...");
                    return "Test1";
            }
            else {
                    System.out.println(" returning Test2...");
                    return "Test2";
            }
      }
}
```

List 3.21 shows around advice implementation for this example.

List 3.21: MyAroundAdvice.java

```
package com.santosh.spring;

import org.aopalliance.intercept.*;

public class MyAroundAdvice implements MethodInterceptor {

  public Object invoke (MethodInvocation mi) throws Throwable {

    //All the pre processing (before advice)
    try{
      /*
        delegate the request to proceed executing the
        further interceptor chain and target method
      */
      System.out.println("In invoke() method before calling proceed()");

      Object o=mi.proceed();

      //after returning advice
      /*
      A simple test logic to demonstrate that around advice
      allows us to change the return value
      */
```

```
        if (o.equals("Test1")) {
          System.out.println("In   invoke()   method   after   executing   proceed()
successfully");
          System.out.println(" Return value from the target method is Test1, changing
return value...");
          return "Method returned Test1 but advice has changed the result";
        }
        System.out.println("In   invoke()   method   after   executing   proceed()
successfully");
        return o;
      }//try
      catch(MyException1 e){
        //after throwing advice
        System.out.println("In invoke() method, proceed() thrown MyException1");
        System.out.println(" Handling MyException1 and returning Hello...");
        return "Hello, there was an exception";
      }
    }
}//class
```

Now configure a proxy for the MyBusinessObject. List 3.22 shows the spring XML configuration file for this example.

List 3.22: mybeans.xml

```
<beans xmlns="http://www.springframework.org/schema/beans"
xmlns:xsi="http://www.w3.org/2001/XMLSchema-instance"
xsi:schemaLocation="http://www.springframework.org/schema/beans
http://www.springframework.org/schema/beans/spring-beans-2.0.xsd">

  <bean id="myser" class="com.santosh.spring.MyBusinessObject"/>
  <bean id="around" class="com.santosh.spring.MyAroundAdvice"/>

  <bean id="myServices"
  class="org.springframework.aop.framework.ProxyFactoryBean">
    <property name="targetName" value="myser"/>
    <property name="interceptorNames">
      <list>
        <value>around</value>
      </list>
    </property>
  </bean>
</beans>
```

List 3.23 shows the test case for MyBusinessObject.

List 3.23: MyBusinessObjectTestCase.java

```
import org.springframework.beans.factory.*;
import org.springframework.beans.factory.xml.*;
import org.springframework.core.io.*;

import com.santosh.spring.MyBusinessObject;
import com.santosh.spring.MyException1;
import com.santosh.spring.MyException2;

public class MyBusinessObjectTestCase {

  public static void main(String s[]) throws Exception {

    BeanFactory beans=new XmlBeanFactory( new FileSystemResource("mybeans.xml"));

    MyBusinessObject bo=(MyBusinessObject) beans.getBean("myServices");

    System.out.println("\nTesting flow when MyException1 is thrown by businessService
3()...");
    System.out.println(bo.businessService3(0));

    System.out.println("\n");

    try{
      System.out.println("Testing flow when MyException2 is thrown by businessService
3()...");
      System.out.println(bo.businessService3(1));
    }
    catch(MyException2 e){
      System.out.println(e);
    }
    System.out.println("\n");
    System.out.println("Testing flow when businessService3() returns Test1...");
    System.out.println(bo.businessService3(2));
    System.out.println("\n");
    System.out.println("Testing flow when businessService3() returns Test2...");
    System.out.println(bo.businessService3(3));
  }//main
}//class
```

After writing all the files of this example compile the java files to find the files as shown in Fig. 3.19.

The MyException1 and MyException2 used in this example are the same as in the previous example. The code for these two exception classes can be found under Lists 3.15 and 3.16 respectively. And the log4j.properties is as shown in List 3.7.

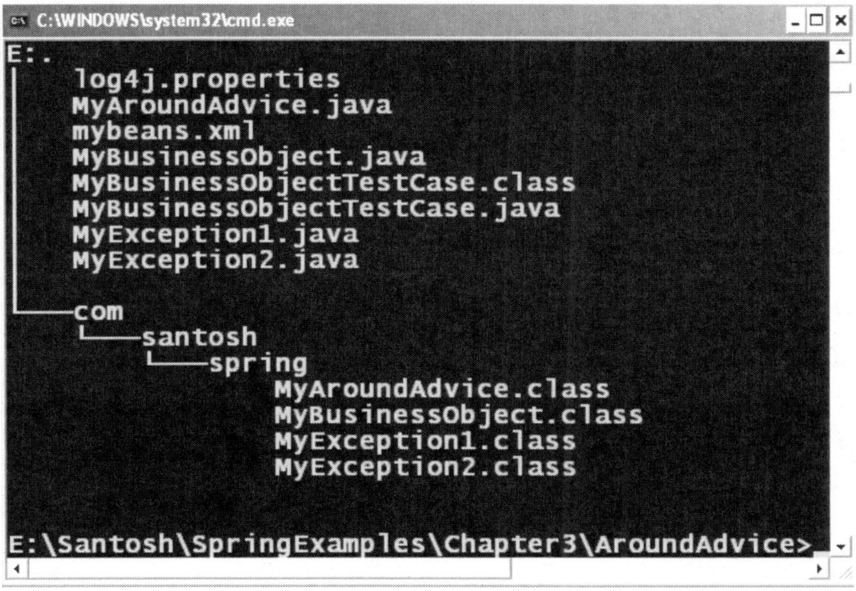

FIGURE 3.19 Tree structure showing files of AroundAdvice example

Now, execute MyBusinessObjectTestCase to find the example in action. The output of the test case execution is shown in Fig. 3.20.

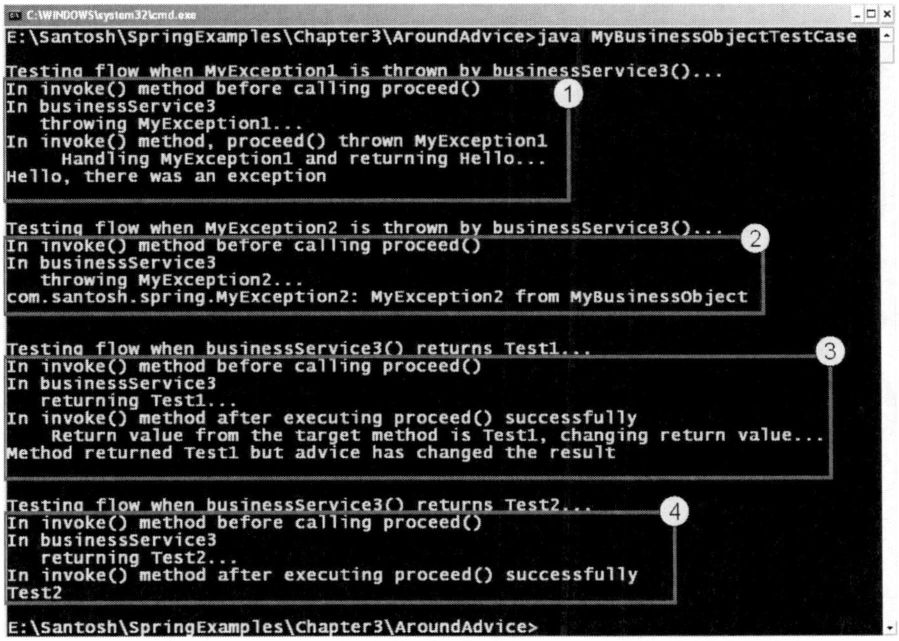

FIGURE 3.20 Output of MyBusinessObjectTestCase

The following important points can be observed from the output shown in the preceding figure.

1. When businessService3() method is throwing MyException1, around advice has handled the exception and returned a string ***'Hello, there was an exception'*** instead of throwing the exception to the client.
2. When businessService3() method is throwing MyException2, around advice is not handling the exception. Instead it is transmitted to the client.
3. As discussed earlier, the around advice is able to access the return value and change the value. Here in this case this is practically demonstrated. When businessService3() method is returning ***'Test1',*** the around advice has changed it to ***'Method returned Test1 but advice has changed the result'***.
4. In this case the businessService3() method is returning a value ***'Test2',*** which is not equals to *'Test1'* thus the around advice is just transmitting the return value to the client, without changing the return value.

Summary

In this chapter, we have learnt about the problems in using the OOP methodology for developing huge enterprise applications and how AOP solves the problem. We have also learnt about the support provided under Spring Framework to implement AOP applications. We have then moved on to learn about the low-level approach of Spring AOP. Thereafter we have learnt about the four advices (before, after returning, throws, and around advices), and worked with these advices using Spring 1.2 style programming. The following are the important points to recall from the discussions in this chapter.

- Aspect Oriented Programming (AOP) is a programming methodology that allows the developers to build the core concerns without making them aware of secondary requirements.
- The AOP methodology allows developers to implement the individual concerns in a loosely coupled fashion and weave them to build the final system.
- AOP framework is one of the key elements of Spring framework, which provides support for AOP-based application development.
- Spring AOP is a proxy-based framework implemented purely in Java.
- Spring AOP is developed based on AOP Alliance API, which enables us to easily integrate with other AOP implementations.
- Spring AOP supports only method interceptions and not field interceptions.
- The Spring Framework itself uses AOP to provide most of the infrastructure logics as declarative services.

In this chapter up to now in all the examples used to demonstrate the various advices, we have considered all the method invocations (join points) on the proxy object that wraps the target object as pointcut. But most of the times we want to apply the advices specific to some join points. The next chapter explains how to configure the pointcuts using Spring 1.2 style programming.

Working with Spring Pointcut and Advisors

4 CHAPTER

Objectives

In this chapter, we will cover:

- Spring pointcut and advisor API
- How to configure the various pointcuts and advisors using the Spring 1.2 style AOP programming

4.1 SPRING POINTCUT AND ADVISOR API

In case of Spring AOP the pointcuts are defined as objects. Thus it allows us to define custom pointcuts. Spring Pointcut API allows us to define a pointcut to apply an advice for a particular class and method (join point). The org.springframework.aop.Pointcut interface is the central part of the spring framework pointcut API. The Pointcut interface declares two methods—ClassFilter and MethodMatcher. The method signatures are as shown in the following code snippets.

Code Snippet

```
public ClassFilter getClassFilter()
public MethodMatcher get MethodMatcher()
```

This defines that each Pointcut object is associated with one ClassFilter and one MethodMatcher. The ClassFilter is used to match the target class and decide whether the advice attached with this pointcut is applicable to the given class or not. This interface includes only one method.

Code Snippet

```
public boolean matches(java.lang.Class targetClass)
```

The *matches()* method determines whether the pointcut is defined for the given class or not. If this returns true then the pointcut is defined for the given targetClass. Meaning this specifies whether the joinpoints of the given class can be a pointcut. Further the MethodMatcher determines whether the advice is to be applied for the given method of the targetClass and optionally with its arguments. The MethodMatcher interface declares three methods as shown below.

```
public interface MethodMatcher {
    public boolean isRuntime();
    public boolean matches(Method m, Class targetClass);
    public boolean matches(Method m, Class targetClass, Object[] arguments);
 }
```

The *isRuntime()* method is used to find whether the pointcut is static or dynamic. That is, if this pointcut takes method runtime argument values into consideration to determine the joinpoint as pointcut to apply advice or not. The static and dynamic pointcuts are explained in detail in the next section. If *isRuntime()* method returns 'false' then the *matches(Method, Class)* method is invoked to find whether the pointcut matches the given method. This is done while creating an AOP proxy instead for every method invocation. Since this does not take target method arguments into consideration it matches the given method forever. If *isRuntime()* method returns 'true' then the *matches(Method, Class, Object[])* method is invoked to find whether the pointcut matches the given method with the given target method arguments. This is done for every method invocation. Since this type of pointcut takes target method argument values into consideration thus it may not match the given method forever.

4.2 TYPES OF POINTCUTS

As described in the preceding section the spring pointcut API includes abstraction for defining two types of pointcuts:

1. Static Pointcut
2. Dynamic Pointcut

Let us discuss these two types of pointcuts in detail.

4.2.1 Static Pointcut

The Static pointcuts are evaluated only once while generating the proxy. Thus these pointcuts are known as static pointcut. The Static pointcut is used when an advice is to be always applied at specified joinpoint without considering the runtime target method arguments. That is, for this pointcut, runtime arguments are not necessary for finding whether the advice should be applied or not. The static pointcuts are more preferred than dynamic pointcuts since these are evaluated only once, that too at the time of creating the proxy. As the static pointcuts are not evaluated at each method invocation it gets free from the runtime overheads of finding the advice that has to be applied. The Spring AOP API includes a convenient class *org.springframework.aop.support.StaticMethodMatcherPointcut* for creating custom static pointcuts. Moreover, to meet the most general requirements A Spring AOP API includes built-in static pointcuts. The following subsections explain how to use built-in static pointcuts.

4.2.1.1 NameMatchMethodPointcut

The NameMatchMethodPointcut is the basic static pointcut, which matches by simple method name. This is useful if we want to define a joinpoint with simple method name matching where the methods are not overloaded and a fine-grained control is not required. Additionally, a wildcard character (*) can be used at the beginning or ending of the name to match all the methods ending with the given name or starting with the given name, respectively. For example, if we want to define a pointcut for a withdraw() method then the bean declaration of pointcut will be as shown in the following code snippet.

Code Snippet

```
<bean id="mypointcut"
class="org.springframework.aop.support.NameMatchMethodPointcut">
  <property name="mappedName">
    <value>withdraw</value>
  </property>
</bean>
```

Similarly, if we want to match all the get methods then the *mappedName* value can be *get**.

4.2.1.1.1 Working with NameMatchMethodPointcut

To demonstrate the working model of NameMatchMethodPointcut instead of writing a separate example we will modify our 'before advice' example configurations. To demonstrate the 'before advice' we have designed AccountServices, which includes withdraw and deposit services, where the logging advice was provided for both the methods. Now we will configure the application so that the logging advice is applied only for the withdraw method. For this we just need to change the spring XML configuration file (that is, mybeans.xml) as shown in List 4.1.

List 4.1: mybeans.xml

```
<beans xmlns="http://www.springframework.org/schema/beans"
xmlns:xsi="http://www.w3.org/2001/XMLSchema-instance"
xsi:schemaLocation="http://www.springframework.org/schema/beans
http://www.springframework.org/schema/beans/spring-beans-2.0.xsd">

  <bean id="accdao"
              class="com.santosh.spring.AccountDAOTestImpl"/>
  <bean id="accservices"
              class="com.santosh.spring.AccountServicesImpl">
    <constructor-arg>
      <ref local="accdao"/>
    </constructor-arg>
  </bean>
  <bean id="logging" class="com.santosh.spring.LoggingAdvice"/>

  <bean id="accountServices"
    class="org.springframework.aop.framework.ProxyFactoryBean">
    <property name="targetName">
      <value>accservices</value>
    </property>
    <property name="interceptorNames">
      <list>
        <value>loggingAdvisor</value>
      </list>
```

```
        </property>
    </bean>

    <bean id="loggingAdvisor"
    class="org.springframework.aop.support.DefaultPointcutAdvisor">
        <property name="advice">
            <ref local="logging"/>
        </property>
        <property name="pointcut">
            <ref local="mypointcut"/>
        </property>
    </bean>
    <bean id="mypointcut"
class="org.springframework.aop.support.NameMatchMethodPointcut">
        <property name="mappedName">
            <value>withdraw</value>
        </property>
    </bean>
</beans>
```

Use the other files as described under the section **working with before advice, that is,** as described under Lists 3.1 through 3.9 (except mybeans.xml of List 3.8) and arrange all the files as shown in Fig. 4.1.

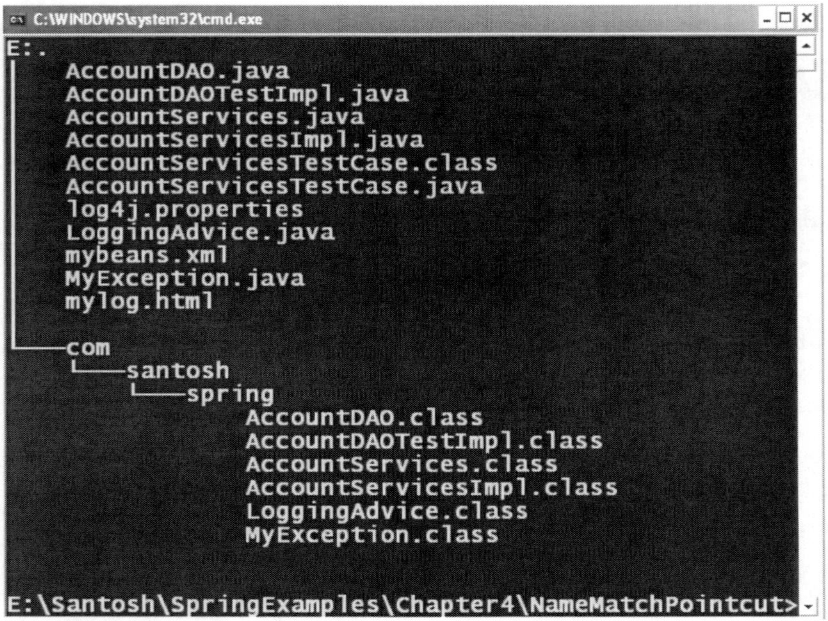

FIGURE 4.1 Tree structure showing files of NameMatchPointcut example

Now execute the AccountServicesTestCase. You will find the output as shown in Fig. 4.2.

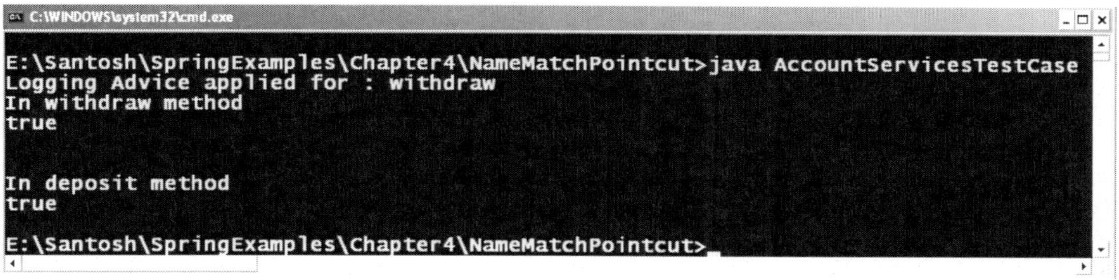

FIGURE 4.2 Output of AccountServicesTestCase

Observe the output—the logging advice is provided only for withdraw but not for the deposit method. Earlier, before configuring this pointcut the advice was provided for both the methods. The output can be found in Fig. 3.7.

The advisor encapsulates a pointcut definition and advice which helps the proxy in deciding whether an advice has to be applied for a joinpoint or not. In this example, we have configured the NameMatchMethodPointcut and then injected it into the DefaultPointcutAdvisor along with the advice. Alternatively, we can use the Spring AOP API provided utility advisor NameMatchMethod PointcutAdvisor to configure the same. The following code snippet shows the mybeans.xml which uses NameMatchMethodPointcutAdvisor to configure the pointcut and advisor equivalent to the configuration shown in List 4.1.

Code Snippet

```
<beans xmlns="http://www.springframework.org/schema/beans"
xmlns:xsi="http://www.w3.org/2001/XMLSchema-instance"
xsi:schemaLocation="http://www.springframework.org/schema/beans
http://www.springframework.org/schema/beans/spring-beans-2.0.xsd">

  <bean id="accdao"
      class="com.santosh.spring.AccountDAOTestImpl"/>
  <bean id="accservices"
      class="com.santosh.spring.AccountServicesImpl">
    <constructor-arg>
      <ref local="accdao"/>
    </constructor-arg>
  </bean>
  <bean id="logging" class="com.santosh.spring.LoggingAdvice"/>

  <bean id="accountServices"
      class="org.springframework.aop.framework.ProxyFactoryBean">
    <property name="targetName">
      <value>accservices</value>
    </property>
```

```
    <property name="interceptorNames">
      <list>
        <value>loggingAdvisor</value>
      </list>
    </property>
  </bean>

  <bean id="loggingAdvisor"
class="org.springframework.aop.support.NameMatchMethodPointcutAdvisor">
    <property name="advice">
      <ref local="logging"/>
    </property>
    <property name="mappedName">
      <value>withdraw</value>
    </property>
  </bean>
</beans>
```

In this sub-section you have learnt the NameMatchMethodPointcut that allows us to configure the pointcut to match with the given method name or pattern that can use * to match the method names. The following subsection describes another built-in static pointcut with more flexible option to define pointcut.

4.2.2 Regular Expression Method Pointcut

The NameMatchMethodPointcut discussed in the preceding subsection was comfortable to configure the pointcut definition based on the method name or pattern that can use * to match the method names. But the NameMatchMethodPointcut does not provide us fine-grained control to describe the method name patterns, and it does not support to handle overloaded methods. The regular expression method pointcut allows us to define pointcut using regular expression patterns. The *org.springframework.aop.support.AbstractRegexpMethodPointcut* is the abstract base regular expression pointcut class *JdkRegexpMethodPointcut* and *Perl5RegexpMethodPointcut* are the two subclasses of this pointcut. The *org.springframework.aop.support.JdkRegexpMethodPointcut* allows preparing the pattern using JDK regular expression syntax and *org.springframework.aop.support. Perl5RegexpMethodPointcut* allows preparing the pattern using Perl regular expression syntax. Here we will limit our discussion to the JDK regular expression.

Table 4.1 describes some important constructs of JDK regular-expression.

TABLE 4.1 Important constructs of JDK regular-expression

Construct	*Description*
\d	Matches a digit, that is characters 0-9. Equivalent to [0-9]
\D	Matches a non-digit character. Equivalent to [^0-9]
\s	Matches a white space character. White space includes tab, new line, and space.
a	Matches character 'a'.
.	Matches any character.
*	The preceding character can appear for zero or more times.
+	The preceding character can appear for one or more times.
?	The preceding character can appear for zero or one times.
{n}	The preceding character should appear exactly for n times
{n,m}	The preceding character should appear for at least n times and not more than m times.
\	escapes the successive character.
[abc]	Matches characters a, d, or c.
[^abc]	Matches any character except a, b, and c.
[a-z]	Matches any character a through z.
[a-d]	Matches any character a through d.
[a-z A-Z]	Matches any character a through z, or A through Z.
\n	Matches a new line character.

We can build patterns using the constructs as explained in Table 4.1. The following code snippet shows the configuration of the JdkRegexpMethodPointcut.

Code Snippet

```
<bean id="mypointcut"
class="org.springframework.aop.support.JdkRegexpMethodPointcut">
  <property name="pattern">
    <value>.*get.*</value>
  </property>
</bean>
```

The preceding code snippet shows the configuration that matches all the getter methods. Apart from configuring a single pattern JdkRegexpMethodPointcut allows us to configure multiple patterns. The following code snippet shows the configuration of multiple patterns.

Code Snippet

```
<bean id="mypointcut"
class="org.springframework.aop.support.JdkRegexpMethodPointcut">
  <property name="patterns">
    <list>
      <value>.*get.*</value>
      <value>.*set.*</value>
    </list>
  </property>
</bean>
```

As done with the NameMatchMethodPointcut we need to inject the pointcut into the advisor along with advice, which can be added into the interceptor list.

4.2.3 Dynamic Pointcuts

The dynamic pointcuts are evaluated once while generating the proxy and further for each of the request for final evaluation. Thus these pointcuts are known as dynamic pointcuts. The dynamic pointcut is used for advice that has to be decided to apply at joinpoint after considering the runtime target method arguments. Dynamic pointcut evaluates for every method invocation and the result cannot be cached since this takes the target method arguments into consideration. This makes dynamic pointcuts costlier than static pointcuts. Thus static pointcuts are more preferred than dynamic pointcuts. To meet the most general requirements Spring AOP API includes built-in dynamic pointcuts. The following sections explain how to use built-in dynamic pointcuts.

4.2.3.1 Control Flow Pointcut

The Control flow pointcut allows us to define a method pointcut that applies advice only when a method is invoked from a specific class or a specific method in a class. For example, the advice is applied only when *withdraw()* method is invoked from *WithdrawService* class, and not applicable when called from any other class like *TransferAmountService* etc.
The following code snippet shows the configuration of ControlFlowPointcut.

Code Snippet

```
<bean id="mypointcut"
      class="org.springframework.aop.support.ControlFlowPointcut">
   <constructor-arg>
      <value>com.santosh.spring.WithdrawService</value>
   </ constructor-arg>
</bean>
```

> **Note:** Apart from the built-in classes, we can even define custom pointcuts since spring pointcuts are defined as classes instead of language constructs. To define a custom pointcut we can implement *Pointcut* interface along with *ClassFilter* and *MethodMatcher* or extend any existing implementations.

Summary

In this chapter you have learnt the Spring 1.2 low-level approach of creating pointcuts. With this we will end the discussion on the Spring 1.2 low-level approach of programming AOP applications. As discussed earlier, Spring Framework 2.0 includes support for two new high-level approach of AOP support—Schema-based and @AspectJ style. Let us learn these simple and useful approaches of programming Spring AOP applications. The next chapter discusses Schema-based and @AspectJ style approaches.

Understanding Spring 2.0 AOP Support

5

CHAPTER

Objectives

In this chapter we will cover:

- Support for high-level approaches of AOP
- Schema-based approach
- @AspectJ style approach

5.1 SCHEMA-BASED AOP SUPPORT

The XML Schema-based approach of defining aspects is the new feature in Spring 2.0 framework. This approach defines the aspects using the 'aop' namespace elements in the Spring XML beans configuration file. This allows us to use to define the pointcuts using the expressions supported with the AspectJ designators. The Schema-based approach of defining the aspects provides the following benefits:

1. We can continue with J2SE 1.4 standards.
2. The advices can be designed completely free from the spring or any other framework API.
3. Any existing class and any method of it can be defined as an advice.

In this case, we need to refer to the XML Schema definition of spring beans configuration file instead of DTD. The following code snippet shows the namespace declarations in the spring beans XML configuration file.

Code Snippet

```
<beans  xmlns="http://www.springframework.org/schema/beans"
xmlns:xsi="http://www.w3.org/2001/XMLSchema-instance"
xsi:schemaLocation="http://www.springframework.org/schema/beans
http://www.springframework.org/schema/beans/spring-beans-2.0.xsd
http://www.springframework.org/schema/aop
http://www.springframework.org/schema/aop/spring-aop-2.0.xsd"
xmlns:aop="http://www.springframework.org/schema/aop">
```

In order to use this approach all we need is to learn the new tags defined under the AOP namespace and the AspectJ designators to build the pointcut expressions. The new 'aop' namespace tags includes the tags to define the aspect, pointcut, advice, and advisor, where all these tags need to be enclosed into the <aop:config> element. This means that the <aop:config> element is the top most element which allows all the AOP declarations. The following sections explain all these elements with relevant examples, starting with pointcut.

> **Note:** In the following sections we will concentrate on the schema-based syntax of defining the pointcut and advice, etc., instead of once again discussing about what is pointcut, advice, or other details since all these are explained in the previous chapter.

5.2 DECLARING POINTCUT

In the Schema-based approach, pointcut is declared using <aop:pointcut> element in spring beans XML configuration file. This can be declared directly inside <aop:config> so that it is shared across multiple advisors and aspects. Alternatively, <aop:pointcut> can be declared inside <aop:aspect> which makes the pointcut available only for that aspect. The following code snippet shows the syntax of the pointcut element.

Code Snippet

```
<aop:pointcut attributes/>
```

The attributes of <aop:pointcut> element are:

Attribute Name	*Description*
id	Holds the unique identifier for a pointcut
expression	Takes the pointcut expression of the specified type
type	Specifies the type of pointcut expression, allowable values are **aspectj** and **regex**

The syntax to build the expression of regex type is the same as used in case of regular expression pointcut learnt in section 4.2.2 of the previous chapter. To build aspectj type of expressions we can use the designators defined under AspectJ 5.

> **Note:** Not all the pointcut designators given under the AspectJ are supported by spring. The designators that are supported by spring are as follows:

1. **execution**
   The execution designator is used for matching method execution joinpoints that is used to match the method joinpoint considering its modifier, return type, declaring type, method name, argument types, and throws clause. The following code snippet shows the syntax of *execution* designator.

Code Snippet

```
execution(modifiers-pattern? return-type-pattern declaring-type-pattern? name-
pattern(param-pattern) throws-pattern?)
```

- **modifiers-pattern**: This part in execution designator is optional, if used this specifies what the modifiers of the method must be. For example, *public* specifies that the method should be public.

- **return-type-pattern:** This part of execution designator mandatory to specify, this determines what the methods return type should be. Using * (wildcard character) in return-type-pattern matches the methods with any return type.
- **declaring-type-pattern**: This part in execution designator is optional and specifies where the method is supposed to be declared.
- **name-pattern**: This matches the method name. We can use * (wildcard character) as all or part of the name pattern.
- **param-pattern:** This part of the execution designator determines what the method arguments should be, empty braces after name-pattern. That is, () matches a method that takes no-arguments, (*) matches a method with one argument of any type, (*, int) matches a method with two arguments where the first can be of any type and second should be int, (..) matches a method with any number of arguments.
- **throws-pattern:** This part in execution designator is optional. If used this specifies what the throws clause of the method must be.

The following are some of the examples for *execution* designator:
a. execution(public * com.santosh.spring.AccountServices.withdraw(..))
The above declaration matches public, withdraw methods declared in AccountServices

b. execution(public * withdraw(..))
The above declaration matches public, withdraw methods declared in any class

c. execution(public * com.santosh.spring.* *(..))
The above declaration matches all the public methods declared in any type packaged into com.santosh.spring package.

2. **within**
The *within* designator is used for matching all method joinpoints within the types that matches the specified type-pattern. The following code snippet shows the syntax of the *witthin* designator.

Code Snippet

```
within(type-pattern)
```

The **type-pattern** in the *within* designator specifies the pattern that matches the types whose each joinpoint has to be captured.

The following are some of the examples for the *within* designator:
a. within(com.santosh.spring.MyServices)
The above declaration matches all the joinpoints in com.santosh.spring.MyServices type

b. within(com.santosh.spring.MyServices+)
The above declaration matches all the joinpoints in com.santosh.spring.MyServices and its subtypes.

3. **this**

   The *this* designator is used for matching all method joinpoints that have a *this* (in java language *this* is a keyword) object associated with them that is of specified type. That is matches all the method invocations from the specified type. The following snippet shows the syntax of *this* designator.

Code Snippet

```
this(type)
```

The following is the example for *this* designator:

a. this(com.santosh.spring.MyServices)

The above declaration matches all the method invocations done from com.santosh.spring. MyServices type

> **Note:** The argument of *this()* cannot take * (or) .. (or) + wildcard characters.

4. **target**

   The *target* designator is used for matching all method joinpoints that are invoked on the object associated with them that is of a specified type. The following code snippet shows the syntax of *target* designator

Code Snippet

```
target(type)
```

The following is the example for *target* designator:

a. target(com.santosh.spring.MyServices)

The above declaration matches all the method invocations done on com.santosh.spring.My Services type or its subtype objects.

> **Note:** The argument of *target()* cannot take * (or) .. (or) + wildcard characters.

5. **args**

   The *args* designator is used to match all method joinpoints based on the argument types of the method joinpoint. The following code snippet shows the syntax of the *target* designator.

Code Snippet

```
args(param-pattern)
```

Where the **param-pattern** in the *args* designator determines what the method arguments should be.

The **args()** matches a method that takes no-arguments.

The **args(*)** matches a method with one argument of any type.

The **args(*, int)** matches a method with two arguments where the first can be of any type and second should be int.

The **args(..)** matches a method with any number of arguments.

The following are some of the examples for the *args* designator:

a. args(*, String)

The above declaration matches methods with two arguments where the first can be of any type and the second should be String.

b. args(.. , String)

The above declaration matches methods with any number of arguments but the last argument should be String.

Now, as we have discussed all the aspectj designators that are supported by Spring AOP, it is time to look at some examples that show the pointcut definitions. The following code snippet shows some sample pointcut declarations in the spring beans XML configuration file.

Code Snippet

```
<!–Pointcut that matches all the setter method of com.santosh.spring.MyServices type
that takes only one argument of any type -->
<aop:pointcut id="matchMySrvicesSetter" type="aspectj" expression=" execution(public
* com.santosh.spring.MyServices.set*(*))"/>

<!–Pointcut that matches all the methods of com.santosh.spring.MyServices type -->
<aop:pointcut id="matchMySrvices" type="aspectj" expression=" within(com.santosh.
spring.MyServices)"/>

<!–Pointcut that matches all the method of any type that takes only one 'int' argument
-->
<aop:pointcut id="matchAllIntArgs" type="aspectj" expression=" args(int)"/>
```

5.3 DECLARING ASPECT

In the schema-based approach aspect is declared using <aop:aspect> element in spring beans configuration file. This is declared directly inside the <aop:config> element. The following code snippet shows the syntax of the aspect element.

Code Snippet

```
<aop:aspect attributes> [body content] </aop:aspect>
```

The attributes of the <aop:aspect> element are:

Attribute Name	*Description*
id	Holds the unique identifier for an aspect.
ref	Takes the name of the bean that encapsulates the aspect.
order	This is an optional attribute. If used it specifies the order of the execution of this aspect when multiple advice executes at a specific joinpoint.

The body content of <aop:aspect> element allows zero or more child tags listed below in any combination

- <aop:pointcut>
- <aop:before>
- <aop:after>
- <aop:after-returning>
- <aop:after-throwing> and
- <aop:around>

5.4 DECLARING ADVICES

The Schema-based approach allows us to define five types of advices listed below.

1. Before Advice
2. After Returning Advice
3. After Throwing Advice
4. After Advice
5. Around Advice

Let us discuss all these advice declarations as supported by the Schema-based approach.

5.5 BEFORE ADVICE

As discussed earlier the before advice executes before the joinpoint execution. The following code snippet shows the syntax of aop before element that is used to declare before advice in Schema-based approach.

Code Snippet

```
<aop:before attributes/>
```

The attributes of <aop:before> element are:

Attribute Name	*Description*
pointcut	Takes the pointcut expression of aspectj type. The designators are explained under Section 5.2.
pointcut-ref	Takes the name of an associated pointcut definition, that is, the id of the pointcut defined using <aop:pointcut> element as described under Section 5.2.
method	Takes the name of the method that has to be invoked before the target method invocation, that is, the method that defines the logic of the advice.
arg-names	Takes the comma-separated list of advice methods argument names that will be matched from pointcut parameters.

Now, as we have learnt about the before advice, pointcut, and aspect syntaxes in the preceding sections, it is time to workout one simple example that will throw more light on the discussion.

5.5.1 Working with Schema-based Approach before Advice

In this example we will configure a logging advice as a before advice to the MyBusinessServices method invocations. List 5.1 shows the MyBusinessServices.java.

List 5.1: MyBusinessServices.java

```
package com.santosh.spring;

public class MyBusinessObject {

        public void businessService1() {
           System.out.println("In businessService1");
        }
}
```

List 5.2 shows the simple aspect class that includes a logging advice.

List 5.2: Logging.java

```
package com.santosh.spring;

public class Logging {

        public void log () {
           System.out.println("In log method of Logging");
        }//log
}//class
```

In the preceding list it can be observed that the logging class is independent of spring API compared to the before advice which we have written in the case of Spring 1.2 style of defining before advice (refer to List 3.6). Now we need to configure the aspect. List 5.3 shows the Spring beans XML configuration file which includes Schema-based aspect definitions.

List 5.3: mybeans.xml

```
<beans xmlns="http://www.springframework.org/schema/beans"
xmlns:xsi="http://www.w3.org/2001/XMLSchema-instance"
xsi:schemaLocation="http://www.springframework.org/schema/beans
http://www.springframework.org/schema/beans/spring-beans-2.0.xsd
http://www.springframework.org/schema/aop http://www.springframework.org/schema/aop/
spring-aop-2.0.xsd"
xmlns:aop="http://www.springframework.org/schema/aop">

     <bean id="myServices"
           class="com.santosh.spring.MyBusinessObject"/>
     <bean id="logging" class="com.santosh.spring.Logging"/>

     <aop:config>
        <aop:aspect id="loggingAspect" ref="logging">
           <aop:before method="log"
           pointcut="within(com.santosh.spring.MyBusinessObject)"/>
        </aop:aspect>
     </aop:config>
</beans>
```

Now, to test this configuration we need to write a simple test case that can access the myServices bean and invoke the businessService1() method. List 5.4 shows a simple test case.

List 5.4: MyBusinessObjectTestCase.java

```
import org.springframework.context.*;
import org.springframework.context.support.*;

import com.santosh.spring.MyBusinessObject;

public class MyBusinessObjectTestCase {

   public static void main(String s[]) throws Exception {

      ApplicationContext beans=
            new ClassPathXmlApplicationContext("mybeans.xml");

      MyBusinessObject bo=
              (MyBusinessObject) beans.getBean("myServices");

      System.out.println("Invoking businessService1()...");
      bo.businessService1();
   }//main
}//class
```

Use log4j.properties as used with all the other examples in this chapter. Now compile the java files and arrange the files as shown in Fig. 5.1.

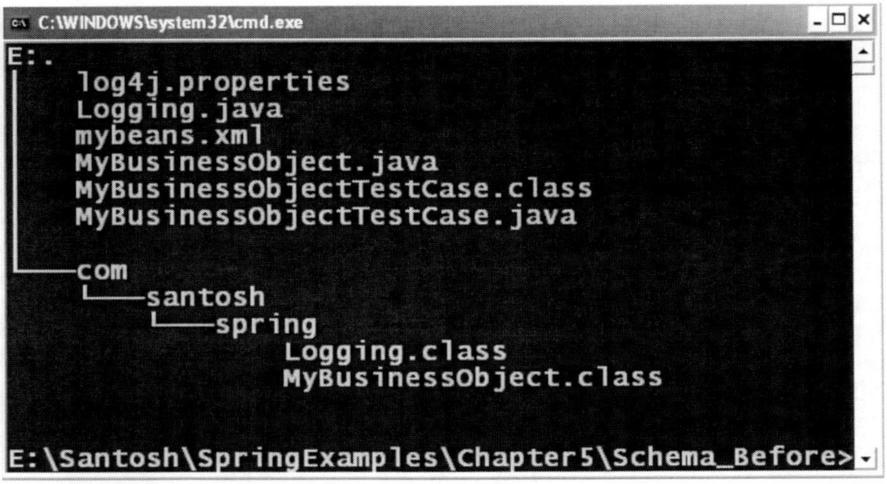

FIGURE 5.1 Tree structure showing files of Schema based AOP example

Now, execute the MyBusinessObjectTestCase to find the configurations in action. Note that to run this example you need the following jar files in classpath:

- spring.jar
- commons-logging.jar
- log4j-1.2.14.jar
- aspectjrt.jar
- aspectjweaver.jar
- cglib-nodep-2.1_3.jar

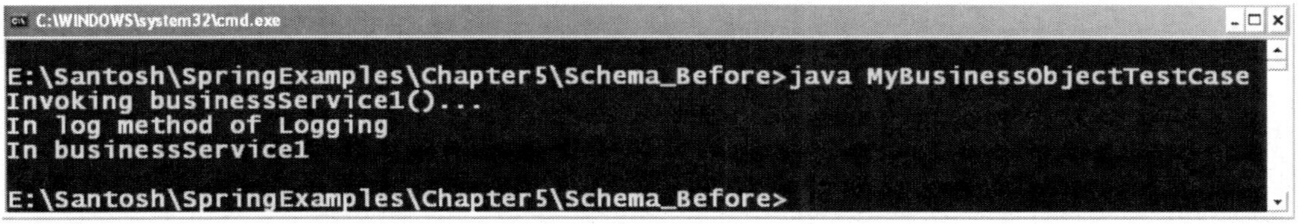

FIGURE 5.2 Output of MyBusinessObjectTestCase

Figure 5.2 shows the output of the MyBusinessObjectTestCase where you can find that the log() method of logging class is invoked just before invocation of the businessServive1() method on the MyBusinessObject instance. In this example we have designed log() method as a no-argument method but it can be defined with org.aspectj.lang.JoinPoint as argument, which enables us to get the details of the joinpoint for which the advice is being provided. The *org.aspectj.lang.JoinPoint* type includes methods that allow us to retrieve the target method description. The methods declared in *org.aspectj.lang.Joinpoint* interface are:

Method Name	***Description***
getArgs()	Returns an object array that gives the values of the target method invocation arguments
getSignature()	Returns *org.aspectj.lang.Signature* type of object that allows to get all the details related to target method signature like modifiers, method name, declaring type etc
getThis()	Returns the joinpoint object
getTarget()	Returns the target object

5.6 AFTER RETURNING ADVICE

As discussed earlier the after returning advice executes after the joinpoint execution completes with normal termination. The following code snippet shows the syntax of aop element that is used to declare after-returning advice in Schema-based approach.

Code Snippet

```
<aop:after-returning attributes/>
```

The attributes of <aop:after-returning > element are:

Attribute Name	*Description*
pointcut	Takes the pointcut expression of aspectj type—the designators are explained under Section 5.2.
pointcut-ref	Takes the name of an associated pointcut definition, that is, the ID of the pointcut defined using <aop:pointcut> element as described under Section 5.2.
method	Takes the name of the method that has to be invoked after the target method invocation completes with normal termination, that is, the method that defines the logic of the advice.
arg-names	Takes the comma-separated list of advice methods argument names that will be matched from pointcut parameters.
returning	Takes the name of the method parameter to which the return value must be passed.

5.6.1 Working with Schema-based Approach after Returning Advice

To find the after returning advice Schema-based approach configuration in action we will modify our previous example. This can be done by just changing the configuration file. List 5.5 shows the modified spring beans XML configuration file.

List 5.5: mybeans.xml

```
<beans xmlns="http://www.springframework.org/schema/beans"
xmlns:xsi="http://www.w3.org/2001/XMLSchema-instance"
xsi:schemaLocation="http://www.springframework.org/schema/beans

http://www.springframework.org/schema/beans/spring-beans-2.0.xsd
http://www.springframework.org/schema/aop http://www.springframework.org/schema/aop/
spring-aop-2.0.xsd"
xmlns:aop="http://www.springframework.org/schema/aop">

  <bean id="myServices"
        class="com.santosh.spring.MyBusinessObject"/>
  <bean id="logging" class="com.santosh.spring.Logging"/>

  <aop:config>
    <aop:aspect id="loggingAspect" ref="logging">
      <aop:after-returning method="log"
      pointcut="within(com.santosh.spring.MyBusinessObject)"/>
    </aop:aspect>
  </aop:config>
</beans>
```

Now, execute the MyBusinessObjectTestCase to find the output as shown in Fig. 5.3.

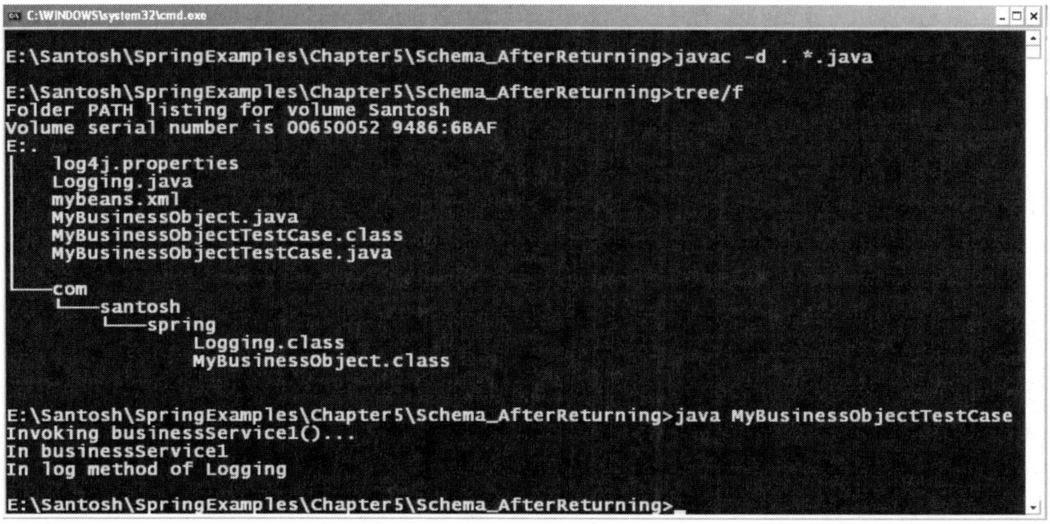

FIGURE 5.3 Output of MyBusinessObjectTestCase

Figure 5.3 shows the output of the MyBusinessObjectTestCase when executed with the spring beans XML configuration file listed under List 5.5. We can observe that this time the log() method of logging is invoked after the execution of businessService1() method of MyBusinessObject.

5.6.2 After Throwing Advice

As discussed earlier the after throwing advice executes after the joinpoint execution completes with abnormal termination. The following code snippet shows the syntax of aop element that is used to declare after-throwing advice in Schema-based approach.

Code Snippet

```
<aop:after-throwing attributes/>
```

The attributes of <aop:after-throwing> element are:

Attribute Name	*Description*
pointcut	Takes the pointcut expression of aspectj type. The designators are explained under Section 5.2.
pointcut-ref	Takes the name of an associated pointcut definition, that is, the ID of the pointcut defined using <aop:pointcut> element as described under Section 5.2.
method	Takes the name of the method that has to be invoked after the target method invocation completes with abnormal termination, that is, the method that defines the logic of the advice.
arg-names	Takes the comma-separated list of advice methods argument names that will be matched from pointcut parameters.
throwing	Takes the name of the method parameter to which the thrown exception must be passed.

The following code snippet shows the spring beans XML configuration file configuring the after throwing advice.

Code Snippet

```
<beans xmlns="http://www.springframework.org/schema/beans"
xmlns:xsi="http://www.w3.org/2001/XMLSchema-instance"
xsi:schemaLocation="http://www.springframework.org/schema/beans
http://www.springframework.org/schema/beans/spring-beans-2.0.xsd
http://www.springframework.org/schema/aop
http://www.springframework.org/schema/aop/spring-aop-2.0.xsd"
xmlns:aop="http://www.springframework.org/schema/aop">

  <bean id="myServices"
        class="com.santosh.spring.MyBusinessObject"/>
  <bean id="exceptionHandler"
      class="com.santosh.spring.MyExceptionHandler"/>

  <aop:config>
    <aop:aspect id="exceptionHandlingAspect"
                ref="exceptionHandler">
      <aop:after-throwing method="handleException"
      pointcut="within(com.santosh.spring.MyBusinessObject)"/>
    </aop:aspect>
  </aop:config>
</beans>
```

As per the configuration in the preceding code snippet, in case of any exception raised by the MyBusinessObject methods the handleException() method of MyExceptionHandler is invoked.

5.6.3 After Advice

The after advice is new in Spring 2.0. It does not have an equivalent in the basic Spring 1.2 AOP style. The after advice executes after the joinpoint execution irrespective of how the joinpoint (method) execution exists, that is, whether it completes with normal or abnormal termination. This advice is considered as finally advice since it acts the same as finally block, that is, being executed in case of normal or abnormal termination of try block. The following code snippet shows the syntax of the element used to configure the after advice.

Code Snippet

```
<aop:after attributes/>
```

The attributes of <aop:after> element are:

Attribute Name	*Description*
pointcut	Takes the pointcut expression of aspectj type. The designators are explained under Section 5.2.
pointcut-ref	Takes the name of an associated pointcut definition, that is, the ID of the pointcut defined using <aop:pointcut> element as described under Section 5.2.
method	Takes the name of the method that has to be invoked after the target method invocation, that is, the method that defines the logic of the advice.
arg-names	Takes the comma-separated list of advice methods argument names that will be matched from pointcut parameters.

The following code snippet shows the spring beans XML configuration file configuring the after advice.

Code Snippet

```
<beans  xmlns="http://www.springframework.org/schema/beans"
xmlns:xsi="http://www.w3.org/2001/XMLSchema-instance"
xsi:schemaLocation="http://www.springframework.org/schema/beans
http://www.springframework.org/schema/beans/spring-beans-2.0.xsd
http://www.springframework.org/schema/aop
http://www.springframework.org/schema/aop/spring-aop-2.0.xsd"
xmlns:aop="http://www.springframework.org/schema/aop">

  <bean id="myServices"
        class="com.santosh.spring.MyBusinessObject"/>
  <bean id="methodFinalizer"
      class="com.santosh.spring.MyMethodFinalizer"/>

  <aop:config>
    <aop:aspect id=" methodFinalizerAspect"
          ref=" methodFinalizer">
      <aop:after method="myFinalizer"
      pointcut="within(com.santosh.spring.MyBusinessObject)"/>
    </aop:aspect>
  </aop:config>
</beans>
```

As per the configuration in the preceding code snippet, irrespective of the execution results of the MyBusinessObject methods, the myFinalizer() method of MyMethodFinalizer is invoked.

5.6.4 Around Advice

As discussed earlier the around advice can surround the joinpoint providing the advice before and after executing the joinpoint and even controls the joinpoint invocation. The advice method used for this type of advice must be defined with the first argument as of org.aspectj.lang.ProceedingJoinPoint type and return type should be java.lang.Object. The ProceedingJoinPoint allows us to invoke the proceed() method that proceeds to invoke the target method. The following code snippet shows the syntax of aop element that is used to declare around advice in Schema-based approach.

Code Snippet

```
  <aop:around attributes/>
```

The attributes of <aop:around> element are:

Attribute Name	*Description*
pointcut	Takes the pointcut expression of aspectj type. The designators are explained under Section 5.2.
pointcut-ref	Takes the name of an associated pointcut definition, that is, the ID of the pointcut defined using <aop:pointcut> element as described under Section 5.2.
method	Takes the name of the method that has to surround the target method invocation.
arg-names	Takes the comma-separated list of advice methods argument names that will be matched from pointcut parameters.

The following code snippet shows the spring beans XML configuration file configuring the around advice.

Code Snippet

```
<beans xmlns="http://www.springframework.org/schema/beans"
xmlns:xsi="http://www.w3.org/2001/XMLSchema-instance"
xsi:schemaLocation="http://www.springframework.org/schema/beans
http://www.springframework.org/schema/beans/spring-beans-2.0.xsd
http://www.springframework.org/schema/aop
http://www.springframework.org/schema/aop/spring-aop-2.0.xsd"
xmlns:aop="http://www.springframework.org/schema/aop">

  <bean id="myServices"
        class="com.santosh.spring.MyBusinessObject"/>
  <bean id="myTransactionAdvice"
       class="com.santosh.spring.MyTransactionAdvice"/>

  <aop:config>
    <aop:aspect id=" myTransactionAspect"
                ref="myTransactionAdvice ">
      <aop:around method="handleTransactions"
      pointcut="within(com.santosh.spring.MyBusinessObject)"/>
    </aop:aspect>
  </aop:config>
</beans>
```

As per the configuration in the preceding code snippet the handleTransaction() method of MyTransactionAdvice surrounds the joinpoints in MyBusinessObject providing the advice before and after executing the methods in MyBusinessObject. The following code snippet shows the MyTransactionAdvice Java source.

Code Snippet

```
package com.santosh.spring;

import org.aspectj.lang.*;

public class MyTransactionAdvice {
```

(Contd.)

```
    public Object handleTransactions(ProceedingJoinPoint pj) {
      //pre processing (before advice)
      //Start the transaction and do other necessary initializations
      try{
        /*
          Delegate the request to proceed executing the
          further interceptor chain and target method
        */
        Object o=mi.proceed();

        //after returning advice
        //end the transaction (may be commit())
        return o;
      }//try
      catch(Throwable e){
        //after throwing advice
        //end the transaction (may be rollback)
        //return some value or throw exception
      }
    }
}
```

It can be observed from the preceding code snippet that the handleTransactions() method that is configured as an around advice is defined with ProceedingJoinPoint as argument and java.lang.Object as return type. In this section, we have learnt how to configure different types of advices as per the Schema-based approach. With this we complete the discussion on the Schema-based approach of defining aspects. The next section explains the @AspectJ annotation style of defining aspects.

5.7 @ASPECTJ STYLE AOP SUPPORT

The @AspectJ style of declaring aspects in a regular Java class using annotations is new in Spring 2.0 and applicable only if we are implementing a project compliant to Java SE 5 or higher language standards. The Spring 2.0 uses the @AspectJ annotations given under the AspectJ 5 release. Moreover, Spring 2.0 understands the @AspectJ annotations as AspectJ 5, using a library supplied by AspectJ for pointcut parsing and matching. In this case while writing the java classes we can use some annotations and define the pointcuts, advices, and aspects. To use @AspectJ aspects with spring framework we need to enable spring support for using @AspectJ style by declaring aspectj-autoproxy. This declaration configures spring runtime to determine whether a bean is advised by one or more aspects. If it is then it will automatically generate a proxy for that bean to intercept method invocations and ensure that the advice is executed as configured.

To enable the spring support for configuring Spring AOP based on @AspectJ aspects we have to include the following element in the spring beans configuration xml file:

```
<aop:aspectj-autoproxy/>
```

In case we are not using Schema-based configuration but we want to use DTD then declare the following bean:

```
<bean
class="org.springframework.aop.aspectj.annotation.AnnotationAwareAspectJAutoProxy
Creator"/>
```

Let us discuss how to declare pointcut in @AspectJ style AOP support.

5.7.1 Declaring Pointcut

The pointcut declaration in @AspectJ AOP style has two parts—the pointcut signature provided by a regular method definition and the expression that decides exactly which method we are interested to intercept. The pointcut expression is declared using @Pointcut annotation defined under *org.aspectj.lang.annotation* package.

> **Note:** The method serving as a pointcut signature should be declared with a return type as *void.*

Code Snippet

```
@Pointcut("within(com.santosh.spring.MyServices)")
public void myPointcut(){}
```

The above code snippet declares the pointcut that can be identified by 'myPointcut' name. The @Pointcut annotation takes an attribute to describe the expression. We use AspectJ designators to prepare expression. Here the pointcut expression describes to match all the method invocations on com.santosh.spring.MyServices type of object.

5.7.2 Declaring Aspect

The aspect with the @AspectJ style of AOP is declared using @Aspect annotation with any bean defined in our application. The @Aspect annotation is packed into the *org.aspectj.lang.annotation* package.

Code Snippet

```
@Aspect
public class MyAspect {…}
```

5.7.3 Declaring Advices

The @AspectJ style of Spring AOP allows us to define five types of advices listed below:

1. Before Advice
2. After Returning Advice
3. After Throwing Advice
4. After Advice
5. Around Advice

Let us discuss all these advice declarations as supported by the @AspectJ style of AOP support.

5.7.4 Before Advice

As discussed earlier, the before advice executes before the joinpoint execution. In this style the before advice is declared using @Before annotation declared in the package *org.aspactj.lang.annotation.* The following code snippet shows the sample code that defines the before advice in @AspectJ style.

Code Snippet

```
package com.santosh.spring;

import org.aspectj.lang.annotation.*;

@Aspect
public class MyAspect {

  @Pointcut("within(com.santosh.spring.MyServices)")
  public void myPointcut(){…}

  @Before("com.santosh.spring.MyAspect.myPointcut()")
  public void myBeforeAdvice(){…}

}
```

As discussed earlier in the Schema based approach if we want to get the target method description like the method signature and argument values we can define the advice method with an argument type as *org.aspectj.lang.JoinPoint.* The following code snippet shows the advice method with JoinPoint argument.

Code Snippet

```
package com.santosh.spring;

import org.aspectj.lang.annotation.*;

@Aspect
public class MyAspect {

  @Pointcut("within(com.santosh.spring.MyServices)")
  public void myPointcut(){…}

  @Before("com.santosh.spring.MyAspect.myPointcut()")
  public void myBeforeAdvice(JoinPoint jp){

    System.out.println("Method Name: "+jp.getSignature().getName());
    System.out.println("Number of arguments: "+jp.getArgs().length);
    System.out.println("Arguments:");
    Object args[]=jp.getArgs();
    for (int i=0; i<args.length; i++)
      System.out.println("Argument "+(i+1)+":"+ args[i]);
  }
}
```

5.7.4.1 After Returning Advice

As described while discussing the Schema-based AOP approach, the after returning advice executes after the joinpoint execution completes with normal termination. This advice is declared using @AfterReturning annotation declared in the package *org.aspactj.lang.annotation.* The following code snippet shows the declaration of after returning advice.

Code Snippet

```
package com.santosh.spring;
import org.aspectj.lang.annotation.*;

@Aspect
public class MyAspect {

  @Pointcut("within(com.santosh.spring.MyServices)")
  public void myPointcut(){…}

  @AfterReturning("com.santosh.spring.MyAspect.myPointcut()")
  public void myAfterReturningAdvice(){…}
}
```

This is the same as discussed with the before advice. We can declare the first argument of advice method of type *org.aspectj.lang.JoinPoint* to get the target method description, and this is applicable for all the advices.

In the preceding code snippet the advice is referring to the pointcut declared separately. Instead we can directly define the pointcut expression while declaring the advice as shown below:

```
  @AfterReturning("within(com.santosh.spring.MyServices)")
  public void myAfterReturningAdvice(){…}
```

To collect the return value of the target method executed, the advice can be declared as shown below:

```
  @AfterReturning(
    pointcut= "within(com.santosh.spring.MyServices)",
    returning="returnValue")
  public void myAfterReturningAdvice(Object returnValue){…}
```

Here the return value of the target method executed is passed to the returnValue parameter of the advice method.

5.7.4.2 After Throwing Advice

As described while discussing the Schema-based AOP approach, the after throwing advice executes after the joinpoint execution completes with abnormal termination. This advice is declared using @AfterThrowing annotation declared in the package *org.aspactj.lang.annotation.* The following code snippet shows the declaration of the after throwing advice.

Code Snippet

```
package com.santosh.spring;
import org.aspectj.lang.annotation.*;

@Aspect
public class MyAspect {

  @AfterThrowing("within(com.santosh.spring.MyServices)")
  public void myAfterThrowingAdvice(){...}
}
```

To collect the exception thrown by the target method executed, the advice can be declared as shown below:

```
@AfterThrowing(
  pointcut= "within(com.santosh.spring.MyServices)",
  throwing="exception")
public void myAfterThrowingAdvice(MyException exception){...}
```

Here the exception thrown by the target method executed is passed to the exception parameter of the advice method.

5.7.4.3 After advice

As discussed with the Schema-based AOP approach, the after advice executes after the joinpoint execution irrespective of how the joinpoint (method) execution exists, that is, does it complete with normal or abnormal termination, and is it considered as finally advice. This advice is declared using @After annotation declared in the package *org.aspactj.lang.annotation.* The following code snippet shows the declaration of after throwing advice.

Code Snippet

```
package com.santosh.spring;
import org.aspectj.lang.annotation.*;

@Aspect
public class MyAspect {

  @After("within(com.santosh.spring.MyServices)")
  public void myAfterAdvice(){...}
}
```

5.7.4.4 Around advice

As discussed with the around advice under the Schema-based AOP approach the around advice can surround the joinpoint providing the advice before and after executing the joinpoint, even controlling the joinpoint invocation. The advice method used for this type of advice must be defined with the first argument as of *org.aspectj.lang.ProceedingJoinPoint* type, and the return type should be java.lang.Object. The *ProceedingJoinPoint* allows us to invoke the proceed() method that proceeds to invoke the target method. This advice is declared using @Around annotation declared in the package *org.aspectj.lang.annotation.* The following code snippet shows the declaration of after throwing advice.

Code Snippet

```
package com.santosh.spring;
import org.aspectj.lang.annotation.*;

@Aspect
public class MyAspect {

@Around("within(com.santosh.spring.MyServices)")
public Object myAdoundAdvice(ProceedingJoinPoint pjp) {

     //do all the processings that has to executed before the joinpoint execution

     Object o=pjp.procced();

     //do all the post processings i.e. the processings that has to be executed after
     the joinpoint execution

     return o;
  }
}
```

You can workout the @AspectJ style syntax explained in this section with the same examples used for demonstrating the respecting advices in Spring 1.2 AOP and Schema-based AOP style with the relevant changes.

Summary

In this chapter we have learnt the Schema-based AOP style and @AspectJ style of programming Spring AOP applications.

JDBC and DAO Module

6

CHAPTER

Objectives

In this chapter we will cover:

- DAO design patterns
- Shortcomings in implementing the DAO and the Spring provided solution for those shortcomings
- Simplified Spring JDBC abstraction framework

6.1 DATA ACCESS OBJECT (DAO)

6.1.1 Context

We have to implement a system that accesses multiple persistent storages, such as a database, flat text files, XML document, etc. And we have tried to implement the persistence logic to access the persistence storages along with the business logic in the business process components. Since the data access logic varies depending on the data store type we have found that this approach is complicated in implementing, testing, and maintaining.

6.1.2 Problem

We want to separate the persistence logic or integration logic (that is, logic to integrate our system with the backend system) from the business logic.

6.1.3 Forces

The following are the characteristics of the forces in developing a system that applies the Data Access Object (DAO) pattern:

- Want to reuse the persistence logic
- Want to abstract the data access logic and backend system exception handling from business logic components
- Want to reduce the number interactions to the data store

6.1.4 Solution

Design a DAO that takes the responsibility of communicating with the backend system and present the data to the business objects/components in our application understandable format.

Now as we have learnt the basics of DAO design pattern, we will write a sample code. The example below represents the employee details stored in the backend persistence store.

6.1.5 Sample Code

It is ever a better practice to design DAO using the 'Program to an Interface' (P2I) principal. The 'Program to an Interface' principal states that concrete implementations must implement an interface, which is used in the program that wants to use the implementation rather than the implementation class itself. Therefore, you can easily substitute a different implementation with little or no impact on client code. Following this principal we will first define an interface for Employee DAO. List 6.1 shows the Employee DAO interface named EmpDAO declaring some data access methods. The EmpDAO includes methods for creating a new employee, getting employee details by employee number, getting all the employees by department number, etc.

List 6.1: EmpDAO.java

```
package com.santosh.spring.dao;

import java.util.List;
import com.santosh.spring.Employee;

public interface EmpDAO {

  void createEmp(Employee e);

  Employee getEmpById(int eno);
  List getEmpsByDept(int dno);

  void updateEmp(Employee e);
}
```

Now, we will provide implementation for the Employee DAO interface designed in List 6.1. List 6.2 shows a concrete implementation for the Employee DAO accessing the data from the backend oracle database.

List 6.2: OracleEmpDAO.java

```
package com.santosh.spring.dao;

import java.util.List;
import java.sql.*;
import com.santosh.spring.db.util.DBUtil;
import com.santosh.spring.Employee;

public class OracleEmpDAO implements EmpDAO {
  /*
  Implement all the methods declared in EmpDAO, and while implementing here we need
  to consider the backend system as Oracle DB
  So need to write SQL statements according to Oracle, and understand the error-codes
  defined by oracle.
  */
  public void createEmp(Employee e){

    Connection con=null;
    try{
```

```
        //DBUtil is a helper class that retrieves the Connection from Pool
        con=DBUtil.getConnection();
        PreparedStatement ps=con.prepareStatement(
          "insert into emp(empno,ename,sal,deptno,job,hiredate)
                                                  values(?,?,?,?,?,?)");
        //Set the values to PreparedStatement
        ps.setInt(1,e.getEmpno());
        ps.setString(2,e.getName());
        ps.setDouble(3,e.getSalary());
        ps.setInt(4,e.getDeptno());
        ps.setString(5,e.getJob());
        ps.setDate(6,e.getHiredate());
        //Now, execute the statement
        int count=ps.executeUpdate();
        if (count==1 || count==Statement.SUCCESS_NO_INFO)
          return;
        else
          throw new MyDAOException("Unable to insert a new record reason unknown");
    }//try
    catch(SQLException seqe){
      //Resolve the SQLException to understand the error, using the Error Code
      //and then throw an application specific exception describing the problem
      //For example
      throw new MyDAOException("<exception description goes here>");
    }//catch
    finally{
      try{
          con.close();
      }//try
      catch(SQLException e){
          throw new MyDAOException(e.getMessage());
      }//catch
    }//finally
}//createEmp

public Employee getEmpById(int eno){

    Connection con=null;
    Employee emp=null;
    try{
        //DBUtil is a helper class that retrieves the Connection from Pool
        con=DBUtil.getConnection();
        PreparedStatement ps=con.prepareStatement(
          "select ename,sal,deptno,job,hiredate from emp where empno=?");
        //Set the values to PreparedStatement
        ps.setInt(1,eno);
        //Now, execute the statement
```

```
            ResultSet rs=ps.executeQuery();
            if (rs.next()){
                emp=new Employee();
                emp.setEmpno(eno);
                emp.setName(rs.getString(1));
                emp.setSalary(rs.getDouble(2));
                emp.setDeptno(rs.getInt(3));
                emp.setJob(rs.getString(4));
                emp.setHiredate(rs.getDate(5));
            }
            return emp;
        }//try
        catch(SQLException seqe){
            //Resolve the SQLException to understand the error, using the Error Code
            //and then throw an application specific exception describing the problem
            //For example
            throw new MyDAOException("<exception description goes here>");
        }//catch
        finally{
            try{
                con.close();
            }//try
            catch(SQLException e){
                throw new MyDAOException(e.getMessage());
            }//catch
        }//finally
    }//getEmpById

    public List getEmpsByDept(int dno){

        Connection con=null;
        List emps=null;
        try{
            //DBUtil is a helper class that retrieves the Connection from Pool
            con=DBUtil.getConnection();
            PreparedStatement ps=con.prepareStatement(
              "select ename,sal,empno,job,hiredate from emp where deptno=?");
            //Set the values to PreparedStatement
            ps.setInt(1,dno);
            //Now, execute the statement
            ResultSet rs=ps.executeQuery();
            emps=new ArrayList();
            while (rs.next()){
                Employee emp=new Employee();
                emp.setDeptno(dno);

                emp.setName(rs.getString(1));
                emp.setSalary(rs.getDouble(2));
```

```
            emp.setEmpno(rs.getInt(3));
            emp.setJob(rs.getString(4));
            emp.setHiredate(rs.getDate(5));
            emps.add(emp);
        }
        return emps;
    }//try
    catch(SQLException seqe){
        //Resolve the SQLException to understand the error, using the Error Code
        //and then throw an application specific exception describing the problem
        //For example
        throw new MyDAOException("<exception description goes here>");
    }//catch
    finally{
        try{
            con.close();
        }//try
        catch(SQLException e){
            throw new MyDAOException(e.getMessage());
        }//catch
    }//finally
}//getEmpByDeptno

public void updateEmp(Employee e){

    Connection con=null;
    try{
        //DBUtil is a helper class that retrieves the Connection from Pool
        con=DBUtil.getConnection();
        PreparedStatement ps=con.prepareStatement(
        "update emp set ename=?,sal=?,deptno=?,job=?,hiredate=? where empno=?");
        //Set the values to PreparedStatement
        ps.setString(1,e.getName());
        ps.setDouble(2,e.getSalary());
        ps.setInt(3,e.getDeptno());
        ps.setString(4,e.getJob());
        ps.setDate(5,e.getHiredate());
        ps.setInt(6,e.getEmpno());
        //Now, execute the statement
        int count=ps.executeUpdate();
        if (count==1 || count==Statement.SUCCESS_NO_INFO)
          return;
        else
          throw new MyDAOException("Unable to update the details,
                                                         reason unknown");
    }//try
    catch(SQLException seqe){
```

```
            //Resolve the SQLException to understand the error, using the Error Code
            //and then throw an application specific exception describing the problem
            //For example
            throw new MyDAOException("<exception description goes here>");
        }//catch
        finally{
            try{
                con.close();
            }//try
            catch(SQLException e){
              throw new MyDAOException(e.getMessage());
            }//catch
        }//finally
    }//updateEmp
}
```

Moreover, in the business objects, or application services components we can create the required DAO object and use it. Generally to make the business components independent of DAO implementations we can design a DAO Factory (that is, a Factory class to create a DAO). Using the DAO factory to pull the concrete DAO implementation object into the business object provides great flexibility. It is easy to modify the DAO implementation without affecting the business objects, as long as the contract established by the DAO interface remains unchanged. List 6.3 shows a sample code for a simple DAO factory.

List 6.3

```
package com.santosh.dao.factory;
public class MyDAOFactory {
    private static MyDAOFactory daoFactory;

  static{
   daoFactory = new MyDAOFactory();
  }
  private MyDAOFactory(){}

  public MyDAOFactory getInstance(){
   return daoFactory;
  }

  public EmpDAO getEmpDAO(){
   return new OracleEmpDAO();
  }
}
```

As we have developed a DAO factory it is now time to see how DAO fits into the business objects. In the preceding sections we learnt that DAOs work together with the business objects to fetch and store the persistent business data. List 6.4 shows the code in business components that interacts with the EmpDAO.

List 6.4

```
EmpDAO ed=DAOFactory.getEmpDAO();
ed.createEmp(e);
```

Form the preceding sample code that demonstrates how to implement the DAO and use it in the business components, the following key points can be identified:

- The DAO methods encapsulate all interactions with the persistence store. To interact with the persistence store it may use JDBC API or an O/R mapping solution like Hibernate or the proprietary APIs of the persistence store, etc.
- The DAO methods wrap the retrieved data in a persistence API neutral transfer object and return it to the business tier for further processing. In the above list, while getting the employee details the data was encapsulated in the ResultSet (JDBC API) that was extracted and encapsulated into com.santosh.spring.Employee object which is persistence API neutral transfer object.
- The DAO objects are stateless in nature. These methods' only task is to access and change persistent data for the business objects.
- The DAO methods catch any exceptions reported in the process of communicating with the persistence store by the underlying persistence API as SQLException when using JDBC, HibernateException when using Hibernate, etc. Thereafter, the DAO objects notify the business objects of such an exception by persistence API neutral custom-build exceptions as shown in List 6.4 and throw MyDAOException.

From this discussion it can be identified that the DAO layer provides a consistent data access API for the business tier abstracting low-level data access API like JDBC, Hibernate, and data store-specific proprietary API.

This section explained the DAO design pattern and its importance. The next section discusses DAO support in Spring framework.

6.2 DAO SUPPORT IN SPRING FRAMEWORK

As discussed above, DAO is used to separate persistence from business logic, which provides a number of benefits as explained in the above section. One of the key benefits is that it provides an easy way to change the data store and data access API without affecting the business objects, as long as the contract established by the DAO interface remains unchanged. But to achieve this while implementing the DAO there are some important things that need to be taken care of as we need to design consistent exceptions that can be thrown to the business components accessing the DAOs. In case of any abnormal conditions risen instead of throwing a data access API defined exception like SQLException and HibernateException, we want to translate the exception into the application-specific exception and throw it to the business objects.

For example, considering the DAOs implemented using JDBC API to access the persistence store here we want to use JDBC drivers to communicate with data store as we know that the JDBC drivers report all error situations by raising the SQLException. The SQLException is a checked exception; therefore we are forced to handle it even though it is not possible to recover from the majority of these exceptions, which unnecessarily results in confusing the application code. Moreover, the error code and message obtained from the SQLException object are database vendor-specific, so it is a better practice to translate these exceptions into application-specific exceptions in the DAO layer instead of extending to the business layer and making the business layer depend on the data access API.

To simplify these issues, Spring framework includes support for DAO. The Spring framework support for DAO includes a consistent exception hierarchy and a convenient translation from data access API-specific exceptions to the spring DAO exception hierarchy packaged into org.springframework.dao package with DataAccessException as the base exception. All these exceptions are unchecked. Moreover, to perform this translation transparently Spring framework includes templates for the most of the generally used data access APIs like JDBC, Hibernate, JDO, JPA (Java Persistence API), iBatis, and Oracle Toplink. The exceptions packaged under the org.springframework.dao package are described in Table 6.1.

TABLE 6.1 Spring DAO Exception

Exception class	*Description*
DataAccessException	The base exception for all the data access exceptions.
CleanupFailureDataAccessException	Exception to describe that the cleanup process is failed after the data access operation. But the data access operation is executed successfully.
ConcurrencyFailureException	Exception to describe the concurrency failure.
DataAccessResourceFailureException	Exception thrown when a resource fails completely. For example we cannot connect to a database using JDBC.
DataIntegrityViolationException	Exception thrown when an attempt to insert or update data results in violation of an integrity constraint.
DataRetrievalFailureException	Exception thrown if certain expected data could not be retrieved. For example, when looking up specific data via a known identifier.
InvalidDataAccessApiUsageException	Exception thrown on incorrect usage of the API, such as failing to compile a query object that needed compilation before execution.
InvalidDataAccessResourceUsageException	Root for exceptions thrown when we use a data access resource incorrectly. Thrown for example on specifying bad SQL when using a RDBMS. Resource-specific subclasses are supplied by concrete data access packages.
PermissionDeniedDataAccessException	Exception thrown when the underlying resource denied permission to access a specific element, such as a specific database table.
UncategorizedDataAccessException	Normal superclass when we cannot distinguish anything more specific than 'something went wrong with the underlying resource': for example, a SQLException from JDBC we cannot pinpoint more precisely.

Apart from the support described above to work easily with a variety of data access APIs such as JDBC, Hibernate, JDO, etc., in a consistent way. Spring framework includes a set of abstract DAO classes that can be extended by our DAO implementations. The abstract DAO classes are described in Table 6.2.

All the abstract DAO support classes described in Table 6.2 are derived from the base class org.springframework.dao.support.DaoSupport class. We will discuss these DAO support classes with practical implementations further in this book when we learn data access using spring support.

In this section we learnt about the difficulties in implementing the DAO and the DAO support in Spring. The following section describes some other shortcomings of DAO pattern and the solution for those problems in Spring.

TABLE 6.2 Spring built-in DAO Support classes

DAO Support Class	*Description*
JdbcDaoSupport	Convenient class for subclassing JDBC DAO implementations, this provides a JdbcTemplate based on the given DataSource to the subclasses. The main intention of using this class as superclass for DAO implementations is for JdbcTemplate usage but it can also be used when working with DataSourceUtils directly or with RDBMS operation classes.
HibernateDaoSupport	Convenient class for subclassing Hibernate DAO implementations, this provides a HibernateTemplate instance initialized based on the given SessionFactory to the subclasses.
JdoDaoSupport	Convenient class for subclassing JDO DAO implementations, this provides a JdoTemplate instance initialized based on the given PersistenceManagerFactory to the subclasses.
JpaDaoSupport	Convenient class for subclassing JPA DAO implementations, this provides a JpaTemplate instance initialized based on the given EntityManagerFactory to the subclasses.

6.3 INTRODUCING SPRING JDBC MODULE

As discussed in the above section the DAO pattern provides a clear separation between the persistence store and business layer and in addition to this DAO support in Spring framework includes some consistent exception providing the convenience to throw low-level data access API independent exceptions to the business components. But still when we are using JDBC API as a low-level data access API to implement the DAOs there are some shortcomings, which can be found from the sample code of DAO implementation shown in List 6.2. The shortcomings are listed below:

- **Code Duplication:** As evident from List 6.2, code duplication with the code related to exception handling, getting the connection, preparing a JDBC statement, etc., is a major problem while using JDBC API directly to access database. As we know that writing boilerplate code over and over again is a clear violation of the basic object-oriented (OO) principle of code reuse. This has some side effects in terms of project cost, timelines, and effort.
- **Resource Leakage:** As shown in List 6.2, in the implementation of OracleEmpDAO class, all DAO methods must hand over control of obtained database resources like connection, statements, and result sets. This is a risky plan because a beginner programmer can very easily skip those code fragments. As a result, resources would run out and bring the system to stop.
- **Error Handling:** When using JDBC directly we need to handle SQLException since the JDBC drivers report all error situations by raising the SQLException. Most of these exceptions are not possible to be recovered. Moreover, the error code and message obtained from the SQLException object are database vendor-specific, so it is difficult to write portable DAO error messaging code.

To solve the above described problems we need to identify the parts of code that remain fixed and then encapsulate them into some reusable objects. The Spring framework provides a solution for these problems by giving a thin, robust, and highly extensible JDBC abstraction framework. The JDBC abstraction framework provided under Spring framework as a value-added service takes care of all the low-level details like retrieving connection, preparing the statement object, executing the query, and releasing the database resources. While using the JDBC abstraction framework of Spring framework for data access the application developer needs to specify the SQL statement to execute and read the results. Since all the low-level logic have been written once and correctly into the abstraction layer provided by Spring JDBC framework this helps to eliminate the shortcomings found in using JDBC API to implement DAOs, which are described above.

As we have discussed about the overview of the Spring JDBC abstraction framework including the discussion like what is the importance of the Spring JDBC framework, now it is time to discuss the Spring JDBC framework in detail. As the basic element of Spring JDBC framework is JdbcTemplate we will start by learning about the JdbcTemplate. The following section explains the JdbcTemplate.

6.4 WHAT IS JDBCTEMPLATE?

The JdbcTemplate is the basic element and a central class of the Spring JDBC abstraction framework which includes the most common logic (that is, the parts of code that remains fixed) in using JDBC API to access data like handling the creation of connection, statement creation, statement execution, and release of resource. This also catches the JDBC exceptions and converts them to the standard and more explanatory exceptions defined in the org.springframework.dao package. JdbcTemplate is designed following a core template pattern. While using the JdbcTemplate the application developer has to only provide code to prepare the SQL statement and extract results. The JdbcTemplate can be used to execute all types of SQL statements and stored procedure calls.

It is important to know that the JdbcTemplate class instances are threadsafe once configured. Meaning you can configure a single instance of a JdbcTemplate and then safely inject this shared reference into multiple DAOs.

The JdbcTemplate central class of Spring JDBC abstraction framework is packaged into org.springframework.jdbc.core package. It is a non-abstract class and can be instantiated using any of the following three constructors.

- **JdbcTemplate() :** Constructs a new JdbcTemplate object. This constructor is provided to allow Java Bean style of instantiation.

> **Note:** When constructing an object using this constructor we need to use setDataSource() method to set the DataSource before using this object to execute the statements.

- **JdbcTemplate(DataSource) :** Constructs a new JdbcTemplate object initializing it with the given DataSource to obtain connections for executing the requested statements.
- **JdbcTemplate(DataSource, boolean) :** Constructs a new JdbcTemplate object initializing it with the given DataSource to object connections for executing the requested statements, and the Boolean value describing the lazy initialization of the SQL Exception translator. If the Boolean value is *true* then the exception translator will not be initialized immediately. Instead it waits until this JdbcTemplate object is used to execute the statement. If the Boolean argument value is *false* then the exception translator is initialized while constructing this object. Using

the JdbcTemplate (DataSource) constructor is the same as using the JdbcTemplate(DataSource, boolean) constructor with the second argument as *true*. That means when a single argument constructor of JdbcTemplate is used the exception translator is not immediately initialized.

Now, as we know how to construct the JdbcTemplate object it is time to learn how to use JdbcTemplate for execution of different types of SQL statements. First, we will start by learning how to execute SQL DML (Data Manipulating Language) statement. The following section explains how to use JdbcTemplate to execute SQL DML (Data Manipulating Language) statements.

6.5 USING JDBCTEMPLATE TO EXECUTE SQL DML STATEMENTS

JdbcTemplate provides update() methods for executing single SQL DML statement. It supports JDBC Statement and PreparedStatement style of executing the SQL statements. The various update() methods available in JdbcTemplate for executing single SQL statement are shown in Table 6.3.

TABLE 6.3 JdbcTemplate methods for executing SQL DML statements

Method	*Description*
public int update(String sql_st)	Executes the given SQL statement using the JDBC Statement object of the JDBC Connection obtained using the DataSource set to this JdbcTemplate object, and returns the update count describing the number of records affected by the statement.
public int update(String sql_st, Object[] params)	Executes the given SQL statement using the JDBC PreparedStatement object of the JDBC Connection obtained using the DataSource set to this JdbcTemplate object. The *sql_st* SQL statement can contain bind parameters (that is, '?' same as the SQL statements used with PreparedStatement). The bind parameters are set with the given arguments to execute the statement. This method returns the update count describing the number of records affected by the statement.
public int update(String sql_st, Object[] params, int[] paramTypes)	Executes the given SQL statement using the JDBC PreparedStatement object of the JDBC Connection obtained using the DataSource set to this JdbcTemplate object. The *sql_st* SQL statement can contain bind parameters (that is, '?' same as the SQL statements used with PreparedStatement). The bind parameters are set with the given arguments to execute the statement. While setting the bind parameters instead of using setObject() a generic method like the above described update() method, this method uses the parameter types described under the third argument *paramTypes,* the paramTypes are the constants from java.sql.Types. This method returns the update count describing the number of records affected by the statement.
public int update(String sql_st, PreparedStatementSetter pss)	Executes the given SQL statement using the JDBC PreparedStatement same as of the above described methods. This method uses the given Prepared-StatementSetter object to set the bind parameters. The PreparedStatementSetter is a helper that sets the parameters of the PreparedStatement, this contains only one method named setValues, that takes PreparedStatement as an argument. This method returns the update count describing the number of records affected by the statement.

(Contd.)

public int update(PreparedStatementCreator psc)	Executes the PreparedStatement that is obtained using the given Prepared StatementCreator. The PreparedStatementCreator contains only one method named createPreparedStatement with an argument of java.sql.Connection type and returns type as java.sql.PreparedStatement. This method returns the update count describing the number of records affected by the statement.
public int update(PreparedStatementCreator psc, KeyHolder kh)	Executes the PreparedStatement that is obtained using the given Prepared-StatementCreator. The PreparedStatementCreator contains only one method named createPreparedStatement with an argument of java.sql.Connection type and returns type as java.sql.PreparedStatement. This method returns the update count describing the number of records affected by the statement. Note that the PreparedStatementCreator has to create a PreparedStatement with activated extraction of generated keys, which is a new feature in JDBC 3.0. That is, the PreparedStatement has to be constructed using the prepareStatement() method of connection with two arguments where the second argument describes Statement.RETURN_GENERATED_KEYS or int[] describes the generated key column indexes or String[]describes the generated key column names.

As we have learnt about the various methods in JdbcTemplate to execute a single DML statement let us find them in action with a simple example.

6.5.1 Example

This example demonstrates all the update methods of JdbcTemplate described in Table 6.3. To make this example simple we use 'dept' table, which is well known. The following SQL Script shows the table description.

SQL Script

```
Create table dept (
deptno number(2) primary key,
dname varchar2(20),
loc varchar2(20) );
```

List 6.5 shows the DAO interface with minimum methods representing the Dept table data. This DAO contains only the methods for creating, updating, and deleting the Dept table records because here we want to look at the implementation of DAO using JdbcTemplate for executing SQL DML statement. Later you can enhance the same interface and class to represent data retrieval statements after you complete the next coming sections that describe how to use JdbcTemplate for executing SQL queries.

List 6.5: DeptDAO.java

```
package com.santosh.spring.jdbc;

public interface DeptDAO {
  int createDept(Dept d);
  void changeLocation(int dno, String newloc);
  void changeDeptDetails(Dept d);
  void removeDept(int dno);
}
```

List 6.6 shows the implementation of DeptDAO. This implementation uses the Spring JDBC abstraction framework to communicate with the database.

List 6.6: DeptDAODBImpl.java

```
package com.santosh.spring.jdbc;

import org.springframework.jdbc.core.*;
import java.util.*;

public class DeptDAODBImpl implements DeptDAO {

    JdbcTemplate jt;

    public DeptDAODBImpl(JdbcTemplate jt){
        this.jt=jt;
    }//cons

    public void changeLocation(int dno, String loc){
        jt.update("update dept set loc=? where deptno=?",
                  new Object[]{loc,new Integer(dno)});
    }

    public void changeDeptDetails(Dept d){
        MyPreparedStatementSetter mpss= new MyPreparedStatementSetter(d);
        jt.update("update dept set dname=?,loc=? where deptno=?", mpss);
    }

    public void removeDept(int dno){
        jt.update("delete from dept where deptno="+dno);
    }
    public int createDept(Dept d) {
        MyPreparedStatementCreator mpsc=new MyPreparedStatementCreator(d);
        return jt.update(mpsc);
    }
}//class
```

List 6.7 shows the Dept transfer object used to exchange the persistence data (Dept details) between the business components and DAOs.

List 6.7: Dept.java

```
package com.santosh.spring.jdbc;

public class Dept implements java.io.Serializable {
  public int deptno;
  public String dname,loc;
}
```

List 6.8 shows the PreparedStatementCreator implementation MyPreparedStatementCreator, which is designed to insert a new dept record.

List 6.8: MyPreparedStatementCreator.java

```
package com.santosh.spring.jdbc;

import org.springframework.jdbc.core.*;
import java.sql.*;

public class MyPreparedStatementCreator implements PreparedStatementCreator {

    Dept d;

    public MyPreparedStatementCreator(Dept d){
        this.d=d;
    }

    public PreparedStatement createPreparedStatement(Connection con)
                                                throws SQLException {

        PreparedStatement ps=con.prepareStatement("insert into dept values(?,?,?)");
        ps.setInt(1,d.deptno);
        ps.setString(2,d.dname);
        ps.setString(3,d.loc);
        return ps;
    }
}//class
```

List 6.9 shows the PreparedStatementSetter implementation MyPreparedStatementSetter, which is designed to set the dept details for updating the department name and location for the given department number.

List 6.9: MyPreparedStatementSetter.java

```
package com.santosh.spring.jdbc;

import org.springframework.jdbc.core.*;
import java.sql.*;

public class MyPreparedStatementSetter implements PreparedStatementSetter {

    Dept d;
    public MyPreparedStatementSetter(Dept d){
        this.d=d;
    }
    public void setValues(PreparedStatement ps) throws SQLException {
        ps.setString(1,d.dname);
        ps.setString(2,d.loc);
        ps.setInt(3,d.deptno);
    }
}//class
```

List 6.10 shows the log4j.properties file, which includes only one property that describes to off the logging for this application.

List 6.10: log4j.properties

```
log4j.rootLogger= OFF
```

After writing all the code shown in the above Lists we now want to configure a spring beans XML configuration file. List 6.11 shows the spring beans XML configuration file for this application. The XML configuration file includes the configurations for DataSource, JdbcTemplate and DeptDAODBImpl.

List 6.11: mybeans.xml

```
<beans xmlns="http://www.springframework.org/schema/beans"
xmlns:xsi= "http://www.w3.org/2001/XMLSchema-instance"
xsi:schemaLocation="http://www.springframework.org/schema/beans
http://www.springframework.org/schema/beans/spring-beans-2.0.xsd">

    <!--Configuring DataSource-->
    <bean id="datasource" class="org.apache.commons.dbcp.BasicDataSource">
        <property name="driverClassName">
            <value>oracle.jdbc.driver.OracleDriver</value>
        </property>
        <property name="url">
            <value>jdbc:oracle:thin:@localhost:1521:sandb</value>
        </property>
        <property name="username">
            <value>scott</value>
        </property>
        <property name="password">
            <value>tiger</value>
        </property>
    </bean>

    <!--Configuring JdbcTemplate-->
    <bean id="jdbctemp" class="org.springframework.jdbc.core.JdbcTemplate">
        <constructor-arg>
            <ref local="datasource"/>
        </constructor-arg>
    </bean>

    <!--Configuring DeptDAO-->
    <bean id="deptdao" class="com.santosh.spring.jdbc.DeptDAODBImpl">
        <constructor-arg>
            <ref local="jdbctemp"/>
        </constructor-arg>
    </bean>
</beans>
```

With this the configuration is completed. Now, after preparing the DAO and its implementation we want to test the configurations. List 6.12 shows a simple test case for the DeptDAO.

List 6.12: DeptDAOTestCase.java

```
import com.santosh.spring.jdbc.DeptDAO;
import com.santosh.spring.jdbc.DeptDAODBImpl;
import com.santosh.spring.jdbc.Dept;

import org.springframework.beans.factory.*;
import org.springframework.beans.factory.xml.*;
import org.springframework.core.io.*;

public class DeptDAOTestCase {

    BeanFactory beans;
    DeptDAO deptDAO;

    public DeptDAOTestCase(){

        beans=new XmlBeanFactory( new FileSystemResource("mybeans.xml"));
        deptDAO=(DeptDAO)beans.getBean("deptdao");
    }

    public static void main(String s[]) throws Exception {

        DeptDAOTestCase dtc=new DeptDAOTestCase();

        dtc.testCreateDept();
        System.out.println();
        dtc.testChangeLocation();
        System.out.println();
        dtc.testChangeDeptDetails();
        System.out.println();
        dtc.testRemoveDept();
    }//main

    public void testCreateDept(){

        System.out.println("Testing createDept method of DeptDAO...");
        Dept newDept=new Dept();
        newDept.deptno=50;
        newDept.dname="New Department";
        newDept.loc="Hyderabad";

        deptDAO.createDept(newDept);
        System.out.println("CreateDept successful");
    }

    public void testChangeLocation(){

        System.out.println("Testing changeLocation method of DeptDAO...");

        deptDAO.changeLocation(40, "Hyderabad");
```

```
        System.out.println("Location of Department 40 changed to Hyderabad
successfully");
    }
    public void testChangeDeptDetails(){
        System.out.println("Testing changeLocation method of DeptDAO...");
        Dept dept=new Dept();
        dept.deptno=50;
        dept.dname="New Department";
        dept.loc="Hyderabad";
        deptDAO.changeDeptDetails(dept);
        System.out.println("Location and Name of Department 40 changed to 'Hyderabad'
and 'New Department' successfully");
    }
    public void testRemoveDept(){
        System.out.println("Testing removeDept method of DeptDAO...");
        deptDAO.removeDept(50);
        System.out.println("Department with deptno 50 removed successfully");
    }
}//class
```

Now it is time to compile and run this example. To compile and run this example set the classpath to the following jar files:

- spring.jar
- commons-logging.jar
- commons-pool.jar
- commons-dbcp.jar
- log4j-1.2.14.jar and
- classes12.zip

Figure 6.1 shows the directories, the compiled files, and the result of executing the DAO test.

As you have learnt how to use JdbcTemplate to execute SQL DML statements, that is, using update() methods, we now want to learn how to execute Data Retrieval Statements like select and read the results. The following section explains how to use JdbcTemplate for executing the SQL Data Retrieval Statements.

6.6 USING JDBCTEMPLATE TO EXECUTE SQL SELECT QUERIES

We have learnt in the above section how to use JdbcTemplate for executing SQL DML statements, but it is not enough to just be able to store data; we even want to read the data from database. The JdbcTemplate provides simple ways to query the database. Using JdbcTemplate to query the database includes two simple steps described below:

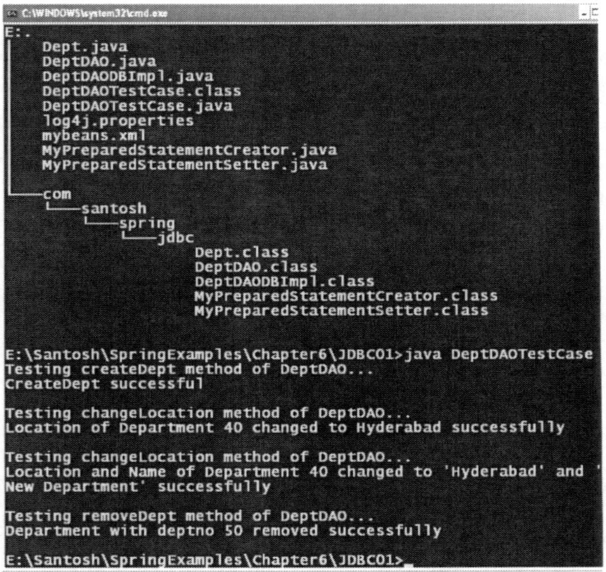

FIGURE 6.1 Output of DeptDAOTestCase

1. Prepare an SQL query and execute
2. Read the results

JdbcTemplate class includes query() methods to prepare and execute the SQL queries. The Spring JDBC abstraction framework provides three different types of callbacks to read the results after executing the SQL query using query() methods. The three callbacks of Spring JDBC abstraction framework to retrieve the data are:

- ResultSetExtractor
- RowCallbackHandler
- RowMapper

All the above three callbacks are described in detail in the following sections.

6.6.1 The ResultSetExtractor

The ResultSetExtractor is a callback interface used by JdbcTemplate's query methods. This interface contains only one method with the signature shown in the following code snippet.

Code Snippet

```
public Object extractData(ResultSet rs)
  throws SQLException, DataAccessException
```

The implementation classes of this interface needs to implement the extractData() method, which takes the responsibility of extracting results from a ResultSet, but it does not need to worry about handling the SQLException raised while extracting the results. The SQLException will be caught and handled by the JdbcTemplate calling this implementation. The extractData() method can return a type of object that can represent the data extracted from the ResultSet. The implementations of this interface are generally designed as stateless to make it reusable and reduce the memory requirements, but this can be designed stateful also, which is required when it accesses some stateful resources like output stream when reading the BLOB/CLOB content. The following code snippet shows the sample code of ResultSetExtractor implementation.

Code Snippet

```
public class DeptExtractor implements ResultSetExtractor {

    public Object extractData(ResultSet rs) throws SQLException {

        List depts=new ArrayList();
        while(rs.next()){
            Dept d=new Dept();
            d.deptno=rs.getInt(1);
            d.dname=rs.getString(2);
            d.loc=rs.getString(3);
            depts.add(d);
        }//if
        return depts;
    }//extractData
}
```

As shown in the preceding code snippet the extractData() method of ResultSetExtractor is given with a ResultSet obtained by the query() method of JdbcTemplate after executing the given SQL query. The extractData() method is responsible to extract all the data from ResultSet iterating over it and return an object representing the result, which is returned to the DAO calling the query() method. As described earlier, the ResultSetExtractor implementation is generally stateless unless it stores the result and represents after the execution of the query. Moreover, the other point to be considered is that the extractData() method includes throws SQLException that means the extractData() method implementation does not require to handle SQLException, but throw it to be handled by the query() method of JdbcTemplate instead making the implementation free from the tedious exception handling code.

This section has explained one approach of reading the results, that is, using ResultSetExtractor which requires iterating through the ResultSet and extract all the data. But in general we want to process results on a per-row basis. The following section explains the other approach of reading the result using RowCallbackHandler that can meet this requirement.

6.6.2 The RowCallbackHandler

The RowCallbackHandler is a callback interface used by JdbcTemplate's query methods. This interface contains only one method with the signature shown in the following code snippet.

Code Snippet

```
public void processRow(ResultSet rs) throws SQLException
```

The implementation classes of this interface needs to implement the processRow() method, which takes the responsibility to process each row of data in the ResultSet. The processRow() method should not call next() on the ResultSet. It requires to extract values of the current row and process the data on per-row basis. Usually the processRow() method does not need to worry about handling the SQLException raised while reading the results. The SQLException will be caught and handled by the JdbcTemplate calling this implementation. The processRow() method cannot return any result. It is generally implemented to process the result like preparing the XML document with the result data. If required it can store the result in its instance variable and then make it available to the DAO but for this it requires to be designed as stateful. The following code snippet shows the sample code of RowCallbackHandler implementation.

Code Snippet

```
public class DeptResults implements RowCallbackHandler {

    public List depts;
    public RowCallbackHandler(){
        depts=new ArrayList();
    }
    public void processRow(ResultSet rs) throws SQLException {
        Dept d=new Dept();
        d.deptno=rs.getInt(1);
        d.dname=rs.getString(2);
        d.loc=rs.getString(3);
        depts.add(d);
    }//processRow
}
```

As shown in the preceding code snippet the processRow() method is implemented to read the values from the current row without invoking next() method and store the result in the instance variable named 'depts' which can be further collected by the DAO. The following code snippet shows the piece of DAO code that shows how this works.

Code Snippet

```
public List getAllDepartments(){
    String sql_query=Ōselect * from deptŌ;
    DeptResults ds=new DeptResults();
    jdbcTemplate.query(sql_query, ds);
    return ds.depts;
}
```

From the above code snippet it can be understood that the RowCallbackHandler has to be stateful and can be used in a single thread environment. Using it in a multithreaded environment may return improper results. It is even a better practice to implement RowCallbackHandler as an anonymous inner class, which provides access to the variables of the surrounding method, that is, the DAO methods. The following code snippet shows the RowCallbackHandler implemented as anonymous inner class.

Code Snippet

```
public List getAllDepartments(){
    String sql_query=Őselect * from deptŐ;
    final List depts=new ArrayList();

    jdbcTemplate.query(sql_query, new RowCallbackHandler () {
        public void processRow(ResultSet rs) throws SQLException {
            Dept d=new Dept();
            d.deptno=rs.getInt(1);
            d.dname=rs.getString(2);
            d.loc=rs.getString(3);
            depts.add(d);
        }//processRow
    });
    return depts;
}
```

This section explained how to use RowCallbackHandler to read results, which provides a per-row basis of reading the results. But this approach forces us to design the implementation as stateful which may be costlier in some cases and to handle such situations Spring JDBC framework supports another approach, that is, RowMapper. The following section explains how to work with RowMapper to read the results.

6.6.3 The RowMapper

The RowMapper is another callback interface used by JdbcTemplate's query methods. This interface contains only one method with the signature shown in the following code snippet.

Code Snippet

```
public Object mapRow(ResultSet rs, int rowNum) throws SQLException
```

The implementation classes of this interface needs to implement the mapRow() method, which takes the responsibility to process each row of data in the ResultSet. The mapRow() method should not call next() on the ResultSet. It requires to extract values of the current row, process the data on per-row basis and map the current row values. As usual, the MapRow() method also does not need to worry about handling the SQLException raised while reading the results. The SQLException will be caught and handled by the JdbcTemplate calling this implementation. The mapRow() method can return an Object representing the result object for the current row. In general the implementations of this interface are designed as stateless to make it reusable and reduce the memory requirements. The following code snippet shows the sample code of RowMapper implementation.

Code Snippet

```
public class DeptResultMapper implements RowMapper {

    public Object mapRow(ResultSet rs, int rowNum) throws SQLException {
        Dept d=new Dept();
        d.deptno=rs.getInt(1);
        d.dname=rs.getString(2);
        d.loc=rs.getString(3);
        return d;
    }
}
```

As shown in the preceding code snippet the mapRow() method is implemented to read the values from the current row without invoking next() method and return the Dept object representing the values of the current row. The following code snippet shows the piece of DAO code that shows how this works.

Code Snippet

```
DeptResultMapper ds;
public void setDeptResultMapper(DeptResultMapper ds){this.ds=ds;}

public List getAllDepartments(){
    String sql_query="select * from dept";
    List depts=jdbcTemplate.query(sql_query, ds);
    return ds.depts;
}
```

This section has explained about the RowMapper and how it can be used to read the results. Moreover, the preceding three sections has explained the three possible approaches to read the results. Now it is time to look at the various query() methods of JdbcTemplate that can be used to execute the SQL query and allows to read the results using any one of the above explained three approaches. The following section explains you the various query() methods of JdbcTemplate.

6.6.4 JdbcTemplate Query() Methods

As in the above section you have learnt about the different callbacks to read the results. Here we will look at the various query() methods of JdbcTemplate that allows us to execute the SQL query and read the results using any one of the callback. Table 6.4 shows the various query() methods of JdbcTemplate.

TABLE 6.4 JdbcTemplate methods for querying results

Method	*Description*
public Object query(String sql, ResultSetExtractor res)	Executes the given SQL query using the JDBC Statement and allows to read the results with a ResultSetExtractor
public void query(String sql, RowCallbackHandler rch)	Executes the given SQL query using the JDBC Statement and allows reading the results with a RowCallbackHandler.

(*Contd.*)

	Note: This methods return type is List in the earlier versions of Spring (that is, up to Spring 2.0). Where it returns the result List in case if the callback implements ResultReader, that is subtype of RowCallbackHandler or else 'null'. In Spring Framework 2.0 ResultReader the subtype of RowCallbackHandler is removed. Thus the return type of this method is changed to void.
public List query(String sql, RowMapper rm)	Executes the given SQL query using the JDBC Statement and allows to read the results with a RowMapper.
public Object query(String sql, Object[] params, ResultSetExtractor res)	Executes the given SQL query using the JDBC PreparedStatement. The SQL statement can contain bind parameters (that is, '?', same as the SQL statements used with PreparedStatement). This method uses the given Object[] 'params' to set the bind parameters, and allows to read the results with a ResultSetExtractor.
public void query(String sql, Object[] params, RowCallbackHandler rch)	Executes the given SQL query using the JDBC PreparedStatement. This method uses the given Object[] 'params' to set the bind parameters and allows to read the results with a RowCallbackHandler.
public List query(String sql, Object[] params, RowMapper rm)	Executes the given SQL query using the JDBC PreparedStatement. This method uses the given Object[] 'params' to set the bind parameters and allows to read the results with a RowMapper.
public Object query(String sql, Object[] params, int[] paramTypes, ResultSetExtractor res)	Executes the given SQL query using the JDBC PreparedStatement object of the JDBC Connection obtained using the DataSource set to this JdbcTemplate object. The bind parameters are set with the given arguments to execute the statement. While setting the bind parameters instead of using setObject() a generic method like the above described update() method, this method uses the parameter types described under the third argument *paramType*. The paramTypes are the constants from java.sql.Types. This method allows reading the results with a ResultSetExtractor.
public void query(String sql, Object[] params, int[] paramTypes, RowCallbackHandler rch)	This method is the same as the above method but this allows us to read the result with RowCallbackHandler.
public List query(String sql, Object[] params, int[] paramTypes, RowMapper rm)	This method is the same as the above method but this allows us to read the result with RowMapper.
public Object query(String sql, PreparedStatementSetter pss, ResultSetExtractor res)	Executes the given SQL query using the JDBC PreparedStatement same as the above described methods. This method uses the given PreparedStatementSetter object to set the bind parameters. The PreparedStatementSetter is a helper that sets the parameters of the PreparedStatement. This contains only one method named setValues, that takes PreparedStatement as an argument. This method allows us to read the result with ResultSetExtractor.
public void query(String sql, PreparedStatementSetter pss, RowCallbackHandler rch)	This method is the same as the above method but this allows us to read the result with RowCallbackHandler.
public List query(String sql, PreparedStatementSetter pss, RowMapper rm)	This method is the same as the above method but this allows us to read the result with RowMapper.

(*Contd.*)

public Object query (PreparedStatementCreator psc, ResultSetExtractor res)	Executes the PreparedStatement that is obtained using the given Prepared-StatementCreator. The PreparedStatementCreator contains only one method named createPreparedStatement with an argument of java.sql.Connection type and return type as java.sql.PreparedStatement. This method allows us to read the result with ResultSetExtractor.
public void query (PreparedStatementCreator psc, RowCallbackHandler rch)	This method is the same as the above method but this allows us to read the result with RowCallbackHandler.
public List query (PreparedStatementCreator psc, RowMapper rm)	This method is the same as the above method but this allows us to read the result with RowMapper.

Table 6.6 has listed all the query() methods of JdbcTemplate that allows us to read the results using the callbacks. As we have learnt about the three callbacks and the various query() methods it is time to look at an example that can explain all the preceding discussions in action.

6.6.5 Modifying DeptDAO to Read Dept Details

To find the query() methods and callbacks learnt in the preceding sections instead of writing a new DAO we can enhance the features of DeptDAO demonstrated in the previous example. First of all we will add three new methods in DeptDAO interface. List 6.12 shows the DeptDAO with the new methods added (shown in bold).

List 6.12: DeptDAO.java

```
package com.santosh.spring.jdbc;

public interface DeptDAO {
     int createDept(Dept d);
     void changeLocation(int dno, String newloc);
     void changeDeptDetails(Dept d);
     void removeDept(int dno);

     String getDeptName(int dno);
     Dept getDeptDetails(int dno);
     java.util.List<Dept> getAllDepartments();
}
```

Now, add the implementations for these three methods in DeptDAODBImpl class. List 6.13 shows the modified version of DeptDAODBImpl class that is added with new methods of implementation shown in bold.

List 6.13: DeptDAODBImpl.java

```
package com.santosh.spring.jdbc;

import org.springframework.jdbc.core.*;
import java.util.*;
import java.sql.*;
```

```
public class DeptDAODBImpl implements DeptDAO {

    JdbcTemplate jt;

    public DeptDAODBImpl(JdbcTemplate jt){
        this.jt=jt;
    }//cons

    public void changeLocation(int dno, String loc){
        jt.update("update dept set loc=? where deptno=?",new Object[]{loc,new
Integer(dno)});
    }

    public void changeDeptDetails(Dept d){
        MyPreparedStatementSetter mpss= new MyPreparedStatementSetter(d);
        jt.update("update dept set dname=?,loc=? where deptno=?",mpss);
    }

    public void removeDept(int dno){
        jt.update("delete from dept where deptno="+dno);
    }

    public int createDept(Dept d) {
        MyPreparedStatementCreator mpsc=new MyPreparedStatementCreator(d);
        return jt.update(mpsc);
  }

    /*Implementation for getDeptName method*/
    public String getDeptName(int dno){
        return (String) jt.query("select dname from dept where deptno="+dno,
            new ResultSetExtractor(){
                public Object extractData(ResultSet rs)throws SQLException{
                    if (rs.next()) return rs.getString(1);
                    else return null;
                }
        });
    }

    /*Implementation for getDeptDetails method*/
    public Dept getDeptDetails(int dno){
        final Dept dept=new Dept();
        jt.query("select * from dept where deptno="+dno,
            new RowCallbackHandler(){
                public void processRow(ResultSet rs)throws SQLException {
                    dept.deptno=rs.getInt(1);
                    dept.dname=rs.getString(2);
                    dept.loc=rs.getString(3);
                }
            });
```

```
        return dept;
    }

    /*Implementation for getAllDepartments method*/
    public List<Dept> getAllDepartments(){
        return (List<Dept>)jt.query("select * from dept", new DeptMapper());
    }
}//class
```

In List 6.13, all the three new methods are given with an implementation as here we want to show all the three callbacks in action so we have used all the three, and two of them are implemented as anonymous inner classes and one as an outer class named DeptMapper. List 6.14 shows the DeptMapper, which is an implementation of RowMapper.

List 6.14: DeptMapper.java

```
package com.santosh.spring.jdbc;

import org.springframework.jdbc.core.*;
import java.sql.*;

public class DeptMapper implements RowMapper {

  public Object mapRow(ResultSet rs, int i) throws SQLException {
    Dept d=new Dept();
    d.deptno=rs.getInt(1);
    d.dname=rs.getString(2);
    d.loc=rs.getString(3);
    return d;
  }//mapRow
}//class
```

After doing the above two additions we want to test these implementations and List 6.15 shows the Test Case for the new methods added in the DeptDAO.

List 6.15: DeptDAOReadTestCase.java

```
import com.santosh.spring.jdbc.DeptDAO;
import com.santosh.spring.jdbc.Dept;

import org.springframework.beans.factory.*;
import org.springframework.beans.factory.xml.*;
import org.springframework.core.io.*;
import java.util.*;

public class DeptDAOReadTestCase {
```

```
BeanFactory beans;
DeptDAO deptDAO;

public DeptDAOReadTestCase(){

  beans=new XmlBeanFactory( new FileSystemResource("mybeans.xml"));
  deptDAO=(DeptDAO)beans.getBean("deptdao");
}

public static void main(String s[]) throws Exception {

  DeptDAOReadTestCase dtc=new DeptDAOReadTestCase();

  dtc.testGetDeptName();
  System.out.println();
  dtc.testGetDeptDetails();
  System.out.println();
  dtc.testGetAllDepartments();
}//main

public void testGetDeptName(){

  System.out.println("Testing getDeptName method of DeptDAO...");
  String dname=deptDAO.getDeptName(20);
  if (dname==null)
    System.out.println("Department not found");
  else
    System.out.println("Department name of department "+20+" is "+dname);

}

public void testGetDeptDetails(){

  System.out.println("Testing getDeptDetails method of DeptDAO...");
  Dept dept=deptDAO.getDeptDetails(20);
  System.out.println("Details of Department 20:");
  System.out.println("\tName : "+dept.dname);
  System.out.println("\tLocation : "+dept.loc);
}

public void testGetAllDepartments(){

  System.out.println("Testing getAllDepartments method of DeptDAO...");
  List<Dept> depts=deptDAO.getAllDepartments();
  for (Dept dept: depts){
```

```
            System.out.println("Details of Department "+dept.deptno+":");
            System.out.println("\tName : "+dept.dname);
            System.out.println("\tLocation : "+dept.loc);
            System.out.println();
        }
    }
}//class
```

The output of the preceding test case is shown in Fig. 6.3 shown below.

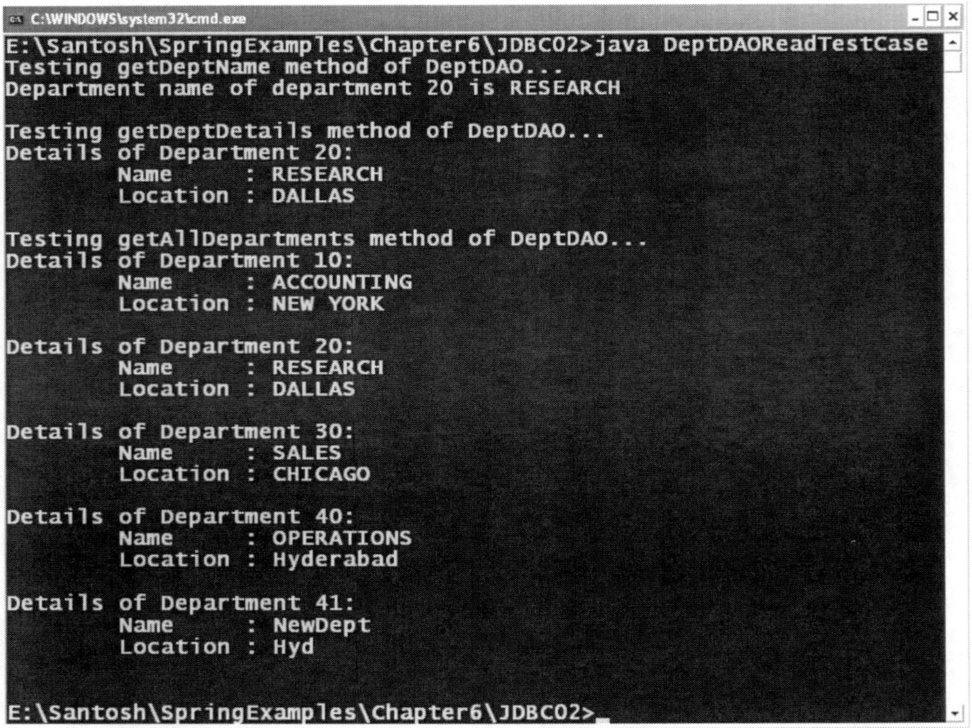

FIGURE 6.3 Output of DeptDAOReadTestCase

In the preceding example, we developed DeptMapper which is an implementation of RowMapper. Instead Spring JDBC framework includes two useful implementations for RowMapper that can be directly used into our application. The default available RowMapper implementations are:

- **SingleColumnRowMapper**
- **ColumnMapRowMapper**

6.6.6 The SingleColumnMapper

The org.springframework.jdbc.core.SingleColumnRowMapper is a utility class under the Spring JDBC framework. This class implements RowMapper. This class converts a single column into a single result value per row. The default implementation works on a ResultSet that just contains a single column. The value for the single column will be extracted from the ResultSet and converted into the specified target type. The type of the result value for each row can be specified through the constructor or by explicitly calling setRequiredType() method of SingleColumnRowMapper. The following code snippet shows the sample code to use SingleColumnRowMapper.

Code Snippet

```
public List<String> getDeptNames(){
  String sql_query="select dname from dept";
  SingleColumnRowMapper scm=new SingleColumnRowMapper (String.class);
  return (List<String>)jdbcTemplate.query(sql_query, scm);
}
```

6.6.7 The ColumnMapRowMapper

The org.springframework.jdbc.core.ColumnMapRowMapper is another utility class under the Spring JDBC framework, this class also implements RowMapper. This class creates a java.util.Map value per row. The Map represents all columns as key-value pairs, one entry for each column, with column name as a key which is case insensitive. The following code snippet shows the sample code to use ColumnMapRowMapper.

Code Snippet

```
public List<Map> getDeptDetails(){
  String sql_query="select * from dept";
  ColumnMapRowMapper cm=new ColumnMapRowMapper ();
  return (List<Map>)jdbcTemplate.query(sql_query, cm);
}
```

We have learnt the basic approach of reading the results of the queries executed using the JdbcTemplate's query() methods. Now we need to look at the other conveniences provided by JdbcTemplate for reading the simple results. The following section explains the various conveniences provided by JdbcTemplate to read simple results.

6.6.8 JdbcTemplate Conveniences to Read Results

Apart from using the callbacks to read the query results JdbcTemplate provides several convenience methods that provide an easy way for accessing data in the database. These convenience methods provide a direct use without the need to create or use additional framework-specific callback objects. They provide basic options for executing queries and read the results. Table 6.5 shows the convenience methods of JdbcTemplate.

TABLE 6.5 JdbcTemplate convenience method for querying data

Method	*Description*
public int queryForInt(String sql_query)	Convenience method that executes the given SQL query using a JDBC Statement object. The SQL query should result in a single row and single column of int type.
public int queryForInt(String sql_query, Object[] params)	Convenience method that executes the given SQL query using a Prepared Statement with the given params. The SQL query should result in a single row and single column of int type.
public int queryForInt(String sql_query, Object[] params, int[] paramTypes)	Same as the preceding method but this facilitates to describe the parameter types in addition.
public long queryForLong (String sql_query)	Convenience method that executes the given SQL query using a JDBC Statement object. The SQL query should result in a single row and single column of long type.
public long queryForLong (String sql_query, Object[] params)	Convenience method that executes the given SQL query using a Prepared Statement with the given params. The SQL query should result in a single row and single column of long type.
public long queryForLong (String sql_query, Object[] params, int[] paramTypes)	Same as the preceding method but this facilitates to describe the parameter types in addition.
public List queryForList(String sql_query)	Convenience method that executes the given SQL query using a JDBC Statement object. The SQL query should result in one or more rows with one or more columns of any type. Returns a List of Map objects. One Map object is created for each row, one entry for each column with column name as a key and its values as an entry value.
public List queryForList(String sql_query, Class elementType)	Convenience method that executes the given SQL query using a JDBC Statement object. The SQL query should result in one or more rows with one column compatible to the given elementType. Returns a List of given element Type of objects.
public List queryForList(String sql_query, Object[] params)	Convenience method that executes the given SQL query using a Prepared Statement with the given params. The SQL query should result in one or more rows with one or more column of any type. Returns a List of Map objects. One Map object is created for each row, one entry for each column with column name as a key and its values as an entry value.
public List queryForList(String sql_query, Object[] params, Class elementType)	Convenience method that executes the given SQL query using a Prepared Statement with the given params. The SQL query should result in one or more rows with one column compatible to the given elementType. Returns a List of given elementType of objects.
public List queryForList(String sql_query, Object[] params, int[] paramTypes)	Same as queryForList(String sql_query, Object[] params) method but this facilitates the description of the parameter types in addition.
public List queryForList(String sql_query, Object[] params, int[] paramTypes, Class elementType)	Same as queryForList(String sql_query, Object[] params, Class elementType) method but this facilitates the description of the parameter types in addition.

(Contd.)

public Map queryForMap (String sql_query)	Convenience method that executes the given SQL query using a statement. The SQL query should result in a single row with one or more column of any type. Returns a Map object with one entry for each column with column name as a key and its values as an entry value.
public Map queryForMap (String sql_query, Object[] params)	Convenience method that executes the given SQL query using a Prepared Statement with the given params. The SQL query should result in a single row with one or more column of any type. Returns a Map object with one entry for each column with column name as a key and its values as an entry value.
public Map queryForMap (String sql_query, Object[] params, int[] paramTypes)	Same as the preceding method but this facilitates the description of the parameter types in addition.
public Object queryForObject (String sql_query, Class type)	Convenience method that executes the given SQL query using a statement. The SQL query should result in a single row with a single column compatible to the given type.
public Object queryForObject (String sql_query, Object[] params, Class type)	Convenience method that executes the given SQL query using a Prepared Statement with the given params. The SQL query should result in a single row with a single column compatible to the given type.
public Object queryForObject (String sql_query, Object[] params, int[] paramTypes, Class type)	Same as the preceding method but this facilitates the description of the parameter types in addition.

After learning the convenience methods we now want to see some of these methods in action. The following section shows how to use these methods in application.

6.6.9 Using JdbcTemplate Conveniences to Read Results

In the preceding section you learnt convenience methods of JdbcTemplate to read results. To throw more light on these methods this section explains an example by putting some of these methods in action. This will explain how to use the other overloaded methods. To demonstrate these methods in this example we will design a partial DAO that represents employee details (emp table) here. As our interest is to learn how to read results using the JdbcTemplate convenience methods that is the reason we want to limit the DAO methods to only a few methods that read the employee details. List 6.16 shows the EmployeeDAO interface.

List 6.16: EmployeeDAO.java

```
package com.santosh.spring.jdbc;

import java.util.*;

public interface EmployeeDAO {

  int getDeptNo(int empno);
  String getName(int empno);
  double getSalary(int empno);

  Map getEmployeeDetails(int empno);
  List getEmployeeDetails();
}
```

List 6.16 shows the EmployeeDAO with five methods that allow to access employee details like methods to get the department number, name, salary of the given employee, one method to get all the details of a particular employee with the given employee number, and the method for getting all the employees details. List 6.17 shows the implementation of this DAO.

List 6.17: EmployeeDAODBImpl.java

```
package com.santosh.spring.jdbc;

import java.util.*;
import java.sql.*;
import org.springframework.jdbc.core.*;

public class EmployeeDAODBImpl implements EmployeeDAO {

  private JdbcTemplate jdbcTemplate;

  public EmployeeDAODBImpl(JdbcTemplate jt){

    jdbcTemplate=jt;
  }

  public int getDeptNo(int empno){
    return jdbcTemplate.queryForInt(
                  "select deptno from emp where empno="+empno);
  }

  public String getName(int empno){
    return (String) jdbcTemplate.queryForObject(
                  "select ename from emp where empno="+empno, String.class);
  }
  public double getSalary(int empno){
    return (Double) jdbcTemplate.queryForObject(
                  "select sal from emp where empno=?",
                  new Object[]{empno}, Double.class);
  }

  public Map getEmployeeDetails(int empno){
    return jdbcTemplate.queryForMap(
                  "select ename, deptno, sal from emp where empno=?",
                  new Object[]{empno});
  }

  public List getEmployeeDetails() {
    return jdbcTemplate.queryForList(
                    "select empno, ename, deptno, sal from emp");
  }
}//class
```

List 6.17 shows the implementation of EmployeeDAO that uses the convenience method of JdbcTemplate explained in the preceding section. List 6.18 shows the spring beans XML configuration file to test this DAO implementation.

List 6.18: mybeans.pxml

```
<beans xmlns="http://www.springframework.org/schema/beans"
xmlns:xsi="http://www.w3.org/2001/XMLSchema-instance"
xsi:schemaLocation="http://www.springframework.org/schema/beans          http://
www.springframework.org/schema/beans/spring-beans-2.0.xsd">
  <bean id="datasource" class="org.apache.commons.dbcp.BasicDataSource">
    <property name="driverClassName">
      <value>oracle.jdbc.driver.OracleDriver</value>
    </property>
    <property name="url">
      <value>jdbc:oracle:thin:@localhost:1521:sandb</value>
    </property>
    <property name="username">
      <value>scott</value>
    </property>
    <property name="password">
      <value>tiger</value>
    </property>
  </bean>

  <bean id="jdbctempl" class="org.springframework.jdbc.core.JdbcTemplate">
    <constructor-arg>
      <ref local="datasource"/>
    </constructor-arg>
  </bean>

  <bean id="empDAO" class="com.santosh.spring.jdbc.EmployeeDAODBImpl">
    <constructor-arg>
      <ref local="jdbctempl"/>
    </constructor-arg>
  </bean>
</beans>
```

List 6.19 shows a simple test case to test the DAO implementation shown in List 6.17.

List 6.19: EmployeeDAOTestCase.java

```
import org.springframework.beans.factory.*;
import org.springframework.beans.factory.xml.*;
import org.springframework.core.io.*;
import com.santosh.spring.jdbc.EmployeeDAO;
import java.util.Map;
```

```
import java.util.Set;
import java.util.List;

public class EmployeeDAOTestCase {
  BeanFactory beans;
  EmployeeDAO employeeDAO;

  public EmployeeDAOTestCase(){

    beans=new XmlBeanFactory(new FileSystemResource("mybeans.xml"));
    employeeDAO=(EmployeeDAO)beans.getBean("empDAO");
  }
  public static void main(String s[]) throws Exception {
    EmployeeDAOTestCase etc=new EmployeeDAOTestCase();

    etc.testGetDeptNo();
    System.out.println();
    etc.testGetName();
    System.out.println();
    etc.testGetSalary();
    System.out.println();
    etc.testGetEmployeeDetails();
    System.out.println();
    etc.testGetEmployeeDetails1();
  }//main

  public void testGetDeptNo(){
    System.out.println("Testing getDeptNo method of EmployeeDAO...");
    int dno=employeeDAO.getDeptNo(7839);
    System.out.println("response of getDeptno(7839) : "+ dno);
  }

  public void testGetName(){
    System.out.println("Testing getName method of EmployeeDAO...");
    String name=employeeDAO.getName(7839);
    System.out.println("response of getName(7839) : "+ name);
  }
  public void testGetSalary(){
    System.out.println("Testing getSalary method of EmployeeDAO...");
```

```
        double sal=employeeDAO.getSalary(7839);
        System.out.println("response of getSalary(7839) : "+ sal);
    }
    public void testGetEmployeeDetails(){
        System.out.println(
                "Testing getEmployeeDetails(7839) method of EmployeeDAO...");
        Map empDetails=employeeDAO.getEmployeeDetails(7839);
        Set<String> keys=empDetails.keySet();
        System.out.println("Employee Details of emp 7839");
        for (String key: keys){
            System.out.println("\t"+key+":"+empDetails.get(key));
        }
    }
    public void testGetEmployeeDetails1() {
            System.out.println(
                    "Testing getEmployeeDetails() method of EmployeeDAO...");
        List<Map> emps=(List<Map>)employeeDAO.getEmployeeDetails();
        System.out.println("getEmployeeDetails() has returned a List with "+
                        emps.size()+" elements");
        System.out.println("EmpNo\tName\tSalary\tDeptNo");
        System.out.println(".............");
        for (Map empDetails: emps){
            System.out.print(empDetails.get("EMPNO")+"\t");
            System.out.print(empDetails.get("ENAME")+"\t");
            System.out.print(empDetails.get("SAL")+"\t");
            System.out.print(empDetails.get("DEPTNO")+"\n");
        }
    }
}
```

Now after writing the files shown in the Lists 6.16 through 6.19 compile the java files and execute the test case listed in List 6.19 as shown in Fig 6.4.

Figure 6.4 shows the test results of the EmployeeDAO implementation that used JdbcTemplate's convenience query() methods. In this section you have learnt how to read the data using the JdbcTemplate of the Spring JDBC abstraction framework. Now it is time to look at some advanced options like calling stored procedures, executing the batch updates, etc., using JdbcTemplate. The following section of this chapter explains these topics one after the other. The next section explains how to call stored procedures using JdbcTemplate.

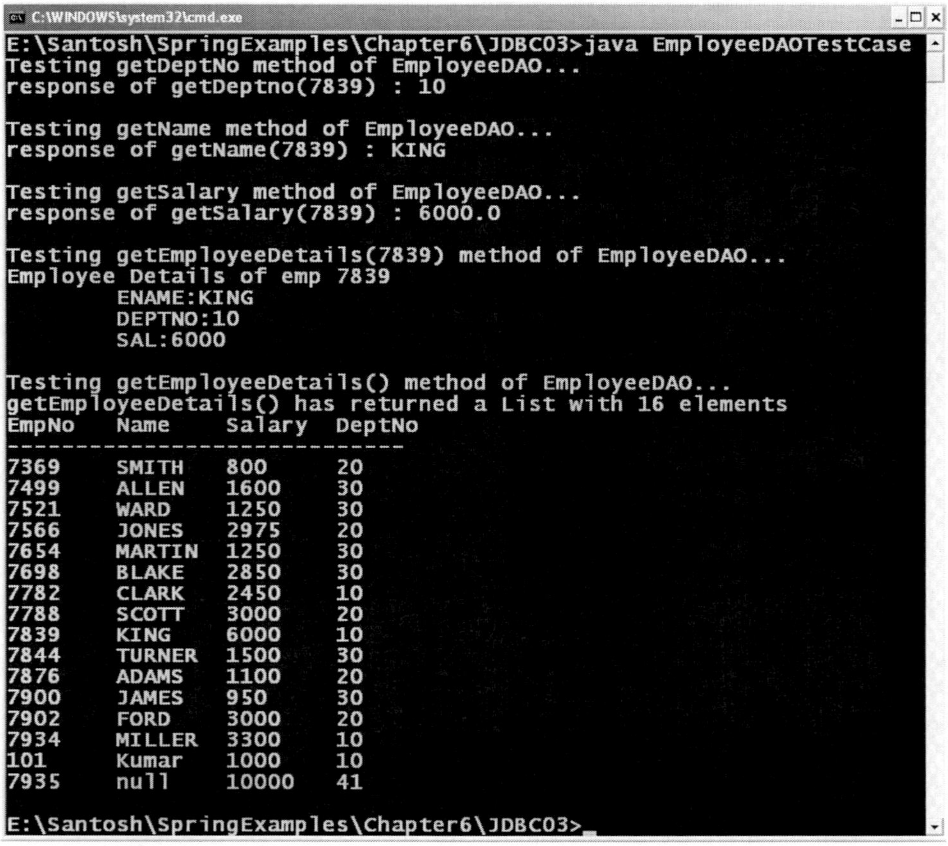

```
C:\WINDOWS\system32\cmd.exe
E:\Santosh\SpringExamples\Chapter6\JDBC03>java EmployeeDAOTestCase
Testing getDeptNo method of EmployeeDAO...
response of getDeptno(7839) : 10

Testing getName method of EmployeeDAO...
response of getName(7839) : KING

Testing getSalary method of EmployeeDAO...
response of getSalary(7839) : 6000.0

Testing getEmployeeDetails(7839) method of EmployeeDAO...
Employee Details of emp 7839
        ENAME:KING
        DEPTNO:10
        SAL:6000

Testing getEmployeeDetails() method of EmployeeDAO...
getEmployeeDetails() has returned a List with 16 elements
EmpNo   Name    Salary  DeptNo
-----------------------------
7369    SMITH   800     20
7499    ALLEN   1600    30
7521    WARD    1250    30
7566    JONES   2975    20
7654    MARTIN  1250    30
7698    BLAKE   2850    30
7782    CLARK   2450    10
7788    SCOTT   3000    20
7839    KING    6000    10
7844    TURNER  1500    30
7876    ADAMS   1100    20
7900    JAMES   950     30
7902    FORD    3000    20
7934    MILLER  3300    10
101     Kumar   1000    10
7935    null    10000   41

E:\Santosh\SpringExamples\Chapter6\JDBC03>
```

FIGURE 6.4 Output of EmployeeDAOTestCase

6.7 CALLING STORED PROCEDURE USING JDBCTEMPLATE

As we know that stored procedure is a subroutine in the database available to the applications accessing database and is called using CallableStatement from the Java programs. Procedures are stored in DB. The procedures called by the CallableStatement are the database programs which contains the database interface.

- The stored procedures contains input, output, or both the input and output parameters.
- After the execution of the SQL statements, the stored procedures return a value through the OUT parameters.
- The stored procedures can return multiple ResultSets.

The stored procedures allow us to make a single call to the database but they are generally a group of SQL statements. The bounded SQL statements are executed statically for better performance. The ored procedure encapsulates the values within three types of parameters such as IN, OUT, and IN OUT. The following parameters can be declared while creating a procedure for the database.

- **IN–**The IN parameter can be referenced by the procedure. The value of the parameter cannot be overwritten by the procedure.
- **OUT–**This parameter cannot be referenced by the procedure, but the value of the parameter can be overwritten by the procedure.
- **IN OUT–**The parameter can be referenced by the procedure and the value of the parameter can be overwritten by the procedure.

The syntax used for creating a procedure is:

```
Create or [Replace] Procedure procedure_name
  [(parameter [, parameter])]
IS
  [Declarations]
BEGIN
  executables
  [EXCEPTION exceptions]
END [Procedure_name]
```

The Spring JDBC framework provides a support for calling stored procedures, JdbcTemplate includes a method named call to execute the procedure or function. The following snippet shows the method signature of call method of JdbcTemplate.

```
public Map call(CallableStatementCreator csc, List declaredParameters)
```

The first argument of the call() method is a CallableStatementCreator, which is a callback interface used by the JdbcTemplate to get the CallableStatement to execute. The CallableStatementCreator interface contains only one method with the signature shown in the following code snippet.

Code Snippet

```
public CallableStatement createCallableStatement(Connection con) throws SQLException
```

The implementation classes of this interface needs to implement the createCallableStatement() method, which takes the responsibility to create a CallableStatement using the given JDBC Connection object and set the parameters. The createCallableStatement() method does not need to worry about handling the SQLException raised while preparing the CallableStatement and setting the parameters. The SQLException will be caught and handled by the JdbcTemplate calling this implementation.

The second argument of the call() method is a java.util.List, which encapsulates the list of declared SqlParameter objects.

As we have learnt about the procedure and the Spring JDBC framework support for calling a procedure it is time to look at an example that can show this in action. List 6.20 shows the simple stored procedure.

List 6.20: getDeptName (stored procedure)

```
create or replace procedure getDeptName (dno number, name OUT varchar2) as
  begin
    select dname into name from dept where deptno=dno;
  end;
```

The stored procedure shown in List 6.20 takes one IN and OUT parameters. The getDeptName procedure takes the department number and gives out the name of the department number through the OUT parameter of the procedure. Now we will write a CallableStatementCreator callback to prepare a CallableStatement that can execute the stored procedure shown in List 6.20. List 6.21 shows the CallableStatementCreator implementation.

List 6.21: MyCallableStatementCreator.java

```
package com.santosh.spring.jdbc;

import org.springframework.jdbc.core.*;
import java.sql.*;

public class MyCallableStatementCreator implements CallableStatementCreator {

  private int deptno;
  public MyCallableStatementCreator(int dno) {deptno=dno;}

  public CallableStatement createCallableStatement(Connection con)
                                                   throws SQLException {

    CallableStatement cs=con.prepareCall("{call getDeptName(?,?)}");
    cs.setInt(1,deptno);
    cs.registerOutParameter(2,Types.LONGVARCHAR);
    return cs;
  }
}//class
```

List 6.21 shows the CallableStatementCreator implementation that prepares a CallableStatement that executes the getDeptName procedure shown in List 6.20. List 6.22 shows the test case that uses JdbcTemplate to execute the procedure using this callback.

List 6.22: CallProcedureTestCase.java

```
import org.springframework.beans.factory.*;
import org.springframework.beans.factory.xml.*;
import org.springframework.core.io.*;
import org.springframework.jdbc.core.JdbcTemplate;
import org.springframework.jdbc.core.SqlParameter;
import org.springframework.jdbc.core.SqlOutParameter;
```

```
import java.sql.Types;
import java.util.Map;
import java.util.ArrayList;
import com.santosh.spring.jdbc.MyCallableStatementCreator;

public class CallProcedureTestCase {

  public static void main(String s[]) throws Exception {

    BeanFactory beans=new XmlBeanFactory(
                          new FileSystemResource("mybeans.xml"));
    JdbcTemplate jdbcTemplate=(JdbcTemplate)beans.getBean("jdbctemp1");

    ArrayList parameters=new ArrayList();
    parameters.add(new SqlParameter(Types.INTEGER));
    parameters.add(new SqlOutParameter("name",Types.LONGVARCHAR));

    Map m=jdbcTemplate.call(
          new MyCallableStatementCreator(new Integer(s[0])), parameters);
    System.out.println("The department name of dept "+new Integer(s[0])+
                        " is : "+ m.get("name"));
  }//main
}//class
```

List 6.22 shows the test case to call the procedure, which includes creating a list of SqlParameter objects and then invoke call() method of JdbcTemplate using appropriate arguments. Figure 6.5 shows the output of the preceding test case when executed with different inputs (that is, department numbers).

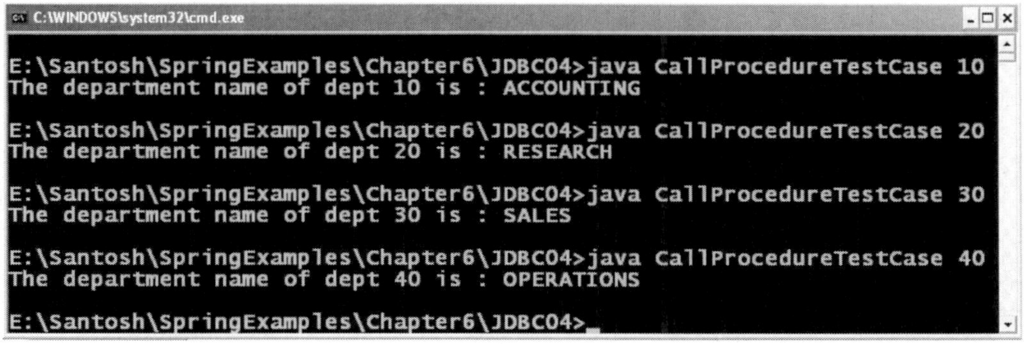

FIGURE 6.4 Outputs of CallProcedureTestCase

In this section we learnt how to call stored procedures with simple in and out parameters, using JdbcTemplate. The next section explains how to execute a stored procedure that returns a CURSOR (that is, ResultSet type), using JdbcTemplate.

6.8 WORKING WITH CURSOR

A cursor defines the runtime execution environment for a query where the result of the query execution can be captured. That is, we can open the cursor and execute the queries in that environment so that we can read the output of the query from the cursor. The syntax used to create a cursor is as follows:

```
create or replace package package_name as
  TYPE type_name IS REF CURSOR;
END;
```

As we have seen how to create a database CURSOR let us learn how to access CURSOR type value using JdbcTemplate. Let us start with creating a cursor. The following code snippet shows the CURSOR declaration:

Code Snippet

```
create or replace package mypack as
type mycursor is ref cursor;
end;
```

The preceding code snippet declares a cursor type with a name 'mycursor' under the package 'mypack'. Now, create a procedure that can return cursor type created in the preceding code snippet.

Code Snippet

```
create or replace procedure getEmpdetails(
empdetails out mypack.mycursor,
dno number) as
begin
  open empdetails for
  select empno, ename, sal from emp where deptno=dno;
end;
```

The preceding code snippet shows procedure 'getEmpdetails' that includes an OUT parameter of 'mypack.mycursor' type, and an IN parameter of 'number' type. This procedure a ResultSet that includes the empno, ename, and sal of all the employees with the given department number. The following code snippet shows how to use JdbcTemplate to execute this procedure and access the ResultSet.

Code Snippet

```
package com.santosh.spring;
import oracle.jdbc.driver.OracleTypes;
import org.springframework.jdbc.core.*;
import java.util.*;
import java.sql.*;

public class JdbcTemplateCursorTestCase {
  public static void main(String[] args) {
```

```
    RowMapper mapper=new RowMapper() {
      public Object mapRow(ResultSet rs, int i)
                        throws SQLException {
            Emp e=new Emp();
            e.empno=rs.getInt(1);
            e.ename=rs.getString(2);
            e.sal=rs.getDouble(3);
            return e;
          }//mapRow
      }//class

    ArrayList parameters=new ArrayList();
    parameters.add(new SqlOutParameter(
              "emps", OracleTypes.CURSOR, mapper));
    parameters.add(new SqlParameter(Types.INTEGER));

    CallableStatementCreator csc=
      new CallableStatementCreator(){
        public CallableStatement createCallableStatement(
                              Connection con) throws SQLException {
          CallableStatement cs=con.prepareCall("{call getEmpdetails(?,?)}");
          cs.registerOutParameter(1, OracleTypes.CURSOR);
          cs.setInt(2, 10);
          return cs;
        }
    }
  Map m=jt.call(csc, parameters);
  List<Emp> l=(List<Emp>)m.get("emps");

      for (Emp e:l){
      System.out.print(e.empno+"\t");
      System.out.print(e.sal+"\t");
      System.out.print(e.ename);
    }
  }
}
```

In this section we learnt how to read ResultSet returned by a stored procedure. The next section explains how to execute batch statements using JdbcTemplate.

6.9 BATCH UPDATES USING JDBCTEMPLATE

As we know the Batch update option allows submitting multiple DML/DDL operations to a data source for processing at once. Submitting multiple DML/DDL queries together, instead of individually improves the performance. The batch update support in JDBC is introduced in JDBC 2.0 specifications, that is, the ability of remembering the list of commands by Statement and

PreparedStatement is added in JDBC 2.0. This section explains how to use such an important batch update option with JdbcTemplate. The JdbcTemplate includes a support for executing the batch of statements through a JDBC Statement and PreparedStatement. The JdbcTemplate includes two overloaded batchUpdate() methods in support of this feature—one for executing a batch of SQL statements using JDBC Statement and the other for executing the SQL statement for multiple times with different parameters using PreparedStatement. The method signatures of these two methods are shown in the following code snippet.

Code Snippet

```
public int[] batchUpdate(String[] sql) throws DataAccessException

public int[] batchUpdate(String sql, BatchPreparedStatementSetter pss)
                                                throws DataAccessException
```

The preceding code snippet shows the batchUpdate methods of JdbcTemplate. The first one is used to issue multiple SQL updates on a single statement using JDBC 2.0 batch update option. If the JDBC driver does not support batch updates then it executes the given SQL updates as separate updates on a single JDBC Statement object. The following sample code shows how to use this method.

Sample Code

```
jdbcTemplate.batchUpdate (new String[]{
                          "update emp set sal=sal*1.3 where empno=7839",
                          "update emp set sal=sal*1.1 where empno=7782",
                          "update dept set loc='Hyderabad' where deptno=10"});
```

The other batchUpdate method of JdbcTemplate allows issuing multiple updates on a single PreparedStatement, using JDBC 2.0 batch updates feature and a BatchPreparedStatementSetter to set values. If the JDBC driver does not support batch updates then this executes the updates as a separate updates on a single PreparedStatement object. The following sample code shows how to use this method.

Sample Code

```
jdbcTemplate.batchUpdate ("update emp set sal*=? where empno=?",
        new BatchPreparedStatementSetter(){
          public int getBatchSize(){return 2;}
          public void setValues(PreparedStatement ps, int i){
            if (i==1){
                 ps.setDouble(1, 1.3);
                 ps.setInt(2, 7839);
            } else {
              ps.setDouble(1, 1.1);
              ps.setInt(2, 7782);
            }//else
        }//setValues
    });
```

The preceding sample code shows how to use batchUpdate() method with String and BatchPrepared StatementSetter for executing a SQL statement for multiple times with different parameter values. Here in the above shown sample code we have designed a anonymous inner class for implementing BatchPreparedStatementSetter; instead we can go for a separate top class to implement the Batch PreparedStatementSetter.

In this section you learnt how to execute batch statements using a JdbcTemplate. And by now from all the above sections you learnt how to use JdbcTemplate for executing SQL DML statements, executing SQL queries to access the database, calling the procedures, and finally execute batch statements. Even though it is simple to use JdbcTemplate for accessing and storing the data in the database as learnt in the preceding sections, there are some cases where we want more high-level abstraction and an object-oriented approach to do this. The following section explains the spring JDBC framework solution for this requirement.

6.10 UNDERSTANDING RDBMS OPERATION CLASSES

We have learnt in the preceding sections about the JdbcTemplate to store and access the data, which is a very straightforward and simple approach. Using JdbcTemplate was even very descriptive making the DAO implementations easier to read and understand. However, in some cases we don't want to build the SQL statements into all the DAO implementations and wanted a more object-oriented approach to access the database. To meet this requirement Spring JDBC abstraction framework includes RDBMS operation classes, which provide a high-level object-oriented abstraction to represent the RDBMS queries, updates, and stored procedures as threadsafe, reusable objects. All the RDBMS operation classes are packaged into org.springframework.jdbc.object package. The org.springframe work.jdbc.object.RdbmsOperation class is the root of the RDBMS operation classes. The Rdbms Operation class is a multithreaded, reusable type representing an SQL query, update or stored procedure. The direct built-in subclasses are SqlCall and SqlOperation, the following diagram shows the basic classes of the RDBMS operations.

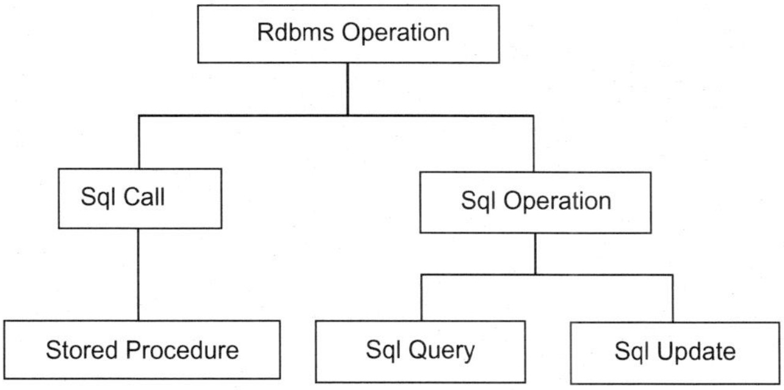

FIGURE 6.5 The hierarchy of the basic RDBMS operation classes

The SqlCall is used for representing and executing the stored procedures. The SqlOperation is used to represent the SQL query and updates using its subtypes SqlQuery and SqlUpdate respectively. The following sections explain how to use all these classes in detail. Let us start with the SqlQuery, which is used to represent the SQL query to access the database.

6.10.1 The SqlQuery Operation Class

The org.springframework.jdbc.object.SqlQuery is an abstract class that provides an abstraction to represent a reusable SQL query to access the database. The SqlQuery class includes a number of convenient execute() methods for executing the query represented by this object. The SqlQuery instance if threadsafe once if it is initialized, meaning once the SqlQuery instance is created and configured using its setter methods it can be used safely from multiple threads. The most widely and easy to use subclass of this class is MappingSqlQuery packaged under the org.springframework.jdbc. object package. The MappingSqlQuery class simplifies the MappingSqlQueryWithParameters by reducing parameters and context details. The subclasses of MappingSqlQuery do not need to worry about parameters. The subclass of MappingSqlQuery needs to implement the abstract mapRow() method to convert each row of the result into an object that has to be included into the result list of this object. The following code snippet shows the signature of the mapRow() method of MappingSqlQuery class.

Code Snippet

```
public abstract Object mapRow(ResultSet rs, int rowNum) throws SQLException
```

From the preceding code snippet of the mapRow() method it is evident that the method can throw an SQLException meaning while converting the current row of the ResultSet into an object we do not require to handle the SQLException. After learning about this operation class to make it more understandable we will look into a sample program that can throw more light on this topic. The following section explains you a sample program to demonstrate how to use MappingSqlQuery.

6.10.1.1 Using SqlQuery

As explained in the preceding section that MappingSqlQuery is the easiest option to use SqlQuery operation, and since it is the convenient one this is more preferred to use. Because of this reason in this example we will use MappingSqlQuery to define a subclass whose object represents an employee query. List 6.23 shows the EmployeeQuery class, which is a subtype of MappingSqlQuery.

List 6.23: EmployeeQuery.java

```
package com.santosh.spring.jdbc;

import java.sql.ResultSet;
import java.sql.Types;
import java.sql.SQLException;
import javax.sql.DataSource;
import org.springframework.jdbc.object.MappingSqlQuery;
import org.springframework.jdbc.core.SqlParameter;

public class EmployeeQuery extends MappingSqlQuery {

  private static String EMPLOYEE_SQL_QUERY=
                "select empno, ename, sal, deptno from emp where empno=?";
```

```
  public EmployeeQuery (DataSource ds) {
    super(ds, EMPLOYEE_SQL_QUERY);
    declareParameter(new SqlParameter(Types.INTEGER));
  }

  public Object mapRow(ResultSet rs, int rowNum)throws SQLException{

    Employee e=new Employee();
    e.setEmpno(rs.getInt(1));
    e.setEname(rs.getString(2));
    e.setSal(rs.getDouble(3));
    e.setDeptno(rs.getInt(4));
    return e;
  }
}
```

List 6.23 shows the implementation of MappingSqlQuery to represent an employee query that results in an Employee object; as a result a record is found with the given employee number. List 6.24 shows the Employee class that represents employee details like empno, name, salary, and deptno.

List 6.24: Employee.java

```
package com.santosh.spring.jdbc;

public class Employee {
  private int empno, deptno;
  private String ename;
  private double sal;

  public int getEmpno(){return empno;}
  public void setEmpno(int i){empno=i;}

  public int getDeptno(){return deptno;}
  public void setDeptno(int i){deptno=i;}

  public String getEname(){return ename;}
  public void setEname(String i){ename=i;}

  public double getSal(){return sal;}
  public void setSal(double i){sal=i;}
}//class
```

List 6.24 shows the spring beans XML configuration file to test the EmployeeQuery listed under List 6.23.

List 6.25: mybeans.xml

```
<beans xmlns="http://www.springframework.org/schema/beans"
xmlns:xsi="http://www.w3.org/2001/XMLSchema-instance"
xsi:schemaLocation="http://www.springframework.org/schema/beans
http://www.springframework.org/schema/beans/spring-beans-2.0.xsd">

  <bean id="datasource" class="org.apache.commons.dbcp.BasicDataSource">
    <property name="driverClassName">
      <value>oracle.jdbc.driver.OracleDriver</value>
    </property>
    <property name="url">
      <value>jdbc:oracle:thin:@localhost:1521:sandb</value>
    </property>
    <property name="username">
      <value>scott</value>
    </property>
    <property name="password">
      <value>tiger</value>
    </property>
  </bean>

  <bean id="employeeQuery" class="com.santosh.spring.jdbc.EmployeeQuery">
    <constructor-arg>
      <ref local="datasource"/>
    </constructor-arg>
  </bean>
</beans>
```

We need to write a simple test case to test the EmployeeQuery. List 6.26 shows the test case that tests the EmployeeQuery.

List 6.26: EmployeeQueryTestCase.java

```
import org.springframework.beans.factory.*;
import org.springframework.beans.factory.xml.*;
import org.springframework.core.io.*;
import com.santosh.spring.jdbc.Employee;
import com.santosh.spring.jdbc.EmployeeQuery;
import java.util.List;

public class EmployeeQueryTestCase {

  public static void main(String s[]) throws Exception {

    BeanFactory beans=new XmlBeanFactory(
                        new FileSystemResource("mybeans.xml"));
```

```
        EmployeeQuery employeeQuery=(EmployeeQuery)
                                        beans.getBean("employeeQuery");

        List emps=employeeQuery.execute(Integer.parseInt(s[0]));
        Employee emp=(Employee) emps.get(0);

        System.out.println("EmployeeDetails:");
        System.out.println("\tEmpno:"+emp.getEmpno());
        System.out.println("\tName:"+emp.getEname());
        System.out.println("\tSalary:"+emp.getSal());
        System.out.println("\tDeptno:"+emp.getDeptno());
    }//main
}//class
```

Now compile and execute the EmployeeQueryTestCase to find EmployeeQuery in action. Figure 6.6 shows the output of the EmployeeQueryTestCase for the employee with empno 7839.

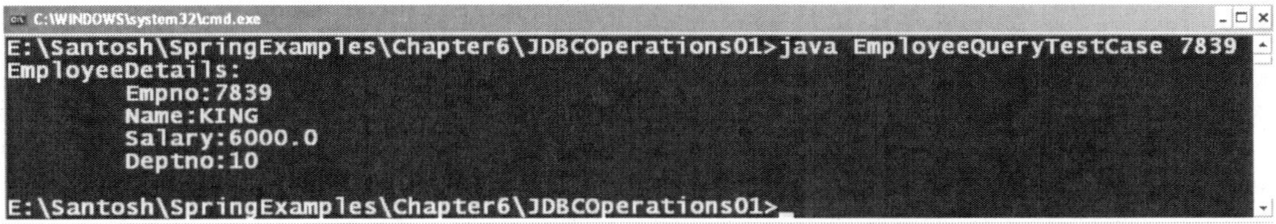

FIGURE 6.6 Output of EmployeeQueryTestCase

In this section you learnt how to use SqlQuery to represent a reusable SQL query to access the database. Apart from being able to represent reusable SQL queries to access the database we want the similar high-level approach to represent SQL updates. The following section explains SqlUpdate that represents reusable SQL updates.

6.10.2 The SqlUpdate Operation Class

The org.springframework.jdbc.object.SqlUpdate is an abstract class that provides an abstraction to represent a reusable SQL DML statement to update the database. The SqlUpdate class includes number of convenient update() methods for executing the update represented by this object. The SqlUpdate instance is threadsafe once it is initialized, meaning once the SqlUpdate instance is created and configured using its setter methods it can be used safely from multiple threads. The SqlUpdate class is a concrete class. The required SqlUpdate can be sub-classed and it is required for adding custom update methods to provide a convenience to execute the statement represented by this object. The SqlUpdate class includes four constructors for creating the SqlUpdate object. Table 6.6 shows all the four SqlUpdate constructors.

TABLE 6.6 Constructors of SqlUpdate class

Constructor	*Description*
public sqlUpdate()	This constructor is included to allow using this class as a JavaBean. When SqlUpdate object is constructed using this constructor the DataSource and SQL statement must be supplied using the respective setter methods before compilation and use.
public sqlUpdate(DataSource ds, String sql)	This constructor creates an object with a given DataSource and SQL statement.
public sqlUpdate(DataSource ds, String sql, int[] types)	This constructor creates an object with a given DataSource, SQL statement and the anonymous parameters as defined in the java.sql.Types.
public sqlUpdate(DataSource ds, String sql, int[] types, int maxRowsAffected)	This constructor creates an object with a given DataSource, SQL statement, the anonymous parameters as defined in the java.sql.Types, and the maximum number of rows that may be affected by the update. When using any of the above three constructors the maximum number of rows is set to 0, which does not limit the number of rows affected.

Now, as we have learnt about the SqlUpdate class we want to put this in action to find how this can be used. The following section shows how to use SqlUpdate.

6.10.2.1 Using SqlUpdate

As explained in the preceding section the SqlUpdate is a concrete class and can be used directly or can be sub-classed. The following sample code shows creating a SqlUpdate object to represent setting salary statement.

Code Snippet

```
SqlUpdate updateSal= new SqlUpdate(ds, "update emp set sal=? where empno=?");
updateSal.declaredParameter(new SqlParameter(Types.DOUBLE));
updateSal.declaredParameter(new SqlParameter(Types.INTEGER));
updateSal.compile();

Object[] params=new Object[]{6000.00, 7839};
int count=updateSal.update(params);

params=new Object[]{3000.00, 7788};
count=updateSal.update(params);
```

The preceding code snippet creates a SqlUpdate object that represents emp update statement that sets a new salary for the given employee. It declares two parameters of double and integer types respectively. To make it more convenient to use we can define a subclass for the SqlUpdate and encapsulate all the statement and parameter details. List 6.27 shows how to rewrite the preceding code as a subclass of SqlUpdate.

List 6.27: UpdateEmpSalary.java

```
package com.santosh.spring.jdbc;

import java.sql.Types;
import java.sql.SQLException;
import javax.sql.DataSource;
import org.springframework.jdbc.object.SqlUpdate;
import org.springframework.jdbc.core.SqlParameter;

public class UpdateEmpSalary extends SqlUpdate {

  private static String EMPLOYEE_SQL_UPDATE=
                              "update emp set sal=? where empno=?";

  public UpdateEmpSalary (DataSource ds) {
    super(ds, EMPLOYEE_SQL_UPDATE);
    declareParameter(new SqlParameter(Types.DOUBLE));
    declareParameter(new SqlParameter(Types.INTEGER));
    compile();
  }

  public int update(double sal, int empno){

    Object[] o=new Object[]{sal,empno};
    return update(o);
  }
}
```

Now the following sample code shows how to access the UpdateEmpSalary to update the salary of employee 7839 and 7788 to 6000 and 3000 respectively.

Code Snippet

```
BeanFactory beans=new XmlBeanFactory(new FileSystemResource("mybeans.xml"));
UpdateEmpSalary ue=(UpdateEmpSalary) beans.getBean("UpdateEmpSalary");

ue.update(7839, 6000);
ue.update(7788, 3000);
```

In this section you learnt how to use SqlUpdate to represent reusable SQL DML statement that can update the database. The next section explains how to use the RDBMS operation class to represent the stored procedure.

6.10.3 The SqlCall Operation Class

The org.springframework.jdbc.object.SqlCall is an abstract class that provides an abstraction to represent a SQL-based call such as a stored procedure or a stored function. The SqlCall class has one direct subclass named StoredProcedure. The StoredProcedure class is an abstract class, which provides an abstraction for representing the RDBMS stored procedures. This class is declared abstract and most of its methods are declared protected to avoid the use of these methods other than through its subclass. The subclass of StoredProcedure can overload the execute() methods and delegate the request to any one of the execute() methods defined in StoredProcedure class. List 6.28 shows the StoredProcedure implementation class that represents the procedure shown in List 6.20.

List 6.28: GetDeptNameProcedure.java

```
package com.santosh.spring.jdbc;

import java.util.Map;
import java.util.HashMap;
import java.sql.Types;
import javax.sql.DataSource;
import org.springframework.jdbc.object.StoredProcedure;
import org.springframework.jdbc.core.SqlParameter;
import org.springframework.jdbc.core.SqlOutParameter;

public class GetDeptNameProcedure extends StoredProcedure {

  private static String DEPT_PROCEDURE="getDeptName";

  public GetDeptNameProcedure (DataSource ds) {
    super(ds, DEPT_PROCEDURE);
    declareParameter(new SqlParameter("dno",Types.INTEGER));
    declareParameter(new SqlOutParameter("name",Types.LONGVARCHAR));
    compile();
  }
  public String execute(int deptno){
    Map m=new HashMap();
    m.put("dno",deptno);
    m= execute(m);
    return (String)m.get("name");
  }
}
```

List 6.28 shows GetDeptNameProcedure class that represents the getDeptName stored procedure. The getDeptName procedure has one IN parameter and one OUT parameter. This class implements an additional execute(int) method that delegates the request to the execute(Map) and collects the output to return it to the client. List 6.29 shows how to use the StoredProcedure implementation shown in the above List.

List 6.29: CallProcedureTestCase.java

```
import org.springframework.beans.factory.*;
import org.springframework.beans.factory.xml.*;
import org.springframework.core.io.*;
import org.springframework.jdbc.core.SqlParameter;
import org.springframework.jdbc.core.SqlOutParameter;
import com.santosh.spring.jdbc.GetDeptNameProcedure;

public class CallProcedureTestCase {

  public static void main(String s[]) throws Exception {

      BeanFactory beans=new XmlBeanFactory(
                                new FileSystemResource("mybeans.xml"));
      GetDeptNameProcedure gd=(GetDeptNameProcedure)
                                beans.getBean("GetDeptNameProcedure");

      String name=gd.execute(new Integer(s[0]));
      System.out.println("The department name of dept "+new Integer(s[0])+
                       " is : "+ name);
    }//main
}//class
```

List 6.30 shows the spring beans XML configuration file to test the StoredProcedure implementation.

List 6.30: mybeans.xml

```
<beans xmlns="http://www.springframework.org/schema/beans"
xmlns:xsi="http://www.w3.org/2001/XMLSchema-instance"
xsi:schemaLocation="http://www.springframework.org/schema/beans
http://www.springframework.org/schema/beans/spring-beans-2.0.xsd">

  <bean id="datasource" class="org.apache.commons.dbcp.BasicDataSource">
    <property name="driverClassName">
      <value>oracle.jdbc.driver.OracleDriver</value>
  </property>
  <property name="url">
      <value>jdbc:oracle:thin:@localhost:1521:sandb</value>
  </property>
  <property name="username">
    <value>scott</value>
  </property>
  <property name="password">
    <value>tiger</value>
  </property>
```

```
    </bean>

    <bean id="GetDeptNameProcedure"
          class="com.santosh.spring.jdbc.GetDeptNameProcedure">
        <constructor-arg>
            <ref local="datasource"/>
        </constructor-arg>
    </bean>
</beans>
```

Now, after writing the XML configuration file shown in List 6.30 compile and execute the CallProcedureTestCase. Figure 6.7 shows the output of the CallProcedureTestCase execution with different department numbers.

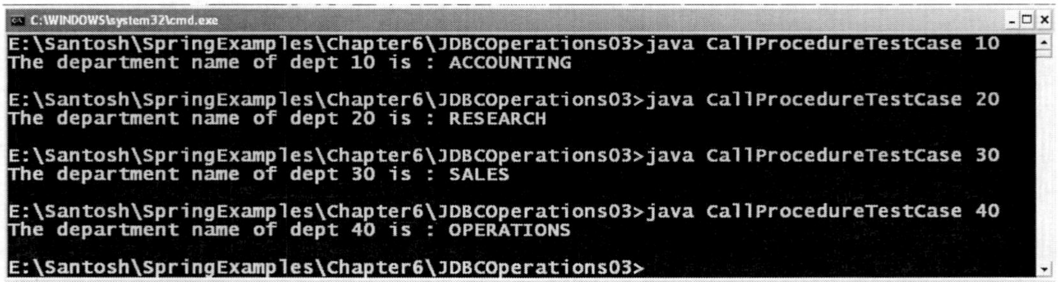

FIGURE 6.7 Output of CallProcedureTestCase

In this section you learnt how to use RDBMS operation class StoredProcedure to represent a stored procedure. This completes the discussion related to the RDBMS operation classes and the Spring JDBC abstraction framework.

Summary

In this chapter you learnt about the DAO design pattern and its shortcomings and also how to handle these shortcomings using the Spring DAO service. Later in this chapter you learnt Spring JDBC abstraction framework in detail and also learnt how to use the JdbcTemplate to perform the database read and update operations with SQL statements, calling stored procedures, using batch updates. The last part of this chapter explained the Spring JDBC frameworks RDBMS operational classes, which provides a more high-level and object-oriented approach to access and update the database. In the next chapter you will learn the problems with accessing data from database with complex RDBMS designs and the solutions for those problems in the form of ORM, and all about Hibernate.

Understanding Hibernate

7

CHAPTER

Objectives

In the previous chapter we introduced the DAO design pattern and even understood the convenience provided by the Spring Framework in implementing the DAO to overcome the shortcomings of using the JDBC as its low-level data access API. We identified that using the JdbcTemplate of Spring JDBC abstraction framework was very descriptive, making the DAO implementations easier to read and understand. Later, we discussed Spring JDBC RDBMS operation classes which eliminate the need to build SQL statements into all the DAO implementations and provide a high level object-oriented abstraction to represent the RDBMS queries, updates, and stored procedures as thread-safe, reusable objects. Even then it is identified that implementing the DAOs for storing and retrieving data with a complex object hierarchy in relational data storages such as RDMBS, involves huge boilerplate code for solving the mismatches between the relational and object-oriented environments. Object/Relational Mapping (ORM) bridges the gap between object and relational schemas, allowing our application to persist objects directly without having need for converting objects to and from a relational format. There are many ORM solutions currently available for various object-oriented programming languages especially for Java.

Hibernate is one of the ORM solutions for Java. In this chapter we will cover:

- The need of ORM
- How Hibernate forms a bridge between object-oriented and relational environment.

7.1 WHAT IS ORM?

Object/Relational Mapping (ORM) is the process of persisting objects in a relational data store such as RDBMS. ORM bridges the gap between object and relational environments, allowing object-oriented applications to persist objects easily without implementing the boilerplate code for solving the mismatches between the object-oriented and relational environments which includes converting objects to and from a relational format. In simple language, ORM simplifies the job of implementing the data access layer of a complex enterprise applications using relational data stores as its persistence store.

7.2 WHAT ARE THE MAIN FEATURES OF ORM?

An ORM conveniently helps to implement the data access layer for enterprise applications implemented using object-oriented programming language and using a relational data store as its persistence store. In general, an ORM provides the following facilities:

- A high-level API for creating, reading, updating, and deleting the persistence objects.
- An object-oriented query language for querying the persistence objects.
- A metadata format for mapping persistence objects to relational elements.
- A caching mechanism with proper locking modes.
- A support for mapping the complex domain object model to the database model.

7.3 WHY OBJECT/RELATIONAL MAPPING (ORM)?

Enterprise-level applications implemented using object-oriented programming languages (such as Java, C++, or C #) manage the data in the form of objects. Moreover, most of these applications use relational data stores such as RDBMS to maintain persistence data, where relational data stores manage the data in the form of tables with rows and columns. In such a context, it is identified that storing the complex object hierarchy in relational database, mapping the objects to tables involves huge code in implementing the data access layer to fill the gap between the object and relational models. Object and relational model capabilities and the approach of viewing the data is different as stated above, which causes mismatch problems such as granularity, inheritance, relations, identity and object tree navigation.

In such a context, implementing the data access layer using low-level API such as JDBC includes huge boilerplate code, which affects the productivity of the system increasing the cost of the application development. Even lack of experience in the team effects the performance and this may even cause a problem of data integrity. Therefore, to solve these problems we need a customizable generic system that can take the responsibility of filling the gap between the object and relational models for our application. This requirement has resulted to introduce ORM, which provides lots of convenience to persist the objects in relational databases. Meaning, using ORM implementations such as Hibernate to implement the data access layer requires far less time writing code that bridges object-oriented applications with relational databases, so that we can get our system to production faster, with more features. As of now there are a number of ORM implementations in Java like Hibernate, JPA (Java Persistence API), JDO (Java Data Objects), etc. Hibernate is one of those ORM implementations with high performance and additional features like dual cache support, object-oriented query language (HQL) support for querying objects, transaction support. Let us start learning how to use Hibernate to solve various mismatch problems.

7.4 UNDERSTANDING HIBERNATE ARCHITECTURE

In the preceding sections we learnt that Hibernate is one of the efficient ORM implementations in Java which helps us to quickly implement a reliable data access layer allowing us to concentrate on other tiers of the application. Now, to take the benefits of Hibernate in implementing the data access layer of our system we need to understand the various elements of Hibernate system and its functioning to effectively use them for our requirements. In this section we will arrange all the important elements of the Hibernate system into architecture and discuss about all the important elements. Figure 7.1 shows the Hibernate architecture.

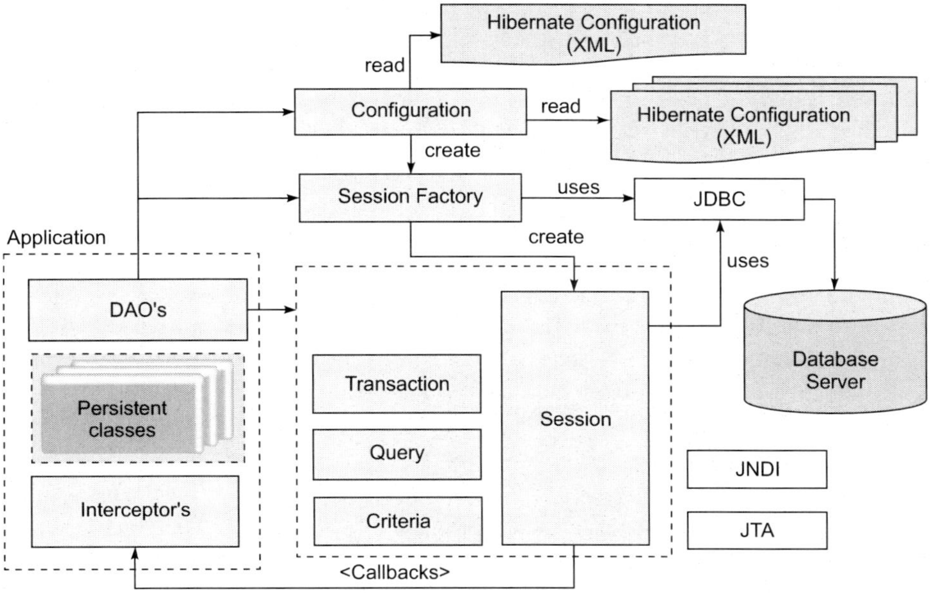

FIGURE 7.1 Architecture showing the basic elements of Hibernate

The basic elements of Hibernate architecture are described in the following section.

7.4.1 Configuration

The org.hibernate.cfg.Configuration class is the basic element of the Hibernate API that allows us to build SessionFactory. That means we can refer to configuration as a factory class that produces SessionFactory instances. The configuration object encapsulates the Hibernate configuration details such as connection properties and dialect, and mapping details described in the Hibernate mapping documents, which are used to build the SessionFactory. Meaning that the Configuration class provides us the convenience to describe the various configurations required for preparing the SessionFactory. As shown in the preceding architecture, the Configuration object takes the responsibility to read the Hibernate configuration and mapping XML documents, resolves them and loads the details into built-in hibernate objects. Therefore to avoid reading the same XML documents for multiple times we generally create a single Configuration object in an application and set all the properties as per the requirements. We can even use hibernate.properties file to specify the default values for a new Configuration object.

7.4.2 SessionFactory

The org.hibernate.SessionFactory interface provides an abstraction for the application to obtain Hibernate Session objects. The SessionFactory object caches the various objects such as

PreparedStatement, configuration settings, EntityPersister & CollectionPersister that describes the mappings, and compiled queries (that is, named queries). Creating a SessionFactory object involves a huge process that include the following operations:

- Start the cache (second level)
- Initialize the identifier generators
- Initialize the EntityPersisters for the mappings described by configuration
- Prepare the CollectionPersisters
- Pre-compile and cache the named queries (HQL and SQL)
- Obtain the JTA TransactionManager

As described above, the SessionFactory initialization process includes various operations that consumes huge resources and extra time. Thus it is generally recommended to use a single SessionFactory per JVM instance (or our application). Moreover, SessionFactory is immutable towards the application, meaning that is thread-safe. Thus there is no problem is using a single SessionFactory for an application with multiple threads also. The successfully initialized SessionFactory can be used to create a Hibernate Session. We can open multiple sessions using a single SessionFactory.

7.4.3 Session

The org.hibernate.Session is a central interface between the application and Hibernate system. The Hibernate Session operates using a single JDBC Connection, which can be injected by the application while constructing its object; otherwise the connection is retrieved by using the connection manager when it is required for the first time. Therefore, the Hibernate session needs to be used in a threadsafe environment. It is recommended to obtain a separate Session for each thread or transaction. The Session interface provides an abstraction for Java application to perform CRUD (Create Read Update Delete) operations on the instances of mapped persistent classes. To do this it includes various convenience methods such as load() method for reading the persistent state, save(), saveOrUpdate(), merge() and update() methods for persisting the entity instances, delete() for deleting the persistent data. Note that after we complete the use of Session, it has to be closed to release all the resources such as cached entity objects, cached collections, proxies, and JDBC connection.

7.4.4 Query

The org.hibernate.Query interface provides an abstraction for executing the Hibernate query and retrieving the results. The Query object represents one Hibernate query, that is, the Query built using Hibernate Query Language (HQL). We will learn about this interface and HQL in detail in Chapter 9.

7.4.5 Criteria

The org.hibernate.Criteria is the central interface for using the Criterion API and it provides a simplified API for using a programmatic approach of searching the persistent objects, alternative to the HQL and SQL. We will discuss about the Criteria interface and the Criterion API in detail in Chapter 9.

7.4.6 Hibernate Configuration

Hibernate allows us to add configuration parameters and mapping files location to the configuration object using its properties in a programmatic approach. Instead of configuring the properties each time in the application code we can use a hibernate.properties file to add the configuration parameters. However, the hibernate.properties file allows us to configure only the configuration parameters. Thus we need to add the mapping files location using the configuration properties. Alternatively, we can use the XML configuration file to specify the configuration parameters and the location of persistent mapping of XML documents. In general it is more comfortable to use an XML configuration rather than properties file or even programmatic property configuration. We can prepare different XML configuration files and switch them programmatically to use different configuration parameters and mapping files depending on the database and sometimes based on working environment such as development or production. We will learn the various elements and attributes of configuration file as we go through various examples.

7.4.7 Hibernate Mappings

The ORM implementations need to basically perform various services like creating, reading, updating, and deleting the persistence objects. To perform this, ORM frameworks requires metadata information for the persistent types. Some ORM frameworks require that persistent objects inherit from a base class or perform post-processing of bytecode. However, Hibernate is a non-invasive ORM service, meaning Hibernate does not require the persistent classes to inherit from a framework-defined base type. Instead, it needs only a small amount of metadata for each persistent class. This metadata is described by using the mapping XML documents. We will learn about the elements and attributes of this mapping file in the coming sections.

7.4.8 Persistent Classes

Persistent classes are the entity classes in an application. The persistent class objects are managed to be in a persistent state by the Hibernate persistence manager. Note that all the instances of the persistent classes need not to be in persistent state; instead they can be in transient or detached state. In Hibernate the persistent classes are simple plain Java classes, meaning that Hibernate is a non-invasive ORM service not requiring the persistent classes to inherit from a framework-defined base type. However, we need to configure metadata for each persistent class in the form of XML mapping file. For maximum portability the following rules are followed while implementing persistent classes:

1. Implement as a non-final class
2. Implement a no-argument constructor
3. Define an identifier property
4. Declare setter and getter methods for persistent fields
5. Implement equals() and hashCode() methods

Let us discuss in detail the reasons to follow the above mentioned rules.

7.4.8.1 Implementing persistent class as a non-final class

The Hibernate builds dynamic proxies for the persistent classes to manage the lazy loading feature and synchronizing the persistent objects with the database. The dynamic proxy is build, implementing the interface that is a super type of persistent class (if specified using 'proxy' attribute in hibernate mapping file), or extending the persistent class. This means that implementing the persistent class as non-final is not mandatory. We can even use a final class that does not implement an interface also as a persistent class, but we need to configure its objects to be loaded using the eager fetching mechanism, which means that we cannot use the lazy association fetching, which limits our options for performance tuning.

> **Note:** The non-final persistent class should not declare the persistent field methods as final if we have any final method as then also we cannot use the lazy association fetching mechanism.

7.4.8.2 Implementing a no-argument constructor

The persistent classes should have a no-argument constructor at least with a package visibility for the following two reasons:

- Hibernate uses the CGLIB API to generate dynamic proxy for the persistent class (that is, runtime proxy as subtype of persistent class)
- Hibernate uses the Constructor.newInstance() method to instantiate persistent classes

7.4.8.3 Defining an identifier property

The identifier property is one of the persistent fields of the persistent class. This property maps to the primary key column of the database table. Even though this is optional it is strongly recommended to define the identifier property. The following functionalities of Hibernate are available only for the persistent classes that implements identifier property:

- Cascade Update or Cascade Merge
- Session.saveOrUpdate()
- Session.merge()

To use these functionalities of Hibernate the persistent class is strongly recommended to declare an identifier property.

7.4.8.4 Declaring setter and getter methods for persistent fields

Hibernate uses JavaBeans style properties, and recognizes method names of the form getXXX, isXXX, and setXXX to access the persistent fields. These setter and getter methods can be declared with any access specifier such as public, protected, or private.

7.4.8.5 Implementing equals() and hashCode() methods

Implementing equals() and hashCode() methods in a persistent class is not mandatory since Hibernate is intelligent to maintain unique persistent objects based on the persistent identity within a session scope. Thus we want to implement equals() and hashcode() methods in the following cases:

- We want to put instances of persistent classes retrieved from different sessions in a Set.
- We want to use reattachment of detached instances

The most common way to implement the equals() method is by comparing the identifier value of the objects. But this approach is not applicable for the persistent classes configured to use identifier generator since Hibernate will only assign the identifier values to objects that are persistent. Meaning that a newly created instance will not have any identifier value which again means that if an object is unsaved and currently it is in a Set, saving it will assign an identifier value to the object which may change its hash code, breaking the Set's contract.

7.5 USING HIBERNATE TO PERFORM BASIC PERSISTENT OPERATIONS

In the preceding sections of this chapter we understood the basic elements of Hibernate system and even seen its arrangement. Now, to use Hibernate in an application to perform various persistent operations we need to implement some basic steps. The basic steps involved in using the Hibernate in a Java application are:

Step 1: Prepare Configuration object
Step 2: Build SessionFactory
Step 3: Obtain a Session
Step 4: Perform persistence operations
Step 5: Close the Session

Let us learn these steps in detail.

7.5.1 Step 1: Prepare Configuration Object

As discussed earlier the org.hibernate.cfg.Configuration object encapsulates the Hibernate configuration details such as connection properties and dialect, and mapping details described in the Hibernate mapping documents, which are used to build the SessionFactory. To do this we can use configuration properties in a programmatic approach or use an XML configuration file in a declarative approach. We can create a Hibernate Configuration object using its no-argument constructor, as shown in the following code snippet.

Code Snippet

```
Configuration cfg=new Configuration();
```

A new configuration object created using its constructor is by default initialized with the properties specified in hibernate.properties file if it is available in the classpath. Once after instantiating the configuration object we need to configure it with the configuration parameters and mapping documents. To do this we can use the programmatic or declarative approach. Let us look at both the approaches. In using the programmatic approach we use its methods such as setProperties(), addResource(), addClass(), etc., and programmatically configure the parameters. The following code snippet shows the code that prepares the Hibernate Configuration object using the programmatic approach.

Code Snippet

```
Configuration cfg=new Configuration();
Properties props=new Properties();
//set the hibernate configuration parameters into the Properties

cfg.setProperties(props);
cfg.addResource("Emp.hbm.xml");
//similarly add all the other resources and other configurations
//Now, configuration object is ready to build session factory
```

As shown in the preceding code snippet we can use the various add and setter methods of Configuration object to set the configuration parameters and mapping details. This approach results in the implementation of huge code for initializing the configuration object and is not convenient to change configuration details. To avoid these problems we can use the Hibernate XML configuration file, which is the most preferred approach, to configure the configuration parameters and mapping documents, that is, the declarative approach. The configure() methods described in Table 7. 1 can be used to configure the configuration object using this approach.

TABLE 7.1 The configure() methods of Hibernate Configuration object

Method	*Description*
configure()	Uses the configuration parameters and mapping document locations specified in Hibernate XML configuration file named hibernate.cfg.xml. The hibernate.cfg.xml file is located using the Class loader.
configure(String configFileName)	Uses the configuration parameters and mapping document locations specified in Hibernate XML configuration file located using the given resource path (configFileName). The configuration file is also located using the Class loader.
configure(File configFile)	Uses the configuration parameters and mapping document locations specified in Hibernate XML configuration file located using the given configFile.
configure(URL configFile)	Uses the configuration parameters and mapping document locations specified in Hibernate XML configuration file located using the given URL.
configure(org.w3c.dom.Document configDocument)	Uses the configuration parameters and mapping document locations specified in Hibernate XML configuration content described by the given DOM Document object tree.

All the configure() methods described in Table 7.1 return Configuration object. These methods are programmed to return 'this' reference, that means these methods return the reference of an object that is used to invoke it. This is known as Method Chaining programming style. This type of programming style is more used in implementing applications using Smalltalk.

In general, most of the time we use the default XML configuration file name, hibernate.cfg.xml. The following code snippet shows the code for preparing the Configuration object using the hibernate.cfg.xml file.

Code Snippet

```
Configuration cfg=new Configuration();
cfg.configure();
//Now, configuration object is ready to build session factory
```

As described in Table 7.1 the configure() method locates the hibernate.cfg.xml file in order to load the configuration parameters and the mapping files location. However, as described earlier, using the XML configuration file gives us an opportunity to switch between the configuration parameters and mapping documents based on the database and working environment. In such a case we want to use the configure() method overloaded with a single argument. We can use a XML configuration file with a different file name as shown in the code snippet below.

Code Snippet

```
Configuration cfg=new Configuration();
cfg.configure("myconfigs/adminmodule.cfg.xml");
//Now, configuration object is ready to build session factory
```

Similarly, we can use any other configure() method for preparing the configuration object. Moreover, we can use both the Hibernate XML configuration file and the programmatic approach to prepare a configuration object. After preparing the configuration object now that we can use it to build the SessionFactory, let us move to the next step which explains about building SessionFactory.

> **Note:** This step is recommended to be performed only once for an application, at startup. That is while initializing the application.

7.5.2 Step 2: Build SessionFactory

After successfully preparing the Configuration object by setting all the configuration parameters and mapping documents location, the Configuration object is used to create the SessionFactory. To do this we use the buildSessionFactory() method of configuration, which creates a new SessionFactory using the configuration parameters and mappings in this configuration. After creating the SessionFactory the configuration object can be discarded. The following code snippet shows the code for building a SessionFactory.

Code Snippet

```
Configuration cfg=new Configuration();
cfg.configure();
SessionFactory factory=cfg.buildSessionFactory();
```

As discussed earlier, the SessionFactory object caches various objects, such as PreparedStatement, configuration settings, EntityPersister and CollectionPersister that describes the mappings, and compiled queries (that is, named queries). Moreover, creating a SessionFactory object, that is, invoking a buildSessionFactory() method of configuration object, involves various processes that include starting the cache (second level) and initializing the identifier generators.

> **Note:** The SessionFactory initialization process is expensive, since it includes various operations that consume huge resources and extra time. Thus it is generally recommended to use a single SessionFactory per JVM instance (or our application). Thus this step is also recommended to perform at the startup of the application, that is, initialization of our application.

After initializing the SessionFactory which we use to open Hibernate Session we can open multiple Sessions on a single SessionFactory object so that all the Sessions can access the configuration and metadata mappings of persistent classes instead of loading them separately for each Session. Optionally, we can use SessionFactory to maintain second-level cache that allows the Sessions opened on it, to share the persistent objects (obviously with a proper locking mechanism).

Now, let us learn how to open the Session using the SessionFactory and perform persistent operations.

7.5.3 Step 3: Obtain a Session

The Hibernate Session works on top of a SessionFactory, meaning a Session is bound to a SessionFactory. The SessionFactory object is used to open a Hibernate Session. To do this we use any one of the openSession() methods of SessionFactory described in Table 7.2.

TABLE 7.2 Method of SessionFactory object to open a new session

Method	*Description*
openSession()	Prepares a new Session that obtains a JDBC Connection object using the ConnectionManager.
openSession(Connection)	Prepares a new Session that uses the given connection.
openSession(Interceptor)	Prepares a new Session that obtains a JBDC Connection object using the ConnectionManager. The Session is registered with the given Interceptor.
openSession(Connection, Interceptor)	Prepares a new Session that uses the given JDBC Connection object. The Session is registered with the given Interceptor.

Note: The second-level cache will be disabled if we supply a JDBC connection as an argument to openSession() method. Hibernate will not be able to track any statements that are executed in the same transaction.

The following code snippet shows the code for creating a new Session.

Code Snippet

```
Configuration cfg=new Configuration();
cfg.configure();
SessionFactory factory=cfg.buildSessionFactory();
Session session=factory.openSession();
```

The openSession() method described above is used to open a new Session. However, in some cases, especially in the managed environments, where multiple components are involved in processing the request in a single transaction, we want to work with a single Session to execute the persistent operations. The getCurrentSession() method can be used in such an environments. The getCurrentSession() method obtains the Session associated with the current JTA transaction; if a Session is not already associated with the current JTA transaction, a new Session will be opened and it will be associated with the JTA transaction. If Hibernate has no access to the TransactionManager or if the application is not associated with any transaction, the getCurrentSession() method throws an HibernateException. The following code snippet shows the code for locating the Session associated with the current transaction.

Code Snippet

```
Configuration cfg=new Configuration();
cfg.configure();
SessionFactory factory=cfg.buildSessionFactory();
Session session=factory.getCurrentSession();
```

The preceding code snippet shows the statements to get the Session associated with the current JTA transaction. If there is no Hibernate Session associated with the current JTA transaction then a new Session is created and associated to the current transaction. After obtaining the Session we can use it to perform persistence operations. Let us learn about the various methods for performing persistence operations.

7.5.4 Step 4: Perform Persistence Operations

The Session interface provides an abstraction for Java application to perform the basic CRUD (Create Read Update Delete) operations on the instances of mapped persistent classes. To do this it includes various convenience methods as described below in Table 7.3.

TABLE 7.3 Convenience methods of Session

Method	*Description*
Object load(Class entityClass, Serializable id)	Locates the persistent instance of the given entity class with the given identifier, if the persistent instance is not available in the cache then it loads the instance from the database and returns it to caller.
Object load(String entityName, Serializable id)	Locates the persistent instance of the entity class identified with the given name and identifier, if the persistent instance is not available in the cache then it loads the instance from the database and returns it to caller.
void load(Object object, Serializable id)	Reads the persistent state located with the given identifier into the given transient instance.
Serializable save(Object object)	Generates an identifier, associates it to the given transient instance, and persist.
void update(Object object)	Update the persistent instance with the identifier of the given object.
void saveOrUpdate(Object object)	Either save or update the given instance, depending upon resolution of the unsaved-value checks.

The methods of Session interface described in Table 7.3 allows the Java application to use Hibernate for performing basic CRUD operations but most of the time we have a requirement to query for persistent objects. To support this requirement Hibernate includes two interfaces—Query and Criteria. You will learn about Query and Criteria interfaces in the next chapter.

7.5.5 Step 5: Close the Session

After we complete the use of Session, it has to be closed to release all the resources such as cached entity objects, collections, proxies, and a JDBC connection. That means the Hibernate Session encapsulates two important types of state, one is the cache of the entity objects, and second a JDBC connection. To close a Hibernate Session we can use its close() method. The following code snippet shows the code for closing the session.

Code Snippet

```
//get the SessionFactory object reference
Session session=factory.openSession();
//Use session for performing persistence operations

//after the use of session, now closing the session
session.close();
```

The close() method of Session ends the Hibernate Session by cleaning up the cache (releasing all the cached objects) and disconnecting the JDBC connection. In general, a session is used to process a single request, meaning open a session to handle the request and close it at the end of request handling. However, in some cases we want to maintain a long session that spans over multiple requests. Maintaining a long session allows us to reuse the persistent objects over multiple database transactions, and avoids the need to re-associate detached instances created or retrieved in previous database transactions. But as we know, holding the JDBC connection open across multiple requests is not recommended since it is an expensive resource. Thus if we want to maintain the Hibernate Session for long periods making it to span over multiple requests for reusing persistent instances we want to disconnect the session's JDBC connection for each request without closing the session. A Hibernate Session interface includes methods disconnect() and reconnect() in support of this type of requirement. The disconnect() method closes the session's JDBC connection without closing the session. And the reconnect() method opens a new connection for this session. The reconnect() method is overloaded. One is no-argument method that obtains the connection using the ConnectionManager and the second takes the java.sql.Connection argument which connects the session to the given JDBC Connection. The following code snippet shows the use of disconnect() and reconnect() methods.

Code Snippet

```
Session session=null;

//Here include the code to get the Session object reference
//from ThreadLocal or HttpSession (if we are working in web environment with Servlets)

session.reconnect(); // this obtains the JDBC Connection for this session

//use the session to handle this request

session.disconnect(); //this closes the session's JDBC Connection
```

> **Note:** Hibernate Session is not threadsafe. So, thus while maintaining the long session be careful to make sure that the two concurrent threads do not operate using the same Hibernate Session. And even remember that while working with servlets the HttpSession is not threadsafe since the servlet container allows multiple requests from the same user to be processed concurrently.

This completes the discussion on the basic steps involved in using Hibernate in our applications. Now, after learning the basic interfaces of Hibernate and its important methods let us look at an example to get a clear picture of this discussion.

7.6 WORKING WITH HIBERNATE TO PERFORM BASIC CRUD OPERATIONS

In this example we will put the basic steps involved in performing the CRUD operations using Hibernate. To do this we use Employee persistent class which is a simple POJO (Plain Old Java Object) class, with a no argument constructor (default constructor) and setter and getter methods for the persistent fields. List 7.1 shows the code for Employee persistent class.

List 7.1: Employee.java

```
package com.santosh.hibernate;
import java.util.Date;

public class Employee{
  private int empno, deptno;
  private String ename, job;
  private double sal;
  private Date hiredate;

  public int getEmpno(){return empno;}
  public void setEmpno(int empno){this.empno=empno;}

  public int getDeptno(){return deptno;}
  public void setDeptno(int deptno){this.deptno=deptno;}

  public String getEname(){return ename;}
  public void setEname(String ename){this.ename=ename;}

  public double getSal(){return sal;}
  public void setSal(double sal){this.sal=sal;}

  public String getJob(){return job;}
  public void setJob(String job){this.job=job;}

  public Date getHiredate(){return hiredate;}
  public void setHiredate(Date hiredate){this.hiredate=hiredate;}
}//class
```

The Employee persistent class shown in the preceding code declares six persistent fields empno, deptno, ename, sal, job, and hiredate of types int, int, String, double, String, java.util.Date respectively. As discussed earlier, Hibernate requires a small amount of metadata description for persistent class, which is specified using the Hibernate mapping XML file. List 7.2 shows the Hibernate mapping for Employee persistent class.

List 7.2: Employee.hbm.xml

```
<!DOCTYPE hibernate-mapping PUBLIC
 "-//Hibernate/Hibernate Mapping DTD 3.0//EN"
 "http://hibernate.sourceforge.net/hibernate-mapping-3.0.dtd">

<hibernate-mapping>
  <class name="com.santosh.hibernate.Employee" table="emp" lazy="false">
```

```
    <id name="empno" type="int">
      <column name="empno"/>
      <generator class="increment"/>
    </id>

    <property name="ename" column="ename"/>
    <property name="sal"/>
    <property name="job"/>
    <property name="hiredate"/>
    <property name="deptno"/>
  </class>
</hibernate-mapping>
```

List 7.2 shows the code for Employee.hbm.xml file that is, the Hibernate mapping XML file to describe the mappings for Employee persistent class. It is recommended to save the mapping configuration with a file named <persistent class general name>.hbm.xml. For example, for com.santosh.hibernate.Employee class we use Employee.hbm.xml file. However, it is not mandatory to follow this convention; instead we can use any file name. Now, let us configure the Hibernate system by specifying the configuration parameters such as connection details and mapping locations.

List 7.3: hibernate.cfg.xml

```
<!DOCTYPE hibernate-configuration PUBLIC
  "-//Hibernate/Hibernate Configuration DTD 3.0//EN"
  "http://hibernate.sourceforge.net/hibernate-configuration-3.0.dtd">

<hibernate-configuration>
  <session-factory>
    <property name="connection.driver_class">
      oracle.jdbc.driver.OracleDriver
    </property>
    <property name="connection.url">
      jdbc:oracle:thin:@seminal1:1521:sandb
    </property>
    <property name="connection.user">scott</property>
    <property name="connection.password">tiger</property>
    <property name="dialect">org.hibernate.dialect.OracleDialect</property>

    <mapping resource="Employee.hbm.xml"/>
  </session-factory>
</hibernate-configuration>
```

List 7.3 shows the configuration to use oracle JDBC thin driver to connect to database for performing persistence operations. Here we have configured dialect to OracleDialect since we are working with Oracle8i see Appendix-B for more details. And even it is describing one mapping resource file Employee.hbm.xml file. Now, we want to test the configurations. List 7.4 shows the code for testing basic CRUD operations.

List 7.4: HibernateBasicTestCase.java

```
import org.hibernate.cfg.*;
import org.hibernate.*;
import org.apache.log4j.Logger;
import org.apache.log4j.Level;
import java.util.Date;
import com.santosh.hibernate.Employee;

public class HibernateBasicTestCase {

  private SessionFactory factory;

  public void createEmployee(Employee emp){
    Session session=null;
    Transaction tx=null;
    try{
      //Open a new Session
      session=factory.openSession();
      tx=session.beginTransaction();
      session.save(emp);
      tx.commit();
      System.out.println(
      "Employee Created with empno: "+ emp.getEmpno());
    }//try
    catch(HibernateException hibernateException){
      tx.rollback();
      //TO DO: Handle the exception
      System.out.println("Exception in creating an Employee");
    }
    finally {
      //Closing the session
      session.close();
    }
  }

  public void updateEmployee(Employee emp){
    Session session=null;
    Transaction tx=null;
    try{
      //Open a new Session
      session=factory.openSession();
      tx=session.beginTransaction();
      session.update(emp);
      tx.commit();
```

```
      System.out.println("Employee updated");
    }//try
    catch(HibernateException hibernateException){
      tx.rollback();
      //TO DO: Handle the exception
      System.out.println("Exception in updating Employee");
    }
    finally {
      //Closing the session
      session.close();
    }
  }

  public Employee getEmployee(int empno){
    Session session=null;
    try{
      //Open a new Session
      session=factory.openSession();
      Employee emp=(Employee)session.load(Employee.class,
        new Integer(empno));
      return emp;
    }//try
    catch(HibernateException hibernateException){
      //TO DO: Handle the exception
      System.out.println("Exception in loading Employee");
      return null;
    }
    finally {
      //Closing the session
      session.close();
    }
  }

  public void removeEmployee(Employee emp){
    Session session=null;
    Transaction tx=null;
    try{
      //Open a new Session
      session=factory.openSession();
      tx=session.beginTransaction();
      session.delete(emp);
      tx.commit();
      System.out.println("Employee Removed");
    }//try
    catch(HibernateException hibernateException){
```

```
            tx.rollback();
            //TO DO: Handle the exception
            System.out.println("Exception in removing Employee");
        }
        finally {
            //Closing the session
            session.close();
        }
    }

    public static void main(String[] args) throws Exception{

        Logger.getRootLogger().setLevel(Level.OFF);

        HibernateBasicTestCase test=new HibernateBasicTestCase();

        //Preparing Configuration object
        Configuration cfg=new Configuration();
        cfg.configure();

        //Building SessionFactory
        test.factory=cfg.buildSessionFactory();

        //Creating a new Persistent State
        Employee emp=new Employee();
        emp.setEname("MARK");
        emp.setSal(500);
        emp.setJob("CLERK");
        emp.setHiredate(new Date());
        emp.setDeptno(20);

        test.createEmployee(emp);

        System.out.println();

        //Updating the Persistent State
        emp.setJob("MANAGER");
        emp.setSal(1000);

        test.updateEmployee(emp);

        System.out.println();

        //Getting an Employee
        emp=test.getEmployee(Integer.parseInt(args[0]));
```

```
        if (emp!=null){
            System.out.println("Employee Details of empno: "+ emp.getEmpno());
            System.out.println("Name : "+ emp.getEname());
            System.out.println("Salary : "+ emp.getSal());
            System.out.println("Hiredate: "+ emp.getHiredate());
        }

        System.out.println();

        //Removing an Employee
        if (emp!=null)
            test.removeEmployee(emp);
    }
}
```

The preceding code shows the steps involved in using Hibernate for performing basic CRUD operations on persistent object. To execute this test case we need to set the following jar files into classpath:

- hibernate3.jar
- asm.jar
- cglib-2.1.jar
- commons-logging-1.0.4.jar
- commons-collections-2.1.1.jar
- dom4j-1.6.jar
- ehcache-1.1.jar
- jta.jar
- log4j-1.2.9.jar
- ojdbc14.jar / classes12.jar

All the above jar files except ojdbc14.jar/classes12.jar file can be found in Hibernate distribution downloads. We can download hibernate distribution from http://www.hibernate.org site. Figure 7.2 shows the output of the HibernateBasicTestCase execution.

Figure 7.2 shows the command setting the classpath, compiling the Java source files (persistent class and test case), and the execution of test case.

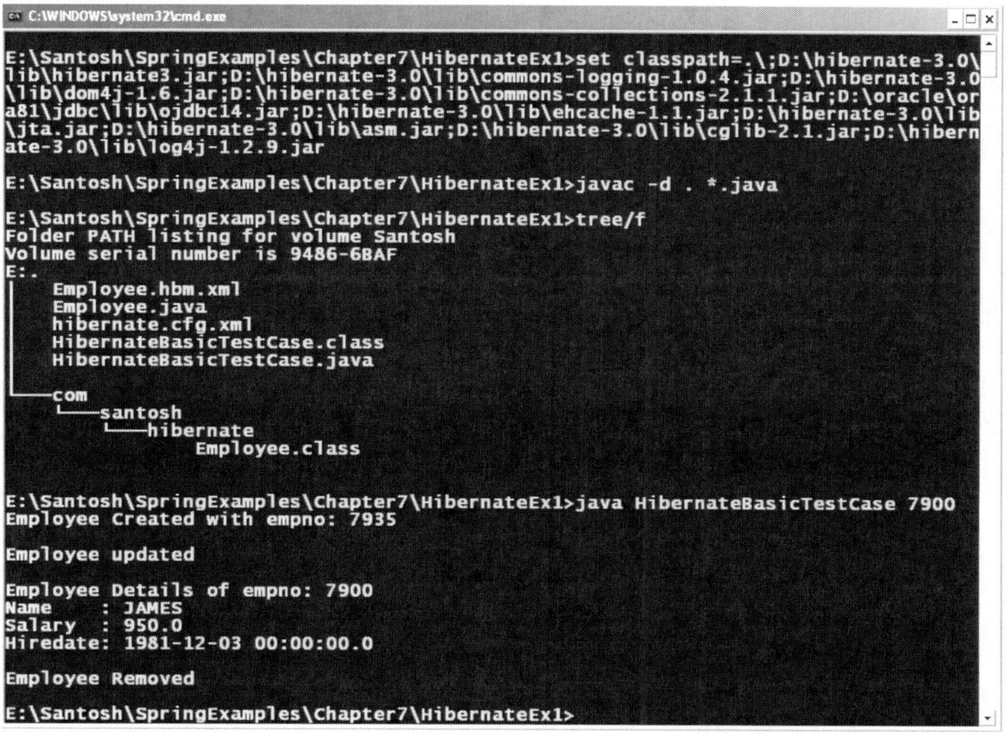

FIGURE 7.2 Output of HibernateBasicTestCase

Summary

In this chapter we learnt about ORM and its need. Later, we understood that Hibernate is one of the ORM implementations of ORM. Then we discussed the important elements of Hibernate architecture followed by the steps involved in using hibernate for performing persistence operations. Finally, we went through an example to demonstrate the use of Hibernate API for performing basic CRUD operations of persistent objects. In the next chapter we will discuss various configurations for mapping mismatches between object and relational environment, such as relationships, value object mapping, and subclass mappings.

Understanding Persistent Classes Mapping

8 CHAPTER

Objectives

In this chapter we will cover:

- Hibernate mapping configurations to map persistent classes solving the mismatch problems such as granularity, subtypes, and relationships
- Problem of granularity

8.1 PROBLEM OF GRANULARITY

While designing our domain object model, few of the entity classes (persistent classes) needs to be coarse-grained classes, for example PersonalDetails—an entity class to represent the personal details of employee, with properties such as *permanentAddress* and *presentAddress* of Address type (Java class), that is, dependent type. While mapping such an entity class properties to the database table columns, if the table is designed with an ADDRESS SQL UDT (User Defined data Types) then we can find a direct mapping. However, the support for UDT, which is one of the object-relational extensions to traditional SQL, has various problems in most of the database management systems. The UDT support is an unclear feature with most database management systems. Using UDT causes portability problems, because of the poor support from SQL standard for the user-defined data types. Thus using user-defined data types is not generally recommended.

That means, we cannot store the Address type into a single column of an equivalent user-defined SQL data type. Thus to store the address details we need to design a table with several columns of common types such as permanent_street, permanent_city, permanent_state, permanent_state, permanent_pin, and similarly four fields for present address. And in our object model, we could use the same approach, representing the two addresses as eight properties of the PersonalDetails class. But we would much prefer to design the PersonalDetails with two properties *permanentAddress* and *presentAddress* of Address type as described earlier, since this object model is more understandable and provides greater code reuse. Therefore, this causes a mismatch between the domain object model entity class and database table.

Hibernate as an ORM fills this gap between the object-oriented environment and relational environment. The <component> tag of hibernate mapping XML file is used to configure the persistent classes with the dependent objects. For example, the following code snippet shows the hibernate mapping for PersonalDetails.

Code Snippet

```
<class name="com.santosh.hibernate.PersonalDetails"
     table="personalDetails">
  <id name="pid">
    <column name="pid"/>
    <generator class="increment"/>
  </id>

  <component  name="permanentAddress"
              class="com.santosh.hibernate.Address">
    <property name="street" column="permanent_street"/>
    <property name="city" column="permanent_city"/>
    <property name="state" column="permanent_state"/>
    <property name="pin" column="permanent_pin"/>
  </component>
  <component  name="presentAddress"
              class="com.santosh.hibernate.Address">
    <property name="street" column="present_street"/>
    <property name="city" column="present_city"/>
    <property name="state" column="present_state"/>
    <property name="pin" column="present_pin"/>
  </component>

  <!–declare other properties –>
</class>
```

The preceding code snippet shows the code for personalDetails Hibernate mapping declaring two Address component type properties permanentAddress and presentAddress. The Address component type is implemented representing four properties such as street, city, state, and pin. The personalDetails can even have other properties. Now, let us implement an example to throw more light on this topic.

8.2 WORKING WITH COMPONENT TYPES

To demonstrate the component type we map Address as a value type and PersonalDetails as persistent class. In this case we use the mapping document to tell Hibernate that the Address is a value type. List 8.1 shows the code for PersonalDetails persistent class.

List 8.1: PersonalDetails.java

```
package com.santosh.hibernate;

public class PersonalDetails {

  public int getPid(){return pid;}
  private void setPid(int i){pid=i;}

  public String getFirstName(){return fname;}
  public void setFirstName(String s){ fname=s;}

  public String getLastName(){return lname;}
  public void setLastName(String s){lname=s;}

  public Address getPermanentAddress(){return permanentAddress;}
  public Address getPresentAddress(){return presentAddress;}

  public void setPermanentAddress(Address addr){permanentAddress=addr;}
  public void setPresentAddress(Address addr){presentAddress=addr;}

  private int pid;
  private String fname,lname;
  private Address permanentAddress, presentAddress;
}
```

List 8.1 shows the code for PersonalDetails persistent class with five properties—two of them being of component types. The permanentAddress and presentAddress properties are of user defined type, that is, Address class, which encapsulates the address details. List 8.2 shows Address class.

List 8.2: Address.java

```
package com.santosh.hibernate;
public class Address{

public String getStreet(){return street;}
public void setStreet(String s){ street=s;}

public String getCity(){return city;}
public void setCity(String s){ city=s;}

public String getState(){return state;}
public void setState(String s){ state=s;}

public int getPin(){return pin;}
public void setPin(String pin){ this.pin=pin;}

  private String street, city, state;
  private int pin;
}
```

List 8.2 shows the Address representing four properties, which is used as a component in PersonalDetails to represent permanentAddress and presentAddress. Now, we need to map the PersonalDetails persistent class describing the composition between PersonalDetails and Address in the mapping document.

List 8.3: PersonalDetails.hbm.xml

```
<!DOCTYPE hibernate-mapping PUBLIC
    "-//Hibernate/Hibernate Mapping DTD 3.0//EN"
    "http://hibernate.sourceforge.net/hibernate-mapping-3.0.dtd">

<hibernate-mapping>
  <class name="com.santosh.hibernate.PersonalDetails"
      table="personalDetails">
    <id name="pid">
      <column name="pid"/>
      <generator class="increment"/>
    </id>

    <property name="firstName" column="firstName"/>
    <property name="lastName" column="lastName"/>

    <component name="permanentAddress"
               class="com.santosh.hibernate.Address">
      <property name="street" column="permanent_street"/>
      <property name="city" column="permanent_city"/>
      <property name="state" column="permanent_state"/>
      <property name="pin" column="permanent_pin"/>
    </component>
    <component name="presentAddress"
               class="com.santosh.hibernate.Address">
      <property name="street" column="present_street"/>
      <property name="city" column="present_city"/>
      <property name="state" column="present_state"/>
      <property name="pin" column="present_pin"/>
    </component>
  </class>
</hibernate-mapping>
```

List 8.3 shows the mapping for PersonalDetails; it declares the unidirectional composition between the PersonalDetails and Address. To work with this mapping let us implement the hibernate XML configuration file.

List 8.4: hibernate.cfg.xml

```
<!DOCTYPE hibernate-configuration PUBLIC
  "-//Hibernate/Hibernate Configuration DTD 3.0//EN"
  "http://hibernate.sourceforge.net/hibernate-configuration-3.0.dtd">

<hibernate-configuration>
  <session-factory>
    <property name="connection.driver_class">
      oracle.jdbc.driver.OracleDriver
    </property>
    <property name="connection.url">
      jdbc:oracle:thin:@seminal1:1521:sandb
    </property>
    <property name="connection.user">scott</property>
    <property name="connection.password">tiger</property>

    <mapping resource="PersonalDetails.hbm.xml"/>

  </session-factory>
</hibernate-configuration>
```

Now, let us implement a test case to test the configurations. The test case loads the PersonalDetails entity object using hibernate session.

List 8.5: PersonalDetailsTestCase.java

```
import org.hibernate.cfg.*;
import org.hibernate.*;
import org.apache.log4j.Logger;
import org.apache.log4j.Level;
import com.santosh.hibernate.PersonalDetails;
import com.santosh.hibernate.Address;

public class PersonalDetailsTestCase {

  public static void main(String[] args) throws Exception{

    Logger.getRootLogger().setLevel(Level.OFF);

    //Preparing Configuration object
    Configuration cfg=new Configuration();
    cfg.configure();

    //Building SessionFactory
    SessionFactory factory=cfg.buildSessionFactory();
```

```
        //Open a new Session
        Session session=factory.openSession();

        PersonalDetails personalDetails=(PersonalDetails)
                 session.load( PersonalDetails.class,
                               Integer.parseInt(args[0]));
        System.out.println("FirstName     : "+ personalDetails.getFirstName());
        System.out.println("LastName      : "+ personalDetails.getLastName());
        System.out.println();
        Address permanentAddress=
                     personalDetails.getPermanentAddress();
        System.out.println("PermanentAddress:");
        System.out.println("\tStreet    : "+ permanentAddress.getStreet());
        System.out.println("\tCity      : "+ permanentAddress.getCity());
        System.out.println("\tState     : "+ permanentAddress.getState());
        System.out.println("\tPin       : "+ permanentAddress.getPin());

        Address presentAddress=
                 personalDetails.getPresentAddress();
        System.out.println("\nPresentAddress:");
        System.out.println("\tStreet    : "+ presentAddress.getStreet());
        System.out.println("\tCity      : "+ presentAddress.getCity());
        System.out.println("\tState     : "+ presentAddress.getState());
        System.out.println("\tPin       : "+ presentAddress.getPin());
    }
}
```

To run this test case we need to create a database table with sample data. The following code snippet shows the SQL commands to create personaldetails table with a sample record.

Code Snippet

```
drop table personaldetails;

create table personaldetails(
pid number,
firstname varchar2(20),
lastname varchar2(20),
permanent_street varchar2(20),
permanent_city varchar2(20),
permanent_state varchar2(20),
permanent_pin number,
present_street varchar2(20),
present_city varchar2(20),
present_state varchar2(20),
present_pin number);
```

```
insert into personaldetails values(
7369, 'Smith', 'John',
'Ameerpet', 'Hyderabad', 'AP', '500049',
'My Street', 'My City', 'Delhi', '200049');
```

Now, compile and execute the test case to load the personaldetails along with the address details. Figure 8.1 following figure shows the result of executing the PersonalDetailsTestCase with a first argument value as 7396.

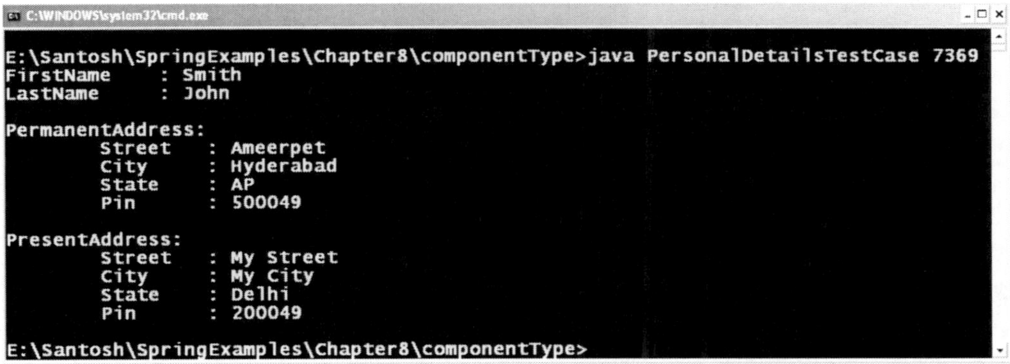

FIGURE 8.1 Output of PersonalDetailsTestcase

In this example, we implemented the composition association as *unidirectional*. That is we can navigate from PersonalDetails to Address but not from Address to User. Hibernate supports both unidirectional and bidirectional compositions. We use <parent> element in <component> tag to map a property to the owning entity, that is, to define the bidirectional composition. For example, the PersonalDetails.hbm.xml mapping file shown in List 8.3 can be modified to use bidirectional composition mapping adding the <parent> tag as shown in List 8.6.

List 8.6: PersonalDetails.hbm.xml

```
<!DOCTYPE hibernate-mapping PUBLIC
    "-//Hibernate/Hibernate Mapping DTD 3.0//EN"
    "http://hibernate.sourceforge.net/hibernate-mapping-3.0.dtd">

<hibernate-mapping>
  <class name="com.santosh.hibernate.PersonalDetails"
      table="personalDetails">
    <id name="pid">
      <column name="pid"/>
      <generator class="increment"/>
    </id>

    <property name="firstName" column="firstName"/>
    <property name="lastName" column="lastName"/>
```

```
    <component name="permanentAddress"
          class="com.santosh.hibernate.Address">
      <parent name="personalDetails"/>
      <property name="street" column="permanent_street"/>
      <property name="city" column="permanent_city"/>
      <property name="state" column="permanent_state"/>
      <property name="pin" column="permanent_pin"/>
    </component>
    <component name="presentAddress"
          class="com.santosh.hibernate.Address">
      <parent name="personalDetails"/>
      <property name="street" column="present_street"/>
      <property name="city" column="present_city"/>
      <property name="state" column="present_state"/>
      <property name="pin" column="present_pin"/>
    </component>
  </class>
</hibernate-mapping>
```

In this example we configured a <parent> element to map the property named *personalDetails* of PersonalDetails type to the owning entity. Thus the Address class should be added with the personalDetails property. List 8.7 shows the Address class with personalDetails property.

List 8.7: Address.java

```
package com.santosh.hibernate;

public class Address{

  public String getStreet(){return street;}
  public void setStreet(String s){ street=s;}

  public String getCity(){return city;}
  public void setCity(String s){ city=s;}

  public String getState(){return state;}
  public void setState(String s){ state=s;}

  public int getPin(){return pin;}
  public void setPin(int pin){ this.pin=pin;}

  public PersonalDetails getPersonalDetails(){return personalDetails;}
  public void setPersonalDetails(PersonalDetails pd){ personalDetails=pd;}

  private String street, city, state;
  private int pin;
  private PersonalDetails personalDetails;
}
```

Now, let us test the configuration. List 8.8 shows the test case to test the bidirectional composition mapping between the PersonalDetails and Address.

List 8.8: BidirectionalCompositionTestCase.java

```
import org.hibernate.cfg.*;
import org.hibernate.*;
import org.apache.log4j.Logger;
import org.apache.log4j.Level;
import com.santosh.hibernate.PersonalDetails;
import com.santosh.hibernate.Address;

public class BidirectionalCompositionTestCase {

  public static void main(String[] args) throws Exception{

    Logger.getRootLogger().setLevel(Level.OFF);

    //Preparing Configuration object
    Configuration cfg=new Configuration();
    cfg.configure();

    //Building SessionFactory
    SessionFactory factory=cfg.buildSessionFactory();

    //Open a new Session
    Session session=factory.openSession();

    PersonalDetails personalDetails=(PersonalDetails)
           session.load( PersonalDetails.class,
                        Integer.parseInt(args[0]));
    System.out.println("FirstName    : "+ personalDetails.getFirstName());
    System.out.println("LastName     : "+ personalDetails.getLastName());
    System.out.println();

    System.out.println("Obtaining Address from PersonalDetails:\n");
    Address permanentAddress=
           personalDetails.getPermanentAddress();
    System.out.println("PermanentAddress:");
    System.out.println("\tStreet   : "+ permanentAddress.getStreet());
    System.out.println("\tCity     : "+ permanentAddress.getCity());
    System.out.println("\tState    : "+ permanentAddress.getState());
    System.out.println("\tPin      : "+ permanentAddress.getPin());

    System.out.println("\nObtaining PersonalDetails from Address:");
    PersonalDetails personalDetails1=
```

```
                    permanentAddress.getPersonalDetails();
    System.out.println("FirstName    : "+ personalDetails1.getFirstName());
    System.out.println("LastName     : "+ personalDetails1.getLastName());

    System.out.println("\nThe reference obtained from Address refers to its owning
entity, to test this we can equate the references 'personalDetails' and
'personalDetails1'; Result="+(personalDetails==personalDetails1));
  }
}
```

Now compile the java files and execute the Test Case shown in List 8.8. To run this example, in addition to the preceding three lists use the files PersonalDetails.java and hibernate.cfg.xml of Lists 8.1 and 8.4 respectively. Figure 8.2 shows the output of the BidirectionalCompositionTestCase.

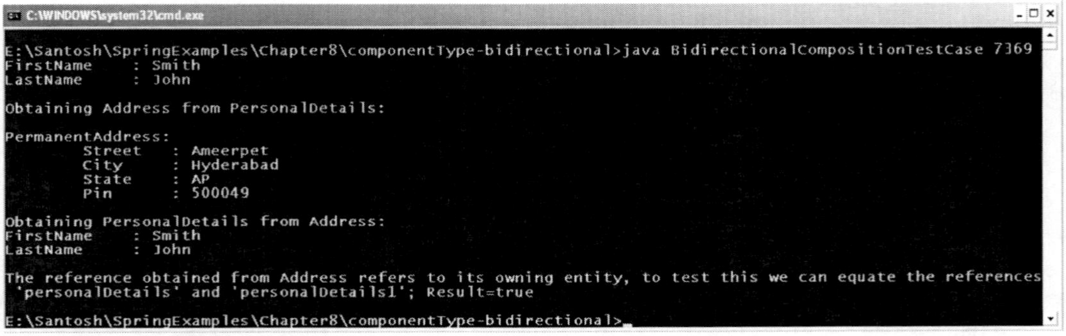

FIGURE 8.2 Output of BidirectionalCompositionTestCase

In this section we learnt about the support for implementing a rich domain model with coarse-grained entity classes, that is, the support for composition—both unidirectional and bidirectional. However, support for this is not enough for implementing a rich domain model, since we use class inheritance and polymorphism that are essential elements of object-oriented models to implement a rich domain model. Let us lean about the subtype's problem and how to map the class inheritance.

8.3 PROBLEM OF SUBTYPE'S

While implementing a complex object-oriented domain model we come across inheritance to abstract the details with several concrete subclasses and avoid unnecessary memory wastage. For example, we want to model employee details for an organization that has two types of employees—hourly and salaried. Some of the important properties for each of these types of employees are; empno, name, hourly_rate, and max_hours_par_day for hourly employees, and empno, name, and annual_salary for salaried employees. Notice that both the employee types have empno and name properties in common. In addition, each type has one or more properties distinct from the properties of the other types. For example, hourly_rate is unique to hourly employees. In this situation if we want to design a conceptual model in an object-oriented environment, we consider the following class design:

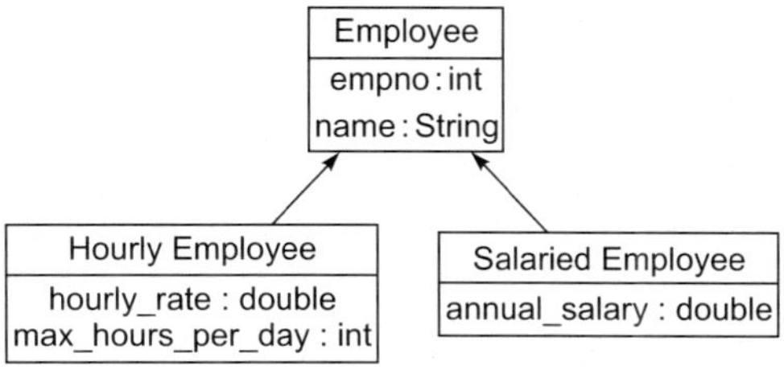

FIGURE 8.3 Employee hierarchy class diagram

As shown in Fig. 8.3 we define a supertype (possibly abstract) called Employee, and subtypes for hourly employees and salaried employees.

The relational environment does not directly support inheritance. However, we can consider the following three choices to define this conceptual model in a database.

1. Define a single table called EMPLOYEE_DETAILS with columns to contain the properties of both the employee types. Defining the columns of subtype properties to be nullable.
2. Define a table called EMPLOYEE_DETAILS with the columns for common properties, and a separate table for each employee type with the columns for the respective employee type, representing the inheritance relation as a foreign key association.
3. Define a separate table for both the employee types such as HOURLY_EMPLOYEE and SALARIED_EMPLOYEE.

This difference in defining the inheritance hierarchy results in a mismatch between object-oriented and relational environments. Hibernate handles this mismatch problem allowing us to map the inheritance hierarchy. Hibernate supports three different approaches of inheritance hierarchy mapping:

1. Table per class hierarchy
2. Table per subclass
3. Table per concrete class

Now, let us discuss each of these approaches.

8.3.1 Table Per Class Hierarchy

In this approach we map the entire class hierarchy to a single table, that is, a single table is used to represent the entire class hierarchy. This table includes columns for the properties of all classes in the hierarchy. This approach of inheritance mapping is basic, easier to use, and efficient compared to the other two approaches. This way of configuring the subclasses is best to use when we are designing our application top-down approach; that means we design the domain model and then design a SQL schema accordingly. However, this approach suffers from one major problem—the columns for properties declared by subclasses must be declared to accept null values, that is, these columns cannot be declared with NOT NULL constraint. This limitation may cause serious problems for data integrity. Figure 8.4 shows this type of mapping.

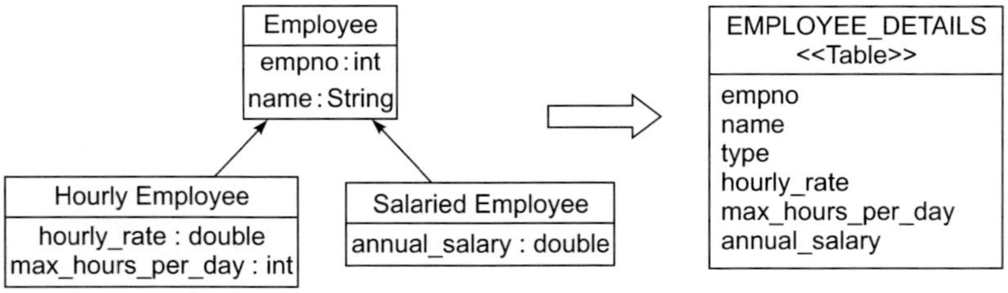

FIGURE 8.4 Table per class hierarchy mapping

In this approach we use the *discriminator* column value to identify the concrete subclass represented by a row. We use <subclass> element to describe the subclass along with its properties, and <discriminator> element to describe the discriminator column of the table. The following code snippet shows the mapping for the Employee class hierarchy.

Code Snippet

```
<hibernate-mapping package="com.santosh.hibernate">

  <class name="Employee" table="EMPLOYEE_DETAILS">
    <id name="empno" type="int">
      <column name="empno"/>
      <generator class="increment"/>
    </id>
    <discriminator column="type"/>

    <property name="name" column="name"/>

    <subclass name="HourlyEmployee" discriminator-value="hourly">
      <property name="maxHoursPerDay" column="max_hours_per_day"/>
      <property name="hourlyRate" column="hourly_rate"/>
    </subclass>

    <subclass name="SalariedEmployee" discriminator-value="salaried">
      <property name="annualSalary" column="annual_salary"/>
    </subclass>
  </class>
</hibernate-mapping>
```

In the preceding code snippet the <class> element is used to map the root class Employee of the inheritance hierarchy to the table EMPLOYEE_DETAILS table. As described earlier, we need to use a special column to distinguish between the subclasses, we use <discriminator> element to do this, and here we configured a column names 'type' whose value is expected to be hourly or salaried. We have even defined two subclasses named HourlyEmployee and SalariedEmployee using the <subclass> elements. Note that the columns mapped to the properties of subclasses should accept null values, that is, the columns cannot be defined with NOT NULL constraint. Let us implement a sample code for understanding this configuration.

8.3.2 Implementing Table Per Class Hierarchy

To demonstrate the working model of the table per class hierarchy mapping we will design the Employee class hierarchy shown in Fig. 8.3. List 8.9 shows the Employee class.

List 8.9: Employee.java

```
package com.santosh.hibernate;

public abstract class Employee{
  private int empno;
  private String name;

  public int getEmpno(){return empno;}
  public void setEmpno(int empno){this.empno=empno;}

  public String getName(){return name;}
  public void setName(String name){this.name=name;}

  public String toString(){
    return "Employee";
  }
}
```

List 8.9 shows the code for the Employee class that is the root class of the employee class inheritance hierarchy, declaring empno and name properties. Now, let us implement the HourlyEmployee, one of the subclasses of Employee.

List 8.10: HourlyEmployee.java

```
package com.santosh.hibernate;

public class HourlyEmployee extends Employee{
  private int maxHoursPerDay;
  private double hourlyRate;

  public double getHourlyRate(){return hourlyRate;}
  public void setHourlyRate(double hourlyRate){this.hourlyRate=hourlyRate;}

  public int getMaxHoursPerDay(){return maxHoursPerDay;}
  public void setMaxHoursPerDay(int maxHoursPerDay){
            this.maxHoursPerDay=maxHoursPerDay;}

  public String toString(){
    return "HourlyEmployee";
  }
}
```

The HourlyEmployee class is used to represent the hourly employee. Similarly, we want to implement the subclass of Employee for representing the salaried employee.

List 8.11: SalariedEmployee.java

```
package com.santosh.hibernate;

public class SalariedEmployee extends Employee{
  private double annualSalary;

  public double getAnnualSalary(){return annualSalary;}
  public void setAnnualSalary(double annualSalary){
             this.annualSalary=annualSalary;}

  public String toString(){
    return "SalariedEmployee";
  }
}
```

Now, let us configure this inheritance hierarchy. List 8.12 shows the mapping configuration file.

List 8.12: Employee.hbm.xml

```
<!DOCTYPE hibernate-mapping PUBLIC
    "-//Hibernate/Hibernate Mapping DTD 3.0//EN"
    "http://hibernate.sourceforge.net/hibernate-mapping-3.0.dtd">

<hibernate-mapping package="com.santosh.hibernate">

  <class name="Employee" table="EMPLOYEE_DETAILS">
    <id name="empno" type="int">
      <column name="empno"/>
      <generator class="increment"/>
    </id>
    <discriminator column="type"/>

    <property name="name" column="name"/>

    <subclass name="HourlyEmployee" discriminator-value="hourly">
      <property name="maxHoursPerDay" column="max_hours_per_day"/>
      <property name="hourlyRate" column="hourly_rate"/>
    </subclass>

    <subclass name="SalariedEmployee" discriminator-value="salaried">
      <property name="annualSalary" column="annual_salary"/>
    </subclass>
  </class>
</hibernate-mapping>
```

List 8.12 shows the code for hibernate mapping file that maps the employee class hierarchy with two subclasses, HourlyEmployee and SalariedEmployee. List 8.13 shows the code for hibernate configuration file.

List 8.13: hibernate.cfg.xml

```
<!DOCTYPE hibernate-configuration PUBLIC
  "-//Hibernate/Hibernate Configuration DTD 3.0//EN"
  "http://hibernate.sourceforge.net/hibernate-configuration-3.0.dtd">

<hibernate-configuration>
  <session-factory>
    <property name="connection.driver_class">
      oracle.jdbc.driver.OracleDriver
    </property>
    <property name="connection.url">
      jdbc:oracle:thin:@seminal1:1521:sandb
    </property>
    <property name="connection.user">scott</property>
    <property name="connection.password">tiger</property>

    <mapping resource="Employee.hbm.xml"/>

  </session-factory>
</hibernate-configuration>
```

To test this mapping, let us implement a test case that loads the employee details row.

List 8.14: EmployeeTestCase.java

```
import org.hibernate.cfg.*;
import org.hibernate.*;
import org.apache.log4j.Logger;
import org.apache.log4j.Level;
import com.santosh.hibernate.Employee;

public class EmployeeTestCase {

  public static void main(String[] args) throws Exception{

    Logger.getRootLogger().setLevel(Level.OFF);

    Configuration cfg=new Configuration().configure();

    SessionFactory factory=cfg.buildSessionFactory();

    Session session=factory.openSession();
```

```
        Employee employee=(Employee)
                session.load( Employee.class,
                        Integer.parseInt(args[0]));

        System.out.println("This employee is : "+employee);
    }
}
```

To execute this test case create EMPLOYEE_DETAILS table in database and insert some records using the SQL statements shown in the code snippet below.

Code Snippet

```
create  table EMPLOYEE_DETAILS(
empno number primary key,
name varchar2(20),
type varchar2(8),
hourly_rate number(10,2),
max_hours_per_day number,
annual_salary number(10,2));

insert into EMPLOYEE_DETAILS values(101, 'Tom', 'salaried', null, null, 500000);
insert into EMPLOYEE_DETAILS values(102, 'John', 'hourly', 1000, 8, null);
```

Figure 8.5 shows the output of the test case.

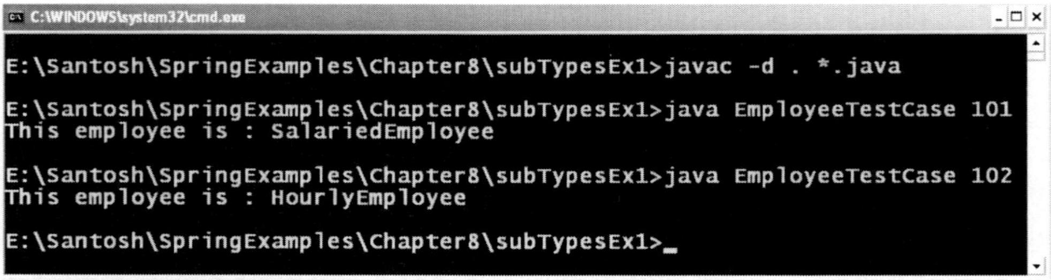

FIGURE 8.5 Output of EmployeeTestCase

As per the records inserted in the database using the SQL statements shown in the preceding code snippet the employee with empno 101 is a salaried employee and 102 is an hourly employee.

> **Note:** We can also use <subclass> mapping element in a separate mapping file as a top-level element instead of <class>. In such as case we have to declare the class that is extended, for example <subclass name="SalariedEmployee" extends="Employee">. It is important to configure that the superclass mapping must be loaded before the subclass mapping file. This is useful when we want to extend a class hierarchy without modifying the mapping file of the superclass.

8.3.3 Table Per Subclass

In this approach we map the class hierarchy to multiple tables associated with the relational foreign key. All the classes in the hierarchy that declares the persistent properties (including abstract classes) are mapped to a separate table. Figure 8.6 shows the mapping:

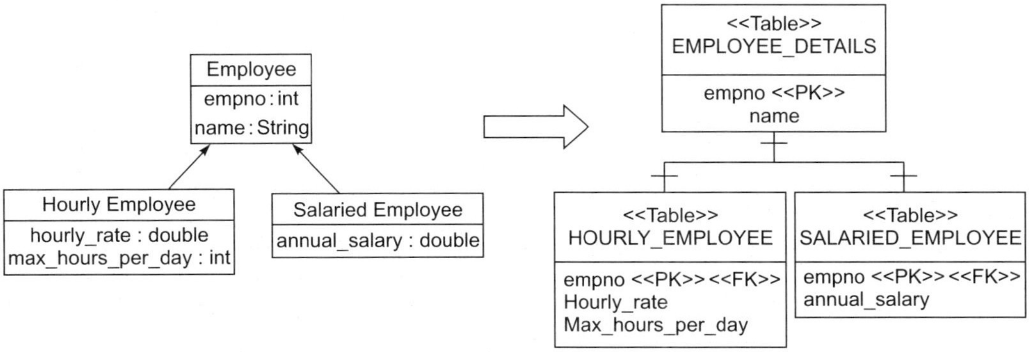

FIGURE 8.6 Table per subclass mapping

As shown in Fig. 8.6, we define a table called EMPLOYEE_DETAILS with the columns for common properties represented by Employee class such as empno and name. We even define a separate table for each employee type with the columns for the respective employee type, such as HOURLY_EMPLOYEE table for HourlyEmployee class and SALARIED_EMPLOYEE table for SalariedEmployee class, representing the inheritance relation as a foreign key association. The main benefits of this approach of inheritance mapping are; the relational model is completely normalized, integrity constraint definitions are straightforward.

In Hibernate, we use <joined-subclass> element to indicate the table per subclass mapping. The <joined-subclass> includes two important attributes to specify the subclass and related table name. The <joined-subclass> encloses the mapping definition for all the properties declared in the joined subclass. List 8.15 shows the hibernate mapping file describing the table per subclass mapping.

List 8.15: Employee.hbm.xml

```
<!DOCTYPE hibernate-mapping PUBLIC
    "-//Hibernate/Hibernate Mapping DTD 3.0//EN"
    "http://hibernate.sourceforge.net/hibernate-mapping-3.0.dtd">

<hibernate-mapping package="com.santosh.hibernate">

  <class name="Employee" table="EMPLOYEE_DETAILS">
    <id name="empno" type="int">
      <column name="empno"/>
      <generator class="increment"/>
    </id>

    <property name="name" column="name"/>
```

```
    <joined-subclass name="HourlyEmployee" table="HOURLY_EMPLOYEE">
         <key column="empno"/>

      <property name="maxHoursPerDay" column="max_hours_per_day"/>
      <property name="hourlyRate" column="hourly_rate"/>
    </joined-subclass>

    <joined-subclass name="SalariedEmployee" table="SALARIED_EMPLOYEE">
         <key column="empno"/>

      <property name="annualSalary" column="annual_salary"/>
    </joined-subclass>
  </class>
</hibernate-mapping>
```

In List 8.15 we configured the root class of the hierarchy using <class> element defining a mapping for id property empno, and one common property 'name' to the NAME column of EMPLOYEE_DETAILS. We even defined two subclasses, HourlyEmployee mapping to HOURLY_EMPLOYEE table and SalariedEmployee mapping to SALARIED_EMPLOYEE table.

> **Note:** Both the joined subclasses declares <key> element defining the foreign key mapping to the ID column of the root table (in this case EMPLOYEE_DETAILS). Use the SQL schema shown in the following code snippet to create the database tables and insert dummy data.

Code Snippet

```
drop table EMPLOYEE_DETAILS;
drop table HOURLY_EMPLOYEE;
drop table SALARIED_EMPLOYEE;

create  table EMPLOYEE_DETAILS(
empno number primary key,
name varchar2(20));

create table HOURLY_EMPLOYEE(
empno number primary key,
hourly_rate number(10,2),
max_hours_per_day number);

create table SALARIED_EMPLOYEE(
empno number primary key,
annual_salary number(10,2));

insert into EMPLOYEE_DETAILS values(101, 'Tom');
insert into SALARIED_EMPLOYEE values(101, 500000);

insert into EMPLOYEE_DETAILS values(102, 'John');
insert into HOURLY_EMPLOYEE values(102, 1000, 8);
```

Now use the Persistent Java classes, hibernate configuration XML file, and Test Case of the example demonstrating the table per class hierarchy, to test the table per subclass mapping shown under List 8.15.

> **Note:** We can also use <joined-subclass> mapping element in a separate mapping file as a top-level element, instead of <class>. In such a case we have to declare the class that is extended, for example, <joined-subclass name="SalariedEmployee" extends="Employee">. It is important to configure that the superclass mapping must be loaded before the subclass mapping file. This is useful when we want to extend a class hierarchy without modifying the mapping file of the superclass.

Now, let us discuss the third approach of inheritance mapping.

8.3.4 Table Per Concrete Class

In this approach we map the class hierarchy to a multiple tables with no relation. We use one table for each concrete (non-abstract) class in the hierarchy, declaring the columns for all the persistent properties declared by the class and inherited from its superclass. Figure 8.7 shows the mapping.

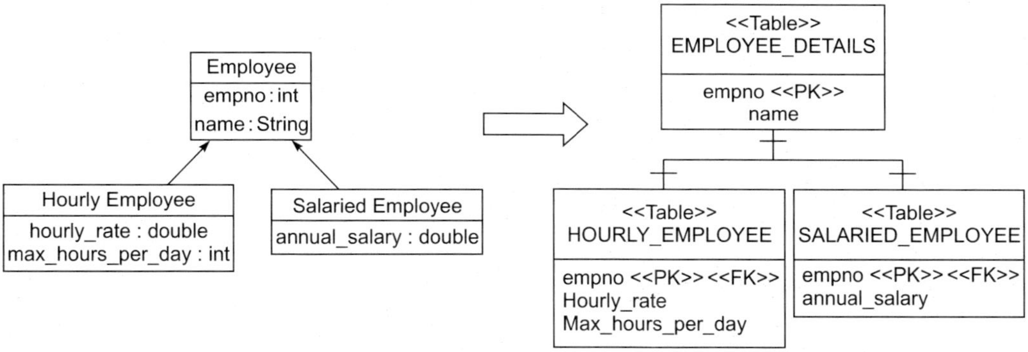

FIGURE 8.7 Table per concrete class

As shown in Fig. 8.7 we define one table per concrete class; in this case for each employee type, that is, HourlyEmployee and SalariedEmployee. The table called HOURLY_EMPLOYEE is defined with the columns for common properties represented by Employee class and the properties represented by HourlyEmployee class. The table called SALARIED_EMPLOYEE is defined with the columns for common properties represented by Employee class and the properties represented by SalariedEmployee class. This mapping strategy does not require any special Hibernate mapping declaration; simply create a new <class> declaration for each concrete class, specifying a different table attribute for each.

This type of mapping is useful for the top level of our class hierarchy where polymorphism is not generally required. The main problem with this approach is that it does not support polymorphic associations properly. We know that associations are represented as foreign key relationships in the database. As shown in Fig. 8.6, the subclasses are all mapped to different tables, thus a polymorphic association to their superclass (Employee class in our example) cannot be represented as a simple foreign key relationship. For example, if Employee is associated with Dept then we need to define foreign key reference in both the tables—HOURLY_EMPLOYEE and SALARIED_EMPLOYEE to the DEPT table.

In this section we learnt the details of mapping an inheritance hierarchy. In the next section we will discuss the problem of mapping associations between entities, which is another major mismatch between object-oriented and relational environments.

8.4 PROBLEM OF RELATIONSHIPS

In our object-oriented domain model various objects relate to one another in some approach, using object reference or collection of object references, that is, an association relation between the object classes. For example, we might design Employee object to represent the employee details. Each Employee object might be associated with one PersonalDetails object; similarly, we might even design Dept object to represent department details where a Dept object might be associated with many number of Employee objects. Figure 8.8 shows the class diagram of this example.

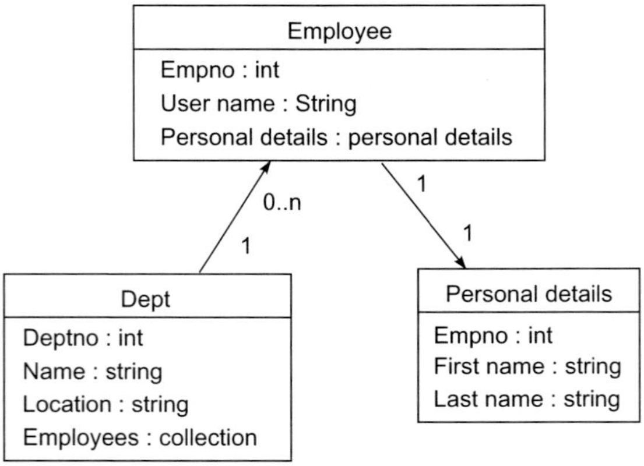

FIGURE 8.8 Class diagram

From Fig. 8.8 we can observe that an association is shown as a solid line between the participating classes. The end of an association where it connects to a class is called an *association role*. Each role has a multiplicity, which indicates how many objects participate in a given relationship. In a class diagram, a multiplicity specification is shown as a text string representing an interval (or intervals) of integers in the format *lower-bound..upper-bound*. The most common multiplicities in practice are 0..1, 1 and * (* character indicates an infinite upper bound). The following are the possible relationships based on the multiplicity:

- **One-to-One**: In this case one entity object is exactly related to one object of another entity. An example of this is the relationship between an employee and his PersonalDetails.
- **One-to-Many**: In this type of relation one entity object is related to many objects of another entity. An example of this is the relationship between a department and the employees working in that department.
- **Many-to-One:** In this type of relation many objects of an entity are related to one object of another entity. An example of this is the relationship between employees and their project. There may be many employees working for a single project.

- **Many-to-Many:** In this type of relation many objects of an entity are related to many objects of another entity. An example of this is the relationship between employees and courses. There may be many employees registered for one course and likewise an employee can register for multiple courses.

> **Note:** The object references are unidirectional, that is the association is from one object to another; meaning only the owning side of the relationship is aware of it. For example, if we declare an object reference of PersonalDetails class in Employee class, we can navigate from Employee object to PersonalDetails object but not in the other direction. If we want to design objects navigable in both the directions, we must define two associations, one in each of the associated classes.

On the other hand in the relational environment we define the relations using a foreign key. The foreign key associations are not by nature directional. Actually, navigation has no meaning for a relational data model, since we can create random data associations with table joins and projection. And the table associations are always one-to-one and one-to-many. Moreover, to define a many-to-many relation we need to introduce a link table, which does not appear in the object model.

These slight differences between the entity association in the object-oriented and relational environments causes the mismatch problem while mapping an object domain model to the relational environment. This is one of the most difficult problems involved in implementing an ORM solution. Hibernate includes a rich association model for association management. Unlike other managed relationships as EJB CMP model, Hibernate associations are all unidirectional, since as discussed above, the associations between the objects are always unidirectional. Moreover, Hibernate claims to persist plain Java objects. Hibernate association model supports to manage all the four types of associations described above. So let us learn how to map the various associations in Hibernate.

8.4.1 One-to-One

This type of association relates one entity object exactly to one object of another entity. An example of this type of association is the relationship between an Employee and his PersonalDetails. Figure 8.9 shows class diagram of this example.

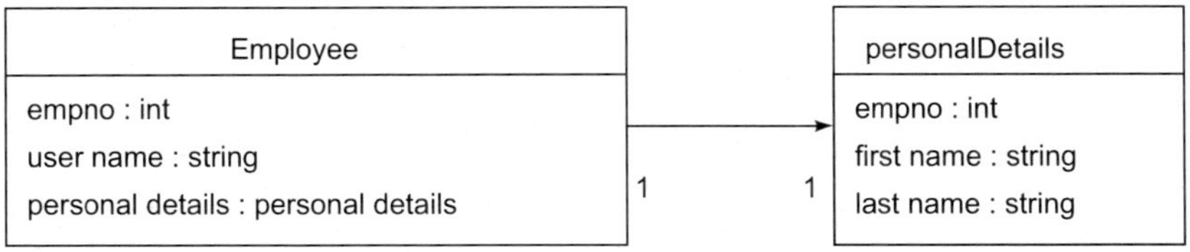

FIGURE 8.9 One to One relation Class Diagram

List 8.16 shows the code for Employee class.

List 8.16: Employee.java

```
package com.santosh.hibernate;

public class Employee{
  private int empno;
  private String userName;
  private PersonalDetails personalDetails;

  public int getEmpno(){return empno;}
  public void setEmpno(int empno){this.empno=empno;}

  public String getUserName(){return userName;}
  public void setUserName(String ueserName){this.userName=userName;}

  public PersonalDetails getPersonalDetails(){return personalDetails;}
  public void setPersonalDetails(PersonalDetails personalDetails){
    this.personalDetails=personalDetails;
  }
}//class
```

List 8.16 shows the code for Employee persistent class that declares two persistent fields including empno Id field. It even declares a relationship property named personalDetails of PersonalDetails type. List 8.17 shows the code for PersonalDetails class.

List 8.17: PersonalDetails.java

```
package com.santosh.hibernate;

public class PersonalDetails{
  private int empno;
  private String firstName, lastName;

  public int getEmpno(){return empno;}
  public void setEmpno(int empno){this.empno=empno;}

  public String getFirstName(){return firstName;}
  public void setFirstName(String firstName){this.firstName=firstName;}

  public String getLastName(){return lastName;}
  public void setLastName(String lastName){this.lastName=lastName;}
}//class
```

Now, we want to tell Hibernate about the relationship that we have between the Employee and PersonalDetails. To map this relation we use <one-to-one> element in hibernate mapping file for Employee persistent class, as shown below:

```
<one-to-one name="personalDetails" class="PersonalDetails"/>
```

The preceding tag informs Hibernate that personalDetails property represents the one to one relation to PersonalDetails from the declaring entity, that is, Employee. List 8.18 shows the complete code for Employee.hbm.xml file.

List 8.18: Employee.hbm.xml

```
<!DOCTYPE hibernate-mapping PUBLIC
    "-//Hibernate/Hibernate Mapping DTD 3.0//EN"
    "http://hibernate.sourceforge.net/hibernate-mapping-3.0.dtd">

<hibernate-mapping package="com.santosh.hibernate">

  <class name="Employee" table="EMPLOYEE">
    <id name="empno" type="int">
      <column name="empno"/>
      <generator class="increment"/>
    </id>

    <property name="userName"/>

    <one-to-one name="personalDetails" class="PersonalDetails"/>
  </class>
</hibernate-mapping>
```

List 8.18 shows the hibernate mapping file for Employee persistent class declaring a relationship filed associating the Employee entity to PersonalDetails entity. List 8.19 shows the code for PersonalDetails hibernate mapping file.

List 8.19: PersonalDetails.hbm.xml

```
<!DOCTYPE hibernate-mapping PUBLIC
    "-//Hibernate/Hibernate Mapping DTD 3.0//EN"
    "http://hibernate.sourceforge.net/hibernate-mapping-3.0.dtd">

<hibernate-mapping package="com.santosh.hibernate">

  <class name="PersonalDetails" table="personaldetails">
    <id name="empno" type="int">
      <column name="empno"/>
      <generator class="increment"/>
    </id>

    <property name="firstName"/>
    <property name="lastName"/>

  </class>
</hibernate-mapping>
```

As we are defining a unidirectional relationship, we don't have any relationship specific configurations in PersonalDetails hibernate mapping file. Now to test the Employee to PersonalDetails relationship mapping we can use the following test case.

List 8.20: EmployeeTestCase.java

```
import org.hibernate.cfg.*;
import org.hibernate.*;
import org.apache.log4j.Logger;
import org.apache.log4j.Level;
import com.santosh.hibernate.Employee;
import com.santosh.hibernate.PersonalDetails;

public class EmployeeTestCase {

  public static void main(String[] args) throws Exception{

    Logger.getRootLogger().setLevel(Level.OFF);

    //Preparing Configuration object
    Configuration cfg=new Configuration().configure();
    cfg.addResource("Employee.hbm.xml");
    cfg.addResource("PersonalDetails.hbm.xml");

    //Building SessionFactory
    SessionFactory factory=cfg.buildSessionFactory();

    //Open a new Session
    Session session=factory.openSession();

    Employee employee=(Employee)
          session.load( Employee.class,
                        Integer.parseInt(args[0]));

    System.out.println("UserName  : "+employee.getUserName());
    PersonalDetails personalDetails=employee.getPersonalDetails();
    System.out.println("FirstName : "+personalDetails.getFirstName());
    System.out.println("LastName  : "+personalDetails.getLastName());
    session.close();
  }
}
```

List 8.10 shows a simple test case to test the Employee to PersonalDetails relationship; it loads the Employee persistent object using Hibernate session and then retrieves the PersonalDetails object using the Employee object. This test case displays the username, firstname, and lastname of the given employee. To execute this test case we require a hibernate.cgf.xml file. List 8.21 shows the code for hibernate.cgf.xml file.

List 8.21: hibernate.cgf.xml

```
<!—hibernate.cfg.xml—>
<!DOCTYPE hibernate-configuration PUBLIC
  "-//Hibernate/Hibernate Configuration DTD 3.0//EN"
  "http://hibernate.sourceforge.net/hibernate-configuration-3.0.dtd">

<hibernate-configuration>
  <session-factory>
    <property name="connection.driver_class">
      oracle.jdbc.driver.OracleDriver
    </property>
    <property name="connection.url">
      jdbc:oracle:thin:@seminal1:1521:sandb
    </property>
    <property name="connection.user">scott</property>
    <property name="connection.password">tiger</property>

  </session-factory>
</hibernate-configuration>
```

Now, create the database using the SQL statements given below:

SQL Script

```
drop table employee;
drop table personaldetails;

create table employee(
empno number,
userName varchar2(20),
deptno number);

create table personaldetails(
empno number,
firstname varchar2(20),
lastname varchar2(20));

insert into employee values(101, 'Tom26', 10);

insert into personaldetails values(101, 'Tom', 'Cat');

commit;
```

Figure 8.10 shows the output of the EmployeeTestCase.

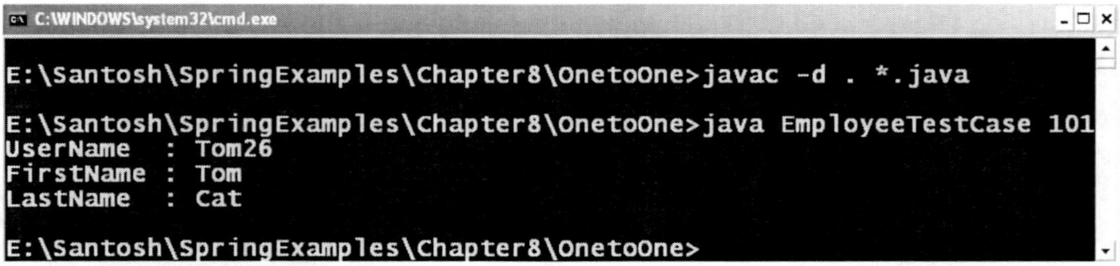

FIGURE 8.10 Output of EmployeeTestCase

In this example we have navigated from Employee to PersonalDetails. If we have to navigate from PersonalDetails to Employee also, we want to define a bidirectional relationship. To do this we want to declare relationship field in PersonalDetails entity, and declare the relationship using <one-to-one> in PersonalDetails.hbm.xml file. See following code snippet.

Code Snippet

```
PersonalDetails.java

package com.santosh.hibernate;

public class PersonalDetails{
  private int empno;
  private String firstName, lastName;
  private Employee employee;

  public void setEmployeeDetails(Employee employee){
    this.employee=employee;
  }
  pubic Employee getEmployeeDetails(){
    return employee;
  }
  ...
}//class

PersonalDetails.hbm.xml

<hibernate-mapping package="com.santosh.hibernate">
  <class name="PersonalDetails" table="personaldetails">
    <id name="empno" type="int">
      <column name="empno"/>
      <generator class="increment"/>
    </id>
```

```
    <property name="firstName"/>
    <property name="lastName"/>

    <one-to-one name="employeeDetails" class="Employee"/>

  </class>
</hibernate-mapping>
```

The preceding code snippet declares a relationship property named employeeDetails in PersonalDetails class that relates to the Employee entity.

8.4.2 One-to-Many

This type of association relates one entity object to many objects of another entity. An example of this type of association is the relationship between a department and the employees working in that department. Figure 8.11 shows class diagram of this example.

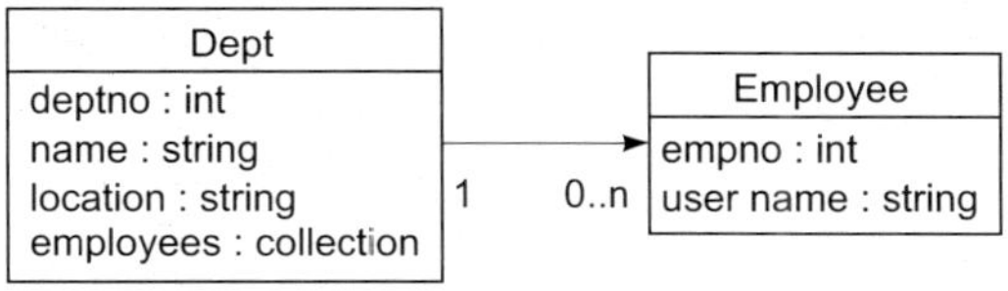

FIGURE 8.11 One-to-Many relation class diagram

Figure 8.11 shows the class diagram describing the one-to-many relation between Dept and Employee, where many employees work in a single department. List 8.22 shows the code for Dept class.

List 8.22: Dept.java

```
package com.santosh.hibernate;

import java.util.*;

public class Dept{
  private int deptno;
  private String name, loc;
  private Collection<Employee> employees;

  public int getDeptno(){return deptno;}
  public void setDeptno(int deptno){this.deptno=deptno;}

  public String getName(){return name;}
  public void setName(String name){this.name=name;}

  public String getLoc(){return loc;}
  public void setLoc(String loc){this.loc=loc;}
```

```
    public Collection<Employee> getEmployees(){return employees;}
    public void setEmployees(Collection<Employee> employees){
        this.employees=employees;
    }
}//class
```

To map the one-to-many relation we use <one-to-many> element within hibernate collection element such as <set> or <list> in hibernate mapping file of Dept persistent class, as shown below:

```
<set name="employees">
    <key column="deptno"/>
    <one-to-many class="Employee"/>
</set>
```

The <set> element informs Hibernate that the Dept class has a property named employees, and that it's a Set containing instances of the Employee class, representing the one to many relation to Employee from the declaring entity i.e. Dept. The <key> element specifies the foreign key from the collection table to the parent table. In this example the collections table is the table mapped to Employee class and the parent table is the table mapped to Dept class. Here the employee table has a deptno column referring the id column (that is, deptno) of dept table. List 8.23 shows the complete code for Dept.hbm.xml file.

List 8.23: Dept.hbm.xml

```
<!DOCTYPE hibernate-mapping PUBLIC
      "-//Hibernate/Hibernate Mapping DTD 3.0//EN"
      "http://hibernate.sourceforge.net/hibernate-mapping-3.0.dtd">

<hibernate-mapping package="com.santosh.hibernate">

    <class name="Dept" table="DEPT">
        <id name="deptno" type="int">
            <column name="deptno"/>
            <generator class="increment"/>
        </id>

        <property name="name" column="dname"/>
        <property name="loc"/>

        <set name="employees">
            <key column="deptno"/>
            <one-to-many class="Employee"/>
        </set>
    </class>
</hibernate-mapping>
```

Now to test the Dept to Employee relationship mapping we can use the following test case:

List 8.24: DeptTestCase.java

```
import org.hibernate.cfg.*;
import org.hibernate.*;
import org.apache.log4j.Logger;
import org.apache.log4j.Level;
import com.santosh.hibernate.Employee;
import com.santosh.hibernate.Dept;
import java.util.*;

public class DeptTestCase {

  public static void main(String[] args) throws Exception{

    Logger.getRootLogger().setLevel(Level.OFF);

    //Preparing Configuration object
    Configuration cfg=new Configuration().configure();
    cfg.addResource("Employee.hbm.xml");
    cfg.addResource("Dept.hbm.xml");

    //Building SessionFactory
    SessionFactory factory=cfg.buildSessionFactory();

    //Open a new Session
    Session session=factory.openSession();

    Dept dept=(Dept)
              session.load( Dept.class,
                            Integer.parseInt(args[0]));

    System.out.println("Department Name   : "+dept.getName()+"\n");

    Collection<Employee> employees=dept.getEmployees();
    System.out.println("Empno\tUserName");
    System.out.println(".............");
    for (Employee employee: employees) {
      System.out.print(employee.getEmpno()+"\t");
      System.out.println(employee.getUserName());
    }
    session.close();
  }
}
```

The following code snippet shows the SQL statements to create a database for the mapping described above.

SQL Script

```
drop table employee;

create table employee(
empno number,
userName varchar2(20),
deptno number);

create table dept(
deptno number,
dname varchar2(20),
loc varchar2(20));

insert into employee values(101, 'Santosh', 10);
insert into employee values(102, 'Subash', 10);
insert into employee values(103, 'Sai', 20);
insert into employee values(104, 'kumar', 20);
insert into employee values(105, 'Chandra', 20);
insert into employee values(106, 'Tom', 30);

commit;
```

Figure 8.12 shows the output of the DeptTestCase.

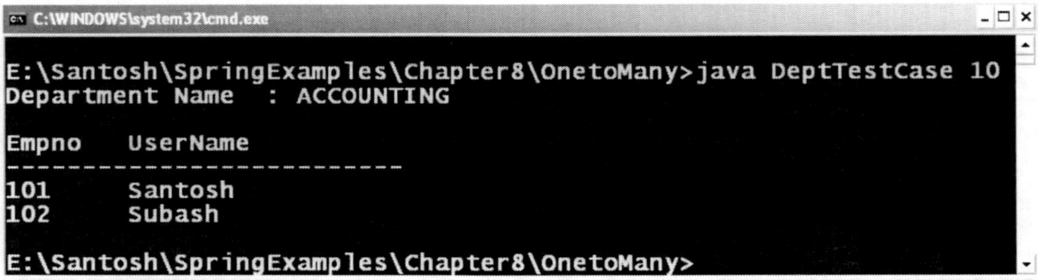

FIGURE 8.12 Output of DeptTestCase

In this example we have navigated from Dept to Employee. If we have to navigate from Employee to Dept, we want to define a many-to-one relationship. The following section explains how to configure a many-to-one relationship.

8.4.3 Many-to-One

This type of association relates many objects of an entity to one object of another entity. An example of this type of association is the relationship between Employee and a Department with many employees. Figure 8.13 shows class diagram of this example.

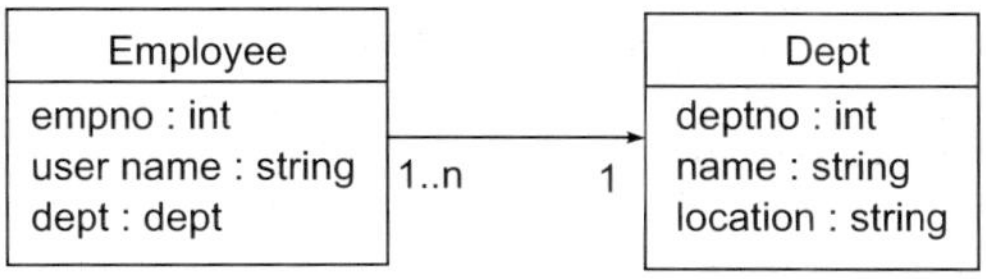

FIGURE 8.13 Many-to-One class diagram

Figure 8.13 shows the class diagram describing the many-to-one relation between Employee and Dept, where many employees work in a single department. List 8.25 shows the code for Employee class.

List 8.25: Employee.java

```
package com.santosh.hibernate;

public class Employee{
  private int empno;
  private String userName;
  private Dept dept;

  public int getEmpno(){return empno;}
  public void setEmpno(int empno){this.empno=empno;}

  public String getUserName(){return userName;}
  public void setUserName(String userName){this.userName=userName;}

  public Dept getDept(){return dept;}
  public void setDept(Dept dept){this.dept=dept;}
}//class
```

To map the many-to-one relation we use <many-to-one> element in hibernate mapping file of Employee persistent class, as shown below:

<many-to-one name="dept" column="deptno"/>

The above described <many-to-one> element informs Hibernate that the Employee class has a property named dept, representing the many-to-one relation to Dept from the declaring entity, that is, Employee. The *column* attribute specifies the foreign key from the declaring to the referring table. In this example, the declaring table is the table mapped to Dept class and its referring table is the table mapped to Employee class. Here the employee table has a deptno column referring the id column (that is, deptno) of dept table. List 8.26 shows the complete code for Employee.hbm.xml file.

List 8.26: Employee.hbm.xml

```
<!DOCTYPE hibernate-mapping PUBLIC
    "-//Hibernate/Hibernate Mapping DTD 3.0//EN"
    "http://hibernate.sourceforge.net/hibernate-mapping-3.0.dtd">
```

```
<hibernate-mapping package="com.santosh.hibernate">

  <class name="Employee" table="EMPLOYEE">
    <id name="empno" type="int">
      <column name="empno"/>
      <generator class="increment"/>
    </id>

    <property name="userName"/>
    <many-to-one name="dept" column="deptno"/>
  </class>
</hibernate-mapping>
```

List 8.26 shows the code for hibernate mapping file of Employee entity, which declares a relationship property named dept that relates to the Dept entity. Now, let us learn how to map a Many-to-Many relationship.

8.4.4 Many-to-Many

This type of relation relates many objects of an entity to many objects of another entity. For example, a relationship between students and courses, where there may be many students registered for one course or a student can register for multiple courses. Figure 8.14 shows the class diagram for this example.

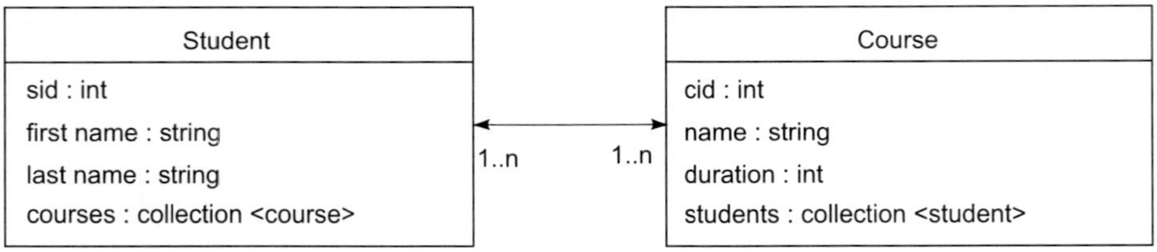

FIGURE 8.14 Class diagram showing Many-to-Many relationship

Figure 8.14 shows the class diagram describing the many-to-many relation between Student and Course, where a Student object holds a collection of Course objects, and similarly a Course object holds a collection of Student objects. As discussed earlier, that the table associations are always one-to-one and one-to-many, we cannot directly associate two tables defining many-to-many relationships.

To define a many-to-many relationship in the database environment we use a link table (also known as collection table), instead of directly relating the tables using the foreign key like one-to-one or one-to-many associations. Figure 8.15 shows the database table schema for students and courses with a many-to-many relationship.

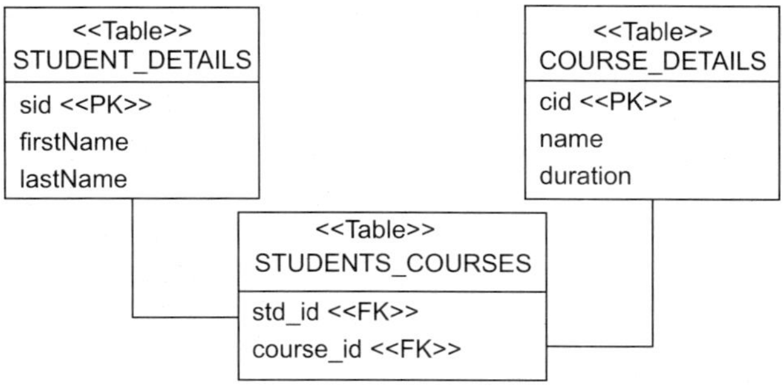

FIGURE 8.15 Table schema for Many-to-Many relationship

Figure 8.15 shows a many-to-many table schema for Student and Course entities where the Student entity maps to STUDENT_DETAILS table and Course entity maps to COURSE_DETAILS table. We do not have an entity class for the link table (in this case STUDENTS_COURSES). The STUDENTS_COURSES table declares a foreign key column named *std_id* referring the STUDENT_DETAILS table; it even declares another foreign key column named *course_id* referring the COURSES_DETAILS table.

Now, let us implement the entity classes Student and Course for STUDENT_DETAILS and COURSE_DETAILS tables, respectively. List 8.27 shows the code for Student.

List 8.27: Student.java

```
package com.santosh.hibernate;

public class Student {

  public int getSid(){return  sid;}
  public void setSid(int i){sid=i;}

  public String getFirstName(){return fname;}
  public void setFirstName(String s){fname=s;}

  public String getLastName(){return lname;}
  public void setLastName(String s){lname=s;}

  public java.util.Collection<Course> getCourses(){
    return courses;
  }
  public void setCourses(java.util.Collection<Course> courses){
    this.courses=courses;
  }

  int sid;
  String fname, lname;
  java.util.Collection<Course> courses;
}
```

List 8.27 shows the code for Student entity declaring three persistent fields named sid, firstName and lastName, and one relationship field named courses relating the Student object to collection of Course objects. List 8.28 shows the code of persistent class for COURSE_DETAILS.

List 8.28: Course.java

```
package com.santosh.hibernate;

public class Course {

  public int getCid(){return  cid;}
  public void setCid(int cid){this.cid=cid;}

  public String getName(){return name;}
  public void setName(String s){name=s;}

  public int getDuration(){return duration;}
  public void setDuration(int d){duration=d;}

  int cid, duration;
  String name;
}
```

List 8.28 shows the code for Course entity declaring three persistent fields named cid, name and duration. As we have created the entity class for student and course now we want to write hibernate mapping files for both the persistent classes, which will define the persistent field and relationship mapping. List 8.29 shows the code for Student hibernate mapping.

List 8.29: Student.hbm.xml

```
<!DOCTYPE hibernate-mapping PUBLIC
    "-//Hibernate/Hibernate Mapping DTD 3.0//EN"
    "http://hibernate.sourceforge.net/hibernate-mapping-3.0.dtd">

<hibernate-mapping package="com.santosh.hibernate">
  <class name="Student" table="STUDENT_DETAILS">
    <id name="sid">
      <column name="sid"/>
      <generator class="increment"/>
    </id>

    <property name="firstName"/>
    <property name="lastName"/>

    <set name="courses" table="STUDENTS_COURSES">
      <key column="std_id"/>
      <many-to-many class="Course" column="course_id"/>
    </set>
  </class>
</hibernate-mapping>
```

List 8.29 shows the code of a hibernate mapping file for Student persistent class. The <set> element in the preceding mapping file informs Hibernate that the Student class has a property named courses, and that its a Set containing instances of the Course class. The *table* attribute of the <set> element specifies the table name used to store the student to course mappings (that is, link table) for the many-to-many mappings. Here in this example this table is named as STUDENTS_COURSES. Note that the table attribute of the <set> element is applicable only when it is used to define many-to-many associations or when value objects. The <key> element specifies the foreign key from the collection (link table) to the parent table. In this example, the collections table is STUDENTS_COURSES and the parent table is the table mapped to Student class, that is, STUDENT_DETAILS. That means here the STUDENTS_COURSES table has a column named *std_id* referring the id column (that is, sid) of STUDENT_DETAILS table.

The <many-to-many> element defines the relationship mapping. Unlike the <one-to-many> element, *column* attribute is mandatory. The *column* attribute specifies the column name in the link table that stores the id of the Course. As we have defined the mapping for Student persistent class, let us write a mapping file for Course persistent class.

List 8.30: Course.hbm.xml

```
<!--hibernate mapping file-->
<!DOCTYPE hibernate-mapping PUBLIC
    "-//Hibernate/Hibernate Mapping DTD 3.0//EN"
    "http://hibernate.sourceforge.net/hibernate-mapping-3.0.dtd">

<hibernate-mapping package="com.santosh.hibernate">
  <class name="Course" table="COURSE_DETAILS">
    <id name="cid">
      <column name="cid"/>
      <generator class="increment"/>
    </id>
    <property name="name" column="name"/>
    <property name="duration" column="duration"/>

  </class>
</hibernate-mapping>
```

Now, let us implement a test case for testing this relationship mapping. List 8.31 shows the code for the StudentTestCase.

List 8.31: StudentTestCase.java

```
import org.hibernate.*;
import org.hibernate.cfg.*;
import org.apache.log4j.Logger;
import org.apache.log4j.Level;
import java.util.*;
import com.santosh.hibernate.Student;
```

```
import com.santosh.hibernate.Course;

public class StudentTestCase {

  public static void main(String s[]) throws Exception {

    Logger.getRootLogger().setLevel(Level.OFF);

    Configuration cfg=new Configuration().configure();
    cfg.addResource("Student.hbm.xml");
    cfg.addResource("Course.hbm.xml");

    SessionFactory sf= cfg.buildSessionFactory();
    Session sess=sf.openSession();

    Student student=(Student) sess.load(Student.class, new Integer(s[0]));

    System.out.println("First Name : "+student.getFirstName());

    System.out.println("This student has registered for the following courses:");

    Collection<Course> courses=(Collection<Course>) student.getCourses();

    System.out.println("CourseID\tName");
    System.out.println("..................");
    for(Course course:courses){
      System.out.print(course.getCid()+"\t\t");
      System.out.println(course.getName());
    }
    sess.close();
  }//main
}//class
```

To execute this test case we need a hibernate configuration file (see List 8.21) and we even need to create the database. The following snippet shows the SQL statements to create database.

SQL Script

```
drop table STUDENT_DETAILS;
drop table COURSE_DETAILS;
drop table STUDENTS_COURSES;

create table STUDENT_DETAILS(
sid number, firstname varchar2(20), lastname varchar2(20));

create table COURSE_DETAILS(cid number, name varchar2(20), duration number);
```

```
create table STUDENTS_COURSES(std_id number, course_id number);

insert into STUDENT_DETAILS values(1001, 'Subash', 'V');
insert into STUDENT_DETAILS values(1002, 'Sai', 'Kumar');
insert into STUDENT_DETAILS values(1003, 'Tom', 'T');
insert into STUDENT_DETAILS values(1004, 'Shankar', 'N');
insert into STUDENT_DETAILS values(1005, 'John', 'T');

insert into COURSE_DETAILS values(11, 'Core Java', 60);
insert into COURSE_DETAILS values(12, 'Spring', 40);
insert into COURSE_DETAILS values(13, 'J2EE', 90);
insert into COURSE_DETAILS values(14, 'Hibernate', 30);

insert into STUDENTS_COURSES values(1001, 11);
insert into STUDENTS_COURSES values(1001, 13);
insert into STUDENTS_COURSES values(1002, 12);
insert into STUDENTS_COURSES values(1002, 13);
insert into STUDENTS_COURSES values(1002, 14);
insert into STUDENTS_COURSES values(1003, 11);
insert into STUDENTS_COURSES values(1004, 12);
insert into STUDENTS_COURSES values(1004, 14);
insert into STUDENTS_COURSES values(1005, 14);

commit;
```

After creating the database compile all the three Java files (Student.java shown in List 8.27, Course.java shown in List 8.28, and StudentTestCase.java shown in List 8.31) and execute the StudentTestCase.

Figure 8.16 shows the outputs of StudentTestCase for different student ids, retrieving the courses that the student registered for. In this example we have defined a relationship filed in Student entity; however, we can even define the relationship field in Course entity also by making the relationship bidirectional. In such a case we use the same <set> with <many-to-many> elements in the Course.hbm.xml file. In this case we want to use *inverse* attribute of <set> element. The following code snippet shows the elements for relationship field mapping in Course.hbm.xml.

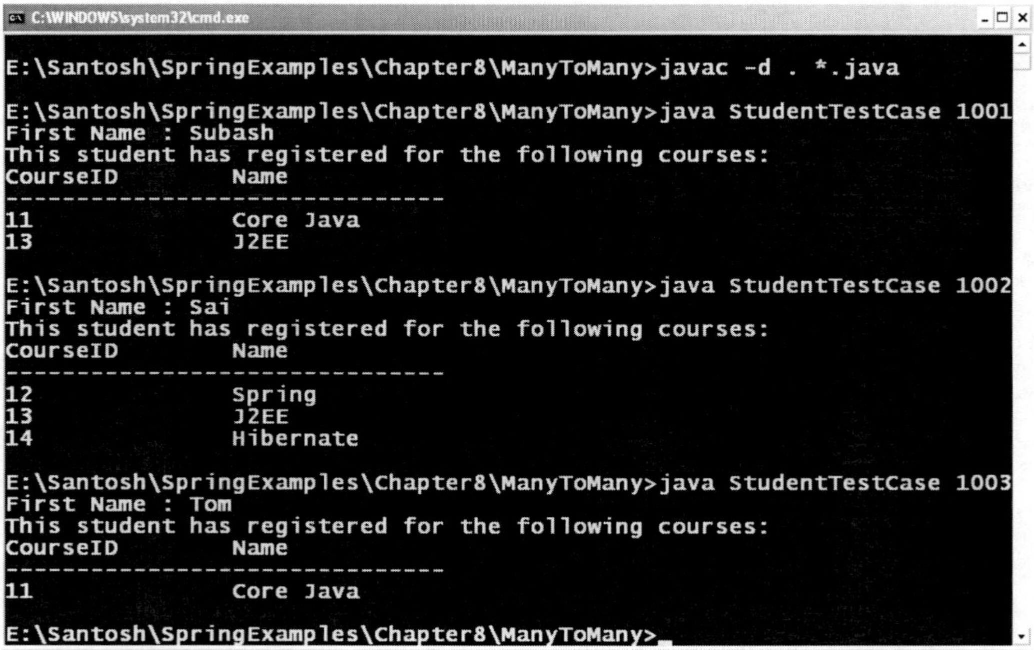

FIGURE 8.16 Output of StudentTestCase showing many-to-many relationship

Code Snippet

```
<set name="students" inverse="true">
  <key column="course_id"/>
  <many-to-many class="Student"/>
</set>
```

Apart from the preceding mapping definition we need to declare the property named students of Collection/Set type in course class. While defining the bidirectional relationship, specifying the inverse is significant since the non-inverse end of the relationship will control the link table.

Summary

In this chapter we have learnt about the Hibernate mapping configurations to map persistent classes solving the mismatch problems such as granularity, subtypes, and relationships. In the next chapter we will discuss on how to query the persistent objects using Hibernate Query Language.

Understanding Hibernate Query Language (HQL) and Criterion API

9 CHAPTER

Objectives

In the previous chapters we discussed mapping persistent objects and performed basic CRUD operations using Hibernate. Retrieving persistent objects from the database is one of the CRUD operations. Up till now we used Hibernate API to retrieve persistent objects using an identifier. However, in most of the cases we wanted to retrieve persistent objects using different conditions such as getting all the employee objects whose name starts with the character 'A'. Hibernate provides a most powerful query language named Hibernate Query Language (HQL) to meet this requirement. Hibernate even provides a Criterion API that provides a type-safe and object-oriented way to retrieve persistent objects. Moreover, it supports the use of native SQL queries to retrieve objects from the database. In this chapter we will cover:

- How to use HQL and Hibernate Criterion API to query the persistent objects
- Importance of HQL and how to use it to retrieve persistent objects

9.1 INTRODUCING HQL

The Hibernate Query Language (HQL) is an object-oriented query language for retrieving persistent objects. As discussed earlier, Hibernate includes get() and load() methods to retrieve the persistent objects by a primary key. Retrieving a single persistent object using its primary key is a basic approach, but in many situations we either do not know the primary key, or we need more than one persistent object as a result by specifying one or more search conditions. Moreover, in some situations we want to retrieve a few properties of a persistent object or objects, without the overhead of loading the persistent objects itself in a transactional scope. In all these cases we need to prepare a query. As we know that SQL is more familiar and standardized to use for querying data from relational databases. We can use SQL to prepare queries for retrieving persistent objects mapped to relational database tables giving the responsibility to the ORM for mapping the JDBC ResultSet's to persistent objects graph, but using SQL to in this case results with the following shortcomings:

- SQL is standardized but its vendor-dependent features limit the portability of SQL statements between databases. Thus we may require changing the statements each time we want to migrate from one database to another.
- SQL is designed more specifically to work with relational database tables but not objects. Thus while working with SQL statements we need to use the database table and column names instead of the persistent class and property names.

To overcome these issues Hibernate introduces its own object-oriented query language called Hibernate Query Language (HQL). HQL is a query-specification language for preparing dynamic and static queries expressed through metadata. HQL queries are compiled to SQL of a database or any other native query language the target database supports. This allows the execution of queries to be shifted to the native language facilities provided by the database. The HQL is intentionally designed similar to SQL so that it can be easily learnt with the basic knowledge of SQL thus minimizing the learning curve. As mentioned earlier, HQL is a powerful query language with most advanced features for retrieving persistent objects using complex conditions. HQL is also known as object-oriented extension to SQL bridging the gap between the object-oriented systems and relational databases. Up till Hibernate 2.x HQL is an exclusively query language used only for object retrieval, not for updating, inserting, or deleting data (that is, it does not supports data manipulation language statements like SQL). However, in Hibernate 3, HQL is enhanced to support data manipulation language statements such as insert, update, and delete. Using HQL for querying persistent objects instead of native SQL provides the following benefits:

- As described earlier we use persistent classes and properties in HQL queries instead of the database tables and column names like in SQL. This makes HQL queries database independent, and so improves portability.
- HQL allows us to apply restrictions to properties of associated objects related by reference or held in collections, which enables us to navigate the object graph using query language.
- HQL provides a support for ordering the result persistent objects.
- HQL is more object-oriented which makes us write HQL queries more easily than SQL. This even benefits us by returning results as objects.
- HQL supports pagination.

As we have understood the need of introducing HQL and its importance, we need to further learn the HQL syntax for preparing queries. Before we start understanding the HQL queries let us discuss on the Hibernate API used to execute the HQL queries and get results.

9.2 USING HIBERNATE API TO EXECUTE HQL QUERIES

There are a number of options in HQL for preparing queries that can retrieve persistent objects or specific persistent object properties as per our requirement, but the general steps involved in executing them are the same. The following three steps are involved in executing the HQL query:

Step 1: Obtain an instance of org.hibernate.Query
Step 2: Customize the Query object
Step 3: Execute the Query

> **Note:** The three steps listed above that uses Hibernate Query API to execute the HQL is new in Hibernate 3.0. I, in Hibernate 2.x we simply use list(String HQLQuery) or iterate(String HQLQuery) methods of Session to execute the HQL query.

Let us discuss these steps in detail.

9.2.1 Obtaining a Query Instance

The org.hibernate.Query is an abstraction, providing object-oriented representation of a HQL query. A Query instance is obtained by calling Session.createQuery() or Session.getNamedQuery() method. The createQuery() method is used to create a new instance of Query for the given HQL query, the HQL query is specified as an argument of the createQuery() method. The getNamedQuery() method is used to obtain an instance of Query for a named query string defined in the mapping file (we will learn about the Named queries later in this chapter). As described earlier, the HQL query is compiled to SQL. If we want to view the converted SQL statements we can configure show_sql named property value to 'true'. To set this property in the Hibernate XML configuration file we use the following tag:

```
<property name="show_sql">true</property>
```

Setting this property in the configuration, results in writing the generated SQL statement to the standard output console. This is useful in debugging the HQL statements. Now, after obtaining the Query object we can customize it, if necessary, before executing the Query.

9.2.2 Customizing the Query Object

After obtaining a Query object we may want to customize it by setting query parameters, cache mode, flush mode, fetch size, an upper limit for the result set size, etc. The Query object supports the following methods for customization shown in Table 9.1.

TABLE 9.1 Query customization methods

Method Name	*Description*
setMaxResults(int maxResults)	Specifies the maximum number of rows to retrieve. If not set, there is no limit to the number of rows retrieved.
setFirstResult(int firstResult)	Specifies the index of the first row to retrieve from. If not set, rows will be retrieved beginning from row 0.
setReadOnly(boolean readOnly)	Specifies whether the persistent objects retrieved by this query will be loaded in a read-only mode. If the persistent objects are loaded in read-only mode then Hibernate will never dirty-check them or make changes persistent.
setCacheable(boolean cacheable)	Specify whether to enable caching of this query result set, that is whether to cache the query results.
setCacheRegion(String cacheRegion)	Specify the name of the cache region where the query is to be stored. The *cache Region* specifies the name of a query cache region, or null for the default query cache.
setCacheMode(CacheMode cacheMode)	Specifies the cache mode for this query. This overrides the current session cache mode, just for this query. Hibernate supports the following cache modes:

(Contd.)

	CacheMode.GET: In this mode, the session may read items from the cache, but will not add items, except to invalidate items when updates occur. **CacheMode.PUT**: In this mode, the session will never read items from the cache, but will add items to the cache as it reads them from the database. **CacheMode.REFRESH**: In this mode, the session will never read items from the cache, but will add items to the cache as it reads them from the database. **CacheMode.IGNORE**: In this mode, the session will never interact with the cache, except to invalidate cache items when updates occur. **CacheMode.NORMAL**: In this mode, the session may read items from the cache, and add items to the cache.
setTimeout(int timeout)	Specifies a timeout for the underlying JDBC query.
setFetchSize(int fetchSize)	Specifies a fetch size for the underlying JDBC query.
setLockMode(String alias, LockMode lockMode)	Set the lockmode for the objects identified by the given alias that appears in the FROM clause. Hibernate supports the following lock modes: **LockMode.NONE**: Specifies that no lock is required. If an object is requested with this lock mode, a READ lock will be obtained if it is necessary to actually read the state from the database, rather than pull it from a cache. This is the default lock mode. **LockMode.READ**: Specifies a shared lock. Objects in this lock mode were read from the database in the current transaction, rather than being pulled from a cache. **LockMode.UPGRADE**: Specifies an upgrade lock. Objects loaded in this lock mode are materialized using an SQL select for update. **LockMode.WRITE**: Specifies a WRITE lock. This lock mode is obtained when an object is updated or inserted. This is not a valid mode for load() or lock().
setFlushMode(FlushMode flushMode)	Specifies the flush mode for this query. This overrides the current session flush mode, just for this query.

Apart from the customizations explained above we may require to set the parameters (positional or named) we will discuss about the parameter in-detail in Section 9.6.3. Now, after customizing the Query object we have to prepare it for execution.

9.2.3 Executing the Query

After preparing the Query object by setting all the custom properties we now want to execute the Query. We use list(), scroll(), iterate() or uniqueResult() methods of Query to execute the HQL query represented by it. We can re-execute the Query by subsequent invocations, since the lifespan of a Query object is bound by the lifespan of the Session that created it. The Query execution methods are described below:

- The list() method returns the query results as a java.util.List. If the query contains multiple results per row, the results are returned in an instance of Object[].
- The scroll() method returns the query results as ScrollableResults. Note that the scrollability of the returned results depends upon JDBC driver support for scrollable ResultSets.
- The iterate() method returns the query results in the form of java.util.Iterator. If the query contains multiple results per row, the results are returned in an instance of Object[]. The persistent objects returned as results are initialized on demand, initially query returns identifiers only.

- The uniqueResult() method is a convenience method to execute a Query that returns a single instance, or null if the query returns no results. Note that this method throws Hibernate Exception, in case if there are more than one objects resulted executing the query.

As mentioned earlier, HQL from Hibernate 3 onwards, also supports Data Manipulating Language operations such as update and delete. And in support of this feature we have the executeUpdate() method. The executUpdate() method returns the number of entities affected by this query, and throws HibernateException if the Query object is representing a select query. Now, as we have learnt about the basic steps for executing the queries, let us learn how to build HQL queries.

9.3 PREPARING HQL QUERIES TO RETRIEVE PERSISTENT OBJECTS

The HQL select query used to retrieve persistent objects is defined as:

Syntax

```
[select_clause] from_clause [where_clause] [groupby_clause] [orderby_clause]
```

> **Note:** The square brackets '[...]' indicate an optional term.

As shown in the preceding syntax, the HQL select query consists of the following five clauses

- The **select_clause**: Specifies the output type, that is, the type of objects or values to be selected.
- The **from_clause**: This portion of the HQL query is used to declare the identification variables (objects) that will be selected by the query. These identification variables can be used by the query in the expressions specified in the other clauses of the query. The from_clause is the only portion of a HQL query that is mandatory.
- The **where_clause**: Specifies the restrictions on the results that are returned by the query. We can use a combination of logical and boolean expressions to compose the where_clause. In addition, we can also use collection commands to work with collections.
- The **groupby_clause**: Allows query results to be aggregated in terms of groups.
- The **orderby_clause**: Specifies the order of the results that are returned by the query.

Now, let us have a close look on each clause for preparing HQL queries using the various constructs of HQL. As described above the from_clause is the only portion of a HQL query that is mandatory, so let us start with the from_clause.

9.3.1 THE FROM CLAUSE

The FROM clause of an HQL query is used to declare the identification variables (objects) that will be selected by the query. These identification variables can be used by the query in the expressions specified in the other clauses of the query. The identification variables designate instances of a particular entity type. The following sample query shows the simplest form of HQL query:

```
from Employee
```

This query returns all the Employee objects in the database, along with all the associated objects and non-lazy collections. Note that the HQL constructs are not case-sensitive. The following listing shows the test case executing simple HQL from clause query:

List 9.1: BasicHQLFromTestCase.java

```
import org.hibernate.cfg.*;
import org.hibernate.*;
import org.apache.log4j.Logger;
import org.apache.log4j.Level;
import com.santosh.hibernate.Employee;
import com.santosh.hibernate.Dept;
import java.util.*;

public class BasicHQLFromTestCase {

  public static void main(String[] args) throws Exception{

    Logger.getRootLogger().setLevel(Level.OFF);

    //Preparing Configuration object
    Configuration cfg=new Configuration().configure();
    cfg.addResource("Employee.hbm.xml");
    cfg.addResource("Dept.hbm.xml");

    //Building SessionFactory
    SessionFactory factory=cfg.buildSessionFactory();

    //Open a new Session
    Session session=factory.openSession();

    Query q=session.createQuery("from Employee");
    List<Employee> employees=q.list();
    System.out.println("Empno\tUserName");
    System.out.println("...............");
    for(Employee employee: employees){
          System.out.print(employee.getEmpno()+"\t");
          System.out.print(employee.getUserName()+"\n");
    }
    session.close();
  }
}
```

To execute this program use the persistent classes, hibernate mapping and configuration files created to demonstrate the examples in Chapter 8. Figure 9.1 shows the output of the BasicHQLFromTestCase.

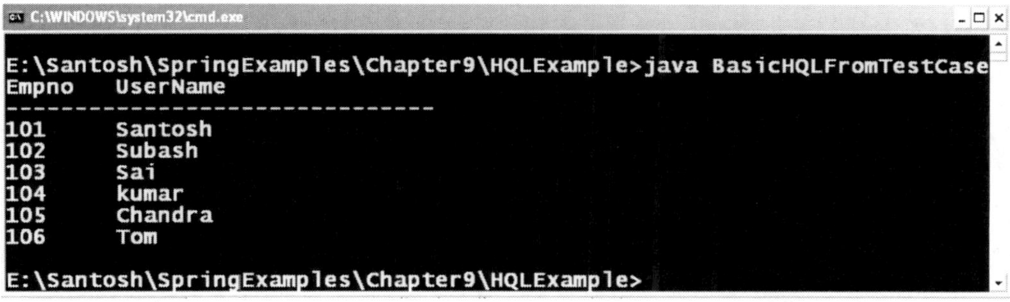

FIGURE 9.1 Output of BasicHQLFromTestCase

In the query used with the above example we have not specified any identification variable, however, if we want to use the declaration in other clauses or in the same then we want to specify an identification variable for the declaration as shown below.

```
from Employee AS e where e.deptno=10
```

This query returns all the Employee objects in the database with a department 10. In this query we have specified an identification variable named 'e' designating the Employee type, which is used in the where clause to refer to its field named deptno (we will learn about the where clause in detail in the next sections). Using the 'AS' construct to declare the identification variable is optional. The identification variable can be a string of alpha-numeric characters in any case. However, it is a good practice to use an initial lowercase similar to the Java naming standards for local variables. An identification variable must not be a reserved identifier, entity type name, or special characters. The preceding query declares only one identification variable, however, the FROM clause can contain multiple identification variable declarations separated by a comma (,). For example:

```
from Dept d, Employee e
```

This query declares two identification variables called 'd' and 'e' designating Dept and Employee entities respectively. This may be required to query on multiple associated objects. If we declare only one identification variable in the query, we get a list of the queried object. But if we declare multiple identification variable declarations, we get a result List containing Cartesian product of the queried objects. For example, for the above shown query we get a List containing Object[], the length of the result list will be the number of Dept objects multiplied by number of Employee objects. Each Object[] in the result list contains two objects, Dept object at index zero and Employee object at index one. Probably we may not be required with such as result list, thus to query associated objects we want to use joins. The following section explains how to use joins in HQL queries.

9.3.2.1 Joins

As mentioned in the preceding section joins are used to query multiple associated objects using a single HQL query. HQL supports the various types of joins; the following snippet shows the syntax of using the joins in HQL query.

```
base_entity_name [AS] base_entity_identification_variable [LEFT [OUTER] | RIGHT
[OUTER] | INNER | FULL] JOIN [FETCH] association_path_expression identification_
variable
```

Example:

```
FROM Dept d JOIN d.employees e
```

Here the *base_entity_name* specifies the base persistent class name (that is, the persistent class object in which the association is defined). In the above example the base entity name is Dept. The *base_entity_identification_variable* in the syntax specifies the identification variable for the base entity object. In the above example the base identification variable name is d. The *association_path_expression* in the syntax specifies the path expression referring to the association property of collection type or a single entity type. In the example this is d.employees, where employees is a one-to-many mapping field declared in Dept persistent class. As specified earlier, HQL supports various types of joins, and it can be found from the syntax that we can specify LEFT JOIN, RIGHT JOIN, INNER JOIN, FULL JOIN, or INNER JOIN FETCH. In our example we have not specified any prefix for JOIN such as LEFT, RIGHT, INNER, or FULL, in which case Hibernate considers INNER as default. Table 9.3 describes the rules of each of these join types.

TABLE 9.3 JOIN types and there rules

Join Type	*Description*
INNER JOIN	This type of join discards all the unmatched objects on either side of the join.
LEFT [OUTER] JOIN	This type of join returns all the objects from the left side of the join, even if the object on the left side of the join has no matching object on the right side of the join.
RIGHT [OUTER] JOIN	This type of join returns all the objects from the right side of the join, even if the object on the right side of the join has no matching object on the left side of the join.
FULL JOIN	This type of join returns all the objects from either side of the join, irrespective of matching objects on the opposite side of the join.
INNER JOIN FETCH	This type of join is used to retrieve the associated object or a collection of objects irrespective of the lazy property on the association.

List 9.2 shows the code for executing a simple HQL join query.

List 9.2: HQLJoinTestCase1.java

```
import org.hibernate.cfg.*;
import org.hibernate.*;
import org.apache.log4j.Logger;
import org.apache.log4j.Level;
import com.santosh.hibernate.Employee;
import com.santosh.hibernate.Dept;
import java.util.*;

public class HQLJoinTestCase1 {
```

```
  public static void main(String[] args) throws Exception{

    Logger.getRootLogger().setLevel(Level.OFF);

    Configuration cfg=new Configuration().configure();
    cfg.addResource("Employee.hbm.xml");
    cfg.addResource("Dept.hbm.xml");

    SessionFactory factory=cfg.buildSessionFactory();
    Session session=factory.openSession();

    Query q=session.createQuery("FROM Dept d JOIN d.employees e");
    List<Object[]> results=q.list();
    System.out.println("Empno\tDeptno\tDepartmentName");
    System.out.println(".......................");
    for(Object[] result: results){
      Dept dept=(Dept)result[0];
      Employee employee=(Employee)result[1];

      System.out.print(employee.getEmpno()+"\t");
      System.out.print(dept.getDeptno()+"\t");
      System.out.print(dept.getName()+"\n");
    }
    session.close();
  }
}
```

List 9.2 shows the code that executes a simple inner join HQL query and prints the results to demonstrate the output of the join query. In this example, we have used the a HQL query 'FROM Dept d JOIN d.employees e' which returns a List of Object[] objects. Each Object[] has two elements—Dept object and Employee object. See the above table for the rule that is used for selecting the objects when INNER JOIN or simply JOIN is used. To execute this example use the Employee, Dept persistent classes, the respective hibernate mapping files, and hibernate configuration file of the one-to-many example demonstrated in Chapter 8. Figure 9.2 shows the output of this example.

```
C:\WINDOWS\system32\cmd.exe

E:\Santosh\SpringExamples\Chapter9\HQLExample>java HQLJoinTestCase1
Empno   Deptno  DepartmentName
----------------------------------------
101     10      ACCOUNTING
102     10      ACCOUNTING
103     20      RESEARCH
104     20      RESEARCH
105     20      RESEARCH
106     30      SALES

E:\Santosh\SpringExamples\Chapter9\HQLExample>
```

FIGURE 9.2 Output of HQLJoinTestCase1

In this example we have got a List of Object[] objects, describing the Dept and Employee objects. We can also use the join identification variable in SELECT clause of the query to select specific properties of the associated entities. The following section explains the select clause of the HQL query.

9.4 THE SELECT CLAUSE

The select clause of the HQL query specifies the output type, that is, the type of objects or values to be selected. The SELECT clause may contain one or more identification variable, single-valued path expression, an aggregate select expression, or a constructor expression. This section explains all these options, one after another, first starting with identification variables. For example:

```
SELECT d from Dept d
```

This query returns a list of Dept objects, here 'd' is an identification variable denoting Dept entity. If required we can also specify multiple identification variables. As mentioned above, the SELECT clause allows one or more identification variables and even allows us to specify a single-valued expression path. For example:

```
SELECT d.name FROM Dept d
```

This query results a list of String objects describing the Dept names. In this query we have specified a single-valued expression of String type. As mentioned above the SELECT clause can contain one or more single-valued path expressions. That means, if we want to select the department location along with the name then we can add another single-valued path expression in the SELECT clause as shown below.

```
SELECT d.name, d.loc FROM Dept d
```

If the SELECT clause specifies multiple single-valued path expressions or identification variables in any combination, the query returns a list of Object[] objects containing the specified values (objects), where the length of the Object[] array is the number of expressions specified. The preceding query returns list of Object[] objects, each of length two describing the Dept name and location. List 9.3 shows the code executing the query with multiple single-valued path expression:

List 9.3: SelectMultipleScalarValues.java

```
import org.hibernate.cfg.*;
import org.hibernate.*;
import org.apache.log4j.Logger;
import org.apache.log4j.Level;
import java.util.*;

public class SelectMultipleScalarValues {

  public static void main(String[] args) throws Exception{
```

```
        Logger.getRootLogger().setLevel(Level.OFF);

        Configuration cfg=new Configuration().configure();
        cfg.addResource("Dept.hbm.xml");
        SessionFactory factory=cfg.buildSessionFactory();
        Session session=factory.openSession();

        Query q=session.createQuery("SELECT d.name, d.loc FROM Dept d");
        List<Object[]> results=q.list();

        System.out.println("Dept Name\tLocation");
        System.out.println("................");
        for(Object[] result: results){
          System.out.print(result[0]+"    \t");
          System.out.print(result[1]+"\n");
        }
        session.close();
    }
}
```

List 9.3 shows the code executing a HQL query selecting multiple scalar values. We can observe that the query returns a list containing Object[] array with values as specified in the SELECT clause. In most cases we want the result as a list of custom value objects instead of Object[] array. The following code snippet shows a sample code for this requirement:

Code Snippet

```
Query q=session.createQuery("SELECT d.name, d.loc FROM Dept d");

List<Object[]> results=q.list();

  List<DeptMinDetails> myresults=new List<DeptMinDetails>();

  for(Object[] result: results){
    myresults.add(new DeptMinDetails(result[0], result[1]));
  }
//use the myresults list that contains DeptMinDetails objects
```

In the preceding code we have selected multiple single-valued scalar values into a list of Object[]'s, and then we have transformed the results into a list of custom ValueObjects (DeptMinDetails). We may have this requirement for various reasons in an enterprise application. For example we want the results to be used in the presentation tier to render a response using some JSP tags (such as <jsp:getProperty> tag) that supports the retrieval of named properties from an object but not indexed properties. However, to meet this requirement the preceding approach has some issues such as increases in memory requirement and unnecessary list iteration. HQL supports these requirements in a more efficient way, allowing us to specify the constructor expression in select clause. The following section describes how to use the constructor expression in a HQL query.

9.6 USING CONSTRUCTOR EXPRESSION IN SELECT CLAUSE

The HQL SELECT clause allows us to specify a constructor expression for retrieving a list of custom ValueObjects. For example, we want to retrieve a list containing DeptMinDetails objects, each DeptMinDetails describing a Dept name and location. We use a HQL construct named NEW to specify the constructor expression. For example:

```
SELECT  NEW com.santosh.hibernate.DeptMinDetails(d.name, d.loc) FROM Dept d
```

This query returns a list of DeptMinDetails objects. The DeptMinDetails class must have the constructor matching the constructor used in the query. We need a two-argument constructor in the DeptMinDetails class. The constructor expression option is one of the most important features of HQL because as explained in the preceding section retrieving the multiple scalar values as a list of custom ValueObjects is the most common requirement of enterprise applications.

> **Note:**
> - The specified class need not be a persistent class mapped to the database table.
> - The constructor name must be fully qualified.

List 9.4 shows the code executing an HQL query with a SELECT clause containing the constructor expression.

List 9.4: SelectConstructorExpression.java

```
import org.hibernate.cfg.*;
import org.hibernate.*;
import org.apache.log4j.Logger;
import org.apache.log4j.Level;
import com.santosh.hibernate.DeptMinDetails;
import java.util.*;

public class SelectConstructorExpression {

  public static void main(String[] args) throws Exception{

    Logger.getRootLogger().setLevel(Level.OFF);

    Configuration cfg=new Configuration().configure();
    cfg.addResource("Dept.hbm.xml");
    SessionFactory factory=cfg.buildSessionFactory();
    Session session=factory.openSession();

    Query q=session.createQuery(
"select new com.santosh.hibernate.DeptMinDetails(d.name, d.loc) from Dept d");

List<DeptMinDetails> results=q.list();
```

```
    System.out.println("Dept Name\tLocation");
    System.out.println(".................");
    for(DeptMinDetails dept: results){

      System.out.print(dept.getName()+"    \t");
      System.out.print(dept.getLocation()+"\n");
    }
    session.close();
  }
}
```

The preceding code is retrieving the results using HQL query in the form of a list of DeptMinDetails objects and writing the results to the standard output console to demonstrate the results obtained. List 9.5 shows the code for DeptMinDetails.

List 9.5: DeptMinDetails.java

```
package com.santosh.hibernate;

import java.io.Serializable;

public class DeptMinDetails implements Serializable{

  private String name, loc;

  public DeptMinDetails(){}
  public DeptMinDetails(String name, String loc){
        this.name=name;
        this.loc=loc;
  }

  public String getName(){return name;}
  public void setName(String name){this.name=name;}

  public String getLocation(){return loc;}
  public void setLocation(String loc){this.loc=loc;}
}//class
```

The DeptMinDetials is a simple plain Java class as used in the HQL query. This has a two-argument constructor taking the name and location as inputs. Here we have even implemented a no-argument constructor which is not mandatory. The DeptMinDetails class even implements Serializable but the class used in a HQL query need not implement Serializable but is required if we want to use this as a transfer object between tiers such as presentation and remote business tier. To execute the SelectConstructorExpression we even need the Dept persistent class and its hibernate mapping file. Figure 9.3 shows the output of SelectConstructorExpression.

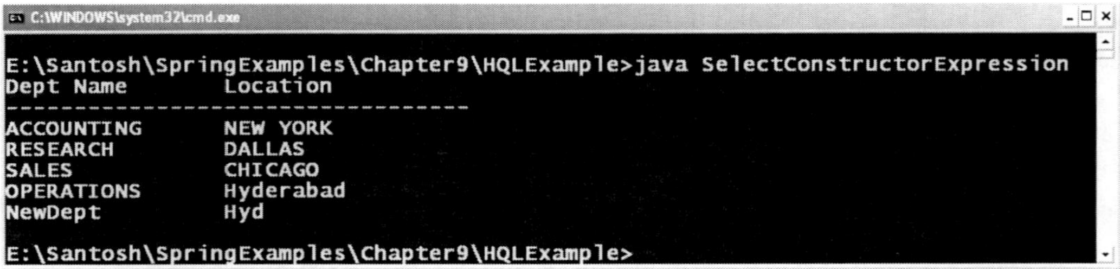

FIGURE 9.3 Output of SelectConstructorExpression

In this section we have learnt how to use constructor expression in the SELECT clause for selecting the data into custom ValueObjects. So far we have seen how to use identification variables, one single-valued path expression, multiple single-valued path expressions and constructor expression. Now let us see the SELECT clause containing aggregate select expression.

9.6.1 Using Aggregate Select Expression in SELECT Clause

The HQL SELECT clause allows us to specify one or more aggregate select expressions for retrieving computed values. For example, we want to get the number of Dept objects, or we want to get the maximum salary among the selected Employee objects. The following five aggregate functions can be used in the SELECT clause of an HQL query: AVG, COUNT, MAX, MIN, and SUM. These functions perform the same operations as their SQL equivalent. All of these functions operate on a path expression. The path expression that is the argument to the aggregate function must be resolved to a persistent field. However, the argument to COUNT may be an identification variable or the path expression argument to COUNT function may be resolved to either a persistent or an association field. Moreover, the path expression argument to functions SUM and AVG must be numeric type otherwise HibernateException is thrown. Table 9.5 describes the five aggregate functions supported by HQL.

TABLE 9.5 HQL aggregate functions

Function	***Description***
COUNT(path_expression)	Returns Integer value specifying the number of values selected by the given path_expression. If there are no values selected then it returns 0. The path_expression can be an identification variable or a persistent or association field.
AVG(path_expression)	Returns a Float value describing the average value of the values selected by the given path_expression.
MIN(path_expression)	Returns the minimum values among the values selected by the given path_expression. The return type of this function is the type of the persistent field that the given path_expression is resolved.
MAX(path_expression)	Returns the maximum values among the values selected by the given path_expression. The return type of this function is the type of the persistent field that the given path_expression is resolved.
SUM(path_expression)	Returns a numeric value describing the sum of the values selected by the given path_expression.

We can use the DISTINCT keyword followed by the expression as an argument to an aggregate function specifying that duplicate values are to be eliminated before the aggregate function is applied. Note that Null values are eliminated before the aggregate function is applied, without considering whether the DISTINCT keyword is specified. Let us look at some examples of using aggregate functions in HQL queries.

```
SELECT COUNT(e) FROM Employee e
```

This query returns the number of Employee objects in the database. As mentioned earlier, we can use DISTINCT keyword to get distinct Employee objects. Note that the HQL constructs are not case-sensitive.

```
SELECT AVG(e.salary) FROM Employee e
```

This query returns a java.lang.Float object that describing the average salary of the employees in the database. Similarly, we can use the other functions in the select clause of the HQL query for retrieving the required results. Apart from the above explained Table 9.6 shows the aggregate functions HQL includes for indexed collections.

TABLE 9.6 HQL aggregate functions for indexed collection

Function	*Description*
elements(path_expression)	Returns the elements of a collection returned by the given path expression.
maxElement(path_expression)	Returns the maximum element in the collection containing the basic types. If the collection returned by the given path expression contains persistent objects then the maximum element is decided based on the ID value of the persistent objects.
minElement(path_expression)	Returns the minimum element in the collection containing the basic types. If the collection returned by the given path expression contains persistent objects then the minimum element is decided based on the ID value of the persistent objects.
maxIndex(path_expression)	Returns the maximum element of a collection returned by the given path expression.
minIndex(path_expression)	Returns the minimum element of a collection returned by the given path expression.
size(path_expression)	Returns the number of elements in a collection returned by the given path expression.

In this section we learnt about the select clause of the HQL query describing the various possible options that a select clause can contain such as one or more identification variables, single-valued path expression, aggregate select expression, or a constructor expression. Now let us learn about the WHERE clause of the HQL query.

9.6.2 The Where Clause

The WHERE clause of HQL query is used to specify restrictions on the results returned by the query. That is, the WHERE clause restricts the result of a select statement. Moreover, the WHERE clause restricts the scope of an update or delete operation (to recall Hibernate 3 supports Data Manipulation Language statements also. We will discuss these statements later in this chapter). The WHERE clause of an HQL query consists of a conditional expression which is a combination of logical and boolean expressions. In addition, we can also use aggregate and collection functions to build the 'where' clause expressions. For example:

```
SELECT d FROM Dept d WHERE d.deptno = 10
```

This query returns a Dept object whose deptno value equals to 10. In this query we have used = (equals) comparison operator to build WHERE clause expression. HQL supports various comparison operators such as = (equals), > (greater than), < (less than), >= (greater than or equals) and <= (less than or equals). In addition, we can also use logical operators such as between, and, or, in, any, exists, like, not and some. For example:

```
SELECT d FROM Dept d WHERE d.name LIKE 'A%'
```

This query returns all the Dept objects whose name starts with a character 'A'. We can even use the aggregate and collection functions explained in the preceding section. For example:

```
SELECT d FROM Dept d WHERE size(d.employees) < 10
```

This query returns all the Dept objects that has less than 10 employees. Similarly, we can use other functions. In this section we have learnt about the WHERE clause of the HQL query and with this we have completed the most important part of the HQL query. We can have GROUP BY clause in a HQL query for aggregating the query results in terms of groups according to a set of properties. We can also have ORDER BY clause to order the results (objects or values) that are returned by the query. For example:

```
SELECT d FROM Dept d ORDER BY d.name
```

This query returns a list of all Dept objects in the database ordering them by Dept name values in ascending order. We can use a DESC construct followed by the order by item as shown below:

```
SELECT d FROM Dept d ORDER BY d.name DESC
```

This query returns a list of all Dept objects in the database ordering them by Dept name values in descending order. So far in all our examples we have prepared static queries but in most of the enterprise applications we need dynamic queries where we can populate the query parameters dynamically. HQL supports two types of input query parameters—positional and named.

9.6.3 Positional Parameters

The positional parameters in HQL query are specified using a '?' character. These are similar to the positional parameters used with JDBC PreparedStatement, the only difference between the HQL positional parameters and JDBC PreparedStatement positional parameters which is the position index in HQL starts from 0 instead of 1. For example:

```
SELECT d FROM Dept d WHERE d.deptno = ?
```

In this query we have specified one positional parameter which is recognized with an index 0. Now we want to set the values for the parameters before executing the query. We use setParameter(int position, Object value) method of Query object to set the parameters. List 9.6 shows the code using the positional parameters.

List 9.6: DynamicHQLQueryEx1.java

```
import org.hibernate.cfg.*;
import org.hibernate.*;
import org.apache.log4j.Logger;
import org.apache.log4j.Level;
import com.santosh.hibernate.Dept;
import java.util.*;

public class DynamicHQLQueryEx1 {

  public static void main(String[] args) throws Exception{

        Logger.getRootLogger().setLevel(Level.OFF);

        Configuration cfg=new Configuration().configure();
        cfg.addResource("Dept.hbm.xml");
        SessionFactory factory=cfg.buildSessionFactory();
        Session session=factory.openSession();

        Query q=session.createQuery(
            "SELECT d.name, d.loc FROM Dept d WHERE d.deptno=?");
        q.setParameter(0, args[0]);

        List<Object[]> results=q.list();
        Object[] result=results.get(0);

        System.out.println("Dept No:"+args[0]);
        System.out.println("Dept Name:"+result[0]);
      System.out.println("Location:"+result[1]);
      session.close();
  }
}
```

In the preceding code we have used setParameter() method for setting the positional parameter. Here we have not specified the parameter type and Query object uses reflection API to determine the parameter type and converts the given value into the respective type. Alternatively, we can use setParameter(int position, Object value, and Type type) method as shown below:

```
q.setParameter(0, new Integer(args[0]), Hibernate.INTEGER);
```

Apart from using setParameter() methods Query object allows us to set the parameters using setXXX methods specific to the parameter type. The following method of Query object can be used as an alternative to the setParameter() methods for setting the positional parameters.

TABLE 9.7 Methods of Query object to set positional parameters

Method	*Description*
setString(int position, String val)	Sets the value of the parameter at a given position to the given Java String value.
setBoolean(int position, boolean val)	Sets the value of the parameter at a given position to the given boolean value.
setByte(int position, byte val)	Sets the value of the parameter at a given position to the given byte value.
setBinary(int position, byte[] val)	Sets the value of the parameter at a given position to the given bytes.
setCharacter(int position, char val)	Sets the value of the parameter at a given position to the given single character.
setShort(int position, short val)	Sets the value of the parameter at a given position to the given short value.
setInteger(int position, int val)	Sets the value of the parameter at a given position to the given int value.
setBigInteger(int position, BigInteger val)	Sets the value of the parameter at a given position to the given Java BigInteger value.
setLong(int position, long val)	Sets the value of the parameter at a given position to the given long value.
setFloat(int position, float val)	Sets the value of the parameter at a given position to the given float value.
setDouble(int position, double val)	Sets the value of the parameter at a given position to the given double value.
setDate(int position, Date date)	Sets the value of the parameter at a given position to the given java.util.Date object.
setCalendar(int position, Calendar val)	Sets the value of the parameter at a given position to the given Java Calendar object.
setEntity(int position, Object val)	Sets the value of the parameter at a given position to the given persistent object.
setLocale(int position, Locale locale)	Sets the value of the parameter at a given position to the given Java Locale.
setBigDecimal(int position, BigDecimal number)	Sets the value of the parameter at a given position to the given Java BigDecimal.

In this section we learnt how to use positional parameters with HQL queries. Let us learn how to use named parameters in HQL query.

9.6.4 Named Parameters

The named parameters are an easier method to deal with the input parameters in HQL queries. Instead of using question marks to specify parameters here we use a name identifier prefixed by the ':' symbol. This makes the parameter setting more descriptive compared to positional parameters. For example:

```
SELECT d FROM Dept d WHERE d.deptno = :departmentNo
```

In this query we have specified one named parameter 'departmentNo'. Now, to set the named parameters we can use setParameter() methods or setter methods specific to each parameter type similar to positional parameters. For example:

```
Query q=session.createQuery("SELECT d.name, d.loc FROM Dept d WHERE d.deptno=
:departmentNo");

q.setParameter("departmentNo", new Integer(args[0]), Hibernate.INTEGER);

List<Object[]> results=q.list();
```

In this code we have one set named parameter 'departmentNo' using setParameter() method. Alternatively, we can even use the parameter type specific setter methods that are similar to the setter methods described for the positional parameters in Table 9.7.

9.4 NAMED QUERIES

So far we have learnt how to prepare HQL queries that can be used to retrieve the persistent objects or values. We generally do not want to hardcode the HQL queries in the application, instead we want to centralize HQL queries into a single file and access from wherever necessary. We can probably think to create an interface with constants describing the HQL query strings that can be accessed from different locations. For example:

```
package com.santosh.hibernate.utils;

public interface MyQueries {
  String GET_ALL_EMPLOYEES="from Employee";
  String GEL_ALL_DEPT_BY_NAME="from Dept d where d.name like :deptNamePattern"
  ...
}
```

The above sample code declares constants in MyQueries interface, which can be used in the application code wherever necessary:

```
public class EmployeeDAOImpl implements EmployeeDAO{
  public List<Employee> getAllEmployees(){
    try {
      ... //code to get Session
      Query q=session.createQuery(MyQueries.GET_ALL_EMPLOYEES);
      return q.list();
    } catch(...){...}
  }
}
```

As shown in the preceding code using an interface with constants can centralize the HQL queries avoiding the HQL queries to hardcode throughout application. However, in this case we have to create the Query object for the same HQL query every time we require it. Hibernate provides us an option called 'named queries' that enables us to externalize the HQL query strings and even cache the Query object avoiding to compile the HQL query every time. We use <query> tag in the Hibernate mapping XML document to configure the HQL named query. For example:

```
<query name="GetDeptByName">
  <![CDATA[ SELECT d FROM Dept d WHERE d.name = :DeptName ]]>
</query>
```

The name attribute of query tag specifies a unique name for the query, which is further used in the application to access the query. We do not have any limitation on the number of HQL named queries. We can define the named queries in a Hibernate mapping XML file of any persistent class. The Query objects for named queries from all the Hibernate mapping files are created and cached while preparing a SessionFactory. That means the compiling named HQL queries into SQL, and then constructing a PreparedStatement for the HQL counterpart SQL statement is done only for one time in an application and that is at the time of constructing a SessionFactory. Now, these Query objects can be located from the cache and executed with the required parameters. To access the named Query from cache we use getNamedQuery() method of Session:

```
Query q=session.getNameQuery("GetDeptByName");
q.setParameter("DeptName", "ACCOUNTING");
List<Dept> result=q.list();
```

The getNamedQuery() method locates the Query object in the second level (that is, SessionFactory) cache with the given name (here we have used GetDeptByName) if found returns it otherwise throws HibernateException. Once after obtaining the Query object we usually set the parameters and then execute it to get the results. In this section we have learnt how to declare the HQL queries externally and reuse the Query objects. So far we have learnt how to prepare the HQL queries and execute them, creating the HQL queries at the time of development and making them to execute is a straightforward manner. However, sometimes we need to create queries dynamically at runtime instead of development time in which case we use string concatenation mechanism to meet the requirement. But this approach is tedious, cumbersome, and error prone. Hibernate 3 provides a simple API named criterion API to create queries dynamically at runtime. The following section explains about the criterion API.

9.5 USING CRITERION API TO BUILD QUERIES

The Criterion API provides a type-safe and object-oriented way to retrieve persistent objects. This provides a simplified API to build queries dynamically at runtime, as an alternative to HQL. The Criterion API is more helpful when we have variable number of conditions in a query. The org.hibernate.Criteria is the basic interface of criterion API for building queries. We use createCriteria() method of Session to create a Criteria object:

```
Criteria c=session.createCriteria("Dept");
  (Or)
Criteria c=session.createCriteria(Dept.class);
```

The preceding code creates a new instance of Criteria for the given entity name or class respectively. To execute the Criteria query is similar to executing the Query, here we use list(), scroll() or uniqueResult() methods of Criteria. For example:

```
Criteria c=session.createCriteria(Dept.class);
List<Dept> depts=c.list();

System.out.println("Deptno\tName");
System.out.println("................");

for(Dept dept: depts) {
  System.out.print(dept.getDeptno()+"\t"); System.out.print(dept.getName()+"\n");
}
```

This code queries all the Dept objects from the database and displays the department number and name on the standard output console. Here we have use list() method to execute the Criteria query. Alternatively, we can use the scroll() method. Moreover, if the criterion query is created to return only a single object or value then we can use the uniqueResult() method. To obtain a particular entity object or objects we need to add some restrictions to the query.

9.5.1 Adding Restrictions to Criterion Query

To narrow the results of the criterion query we want to add restrictions to the query such as we may want to build a query that can return all the Dept objects whose loc property value matches with the given location. We use add() method of Criteria object to add restrictions. The add() method takes org.hibernate.criterion.Criterion type instance as an argument. Hibernate criterion API includes number of built-in implementations for org.hibernate.criterion.Criterion interface. We use the static factory methods of org.hibernate.criterion.Restrictions class to create built-in criterion types. For example:

```
Criteria c=session.createCriteria(Dept.class);
c.add(Restrictions.eq("loc", "Hyderabad"));
List<Dept> depts=c.list();
```

The preceding core generates a query that returns all the Dept objects whose loc property value is "Hyderabad". Similarly, we have static factory methods for various other logical and compression operations. We can repeat the use of add() to add multiple restrictions to a query. Table 9.8 shows the static factory methods of Restrictions class.

TABLE 9.8 Static factory methods of Restrictions class

Method	***Description***
isEmpty(String propertyName)	Creates a Criterion object that constrains the given collection valued property to be empty.
isNotEmpty(String propertyName)	Creates a Criterion object that constrains the given collection valued property to be non-empty.

(Contd.)

isNull(String propertyName)	Creates a Criterion object that constrains the specified property value to be null.
isNotNull(String propertyName)	Creates a Criterion object that constrains the specified property value to be not null.
eq(String propertyName, Object value)	Creates a Criterion object that constrains the specified property value to be equal to the given value.
eqProperty(String propertyName, String otherPropertyName)	Creates a Criterion object that constrains the specified properties values to be equal. That means it checks whether the values of the two properties of an object are equal.
ne(String propertyName, Object value)	Creates a Criterion object that constrains the specified property value to be not equal to the given value.
neProperty(String propertyName, String otherPropertyName)	Creates a Criterion object that constrains the specified properties values to be not equal.
gt(String propertyName, Object value)	Creates a Criterion object that constrains the specified property value to be greater than the given value.
ge(String propertyName, Object value)	Creates a Criterion object that constrains the specified property value to be greater than or equal to the given value.
gtProperty(String propertyName, String otherPropertyName)	Creates a Criterion object that constrains the value of the property specified as a first argument to be greater than the value of the property specified as a second argument.
geProperty(String propertyName, String otherPropertyName)	Creates a Criterion object that constrains the value of the property specified as a first argument to be greater than or equal to the value of the property specified as a second argument.
lt(String propertyName, Object value)	Creates a Criterion object that constrains the specified property value to be less than the given value.
le(String propertyName, Object value)	Creates a Criterion object that constrains the specified property value to be less than or equal to the given value.
ltProperty(String propertyName, String otherPropertyName)	Creates a Criterion object that constrains the value of the property specified as a first argument to be less than the value of the property specified as a second argument.
leProperty(String propertyName, String otherPropertyName)	Creates a Criterion object that constrains the value of the property specified as a first argument to be less than or equal to the value of the property specified as a second argument.
like(String propertyName, Object value)	Creates a Criterion object that constrains the specified property value matching with the given pattern (that is, value).
ilike(String propertyName, Object value)	This is same as like but this operates in a case insensitive mode.
in(String propertyName, Collection values)	Creates a Criterion object that constrains the specified property value to be equal to any of the values in the given Collection.
in(String propertyName, Object[] values)	Creates a Criterion object that constrains the specified property value to be equal to any of the values in the given Object[].
between(String propertyName, Object low, Object high)	Creates a Criterion object that constrains the specified property value to be in between of the given low and high values.
not(Criterion expression)	Creates a Criterion object that constrains the negation of the given expression.

(Contd.)

sizeEq(String propertyName, int size)	Creates a Criterion object that constrains the specified collection valued property size to be equal to the given value.
and(Criterion lhs, Criterion rhs)	Creates a Criterion object that constrains the conjunction of the given left hand side (lhs) and right hand side (rhs) Criterion expressions.
or(Criterion lhs, Criterion rhs)	Creates a Criterion object that constrains the disjunction of the given left hand side (lhs) and right hand side (rhs) Criterion expressions.

Example

```
Criteria c=session.createCriteria(Emp.class);
c.add(Restrictions.and(
    Restrictions.like("name", "A%"),
    Restrictions.eq("deptno", new Integer(40))));
List<Emp> employees=c.list();
```

The preceding core generates a query that returns all the Emp objects whose name starting with a character 'A', and working in department 40. Up to now we have seen how to use criterion API to retrieve all or specific entity objects. However, in most cases we require to set projection to retrieve specific properties instead of the complete entity object.

9.5.2 Setting Projection to Criteria

Projection is used to specify the output type, that is, the type of objects or values to be selected. That means a projection in criterion API enables us to select specific columns of entity or its associated entities. We use setProjection() method of Criteria object to set the projection. The setProjection() method takes org.hibernate.criterion.Projection type instance as argument. Hibernate criterion API includes number of built-in implementations for org.hibernate.criterion.Projection interface. We use the static factory methods of org.hibernate.criterion.Projections class to create built-in Projection types. For example:

Code Snippet

```
Criteria c=session.createCriteria(Dept.class);
c.setProjection(Projections.property("deptno"));
List<Integer> dept_nos=c.list();
```

The preceding code snippet generates a query that returns a list of Integer objects, each object describing a deptno. Table 9.9 describes the static factory methods defined in Projections class.

TABLE 9.9 Methods in Projection class for creating a Projection

Method	*Description*
property(String propertyName)	Creates a Projection object that adds the given property into the select clause.
count(String propertyName)	Creates a Projection object that adds the given property value count into the select clause.
countDistinct(String propertyName)	Creates a Projection object that adds the given property's distinct values count into the select clause.

(*Contd.*)

distinct(Projection proj)	Creates a distinct Projection of the given Projection.
min(String propertyName)	Creates a Projection object that adds the given property's minimum value into the select clause.
max(String propertyName)	Creates a Projection object that adds the given property's maximum into the select clause.
sum(String propertyName)	Creates a Projection object that adds the given property value sum into the select clause.
avg(String propertyName)	Creates a Projection object that adds the given property's average value into the select clause.
rowCount()	Creates a Projection object that adds the queries row count into the select clause.

To add multiple projection elements we want to use ProjectionList as shown in the following code snippet.

Code Snippet

```
Criteria c=session.createCriteria(Dept.class);
c.setProjection(
  Projections.projectionList()
  .add(Projections.property("deptno"))
  .add(Projections.property("name")));

List<Object[]> results=c.list();

System.out.println("Deptno\tName");
System.out.println("..............");

for(Object[] result: results) {
  System.out.print(result[0]+"\t");
  System.out.print(result[1]+"\n");
}
```

The preceding code snippet creates a query that returns a list of Object[] objects. Each Object[] is of length two, deptno at index 0 and name at index 1. Note that the order in which the projection elements are added to the ProjectionList is the same as the order in which the Object[] specifies the values. In this section we learnt how to set projection for a Criterion query.

While retrieving the data using queries we may want to get the results in order. To add order by clause for the criterion based query we use the addOrder(Order) method. The org.hibernate.criterion. Order class implements the following two static factory methods to create an Order object:

- asc(String propertyName)
- desc(String propertyName)

Code Snippet

```
Criteria c=session.createCriteria(Emp.class);
c.addOrder(Order.desc("sal"));
List<Emp> result=c.list();
```

This code snippet creates a query that returns all the Emp objects from the database. The Emp objects are arranged based on the value of its property named sal, in descending order. We can add multiple order by items using addOrder() method for multiple times as shown in the following code snippet.

Code Snippet

```
Criteria c=session.createCriteria(Emp.class);
c.addOrder(Order.desc("sal"));
c.addOrder(Order.desc("deptno"));
List<Emp> result=c.list();
```

This code snippet creates a query that returns all the Emp objects, first ordering them based on its sal and then based on the deptno. Apart from these features Criteria allows us to navigate associations using createCriteria() or createAlias() methods of Criteria object. In addition to all these methods, Criteria object supports the query customization methods as described in Table 9.1. In this section, we have learnt how to use Criterion API to build dynamic queries for retrieving the persistent objects. So far we learnt how to query the persistent objects using HQL and Criterion API, which have their own importances. As mentioned earlier, HQL of Hibernate 3 supports Data Manipulation Language statements also. Let us find how to execute the HQL update statements.

9.6 USING HQL TO PERFORM BULK UPDATE AND DELETE OPERATIONS

HQL from Hibernate 3 onwards supports bulk update and delete operations, which applies to entities of a single entity class together with its subclasses, if any. Only one entity abstract schema type may be specified in the UPDATE clause of UPDATE statement and FROM clause of DELETE statement. The syntax for HQL update and delete is similar to the SQL update and delete statements syntax respectively. However, here we use the entity names and persistent properties instead of table names and column names. For example:

```
UPDATE Emp SET sal = sal*1.1 WHERE deptno=10
```

This query updates the salary of all the employees in department 10; the salary is incremented by 10 percent. To execute this HQL statement we use executeUpdate() method of Query object as shown below:

```
Query q=session.createQuery("UPDATE Emp SET sal=sal*1.1 WHERE deptno=10");
int count=q.executeUpdate();
```

This code executes the HQL update statement; the executeUpdate() method returns the update count, that is, the number of persistent objects that are updated by this query. Similarly, we can execute delete statements. As described earlier, HQL supports positional and named parameters. We can use these types of input parameters for setting some dynamic values to the HQL update and delete statements.

Summary

In this chapter we learnt how to use HQL and Hibernate Criterion API to query persistent objects. We have identified that in most enterprise applications, we want to retrieve persistent objects using different conditions such as getting all the employee objects whose name starts with character 'a' or getting all the Employee objects whose deptno is equal to 10. Hibernate Query Language (HQL) is the most powerful query language to meet this requirement. Hibernate even provides a Criterion API that provides a typesafe and object-oriented way to retrieve persistent objects. In the next chapter we will discuss how Hibernate works with Spring framework.

Implementing Hibernate with Spring

10 CHAPTER

Objectives

In Chapter 6 we discussed the DAO design pattern, which is used to separate the persistence from the business logic providing a consistent data access API for the business tier abstracting the low-level data access API like JDBC, Hibernate, data store-specific proprietary API. One of the key benefits of implementing DAOs in a system is it provides an easy way to change the data store and data access API without affecting the business objects, as long as the contract established by the DAO interface remains unchanged.

In Chapter 7 we introduced the Hibernate framework explaining its importance and architecture overview; in Chapter 8 we learnt the persistent class mapping for various object relational mismatch problems such as granularity, subtypes, and associations. In Chapter 9 we learnt about the powerful object-oriented query language HQL from Hibernate and Criterion API for building dynamic queries. From these chapters we can understand that using an ORM implementation such as Hibernate saves thousands of lines of code in data access layer (that is, with DAOs).

However, as discussed under the **DAO support in Spring** section of Chapter 6, to achieve a clean separation between the business and persistence logic we need to take care of a few important things while implementing the DAO. One of the important challenges in implementing DAOs is to transform the low-level data access API exceptions to application-specific exceptions before throwing an exception to the business objects. Anyhow while using Hibernate with the Spring framework we have support for simplifying this job and as well as some additional services. Apart from Hibernate, Spring supports other ORM implementations such as Java Data Objects (JDO), Java Persistence API (JPA), iBATIS and Oracle TopLink. In this book we will only focus on using Hibernate in Spring environment.

In this chapter we will cover:

- How to use Hibernate in Spring environment
- How to work with transactions in Spring environment
- How to integrate Spring with Hibernate

10.1 USING HIBERNATE WITH SPRING

As discussed in the introduction, Spring supports integration with Hibernate providing the integration points for the Spring applications to access Hibernate services. While using Hibernate as a low-level data access API for implementing DAOs we can identify the following shortcomings:

- **Code Duplication:** Code duplication with the code related to exception handling, getting the session, beginning a transaction, etc., is a major problem in the use of Hibernate directly to access database. As we know that writing boilerplate code over and over again is a clear violation of the basic Object Oriented (OO) principle of code reuse. This has some side effects in terms of project cost, timelines, and effort.
- **Resource Leakage:** While implementing the DAOs, all the DAO methods must close the Hibernate session. This is a risky plan because a beginner programmer can very easily skip these code fragments. As a result, resources would run out and bring the system to stop.
- **Error Handling:** When using Hibernate directly we need to handle HibernateException since Hibernate API report all error situations by raising the HibernateException and its subtypes. Most of these exceptions are not possible to be recovered. Moreover, it is difficult to write portable DAO error messaging code.

To solve the preceding problems we need to identify the parts of code that remains fixed and then encapsulate them into some reusable objects. The Spring framework provides a solution for these problems by giving a HibernateTemplate and other support classes. The Spring frameworks support for Hibernate, includes lots of IoC convenience features addressing many of the Hibernate integration issues. Using Spring Framework support for implementing Hibernate-based DAOs provides a better resource management where Spring context takes the responsibility of initializing and maintaining the SessionFactory, and Session instances. It provides a better transaction management in the form of declarative transactions support. Moreover, this makes testing the DAOs much easier.

10.2 HIBERNATETEMPLATE

Spring framework offers HibernateTemplate to simplify implementation of the Hibernate data access code, addressing the above mentioned shortcomings. The HibernateTemplate includes various methods that reflect the Hibernate Session methods, in addition to the convenience methods that avoid code duplication. It takes the responsibility to manage the Hibernate Session making the application free from implementing the code for opening and closing the Hibernate session accordingly. The other important service it provides is to convert the HibernateException's into DataAccessExceptions. Spring framework includes two HibernateTemplate class—one in the org.springframework.orm.hibernate package which supports to work with Hibernate 2.1 and another in org.springframework.orm.hibernate3 package which supports to work with Hibernate 3. Note that Spring Framework from its 2.5 version onwards supports Hibernate 3.1 or higher version only. Support for Hibernate 2.1 and Hibernate 3.0 is removed. The following constructors of HibernateTemplate can be used to instantiate HibernateTemplate:

- **HibernateTemplate():** Constructs a new HibernateTemplate object. This constructor is provided to allow Java Bean style of instantiation. Note that when constructing an object using this constructor we need to use setSessionFactory() method to set the Hibernate SessionFactory before using any of the method of this object.
- **HibernateTemplate(SessionFactory):** Constructs a new HibernateTemplate object initializing it with the given Hibernate SessionFactory used to create Session for executing the requested statements.
- **HibernateTemplate(SessionFactory, boolean):** Constructs a new HibernateTemplate object initializing it with the given Hibernate SessionFactory used to create Session for executing the

requested statements, and boolean value describes the allowCreate flag. Setting the allowCreate flag to 'true' specifies HibernateTemplate to perform its own Session management instead of participating in a custom Hibernate current session context.

After constructing the HibernateTemplate object we can use its methods that reflect the methods of Hibernate Session to persist and query the persistent objects with the help of the following code snippet. For example:

Code Snippet

```
public class DeptDAOImpl implements DeptDAO{

  HibernateTemplate hibernateTemplate;
  public void setHibernateTemplate(HibernateTemplate hibernateTemplate){
    this.hibernateTemplate=hibernateTemplate
  }

  public void createDept(Dept d){
    hibernateTemplate.save(d);
  }
  public Dept findDeptById(int deptno) {
    return (Dept)hibernateTemplate.load(Dept.class, deptno);
  }
  ...
}
```

The preceding code snippet shows the code for DeptDAOImpl where it uses HibernateTemplate to perform simple create and select operations. The createDept() method is using save() method to persist the Dept object. To observe we do not require to handle HibernateException and even deal with transactions. Similarly, we have implemented findDeptById() method using load() method. In addition to the methods reflecting the Hibernate Session methods, HibernateTemplate provides some convenience methods for executing the HQL queries with or without parameters. For example:

Code Snippet

```
public class DeptDAOImpl implements DeptDAO{

  HibernateTemplate hibernateTemplate;
  public void setHibernateTemplate(HibernateTemplate hibernateTemplate){
    this.hibernateTemplate=hibernateTemplate;
  }

  public List findDeptByName(String name) {
    return hibernateTemplate.find("find Dept d where d.name like '"+name+ "' ");
  }
  public List findDeptByLocation(String location) {
    return hibernateTemplate.find("find Dept d where d.loc=?", location);
```

```
    }
    public List findDeptByNameAndLocation(String name, String location) {
      return hibernateTemplate.find("find Dept d where d.loc=? and d.name like ?",
                           new Object[]{location, name});
    }
    ...
}
```

The preceding code snippet shows the DeptDAOImpl. The findDeptByName() method uses find(String) method of HibernateTemplate to execute static HQL query and retrieve the results. The findDeptByLocation() method uses find(String, Object) to execute an HQL query binding one value to a '?' parameter in the query string. The findDeptByNameAndLocation() method uses find(String, Object[]) method of HibernateTemplate to execute an HQL query binding the multiple parameter values. In this case we have bonded two values. Apart from providing the various convenience methods the HibernateTemplate provides a support for the callback-based approach. The HibernateTemplate provides a method execute() which takes an argument of HibernateCallback object. Its method signature is shown below.

```
public Object execute(HibernateCallback action) throws DataAccessException
```

This method executes the Hibernate action specified by the given HibernateCallback instance in a Session; this transforms any HibernateException thrown by the callback into an appropriate Spring DAO exception. The HibernateCallback interface declares only one method with the following signature:

```
public Object doInHibernate(Session session)
  throws HibernateException, SQLException
```

The doInHibernate() method allows us to implement the Hibernate data access operations using the given Session. Here we do not require to worry about opening or closing the Session, handling transactions, or handling HibernateException. This callback-based approach of using the HibernateTemplate is most useful for executing the methods of Hibernate Session that are not exposed on HibernateTemplate. For example, we may want to prepare and execute a dynamic query using criterion API. It is an event used to execute multiple Hibernate data access operations using a single Session.

Now as we have discussed about how to use HibernateTemplate for executing Hibernate data access operations, let us find how to configure the HibernateTemplate in Spring Beans XML configuration file. List 10.1 shows the code for Spring Bean XML configuration file configuring the HibernateTemplate, DeptDAOImpl and their associated beans.

List 10.1: mybeans-context.xml

```
<beans xmlns="http://www.springframework.org/schema/beans"
xmlns:xsi="http://www.w3.org/2001/XMLSchema-instance"
xsi:schemaLocation="http://www.springframework.org/schema/beans
http://www.springframework.org/schema/beans/spring-beans-2.0.xsd">
```

```
  <bean id="deptDAO" class="com.santosh.hibernate.DeptDAOImpl">
  <property name="hibernateTemplate" ref="hibernateTemplate"/>
  </bean>

  <bean id="hibernateTemplate"
        class="org.springframework.orm.hibernate3.HibernateTemplate">
      <constructor-arg ref="sessionFactory"/>
  </bean>

  <bean id="sessionFactory" factory-bean="configuration"
        factory-method="buildSessionFactory"/>

  <bean id="configuration" class="org.hibernate.cfg.Configuration"
        init-method="configure"/>
</beans>
```

In List 10.1 we defined a bean with id '*configuration*' that represents org.hibernate.cfg. Configuration object. We have even configured an init-method attribute to '*configure*' which specifies the Spring container to invoke configure() method on the Hibernate Configuration object immediately after it is initialized. This bean definition prepares the Hibernate Configuration object that loads the hibernate configurations from hibernate.cfg.xml. Thus to initialize the Spring container using the preceding Spring beans XML configuration file we need a hibernate.cfg.xml file in the classpath. The bean defined with id '*sessionFactory*' creates a org.hibernate.SessionFactory object using the non-static factory method named *buildSessionFactory* of configuration object. The bean defined with id '*hibernateTemplate*' creates an instance of org.springframework.orm.hibernate3.HibernateTemplate using its one argument constructor injecting the Hibernate SessionFactory object. Finally, a bean with id '*deptDAO'* is injected with the HibernateTemplate. In this case we have configured the Hibernate SessionFactory defining the Configuration and external hibernate.cfg.xml file instead. Spring framework includes a utility class for configuring the SessionFactory through Spring configuration file.

10.3 MANAGING HIBERNATE RESOURCE

As discussed in the preceding section Spring Framework includes a utility class for configuring the SessionFactory through Spring configuration file. Since we know that the SessionFactory initialization process includes various operations that consume huge resources and extra time, it is generally recommended to use a single SessionFactory per JVM instance (or our application). Moreover, SessionFactory is immutable towards the application, meaning SessionFactory is threadsafe. Thus there is no problem is using a single SessionFactory for an application with multiple threads also. The utility class provided by Spring Framework for configuring the SessionFactory is org.springframe work.orm.hibernate3.LocalSessionFactoryBean class. The LocalSessionFactoryBean object is constructed using the no-argument constructor and it provides various methods to set the hibernate properties. The following code snippet shows the code for basic configuration of LocalSessionFactory.

Code Snippet

```
<bean id="sessionFactory"
    class=" org.springframework.orm.hibernate3.LocalSessionFactoryBean">
  <property name="dataSource" ref="dataSource"/>
</bean>

<bean id="dataSource" class="org.apache.commons.dbcp.BasicDataSource">
  <property name="driverClassName" value="oracle.jdbc.driver.OracleDriver"/>
  <property name="url" value="jdbc:oracle:thin:@localhost:1521:sandb"/>
  <property name="username" value="scott"/>
  <property name="password" value="tiger"/>
</bean>
```

This configuration defines a LocalSessionFactoryBean injecting the DataSource that should be used to connect to database. We can also set the various hibernate properties as properties to the LocalSessionFactoryBean, which eliminates the need to write a separate hibernate.properties file. For example:

```
<bean id="sessionFactory"
      class=" org.springframework.orm.hibernate3.LocalSessionFactoryBean">
    <property name="dataSource" ref="dataSource"/>
    <property name="hibernateProperties">
      <props>
        <prop key="hibernate. show_sql">true</prop>
      </props>
    </property>
</bean>
```

This configuration defines a SessionFactory configuring a DataSource and a hibernate property named show_sql to 'true'. Similarly, we can configure all the required hibernate properties. The LocalSessionFactoryBean even allows us to configure the Hibernate mapping resources.

```
<bean id="sessionFactory"
      class=" org.springframework.orm.hibernate3.LocalSessionFactoryBean">
    <property name="dataSource" ref="dataSource"/>
    <property name="mappingResources">
      <list>
        <value>mymappings/Employee.hbm.xml</value>
        <value>mymappings/Dept.hbm.xml</value>
      </list>
    </property>
</bean>
```

This bean definition configures the LocalSessionFactory injecting a DataSource and a String[] describing the hibernate mapping files location. Here we have used mappingResources property to specify the mapping files location. Alternatively, we can use mappingJarLocations property to configure one or more jar files that contain the Hibernate mapping XML files.

```
<bean id="sessionFactory"
      class=" org.springframework.orm.hibernate3.LocalSessionFactoryBean">
    <property name="dataSource" ref="dataSource"/>
    <property name="mappingJarLocations">
      <list>
        <value>mymappings/module1Mappings.jar</value>
        <value>mymappings/module2Mappings .jar</value>
      </list>
    </property>
</bean>
```

In this configuration we have configured module1Mappings.jar and module2Mappings.jar files to the mappingJarLocations property, which specifies the LocalSessionFactoryBean to find all the Hibernate mapping XML files in the configured jar files. Instead of packaging the mapping files into jar files and configuring them, we can configure a folder containing the mapping files as shown below:

```
<bean id="sessionFactory"
      class=" org.springframework.orm.hibernate3.LocalSessionFactoryBean">
    <property name="dataSource" ref="dataSource"/>
    <property name="mappingDirectoryLocations">
      <list>
        <value>example/mymappings</value>
      </list>
    </property>
</bean>
```

We have configured example/mymappings folder to the mappingDirectoryLocations describing the LocalSessionFactory that the Hibernate mapping files can be located in example/mymappings folder. We can also configure multiple folders. Similarly, we can configure the Hibernate XML configuration file to the property configLocation. If we want to specify multiple XML configuration files then we use configLocations property. Once after configuring the LocalSessionFactoryBean we can inject it into the HibernateTemplate as shown below:

```
<bean id="sessionFactory"
      class=" org.springframework.orm.hibernate3.LocalSessionFactoryBean">
    <property name="dataSource" ref="dataSource"/>
    <property name="mappingResources">
      <list>
        <value>mymappings/Employee.hbm.xml</value>
        <value>mymappings/Dept.hbm.xml</value>
      </list>
    </property>
</bean>
<bean id="hibernateTemplate"
    class="org.springframework.orm.hibernate3.HibernateTemplate">
    <constructor-arg ref="sessionFactory"/>
</bean>
```

In this section we have learnt how to use LocalSessionFactoryBean to configure the SessionFactory through Spring configuration file. The LocalSessionFactoryBean object can be used to construct HibernateTemplate, which can be injected into our application DAOs so that it can be used for performing the Hibernate data access operations.

10.4 USING HIBERNATEDAOSUPPORT

Spring framework support for accessing Hibernate data access operations includes a convenience HibernateDaoSupport class packaged into org.springframework.orm.hibernate3.support package. We need our DAO classes to subclass from HibernateDaoSupport, to use its conveniences. The HibernateDaoSupport enables us to implement DAOs using the Hibernate data access code directly without wrapping the Hibernate access code in a callback, while still using the Spring Frameworks exception translators for translating the HibernateException's into an appropriate Spring's generic DataAccessException. For example:

Code Snippet

```
public class DeptDAOImpl extends HibernateDaoSupport implements DeptDAO {

   public List findDeptByLocation(String location) throws MyException {
         Session session=getSession();
         try {
               Criteria criteria=session.createCriteria(Dept.class);
               criteria.add(Restrictions.eq("loc", location));
               List result=criteria.list();
               if (result.isEmpty())
                   throw new MyException();
               return result;
         } catch (HibernateException he) {
                 throw convertHibernateAccessException(he);
         }
   }
}
```

To use this code snippet we need to inject Hibernate SessionFactory or HibernateTemplate to these objects using setSessonFactory() or setHibernateTemplate() methods respectively. The HibernateDao Support class provides convenience method getSession() for getting the Hibernate Session, which allows us to execute the Hibernate Session methods directly without using HibernateTemplate callback approach. In the preceding code snippet we have obtained the Hibernate Session and used it to prepare and execute the criteria. The same can be implemented using the HibernateTemplate callback facility as shown below:

Code Snippet

```
public class DeptDAOImpl implements DeptDAO {

  public List findDeptByLocation(String location) {

    return (List) hibernateTemplate.execute(
      new HibernateCallback(){
        public Object doInHibernate(Session session)
                              throws HibernateException, SQLException {

              Criteria criteria=session.createCriteria(Dept.class);
              criteria.add(Restrictions.eq("loc", location));
              List result=criteria.list();
              if (result.isEmpty())
                      throw new MyRuntimeException();
              return result;
        }
      });
    }
}
```

The main advantage of using the HibernateDaoSupport to execute the Hibernate session methods directly instead of using HibernateTemplate callback approach is, it allows us to throw any checked exception from the data access code, which is not allowed while working with HibernateTemplate callback. HibernateDaoSupport, apart from allowing us to get the Hibernate Session and execute the Hibernate data access code directly can even allow us to get the HibernateTemplate using the convenience method getHibernateTemplate() to execute the Hibernate data access operations using HibernateTemplate. List 10.2 shows the Spring beans XML configuration file configuring the DeptDAOImpl implemented as a subtype of HibernateDaoSupport.

List 10.2 Spring beans XML configuration file

```
<bean id="sessionFactory"
      class=" org.springframework.orm.hibernate3.LocalSessionFactoryBean">
    <property name="dataSource" ref="dataSource"/>
    <property name="mappingResources">
      <list>
        <value>mymappings/Employee.hbm.xml</value>
        <value>mymappings/Dept.hbm.xml</value>
      </list>
    </property>
</bean>
<bean id="deptDAO" class="com.santosh.hibernate.DeptDAOImpl">
  <property name="sessionFactory" ref="sessionFactory"/>
</bean>
```

List 10.2 defines two bean configurations, one configuring the SessionFactory and the second configuring the DeptDAOImpl wiring the SessionFactory. In this section we learnt how to use HibernateDaoSupport for access Hibernate data access operations in out application DAO.

10.5 UNDERSTANDING TRANSACTIONS

Transaction is a set of statements executed on a resource or resources as a unit, applied with ACID properties. Transactions are required to provide data integrity, correct application semantics, and a consistent view of data during concurrent access. The transaction ACID (Atomicity Consistency Isolation Durability) properties are:

1. Atomicity
Is the ability to guarantee that either all tasks of a transaction are performed or none of them are performed. This property provides an ability to save (commit) or cancel (rollback) the transaction at any point, controlling all the statements of a transaction.

2. Consistency
This property guarantees that the data is in a legal state when the transaction begins and ends. That is if the data used in the transaction is consistent before starting the transaction then it will be consistent even after the end of the transaction. Where the data that satisfies the integrity constraints of that type then it is known as consistent data or data in legal state.

For example, if an integrity constraint states that all accounts must have a positive balance (that is, minimum as 0), then any transaction violating this rule will be aborted (that is, rollback).

3. Isolation
It is the ability of the transaction to isolate or hide the data used by it from other transactions until the transaction ends. This is done by preparing locks on data.

The problems identified while the concurrent operations on data are:

(i) Dirty Read
Dirty read occurs when a transaction reads data from a row that has been modified by another transaction, but has not yet committed.

(ii) Non-repeatable Read
Non-repeatable reads may occur when the read lock is not acquired while performing the SELECT operation. For example, if we have selected data under transaction T1 and meanwhile, if the same is updated by some other transaction, say T2 then transaction T1 reads two versions of data and this is considered as a non-repeatable read. This is avoided by preparing a read lock by transaction T1 on the data which it has selected.

(iii) Phantom Read
A phantom read occurs when, in the course of a transaction, two identical queries are executed and the collection of rows returned by the second query is different from the first. This can occur when range locks are not acquired while performing a SELECT. That is in a transaction T1 we have executed query Q1 and got some results (say 10 rows) and within the same transaction if we execute the query Q1 and if it results with a different number of rows (say 11 rows) then this problem is referred as phantom read problem. This happens if some other transaction inserts a new record that satisfies query Q1.

Most of resources provide the following isolation levels that control the degree of locking.

(i) READ UNCOMMITED
In this level, dirty reads, non-repeatable reads, and phantom reads may occur.

(ii) READ COMMITED
In this level, dirty reads are not allowed but non-repeatable reads and phantom reads may occur.

(iii) REPEATABLE READ
In this level, dirty reads and non-repeatable reads are not allowed but phantom reads may occur.

(iv) SERIALIZABLE
This isolation level specifies that all transactions occur in a completely isolated fashion. At this isolation level, dirty reads, non-repeatable reads and phantom reads cannot occur.

4. Durability
This property refers to the guarantees that once the user has been notified of the success, that is commit, the transaction will persist all the statements in the transaction or leave the complete transaction unsaved. That is, if a transaction succeeds, the system guarantees that its updates will persist, even if the computer crashes immediately after the commit. Specialized logging allows the system's restart procedure to complete unfinished operations, making the transaction durable.

Now as we have understood what a transaction is and its properties, let us learn the support provided by Spring for transaction management.

10.6 SPRING SUPPORT FOR TRANSACTION MANAGEMENT

Spring framework includes a complete support for transaction management. Spring Framework provides a consistent abstraction for transaction management that provides a generic programming model across different transaction APIs such as JDBC, JTA, Hibernate, JPA, and JDO. It even provides a support for programmatic and declarative transaction management analogous to EJB containers transaction management service, but the Spring Frameworks transaction management abstraction is more flexible than that of the EJB service.

As we know that most enterprise applications deal with two types of transaction managements—local and distributed (or global).

Local Transaction: A transaction whose statements are executed on to a single transactional resource through one resource object (that is, through one session) is known as local transaction. The one best example of local transaction is a transaction managed using JDBC connection.

Distributed Transaction (global transaction): A transaction whose statements are executed on one or more transactional resource through multiple resource objects is known as a distributed or global transaction. We generally use JTA for programming distributed transactions that span over multiple transactional resources. The Local transactions are resource-specific. Thus the resource manager can manage local transactions, whereas to manage distributed transactions we need a transaction Manager that further uses the transactional resource objects participating in the transaction. We have different transaction APIs to program transactions based on the data access API that we use in our application, such as JDBC, Hibernate, and JDO. Spring Framework provides a consistent programming model for transaction management in any environment, which enables us to write the code that can work in different environments with different transaction management strategies once. It even supports a declarative transaction model that makes the application code completely free from transaction management. Now, let us discuss how to use the transaction management convenience provided by the Spring Framework.

10.7 DEFINING TRANSACTION STRATEGY

The transaction strategy in a Spring transaction is defined using the org.springframework.tranascation. PlatformTransactionManager type object, the PlatformTransactionManager object implements three methods:

Code Snippet

```
public interface PlatformTransactionManager {

  TransactionStatus getTransaction(TransactionDefinition definition)
              throws TransactionException;

  void commit(TransactionStatus status) throws TransactionException;

  void rollback(TransactionStatus status) throws TransactionException;
}
```

The getTransaction() method returns a TransactionStatus object, based on the given Transaction Definition. A TransactionStatus is associated with a thread of execution, thus a TransactionStatus object might represent a new or existing transaction. Spring Framework provides the following built-in implementations for PlatformTransactionManager.

TABLE 10.1 Spring framework built-in implementations for PlatformTransactionManager

Class	*Description*
org.springframework.jca.cci.connection. CciLocalTransactionManager	The PlatformTransactionManager implementation that manages local transaction for single CCI Connection Factory. The CCI connections are used to perform operations on an EIS.
org.springframework.jdbc.datasource.Data SourceTransactionManager	The PlatformTransactionManager implementation that manages local transaction for single JDBC Connection, obtained using the specified DataSource. This is used when we use JdbcTemplate for persistence operations.
org.springframework.orm.hibernate3.Hibernate TransactionManager	The PlatformTransactionManager implementation that manages local transaction for single Hibernate Session, obtained using the specified SessionFactory. This is used when we use Hibernate for persistence operations.
org.springframework.orm.jdo.JdoTransaction Manager	The PlatformTransactionManager implementation that manages local transaction for single JDO PersistenceManager, obtained using the specified PersistenceManagerFactory. This is used when we use JDO for persistence operations.

(Contd.)

org.springframework.orm.jpa.JpaTransaction Manager	The PlatformTransactionManager implementation that manages local transaction for single JPA EntityManager, obtained using the specified EntityManagerFactory. This is used when we use JDO for persistence operations.
org.springframework.jms.connection.Jms TransactionManager	The PlatformTransactionManager implementation that manages local transaction for single JMS Session, obtained using the specified ConnectionFactory.
org.springframework.transaction.jta.Jta TransactionManager	The PlatformTransactionManager implementation that manages distributed (global) transaction delegating to the backend JTA provider, which can be a J2EE servers transaction manager or a local JTA provider embedded within the application.

As mentioned, each of these implementations of PlatformTransactionManager provides a gateway for accessing the platform-specific transaction implementations, allowing us to write transactional code in Spring without worrying much about platform-specific transaction implementations. To use any of the above tabled transaction managers we need to declare them in the application context injecting the respective factory object such as DataSource (which can be considered as JDBC Connection factory) for DataSourceTransactionManager, SessionFactory for HibernateTransaction Factory. For example:

```
<bean id="transactionManager"
class=" org.springframework.jdbc.datasource.DataSourceTransactionManager">
  <property name="dataSource" ref="dataSource"/>
</bean>
```

This defines a DataSourceTransactionManager injecting the java.sql.DataSource object using the dataSource property. Similarly, we can define the other transaction manager implementations inject the respective resource factory object.

In this section we learnt how to configure the transaction strategy that our application wants to work with. We identified that the PlatformTransactionManager implementation object returns the Transaction Status object which enables us to work with the platform-specific transaction management (such as Hibernate transactions, JDBC transactions, JTS transactions, etc.) without worrying about the platform-specific transaction API. However, to obtain the TransactionStatus object we need to invoke the getTransaction() method that requires a TransactionDefinition object as input. Let us learn about the TransactionDefinition and its built-in implementations.

10.8 UNDERSTANDING TRANSACTIONDEFINITION

The org.springframework.transaction. TransactionDefinition interface provides an abstraction for representing the transaction properties that are required to customize the transaction. The Transaction Definition object describes the following five properties:

1. Isolation Level
2. Transaction Name
3. Transaction Timeout
4. Read only
5. Propagation Behavior

We have some built-in implementations for TransactionDefinition such as DefaultTransaction Definition and DefaultTransactionAttribute. We generally use DefaultTransactionDefinition while working with programmatic transaction management and DefaultTransactionAttribute while working with Declarative transaction management, which allows us to specify the exceptions that will cause the transaction to rollback, in addition to the above listed properties. Let us now understand each of these properties in detail.

10.8.1 Isolation Level

The Isolation level property specifies the isolation level for this transaction. The isolation level in a Spring-based transaction management can be specified by using the TransactionDefinition object. The default isolation level is always specified by the underlying data source; sometimes we want to specify the isolation level explicitly. The TransactionDefinition implementation provides a setter method to set the transaction isolation. In general most of the implementations have a method named *setIsolationLevel(int isolationLevel)* in order to set the transaction isolation for a transaction, which allows one of the following constants:

TABLE 10.2 Constants describing the isolation levels

Constant	*Description*
TransactionDefinition.ISOLATION_DEFAULT	Specifies to use the default isolation level of the underlying data store.
TransactionDefinition.ISOLATION_READ_UNCOMMITTED	In this level dirty reads, non-repeatable reads, and phantom reads may occur.
TransactionDefinition.ISOLATION_READ_COMMITTED	In this level, dirty reads are not allowed but non-repeatable and phantom reads may occur.
TransactionDefinition.ISOLATION_REPEATABLE_READ	In this level, dirty reads and non-repeatable reads are not allowed but phantom reads may occur.
TransactionDefinition.ISOLATION_SERIALIZABLE	This isolation level specifies that all transactions occur in a completely isolated fashion. At this isolation level, dirty reads, non-repeatable reads, and phantom reads cannot occur.

Alternatively, some implementations of TransactionDefinition such as DefaultTransaction Definition provides a utility method *setIsolationLevelName(String constantName)* to set the isolation level by the name of the corresponding constant in TransactionDefinition. For example, "ISOLATION_DEFAULT".

> **Note:** The specified isolation level will be applicable only when a new transaction is started. T, thus this property is useful with PROPAGATION_REQUIRED, PROPAGATION_REQUIRES_NEW and PROPAGATION_NESTED. Moreover, if the specified isolation level is not supported by the underlying data source, it throws an exception.

10.8.2 Transaction Name

This property specifies the name of the transaction. Only for programmatic transactions are we allowed to set the custom transaction name. If not specified it defaults to none. In case of declarative transactions this is set to fully-qualified class name followed by "." (period), followed by the method name for which this transaction is started. This will be used as transaction name to be shown in a transaction monitor, which is applicable with some transaction monitors such as WebLogic. The TransactionDefinition implementation provides a setter method to set the name, in general most of the implementations have a method named *setName(String)* in order to set the transaction name for this transaction.

10.8.3 Transaction Timeout

This property specifies the timeout as number of seconds to apply for this transaction. The specified timeout will be applicable only when a new transaction is started, thus this property is useful with PROPAGATION_REQUIRED, PROPAGATION_REQUIRES_NEW and PROPAGATION_NESTED. Moreover, the transaction manager that does not support setting the timeouts throws an exception.

10.8.4 Read Only

This property specifies the read-only flag. The read-only flag applies to a transaction context in which this method is operating or if the method is operating in a non-transactional environment, the flag will only apply to managed-resources within the application, such as a Hibernate Session. Note that this flag is a hint for the actual transaction subsystem; it will not necessarily cause failure of write-access attempts.

10.8.5 Propagation Behavior

The propagation behavior property specifies the propagation for this transaction. The propagation behavior in a Spring-based transaction management can be specified by using the Transaction Definition object. The TransactionDefinition implementation provides a setter method to set the transaction propagation behavior, in general most of the implementations have a method named *setPropagationBehavior(int propagationBehavior)* in order to set the propagation behavior for a transaction, which allows one of the following constants:

1. TransactionDefinition.PROPAGATION_NOT_SUPPORTED
2. TransactionDefinition.PROPAGATION_SUPPORTS
3. TransactionDefinition.PROPAGATION_REQUIRED
4. TransactionDefinition.PROPAGATION_REQUIRES_NEW
5. TransactionDefinition.PROPAGATION_MANDATORY
6. TransactionDefinition.PROPAGATION_NEVER
7. TransactionDefinition.PROPAGATION_NESTED

Alternatively, some implementations of TransactionDefinition such as DefaultTransaction Definition provides a utility method *setPropagationBehaviourName(String constantName)* to set the propagation behaviour by the name of the corresponding constant in TransactionDefinition, for example "PROPAGATION_REQUIRED".

Now, let us understand the behavior of the above listed propagation constants.

10.8.5.1 TransactionDefinition.PROPAGATION_NOT_SUPPORTED

This propagation constant specifies that the method cannot be involved in a transaction at all. If the current thread is found associated with a transaction then it is suspended. That means any transactional resources obtained in a method using this behavior will not be associated with a transaction. While using JtaTransactionManager the transaction suspension is not allowed out-of-box. We know that JTA exposes javax.transaction.UserTransaction object for managing the transaction out-of-the-box, which does not allows transaction suspending. The javax.transaction.TransactionManager object allows suspending transaction but making the javax.transaction.TransactionManager object is up to the interest of the server or transaction manager provider.

This type of propagation behavior is used for the methods encapsulation.The operations that do not need the ACID properties, and we do not want to isolate this method operations from other concurrent operations.

10.8.5.2 TransactionDefinition.PROPAGATION_SUPPORTS

This propagation constant specifies that the method does not require a separate transaction but wants to participate in the transaction if any exist, that is, if the current thread is found associated with a transaction. That means a method using this propagation constant continues to run in the transaction if a transaction is in progress, otherwise the method will run with no transaction.

10.8.5.3 TransactionDefinition.PROPAGATION_REQUIRED

This propagation constant specifies that the method should always run in a transaction. If the current thread is found associated with a transaction, the method joins the existing transaction. Otherwise, a new transaction is started to manage the transactional operations of this method. That means this propagation behavior is handy to use, which enables us to participate in the existing transaction or start a new transaction depending on the situation.

10.8.5.4 TransactionDefinition.PROPAGATION_REQUIRES_NEW

This propagation constant specifies that the method should always run in a new transaction. To do this the transaction manager object finds whether the current thread is associated with a transaction, if found, the transaction is suspended for the duration of this method, that is, after the execution of this method it is resumed. Then a new transaction is started. After the execution of the method, the new transaction started for this method execution is ended (that is, resolved to commit or rollback), and then the suspended outer transaction is resumed before returning to the caller method. This propagation behavior is useful when we want our method to run with ACID properties of transaction as a single unit of work, but without including the transactional operations performed by the caller.

10.8.5.5 TransactionDefinition.PROPAGATION_MANDATORY

This propagation constant specifies that the method should always run in a transaction. In this case if the current thread is found associated with a transaction, the method joins in that transaction. Otherwise an IllegalTransactionStateException is thrown to the caller.

10.8.5.6 TransactionDefinition.PROPAGATION_NEVER

This propagation constant specifies that the method will never involve itself in a transaction. In this case if the current thread is found associated with a transaction, an IllegalTransactionStateException is thrown to the caller. Otherwise, the method executes with no transaction.

10.8.5.7 TransactionDefinition.PROPAGATION_NESTED

This propagation constant specifies that the method will always run in a transaction. If the current thread is associated with a transaction then a nested transaction is started. The nested transaction can be committed or rolled back independent of the enclosing transaction. If there is no transaction associated with the current thread, a new transaction is started. Note that the underlying transaction manager should support creating nested transactions, otherwise a NestedTransactionNotSupported Exception is thrown.

Now as we have learnt how to configure the transaction manager and the various properties of TransactionDefinition let us find how to coordinate the resource object with the transactions.

10.9 COORDINATING RESOURCE OBJECT WITH TRANSACTION

In the previous section we learnt about the transaction manager implementations and how to configure them. Now we need to understand how to coordinate the resource object used in the application code (directly or indirectly) with the transactions. Spring provides two approaches to do this:

One is to use the Spring high-level persistence integration APIs such as JdbcTemplate, Hibernate Template, JpaTemplate, JdoTemplate.

The other approach is to use the Spring provided utils classes for obtaining the resource object such as DataSourceUtils for obtaining JCBC Connection, SessionFactoryUtils for obtaining Hibernate Session. For example:

```
Connection con=DataSourceUtils.getConnection(dataSource);
```

Here the *dataSource* is a reference refereeing to the java.sql.DataSource object that can be used to obtain the JDBC Connection. The getConnection() method of DataSourceUtils class finds whether the current thread is associated with any transaction, and a Connection obtained from the specified DataSource is already coordinated with the transaction, if found then it returns that Connection. Otherwise, it creates a new connection using the specified DataSource, optionally coordinating to any existing transaction, making it available for subsequent reuse in that same transaction. This even takes the responsibility to wrap any SQLException raised in this process, into a Spring Framework CannotGetJdbcConnectionException (subtype of DataAccessException). Note that this will also work fine without Spring transaction management as coordinating the resource object with transaction is optional, so we can use it with or without using Spring transaction management. Similarly, we can use SessionFactoryUtil to obtain Hibernate Session, PersistenceManagerFactoryUtil to obtain JDO PersistenceManager, etc.

Now, as we have understood how to coordinate the resource objects to transactions let us start understanding how to use transaction manager to manage our transactions. Spring Framework provides two approaches to work with transactions—programmatic and declarative. Let us start with Programmatic Transaction Management.

10.10 PROGRAMMATIC TRANSACTION MANAGEMENT

In this approach of transaction management the application code gets the complete control on the transaction. This is good to use when we have a small number of transactional operations. Spring Framework provides two ways to use programmatic transaction management:

1. Using a PlatformTransactionManager implementation object directly
2. Using TransactionTemplate

Let us learn both the approaches, first using the PlatformTransactionManager.

10.10.1 Using a PlatformTransactionManager Object Directly

In this case we use the PlatformTransactionManager implementation object directly to manage our transactions programmatically. The various built-in implementations of PlatformTransactionManager are shown under Table 10.1, according to the persistence API used in the application. We need to choose the appropriate implementation. This is a pretty straightforward approach; we simply need to get the required PlatformTransactionManager implementation object, thereafter using the Transaction Definition and TransactionStatus objects we can start and end (commit or rollback) the transaction. The following code snippet shows the sample code.

Code Snippet

```
public class MyServicesImpl implements MyServices {

  PlatformTransactionManager transactionManager;

  public void setTransactionManager(PlatformTransactionManager txManager){
    this.transactionManager=txManager;
  }

  public void myService1() {

    DefaultTransactionDefinition transactionDefinition =
                                   new DefaultTransactionDefinition();

    transactionDefinition.setName("MyTX");
    transactionDefinition.setPropagationBehavior(
                            TransactionDefinition.PROPAGATION_SUPPORTS);

    TransactionStatus status =
                    transactionManager.getTransaction(transactionDefinition);
    try {
        //execute some business logic
    }catch (Exception ex) {
        transactionManager.rollback(status);
```

```
            //do some exception handling or re-throw it to the caller
        }
        transactionManager.commit(status);
    }
}
```

In this code we created a DefaultTransactionDefinition object, initializing it with some properties such as name (setting the transaction name explicitly is possible only with programmatic transactions) and propagationBehavior. Then, we obtained a TransactionStatus from the transactionManager using the TransactionDefinition object. At the end if we identify that the application code is executed successfully, we have committed the transaction using the commit() method of transaction manager object. Otherwise, we have rollbacked the transaction using rollback() method. Instead of directly using the platform-specific transaction manager object directly we can try a simpler way to use programmatic transaction management, using TransactionTemplate—explained in the next section.

10.10.2 Using TransactionTemplate

The org.springframework.transaction.support.TransactionTemplate defines another way of working with the programmatic transactions. It uses a callback approach that makes the application code free from the boilerplate code for obtaining and releasing transactional resources. In this case we have to implement the TransactionCallback encapsulating the application code that must execute in a transactional context. Thereafter, invoke the execute() method of TransactionTemplate passing the TransactionCallback implementation object as shown below.

Code Snippet

```
public class MyServicesImpl implements MyServices {

    TransactionTemplate transactionTemplate;

    public void setTransactionTemplate(TransactionTemplate transactionTemplate){
        this.transactionTemplate = transactionTemplate;
    }

    public void myService1() {

        transactionTemplate.execute( new TransactionCallback() {
            publilc Object doInTransaction(TransactionStatus status)
                                            throws TrnsactionExceptio{
                try {
                    //execute some business logic
                }catch (MyException ex) {
                    status.setRollbackOnly();
                    //do some exception handling or re-throw it to the caller
                }
            }
        });
    }
}
```

In this code snippet we implemented TransactionCallback as an anonymous class encapsulating the business logic that have to be executed in a transactional context, passing its instances as an argument to the execute method of TransactionTemplate. The following code snippet shows the declaration of the MyServicesImpl and TransactionTemplate:

```
<bean id="myServices" class="com.santosh.spring.MyServicesImpl">
  <property name="transactionTemplate" ref=" transactionTemplate"/>
</bean>
<bean id=" transactionTemplate"
class="org.springframework.transaction.support.TransactionTemplate">
  <property name="propagationBehaviorName"
           value="PROPAGATION_SUPPORTS"/>
</bean>
```

This definition defines two Spring beans, the myServices bean creates an instance of com.santosh. spring.MyServicesImpl setting the transactionTemplate property. The transactionTemplate bean creates an instance of org.springframework.transaction.support.TransactionTemplate setting the propagationBehaviourName property to PROPAGATION_SUPPORTS. Similarly, we can set the other properties of the TransactionTemplate.

In this section we learnt how to use the Spring provided generic transaction API for programmatic transaction management. It can be identified that in this approach we need to implement the application code with some Spring provided transaction API which makes the code bounded to Spring API. Spring Framework provides a declarative approach to work with transactions that makes the application code completely independent of the Spring transaction management API.

10.11 DECLARATIVE TRANSACTION MANAGEMENT

One of the important enterprise-level services provided by Spring Framework is the declarative transaction management. The declarative transaction management makes our application code free from the transaction API providing the convenience of specifying the transaction behavior to the individual methods externally, which means that we can change the transaction behavior with almost no changes in the application code. This even provides convenience to decide the transaction behavior of the methods at the time of deploying instead of developing the application code. The declarative transaction management is implemented by Spring Framework using Spring AOP. The declarative transaction management is analogous to the Container Managed Transaction (CMT) service of Enterprise Java Bean (EJB); however, the Spring Framework's declarative transaction management has the following benefits compared to the EJB CMT:

- Spring Framework's declarative transaction management can be configured to work with different platform-specific transaction environments such as JDBC, Hibernate, JPA, JDO, and JTA. Whereas, EJB CMT is tightly bounded to only work with JTA.
- The Spring Framework's declarative transaction management allows us to customize the transaction behavior, using AOP without mixing the customization logic with the core application code. For example, we want to execute some custom logic while rolling back the transaction.

- The Spring Framework's declarative transaction management provides a convenience to declaratively specify the transaction rollback rules. For example, if a method is defined to throw two application exceptions such as MyException1 and MyException2, and we want to specify that only for MyException1 the transaction needs to be rolled back not for MyException2. This is allowed with Spring Framework's declarative transaction management. This feature is not supported with EJB CMT.
- The Spring Framework's declarative transaction management can be applied to any class managed by Spring container. Whereas EJB CMT service can be applied to only EJBs.

Apart from the benefits described above, Spring Framework's declarative transaction management has a limitation; it doesn't support propagation of transaction contexts across remote calls like EJB CMT. In most cases we do not want transactions to span over remote calls, however, sometimes we are in need of this requirement. In such a case it is recommended to use EJB.

10.12 CONFIGURING SPRING FRAMEWORK'S DECLARATIVE TRANSACTION

Configuring Spring Framework's declarative transactions is done using the *tx* namespace tags. Note that the *tx* namespace tags are new in Spring 2.0 and enhanced in Spring 2.5. We use the TransactionProxyFactoryBean for configuring declarative transactions in Spring 1.2; this is still supported with the current version of Spring Framework. The following tags are defined under the *tx* namespace:

- <tx:advice>
- <tx:attribute>
- <tx:method>
- <tx:jta-transaction-manager>
- <tx:annotation-driven>

To use *tx* namespace tags we need to import the spring-*tx* schema and declare its namespace in the Spring beans XML configuration file, as shown below:

Code Snippet

```
<beans xmlns="http://www.springframework.org/schema/beans"
xmlns:aop="http://www.springframework.org/schema/aop"
xmlns:tx="http://www.springframework.org/schema/tx"
xmlns:xsi="http://www.w3.org/2001/XMLSchema-instance"
xsi:schemaLocation="http://www.springframework.org/schema/beans
http://www.springframework.org/schema/beans/spring-beans-2.0.xsd
http://www.springframework.org/schema/aop http://www.springframework.org/schema/aop/
spring-aop-2.0.xsd
http://www.springframework.org/schema/tx
http://www.springframework.org/schema/tx/spring-tx-2.0.xsd">
```

> **Note:** If we are using Spring Framework 2.5 then use spring-tx-2.5.xsd instead of spring-tx-2.0.xsd.

Now, let us discuss all the above listed tags defined under the *tx* namespace:

10.12.1 The <tx:advice> Tag

The <tx:advice> tag defines a transactional advice. The <tx:advice> is associated with the PlatformTransactionManager object that is to be used for managing the transactions for this advice. The <tx:advice> tag allows to define the transactional semantics of any number of methods using its child elements. The transactional semantics includes the propagation settings, isolation level, rollback rules, read-only, and timeout. The <tx:advice> tag allows two attributes 'id' and 'transaction-manager'. The 'id' attribute specifies a unique name for this transactional advice. The 'transaction-manager' attribute specifies the bean name of the PlatformTransactionManager implementation's bean definition in the application context, which is used to drive the transactions. For example:

Code Snippet

```
<beans xmlns="http://www.springframework.org/schema/beans"
xmlns:aop="http://www.springframework.org/schema/aop"
xmlns:tx="http://www.springframework.org/schema/tx"
xmlns:xsi="http://www.w3.org/2001/XMLSchema-instance"
xsi:schemaLocation="http://www.springframework.org/schema/beans
http://www.springframework.org/schema/beans/spring-beans-2.0.xsd
http://www.springframework.org/schema/aop http://www.springframework.org/schema/aop/
spring-aop-2.0.xsd
http://www.springframework.org/schema/tx
http://www.springframework.org/schema/tx/spring-tx-2.0.xsd">

<!—Defining a DataSource—>
  <bean id="dataSource" class="org.apache.commons.dbcp.BasicDataSource">
    <property name="driverClassName" value="oracle.jdbc.driver.OracleDriver"/>
    <property name="url" value="jdbc:oracle:thin:@localhost:1521:sandb"/>
    <property name="username" value="scott"/>
    <property name="password" value="tiger"/>
  </bean>

<!—
  Defining a PlatformTransactionManager implementation object for DataSource
—>
  <bean id="dataSourcetxManager"
    class="org.springframework.jdbc.datasource.DataSourceTransactionManager">
    <property name="dataSource" ref="dataSource"/>
  </bean>

<!—Defining a transactional advice -->
  <tx:advice transaction-manager="dataSourcetxManager" id="mytxAdvice">
    <!—child tags to define the transaction semantics for the method comes here —>
  </tx:advice>

<!—other definitions —>
```

In this configuration we defined a DataSourceTransactionManager bean with an id dataSourcetx Manager injecting the DataSource defined in the same configuration document. We can use any other PlatformTransactionManager implementation as per the transactional resources that our application code is dealing with. Thereafter, the <tx:advice> tag is defined setting its transaction-manager attribute to dataSourcetxManager specifying to use the DataSourceTransactionManager for managing the transactions. The transactional advice is also given with a unique identity mytxAdvice using its 'id' attribute.

The <tx:advice> element takes only one child tag named <tx:attributes>, which can occur maximum for one time. Where the <tx:attributes> element simply encloses one or more <tx:method> tags to define the transactional semantics such as the propagation settings, the isolation level, the rollback rules, read only, and timeout. The following section explains the <tx:method> tag.

10.12.2 The <tx:method> Tag

The <tx:method> tag is used to configure the transactional semantics for a method or methods. The transactional semantics includes propagation, isolation, rollback, read-only, and timeout. The <tx:method> tag allows the following attributes.

TABLE 10.3 Attributes of <tx:method> tag

Attribute Name	*Description*	*Default*
name	Specifies the method name for which these transaction semantics have to be associated. The name can have wildcard character (*) to match the number of methods for which we want the same transaction attributes to be applied. For example, 'set*' matches all the methods whose name starts with set.	No default value: this attribute is mandatory to use.
propagation	Specifies the propagation behavior. Accepts one of the following values: REQUIRED, NEVER, SUPPORTS, MANDATORY, REQUIRES_NEW, NOT_SUPPORTED, and NESTED. See Section 10.8.5 to understand these propagation behaviors.	REQUIRED
isolation	Specifies the isolation level to use with the transactions for the specified methods. Allows one of the following values: DEFAULT, READ_UNCOMMITTED, READ_COMMITTED, REPEATABLE_READ, SERIALIZABLE. See Section 10.8.1.	DEFAULT
timeout	Specifies the transaction timeout in seconds. See Section 10.8.3.	–1
read-only	Specifies whether the transactions should be read only. See Section 10.8.4.	false
rollback-for	Specifies the comma separated class names of the Exceptions for which the transaction has to be rolled back.	No value
no-rollback-for	Specifies the comma separated class names of the Exceptions for which the transaction should not be rolled back.	No value

To recall most of the above attributes are defined using the TransactionDefinition object.

Code Snippet

```
<beans xmlns="http://www.springframework.org/schema/beans"
xmlns:aop="http://www.springframework.org/schema/aop"
xmlns:tx="http://www.springframework.org/schema/tx"
xmlns:xsi="http://www.w3.org/2001/XMLSchema-instance"
xsi:schemaLocation="http://www.springframework.org/schema/beans
http://www.springframework.org/schema/beans/spring-beans-2.0.xsd
http://www.springframework.org/schema/aop http://www.springframework.org/schema/aop/
spring-aop-2.0.xsd
http://www.springframework.org/schema/tx
http://www.springframework.org/schema/tx/spring-tx-2.0.xsd">

<!–Defining a DataSource-->
  <bean id="dataSource" class="org.apache.commons.dbcp.BasicDataSource">
    <property name="driverClassName" value="oracle.jdbc.driver.OracleDriver"/>
    <property name="url" value="jdbc:oracle:thin:@localhost:1521:sandb"/>
    <property name="username" value="scott"/>
    <property name="password" value="tiger"/>
  </bean>

<!--
  Defining a PlatformTransactionManager implementation object for DataSource
–>
  <bean id="dataSourcetxManager"
    class="org.springframework.jdbc.datasource.DataSourceTransactionManager">
    <property name="dataSource" ref="dataSource"/>
  </bean>

<!–Defining a transactional advice -->
  <tx:advice transaction-manager="dataSourcetxManager" id="mytxAdvice">
    <tx:attributes>
      <tx:method name="set*" propagation="REQUIRED"
            rollback-for="com.santosh.spring.exceptions.MyException1"/>
      <tx:method name="get*" propagation="SUPPORTS" read-only="true"
          no-rollback-for="com.santosh.spring.exceptions.MyException1"/>
    </tx:attributes>
  </tx:advice>

<!–other bean definition -->
```

The above configurations define two <tx:method> tags—the first one describing to use the propagation behavior REQUIRED for all the methods whose name starts with set and it even describes that if method throws an application exception com.santosh.spring.exceptions.MyException1, the transaction should be rolled back. The second <tx:method> tag describes to use the propagation behavior SUPPORTS for all the methods whose name starts with get and the transaction should be read-only; it even describes that if method throws an application exception com.santosh.spring.exceptions.MyException1, the transaction should not be rolled back.

Once after configuring the <tx:advice> along with its child tags as shown in the preceding code snippet, we need to configure this advice like any other AOP advice to the Spring beans as shown below:

Code Snippet

```
<aop:config>
  <aop:pointcut id="myPointCut"
      expression="within(com.santosh.spring.services.EmloyeeServices)"/>
  <aop:advisor id="mytxAdvisor" advice-ref="mytxAdvice"
               pointcut-ref=" myPointCut"/>
</aop:config>
```

In this configuration we specified that the transactional advice defined with an id mytxAdvice (explained above) is applicable for all the methods of com.santosh.spring.services.EmployeeServices class (see Chapter 5 for description of how to prepare pointcut expressions).

10.12.3 The <tx:jta-transaction-manager> Tag

The <tx:jta-transaction-manager> is a utility tag that is used to create a default JtaTransactionManager bean with a name "transactionManager", instead of defining a Spring regular bean definition. This tag automatically detects WebLogic, WebSphere an OC4J, creating a WebLogicJtaTransactionManager, WebSphereUowTransactionManager or OC4JJtaTransactionManager, respectively.

> **Note:** This tag creates a default JtaTransactionManager object: it does not allow to customize the properties of JtaTransactionManager that it is creating. If we want to define a JtaTransactionManager with custom properties, use regular Spring bean definition. Note that this tag is new in Spring 2.5 and is not available in Spring 2.0.

10.12.4 The <tx:annotation-driven> Tag

This <tx:annotation-driven> tag is used to specify that the transaction configurations are defined in the bean classes using the @Transactional annotation. That means Spring Framework 2 allows us to define the declarative transactions using the XML-based and annotation-based approach. This tag is required to be included into the Spring beans XML file of the application context when we want to use the annotation-based approach to configure transactions. This tag allows the following attributes.

TABLE 10.4 Attributes of <tx:annotation-driven> tag

Attribute Name	*Description*	*Default*
transaction-manager	Specifies the bean name of the Platform Transaction Manager implementation's bean definition in the application context, which is used to drive the transactions.	TransactionManager
mode	Specifies whether to proxy the beans using Spring AOP framework or waved using the AspectJ transaction aspect. Allows the following two values: proxy or aspectj.	proxy

(Contd.)

proxy-target-class	Specifies a boolean value describing whether to use CGLIB for class based proxies or Java interface based proxies. True specifies to use CGLIB.	false
order	Specifies the order of the execution of the transaction advisor when multiple advices executes at a specific joinpoint.	Ordered.LOWEST_ PRECEDENCE

Let us learn how to configure declarative transactions using the annotation-based approach.

10.13 USING @TRANSACTIONAL ANNOTATION

In addition to configuring declarative transactions using the XML-based approach Spring Framework 2.0 provides support for configuration declarative transactions using Java 5-based annotations. This is a simple-to-use approach enabling us to configure the transaction semantics directly in the Java source code. But this option is available only when we are using Java 5 or a higher version. The @Transactional annotation is defined in org.springframework.transaction.annotation package and can be applied to methods or class. The @Transactional annotation declares the following optional elements:

TABLE 10.5 Elements of @Transactional annotation

Element name	*Description*
isolation	Specifies the transaction isolation level, accepts Isolation enum type value. Defaults to Isolation.DEFAULT.
propagation	Specifies the propagation behavior, accepts Propagation enum type value. Defaults to Propagation.REQUIRED.
readOnly	Specifies the read-only flag for the transaction, describing whether the transaction is read only. Defaults to false.
timeout	Specifies the timeout period for this transaction. Defaults to -1.
rollbackFor	Specifies zero or more exception classes (subtypes of Throwable) for which the transaction has to be rolled back.
rollbackForClassName	Specifies zero or more exception class name for which the transaction has to be rolled back.
noRollbackFor	Specifies zero or more exception classes (subtypes of Throwable) for which the transaction should not be rolled back.
noRollbackForClassName	Specifies zero or more exception class name for which the transaction should not be rolled back.

The following code snippet shows the code using @Transactional annotation.

Code Snippet

```
import org.springframework.transaction.annotation.*;
public class MyServices {
  @Transactional(propagation=Propagation.SUPPORTS,
  isolation=Isolation.READ_COMMITED)
```

```
   public void myService1() {
      ...
   }
   @Transactional(rollbackFor={MyException1.class, MyException2.class})
   public void myService2() throws MyException1, MyException2, MyException3 {
      ...
   }
}
```

In this code we defined myService1() method to use a transaction propagation as SUPPORTS and the isolation level to READ COMMITED, remaining to defaults. And the myService2() method uses the default propagation behavior, isolation level, read-only and timeout, where as it defines that if the method throws MyException1 or MyException2, the transaction should not be rolled back. To specify the Spring container to identify the @Transactional annotation in the POJOs and make the bean instances transactional, we need to add the <tx:annotation-driven> tag in the Spring beans XML configuration file as shown below:

Code Snippet

```
<beans xmlns="http://www.springframework.org/schema/beans"
xmlns:aop="http://www.springframework.org/schema/aop"
xmlns:tx="http://www.springframework.org/schema/tx"
xmlns:xsi="http://www.w3.org/2001/XMLSchema-instance"
xsi:schemaLocation="http://www.springframework.org/schema/beans
http://www.springframework.org/schema/beans/spring-beans-2.0.xsd
http://www.springframework.org/schema/aop http://www.springframework.org/schema/aop/
spring-aop-2.0.xsd
http://www.springframework.org/schema/tx http://www.springframework.org/schema/tx/
spring-tx-2.0.xsd">

   <bean id="dataSource" class="org.apache.commons.dbcp.BasicDataSource">
      <property name="driverClassName"
               value="oracle.jdbc.driver.OracleDriver"/>
      <property name="url" value="jdbc:oracle:thin:@localhost:1521:sandb"/>
      <property name="username" value="scott"/>
      <property name="password" value="tiger"/>
   </bean>

   <bean id="dataSourcetxManager"
   class="org.springframework.jdbc.datasource.DataSourceTransactionManager">
      <property name="dataSource" ref="dataSource"/>
   </bean>

   <tx:annotation-driven transaction-manager="dataSourcetxManager"/>

   <!–other bean definitions -->
</beans>
```

The <tx:annotation-driven> tag in the Spring beans XML configuration file tells the Spring container that it needs to find the @Transactional annotation in the Spring beans and make them transactional by auto proxying them. See Table 10.4 for the various attributes allowed in <tx:annotation-driven> tag.

Summary

In this chapter we learnt how to using Hibernate with Spring Framework in which we learnt that Spring Framework provides us some conveniences that allows elimination of the boiler plate code such as obtaining and closing the Hibernate Session, and handling HibernateExceptions. Later we discussed about the Spring transaction management support; in this part of the chapter we learnt that Spring Framework provides a platform independent transaction management support. We even learnt how to use the Spring programmatic and declarative transaction management support. With this chapter we will end the discussion on Spring services to implement Data Access Layer. In the next chapter we will start learning how to implement web tier and the Spring services provided in implementing web tier.

Getting Started with Spring Web MVC Framework

11 CHAPTER

Objectives

In this chapter we will cover:

- Spring Web MVC framework
- The MVC architecture, its need and the front controller design pattern, which are the prerequisites for understanding the Spring web MVC framework
- Spring Web MVC architecture and its elements

11.1 MVC ARCHITECTURE

N-Tier architecture refers to the architecture of an application that has at least three tiers (that is, three parts) separated logically or physically. This architecture model allows us to design an application with any number of tiers arranged above another, each serving distinct and separate tasks, and each tier interacting only with the tier directly below.

> **Note:**
>
> 1. Tier can be defined as one of two or more levels, or rows arranged one above another. Simply put, a tier refers to a division of the application. Tier and layer are interchangeably used, they mean the same.
> 2. The term logical tiers (or logical layers) mean that tiers are separated in terms of a set of classes but are running in the same process (that is, hosted on the same server), whereas physical tiers (or physical layers) mean that the tiers are separated in a set of classes and are running in different processes generally in different machines.

N-tier architecture is important because each tier in this can be located on physically different servers. Hence they scale out and handle more load. In addition, what each tier does internally is completely hidden to the other tiers and this makes it possible to change or update one tier without recompiling or modifying the others. This is an important feature of n-tier architecture, as additional features or change to a tier can be done without modifying or redeploying the whole application. For example, by separating data access code from the business logic code, if our data store changes we only need to change the data access code. Because business logic code remains the same, the business logic code does not need to be changed or re-compiled.

Once if we decide to use n-tire architecture to develop our project then the first problem we need to solve is identifying the number of tiers our application has to be divided into and their responsibilities. Dividing the system into multiple tiers gives the advantages described above but the more tiers you add, more the performance is affected. It is up to the application architect to know and understand this, and all other factors affecting the system, and be able to make a decision based on this. This decision is usually made depending on the amount of work and documentation that was produced at the analysis phase. Moreover, at present there are number of architectural patterns, each of them explaining the common problems in complex applications and providing solutions for the problem it describes. One of these architectural patterns is Model-View-Controller (MVC).

In case of applications that present a large amount of data to the user, it is recommended to separate data and user interface concerns so that changes to the user interface will not affect data handling, and that the data can be reorganized without changing the user interface. The Model-View-Controller pattern solves this problem by decoupling data access and business logic from data presentation and user interaction, by introducing an intermediate component controller.

The responsibilities of Model, View, and Controller as defined under the MVC pattern are:

Model: This tier is responsible to represent business process and business data of the application.

View: This tier is responsible to prepare the presentation for the client based on the outcome of the request processing. That is, this renders the model data into the client's user interface type.

Controller: This tier is responsible for controlling the request to response flow in the middleware.

Now, if we want to develop a web-based n-tier application following MVC in java then we can follow any one of the two model architectures as described below.

11.1.1 Model-1 Architecture

In this model, the client directly accesses the pages in the web container, and these pages service the entire request and send the response back. While servicing the client requests these pages generally use a model which represents the business logic for the application. These pages are usually implemented using JSP pages, sometimes servlets, and model as Beans. In this architecture, controlling and presentation are mixed into a single component, and hence this model architecture is also known as page-centric architecture. This architecture is shown in Fig. 11.1.

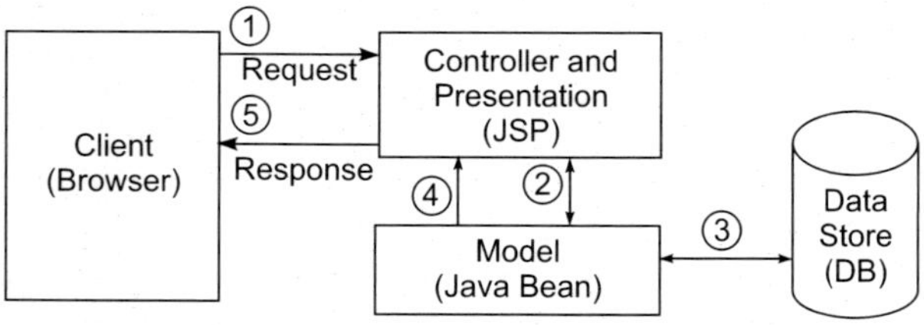

FIGURE 11.1 Model-1 Architecture

11.1.2 Model-2 Architecture

In this model, the client cannot directly access the pages, instead all the requests are made to a controller component generally implemented as a servlet. The controller component then uses the model (which is generally java bean or EJB) to process the client request, and then dispatches the request to view pages (implemented using JSP). These pages prepare the response and send it to the client. This architecture is shown in Fig. 11.2.

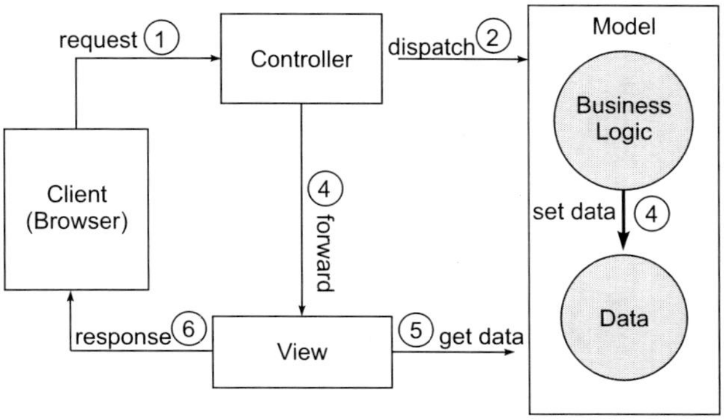

FIGURE 11.2 Model-2 Architecture

Now, as we have learnt about the two models of developing web application in java, it is time to learn the Front controller pattern that solves the most general problem found in developing Model-2 applications.

11.2 FRONT CONTROLLER DESIGN PATTERN

We know that patterns are strategies that allow programmers to share knowledge about the recurring problems and their solutions. Documenting patterns is one way we can reuse and possibly share information on how best it is to solve a specific problem. And a well-known definition for a pattern: A pattern is a tree-part rule, which expresses a relation between a certain context, problem, and solution.

In this section you will learn about one of the common problems found in most of the Model-2 based MVC applications.

11.2.1 Context

We have decided to use the Model-View-Controller (MVC) pattern to separate the user interface logic from the business logic of a Web application. We have reviewed the Page Controller pattern, but page controller classes have complicated logic, or our application determines the navigation between pages dynamically based on configurable rules.

The **Page Controller** pattern describes a separate controller per logical page.

11.2.2 Problem

We want to structure the controller for very complex Web applications in the best possible manner so that we can achieve reuse and flexibility while avoiding code duplication and decentralization problems in page controller.

11.2.3 Forces

The following are the characteristics of the forces from the MVC that applies the Front Controller pattern:

1. If common logic is replicated in different pages in the system, we need to centralize this logic to reduce the amount of code duplication. Removing the duplicated code is critical in improving the overall maintainability of the system.
2. We want to separate system processing logic from the view.
3. The Page Controller pattern describes a separate controller per logical page. This solution breaks down when you need to control or coordinate processing across multiple pages. For example, you have complex configurable navigation which is stored in XML, in your Web application. When a request comes in, the application must look up where to go next, based on its current state.

11.2.4 Solution

Use a Front Controller as the initial point of contact for handling all related requests. The Front Controller solves the decentralization problem present in Page Controller by channeling all requests through a single controller, that is, it centralizes control logic that is otherwise duplicated, and even manages key request handling activities, like protocol handling, context transformation, navigation and routing, and dispatch.

Protocol Handling is a process of handling a protocol-specific request, which involves in resolving the request given in a specific protocol format and preparing a message in a specific protocol format.

Context Transformation is a process of converting the protocol specific data into a more general form, like into our system-defined java bean object or into a general collection object.

Navigation is a process that chooses the object for handling a particular request that can perform the core processing for this request and the view that can present the response to the client.

Dispatch involves in dispatching the request from one part of the application to another, like from request handling object to view processing components.

11.2.5 Benefits of Using this Pattern

- **Centralized control**: Front Controller organizes all of the requests that are made to the Web application. The solution describes to use a single controller instead of the distributed model used in Page Controller, which describes to use a separate controller for each page. This single controller is in the perfect location to enforce application-wide policies, such as security, logging, and usage tracking.
- **Threadsafety**: Because each request involves creating a new command object, the command objects themselves do not need to be threadsafe. This means that we avoid the issues of threadsafety in the command classes. This does not mean that you can avoid threading issues altogether, though, because the code that the commands act upon, the model code, still must be threadsafe.
- **Configurability**: Only one front controller needs to be configured into the Web server; the handler does the rest of the dispatching. This simplifies the configuration of the Web server.

Use of dynamic command objects enables you to add new commands without modifying the existing code.

11.2.3 Issue in Using this Pattern

- **Performance considerations**: Front Controller is a single controller that handles all requests for the Web application. Here it requires determining the type of command that processes the request. If it must retrieve data from XML document (configuration files) to make the decision, performance could be very slow as a result. However, this can be minimized by loading the configurations into memory at the time of initializing the application and avoiding the reading of the XML document multiple number of times.

As we have discussed about the MVC and Front Controller patterns which are important to understand the Spring Web MVC Framework it is time to learn about the Spring Web MVC framework. The following sections explains you the Spring Web MVC framework, starting with Spring Web MVC framework followed by its architecture and various elements of Spring Web MVC framework.

11.3 WHAT IS SPRING WEB MVC FRAMEWORK?

Spring Web MVC Framework is an open-source web application framework which is a part of Spring Framework licensed under the terms of the Apache License, Version 2.0. Spring Web MVC is one of the efficient and high-performance open-source implementation of Model-2 based Model-View-Controller (MVC). Spring Web MVC framework provides utility classes to handle many of the most common tasks in Web application development.

What is a Framework?

Framework is a set of well-defined classes and interfaces that provides services to our application. With a framework, it contains the executing routines and invokes operations on to your extensions through inheritance and other means.

11.4 NEED OF SPRING WEB MVC FRAMEWORK

You know the requirement of web applications and you have learnt from the preceding sections of this chapter about the two development models for developing web applications. Moreover, most of the huge enterprise applications are developed following Model-2 architecture. It can be identified that while developing the web applications following such architecture gives a number of benefits. However, using the basic web technologies like servlets and JSP for developing such a web application is complicated and contains most of the infrastructure logics that results in an increase of the application development cost, development time, and further affects the productivity of the application. To solve these problems we want a readymade solution for the infrastructure logics in developing web applications following Model-2 architecture instead of developing it as a part of our project development, which can reduce the development time and cost, and even improve the performance and productivity of the application. This is where the need for web application frameworks comes and as a reply for this requirement one of the solution is given under the Spring Framework as one of its modules Spring Web MVC Framework. Spring Web MVC Framework has restructured the way Web programmers think about and construct Web application in Java.

11.5 BENEFITS OF SPRING WEB MVC FRAMEWORK

We have a number of benefits in using Spring Web MVC Framework for developing web applications in Java. Before we look into the benefits of Spring Web MVC Framework we need to remember that all the benefits of the MVC approach and Model-2 development model are available when using Spring Web MVC Framework. For example, MVC Model-2 provides a clear separation between the presentation logic (for example, HTML and tag libraries) from the request handling code (using Java servlets, Plain Java Classes and JSP Scriplets, etc.) is also one of the benefits of Spring Web MVC Framework. The web applications developed using Spring Web MVC Framework is easier to develop, understand, and maintain. The following are the added benefits of using Spring Web MVC Framework for developing web applications.

- Spring Web MVC Framework is open-source, which allows us to download the source code and modify it to supports user extensions according to our requirements.
- The other important advantage of Spring Web MVC Framework being open source its code is exposed to the developers (that is, for us) and this enables fast development and maintenance cycle. As a result we can expect fast response from the spring team in fixing the bugs and response to the new requirements in the market.
- Spring Web MVC Framework is implemented using standard java technologies like Java Servlets and JSP. Thus we are allowed to host Spring Web MVC project on any Java enterprise web server by just including the spring jar files into the lib on our web application/project.
- Reduces the development time and cost in developing the controller and view parts of web application developed following MVC architecture and Model-2 development model.
- Spring Web MVC uses XML-based configuration files to collect the configuration details from the application provider.
- Spring Web MVC provides centralized XML file-based configuration. This allows us to configure most of the application properties in XML files rather then hard coding into Java classes, which means that many changes can be made without modifying or recompiling Java code, and the changes can be made by modifying a single file.
- This lets the Java developers focus on implementing the business logic without needing to know about the overall system layout.
- Allows the use of existing business objects as command or form-objects instead of mirroring them in order to extend a particular framework base class.
- Provides customizable navigation and view management. The navigation and view resolution strategies can be configured as a simple URL-based configuration, bean-name based, or to any system specific built resolution strategies. This is more flexible than some web MVC frameworks which mandate a particular technique.
- Spring Web MVC includes a simple yet powerful JSP tag library known as the Spring tag library that provides support for features such as data binding and themes. And the JSP form tag library, introduced in Spring 2.0 makes writing forms in JSP pages much easier.

As we have understood what is a Spring Web MVC and its benefits now it is time to look at the architecture of Spring Web MVC. The following section explains you the Spring Web MVC architecture.

11.6 SPRING WEB MVC ARCHITECTURE

Figure 11.3 shows the basic elements of Spring Web MVC application and the interactions between them, that is, the architecture of Spring Web MVC.

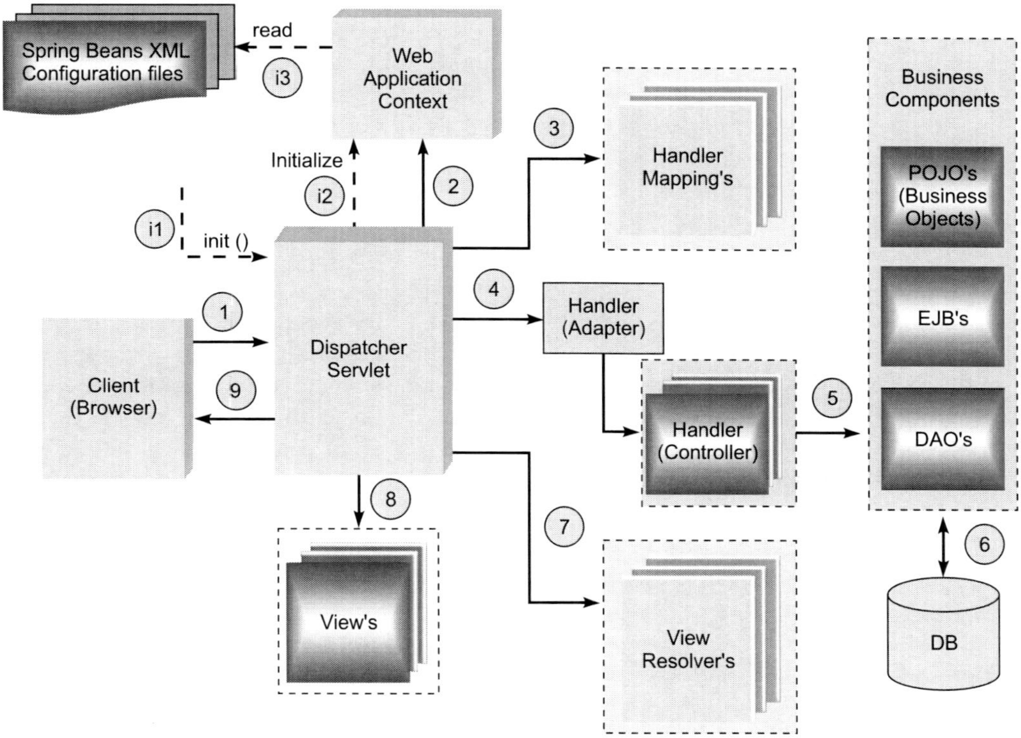

FIGURE 11.3 Spring Web MVC architecture with its basic elements

> **Note:** In the above architecture the dotted arrows shows the initialization process and solid arrows shows the request processing. And the shaded elements are the elements which we need to program.

As shown in Fig. 11.3 the DispatcherServlet is the front controller for the Spring Web MVC application, providing a centralized access for various requests to the application and collaborating with various other objects to complete the request handling and present the response to client. The DispatcherServlet uses the WebApplicationContext object to locate the various objects configured in the Spring Bean XML configuration file. The WebApplicationContext is instantiated and initialized as a part of the DispatcherServlet's initialization process. The WebApplicationContext object is responsible to locate the spring beans XML configuration file and load its details to prepare the context for handling the requests. Now, when a client request is given to DispatcherServlet, it performs the following operations:

- First of all the DispatcherServlet makes the framework objects available to handlers and view objects by setting them into request scope. Here the framework objects are WebApplication Context, LocaleResolver, ThemeResolver, and ThemeSource.
- Checks whether the request is a Multipart request and if it is so then it wraps the request in a MultipartHttpServletRequest object. This is done only if we configure a multipart resolver.
- Requests the configured handler mappings to locate the controller that can handle this request. The handler mappings are invoked in a sorted order one after the other until the controller is located.
- Delegate the request to controller located in the above step with the help of handler adapter.
- Collect the ModelAndView object returned by the controller if it is *null* then end the request processing without continuing the request delegation to view.
- Request the view resolver to locate the view that can prepare the presentation for this request.
- Dispatch the request to the view located by the view resolver in the above step.

The above steps provide the complete overview of the request processing flow in Spring Web MVC application, but we still need to discuss much more about this like about the various handler mappings and how they locate the controller, what are the different types of controllers we have, how to develop and configure view resolver, etc., but discussing all these at this point is not reasonable as it will tend to cause confusion. Thus after we write one simple application and execute it only then can we comfortably understand the various elements of the system in detail. The next chapter explains all the elements of Spring Web MVC architecture in detail. The following section explains the basic Spring Web MVC application.

11.7 WRITING YOUR FIRST SPRING WEB MVC APPLICATION

To make the first example simple we are implementing a login process which is a well-known one. This example consists of a Login.html which provides an entry point for this application by providing login view allowing the user to make a login action. The Login.html is shown in List 11.1.

List 11.1 Login.html

```
<html>
  <body>
      <form action="login.spring"> <pre>
         User Name : <input type="text" name="uname"/>
         Password    : <input type="password" name="pass"/>
               <input type="submit" value="LogIN"/>
       </pre> </form>
  </body>
</html>
```

The request made using the Login.html is received by the DispatcherServlet, which then dispatches the request to the LoginController invoking handleRequest() method. The LoginController class to process the login request is shown in List 11.2.

List 11.2: LoginController.java

```
package com.santosh.spring;

import org.springframework.web.servlet.*;
import org.springframework.web.servlet.mvc.*;

import javax.servlet.http.*;

public class LoginController implements Controller {

  LoginModel loginModel;

  public void setLoginModel(LoginModel lm){
        loginModel=lm;
  }

  public ModelAndView handleRequest(
                        HttpServletRequest req,
                        HttpServletResponse res) throws Exception  {

        String uname= req.getParameter("uname");
        String pass= req.getParameter("pass");

        String type=loginModel.validate(uname, pass);

        if (type==null)
        return new ModelAndView("/Login.html");
        else if(type.equals("admin"))
        return new ModelAndView("/AdminHome.jsp");
        else
        return new ModelAndView("/UserHome.jsp");
  }//handle
}//class
```

As shown in List 11.2 the LoginController handleRequest() method is invoking the validate() method on the LoginModel object where LoginModel is a plain java class designed to perform business logic operation, in this case validating the login details. List 11.3 shows the LoginModel.java.

List 11.3: LoginModel.java

```
package com.santosh.spring;

import org.springframework.jdbc.core.*;
import org.springframework.dao.EmptyResultDataAccessException;

public class LoginModel {

  public LoginModel(JdbcTemplate jt){
        jdbcTemplate=jt;
  }

  public String validate(String uname, String pass) {
        try{
              return (String)jdbcTemplate.queryForObject(
                    "select type from userdetails where username=\'"+
                      uname+"\' and userpass=\'"+pass+"\'", String.class);
        }
        catch(EmptyResultDataAccessException e){
              return null;
        }
  }//validate

  private JdbcTemplate jdbcTemplate;
}//class
```

As we have discussed in the above sections we need to configure the beans (defining controllers) into the Spring Beans XML configuration file. This XML configuration file name should be [servlet-name]-servlet.xml in the WEB-INF directory of our web application. Here in this example we will define the servlet-name for DispatcherServlet declaration as ‘ds’. Thus the file name here is ds-servlet.xml. List 11.4 shows the ds-servlet.xml file for this example.

List 11.4: ds-servlet.xml

```
<beans xmlns="http://www.springframework.org/schema/beans"
xmlns:xsi="http://www.w3.org/2001/XMLSchema-instance"
xsi:schemaLocation="http://www.springframework.org/schema/beans
http://www.springframework.org/schema/beans/spring-beans-2.0.xsd">

  <!–Configuring DataSource-->
  <bean id="datasource" class="org.apache.commons.dbcp.BasicDataSource">
      <property name="driverClassName">
            <value>oracle.jdbc.driver.OracleDriver</value>
      </property>
      <property name="url">
            <value>jdbc:oracle:thin:@localhost:1521:sandb</value>
```

```
        </property>
        <property name="username">
              <value>scott</value>
        </property>
        <property name="password">
              <value>tiger</value>
        </property>
    </bean>

    <!--Configuring JdbcTemplate-->
    <bean id="jdbctemp" class="org.springframework.jdbc.core.JdbcTemplate">
          <constructor-arg>
                <ref local="datasource"/>
          </constructor-arg>
    </bean>

    <bean id="loginModel" class="com.santosh.spring.LoginModel">
        <constructor-arg>
              <ref local="jdbctemp"/>
        </constructor-arg>
    </bean>

    <bean id="logincnt" class="com.santosh.spring.LoginController">
      <property name="loginModel">
            <ref local="loginModel"/>
      </property>
    </bean>

    <bean id="myurlmapping"
class="org.springframework.web.servlet.handler.SimpleUrlHandlerMapping">
          <property name="mappings">
              <props>
                  <prop key="/login.spring">logincnt</prop>
              </props>
          </property>
    </bean>
</beans>
```

List 11.5 shows the AdminHome.jsp, which is presented in case the login details are validated as an admin type user.

List 11.5 AdminHome.jsp

```
<html> <body>
   Welcome to the Admin Home page <br/>
   User Name : <%=request.getParameter("uname")%>
</html> </body>
```

List 11.6 shows the UserHome.jsp, which is presented in case the login details are validated as a user type.

List 11.6 UserHome.jsp

```
<html> <body>
   Welcome to the Non-Admin User Home page <br/>
   User Name : <%=request.getParameter("uname")%>
</html> </body>
```

Finally, as discussed we need to configure DispatcherServlet in web.xml since it is also a normal servlet as any other servlet. We will discuss the DispatcherServlet and its configurations in detail in Chapter 12. List 11.7 shows the web.xml.

List 11.7 web.xml

```
<web-app>
 <servlet>
  <servlet-name>ds</servlet-name>
   <servlet-class>org.springframework.web.servlet.DispatcherServlet</servlet-class>
  <load-on-startup>0</load-on-startup>
 </servlet>
 <servlet-mapping>
  <servlet-name>ds</servlet-name>
  <url-pattern>*.spring</url-pattern>
 </servlet-mapping>
</web-app>
```

11.7.1 Configuring Spring Web MVC Application

Now, as you have written the Spring Web MVC example that explained in List 11.1 through List 11.7 follow the following steps to configure your Spring Web MVC application to see it in action.

Step 1: Set the classpath
Set spring.jar into classpath in addition to your existing classpath.

Step 2: Compile LoginController.java and LoginModel.java, as shown in Fig. 11.4.

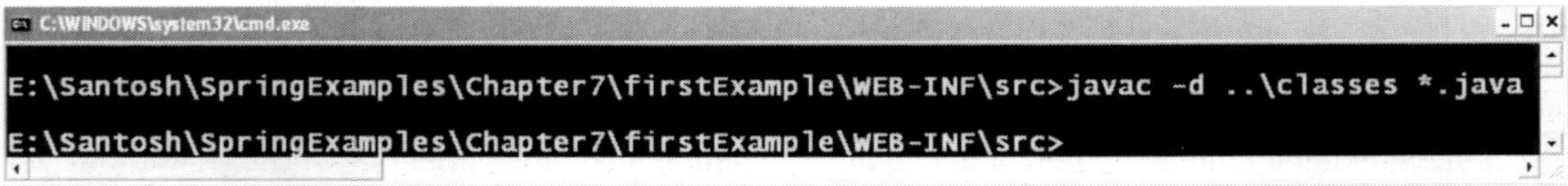

FIGURE 11.4 Compiling all the Java files of this example

Step 3: Arrange the files in the directory structure as shown in Fig. 11.5.

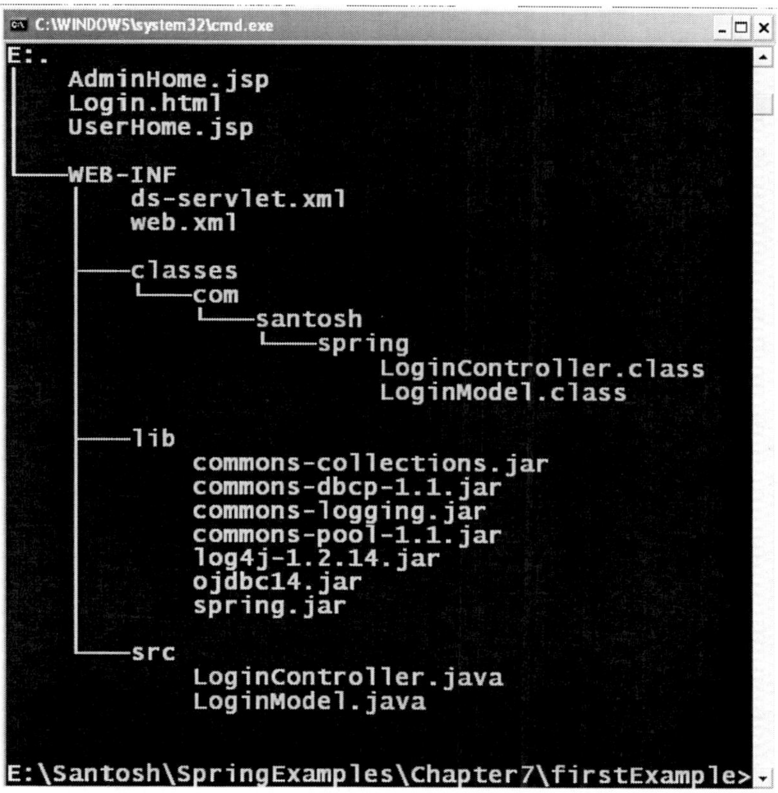

FIGURE 11.5 Tree structure showing the files of the Spring web MVC application

Step 4: Create a table in oracle database and insert some records to test the application.

The following code snippet shows the code to create a userdetails table.

Code Snippet

```
drop table userdetails;

create table userdetails(
 username varchar2(20),
 userpass varchar2(20),
 email varchar2(30),
 address varchar2(30),
 mobile number(10),
 type varchar2(5)
);
```

The following code snippet shows commands to insert some records to test the application.

Code Snippet

```
insert into userdetails values('Santosh', 'kumar', 'to_santoshk@yahoo.com', 'hyd',
9704309999, 'admin');
insert into userdetails values('Subash', 'chandra', 'subbu_lippi@yahoo.com', 'hyd',
1234567890, 'user');
```

Step 5: Deploy the application into any Java Web application server.

Here we are using Tomcat server to demonstrate this example but as described already the Spring Web MVC framework is not server dependent and can be deployed into any Java web application server. You can use any of the deployment options that you have learnt in servlets and JSP to deploy web application in Tomcat. The basic approach is to copy the work_folder into <tomcat_home>/webapps folder.

Step 6: Start the server and run the example.
Start the Tomcat server and browse the example using the URL
http://localhost:8080/firstExample/Login.html. You will find the following screen.

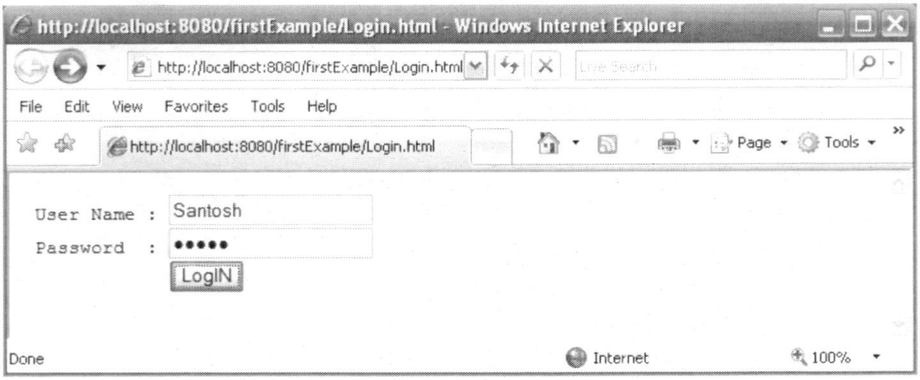

FIGURE 11.6 Home page of Login process

Enter the login details as shown in Fig. 11.6. As per the database created if every thing is successful you will find the view as shown in Fig. 11.7, that is a presentation of AdminHome.jsp.

In case the login details are not valid then the Login page is presented, and if the login details are validated as type 'user' then UserHome.jsp is presented.

In this section we have learnt how to write and configure a basic Spring Web MVC application. We will learn all the elements of spring web MVC architecture in detail in the next chapter.

FIGURE 11.7 Success view of Login request

Summary

In this chapter we learnt the prerequisites for understanding Spring Web MVC framework, including MVC Architecture, Model-1 and 2 architectures, and Front controller design pattern. Then we have discussed the importance of Spring Web MVC framework. In the later part of this chapter we had an overview of the Spring Web MVC framework architecture and even a basic example. In the next chapter you will learn initialization and request processing workflow, and all these elements of Spring Web MVC architecture in detail.

Understanding DispatcherServlet and Request Processing Workflow

12

CHAPTER

Objectives

In this chapter we will cover:

- Elements of Spring Web MVC framework
- Initialization and request processing workflow

12.1 WHAT IS DISPATCHERSERVLET?

The DispatcherServlet of Spring Web MVC framework is an implementation of Front Controller and is a Java Servlet component, that is, it is a Servlet Front for Spring Web MVC applications. DispatcherServlet is the front controller class that receives all incoming HTTP client requests for the Spring Web MVC application. In addition, DispatcherServlet is responsible for initializing the Spring Web MVC framework for our application, and is a servlet implemented as a subtype of HttpServlet just like any other servlet. DispatcherServlet is also required to be configured in our web application like any other servlet, that is, into Web application deployment descriptor (web.xml). The following code snippet shows the declaration of DispatcherServlet in web.xml.

Code Snippet

```
<!—Declaring DispatcherServlet -->
<servlet>
  <servlet-name>ds</servlet-name>
   <servlet-class>org.springframework.web.servlet.DispatcherServlet</servlet-class>
  <load-on-startup>0</load-on-startup>
 </servlet>
```

The preceding code snippet shows the declaration of DispatcherServlet. In addition to this declaration we can configure the initialization parameters to alter the behavior of the DispatcherServlet with respect to locating the Spring Beans XML configuration files and initializing the application context. Table 12.1 describes the various initialization parameters that can be configured to DispatcherServlet.

TABLE 12.1 Initialization Parameters of DispatcherServlet

Parameter Name	***Description***
contextClass	Specifies the web application context class to use. This class must be subtype of *org.springframework.web.context.WebApplicationContext*. Default is ***org.springframework.web.context.support.XmlWebApplicationContext***.
namespace	Specifies the custom namespace for this servlet. This is used by the servlet for building a default context config location. Default is ***<servlet name>-servlet***.
contextConfigLocation	Specifies the context config location. This location string can specify multiple locations separated by any number of commas or spaces. Default is ***/WEB-INF/<namespace>.xml***
publishContext	Specifies whether to put this servlet's WebApplicationContext into ServletContext scope. To make this WebApplicationContext available to all objects in this web application, that is, like other servlets in this application. If this is configured to true then this servlet stores the WebApplicationContext into application scope with *org.springframework.web.servlet.FrameworkServlet.CONTEXT.<servlet name>* as attribute name. Default is ***true***.
publishEvents	Specifies whether this servlet should put a ServletRequestHandledEvent at the end of each request. Default is ***true***.
detectAllHandlerMappings	Specifies whether to detect all HandlerMapping beans in this servlet's context or just a single bean with name *handlerMapping*. Default is ***true***. We need to configure ***false*** if we want this servlet to use a single HandlerMapping, in spite of multiple HandlerMapping beans being defined in the context.
detectAllHandlerAdapters	Specifies whether to detect all HandlerAdapter beans in this servlet's context or just a single bean with name *handlerAdapter*. Default is ***true***. We need to configure ***false*** if we want this servlet to use a single HandlerAdapter, in spite of multiple HandlerAdapter beans being defined in the context.
detectAllHandlerExceptionResolvers	Specifies whether to detect all HandlerExceptionResolver beans in this servlet's context or just a single bean with name *handlerExceptionResolver*. Default is ***true***. We need to configure ***false*** if we want this servlet to use a single HandlerExceptionResolver, in spite of multiple HandlerExceptionResolver beans being defined in the context.
detectAllViewResolvers	Specifies whether to detect all ViewResolver beans in this servlet's context or just a single bean with name *viewResolver*. Default is ***true***. We need to configure ***false*** if we want this servlet to use a single ViewResolver, in spite of multiple ViewResolver beans being defined in the context.
cleanupAfterInclude	Specifies whether to perform cleanup of request attributes after an include request. If this is set to true then all the request attributes are reset to the original state after the DispatcherServlet has processed within an include request. If not only the DispatcherServlet's own request attributes will be reset. Default is ***true***.

The following code snippet shows the declaration of DispatcherServlet configured with a 'contextConfigLocation' init parameter described in Table 12.1.

Code Snippet

```
<!–Declaring DispatcherServlet -->
<servlet>
  <servlet-name>ds</servlet-name>
  <servlet-class>org.springframework.web.servlet.DispatcherServlet</servlet-class>
  <init-param>
    <param-name>contextConfigLocation</param-name>
    <param-value>
      /WEB-INF/myconfigs/applicationBeans.xml
      /WEB-INF/myconfigs/applicationControllers.xml
    </param-value>
  </init-param>
  <load-on-startup>0</load-on-startup>
</servlet>
```

The preceding code snippet declares DispatcherServlet that specifies the servlet to use applicationBeans.xml and applicationControllers.xml documents to initialize WebApplicationContext. After declaring the DispatcherServlet we need to configure mappings for it. In this we need to inform the servlet container to direct the requests that can be handled by the DispatcherServlet. Since the DispatcherServlet has to be configured to receive all the requests to our application, that is, for various services, DispatcherServlet's mapping should be generic. Thus in general we use path or extension mappings. The following code snippet shows the sample mapping for DispatcherServlet.

Code Snippet

```
<servlet-mapping>
  <servlet-name>ds</servlet-name>
  <url-pattern>*.spring</url-pattern>
</servlet-mapping>
```

As per the mapping shown in the preceding code snippet all the request for this context whose servletPath ends with **.spring** extension are dispatched by the web container to the DispatcherServlet. Note that as shown in the preceding code snippet it is not mandatory to configure only **.spring,** instead we are allowed to configure any other extension.

> **Note:** Spring Web MVC framework does not force us to use specific extensions or patterns in URLs; we are free to use whatever paths we like. Moreover, Spring Framework is not bonded to match the handlers only based on URLs. Alternatively, we can define a mapping based on parameters, or HTTP session state, etc. This feature is not supported by most Web MVC frameworks which includes Struts.

In this section we have learnt about the DispatcherServlet and its configuration parameters/Now it is time to learn about the Initialization and Request processing workflow of DispatcherServlet. Let us start by understanding DispatcherServlet's Initialization stage.

12.2 DISPATCHERSERVLET'S INITIALIZATION STAGE

While initializing the DispatcherServlet it creates WebApplicationContext implementation class instance, either user configured custom context class or the default XmlWebAppliationContext. The WebApplicationContext is responsible to locate the Spring Beans XML configuration file, then read, validate the configurations and load the details into configuration objects. The DispatcherServlet uses the WebApplicationContext for accessing various framework objects that are used to execute the workflow for handling the request. The special framework objects that are initialized using the WebApplicationContext are described in Table 12.2.

TABLE 12.2 Spring Web MVC Framework special objects

Types	*Description*
MultipartResolver	The MultipartResolver object is used to resolve multipart requests and is used in multipart file uploads. To configure MultipartResolver we need to define a bean definition with an id '*multipartResolver*' in the spring beans XML configuration file. If no bean is defined with this id in the context, no multipart handling is provided, that is, DispatcherServlet does not take any default.
LocaleResolver	LocaleResolver provides an abstraction for web-based locale resolution strategies that allows for both locale resolution via the request and locale modification via request and response. To configure LocaleResolver we need to define a bean definition with an id '*localeResolver*' in the spring beans XML configuration file. If no bean is defined with this id in the context, the default implementation is AcceptHeaderLocaleResolver, simply using the request's locale provided by the respective HTTP header.
ThemeResolver	ThemeResolver provides an abstraction for resolving themes for the web application, which is useful for creating personalized layouts.
HandlerMapping	The HandlerMapping is responsible to map the incoming request to the handler that can handle the request.
HandlerAdapter	The HandlerAdapter implementation takes the responsibility to identify the type of the handler and invoke its appropriate methods. The use of HandlerAdapter facilitates us to use Plain Old Java Objects (POJOs) with any method encapsulating the handler behavior, as a handler.
HandlerExceptionResolver	The HandlerExceptionResolver is by DispatcherServlet to handle the exceptions thrown by the HandlerInterceptor or handler.
RequestToViewNameTranslator	The RequestToViewNameTranslator id used for translating an incoming request to a view name when no view name is explicitly supplied under the ModelAndView object returned by the HandlerExceptionResolver or handler.
ViewResolver	The ViewResolver is by DispatcherServlet to resolve the view name encapsulated in the ModelAndView object returned by the handler, to locate view object.

All the special framework objects described in Table 12.2 are initialized by the DispatcherServlet using the WebApplicationContext and based on the detectAllXXX initialization parameters configured to this servlet as described in Table 12.1. Once if all these objects are initialized successfully, the DispatcherServlet instance is put into service, which provides an entry point to serve the client requests using the special framework objects.

In this section we learnt about the initialization process of DispatcherServlet that prepares the context for the Spring Web MVC application. The following section explains the workflow of the request processing when Dispatcher Servlet receives the request.

12.3 DESCRIBING THE SPRING WEB MVC REQUEST PROCESSING WORKFLOW

When a DispatcherServlet receives a request it performs various operations to process the request. The brief description of the request processing workflow was explained in the previous chapter This section and the following ones give you a detailed description of the complete workflow of Spring Web MVC request processing. To easily understand the complete request processing workflow of Spring Web MVC we can divide it broadly into the following eight phases.

1. **Phase 1:** Prepare the request context.
2. **Phase 2:** Locate the handler.
3. **Phase 3:** Execute Interceptors preHandle methods.
4. **Phase 4:** Invoke handler.
5. **Phase 5:** Execute Interceptors postHandle methods.
6. **Phase 6:** Handle Exceptions.
7. **Phase 7:** Render the view.
8. **Phase 8:** Execute Interceptors afterCompletion methods.

Figure 12.1 shows the high-level block diagram of the eight phases that the request processing work flow is divided into.

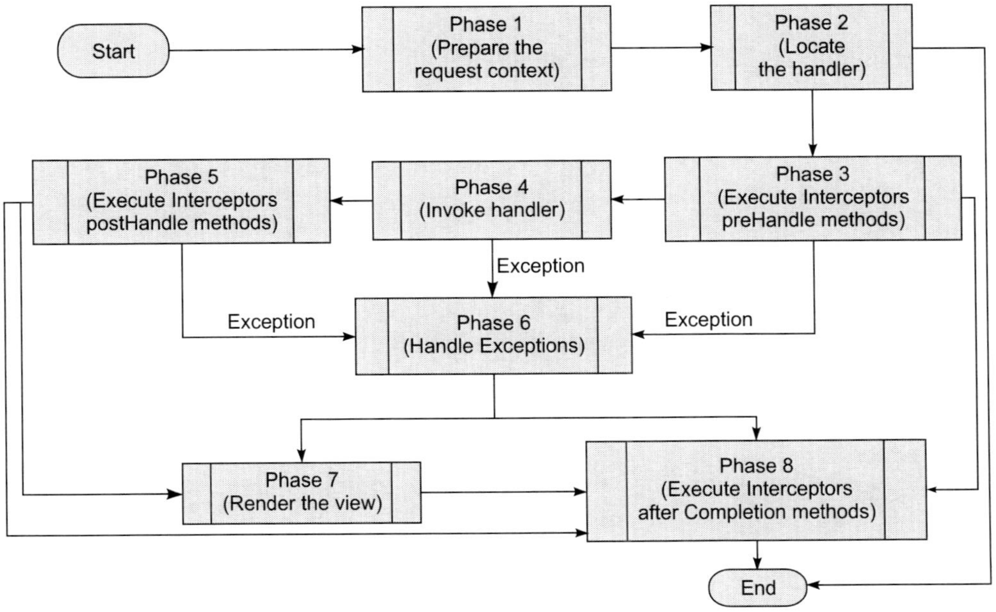

FIGURE 12.1 Flow diagram showing the high-level block diagram of Spring Web MVC request processing workflow

The brief explanation of the eight phases is as follows:

Phase 1: Prepare the request context

The request processing workflow starts by preparing the request context in which the request is set with some framework objects to make them available for the various objects involved in the workflow.

Phase 2: Locate the handler

After the request context is prepared successfully the workflow continues with finding an appropriate handler to handle this request (that is, in Phase 2). This is done with the help of the HandlerMappings configured with the application. If this phase locates a handler then the result of this phase is HandlerExecutionChain and in case the handler cannot be located then the *HttpServlet Response.SC_NOT_FOUND* response error status is set and the request processing is terminated.

Phase 3: Execute Interceptors preHandle methods

After the HandlerExecutionChain is located in Phase 2, the workflow continues with this phase. In this phase the preHandle method on the HandlerInterceptor objects available in the HandlerExecutionChain is located in Phase 2. If the preHandle() method returns false then the workflow moves to Phase 8. If the preHandle() method throws any exception the workflow moves to Phase 6. If all the preHandle() methods return true then the workflow moves to the next phase.

Phase 4: Invoke handler

After the interceptor's preHandle methods are executed successfully returning true then the workflow continues to invoke the handler using an appropriate HandlerAdapter. The outcome of this phase may return ModelAndView object or throw an exception. If the handler throws an exception then the workflow moves to Phase 6, if not it moves to Phase 5.

Phase 5: Execute Interceptors postHandle methods

In this phase, the postHandle method of HandlerInterceptor objects is executed in the reverse order as they are registered. If the postHandle method throws an exception then the workflow moves to Phase 6. If the ModelAndView returned in Phase 4 (that is, by handler) is null then the control moves to Phase 8, if not it moves to to Phase-7.

Phase 6: Handle Exceptions

This phase of workflow is executed if there is an exception while executing the handler or, preHandle or postHandle methods of HandlerInterceptor. This phase is responsible to handle the exception and return ModelAndView if an appropriate HandlerExceptionResolver is located. If this phase results in a valid ModelAndView object reference then the workflow proceeds to Phase 7, if not it does to Phase 8.

Phase 7: Render the view

This phase of the workflow renders a response to the requesting client as per the outcome of Phase 4 or Phase 6, that is, ModelAndView.

Phase 8: Execute Interceptors afterCompletion methods

This is the last phase of the workflow, which is executed in any circumstances once if the workflow completes Phase 2 successfully and the respective HandlerInterceptor preHandle() method returns true (that is, executed in Phase 3). In this phase afterCompletion method of HandlerInterceptor objects are invoked in the reverse order as they are registered, which allows us to do finalizations (doing proper resource cleanup).

As we have discussed all the eight phases briefly it is time to discuss all these phases in detail looking at the various configurations respectively. The following sections throughout this chapter explains, one after the other, all these eight phase in detail. Let us start with the first phase, that is, prepare the request context.

12.4 PHASE 1: PREPARE THE REQUEST CONTEXT

In the first phase of the request processing, the DispatcherServlet prepares the request context by setting the framework objects into the request scope. Here the framework objects are WebApplicationContext, LocaleResolver, ThemeResolver, and ThemeSource. These objects are set into the request scope to make them available to handler and view objects, so that the handler or view objects can use these objects to communicate with the framework and collect some runtime details. Apart from preparing and setting the framework objects into the request scope, DispatcherServlet resolves the request using the MultipartResolver so that if the request contains multipart data then it wraps the request in a MultipartHttpRequestRequest type object. In case if there is any problem in this process the request processing is terminated by throwing an exception. Once if this process is done successfully the request process workflow continues to the next phase, that is, locate the handler. The following section explains the second phase of the request process workflow.

12.5 PHASE 2: LOCATE THE HANDLER

After preparing the request context the DispatcherServlet locates the handler that can handle this request. The DispatcherServlet uses the registered HandlerMapping's and collects the Handler ExecutionChain object. The HandlerExecutionChain object encapsulates the HandlerInterceptor's and the handler object (that is, controller). The following diagram shows the operations performed under this step.

Step 1: Prepare an HandlerMapping Iterator

As shown in the preceding figure the workflow of Phase 2 starts with preparing an Iterator object of the Collection storing the HandlerMapping objects. This Collection object is created while the DispatcherServlet is being initialized, that is, in its initialization phase. Thereafter, the first element is retrieved from the iterator. This cannot be an empty collection since if there is no HandlerMapping configured in the context then DispatcherServlet uses BeanNameUrlHandlerMapping as default handler mapping.

Step 2: Identify the handler

After Step 1 the locate handler workflow invokes the getHandler() method of the current HandlerMapping object in the iteration. If the getHandler() method returns null, which indicates that the current HandlerMapping failed to locate the handler for this request then the workflow proceeds to the next step. If the getHandler() method returns a valid HandlerExecutionChain object reference then the Phase 2 workflow is finished delegating the control to Phase 3.

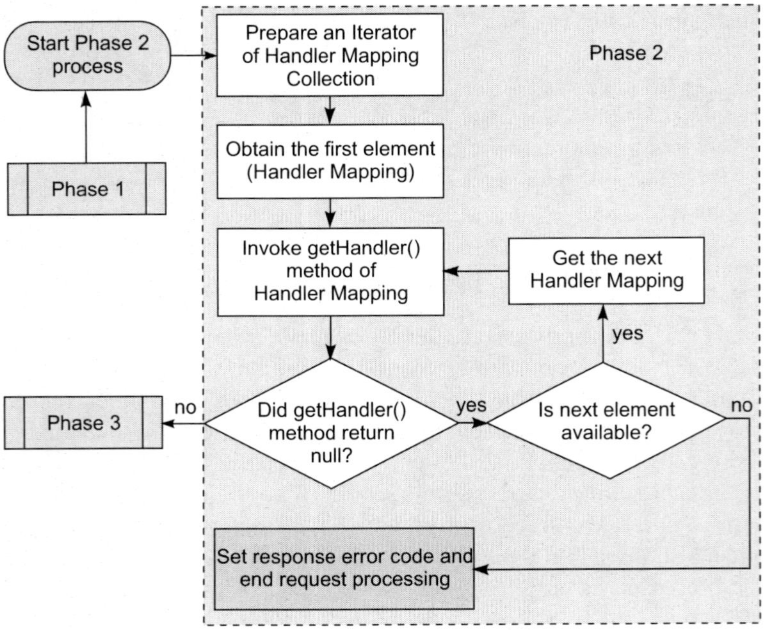

FIGURE 12.2 Flow diagram for Phase 2 of Spring Web MVC request processing workflow

Step 3: Move to next element

If the HandlerMapping in the preceding step fails to locate the handler then the workflow proceeds to get the next HandlerMapping from the iterator prepared in Step 1. If the next element is available then the process moves to Step 2, if not then an *HttpServletResponse.SC_NOT_FOUND* response error status is set and the request processing is terminated.

From the preceding steps it can be understood that the workflow in this phase, invokes the getHandler(HttpServletRequest) method on each of the HandlerMapping until the method returns a valid HandlerExecutionChain object. If all the HandlerMappings fails to determine the handler then a *HttpServletResponse.SC_NOT_FOUND* response error status is set and the request processing is terminated. If the HandlerExecutionChain is located the workflow proceeds to the next phase, in which it invokes the HandlerInterceptors. Before we discuss the next phase we need to learn about the HandlerMappings and its configurations.

12.5.1 The HandlerMappings

The HandlerMapping is responsible for mapping the incoming request to the handler that can handle the request. As discussed in the above section, when the DispatcherServlet receives the request it delegates the request to the HandlerMapping, which identifies the appropriate HandlerExecutionChain that can handle the request. The Spring Web MVC framework provides customizable navigation strategies. Spring provides built-in navigation strategies as determining the handler based on the request URL mapping which is again based on the bean name. Apart from the built-in navigation strategies Spring allows defining system-specific built strategy, which can be done by writing a class implementing the HandlerMapping interface. The Spring built-in HandlerMapping implementations are:

1. BeanNameUrlHandlerMapping
2. SimpleUrlHandlerMapping
3. ControllerClassNameHandlerMapping
4. CommonsPathMapHandlerMapping

Now, let us discuss these handler mappings in detail and learn how to configure each of them.

12.5.1.1 BeanNameUrlHandlerMapping

The org.springframework.web.servlet.handler.BeanNameUrlHandlerMapping is one of the implementation of HandlerMapping interface. This implementation defines the navigation strategy that maps the request URL's servlet-path to the bean names. This handler mapping strategy is very simple but powerful, and is the default when no handler mapping is configured in the application context. The following code snippet shows the sample configuration of this handler mapping.

Code Snippet

```
<beans>
  <beanid="handlerMapping"class="
org.springframework.web.servlet.handler.BeanNameUrlHandlerMapping"/>

  <bean  name="/addEmployee.spring"
         class="com.santosh.spring.AddEmployeeController">
         <!-set the dependencies -->
  </bean>
  <bean name="/removeEmployee.spring"
         class="com.santosh.spring.RemoveEmployeeController">
         <!-set the dependencies -->
  </bean>
</beans>
```

According to the above configuration the request with the URL <context path>/addEmployee.spring will be handled by the AddEmployeeController and the request with the URL <context path>/removeEmployee.spring will be handled by the RemoveEmployeeController.

> **Note:** The BeanNameUrlHandlerMapping is the default handler mapping when no handler mapping is configured in the application context.

We want to configure the BeanNameUrlHandlerMapping explicitly only in two cases. One is when we want to configure multiple handler mappings along with this handler mapping also as one of them. Second is when we want to configure handler interceptors (we will discuss how to configure interceptors in the next sections under Phase 3 of request processing workflow).

12.5.1.2 SimpleUrlHandlerMapping

The org.springframework.web.servlet.handler.SimpleUrlHandlerMapping is one of the implementations of HandlerMapping interface. This implementation defines the navigation strategy that maps the request URLs servlet-path to the mappings configured. That is, it locates the handler (controller) by matching the request URL's servlet path with the key of the given properties or map. In this case we need to inject properties or map object that describes the mappings between the request URL path and handler beans (controllers). The SimpleUrlHandlerMapping supports two options to configure the mappings—one to bean names and other to bean instances.

12.5.1.2.1 Option 1

This is one of the options SimpleUrlHandlerMapping provides us to map the URL path to the handler bean id or name. Here we need to set the 'mappings' property of the SimpleUrlHandlerMapping. The mappings property is defined of java.util.Property type. The following code snippet shows the configuration of SimpleUrlHandlerMapping mapping the paths to bean names.

Code snippet

```
<beans>
  <bean id="handlerMapping" class="
org.springframework.web.servlet.handler.SimpleUrlHandlerMapping">
  <property name="mappings">
    <props>
      <prop key="/addEmployee.spring">addEmp</prop>
      <prop key="/removeEmployee.spring">removeEmp</prop>
      <prop key="/searchEmployee.spring">searchEmp</prop>
    </props>
  </property>
</bean>

<bean id="addEmp" class="com.santosh.spring.AddEmployeeController">
  <!–configure dependencies-->
</bean>
<bean id="removeEmp" class="com.santosh.spring.RemoveEmployeeController">
  <!–configure dependencies-->
</bean>
<bean id="searchEmp" class="com.santosh.spring.SearchEmployeeController">
  <!–configure dependencies-->
</bean>
```

According to the above configuration the request with the URL <context path>/addEmployee.spring will be handled by the AddEmployeeController, the request with the URL <context path>/removeEmployee.spring will be handled by the RemoveEmployeeController, and the request with the URL <context path>/searchEmployee.spring will be handled by the SearchEmployeeController.

This configuration is suitable for configuring non-singleton beans but configuring mappings to bean names for singleton beans is not recommended since the handler mapping in this case has to request the WebApplicationContext for the bean, which is definitely an unnecessary overhead. To configure singleton beans the option described below is most suitable.

12.5.1.2.2 Option 2

In this case a SimpleUrlHandlerMapping provides us to map the URL path to the handler bean object. Here we need to set the 'urlMap' property of the SimpleUrlHandlerMapping. The urlMap property is defined of java.util.Map type. The following code snippet shows the configuration of Simple UrlHandlerMapping mapping the paths to bean objects.

Code Snippet

```
<bean id="handlerMapping" class="
org.springframework.web.servlet.handler.SimpleUrlHandlerMapping ">
  <property name="urlMap">
    <map>
      <entry key="/addEmployee.spring">
        <ref local="addEmp"/>
      </entry>
      <entry key="/removeEmployee.spring">
        <ref local="removeEmp"/>
      </entry>
      <entry key="/searchEmployee.spring">
        <ref local="searchEmp"/>
      </entry>
    </map>
  </property>
</bean>

<bean id="addEmp" class="com.santosh.spring.AddEmployeeController">
  <!–configure dependencies–>
</bean>
<bean id="removeEmp" class="com.santosh.spring.RemoveEmployeeController">
  <!–configure dependencies–>
</bean>
<bean id="searchEmp" class="com.santosh.spring.SearchEmployeeController">
  <!–configure dependencies–>
</bean>
```

According to the above configuration the request with the URL <context path>/addEmployee.spring will be handled by the AddEmployeeController, the request with the URL <context path>/removeEmployee.spring will be handled by the RemoveEmployeeController and the request with the URL <context path>/searchEmployee.spring will be handled by the SearchEmployeeController.

This configuration is suitable for configuring singleton beans.

12.5.1.3 ControllerClassNameHandlerMapping

The *org.springframework.web.servlet.mvc.support.ControllerClassNameHandlerMapping* is the implementation of HandlerMapping interface. This handler mapping implementation is newly introduced in spring 2.0. The ControllerClassNameHandlerMapping follows a simple convention for generating URL path mappings. The convention for simple Controller implementations (those that handle a single request type) is to take the short name of the controller Class, remove the 'Controller' suffix if it exists and return the remaining text, lowercased, as the mapping, with a leading /. For example, if the controller class name is com.santosh.spring.AddEmployeeController then the path is /addemployee*, and for controller class RemoveEmployeeController it is /removeemployee*. The following code snippet shows the sample configuration of ControllerClassNameHandlerMapping.

Code Snippet

```
<bean id="handlerMapping"
class="org.springframework.web.servlet.mvc.support.ControllerClassNameHandlerMapping"/>

<bean id="addEmp" class="com.santosh.spring.AddEmployeeController">
  <!–configure dependencies-->
</bean>
<bean id="removeEmp" class="com.santosh.spring.RemoveEmployeeController">
  <!–configure dependencies-->
</bean>
```

According to the above configuration the request with the URL <context path>/addemployee will be handled by the AddEmployeeController, the request with the URL <context path>/removeemployee will be handled by the RemoveEmployeeController.

12.5.1.4 CommonsPathMapHandlerMapping

The org.springframework.web.servlet.handler.CommonsPathMapHandlerMapping is one of the implementation of HandlerMapping interface. The CommonsPathMapHandlerMapping is designed to recognize Commons Attributes metadata attributes of type PathMap defined in the application Controllers and automatically wires them into the current DispatcherServlet's WebApplication Context. To use this HandlerMapping the controller class must have a class level metadata of the form @org.springframework.web.servlet.handler.commonsattributes.PathMap("/mypath.spring"). We can configure multiple path maps for a single controller. The following code snippet shows the sample controller class with a single path map configuration.

Code Snippet

```
package com.santosh.spring;

import org.springframework.web.servlet.mvc.*;
/**
* @org.springframework.web.servlet.handler.commonsattributes.PathMap(
"/addEmployee.spring")
*/
public class AddEmployeeController implements Controller {

  public void handleRequest(
        HttpServletRequest request,
        HttpServletResponse response)throws Exception {
    ...
  }
  ...
}
```

The preceding code snippet shows the AddEmployeeController, which is an implementation of simple Controller, mapped to '/addEmployee.spring' path.

> **Note:** To use commons attributes path mapping, we must compile application classes with Commons Attributes, and run the Commons Attributes indexer tool on the application classes, which must be in a Jar rather than in WEB-INF/classes as an individual classes.

Now, as we have discussed about the important spring built-in implementations of handler mappings and their configurations and we know that we can configure multiple handler mappings in the application context let us look at how to configure multiple handler mappings in the context.

12.5.1.4 Configuring multiple handler mappings

We can configure multiple handler mappings in an application context. In such a case we need to configure an additional property 'order' that takes 'int' value on each of the handler mapping. The following code snippet shows the multiple handler mappings configuration.

Code Snippet

```
<bean id="handlerMapping1" class=" org.springframework.web.servlet.handler.
ControllerClassNameHandlerMapping">
  <property name="order">
   <value type="int">0</value>
  </property>
</bean>

<bean id="handlerMapping2" class="
org.springframework.web.servlet.handler.BeanNameUrlHandlerMapping">
  <property name="order">
   <value type="int">1</value>
  </property>
</bean>

<bean id="handlerMapping3" class="
org.springframework.web.servlet.handler.SimpleUrlHandlerMapping ">
  <property name="urlMap">
    <map>
      <entry key="/addEmployee.spring">
        <bean class="com.santosh.spring.AddEmployeeController">
          <!–configure dependencies-->
        </bean>
      </entry>
  <entry key="/removeEmployee.spring">
      <ref local="removeEmp"/>
  </entry>
  <entry key="/searchEmployee.spring">
      <ref local="searchEmp"/>
  </entry>
  </map>
  </property>
```

```
  <property name="order">
   <value type="int">3</value>
  </property>
</bean>
<bean id="removeEmp" class="com.santosh.spring.RemoveEmployeeController">
  <!–configure dependencies-->
</bean>
<bean id="searchEmp" class="com.santosh.spring.SearchEmployeeController">
  <!–configure dependencies-->
</bean>
<!–similarly other controller bean declarations –>
```

The preceding code snippet shows how to define three handler mappings where the first preference is given to the ControllerClassNameHandlerMapping, and if it cannot determine the handler by resolving the path then the next handler mapping that is BeanNameUrlHandlerMapping is used, and so on.

> **Note:** If the 'detectAllHandlerMappings' initialization parameter of DispatcherServlet is confi-gured to false then multiple handler mappings are not detected instead only the bean with a name handlerMapping is located as a HandlerMapping.

12.6 PHASE 3: EXECUTE INTERCEPTORS PREHANDLE METHODS

After successfully locating the HandlerExecutionChain in Phase 2 (that is, locate the handler) the DispatcherServlet executes the HandlerInterceptors described by the HandlerExecutionChain returned by the HandlerMapping. The HandlerInterceptor gives us an opportunity to add common pre- and post-processing behavior without needing to modify each handler implementation. The Handler Interceptor is basically similar to a Servlet 2.3 Filter. Applications can register any number of existing or custom interceptors for certain groups of handlers. The HandlerInterceptor is called before the appropriate HandlerAdapter triggers the execution of the handler itself. In this phase the preHandle method of HandlerInterceptor objects is executed to perform handler pre-processings. Figure 12.3 shows the various operations performed in this phase.

The following steps explain the Phase 3 workflow in detail.

Step 1: Prepare counters

As shown in Fig. 12.3 the workflow of Phase 3 starts with setting the interceptorIndex to -1 and the count to 0. The interceptorIndex is used to track the index of the interceptor in the list that has completed the preHandle processing successfully, which is further used in Phase 8 to execute the afterCompletion methods of the respective HandlerInterceptors whereas the count is used to iterate through the list of interceptors. After the counters are prepared if there are any interceptors configured, that is, if the interceptor's length is greater than 0 (zero) then the workflow proceeds to Step 2, if not, it proceeds to the next phase, that is, Phase 4.

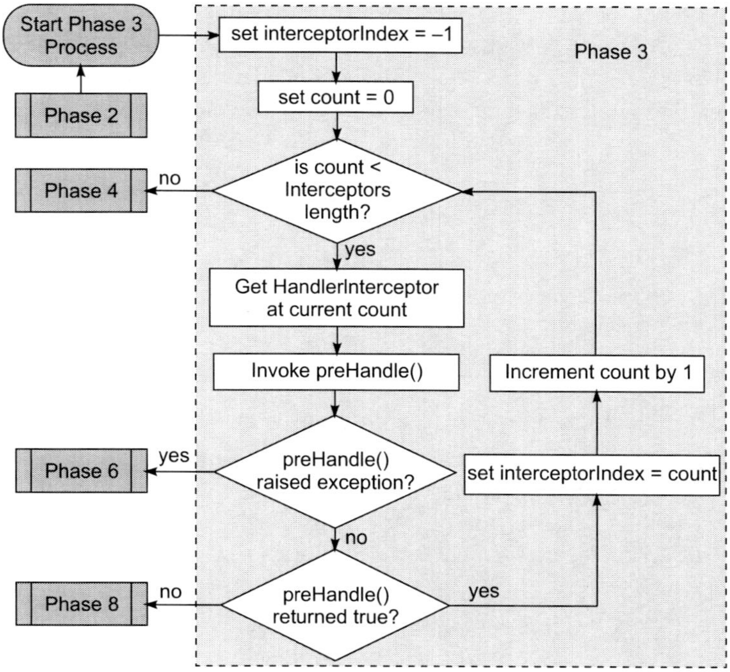

FIGURE 12.3 Flow diagram explaining Phase 3 of Spring Web MVC request processing

Step 2: Obtain HandlerInterceptor

After the counters are prepared successfully, DispatcherServlet obtains the HandlerInterceptor at the current index from the interceptor's list.

Step 3: Invoke interceptors preHandle() method

After obtaining the HandlerInterceptor, DispatcherServlet invokes preHandle() method on the interceptor obtained in the preceding step.

- If the preHandle() method throws an exception then the workflow proceeds to Phase 6 (that is, Handle Exceptions Phase).
- If the preHandle() method executes without throwing an exception but returns *false* then the workflow proceeds to Phase 8 (that is, execute interceptors afterCompletion methods).
- In case the preHandle() method returns *true* then the workflow continues with the next step of this phase.

Step 4: Advance the counters

This step of the Phase 3 workflow executes if the preHandle() method of the current interceptor returns *true* as explained in the preceding step. In this step first the interceptorIndex is set with the current count value indicating that the interceptors up to this index have completed the pre-processing successfully. Then the count is incremented by one. Now, it verifies whether the current count is less than the interceptor's length. If so then the workflow proceeds to Step 2 of this phase, if not the workflow proceeds to Phase 4.

In this section we learnt what is the HandlerInterceptor how the preHandle() method of the HandlerInterceptor participates in Phase 3, where the other two methods postHandle() and afterCompletion() are involved in Phase 5 and Phase 8 of the workflow respectively, which we will learn as we move on through this chapter. But as of now let us discuss how to write and configure the HandlerInterceptor.

12.6.1 Using HandlerInterceptor

Using the HandlerInterceptor includes the following two steps:

Step 1: Write an HandlerInterceptor implementation
Step 2: Configure the interceptor

Let us discuss these steps in detail.

Step 1: Writing a HandlerInterceptor implementation

The HandlerInterceptor can be used for implementing pre-processing aspects, for example, for authorization checks, or common handler behavior like locale or theme changes. The Spring framework includes built-in HandlerInterceptor's implementing the most common pre-processing concerns like locale and theme change. The following are the built-in HandlerInterceptor implementations.

- org.springframework.web.servlet.i18n.LocaleChangeInterceptor
- org.springframework.web.servlet.theme.ThemeChangeInterceptor

Apart from the built-in HandlerInterceptors we can write HandlerInterceptor implementations encapsulating the custom pre- and post-processing logics. The following code snippet shows the implementation methods of HandlerInterceptor.

Code Snippet

```
package com.santosh.spring;

import javax.servlet.http.HttpServletRequest;
import javax.servlet.http.HttpServletResponse;

import org.springframework.web.servlet.HandlerInterceptor;
import org.springframework.web.servlet.ModelAndView;

public class MyHandlerInterceptor implements HandlerInterceptor {

  public boolean preHandle(
      HttpServletRequest request,
      HttpServletResponse response,
      Object handler) throws Exception {

    // DO some preprocessing like check the security etc
```

```
    /* return boolean value accordingly,
    * if you want to continue the interceptor chain then return true
    */
    return false;
  }

  public void postHandle(
      HttpServletRequest request, HttpServletResponse response,
      Object handler, ModelAndView mandv) throws Exception {

    // DO some postprocessing
    //This method is executed in Phase-5
  }

  public void afterCompletion(
      HttpServletRequest request, HttpServletResponse response,
      Object handler, Exception exception)
      throws Exception {
    // DO finalizations
    //This method is executed in Phase-8
  }
}
```

As shown in the preceding code snippet instead of implementing the HandlerInterceptor we can even extend the HandlerInterceptorAdapter class. The HandlerInterceptorAdapter is an abstract class providing an empty implementation for all the three method of the HandlerInterceptor. That is the HandlerInterceptorAdapter is simply an adapter class for the HandlerInterceptor interface.

Step 2: Configuring the interceptors

In general an interceptor chain is defined per HandlerMapping bean. To apply an interceptor chain to a group of handlers, we need to map the interceptors to the HandlerMapping bean using its "interceptors" property of type java.util.List. The following code snippet shows the sample configuration.

Code Snippet

```
<bean id="myinterceptor" class="com.santosh.spring.MyHandlerInterceptor"/>

<bean id="handlerMapping"
class="org.springframework.web.servlet.handler.BeanNameUrlHandlerMapping">
  <property name="interceptors">
    <list>
      <ref local="myinterceptor"/>
    </list>
  </property>
</bean>
```

As discussed earlier an application can register any number of existing or custom interceptors for certain groups of handlers. In case of multiple interceptors being configured they are executed in the same order as they are configured with the handler mapping. As we move on through this chapter we will have an opportunity to learn the built-in interceptors, for example, under the internationalization concept we can learn the configurations of LocaleChangeInterceptor, etc. As of now we will continue with the next phase (that is, Phase 4) of the Spring web MVC request processing workflow.

12.7 PHASE 4: INVOKE HANDLER

In this phase of Spring web MVC request processing workflow the DispatcherServlet delegates the request to the handler that is located by the HandlerMapping in Phase 2. DispatcherServlet uses HandlerAdapter to delegate the request to the handler located to handle this request. Figure 12.4 shows the various operations performed under this phase.

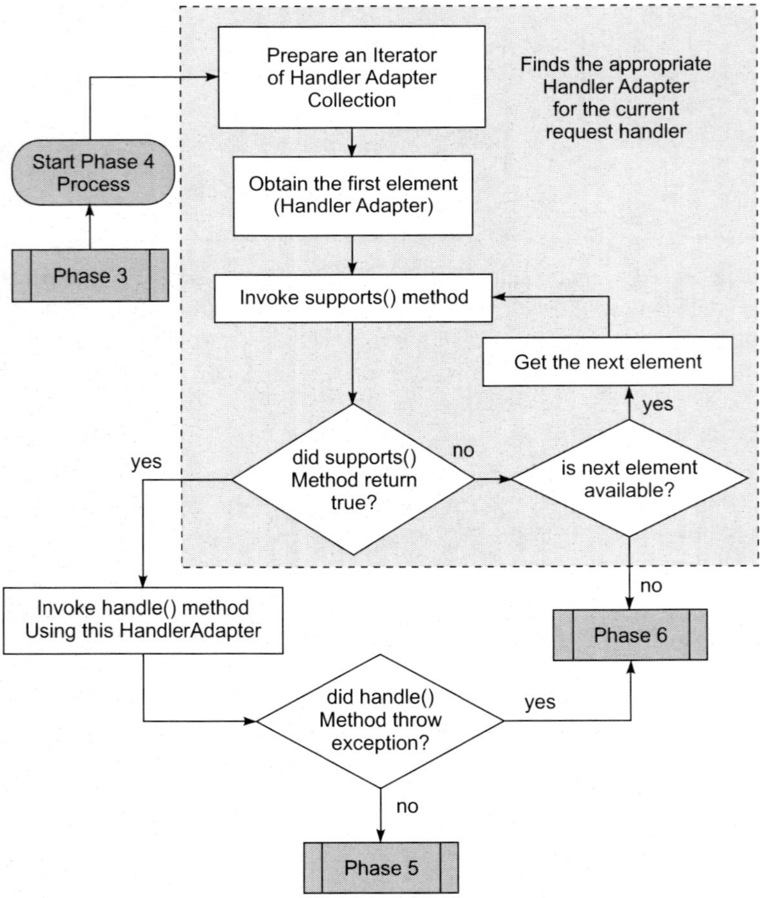

FIGURE 12.4 Flow diagram explaining Phase 4 of Spring Web MVC request processing

The following steps explains the Phase 4 workflow in detail.

Step 1: Prepare a iterator of HandlerAdapter collection

As shown in Fig. 12.4 the Phase 4 workflow starts with preparing an iterator of the collection representing the HandlerAdapter objects configured in the application. The handlerAdapters collection is initialized in the initialization phase of the DispatcherServlet where it finds all HandlerAdapters in the ApplicationContext. If no HandlerAdapter beans are defined in the application then the default is considered as SimpleControllerHandlerAdapter. Thus the handlerAdapters collection contains at least one element.

Step 2: Get HandlerAdapter

In this step the workflow obtains the next element from the iterator prepared in Step 1 and casts it into HandlerAdapter type reference.

Step 3: Find is HandlerAdapter compatible

After getting the HandlerAdapter of the current iteration the workflow continues with finding whether this HandlerAdapter is suitable for the handler located in Phase 2. This is done by invoking supports() method on the HandlerAdapter. If it returns *true* then it indicates that this HandlerAdapter supports the handler. In such a case the workflow continues to the next step. If the supports() method returns *false* then the workflow continues finding whether there is a next element in the handlerAdapter Collection, if found then it moves to Step 2. If not then ServletException is thrown, delegating the workflow to Phase 6.

Step 4: Execute handler

After successfully locating the HandlerAdapter that supports the handler that is located in Phase 2, the workflow proceeds to invoke handle() method of HandlerAdapter which further delegates the request to the handler (may be controller). If the handle() method throws any exception then the workflow proceeds to Phase 6, if not it proceeds to Phase 5 after collecting the ModelAndView object reference returned by the handle() method.

Now, as we have discussed about the workflow of Phase 4, let us discuss HandlerAdapters and some important handler types.

12.7.1 The HandlerAdapter

The HandlerAdapter implementation takes the responsibility of identifying the type of handler and invokes its appropriate methods. The use of HandlerAdapter facilitates us to use Plain Old Java Objects (POJOs) with any method encapsulating the handler behavior, as a handler. Spring provides the built-in HandlerAdapter implementations supporting different types of handlers to work with. The various types of handlers supported by the Spring built-in HandlerAdapter are controller types, HttpRequestHandler types, Servlet types, and ThrowawayController types. The Spring built-in HandlerAdapter implementations are described in Table 12.3.

TABLE 12.3 Spring built-in HandlerAdapter implementations

HandlerAdapter class	*Description*
SimpleControllerHandlerAdapter	HandlerAdapter implementation to handle request using the Controller type of handlers, that is, the handlers that implement Controller interface. This is most commonly used type of handlers in Spring.
ThrowawayControllerHandlerAdapter	HandlerAdapter implementation to handle request using the ThrowawayController type of handlers, that is, the handlers that implement ThrowawayController interface. ThrowawayController is an alternative to the Controller interface, for implementing handlers that are not aware of the Servlet API. The main advantage of this controller is that these are testable without HttpServletRequest and HttpServletResponse mocks, just like WebWork actions.
HttpRequestHandlerAdapter	This is a new HandlerAdapter implementation in Spring 2.0 that supports to handle HttpRequestHandler type of handlers.
SimpleServletHandlerAdapter	HandlerAdapter implementation to handle request using the simple Servlet. This adapter implementation enables us to use any existing servlets to work with the DispatcherServlet.

Note: By default only the SimpleControllerHandlerAdapter and ThrowawayControllerHandler-Adapter handler adapters are available to the DispatcherServlet. Other handler adapters need to be explicitly configured, as normal as other beans in the context Spring Beans XML configuration file of DispatcherServlet.

Apart from the built-in HandlerAdapter's Spring allows defining system-specific built adapters, which can be done by writing a class implementing org.springframework.web.servlet.HandlerAdapter interface. The HandlerAdapter interface declares three methods (supports(), handle() and getLast Modified()) that have to be implemented by the HandlerAdapter implementations to help Dispatcher Servlet in delegating the request to the handlers. Table 12.4 describes the methods of HandlerAdapter.

TABLE 12.4 Methods of HandlerAdapter

Method	*Description*
boolean supports(Object handler)	Specifies whether the given handler type is supported by this adapter, that is, whether this adapter is capable to use the given handler in handling the request. If the adapter understands the given handler type then it returns 'true' else it returns 'false'.
ModelAndView handle(HttpServletRequest request, HttpServletResponse response, Object handler) throws Exception	Handles the request using the given handler. This method is invoked on this adapter if its supports() method for this handler returns true. After the request handling returns ModelAndView object that describes the model data and the view (more about ModelAndView is explained in the next section). This method can return true to describe the DispatcherServlet that the response is generated and thus it does not requires to delegate the request to any view.
long getLastModified(HttpServletRequest request, Object handler)	This is same as of HttpServlet's getLastModified() method. Can return -1 if the given handler does not support to determine the last modified date.

As described above, that the handler adapter should implement all these three methods as described in Table 12.4. The following code snippet shows the sample implementation of HandlerAdapter.

Code Snippet

```
package com.santosh.spring;

import java.util.Map;

import javax.servlet.http.HttpServletRequest;
import javax.servlet.http.HttpServletResponse;

import org.springframework.web.servlet.HandlerAdapter;
import org.springframework.web.servlet.ModelAndView;

public class MyHandlerAdapter implements HandlerAdapter {

  public boolean supports(Object handler) {
    return (handler instanceof com.santosh.spring.MyHandler);
  }

  public ModelAndView handle(
        HttpServletRequest request,
        HttpServletResponse response,
        Object handler) throws Exception {

    MyHandler myHandler=(MyHandler)handler;
    String view=myHandler.process(request, response);
    Map model=(Map)request.getAttribute("model");
    if (view==null) return null;
    else if (model==null) return new ModelAndView(view);
    else  return new ModelAndView(view, model);
  }

  public long getLastModified(HttpServletRequest request, Object handler) {
    return -1;
  }
}
```

The preceding code snippet shows a sample implementation of HandlerAdapter. The MyHandlerAdapter implementation shown in the preceding code snippet is designed to support the handlers of type com.santosh.spring.MyHandler, that is, all the types that implement the MyHandler interface. Moreover, to handle the request the adapter invokes the process() method of the given handler. The process() method can return null or a view name and the model data can be encapsulated into a Map saving into request scope. The following code snippet shows the MyHandler interface that have to be implemented by the handlers to be processed by the MyHandlerAdapter.

Code Snippet

```
package com.santosh.spring;

import javax.servlet.http.HttpServletRequest;
import javax.servlet.http.HttpServletResponse;

public interface MyHandler {

   String process(
      HttpServletRequest request,
      HttpServletResponse response)throws Exception;
}
```

We have implemented the handler adapter to support our own type of handlers. Now, we want to declare the handler adapter as the other adapters making it available to DispatcherServlet. As we know that SimpleControllerHandlerAdapter and ThrowawayControllerHandlerAdapter handler adapters are only by default available to the DispatcherServlet and the other adapters have to be configured explicitly, the following code snippet shows the bean declaration of the MyHandlerAdapter.

Code Snippet

```
<bean class="com.santosh.spring.MyHandlerAdapter"/>
```

The bean definition shown in the preceding code snippet needs to be included into the context Spring Beans XML configuration file.

> **Note:** Even though Spring supports implementing the custom handler adapters that enables handling the request using user defined type of handlers (without making them depend on the spring API), however it is recommended to use the Spring Controller infrastructure to implement the handler. The custom handler adapter option is given to support some situations where we want to use the existing handlers without rewriting them as spring defined controllers.

In this section we learnt about the HandlerAdapter, the various built-in implementations and how to implement custom HandlerAdapter. The most common way to implement handlers is as a controller. The next chapter (that is, Chapter 13) is completely dedicated to explain the various controllers available in Struts framework. It can be identified from the discussion in the preceding sections that the HandlerAdapter uses handler to handle the request and results returning the ModelAndView object. Thus let us learn about the ModelAndView before we continue to learn Phase 5 of the request processing workflow.

12.7.2 About ModelAndView

The ModelAndView is a value object designed to hold model and view making it possible for a handler to return both model and view in a single return value. The ModelAndView object represents a model and view specified by the handler, which are resolved by the DispatcherServlet using the special framework objects as ViewResolver and View. The view is an object that can describe a view name in the form of String which will be resolved by a ViewResolver object to locate View object, alternatively, a View object directly. The model is a Map, enabling to specify multiple objects. All the technologies that are used to render the view may not access the model data in the same way, like JSP/JSTL uses the model data in request, session, or application scope whereas the technologies like Velocity does not have support to access application scoped data and generally does not depend on HTTP-specific constructs to access the model data. Thus, it is ever a better practice to design the controllers independent of view technologies (especially in describing the model data to the view), which enables us to freely use any view technology to render the view and allow to migrate from one view technology to other without affecting the controllers. This is the reason Spring Web MVC framework describes the models as a simple java.util.Map object in the ModelAndView. Now, as we have understood the importance of ModelAndView in Spring Web MVC let us have a close look into the ModelAndView class.

The ModelAndView class includes seven constructors providing the convenience for constructing ModelAndView object with different combinations. Table 12.5 describes all the seven constructors of ModelAndView.

TABLE 12.5 Constructors of ModelAndView class

Constructor	*Description*
ModelAndView()	Constructor for instantiating using bean-style.
ModelAndView(String viewName)	Convenient constructor to use when there is no model data to expose. The argument specifies the view name to be resolved by ViewResolver to locate the View that can render the view.
ModelAndView(View view)	Convenient constructor to use when there is no model data to expose, same as the preceding constructor. The argument specifies the View object that can render the view.
ModelAndView(String viewName, Map model)	Convenient constructor to create new ModelAndView with given a view name and a model Map.
ModelAndView(View view, Map model)	Convenient constructor to create new ModelAndView with given a View object and a model Map.
ModelAndView (String viewName, String modelName, Object modelObject)	Convenient constructor to create new ModelAndView with the given view name and a single model object.
ModelAndView(View view, String modelName, Object modelObject)	Convenient constructor to create new ModelAndView with the given View object and a single model object.

Note: The model data supplied in the form of Map to the ModelAndView is copied into the ModelMap object internally managed by this class. Thus, we should not consider modifying the supplied Map after supplying it to this class, for modifying the model data.

The ModelAndView implements the various methods for setting, and getting its properties. Table 12.6 describes the various methods of ModelAndView.

TABLE 12.6 Methods of ModelAndView object

Method	*Description*
void setViewName(String viewName)	Allows setting a view name, to be resolved by the ViewResolver. If the view name or View is already set, this will override the value.
String getViewName()	Return the view name encapsulated by this ModelAndView. Returns null if this ModelAndView is describing View object.
void setView(View view)	Allows setting a View object. If the view name or View is already set, this will override the value.
View getView()	Return the View object encapsulated by this ModelAndView. Returns null if this ModelAndView is describing a view name.
ModelMap getModelMap()	Returns a ModelMap instance encapsulated by this ModelAndView object.
Map getModel()	Is a utility convenient method returning ModelMap in the form of Map.
addObject(String modelName, Object modelObject)	Allows to add an object with the given name to the model.
addAllObjects(Map modelMap)	Add all entries contained in the given map to the model.
boolean isEmpty()	Return whether this ModelAndView object is empty.
boolean isReference()	Return whether the view part of this ModelAndView is describing view name. Returns true if the view in this ModelAndView is of the form String.
boolean hasView()	Returns boolean describing whether or not this ModelAndView has a view, either as a view name or as a direct View object.

In this section we have discussed about the ModelAndView object and the various methods implemented in this class.

Now as we have discussed about Phase 4 in detail, looking at the various handler adapters available in Spring framework and even about ModelAndView, we want to move our discussion to Phase 5 of the spring web MVC request processing workflow. Before continuing to read the next sections it is recommended to once again have a look on the flow diagram showing the high-level workflow diagram of Spring Web MVC request processing (Fig. 12.1).

12.8 PHASE 5: EXECUTE INTERCEPTORS POSTHANDLE METHODS

As explained in Phase 3 the HandlerInterceptor gives us an opportunity to add common pre- and post-processing behavior without needing to modify each handler implementation. The post-processing operations like changing the logical view name in the ModelAndView based on some inputs/output to support different types of views. In Phase 3 the preHandle method of handler interceptors are executed and in this phase the postHandle methods are executed as the handler execution is completed in Phase 4. Figure 12.5 shows the various operations performed in this phase.

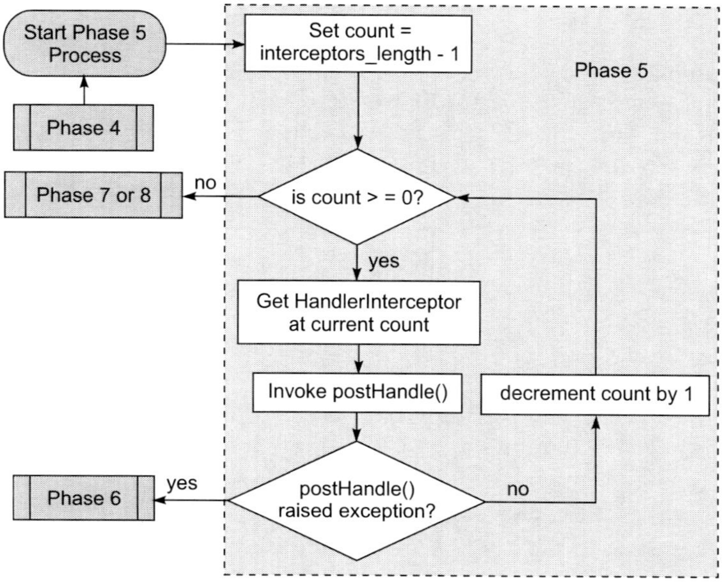

FIGURE 12.5 Flow diagram for Phase 5 of Spring web MVC request processing workflow

The following steps explains the workflow of Phase 5 in detail.

Step 1: Prepare the counter

As shown in Fig. 12.5 the workflow of Phase 5 starts with setting the count to one minus the interceptor's length so that the postHandle method can be invoked on the interceptor's in the reverse order. If the interceptors length is 0 (zero) then the workflow proceeds to Phase 7 or 8 based on whether the handler in Phase 4 has returned a valid ModelAndView object reference or null. If there are any interceptors configured then the workflow proceeds to the next step of this phase.

Step 2: Invoke postHandle method

Here it obtains the HandlerInterceptor at the current count and uses it to invoke postHandle() method. If the postHandle() method throws any exception then the workflow proceeds to Phase 6 to handle the exception. If the postHandle() method execution is successful (that is, normal termination) then count is decremented by 1, if the count is greater than or equal to 0 (zero) then repeat Step 2 (that is, this step) once again. If the count is less than 0 (zero) then the workflow proceeds to Phase 7 or 8 based on the result of Phase 4. That is, if the handler in Phase 4 has returned a valid ModelAndView object reference then workflow proceeds to Phase 7 to render the view, if the handler had returned *null* then the workflow proceeds to Phase 8 considering that the handler had prepared the response.

How to write and configure the HandlerInterceptor is discussed under Phase 3 (Execute Interceptors preHandle methods) refer Section 12.6.1.

12.9 PHASE 6: HANDLE EXCEPTIONS

This phase of the Spring Web MVC request processing workflow is executed only when there is any exception raised while executing Phases 3, 4, and 5, that is, while executing the interceptors preHandle() or postHandle() methods or the handler. DispatcherServlet uses HandlerExceptionResolver to handle the exceptions thrown by the HandlerInterceptor or handler. Spring allows us to configure multiple HandlerExceptionResolver's.

> **Note:** Spring does not take a default type for HandlerExceptionResolver, like which it does with HandlerMapping and HandlerAdapter. Figure 12.6 shows the flow diagram for the Phase 6 of the Spring web MVC request processing workflow.

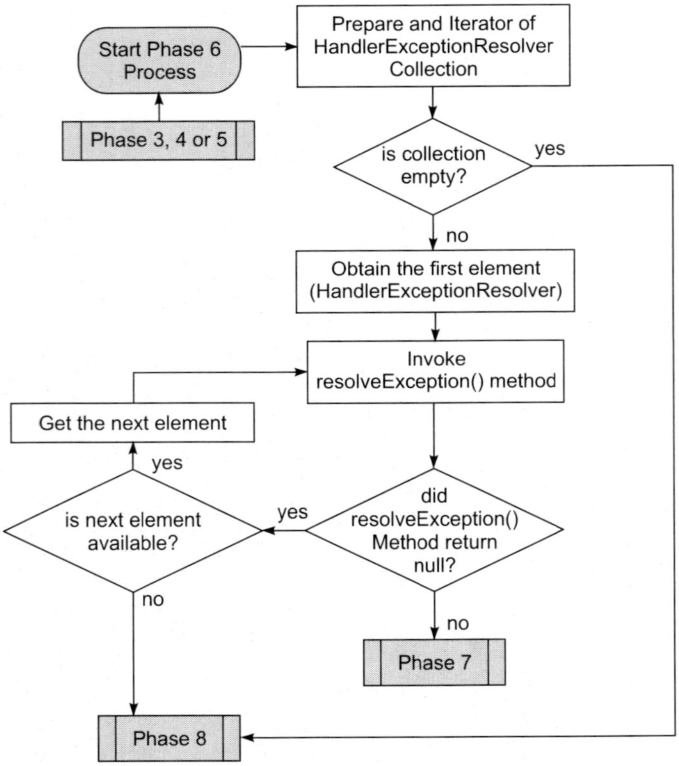

FIGURE 12.6 Flow diagram explaining Phase 6 of Spring Web MVC request processing

The following steps explains the workflow of Phase 6 in detail.

Step 1: Prepare an iterator of exception resolvers

As shown in Fig. 12.6, the workflow of Phase 6 starts with preparing an iterator of the Collection representing HandlerExceptionResolver objects configured in the application. The handlerException Resolvers Collection is initialized in the initialization phase of the DispatcherServlet where it finds all

HandlerExceptionResolver's in the ApplicationContext. If no HandlerExceptionResolver beans are defined in the application then this collection will be empty. If the handlerExceptionResolvers collection is empty then it considers that there are no exception handlers for the application, thus the workflow proceeds to Phase 8 which then ends the request processing by throwing the same exception. If the collection is not empty then the workflow continues to the next step of this phase.

Step 2: Get HandlerExceptionResolver

In this step the workflow obtains the next element from the iterator prepared in Step 1 and casts it into HandlerExceptionResolver type reference.

Step 3: Invoke resolveException() method

After getting the HandlerExceptionResolver of the current iteration the resolveException() method is invoked to handle the exception. If the resolveException() method returns a valid ModelAndView object reference then the workflow proceeds to Phase 7 for rendering a response. If the resolveException() method returns *null* then it finds whether the next element is available in the iterator. If so, then the workflow proceeds to Step 2 of this phase. If the next element is not available, then the workflow proceeds to Phase 8 which then ends the request processing by throwing the same exception.

12.9.1 Configuring HandlerExceptionResolver

Configuring the HandlerExceptionResolver is as normal as other beans. The most commonly used HandlerExceptionResolver implementation is SimpleMappingExceptionResolver. The Simple MappingExceptionResolver allows for mapping exception class names to view names, either for a list of given handlers or for all handlers in the DispatcherServlet. The following code snippet shows the configuration of SimpleMappingExceptionResolver.

Code Snippet

```
<bean id="handlerExceptionResolver"
class="org.springframework.web.servlet.handler.SimpleMappingExceptionResolver">
  <property name="exceptionMappings">
    <props>
      <prop key="
          org.springframework.dao.EmptyResultDataAccessException">
        /SQLError.html
      </prop>
      <prop
key="org.springframework.web.HttpRequestMethodNotSupportedException">
        /MyError.html
      </prop>
    </props>
  </property>
</bean>
```

As shown in the above code snippet the SimpleMappingExceptionResolver is configured with an exceptionMapping property that describes the mapping between the exception type and view page to which the request is to be forwarded when the respective exception is raised in the request handling. Similarly, we can configure multiple exception resolvers. In such a case 'order' property can be used to specify the order in which the resolvers have to be used, just like the HandlerMappings and HandlerAddapters learnt earlier. Now to throw some more light on this configuration we will modify the login process example described in the previous chapter (that is, the first example), the following change and additions are required to do for demonstrating the exception resolver configuration.

1. Change the LoginController class handleRequest() method to throw MyException if the user details are identified to be invalid.
2. Add the exception resolver configuration.
3. Write the exception class, MyException.

Let us do the changes, first modifying the LoginController class handleRequest() method to throw MyException if the LoginModel validate() returns null. List 12.1 shows the complete LoginController class with the modified code in bold.

List 12.1: LoginController.java

```
package com.santosh.spring;

import org.springframework.web.servlet.*;
import org.springframework.web.servlet.mvc.*;
import org.springframework.validation.*;

import javax.servlet.http.*;
import java.io.*;

public class LoginController implements Controller {

  LoginModel loginModel;

  public void setLoginModel(LoginModel lm){
    loginModel=lm;
  }

  public ModelAndView handleRequest(
              HttpServletRequest req,
              HttpServletResponse res) throws Exception {

    String uname= req.getParameter("uname");
    String pass= req.getParameter("pass");

    String type=loginModel.validate(uname, pass);

    if (type==null)
      throw new MyException("User Details are not valid");
      //return new ModelAndView("/Login.html");
    else if(type.equals("admin"))
```

```
        return new ModelAndView("/AdminHome.jsp");
      else
        return new ModelAndView("/UserHome.jsp");
    }//handle
}//class
```

After we do the change in the controller we now want to add the exception resolver configuration in the ds-servlet.xml file. List 12.2 shows the complete ds-servlet.xml file with the newly added coded in bold.

List 12.2: ds-servlet.xml

```
<beans xmlns="http://www.springframework.org/schema/beans"
xmlns:xsi="http://www.w3.org/2001/XMLSchema-instance"
xsi:schemaLocation="http://www.springframework.org/schema/beans
http://www.springframework.org/schema/beans/spring-beans-2.0.xsd">

  <!--Configuring DataSource-->
  <bean id="datasource" class="org.apache.commons.dbcp.BasicDataSource">
    <property name="driverClassName">
      <value>oracle.jdbc.driver.OracleDriver</value>
    </property>
    <property name="url">
      <value>jdbc:oracle:thin:@localhost:1521:sandb</value>
    </property>
    <property name="username">
      <value>scott</value>
    </property>
    <property name="password">
      <value>tiger</value>
    </property>
  </bean>

  <!--Configuring JdbcTemplate-->
  <bean id="jdbctemp" class="org.springframework.jdbc.core.JdbcTemplate">
    <constructor-arg>
      <ref local="datasource"/>
    </constructor-arg>
  </bean>

  <!--Configuring LoginModel-->
  <bean id="loginModel" class="com.santosh.spring.LoginModel">
    <constructor-arg>
      <ref local="jdbctemp"/>
    </constructor-arg>
  </bean>
```

```
  <!--Configuring Controller-->
  <bean id="logincnt" class="com.santosh.spring.LoginController">
    <property name="loginModel">
      <ref local="loginModel"/>
    </property>
  </bean>

  <bean id="myurlmapping"
class="org.springframework.web.servlet.handler.SimpleUrlHandlerMapping">
    <property name="mappings">
      <props>
        <prop key="/login.spring">logincnt</prop>
      </props>
    </property>
  </bean>

  <bean id="handlerExceptionResolver"
class="org.springframework.web.servlet.handler.SimpleMappingExceptionResolver">
    <property name="exceptionMappings">
      <props>
        <prop key="com.santosh.spring.MyException">
          /Error.html
        </prop>
      </props>
    </property>
  </bean>
</beans>
```

Actually, we finished with the configurations but since here we are using a user defined exception type to demonstrate the exception resolver we need to write a simple user defined exception MyException. List 12.3 shows MyException.java file.

List 12.3: MyException.java

```
package com.santosh.spring;

public class MyException extends RuntimeException {
  public MyException(String s){super(s);}
}
```

Finally, we will write a simple dummy Error.html which we have configured to deploy when the fields are not rejected by the validator but are not valid according to the database. List 12.4 shows Error.html.

List 12.4 Error.html

```
<html>
  <body>
    A simple test error page<br/>
    User Details are not valid
  </body>
</html>
```

Now we are ready with the application to test the exception resolver. For a better clarity on the various files required for executing this example look at Fig. 12.7.

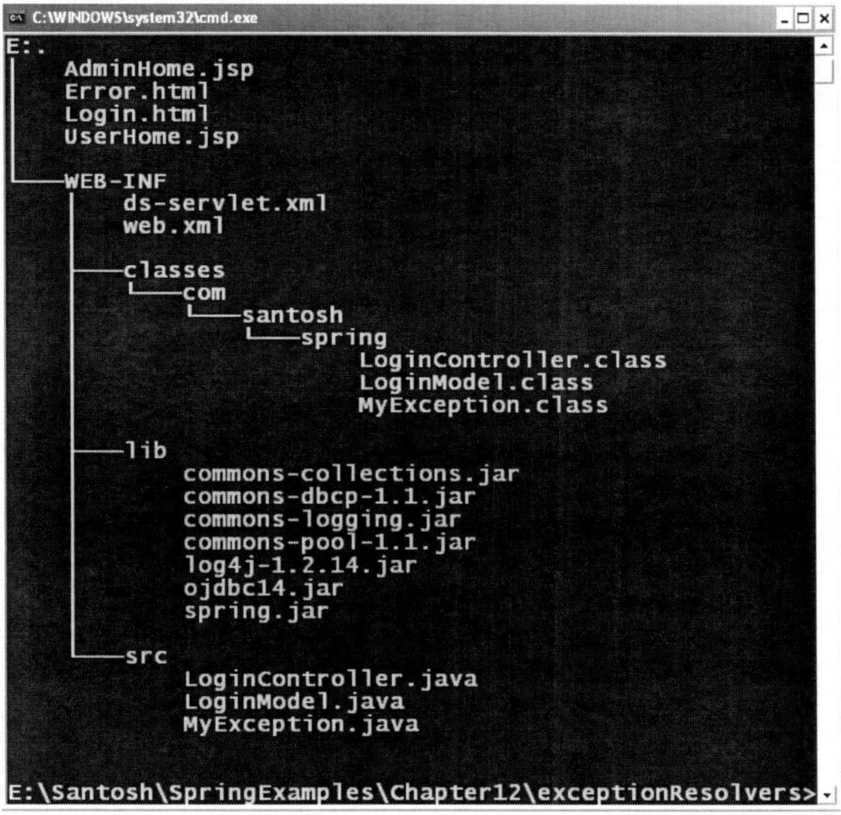

FIGURE 12.7 Tree structure showing the files of exceptionResolvers example

The preceding lists in this section show the code for Error.html, ds-servlet.xml LoginController.java, and MyException.java files while the remaining files Login.html, LoginModel.java, AdminHome.jsp, UserHome.jsp, and web.xml files are as described in the first example demonstrated in Chapter 11. See Lists 11.1, 11.3, 11.5, 11.6, 11.7 for these files.

Now deploy the application and browse the example using the URL http://localhost:8080/exceptionResolvers/Login.html. You will find the view as shown in Fig. 12.8.

Figure 12.8 shows the login page that allows to submit login details, enter some data into the fields so that the validate() method of LoginModel returns *null,* that is, like invalid password, and as per the configurations in this case the Error.html page is presented as shown in Fig. 12.9.

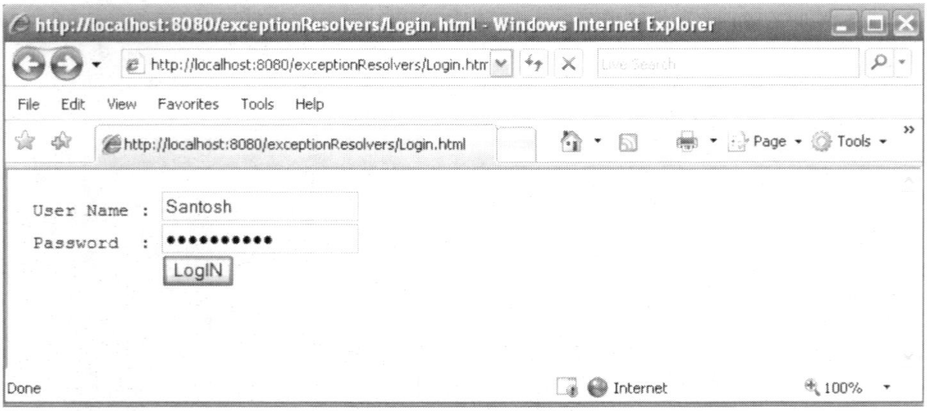

FIGURE 12.8 Login form view

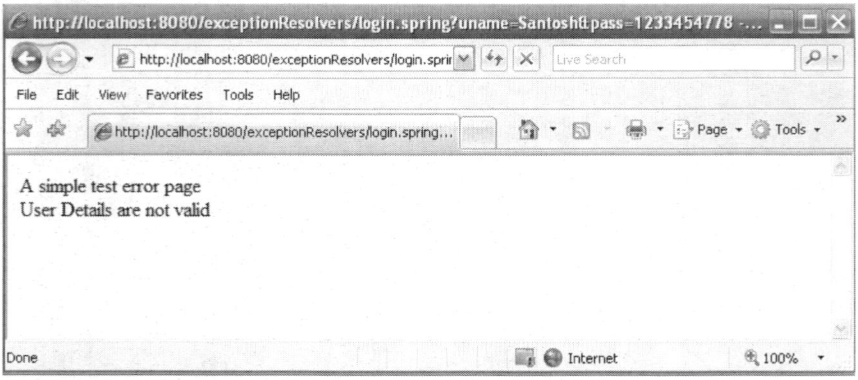

FIGURE 12.9 Error page describing login details are invalid

Figure 12.9 shows the Error.html view which is presented to the client because of MyException being thrown by the controller.

In this section you learnt how Spring framework handles the exceptions and how to configure exception resolvers. You will learn how these messages can be presented along with the complex view content to the client with some Spring tag library in Chapter 14. Now as we have completed with Phase 6 the following section explains the next phase in the Spring web MVC framework workflow is Phase 7, that is, render the view.

12.10 PHASE 7: RENDER THE VIEW

The Spring Web MVC request processing workflow executes this phase only in the following two cases:

- **Case 1:** If the handler in Phase 4 returns a valid (not null) ModelAndView object reference, and Phase 5 is executed successfully (that is, postHandle() method of HandlerInterceptors).
- **Case 2:** If the HandlerExceptionResolver in Phase 6 returns a valid (not null) ModelAndView object reference.

This phase of request processing workflow is responsible to render the response for a request as per the outcome of the request handling done the preceding phases. The workflow associated with this phase shown in Fig. 12.10.

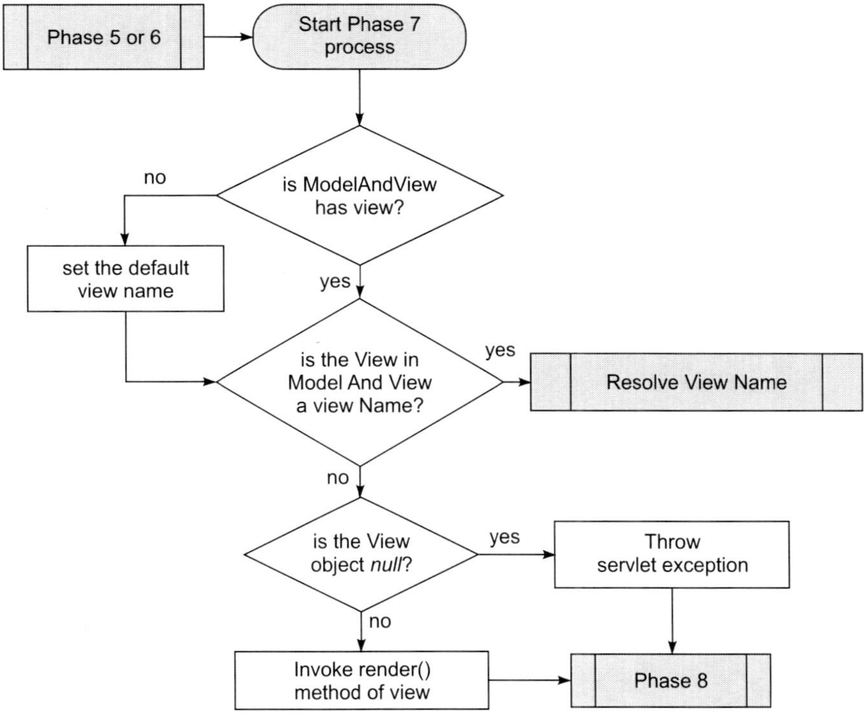

FIGURE 12.10 Flow diagram for Phase 7 of Spring web MVC request processing workflow

The following steps explain this workflow described in the preceding figure in detail.

Step 1: Find the View

As shown in the preceding figure, the workflow of Phase 7 of Spring Web MVC request processing workflow starts with finding for the view in the ModelAndView object produced in the previous phases (Phase 4 or 6). This is done using the *hasView()* method of ModelAndView. If *hasView()* method returns false, that is, the ModelAndView object does not contain a view; then a default view name is set to the ModelAndView object. The default view name is obtained by DispatcherServlet using the

RequestToViewNameTranslator type object configured in this context. If there is no RequestToViewNameTranslator type bean configured in the context then null is set as view name.

Step 2: Find is ModelAndView contains View reference

After the successful execution of Step 1 the workflow continues with finding whether the view in the ModelAndView object is holding a View object reference or a view name. This is done using the *isReference*() method of ModelAndView.

If *isReference*() method returns 'false' and if the view reference is not null then the workflow proceeds to the next step.

If *isReference*() method returns 'true' then the workflow proceeds to resolve the view name. The 'Resolve View Name' process is explained in the next section. If the 'Resolve View Name' process successfully resolves the view name to View object then the workflow proceeds to the next step.

If the view reference is null or the ViewResolver's fails to resolve the view name (that is, if 'Resolve View Name' process returns *null*), the workflow proceeds to Phase 8 by throwing a ServletException.

Step 3: Delegate to view object for rendering

After successfully locating the View object the request is delegated to the view object invoking render() method of View. The view object takes the responsibility to prepare the response, that is, presentation for the client. Thereafter, the workflow proceeds to Phase 8 to perform the finalizations.

In this section we learnt steps involved in using the view object to render the view. The following section explains the workflow associated in using the ViewResolver implementations to resolve the view name to view object.

12.10.1 The 'Resolve View Name' Process

As described in the preceding section if the ModelAndView object describes a view name instead of View object, DispatcherServlet uses the configured ViewResolver objects to resolve the view name to locate View object. As an overview at this point we can simply consider that the ViewResolver object is responsible to locate the View object that can render a view for this request (the various ViewResolver types and their configurations are explained in detail in Chapter 14). Figure 12.11 shows the workflow involved in resolving the view name.

The following steps explain the resolve view name workflow shown in Fig. 12.11.

Step 1: Prepare a ViewResolver Iterator

As shown in Fig 12.11 the workflow starts with the preparation of an iterator of the collection storing the ViewResolver objects. This collection is created while the DispatcherServlet is being initialized. Thereafter the first element is retrieved from the iterator.

Step 2: Resolve View Name

After Step 1 the workflow proceeds to invoke the resolveViewName() method of the current ViewResolver object in the iteration. If the resolveViewName() method returns null, which indicates that the current ViewResolver failed to resolve the view name. In this case the workflow proceeds to the next step. If the resolveViewName() method returns a valid View object reference then the workflow completes returning the same, which is further used to render the view as described in the preceding section.

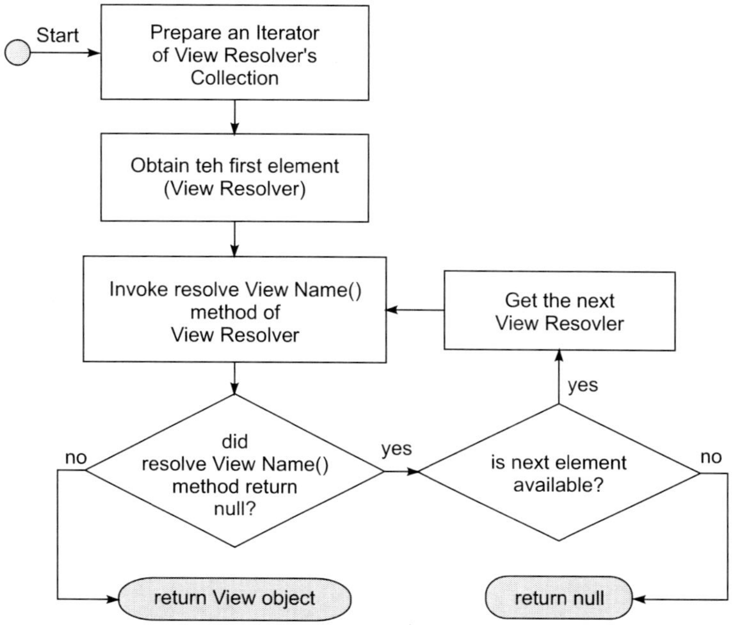

FIGURE 12.11 The 'Resolve View Name' process workflow

Step 3: Move to next element

If the ViewResolver in the preceding step fails to resolve the view name then the workflow proceeds to get the next ViewResolver from the iterator prepared in Step 1. If the next element is available then the process moves to Step 2, if not the workflow completes returning *null*.

In this section we learnt about the workflow involved in resolving the view name, and in the preceding section we discussed the process of using View object for rendering. The various ViewResolver and View implementations provided under Spring are discussed in Chapter 14. Now, let us learn the last phase in handling the request, that is, Phase 8.

12.11 PHASE 8: EXECUTE INTERCEPTORS AFTERCOMPLETION METHODS

As explained in Phase 3, the HandlerInterceptor gives us an opportunity to add common pre- and post-processing behavior without needing to modify each handler implementation. While in Phase 3 the preHandle method of handler interceptors are executed, and in Phase 5 the postHandle methods are executed. In this phase of workflow the afterCompletion method is executed on the Handler Interceptors whose preHandle method has successfully executed and returned 'true' (that is, in Phase 3). The afterCompletion method is called on any outcome of handler execution, thus allowing us to do the resource cleanup. Figure 12.12 shows the various operations performed in this phase.

The following steps explain the workflow shown in Fig. 12.12 in detail.

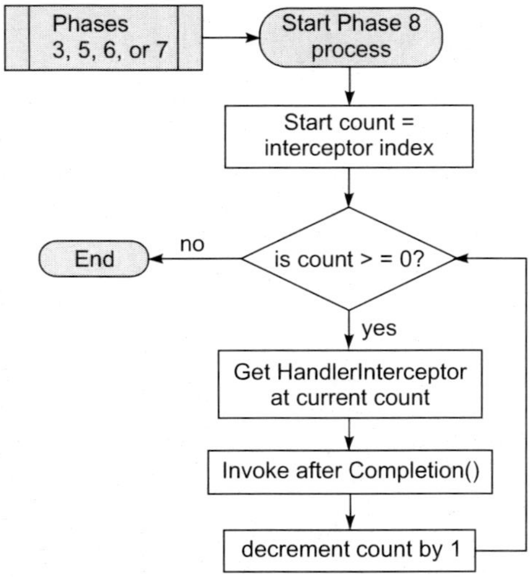

FIGURE 12.12 Flow diagram explaining Phase 8 of Spring Web MVC request processing

Step 1: Prepare counter

As shown in Fig. 12.12, the workflow of Phase 8 starts with setting the count to interceptorIndex value. The interceptorIndex is set in the preprocessing phase, that is, Phase 3 used to track the index of the interceptor in the list that have completed the preHandle processing successfully so that in this phase the afterCompletion methods can be executed only on those HandlerInterceptors. That is, if the workflow reaches to this phase from Phase 5 then the interceptorIndex will be equal to the interceptors' length minus 1 (interceptorsLength-1) since the preHandle method of all the interceptors are executed successfully. Thus the afterCompletion method will be executed on all the interceptors in reverse order as compared to the order in which they are configured. If the workflow reaches to this phase because of any exception raised in the preHandle method or if the preHandle method returns 'false' then the interceptor chain stops executing the preHandle methods and delegates to this phase via Phase 6 or directly. After the counter is prepared if there are any interceptors configured, that is, if the count is greater than or equal to 0 (zero) then the workflow proceeds to Step 2, if not it ends the request processing doing the necessary cleanup operations.

Step 2: Obtain HandlerInterceptor

After the counter is prepared successfully DispatcherServlet obtains the HandlerInterceptor at the current index from the interceptors' list.

Step 3: Invoke interceptors afterCompletion() method

After obtaining the HandlerInterceptor DispatcherServlet invokes afterCompletion method.

Step 4: Change the counter

In this step of the Phase 8 workflow the count is decrease by one and then verifies whether the current count is greater than or equal to 0 (zero). If so then the workflow proceeds to Step 2 of this phase, if not it ends the request processing doing the necessary cleanup operations.

How to write and configure the HandlerInterceptors was discussed under the Phase 3 (Execute Interceptors preHandle methods) refer Section 12.6.1.

With this phase the Spring web MVC request processing workflow ends.

Summary

In this chapter we learnt about the initialization and the request processing workflow of Spring Web MVC application in detail. To understand the complete workflow in detail and the internals of the Spring Web MVC workflow we have divided the workflow into eight phases. Further in this chapter we learnt all these phases individually with the flow diagrams, steps, and code snippets. This chapter is the most important for the developers involved in web tier development using Spring Framework. In the next chapter we will teach the Spring Framework's built-in controllers that help us in developing the handlers for implementing various requirements.

Describing Controllers and Validations

13 CHAPTER

Objectives

In the previous chapter we learnt about the complete workflow of Spring Web MVC request processing, where we understood that one of the various extension points that spring provides to implement custom logic in the workflow is in the form of a handler. As discussed under Phase 4 of the request processing workflow, DispatcherServlet uses HandlerAdapter to invoke the handler, where the handler takes the responsibility to handle the request. Moreover, the most common way to implement the handler in Spring Web MVC application is as a controller. In this chapter we will cover:

- How to implement handlers in the form of controllers using various Spring Framework's built-in controllers that help us in developing the handlers for various requirements by providing the common infrastructures.

13.1 TYPES OF CONTROLLERS

Spring Framework provides various built-in controllers supporting us to implement the most common requirements in the simplest approach leaving the most infrastructures to be implemented by the framework itself, which includes form-specific controllers, command-based controllers, and wizard-style controllers, etc. The most commonly used built-in controller types provided by the Spring Web MVC framework are listed below:

- Controller
- AbstractCommandController
- SimpleFormController
- Wizard Form Controller
- MultiActionController

Now, let us learn each of these in detail concentrating on the aspects like how to configure them and in which situation they have to be used. The following sections explain each of the above listed types in detail, starting with the basic type Controller.

13.2 CONTROLLER INTERFACE

The *org.strutsframework.web.servlet.mvc.Controller* is the base controller interface, representing a component that receives HttpServletRequest and HttpServletResponse instances to handle the request just like a servlet but this participates in Spring Web MVC request processing workflow. This can be compared to the Struts Actions that participate in the Struts framework request processing workflow. The Controller interface declares only one method, handleRequest(). The following snippet shows the method signature of the handlerRequest().

```
public ModelAndView handleRequest(HttpServletRequest, HttpServletResponse)
  throws Exception
```

The implementation of the Controller interface has to implement this method. The DispatcherServlet gets the request and successfully passes through Phases 1, 2, and 3 of its request processing workflow and even successfully delegates the request to the appropriate HandlerAdapter invoking the handle() method. The handler designed of this type will be supported by SimpleControllerHandlerAdapter. The SimpleControllerHandlerAdapter's handle () method simply invokes the handleRequest() method of the handler (in this case controller), which gives the control to our controller component so that we can perform some request handling logic in the Spring web MVC request processing workflow. The handleRequest() method has to return a ModelAndView after the request handling is completed. The ModelAndView object describes the model data and the view description to locate and render the view. If the handleRequest() method returns *null* it informs the DispatcherServlet that the response generation is completed and it needs to skip Phase 6 of the workflow. In the first example of this chapter which was designed to demonstrate the basics flow of Spring web MVC application, we have designed a handler (that LoginController, see List 11.2) of this type to include the system-specific login process into the Spring workflow. As it can be observed from the listing 11.2 implementing Controller interface and including the request handling logic into handleRequest() method defines a very basic approach of handling the request, but in general we need few additional conveniences while handling the request like request data conversion and binding the form data to the value object, etc. To meet these infrastructural requirements Spring web MVC framework includes some built-in implementation classes of Controller like AbstractCommandController, SimpleFormController, etc. These are explained in the following sections.

13.3 ABSTRACTCOMMANDCONTROLLER

As discussed in the above section the handler component in general has some infrastructural requirements to handle the request—the AbstractCommandController class implementing Controller interface provides one of those infrastructural services. The AbstractCommandController takes the responsibility to bind the request data to the command object properties, and if required validates the fields as per the specified rules. The AbstractCommandController implements the handleRequest() method of Controller interface which performs the following operations:

1. Creates an instance for the command class configured.
2. Binds the request data to the command object properties and validates the properties.
3. Prepare a BindException object that represents the validation errors, if any.
4. Delegates the request to handle() method, which we need to implement for adding system specific request handling logic.

The following code snippet shows the handle() method of AbstractCommandController that our handler has to implement.

Code Snippet

```
protected ModelAndView handle(
            HttpServletRequest request,
            HttpServletResponse response,
            Object command, BindException errors)
            throws Exception
```

After learning about the AbstractCommandController and its services let us work with one sample code to put more light on this topic.

13.3.1 Working with AbstractCommandController

This example gives us an opportunity to put some of the concepts which we have learnt in the preceding sections also into action. Here to make the sample code simple and completely related to the technology we take a login use case implementation which can even show the difference between the Controller used in the previous example and AbstractCommandController.

This example consists of a Login.html which provides an entry point for this application by providing login view allowing the user to make a login action. The Login.html is shown in List 13.1.

List 13.1: Login.html

```
<html>
 <body>
   <form action="login.spring"> <pre>
User Name : <input type="text" name="uname"/>
Password : <input type="password" name="pass"/>
     <input type="submit" value="LogIN"/>
   </pre> </form>
 </body>
</html>
```

The request made using the Login.html is received by the DispatcherServlet, which then dispatches the request to the LoginController invoking handle() method. The LoginController class to process the login request is shown in List 13.2.

List 13.2: LoginController.java

```
package com.santosh.spring;

import org.springframework.web.servlet.*;
import org.springframework.web.servlet.mvc.*;
import org.springframework.validation.*;

import javax.servlet.http.*;
import java.io.*;

public class LoginController extends AbstractCommandController {
```

```
  LoginModel loginModel;

  public void setLoginModel(LoginModel lm){
        loginModel=lm;
  }

  public ModelAndView handle(HttpServletRequest req, HttpServletResponse res,
                            Object command, BindException errors)
                                throws Exception {

      String type=loginModel.validate((UserDetails)command);

      if (type==null)
        return new ModelAndView("/Login.html");
      else if(type.equals("admin"))
        return new ModelAndView("/AdminHome.jsp");
      else
        return new ModelAndView("/UserHome.jsp");
  }//handle
}//class
```

As explained earlier, the AbstractCommandController can bind the request data to the command object properties. In this example, as it can be observed from List 13.2 we are using a UserDetails class as a command class. List 13.3 shows the UserDetails.java.

List 13.3: UserDetails.java

```
package com.santosh.spring;

public class UserDetails {

  public String getUname() { return uname; }
  public String getPass() { return pass; }
  public void setUname(String s) { uname=s; }
  public void setPass(String s) { pass=s; }

  private String uname, pass;
}//class
```

As shown in List 13.3, LoginController handle() method is invoking the validate() method on the LoginModel object where LoginModel is a plain java class designed to perform business logic operation. In this case validate the login details. List 13.4 shows the LoginModel.java.

List 13.4: LoginModel.java

```
package com.santosh.spring;

import org.springframework.jdbc.core.*;
import org.springframework.dao.EmptyResultDataAccessException;
```

```
public class LoginModel {

  public LoginModel(JdbcTemplate jt){
        jdbcTemplate=jt;
  }

  public String validate(UserDetails user) {
        try{
              return (String)jdbcTemplate.queryForObject(
                    "select type from userdetails where username=\'"+
    user.getUname()+"\' and userpass=\'"+user.getPass()+
    "\'", String.class);
        }
        catch(EmptyResultDataAccessException e){
              return null;
        }
  }//validate

  private JdbcTemplate jdbcTemplate;
}//class
```

Now, we want to write the Spring Beans XML configuration file. This XML configuration file name should be [servlet-name]-servlet.xml in the WEB-INF directory of our web application. In this example we will define the servlet-name for DispatcherServlet declaration as ‘ds’. Thus the file name here is ds-servlet.xml. List 13.5 shows the ds-servlet.xml file for this example.

List 13.5: ds-servlet.xml

```
<beans xmlns="http://www.springframework.org/schema/beans"
xmlns:xsi="http://www.w3.org/2001/XMLSchema-instance"
xsi:schemaLocation="http://www.springframework.org/schema/beans
http://www.springframework.org/schema/beans/spring-beans-2.0.xsd">

  <!--Configuring DataSource-->
  <bean id="datasource" class="org.apache.commons.dbcp.BasicDataSource">
        <property name="driverClassName">
              <value>oracle.jdbc.driver.OracleDriver</value>
        </property>
        <property name="url">
              <value>jdbc:oracle:thin:@localhost:1521:sandb</value>
        </property>
        <property name="username">
              <value>scott</value>
        </property>
        <property name="password">
              <value>tiger</value>
        </property>
  </bean>
```

```
  <!--Configuring JdbcTemplate-->
  <bean id="jdbctemp" class="org.springframework.jdbc.core.JdbcTemplate">
         <constructor-arg>
                <ref local="datasource"/>
         </constructor-arg>
  </bean>

  <bean id="loginModel" class="com.santosh.spring.LoginModel">
         <constructor-arg>
                <ref local="jdbctemp"/>
         </constructor-arg>
  </bean>

  <bean id="logincnt" class="com.santosh.spring.LoginController">
         <property name="loginModel">
                <ref local="loginModel"/>
         </property>
         <!--configure the command class name-->
         <property name="commandClass">
                <value type="java.lang.Class">
                       com.santosh.spring.UserDetails
                </value>
         </property>
<!--configure the command name, the name to use when binding the instantiated command
class to the request-->
         <property name="commandName">
                <value>UserDetails</value>
         </property>
  </bean>

  <bean id="myurlmapping"
class="org.springframework.web.servlet.handler.SimpleUrlHandlerMapping">
         <property name="mappings">
                <props>
                       <prop key="/login.spring">logincnt</prop>
                </props>
         </property>
  </bean>
</beans>
```

List 13.6 shows the AdminHome.jsp, which is presented in case the login details are validated as an admin type user.

List 13.6: AdminHome.jsp

```
<html> <body>
  Welcome to the Admin Home page <br/>
```

```
  User Name : <%=request.getParameter("uname")%>
</html> </body>
```

List 13.7 shows the UserHome.jsp, which is presented in case the login details are validated as a user type.

List 13.7: UserHome.jsp

```
<html> <body>
  Welcome to the Non-Admin User Home page <br/>
  User Name : <%=request.getParameter("uname")%>
</html> </body>
```

Finally, as discussed we need to configure DispatcherServlet in web.xml since it is also a normal servlet as any other servlet. List 13.8 shows the web.xml.

List 13.8: web.xml

```
<web-app>
 <servlet>
  <servlet-name>ds</servlet-name>
   <servlet-class>org.springframework.web.servlet.DispatcherServlet</servlet-class>
  <load-on-startup>0</load-on-startup>
 </servlet>
 <servlet-mapping>
  <servlet-name>ds</servlet-name>
  <url-pattern>*.spring</url-pattern>
 </servlet-mapping>
</web-app>
```

Now, as you have written the Spring Web MVC example explained in Lists 13.1 through 13.8 follow the following steps to configure your Spring Web MVC application to see it work.

This example uses the 'userdetails' table created for the first example explained in Chapter 11. Now, deploy the application into any Java Web application server. Here we are using Tomcat server to demonstrate this example but as described already Spring Web MVC framework is not server-dependent; it can be deployed into any Java web application server. You can use any of the deployment option that you have learnt in servlets and JSP to deploy web application in Tomcat. The basic approach is to copy the work_folder into <tomcat_home>/webapps folder. After deploying the application start the Tomcat server then browse the example using the URL **http://localhost:8080/commandController/Login.html.** You will find the following screen:

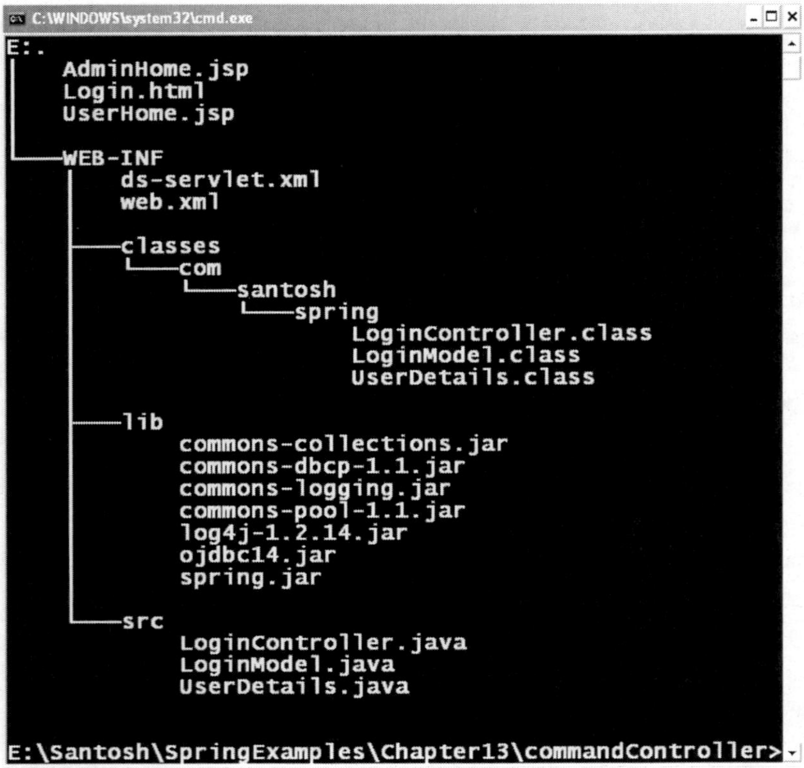

FIGURE 13.1 Tree structure showing files of commandController example

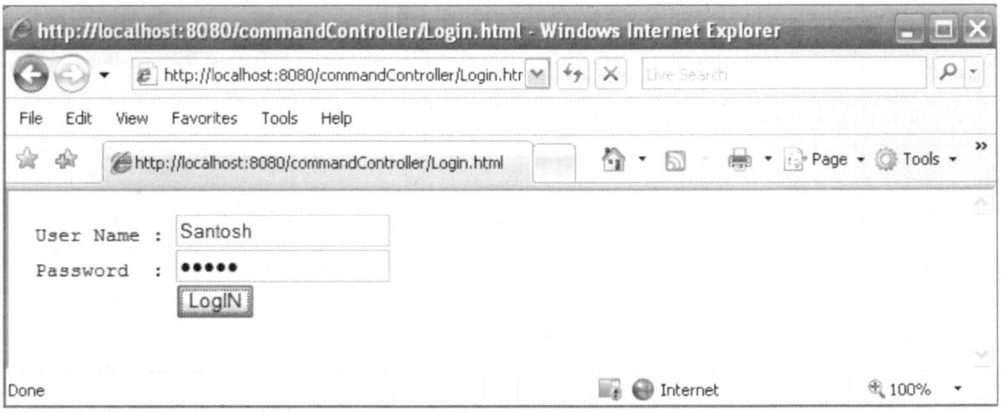

FIGURE 13.2 Login form view

Enter the login details as shown in Fig. 13.2. As per the database created if every thing is successful you will find the view as shown in Fig. 13.3. That is, AdminHome.jsp is presented.

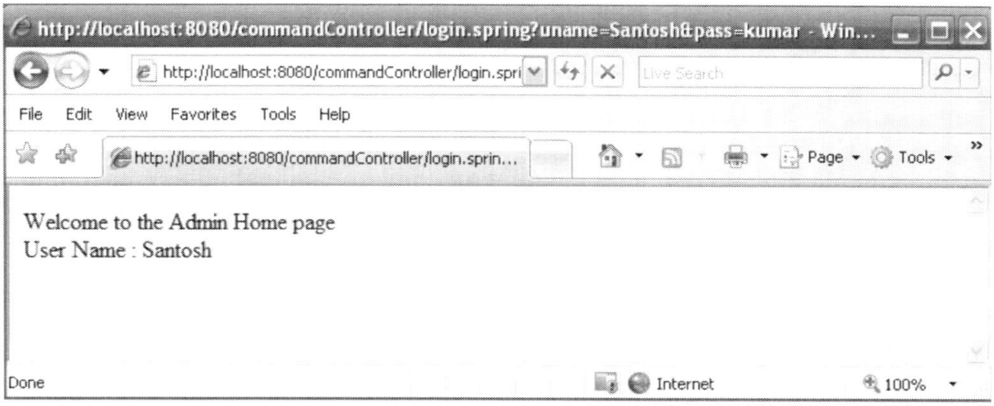

FIGURE 13.3 Login success view

If the login details are not valid then the Login page is presented, whereas if the login details are validated as type 'user' then UserHome.jsp is presented. In this example, we have learnt the how to use command objects along with the AbstractCommandController. In this example we have not configured validations, now if we want to apply validations to the form fields like the username and password should not be empty and password should contain five characters minimum. The following section explains how to configure the validator for the command object.

13.4 UNDERSTANDING VALIDATORS

Validating the request data is the most common requirement while processing the form data. Spring Web MVC framework provides a built-in support for form data validation. The following two steps are involved in using validator for command objects.

Step 1: Write a validator class

The validator class should be a subtype of org.springframework.validation.Validator interface. The Validator interface declares two methods supports() and validate(). The method signatures of both the methods are shown in the code snippet below.

Code Snippet

```
public boolean supports(Class c)
public void validate(Object target, Errors errors)
```

The supports() method takes an argument of java.lang.Class type. This is responsible to find whether this validator is designed to validate the given class type of object. If it finds that it can validate then it returns 'true' which informs the Spring framework that this validator can be used to validate the command object fields. The typical implementation of this method would be to use equals() method of java.lang.Class and find if it is equal to our required class. The following code snippet shows the sample implementation for the UserDetails command object fields as shown in the following snippet.

Code Snippet

```
public boolean supports(Class c) {
    return c.equals(UserDetails.class);
}
```

Thereafter, we want to even implement validate(). The validate() method requires to take the responsibility of validating the fields of the command class object that this validator supports. The validate() method takes two arguments one the target object (that is, the object whose fields is to be validated) and the second is the org.springframework.validation.Errors. The Errors object acts as an out parameter used to write the errors raised in this validate method so that the same can be described to the controller in the form of BindException. To validate the fields we can use the ValidationUtils convenient utility methods. The ValidationUtils is an abstract class and all the ValidationUtils methods are static and thus we do not require creating an instance of ValidationUtils class. The methods available in ValidationUtils class are shown in Table 13.1.

TABLE 13.1 Methods of ValidationUtils

Method	*Description*
public static void rejectIfEmpty(Errors errors, String field, String errorCode)	Rejects the field, adds the given error code for the field into the given errors if the field is empty (that is, null or " ").
public static void rejectIfEmpty(Errors errors, String field, String errorCode, String defaultValue)	Same as the above method but this adds the default message apart from error code to the error message.
public static void rejectIfEmpty(Errors errors, String field, String errorCode, Object[] errorargs, String defaultValue)	Reject the given field with the given error code, error arguments, and default message if the value is empty.
public static void rejectIfEmptyOrWhitespace(Errors errors, String field, String errorCode)	Reject the given field with the given error code if the value is empty or just contains whitespace.
public static void rejectIfEmptyOrWhitespace(Errors errors, String field, String errorCode, String defaultMessage)	Reject the given field with the given error code and default message if the value is empty or just contains whitespace.
public static void rejectIfEmptyOrWhitespace(Errors errors, String field, String errorCode, Object[] errorargs, String defaultMessage)	Reject the given field with the given error code, error arguments, and default message if the value is empty or just contains whitespace.

Step 2: Associate the Validator to the Controller

Once after the validator is written now we want the validator to be used for validating the command object created by the command controller, which we have learnt earlier in this section. To associate the validator to the controller we can use the 'validator' or 'validators' property defined in BaseCommandController which is the super type for AbstractCommandController. The controller can be configured with multiple validators where further it uses the supports() method of validator to choose the suitable validator for this request fields validation. The following code snippet shows the sample declaration of validator in spring beans XML configuration file.

Code Snippet

```
<bean id="logincnt" class="com.santosh.spring.LoginController">
      <!--configure the command class name-->
      <property name="commandClass">
            <value type="java.lang.Class">
                  com.santosh.spring.UserDetails
            </value>
      </property>
      <property name="commandName">
            <value>UserDetails</value>
      </property>
      <property name="validator">
            <bean class="com.santosh.spring.UserValidator"/>
      </property>
</bean>
```

Now, we have learnt how to write and configure validator for our command object fields. To throw more light on this topic we want to look at a practical implementation of the validator.

13.4.1 Working with Validators

To demonstrate the validators we will modify the preceding example (login process), used to demonstrate the AbstractCommandController. The following additions or modifications need to be done to the preceding example to add validations for the UserDetails properties.

1. Write a UserValidator class
2. Modify the handle() method of LoginController to display error messages
3. Modify LoginController bean definition in ds-servlet.xml to assign validator

Let us start doing the above described changes to the login example one after the other. List 13.9 shows the UserValidator.java.

List 13.9: UserValidator.java

```
package com.santosh.spring;

import org.springframework.validation.*;

import javax.servlet.http.*;
import java.io.*;

public class UserValidator implements Validator {

    public boolean supports(Class c) {
    return c.equals(UserDetails.class);
  }

    public void validate(Object target, Errors errors) {

          UserDetails ud = (UserDetails) target;
```

```
        //Rejects the given field if is empty or contains only whitespace
        /*Note:
          The object whose field is being validated does not need to be passed
          because the 'errors' instance can resolve field values by itself
          it will usually hold an internal reference to the target object
        */
        ValidationUtils.rejectIfEmptyOrWhitespace(errors, "uname",
                    "field.required", "The username field cannot be empty");
        ValidationUtils.rejectIfEmptyOrWhitespace(errors, "pass",
                    "field.required", "The password field cannot be empty");

        if (ud.getPass() != null && !ud.getPass().equals("")
                                 && ud.getPass().length()<5) {
          errors.rejectValue("pass", "field.minlength",
                       new Object[]{Integer.valueOf(5)},
                       "The password must contain minimum 5 characters.");
        }//if
    }//validate
}//class
```

As shown in List 13.9 the supports() method returns 'true' in case the Class object given as an argument represents UserDetails class if not 'false'. This describes that the UserValidator's validate() method is used only to validate UserDetails object fields. The validate() method of checking for the three rules is described below:

- uname field cannot be empty
- pass field cannot be empty
- pass field must contain minimum 5 characters

As we have written the UserValidator, we want to modify the LoginController class handle() method to design intelligent to display the error messages to the client. List 13.10 shows the complete LoginController.java with the modified section bold.

List 13.10: LoginController.java

```
package com.santosh.spring;

import org.springframework.web.servlet.*;
import org.springframework.web.servlet.mvc.*;
import org.springframework.validation.*;

import javax.servlet.http.*;
import java.io.*;

public class LoginController extends AbstractCommandController {

  LoginModel loginModel;

  public void setLoginModel(LoginModel lm){
         loginModel=lm;
  }
```

```
    public ModelAndView handle(HttpServletRequest req, HttpServletResponse res,
                               Object command, BindException errors)
                                        throws Exception {

        if (errors.hasErrors()){
               System.out.println("Errors in validation");
               //Code to write the error message to client,
               //this logic is used to demonstrate practically the workflow
               //about the handle method returning null
               PrintWriter out=res.getWriter();
               out.println(
                   "We have found some errors in the data submitted by you :");
               out.println("<br/>Total Number of errors: <b>"+
                                       errors.getErrorCount()+"</b><br/>");
              out.println("The errors associated with uname field are:<br/>");

              java.util.List<FieldError> errors_list=
                                            errors.getFieldErrors("uname");

              for (FieldError error: errors_list)
                      out.println(error.getDefaultMessage()+"<br/>");

              out.println(
                     "<br/>The errors associated with pass field are:<br/>");

               errors_list=errors.getFieldErrors("pass");

              for (FieldError error: errors_list)
                     out.println(error.getDefaultMessage()+"<br/>");

              return null;
        }

        String type=loginModel.validate((UserDetails)command);

        if (type==null)
        return new ModelAndView("/Login.html");
        else if(type.equals("admin"))
        return new ModelAndView("/AdminHome.jsp");
        else
        return new ModelAndView("/UserHome.jsp");
    }//handle
}//class
```

In the preceding code the content in bold characters is the new code added compared to the LoginController class used with the previous example (see List 13.2). In this new code it finds whether there are any fields rejected in the validation and if there are any, then their default values are got and presented to the client. In this case we want to return null informing the Spring framework that it does not require to resolve the view, and apply it to prepare the presentation for client. Now as a last modification we want to associate the validator to the controller. List 13.11 shows the complete ds-servler.xml file with the new added code displayed in bold.

List 13.11: ds-servlet.xml

```
<!--ds-servlet.xml-->
<beans xmlns="http://www.springframework.org/schema/beans"
xmlns:xsi="http://www.w3.org/2001/XMLSchema-instance"
xsi:schemaLocation="http://www.springframework.org/schema/beans
http://www.springframework.org/schema/beans/spring-beans-2.0.xsd">

  <!--Configuring DataSource-->
  <bean id="datasource" class="org.apache.commons.dbcp.BasicDataSource">
        <property name="driverClassName">
              <value>oracle.jdbc.driver.OracleDriver</value>
        </property>
        <property name="url">
              <value>jdbc:oracle:thin:@localhost:1521:sandb</value>
        </property>
      <property name="username">
              <value>scott</value>
      </property>
      <property name="password">
              <value>tiger</value>
      </property>
  </bean>

  <!--Configuring JdbcTemplate-->
  <bean id="jdbctemp" class="org.springframework.jdbc.core.JdbcTemplate">
        <constructor-arg>
              <ref local="datasource"/>
        </constructor-arg>
  </bean>

  <bean id="loginModel" class="com.santosh.spring.LoginModel">
        <constructor-arg>
              <ref local="jdbctemp"/>
        </constructor-arg>
  </bean>

  <bean id="logincnt" class="com.santosh.spring.LoginController">
        <property name="loginModel">
              <ref local="loginModel"/>
        </property>
        <!--configure the command class name-->
        <property name="commandClass">
              <value type="java.lang.Class">
                    com.santosh.spring.UserDetails
```

```
                </value>
        </property>
        <property name="commandName">
                <value>UserDetails</value>
        </property>
        <property name="validator">
                <bean class="com.santosh.spring.UserValidator"/>
        </property>
  </bean>

  <bean id="myurlmapping"
class="org.springframework.web.servlet.handler.SimpleUrlHandlerMapping">
        <property name="mappings">
                <props>
                        <prop key="/login.spring">logincnt</prop>
                </props>
        </property>
  </bean>
</beans>
```

As we have done with all the three changes as shown under Lists 13.9, 13.10, and 13.11, compile the Java files and arrange all the files as shown in Fig. 13.4.

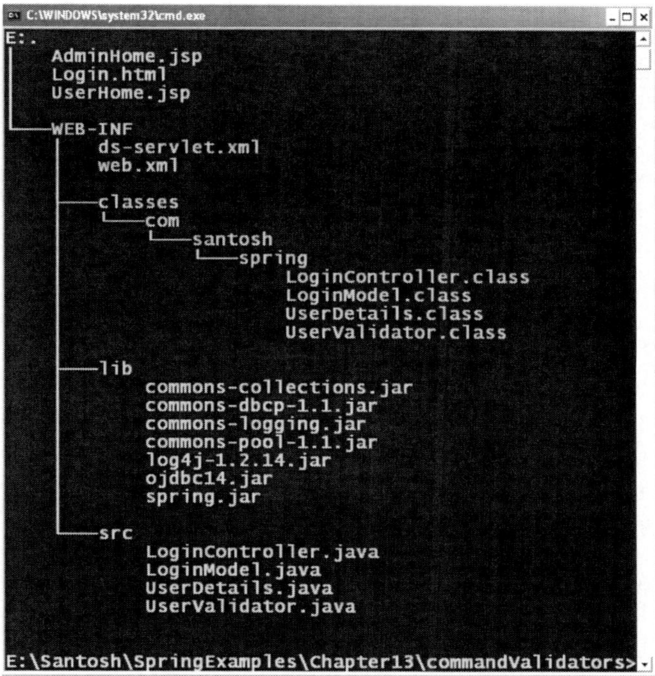

FIGURE 13.4 Tree structure showing all the files of comandValidators example

Deploy the application into the server as usual and browse the application using the URL http://localhost:8080/commandValidators/Login.html. You will find the view as shown in Fig. 13.5.

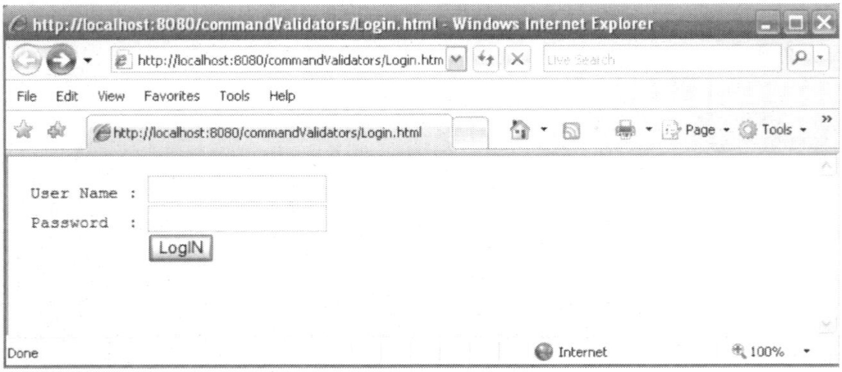

FIGURE 13.5 Login view

Now submit the form with empty field values and observe the output—you will find that both the fields are rejected and the default error messages are presented to the client as shown in Fig. 13.6.

FIGURE 13.6 Error messages for invalid login details

Similarly, test with the other inputs and you will find the respective outputs as explained and implemented. You will learn the Spring error tags to present the error messages in the view page in the next section, render view phase. In this subsection you learnt the AbstractCommandController and the validators, which provide us some infrastructural services while handling the request made as a form submission. In the next subsection you will learn additional requirements of form request handling and the solution for the requirements from Spring framework.

13.5 SIMPLEFORMCONTROLLER

In the preceding section we discussed about AbstractCommandController that implements some of the form processing infrastructure concerns like binding the request parameters data to the command object and validating the fields. But apart from these we have some other set of requirements in handling form requests like prepare the command object and present a new form on request. Process the form data submission in which if the data binding is not successful present the same form if not present some success view after handling the request. The SimpleFormController implements these infrastructure concerns providing us convenience in developing form request processing handlers (controllers). The controller class can simply extend SimpleFormController and do some configurations by injecting properties to get these infrastructures applied for our request handling logic. The following section explains the workflow of the SimpleFormController in detail.

13.5.1 Understanding the SimpleFormController Workflow

The SimpleFormController workflow starts by identifying whether the request is for a new form or a form submission. Figure 13.7 shows this flow.

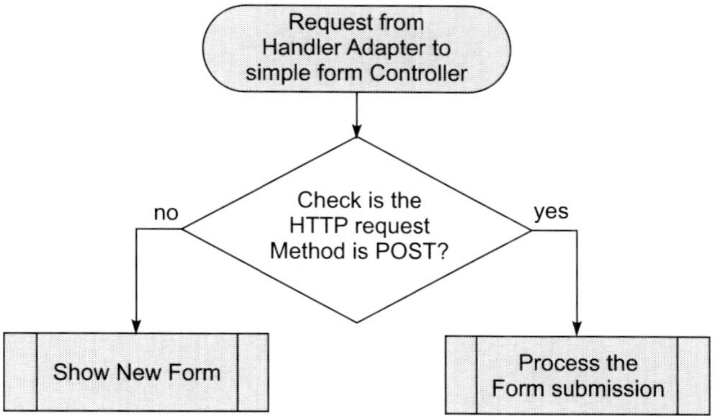

FIGURE 13.7 The high level flow diagram showing the workflow of SimpleFormController

As shown in Fig. 13.7 when SimpleFormController receives the request it identifies whether the request is for a new form or not. This is done by invoking isFormSubmission() method. The default implementation of isFormSubmission() method uses the HTTP request method of this request to find whether the request is for a new form. If the HTTP request method is HTTP POST method then the request is considered for processing the form submission, if not for a new form. However, we have an option to change this behavior by overriding the isFormSubmission() method with the method signature shown below.

Code Snippet

```
protected boolean isFormSubmission(HttpServletRequest request)
```

If the isFormSubmission() method returns true then the request is considered for processing the form submission. As shown in Fig. 13.7, if the request is identified for a new form then **Show New Form** workflow starts, if not then **Process the Form Submission** workflow starts. The following sections will explain these two workflows in detail.

13.5.1.1 The 'Show New Form' workflow

The **Show New Form** workflow starts if the SimpleFormController identifies the request for new form. The flow diagram of the **Show New Form** workflow is shown in Fig. 13.8.

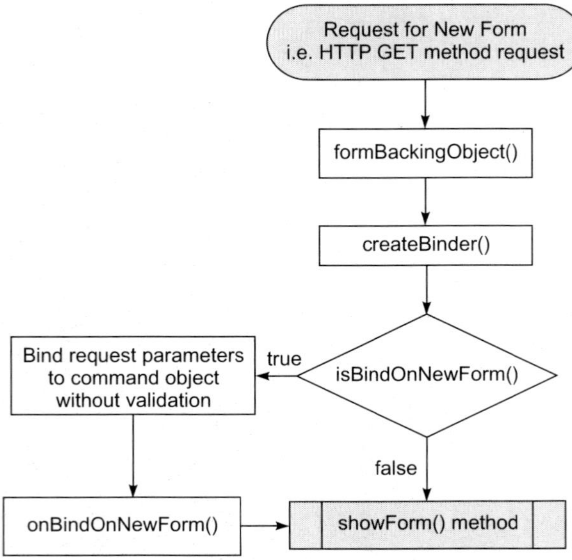

FIGURE 13.8 Flow diagram for the **Show New Form** workflow

Let us discuss the various operations performed under the **Show New Form** workflow as shown in Fig. 13.8.

Step 1: Creating a new command object

As shown in Fig. 13.8 the **Show New Form** workflow starts by creating a new command object. This is done by invoking formBackingObject() method. The default implementation of this method creates a new instance using the no-argument constructor of the configured commandClass. However, we are allowed to change this behavior by overriding the formBackingObject() method with the following method signature.

Code Snippet

```
protected Object formBackingObject(HttpServletRequest request) throws Exception
```

In case if this process fails, that is, if the formBackingObject() method fails to create a command object, or even if the formBackingObject() returns an object which is not an instance of the configured command class then ServletException is thrown terminating the workflow.

Step 2: Create and prepare binder

After the command object is created the next step in the workflow is to create and prepare a data binder. This is done by invoking createBinder() method of controller.

The DataBinder allows for setting property values on to a target object, including support for validation and binding result analysis. This even allows us to customize the binding process by specifying allowed fields, required fields, custom editors, etc.

The default implementation of createBinder() method performs the following operations:

- Creates a new instance of org.springframework.web.bind.ServletRequestDataBinder. Where the ServletRequestDataBinder is a special DataBinder to perform data binding from servlet request parameters to JavaBeans based properties.
- Invokes prepareBinder() method that prepares the given binder, applying the specified MessageCodesResolver, BindingErrorProcessor and PropertyEditorRegistrars.
- Thereafter, finally it invokes initBinder() method which allows us to initialize the binder by registering the binder with custom editors. The method signature of initBinder() is shown in the code snippet below.

Code Snippet

```
protected void initBinder(HttpServletRequest request, ServletRequestDataBinder
binder) throws Exception
```

If we want to configure any custom property editors for the data binder created then the controller can override the initBinder() method.

Step 3: Determine is binding required on new form request

After the data binder is created successfully the next operation is to find whether the request data binding to the command object is necessary for a new form request. This is required before data binding is done as this workflow is to show the new form. To determine whether the request data binding is required the workflow uses isBindOnNewForm() method. To disable or enable the binding on new form request configure the *bindOnNewForm* property. Setting *bindOnNewForm* property to *true* indicates that the request parameters should be bound in case of a request for a new form. The following code snippet shows bindOnNewForm property configuration for a controller.

Code Snippet

```
<bean id="mycontroller" class="com.nit.spring.MyController">
  <property name="bindOnNewForm" value="true"/>
  <!--configure the other properties like commandClass etc -->
</bean>
```

If the *bindOnNewForm* property is set to true then the workflow proceeds to Step 4, if not it moves to Step 5.

Step 4: Bind the request parameters to command object

This step of the **Show New Form** workflow executes only if the bindOnNewForm property of the controller is set to *true*, as explained earlier. In this step controller uses the data binder created in Step 2 to bind the request parameters to the command object created in Step 1. After the request data is bounded the onBindOnNewForm() method is invoked as callback for custom post-processing binding data for a new form request. The default implementation of this method is empty. The following code snippet shows the method signature of onBindOnNewForm() method.

Code Snippet

```
protected void onBindOnNewForm(HttpServletRequest request, Object command) throws
Exception
```

Step 5: Execute the showForm() method

The showForm() method is responsible to prepare ModelAndView for the given viewname, including reference and errors, adding a controller-specific control model. The workflow of the showForm() method is shown Fig. 13.9.

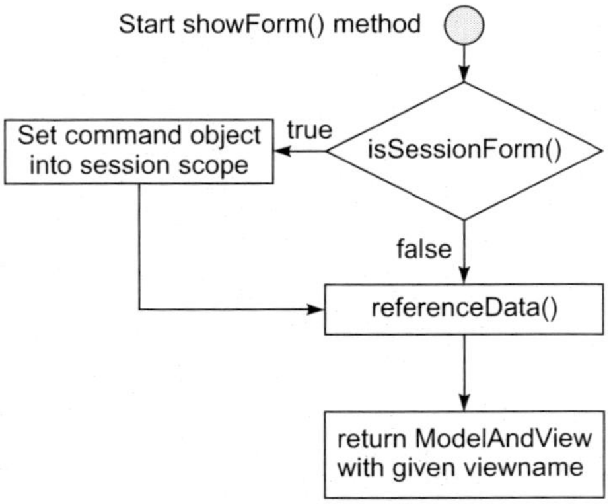

FIGURE 13.9 Flow diagram for showForm() method workflow

As shown in Fig. 13.9 the showForm() workflow includes the following steps of operations.

Step 5.1: Determine whether the command object issessionform

The showForm() method workflow starts by finding whether the controller is configured with the command object that has to be maintained in the session scope. This is done by invoking the isSessionForm() method. To configure the command object to maintain in session scope set the *sessionForm* property of controller to *true*. The following code snippet shows the configuration.

Code Snippet

```
<bean id="mycontroller" class="com.nit.spring.MyController">
   <property name="sessionForm" value="true"/>
   <!--configure the other properties like commandClass etc-->
</bean>
```

If the sessionForm is set to true then the workflow proceeds to Step 5.2, if not, it moves to Step 5.3.

Step 5.2: Bind or re-bind the command object to session scope

As described in the preceding step, this step of the workflow is executed only if the *sessionForm* property is set to *true*. In this step the command object created is set into the session scope with the configure attribute name. We can set the *commandName* property to configure the attribute name.

Step 5.3: Add errors and reference data to ModelAndView

In this step of the showForm() method workflow the controller adds the errors model as starting point, containing form object under *commandName* property value as key, and corresponding errors instance under internal key. Thereafter, the reference data is merged into the model. To get the reference data the controller invokes referenceData() method, by default this method returns *null.* If we want to add any reference data to the model then we can override the referenceData() method with the following method signature.

Code Snippet

```
protected Map referenceData(HttpServletRequest request, Object command, Errors errors)
throws Exception
```

After the reference data is added to the model the showForm() method creates a ModelAndView object with the given viewname, and the final model for trigger rendering of view.

We have discussed the **Show New Form** workflow which is executed in case the request is for the new form. Now we want to learn the second workflow that is workflow for processing the form submission. The following section explains the **Process the Form Submission** workflow.

13.5.1.2 The 'Process the Form Submission' workflow

The **Process the Form Submission** workflow starts if the SimpleFormController identifies the request as being that for processing the form submission. Generally this is done when a HTTP POST method request is done. The flow diagram of the **Process the Form Submission** workflow is shown in Fig. 13.10.

The following steps explain in detail the **Process the Form Submission** workflow shown in Fig. 13.10.

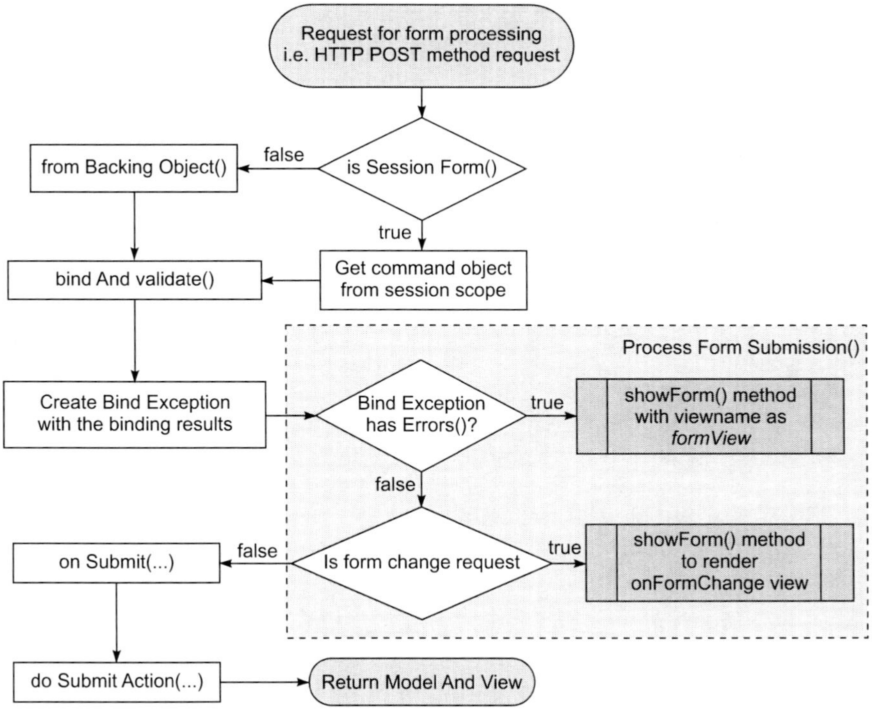

FIGURE 13.10 Flow diagram for Process the Form Submission workflow.

Step 1: Determine whether the isSessionFrom and create/locate command object

The **Process the Form Submission** workflow starts by identifying whether the controller is configured to store its command object in the session scope. As discussed earlier, to configure the command object for maintaining in a session scope set the *sessionForm* property to *true*. If the sessionForm is set to true then the command object is located from the session scope. If the sessionForm is set to *false* a new command object is created using the formBackingObject() method as described under Step 1 of **Show New Form** workflow (see the preceding section).

Step 2: Bind the request parameters to the command object and validate the fields

After the successful execution of Step 1 the workflow continues with this step in which it invokes bindAndValidate() method of controller that performs the following operations.

- First of all the bindAndValidate() method creates a new data binder object. For this it invokes createBinder() method (for detailed description on createBinder() method see Step 2 of **Show New Form** workflow, explained in the preceding section).
- The data binder created successfully is now used to bind the request parameters to the command object. After the request data is bounded the onBind() method is invoked as callback for custom post-processing binding data before the data validation. The default implementation of this method is empty. The following code snippet shows the method signature of onBind() method.

Code Snippet

```
protected void onBind(HttpServletRequest request, Object command) throws Exception
```

- After the request parameters are bound to the command object successfully the bindAndValidate() method finds for the suitable validator and performs the command object data validation. After this process is completed the onBindAndValidate() method is invoked as callback for custom post-processing in terms of binding and validation. The method signature of onBindAndValidate() method is shown in the code snippet below.After this method execution the bindAndValidate() method returns the binder.

Code Snippet

```
protected void onBindAndValidate(HttpServletRequest request, Object command,
BindException errors) throws Exception
```

Step 3: Create BindException

After the execution of the bindAndValidate(), that is, Step 2, the new BindException object is created with the binding results obtained from the binder returned by bindAndValidate() method.

Step 4: Execute processFormSubmission() method

After the successful execution of Step 1, 2, and 3 the **'Process the Form Submission'** workflow executes the processFormSubmission() method which performs the following operations.

- The processFormSubmission() method workflow starts with determining whether the given BindException has errors. If the BindException has errors then the showForm() method is invoked to trigger rendering of formview.

- If the BindException does not has any errors then the workflow continues in finding whether the isFromChangeRequest() is true. If the formChangeRequest is set to *true* then the showForm() method is invoked to trigger rendering of onFormChange view.
- If the BindException does not has any errors and formChangeRequest is not set to *true* then the workflow continues with the onSubmit() method execution, that is, Step 5.

Step 5: Execute onSubmit() method

After the successful binding the request parameters to the command object and validating the fields the onSubmit() method is invoked giving us an opportunity to handle the request. The default implementation of onSubmit() method invokes the doSubmitAction() and then returns a ModelAndView representing the successView.

As we have understood the workflow of SimpleFormController let us write one example to demonstrate how to use SimpleFormController.

13.5.2 Working with SimpleFormController

To demonstrate the use of SimpleFormController and the various configurations, we will design a simple AddEmplyee use case which takes the user details and saves it into the database. List 13.12 shows the AddEmployeeController.java that extends SimpleFormController overriding doSubmitAction() method to handle the request.

List 13.12: AddEmployeeController.java

```
package com.santosh.spring;

import org.springframework.web.servlet.mvc.*;

public class AddEmployeeController extends SimpleFormController {

  EmployeeServices employeeServices;

  public void setEmployeeServices(EmployeeServices es){
        employeeServices=es;
  }
  @Override
  public void doSubmitAction(Object command) throws Exception  {
    employeeServices.create((EmpDetails)command);
  }//doSubmitAction
}//class
```

List 13.13 shows the command class EmpDetails, which is designed to represent empno, deptno, mgr, name, job, sal, comm, etc.

List 13.13: EmpDetails.java

```
package com.santosh.spring;

public class EmpDetails implements java.io.Serializable{

  public EmpDetails(){
        System.out.println("In EmpDetails Constructor, constructing a new instance
for EmpDetails");
  }
  public double getComm() { return comm; }
  public void setComm(double comm) { this.comm = comm; }
  public int getDeptno() { return deptno; }
  public void setDeptno(int deptno) { this.deptno = deptno; }
  public int getEmpno() { return empno; }
  public void setEmpno(int empno) { this.empno = empno; }
  public String getJob() { return job; }
  public void setJob(String job) { this.job = job; }
  public int getMgr() { return mgr; }
  public void setMgr(int mgr) { this.mgr = mgr; }
  public String getName() { return name; }
  public void setName(String name) { this.name = name; }
  public double getSal() { return sal; }
  public void setSal(double sal) { this.sal = sal; }

  private int empno, deptno, mgr;
  private String name, job;
  private double sal, comm;
}//class
```

Now, to add the validations for the EmpDetails fields, we want to write a validator class. List 13.14 shows the EmpValidator.java.

List 13.14: EmpValidator.java

```
package com.santosh.spring;

import org.springframework.validation.*;

public class EmpValidator implements Validator {

  public boolean supports(Class c) {
        boolean flag=c.equals(EmpDetails.class);
        return flag;
   }
```

```
  public void validate(Object target, Errors errors) {
        EmpDetails ud = (EmpDetails) target;

        ValidationUtils.rejectIfEmptyOrWhitespace(errors, "name",
                            "field.required", "The name field cannot be empty");

        if (ud.getDeptno() < 10 ) {
                errors.rejectValue("deptno", "field.minValue",
                            new Object[]{Integer.valueOf(9)},
                            "The deptno should be greater than 9.");
        }
        else if (ud.getDeptno() > 99 ) {
          errors.rejectValue("deptno", "field.maxValue",
                      new Object[]{Integer.valueOf(99)},
                      "The deptno can contain value less than 99.");
        }
    }
}//class
```

To save the employee details into the database we want to use JdbcTemplate. List 13.15 shows the EmployeeServices.java.

List 13.15: EmployeeServices.java

```
package com.santosh.spring;

import org.springframework.jdbc.core.*;
import java.sql.Date;
import java.sql.PreparedStatement;
import java.sql.SQLException;

public class EmployeeServices {

  public EmployeeServices(JdbcTemplate jt){
    jdbcTemplate=jt;
  }

  public void create(final EmpDetails user) {

    jdbcTemplate.update("insert into emp values(?,?,?,?,?,?,?,?)",
      new PreparedStatementSetter(){
        public void setValues(PreparedStatement ps) throws SQLException {
          ps.setInt(1, user.getEmpno());
          ps.setString(2, user.getName());
          ps.setString(3, user.getJob());
          ps.setInt(4, user.getMgr());
```

```
            ps.setDate(5, new Date(System.currentTimeMillis()));
            ps.setDouble(6, user.getSal());
            ps.setDouble(7, user.getComm());
            ps.setInt(8, user.getDeptno());
         }
      });
   }//create
   private JdbcTemplate jdbcTemplate;
}//class
```

Now we want to design the add employee view that allows us to submit employee details to save into database. List 13.16 shows the AddEmployee.jsp.

List 13.16: AddEmployee.jsp

```
<%@taglib uri="http://www.springframework.org/tags/form" prefix="form"%>
<html>
  <body>
    <!– This tags are used to display the error messages
    of properties name and deptno –>
    <i><form:errors path="EmpDetails.name"/><br/><br/>
    <form:errors path="EmpDetails.deptno"/></i>
      <form action="addEmployee.spring" method="post"> <pre>
 Employee Number   : <input type="text" name="empno"/>
 Name              : <input type="text" name="name"/>
 Job               : <input type="text" name="job"/>
 Manager ID        : <input type="text" name="mgr"/>
 Salary            : <input type="text" name="sal"/>
 Commition         : <input type="text" name="comm"/>
 Department No     : <input type="text" name="deptno"/>
        <input type="submit" value="Add Employee"/>
     </pre> </form>
  </body>
</html>
```

List 13.17 shows the AddEmployeeSuccess.jsp that is presented to the client in case the add employee process is successful.

List 13.17: AddEmployeeSuccess.jsp

```
<html>
  <body>
  Employee details added Successfully
  </body>
</html>
```

List 13.18 shows the Home page that includes one hyperlink that allows making a GET method request to addEmployee.spring, which demonstrates the Show New Form workflow.

List 13.18: Home.jsp

```
<html>
  <body>
  <a href="addEmployee.spring">Add Employee</a>
  </body>
</html>
```

The spring beans XML configuration doing the various configurations required for the example is shown in List 13.19.

List 13.19: ds-servlet.xml

```
<beans xmlns="http://www.springframework.org/schema/beans"
xmlns:xsi="http://www.w3.org/2001/XMLSchema-instance"
xsi:schemaLocation="http://www.springframework.org/schema/beans
http://www.springframework.org/schema/beans/spring-beans-2.0.xsd">

  <!–Configuring DataSource–>
  <bean id="datasource" class="org.apache.commons.dbcp.BasicDataSource">
    <property name="driverClassName" value="oracle.jdbc.driver.OracleDriver"/>
    <property name="url" value="jdbc:oracle:thin:@localhost:1521:sandb"/>
    <property name="username" value="scott"/>
    <property name="password" value="tiger"/>
  </bean>

  <!–Configuring JdbcTemplate–>
  <bean id="jdbctemp" class="org.springframework.jdbc.core.JdbcTemplate">
    <constructor-arg>
      <ref local="datasource"/>
    </constructor-arg>
  </bean>

  <bean id="empServices" class="com.santosh.spring.EmployeeServices">
    <constructor-arg>
      <ref local="jdbctemp"/>
    </constructor-arg>
  </bean>

  <bean name="/addEmployee.spring" class="com.santosh.spring.AddEmployeeController">
    <property name="employeeServices">
      <ref local="empServices"/>
    </property>
    <!– configure the command class name –>
    <property name="commandClass">
      <value type="java.lang.Class">
        com.santosh.spring.EmpDetails
```

```
        </value>
      </property>
      <!– configure the command name, the name to use when binding the instantiated
command class to the request –>
      <property name="commandName">
        <value>EmpDetails</value>
      </property>
      <property name="validator">
        <bean class="com.santosh.spring.EmpValidator"/>
      </property>
      <!– <property name="bindOnNewForm" value="true"/>–>
      <property name="sessionForm" value="false"/>

      <property name="formView">
        <value>/AddEmployee.jsp</value>
      </property>
      <property name="successView">
        <value>/AddEmployeeSuccess.jsp</value>
      </property>
    </bean>
</beans>
```

Finally, we want to configure the DispatcherServlet with web applications which can be done using web.xml. List 13.20 shows the web.xml for this example.

List 13.20: web.xml

```
<web-app xmlns="http://java.sun.com/xml/ns/j2ee"
      xmlns:xsi="http://www.w3.org/2001/XMLSchema-instance"
      xsi:schemaLocation="http://java.sun.com/xml/ns/j2ee http://java.sun.com/xml/ns/
j2ee/web-app_2_4.xsd" version="2.4">
 <servlet>
   <servlet-name>ds</servlet-name>
    <servlet-class>org.springframework.web.servlet.DispatcherServlet</servlet-class>
   <load-on-startup>0</load-on-startup>
 </servlet>
 <servlet-mapping>
   <servlet-name>ds</servlet-name>
   <url-pattern>*.spring</url-pattern>
 </servlet-mapping>
</web-app>
```

As we have written all the files required for this example compile the Java files and arrange the files as shown in Fig. 13.11.

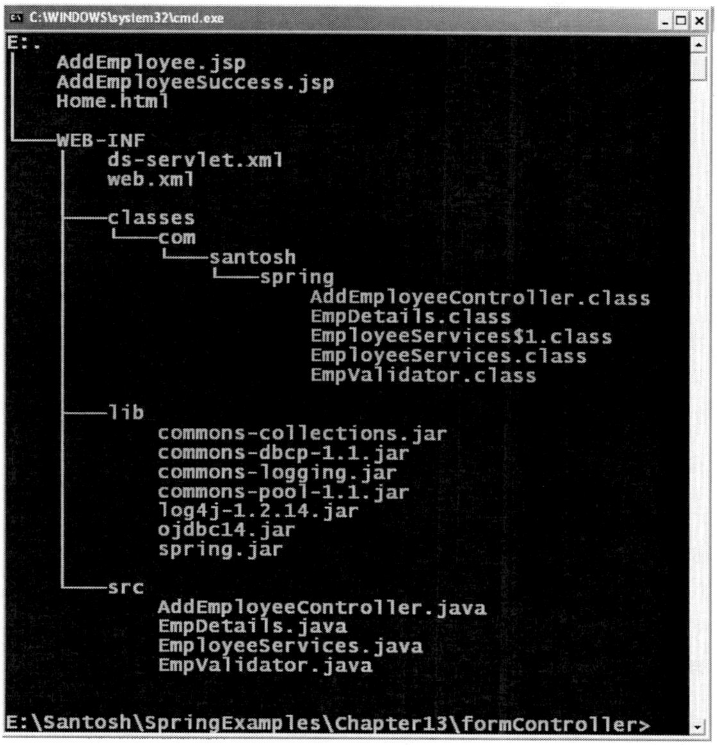

FIGURE 13.11 Directory structure to demonstrate SimpleFormController

Now, deploy the formController example into the Tomcat server (or any other web server) and browse the URL **http://localhost:8080/formController/Home.html** to find the home page as shown in Fig. 13.12.

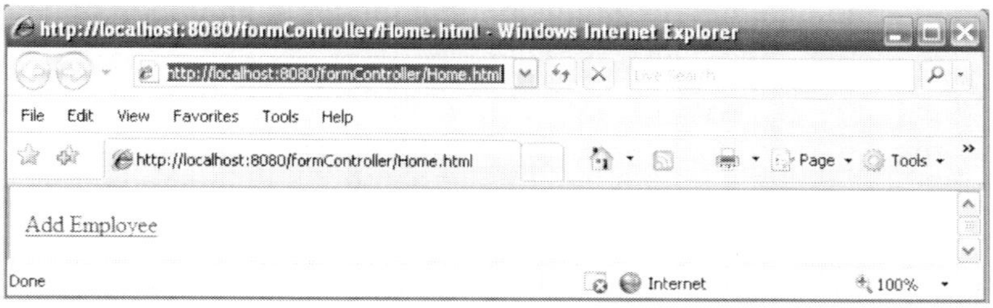

FIGURE 13.12 SimpleFormController examples home page

As shown in Fig. 13.12 the Home.html view gives us an opportunity to make a HTTP GET method request for **/addEmployee.spring** path. As per the configuration done in ds-servlet.xml shown in List 13.19, the **/addEmployee.spring** path is mapped to com.santosh.spring.AddEmployeeController which is a subtype of SimpleFormController. Thus this request results in presenting a new form (form for adding an employee) as discussed under the Section 13.5.1.1.

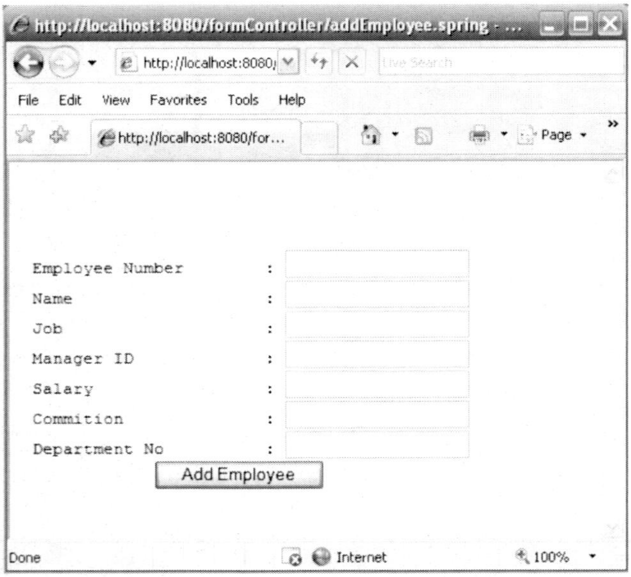

FIGURE 13.13 Form for adding new employee

Figure 13.13 shows the new form for adding an employee. Now enter the data as shown in Fig. 13.14 leaving the 'Name' field as empty and 'Department No' field with some value less than 10 like 9, so that we can find the formView as explained in the 'Process the Form Submission' workflow under the Section 13.5.1.2.

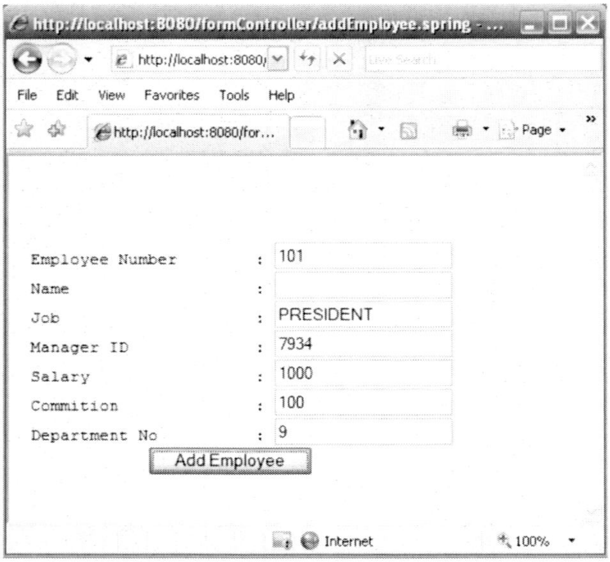

FIGURE 13.14 Add new employee form with data

Figure 13.14 shows the add new employee form with data entered. When this form is submitted as explained earlier, Name and Department No fields are not valid. Thus it presents the same form with error messages describing the errors.

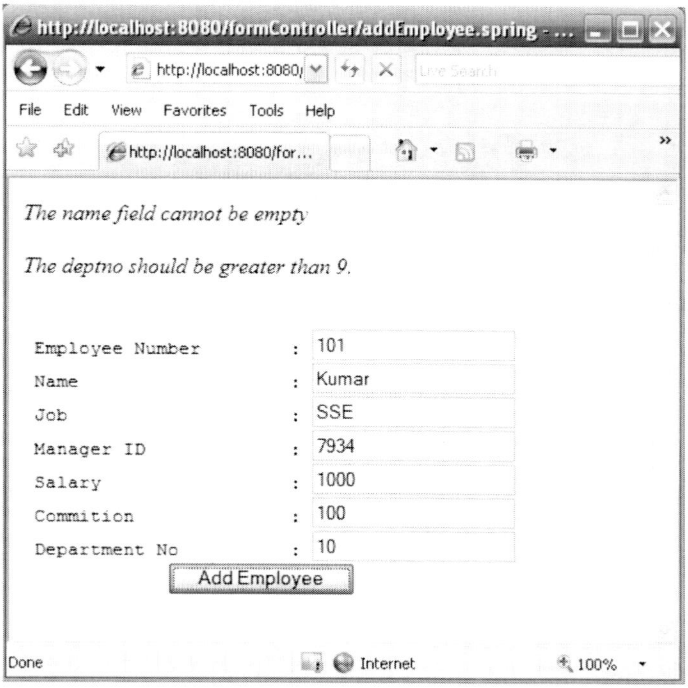

FIGURE 13.15 Add new employee form with error messages

Figure 13.15 shows the error messages for the form details submitted as shown in Fig. 13.14. Now enter some valid details as shown in Fig. 13.15 and submit the form.

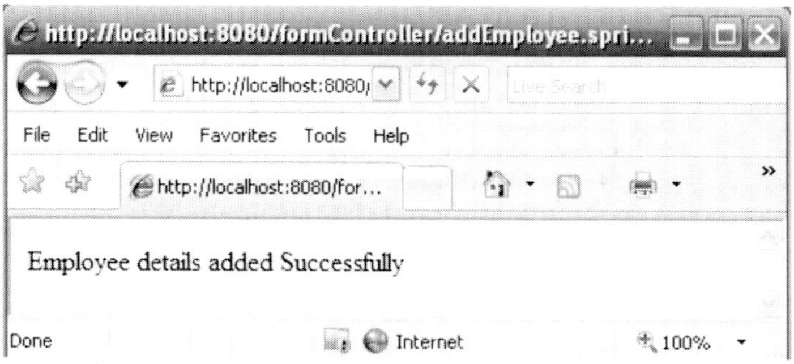

FIGURE 13.16 Add employee success view

Figure 13.16 shows the view presented by AddEmployeeSuccess.jsp, as discussed in the 'Process the Form Submission' workflow. If the data is processed successfully the successView is presented to the client. Here the successView is configured as AddEmployeeSuccess.jsp (see ds-servlet.xml under List 13.19. This example has given us an opportunity to practically demonstrate the various issues in workflow discussed in the preceding sections. Now, after browsing this example find the Tomcat server console and you will find the EmpDetails (command object) being created for each of request.

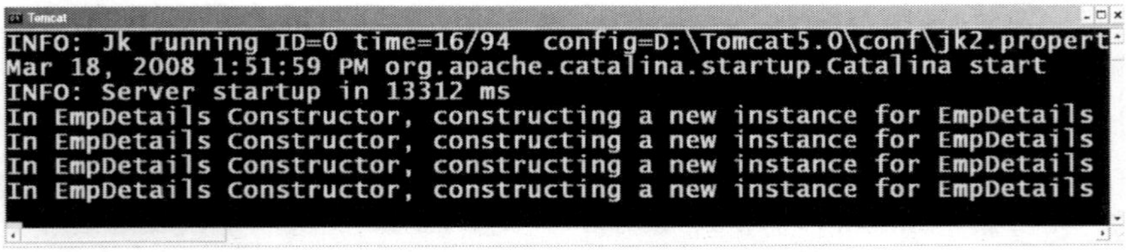

FIGURE 13.17 Tomcat server console

Figure 13.17 shows the Tomcat server console where you can observe that EmpDetails object is created for each request since the controller is configured with sessionForm as false (that is, the default value of sessionForm property is *false*). Now if we want to configure the EmpDetails (command object) to be created per session and maintain the command object in the session scope we want to configure sessionForm property of the controller to *true*, in ds-servlet.xml file. The following code snippet shows the sessionForm property configuration that can be added in the AddEmployeeController bean definition in ds-servlet.xml (List 13.19).

Code Snippet

```
<property name="sessionForm" value="true"/>
```

After configuring the property shown in the preceding code snippet reload the application and run the example. Once again you will find the EmpDetails object being created per session instead of for each of the request.

13.6 WIZARD FORM CONTROLLER

In the preceding section we have seen that the SimpleFormController implements most of the form processing infrastructure concerns like binding the request parameters data to the command object, validating the fields, etc., enabling us to develop a controller for processing a single-page form. However, while implementing some processes like registration and order processing, we require some additional infrastructures that support multiple pages including forms that together fill a command object as one page filling the general details—one personal, and the other address.

The AbstractWizardFormController implements these infrastructure concerns providing us convenience in developing controllers for the wizard style workflow. The AbstractWizardForm Controller is an abstract class packaged into the *org.springframework.web.servlet.mvc* package. The AbstractWizardFormController supports to process multiple pages including finish and cancel actions, and even allows implementing logic to execute while changing the page in the wizard. The AbstractWizardFormController's workflow is almost similar to the workflow of SimpleForm

Controller, in addition this includes the finish, cancel, and page change actions instead of one single submit action. The AbstractWizardFormController allows us to adjust our requirements (that is, customizations) through the various properties it supports. Table 13.2 describes the properties of AbstractWizardFormController.

TABLE 13.2 Properties of AbstractWizardFormController

Property	*Description*
pages	The 'pages' property is of String array type. Specifies the list of view names (wizards) for this controller.
allowDirtyBack	Specifies whether this controller allows navigating to the previous wizards.
allowDirtyForward	Specifies whether the controller moves to the next wizard with validation errors. The default value is false.
pageAttribute	Specifies the property name in the model (that is, command object) that describes the current page number. If this property is configured then the controller sets the current page number to the specified property.

To throw more light on this topic let us look at a simple sample code to demonstrate the multi-wizard process practically.

13.6.1 Working with Wizard Controller

To demonstrate the wizard controller we will implement a simple registration process that takes the inputs from client in three steps here. The first wizard takes general details like username, password, re-password, and email. The second wizard takes the personal details and then the last wizard, that is, the third wizard takes address details.

Let us start developing RegistrationStep1.html, which describes the view for the first wizard.

List 13.21: RegisterationStep1.html

```
<html>
  <body>
    <form name="form1" method="post" action="registration.spring">
      <table border="0" align="left">
        <tr>
          <td colspan="2">
            <div align="center"><strong>Registration Step 1</strong></div>
          </td>
        </tr>
        <tr><td> </td><td> </td></tr>
        <tr>
          <td>User Name</td>
          <td><input name="uname" type="text" id="uname"></td>
        </tr>
        <tr><td>Password</td>
          <td><input name="pass" type="password" id="pass"></td>
```

```
        </tr>
        <tr>
          <td>Re-Password</td>
          <td><input name="repass" type=" password" id="repass"></td>
        </tr>
        <tr>
          <td>Email</td>
          <td><input name="email" type="text" id="email"></td>
        </tr>
        <tr><td> </td><td> </td></tr>
        <tr>
          <td colspan="2"> <div align="center">
              <input type="submit" name="Submit" value="Next &gt;">
          </div> </td>
        </tr>
      </table>
      <input type="hidden" name="_page" value="1"/>
    </form>
  </body>
</html>
```

List 13.22 shows the registration Step 2 view.

List 13.22: RegistrationStep2.html

```
<html>
  <body>
    <form name="form1" method="post" action="registration.spring">
      <table width="41%" border="0" align="left">
        <tr>
          <td colspan="2">
            <div align="center"><strong>Registration Step 2</strong></div>
          </td>
        </tr>
        <tr><td> </td><td> </td></tr>
        <tr>
          <td>First Name</td>
          <td><input name="fname" type="text" id="fname"></td>
        </tr>
        <tr>
          <td>Last Name</td>
          <td><input name="lname" type="text" id="lname"></td>
        </tr>
        <tr>
          <td>Middle Name (Initial)</td>
          <td><input name="initial" type="text" id="initial"></td>
```

```
        </tr>
        <tr>
          <td>DOB</td>
          <td><input name="dob" type="text" id="dob"></td>
        </tr>
        <tr>
          <td>Mobile</td>
          <td><input name="mobile" type="text" id="mobile"></td>
        </tr>
        <tr>
          <td>Phone</td>
          <td><input name="phone" type="text" id="phone"></td>
        </tr>
        <tr><td> </td><td> </td></tr>
        <tr>
          <td colspan="2"><div align="center">
               <input type="submit" name="Submit" value="Next &gt;">
          </div></td>
        </tr>
      </table>
      <input type="hidden" name="_page" value="2"/>
    </form>
  </body>
</html>
```

After writing the wizard 1 and 2 views we will now write the final wizard that finishes the process. List 13.23 shows the RegistrationFinal.html.

List 13.23: RegistrationFinal.html

```
<html>
  <body>
    <form name="form1" method="post" action="registration.spring">
      <table width="41%" border="0" align="left">
        <tr><th colspan="3" align="center">Registration Final Step</th></tr>
        <tr>
          <td colspan="2"><strong>Address:</strong></td><td> </td>
        </tr>
        <tr>
          <td>   </td><td>Address1</td>
          <td><input name="addr1" type="text" id="addr1"></td>
        </tr>
        <tr>
          <td>   </td><td>Street</td>
          <td><input name="street" type="text" id="street"></td>
        </tr>
```

```
        <tr>
          <td>    </td><td>City</td>
          <td><input name="city" type="text" id="city"></td>
        </tr>
        <tr>
          <td>    </td><td>State</td>
          <td><input name="state" type="text" id="state"></td>
        </tr>
        <tr>
          <td>    </td><td>Country</td>
          <td><input name="country" type="text" id="country"></td>
        </tr>
        <tr>
          <td>    </td><td> </td><td> </td>
        </tr>
        <tr>
          <td colspan="3" align="center">
            <input type="submit" value="Finish">
          </td>
        </tr>
      </table>
      <input type="hidden" name="_finish" value="finish"/>
    </form>
  </body>
</html>
```

After creating all the three wizards we will create a controller that can process the wizard navigation and the data after submitting the final wizard. List 13.24 shows the RegistrationController.java, subtype of AbstractWizardFormController implementing the processFinish() method that processes the form data.

List 13.24: RegistrationController.java

```
package com.santosh.spring;

import javax.servlet.http.HttpServletRequest;
import javax.servlet.http.HttpServletResponse;

import org.springframework.validation.BindException;
import org.springframework.web.servlet.ModelAndView;
import org.springframework.web.servlet.mvc.AbstractWizardFormController;

/**
 * @author Santosh
 *
 */
```

```
public class RegistrationController extends AbstractWizardFormController {

  private UserDAO userDAO;
  public RegistrationController(UserDAO userDAO){
    this.userDAO=userDAO;
  }
  protected ModelAndView processFinish(
      HttpServletRequest request,
      HttpServletResponse response, Object command,
      BindException exceptions) throws Exception {

    UserDetails userDetails=(UserDetails)command;
    boolean flag=userDAO.create(userDetails);
    if (flag)
      return new ModelAndView("RegistrationSuccess.jsp");
    return new ModelAndView("RegistrationFail.html");
  }
}
```

It can be observed from the preceding code snippet that the controller depends on the command class (UserDetails) and UserDAO to create a user with the data encapsulated in UserDetails object. Let us implement the UserDetails and UserDAO types that RegisterController depends on. List 13.25 shows the UserDetails.java that is used as a command object.

List 13.25: UserDetails.java

```
package com.santosh.spring;

import java.io.Serializable;
/**
 * @author Santosh
 *
 */
public class UserDetails implements Serializable {

  public String uname, pass, repass, email;
  public String fname, lname, initial, dob, mobile, phone;
  public String addr1, street, city, state, country;

  public String getAddr1() {return addr1;}
  public void setAddr1(String addr1) {this.addr1 = addr1;}
  public String getCity() {return city;}
  public void setCity(String city) {this.city = city;}
  public String getCountry() {return country;}
  public void setCountry(String country) {this.country = country;}
  public String getDob() {return dob;}
```

```
  public void setDob(String dob) {this.dob = dob;}
  public String getEmail() {return email;}
  public void setEmail(String email) {this.email = email;}
  public String getFname() {return fname;}
  public void setFname(String fname) {this.fname = fname;}
  public String getInitial() {return initial;}
  public void setInitial(String initial) {this.initial = initial;}
  public String getLname() {return lname;}
  public void setLname(String lname) {this.lname = lname;}
  public String getMobile() {return mobile;}
  public void setMobile(String mobile) {this.mobile = mobile;}
  public String getPass() {return pass;}
  public void setPass(String pass) {this.pass = pass;}
  public String getPhone() {return phone;}
  public void setPhone(String phone) {this.phone = phone;}
  public String getRepass() {return repass;}
  public void setRepass(String repass) {this.repass = repass;}
  public String getState() {return state;}
  public void setState(String state) {this.state = state;}
  public String getStreet() {return street;}
  public void setStreet(String street) {this.street = street;}
  public String getUname() {return uname;}
  public void setUname(String uname) {this.uname = uname;}
}
```

List 13.26 shows the UserDAO interface that provides an abstraction to access the UserDAOImpl that performs persistence operations for inserting the user details into the database.

List 13.26: UserDAO.java

```
package com.santosh.spring;
/**
 * @author Santosh
 *
 */
public interface UserDAO {
  boolean create(UserDetails userDetails);
}
```

List 13.27 shows the UserDAO interface declaring only one method to create a user account. Now, we will implement this interface that performs persistence operations using Spring JDBC Abstraction Framework's JdbcTemplate.

List 13.27: UserDAOImpl.java

```
package com.santosh.spring;

import java.sql.PreparedStatement;
import java.sql.SQLException;
import java.sql.Statement;
import org.springframework.jdbc.core.JdbcTemplate;
import org.springframework.jdbc.core.PreparedStatementSetter;
/**
 * @author Santosh
 *
 */
public class UserDAOImpl implements UserDAO {

  private JdbcTemplate jdbcTemplate;
  public UserDAOImpl(JdbcTemplate jt){
    jdbcTemplate=jt;
  }
  public boolean create(final UserDetails userDetails) {
    System.out.println("create");
    int count=jdbcTemplate.update("insert into users values
(?,?,?,?,?,?,?,?,?,?,?,?,?,?)",
      new PreparedStatementSetter(){
        public void setValues(PreparedStatement ps)throws SQLException{
          ps.setString(1,userDetails.uname);
          ps.setString(2,userDetails.pass);
          ps.setString(3,userDetails.email);
          ps.setString(4,userDetails.fname);
          ps.setString(5,userDetails.lname);
          ps.setString(6,userDetails.initial);
          ps.setString(7,userDetails.dob);
          ps.setString(8,userDetails.mobile);
          ps.setString(9,userDetails.phone);
          ps.setString(10,userDetails.addr1);
          ps.setString(11,userDetails.street);
          ps.setString(12,userDetails.city);
          ps.setString(13,userDetails.state);
          ps.setString(14,userDetails.country);
        }
      });
    return (count==1 || count==Statement.SUCCESS_NO_INFO);
  }
}
```

List 13.28 shows the simple view that is presented in case the controller fails to insert the user details into the database.

List 13.28: RegistrationFail.html

```
<html>
  <body>Registration Process Failed</body>
</html>
```

List 13.29 shows the simple view that is presented in case the controller successfully inserts the user details into database.

List 13.29: RegistrationSuccess.jsp

```
<html>
  <body>Registration Process Finished</body>
</html>
```

In List 13.29 we have created all the views, controller and its supporting classes as UserDetails, UserDAO, UserDAOImpl required for this example. Now we need to configure the controller and the UserDAO in the spring beans XML configuration file of this context. Up till now in the various examples demonstrated in this chapter we have used ds-servlet.xml (i.e. <servlet-name>-servlet.xml) but we can use any other name for this file and even we can also configure the beans in multiple XML configuration files. Here we will describe this feature in this example. List 13.30 shows the applicationControllers.xml, one of the XML configuration files to be configured to our applications DispatcherServlet.

List 13.30: applicationControllers.xml

```
<beans xmlns="http://www.springframework.org/schema/beans"
xmlns:xsi="http://www.w3.org/2001/XMLSchema-instance"
xsi:schemaLocation="http://www.springframework.org/schema/beans
http://www.springframework.org/schema/beans/spring-beans-2.0.xsd">

  <bean name="/registration.spring"
        class="com.santosh.spring.RegistrationController">
    <constructor-arg>
      <ref bean="userDAO"/>
    </constructor-arg>

    <property name="commandClass">
      <value type="java.lang.Class">
        com.santosh.spring.UserDetails
      </value>
    </property>
    <property name="commandName">
      <value>UserDetails</value>
    </property>
    <property name="sessionForm" value="true"/>
    <property name="pages">
```

```
      <list>
      <value>/RegistrationStep1.html</value>
      <value>/RegistrationStep2.html</value>
      <value>/RegistrationFinal.html</value>
      </list>
    </property>
    <property name="allowDirtyForward">
      <value>false</value>
    </property>
  </bean>
</beans>
```

Now List 13.31 shows applicationDAOs.xml file that declares the UserDAO and its dependencies.

List 13.31: applicationDAOs.xml

```
<beans xmlns="http://www.springframework.org/schema/beans"
xmlns:xsi="http://www.w3.org/2001/XMLSchema-instance"
xsi:schemaLocation="http://www.springframework.org/schema/beans
http://www.springframework.org/schema/beans/spring-beans-2.0.xsd">

  <!–Configuring DataSource–>
  <bean id="datasource" class="org.apache.commons.dbcp.BasicDataSource">
    <property name="driverClassName" value="oracle.jdbc.driver.OracleDriver"/>
    <property name="url" value="jdbc:oracle:thin:@localhost:1521:sandb"/>
    <property name="username" value="scott"/>
    <property name="password" value="tiger"/>
  </bean>

  <!–Configuring JdbcTemplate–>
  <bean id="jdbctemp" class="org.springframework.jdbc.core.JdbcTemplate">
    <constructor-arg>
      <ref local="datasource"/>
    </constructor-arg>
  </bean>

  <bean id="userDAO" class="com.santosh.spring.UserDAOImpl">
    <constructor-arg>
      <ref local="jdbctemp"/>
    </constructor-arg>
  </bean>
</beans>
```

Now finally we need to configure the DispatcherServlet in web.xml file making it available to the web container. List 13.32 shows the web.xml for this application.

List 13.32: web.xml

```
<?xml version="1.0" encoding="UTF-8"?>
<web-app version="2.4"
  xmlns="http://java.sun.com/xml/ns/j2ee"
  xmlns:xsi="http://www.w3.org/2001/XMLSchema-instance"
  xsi:schemaLocation="http://java.sun.com/xml/ns/j2ee
  http://java.sun.com/xml/ns/j2ee/web-app_2_4.xsd">

  <servlet>
    <servlet-name>ds</servlet-name>
    <servlet-class>
      org.springframework.web.servlet.DispatcherServlet
    </servlet-class>
    <init-param>
      <param-name>contextConfigLocation</param-name>
      <param-value>
        /WEB-INF/myconfigs/applicationControllers.xml
        /WEB-INF/myconfigs/applicationDAOs.xml
      </param-value>
    </init-param>
    <load-on-startup>0</load-on-startup>
  </servlet>
  <servlet-mapping>
    <servlet-name>ds</servlet-name>
    <url-pattern>*.spring</url-pattern>
  </servlet-mapping>
</web-app>
```

List 13.32 shows the web.xml configuration file configuring DispatcherServlet for this application; here we are using 'contextConfigLocation' parameter for configuring the Spring Beans XML configuration files location instead of using ds-servlet.xml (that is, <servlet-name>-servlet.xml) as used in the previous examples demonstrated in this chapter. See Chapter 12, Section 12.1 for description on DispatcherServlet initialization parameters.

As we have completed creating all the files required for this examples compile all the java files and arrange the files in the directory structure as shown in Fig. 13.18.

After arranging the files into the directory structure as shown in the preceding figure, deploy the application into any server that includes J2EE Web Container, like Tomcat, Weblogic, etc. Here we use Tomcat server but as we have already mentioned earlier, the Spring Web MVC framework is not dependent on any specific server. To run this example we want to create the 'users' table in the database. List 13.33 shows the create table command that creates the 'users' table.

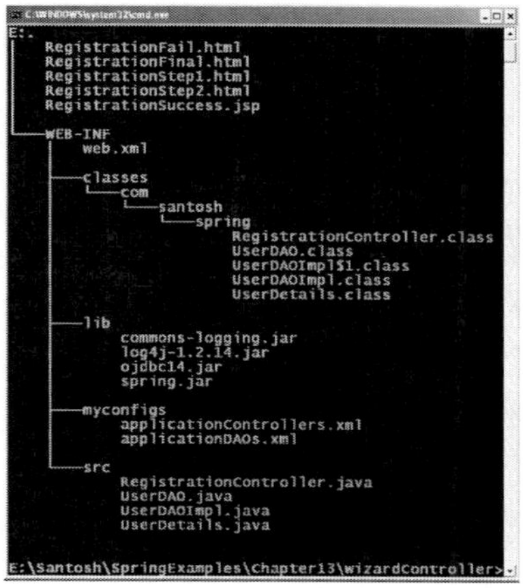

FIGURE 13.18 Directory structure of wizardController example

List 13.33: create users table

```
create table users (
uname varchar2(20), pass varchar2(10), email varchar2(20), fname varchar2(12),
lname varchar2(12), nameInitial varchar2(2), dob varchar2(10), mobile varchar2(12),
phone varchar2(10), addrl varchar2(20), street varchar2(20), city varchar2(15),
state varchar2(10), country varchar2(10));
```

After creating the 'users' table in the database and deploying the application into the server start the server, browse the application using the URL **http://localhost:8080/wizardController/registration.spring.** We will find the controller presenting the first wizard view, that is, RegistrationStep1.html. Enter the details as shown in Fig. 13.19 and submit the request to find the second wizard.

FIGURE 13.19 The first wizard of the total three wizards in registration process

After submitting the details using the first wizard the controller stores the details into the command object saving it into the session scope and then presents the next view as described by the '_page' parameter of this request.

> **Note:** The page numbers starts from 0. As per the pages configured in the applicationControllers.xml file shown in List 13.30, RegistrationStep2.html is the page at the page number 1. Thus when the RegistrationStep1.html submits the form controller presents RegistrationStep2.html view, enter the details as shown in Fig. 13.20 and submit the request to get the final view.

FIGURE 13.20 The second wizard of the total three wizards in registration process

After entering the details as shown in Fig. 13.20 and submitting the request the controller saves the given details in the command object and presents the next view, that is, RegistrationFinal.html. Enter the details as shown in Fig. 13.21 and submit the request to finish the process.

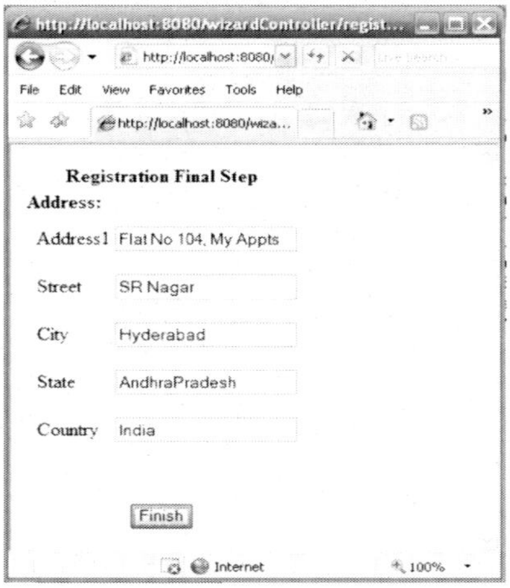

FIGURE 13.21 The final wizard of the registration process

Once the form shown in Fig. 13.21 is submitted the controller executes the logic implemented in the processFinish() method, which uses UserDAO to save the user details into the database. If the controller saves the data successfully, the RegistrationSuccess.jsp is presented otherwise the RegistrationFail.html page is presented.

While working with the wizard controller if we want to implement validations for each page and/or finally for all the pages at the end, override validatePage() method. The validatePage() method signature is shown in the following code snippet.

Code Snippet

```
public void validatePage(Object command, Errors errors, int page, boolean finish)
```

For example, after submitting the first wizard if we want to check whether the submitted password and re-password values are equal, the validatePage() method in the RegistrationController.jsp is shown.

```
public void validatePage(Object command, Errors errors, int page, boolean finish){
  UserDetails ud=(UserDetails)command;

  if (page==1){
    if(!ud.pass.equals(ud.repass)){
      System.out.println("abc");
      errors.rejectValue("pass", "field.pass",
          new Object[]{}, "Password and Repassword must be same");
    }
  }
}
```

In this section we learnt how to implement a controller handling multiple wizards, using the infrastructures provided by the Spring Web MVC built-in controller AbstractWizardFormController. In the next section we will learn how to implement multiple actions into a single controller.

13.7 MULTIACTIONCONTROLLER

The org.springframework.web.servlet.mvc.multiaction.MultiActionController class allows us to combine a set of similar actions into a single controller class in order to simplify the application design by eliminating the need to create separate controller classes for each of the action. That is, this class provides a mechanism for modularizing a set of related actions into a single controller. This is similar to a Struts Frameworks DispatchAction, but more refined. The MultiActionController dispatches the request to a public method that is named by the method name described by the MethodNameResolver it is configured with. As described, the MultiActionController provides an infrastructure for designing a controller class to handle more than a few different types of request with different methods. The method signature of the request handling methods in the subclass of MultiActionController is as shown in the following code snippet.

Code Snippet

```
public (ModelAndView | Map | void) <method_name>(HttpServletRequest request,
HttpServletResponse response [, HttpSession session | Object command]) throws Throw
able
```

As shown in the preceding code snippet the methods return type can be ModelAndView, Map, or void.

- If the return type is Map then the configured org.springframework.web.servlet.RequestToView NameTranslator will be used to determine the view name, that is, view name translation will be used to generate the view name.
- If the return type is *void* then the return value is assumed as *null*, meaning that the handler method is responsible for writing the response directly to the HttpServletResponse.

The following code snippet shows the sample implementation of MultiActionController subclass.

Code Snippet

```
package com.santosh.spring;

import java.util.Collection;

import javax.servlet.http.HttpServletRequest;
import javax.servlet.http.HttpServletResponse;

import org.springframework.web.servlet.ModelAndView;
import org.springframework.web.servlet.mvc.multiaction.MultiActionController;

public class EmployeeSearchController extends MultiActionController {

  public ModelAndView searchByEmpno(
          HttpServletRequest request,
          HttpServletResponse response) throws Exception {
       /*
        * request handling logic for searching employee details
        * with the given empno.
        *
        * prepare ModelAndView object,
        * adding the model (EmpDetails) and the view name
        */
       return mav;
  }

  public ModelAndView searchByEname(
            HttpServletRequest request,
            HttpServletResponse response) throws Exception {
       /*
```

```
     * request handling logic for searching employee details
     * with the given employee name.
     *
     * prepare ModelAndView object,
     * adding the model (EmpDetails) and the view name
     */
    return mav;
  }

  public ModelAndView searchByJob(
            HttpServletRequest request,
            HttpServletResponse response) throws Exception {
    /*
     * request handling logic for searching employee details
     * with the given employee name.
     *
     * prepare ModelAndView object,
     * adding the model (EmpDetails) and the view name
     */
    return mav;
  }

  public ModelAndView searchByDeptno(
      HttpServletRequest request,
      HttpServletResponse response) throws Exception {
    /*
     * request handling logic for searching employee details
     * with the given employee name.
     *
     * prepare ModelAndView object,
     * adding the model (EmpDetails) and the view name
     */
    return mav;
  }
}
```

As shown in the preceding code snippet,to implement multiple actions into a single controller class we can subclass MultiActionController and implement methods for each of the action. The following code snippet shows the configuration of the EmployeeSearchController.

Code Snippet

```
<bean id="empSearchController"
class="com.santosh.spring.EmployeeSearchController">
 <property name="methodNameResolver" ref="myMethodResolver"/>
</bean>
```

The preceding code shows the configuration of EmployeeSearchController with a myMethodResolver (we will learn about different MethodNameResolvers and their configurations in the next section). Apart from this approach of configuration MultiActionController also supports delegation to another object. That is, instead of implementing a subclass of MultiActionController we can implement a plain java class and configure it as a delegate using the *delegate* property of MultiActionController as shown in the following code snippet.

Code Snippet

```
<bean id="empSearchControllerDelegate"
class="com.santosh.spring.EmployeeSearchController"/>

<bean id="empSearchController"
class="org.springframework.web.servlet.mvc.multiaction.MultiActionController">
 <property name="methodNameResolver" ref="myMethodResolver"/>
 <property name="delegate" ref="empSearchControllerDelegate"/>
</bean>
```

As we have learnt the method signatures for the handling different requests, and how to implement and configure MultiActionController and/or its subclass, it is time to look at the MethodName Resolvers that resolves the method name for handling the given request.

13.7.1 MethodNameResolvers

The MethodNameResolver is responsible to identify the method name that handles this request and this is done based on any aspect of the request, such as its URL or a value of configured parameter. The actual approach can be configured using the "methodNameResolver" bean property of a MultiActionController. The Spring web MVC framework includes two important built-in MethodNameResolver implementations:

1. ParameterMethodNameResolver
2. PropertiesMethodNameResolver

Let us learn these MethodNameResolvers in detail.

13.7.1.1 The ParameterMethodNameResolver

The ParameterMethodNameResolver is an implementation of MethodNameResolver that uses a simple strategy for resolving the method name for the given request. As the name suggests, the ParameterMethodNameResolver looks for a given named parameter, whose value is considered the name of the method to invoke. The name of the parameter can be configured using *paramName* property, the default is taken as *action* and to configure the default method name use *defaultMethodName* property. This strategy is generally used with the forms containing multiple submit buttons or a list box whose value decides the action, like we may have a search view in which a search by criteria type is selected from the list box, as by empno, name, deptno, etc. The following code snippet shows the configuration of ParameterMethodNameResolver.

Code Snippet

```
<bean id="myMethodResolver" class="
org.springframework.web.servlet.mvc.multiaction.ParameterMethodNameResolver">
  <property name="paramName" value="submit"/>
  <property name="defaultMethodName" value="inValidRequest"/>
</bean>
```

13.7.1.2 The PropertiesMethodNameResolver

The PropertiesMethodNameResolver is an implementation of MethodNameResolver interface that uses the configured java.util.Properties to resolve the method name for the given request. This allows us to configure java.util.Properties to define the mapping between the URL of incoming requests and the corresponding method name. To configure such a Properties object use the mapping property of PropertiesMethodNameResolver. The following code snippet shows the configuration of PropertiesMethodNameResolver.

Code Snippet

```
<bean id="myMethodResolver" class="
org.springframework.web.servlet.mvc.multiaction.PropertiesMethodNameResolver">
  <property name="mappings">
   <props>
     <prop key="/add.spring">add</prop>
     <prop key="/subtract.spring">subtract</prop>
    </props>
  </property>
</bean>
```

We have learnt how to configure the built-in MethodNameResolver. To throw more light on this topic we will look at an example that can practically demonstrate the use of MultiActionController.

13.7.2 Working with MultiActionController

To demonstrate the MultiActionController in action we implement addition and subtraction actions into a single controller class. Starting with the controller implementation, List 13.34 shows the ArithmeticController.java.

List 13.34: ArithmeticController.java

```
package com.santosh.spring;

import javax.servlet.http.HttpServletRequest;
import javax.servlet.http.HttpServletResponse;
import org.springframework.web.servlet.ModelAndView;
import org.springframework.web.servlet.mvc.multiaction.MultiActionController;

public class ArithmeticController extends MultiActionController {
```

```
    public ModelAndView add(
HttpServletRequest request, HttpServletResponse response)
        throws Exception {

      int op1 = Integer.parseInt(request.getParameter("operand1"));
      int op2 = Integer.parseInt(request.getParameter("operand2"));
      int result = op1 + op2;
      return new ModelAndView("/Home.jsp", "result", result + "");
    }

    public ModelAndView subtract(
HttpServletRequest request, HttpServletResponse response)
        throws Exception {

      int op1 = Integer.parseInt(request.getParameter("operand1"));
      int op2 = Integer.parseInt(request.getParameter("operand2"));
      int result = op1 - op2;
      return new ModelAndView("/Home.jsp", "result", result + "");
    }
}
```

Now, we will design a view that enables us to make a request for addition/subtraction, and even display the results. List 13.35 shows Home.jsp.

List 13.35: Home.jsp

```
<html>
  <body>
    <%if(request.getAttribute("result")!=null){%>
    Result of previous request (<%=request.getParameter("submit")%>):
    <b><%=request.getParameter("operand1")%> , <%=request.getParameter("operand2")%>
is <%=request.getAttribute("result")%></b>
    <%}%>

    <form action="mypath.spring" method="POST">
      Operand1 : <input type="text" name="operand1" />
      <br />
      Operand2 : <input type="text" name="operand2" />
      <br/> <br/>
      <input type="submit" name="submit" value="add"/>
      <input type="submit" name="submit" value="subtract"/>
    </form>
  </body>
</html>
```

Now write a Spring beans XML configuration file configuring controller with the ParameterMethod NameResolver to test the ArithmeticController,. List 13.36 shows the ds-servlet.xml configuration file.

List 13.36: ds-servlet.xml

```
<beans  xmlns="http://www.springframework.org/schema/beans"
xmlns:xsi="http://www.w3.org/2001/XMLSchema-instance"
xsi:schemaLocation="http://www.springframework.org/schema/beans
http://www.springframework.org/schema/beans/spring-beans-2.0.xsd">
  <bean id="myMethodResolver" class="
org.springframework.web.servlet.mvc.multiaction.ParameterMethodNameResolver">
     <property name="paramName" value="submit"/>
  </bean>

  <bean name="/mypath.spring"
       class="com.santosh.spring.ArithmeticController">
     <property name="methodNameResolver" ref="myMethodResolver"/>
  </bean>
</beans>
```

Now, finally configure DispatcherServlet as usual in the web.xml.

List 13.37: web.xml

```
<web-app xmlns="http://java.sun.com/xml/ns/j2ee"
    xmlns:xsi="http://www.w3.org/2001/XMLSchema-instance"
     xsi:schemaLocation="http://java.sun.com/xml/ns/j2ee http://java.sun.com/xml/ns/
j2ee/web-app_2_4.xsd" version="2.4">
 <servlet>
  <servlet-name>ds</servlet-name>
  <servlet-class>org.springframework.web.servlet.DispatcherServlet</servlet-class>
  <load-on-startup>0</load-on-startup>
 </servlet>
 <servlet-mapping>
  <servlet-name>ds</servlet-name>
  <url-pattern>*.spring</url-pattern>
 </servlet-mapping>
</web-app>
```

After writing all the files from List 13.34 through List 13.37 compile the Java files and arrange them in a directory structure as shown in Fig. 13.22.

Now, deploy the multiActionControllerEx into Tomcat server and browse the URL **http://localhost:8080/multiActionControllerEx/Home.jsp** to view the home page which enables us to make request for addition or subtraction. The home page view is shown in Fig. 13.23.

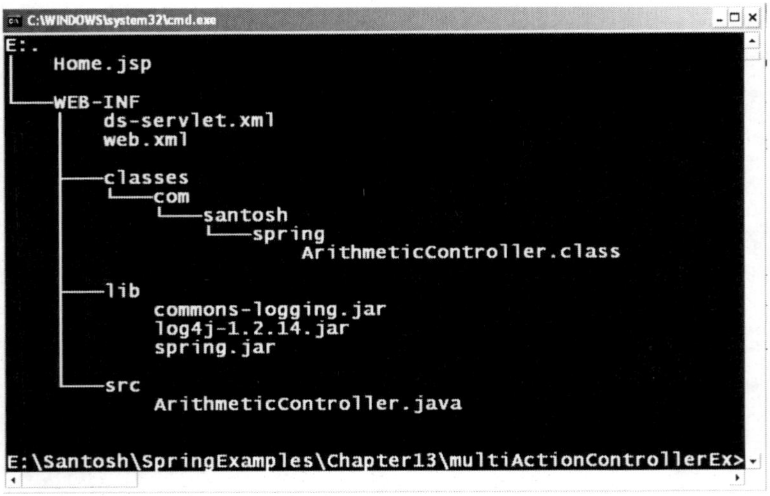

FIGURE 13.22 Directory structure showing files of multiaction controller example

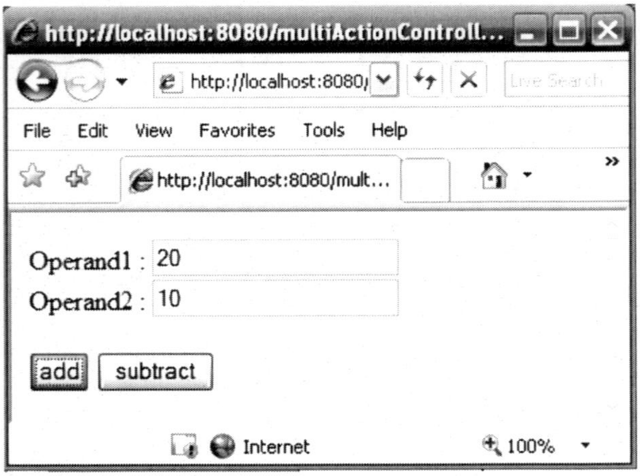

FIGURE 13.23 Home page for multiaction controller example

Enter the numbers as shown in Fig. 13.23 and submit the form using **add** button to execute add() method of ArithmeticController. The result is presented as shown in Fig. 13.24.

Similarly, enter some values and go for subtract button to execute subtract() method of ArithmeticController.

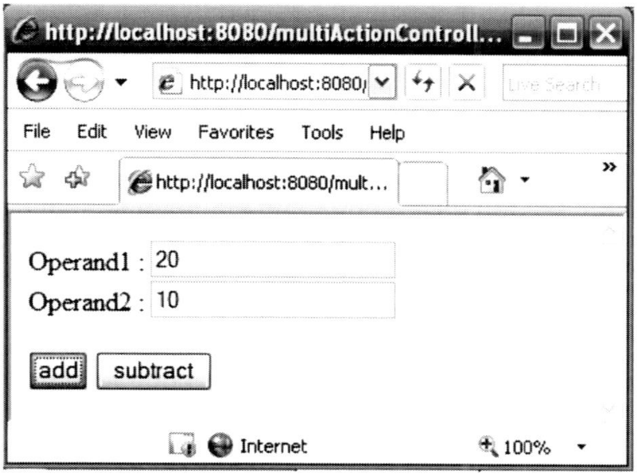

FIGURE 13.24 Output of Addition operation

Summary

In this chapter we learnt the Spring Web MVC framework-provided built-in utility controllers that provide convenience in implementing the controllers for various requirements. The most commonly used controllers that are given under the Spring Web MVC framework are summarized below:

- **AbstractCommandController**–This provides infrastructure to implement controllers that implements form submission request.
- **SimpleFormController**–This is a subtype of AbstractCommandController that includes additional infrastructures for processing form submissions as identifying request for new form to present a new form, and identifying the form submission request to process the form request data.
- **AbstractWizardFormController**–This provides infrastructure to handle multi-wizards request processing.
- **MultiActionController**–This provides infrastructure to implement multiple actions into a single controller class.

All these controllers have been explained in detail with simple independent examples to help you understand how to use the Spring-provided infrastructures to implement your requirements. Apart from the various controllers in this chapter we have also learnt how to validate the form fields using the Spring validator infrastructure. In the next chapter we will learn various view technologies and how to use them to build views for the Spring Web MVC applications.

Describing View-Resolver and View

14 CHAPTER

Objectives

In Chapter 11 we introduced the Spring Web MVC Framework explaining its importance and architecture overview. In Chapter 12 we learnt initialization and request processing workflow of the Spring Web MVC Framework in detail. While discussing about the request processing workflow we understood how to map incoming requests to relevant handlers (controllers), and how to create models (that is, about the ModelAndView) that can be used while rendering views. Thereafter, in the previous chapter we learnt how to implement handlers in the form of controllers using various built-in controllers.

In this chapter we will cover:

- How to render views based on the models returned by handlers (controllers), that is, in the form of ModelAndView object
- The ViewResolver infrastructural element of Spring Web MVC Framework
- Various built-in ViewResolver implementations that Spring provides
- View object that makes the Spring Web MVC application independent of view technology used to render the view
- How to work with some of the view technologies that Spring integrates with, such as JSP/JSTL, Velocity, Tiles, JSF, Excel spreadsheets, and PDF.

14.1 UNDERSTANDING VIEWRESOLVER

As we know that the Model-View-Controller pattern describes how to decouple data access and business logic from data presentation and user interaction, by introducing an intermediate component–controller. Moreover, one of the most important requirements that we need to consider while implementing the MVC pattern is that the controller should be designed independent of the view technology used to render the view providing the convenience to freely use any view technology to render the view. Spring well understands this requirement and in support of this requirement it includes the ViewResolver element in the Web MVC architecture that it implements. The ViewResolver object is responsible to locate the view object that can render a view for this request. As we have discussed in the earlier chapter we know that the DispatcherServlet uses the ViewResolver to resolve the logical view name described by the ModelAndView object to locate the View object (see Phase-7 of the discussion in Chapter 12). Spring provides various built-in ViewResolver implementations that meet most of our requirements in locating the view. The most commonly used Spring provided built-in ViewResolver implementations are listed below:

- UrlBasedViewResolver.
- InternalResourceViewResolver.
- ResourceBundleViewResolver.
- BeanNameViewResolver.
- XmlViewResolver.

Each one of these ViewResolver implementations presents a unique way to transform the logical view name to view objects capable of rendering the view for this request. Apart from the built-in ViewResolver implementations that Spring provides it also allows us to implement custom view resolves for additional view technologies. Let us now learn all the built-in ViewResolver implementations listed above, starting with the UrlBasedViewResolver.

14.1.1 UrlBasedViewResolver

The org.springframework.web.servlet.view.UrlBasedViewResolver is one of the implementations of ViewResolver interface. This implementation defines the view navigation strategy that maps the view name to the URL resources. This view resolver strategy is useful if our view names directly match the unique part of the resource file name. The view names can either be a URL path directly locating the resource, or get added by a specified prefix and/or suffix to form a URL path to locate the resource. The *prefix* and *suffix* properties allow us to configure the prefix and suffix that needs to be added to the view name to prepare the URL path. This view resolver returns a View object of the configured view class for all the resolved views. The view class for this resolver can be configured using *viewClass* property. The UrlBasedViewResolver supports AbstractUrlBasedView subclasses like Internal Resource View, VelocityView, RedirectView, JstlView, etc. The following code snippet shows the sample configuration of this view resolver.

Code Snippet

```
<bean id="viewResolver"
    class="org.springframework.web.servlet.view.UrlBasedViewResolver">
  <property name="prefix" value="/WEB-INF/jsps/"/>
  <property name="suffix" value=".jsp"/>
  <property name="viewClass"
    value="org.springframework.web.servlet.view.InternalResourceView"/>
</bean>
```

As per the preceding configuration the view resolver adds '/WEB-INF/jsps' and '.jsp' as a prefix and suffix respectively to prepare a URL path (For example, if the view name is 'ShowEmployee' then the URL path becomes to '/WEB-INF/jsps/ShowEmployee.jsp'), which is used to locate the resource. If the resource is located, it returns an instance of InternalResourceView which represents the resource at the URL path. This view resolver implementation additionally supports the feature of specifying the forward URLs and redirects the URLs. Forward URLs can be specified using 'forward:' as a prefix to the URL and redirect URLs can be specified using 'redirect:' as a prefix to the URL.

> **Note:** While configuring multiple view resolvers in an application context it is recommended to configure this resolver as a last option since it will attempt to resolve any view name.

14.1.2 InternalResourceViewResolver

The org.springframework.web.servlet.view.InternalResourceViewResolver is a subclass of UrlBased ViewResolver. This is a convenient subclass of UrlBasedViewResolver supporting InternalResourceView and its subtypes as view. This uses the same strategy described for UrlBasedViewResolver to resolve the view name. The following code snippet shows the sample configuration of this view resolver.

Code Snippet

```
<bean id="viewResolver"
  class="org.springframework.web.servlet.view.InternalResourceViewResolver">
  <property name="prefix" value="/WEB-INF/jsps/"/>
  <property name="suffix" value=".jsp"/>
  <property name="viewClass"
    value="org.springframework.web.servlet.view.InternalResourceView"/>
</bean>
```

The preceding configuration looks almost same as the UrlBasedViewResolver; the strategy used is also the same, but as described earlier this is a convenient class to use InternalResourceView and its subtypes, supporting to locate the internal resources (that is, resources in the web application).

Note:

- Configuring a viewClass other than the InternalResourceView or its subclass to the InternalResourceViewResolver will throw an exception.
- Here if the viewClass is not configured then it defaults to **InternalResourceView**.

14.1.3 ResourceBundleViewResolver

The org.springframework.web.servlet.view.ResourceBundleViewResolver is ViewResolver implementation that defines the view navigation strategy, which maps the logical view name to the View using the bean definitions in the given ResourceBundle. This ViewResolver implementation supports internationalization (I18N). Meaning that the ResourceBundleViewResolver can be used to resolve the logical view name to the localized views, that is, like we may want to present the product details using different views—one for each locale that our application supports. For example, a shopping-cart application providing its services in United States of America, France, and Italy wants to present the product details catalog in the form of plain HTML to Americans, in the form of an Excel sheet to the French and in the form of a PDF to the Italians. The ResourceBundleViewResolver helps us in configuring this requirement without costing to write different controllers or adding additional code in controller while configuring the logical view name into the ModelAndView. The following code snippet shows the configuration of the ResourceBundleViewResolver.

Code Snippet

```
<bean id="viewResolver"
  class="org.springframework.web.servlet.view.ResourceBundleViewResolver">
  <property name="basename" value="myviews"/>
</bean>
```

The 'basename' property is used to specify the basename which allows the ResourceBundle ViewResolver to locate the locale-specific properties file using the java.util.PropertyResourceBundle. Here we have configured the basename to 'myviews' which locates the files myviews.properties, myviews_en.properties, myviews_en_US.properties, etc. If the basename property is not configured then it takes 'views' as a default value. Now, as we have configured the resolver and learnt how to configure basename, it is time to understand how to implement the properties files to match the logical view name to the View object. Each of the property file should have an entry with the property name as <logical view name>.class mapping to the class name of the View object that should be used to render the view. The following snippet shows the sample entry into the myviews.properties.

Code Snippet: myviews.properties

```
productDetails.class=org.springframework.web.servlet.view.JstlView
```

The name of the entry shown in the preceding snippet describes to the resolver the use of JstlView for the logical view name 'productDetails'. Apart from this property we may require to configure some other properties according to the view configured. For example, for productDetails as we have configured JstlView we want to additionally configure the URL to specify the location of JSP document that the JstlView has to use to render the view. This is done by setting the productDetails.url (that is, <logical view name>.url) to location of JSP document. The following snippet shows the entries in the property file.

Code Snippet: myviews.properties

```
productDetails.class=org.springframework.web.servlet.view.JstlView
productDetails.url=/WEB-INF/jsps/ProductDetailsView.jsp
```

As shown in the preceding configuration the productDetails.url property results to invoke setUrl() method on the JstlView object setting the value '/WEB-INF/jsps/ProductDetailsView.jsp'. Similarly, to set the properties of the configured view class, we can include an entry into the properties files with the name as <logical view name>.<view property name>.

Although the ResourceBundleViewResolver is powerful in mapping the logical view names to the view based on the locale, in all the cases we may not require resolving the views based on the locale. Alternatively, we may want to locate the views based on the bean name. Let us learn some ViewResolver implementations that allow us to resolve the views based on the bean name.

14.1.4 BeanNameViewResolver

The org.springframework.web.servlet.view.BeanNameViewResolver is a ViewResolver implementation that defines the view navigation strategy which maps the logical view name to the bean names in the application context to resolve the view. Configuring the BeanNameViewResolver is as simple as configuring other beans in the context. The following code snippet shows the BeanNameViewResolver configuration.

Code Snippet

```
<bean id="viewResolver"
  class="org.springframework.web.servlet.view.BeanNameViewResolver"/>
```

Now, when the DispatcherServlet requests this resolver to resolve the view, this resolver will look for a bean name in the application context that matches with the logical view name in the given ModelAndView object. The bean located in this way is expected to be a subtype of View. As discussed above, the BeanNameViewResolver locates the view by matching the logical view name with the bean names in the application context, but in case we have many views it is generally not a better practice to mix the views with the main application context beans. To manage these kinds of situations we can use XmlViewResolver. Let us learn how to configure and work with the XmlViewResolver.

14.1.5 XmlViewResolver

The org.springframework.web.servlet.view.XmlViewResolver is ViewResolver implementation that defines the view navigation strategy which maps the logical view name to the bean names in the Spring Beans XML file configured to its 'location' property for resolving the view. Configuring the XmlViewResolver is as simple as configuring other beans in the context. The following code snippet shows the XmlViewResolver configuration.

Code Snippet

```
<bean id="viewResolver"
  class="org.springframework.web.servlet.view.XmlViewResolver">
  <property name="location" value="/WEB-INF/views/MyViews.xml"/>
</bean>
```

The 'location' attribute specifies the Spring Beans XML configuration file in which the views have to be located. If this property is not configured then the XmlViewResolver by default looks for the definitions in '/WEB-INF/views.xml' file. Moreover, as per the configuration shown in the preceding code snippet, when the DispatcherServlet requests this resolver to resolve the view, this resolver will look for a bean name in the '/WEB-INF/views/MyViews.xml' file that matches with the logical view name in the given ModelAndView object. We have learnt about the various important ViewResolver implementations and how to configure them. Let us now learn how to configure multiple ViewResolvers in the application context.

14.1.6 Configuring Multiple ViewResolvers

We can configure multiple view resolvers in an application context. In such a case we need to configure an additional property 'order' that takes 'int' value on each of the view resolver. The following code snippet shows the multiple view resolver's configuration.

Code Snippet

```
<bean  class="org.springframework.web.servlet.view.XmlViewResolver">
  <property name="location" value="/WEB-INF/views/MyViews.xml"/>
  <property name="order" value="0"/>
</bean>
<bean  class="org.springframework.web.servlet.view.BeanNameViewResolver">
  <property name="order" value="1"/>
</bean>
```

```
<bean  class="org.springframework.web.servlet.view.InternalResourceViewResolver">
  <property name="prefix" value="/"/>
  <property name="suffix" value=".jsp"/>
  <property name="viewClass"
    value="org.springframework.web.servlet.view.JstlView"/>
  <property name="order" value="2"/>
</bean>
```

The preceding code snippet shows how to define three view resolvers where the first preference is given to the XmlViewResolver. If it cannot resolve the view name then the next view resolver (that is BeanNameViewResolver) is used, and so on.

> **Note:** If the 'detectAllViewResolvers' initialization parameter of DispatcherServlet is configured to false then multiple view resolvers are not detected instead only the bean with a name viewResolver is located as a ViewResolver.

So far in the chapter we have discussed the ViewResolver, Spring provided important built-in ViewResolver implementations and even learnt how to configure multiple ViewResolvers. We have understood that the ViewResolver is used by the DispatcherServlet to transform a logical view name to View object capable of rendering the view for this request. Moreover, if the ViewResolver successfully resolves the logical view name then it returns a View object to the DispatcherServlet (see Fig. 12.11). The DispatcherServlet uses this View object to render the view. Now let us learn about the View and its various built-in implementations.

14.2 UNDERSTANDING VIEW

We know that JSP is the most commonly used technology to render the view of web applications implemented in Java. JSP is convenient for implementing the simple views that are rendered into tags like html but when the views are much more complex to implement most of the view designers use templating solutions like Velocity, FreeMarker, and Tiles. Moreover, JSP is preferred for implementing the views that produces the tag based output like HTML, and WML. However, as per the current requirements the web applications need to be capable of producing the outputs not only in the form of HTML or any other XML tags but also binary content like Microsoft Excel sheet, PDF document, etc. Thus, from this discussion it can be understood that implementing the view in Web MVC is not just simply implementing JSP all the time.

Apart from this, as discussed earlier in this chapter one of the most important requirements that we need to consider while implementing MVC pattern is that the controller should be designed independent of the view technology used to render the view providing the convenience to freely use any view technology to render the view. And in support of this requirement the Spring Web MVC uses ModelAndView to describe a model and view in the form of simple plain java object. The view is an object that can describe a view name in the form of String which will be resolved by a ViewResolver object to locate view object, alternatively a view object directly.

The org.springframework.web.servlet.View is an interface that provides a standard abstraction for the DispatcherServlet to interact with the view implementations that are responsible for rendering the content and prepare the presentation for this request. The view interface declares two methods getContentType() and render(). The method signatures of these two methods are shown below.

Code Snippet

```
public String getContentType()

public void render(
  Map model,
  HttpServletRequest request,
  HttpServletResponse response) throws Exception
```

The getContentType() method can be used by the view implementations to return the content type of the view that it is responsible to generate. The render() method is implemented to take the responsibility to render the view using the given model, request, and response objects. As we know that the various technologies that are used to render the view may not access the model data in the same way, like JSP/JSTL uses the model data in request, session, or application scope. Whereas technologies like Velocity does not have support to access application scoped data and generally does not depend on HTTP-specific constructs to access the model data. Thus, it is never a better practice to design the controllers independent of view technologies (especially in describing the model data to the view), which enables us to freely use any view technology to render the view and allow to migrate from one view technology to another without affecting the controllers. This is the reason Spring Web MVC framework describes the models as a simple java.util.Map object. The following code snippet shows the sample implementation of View.

Code Snippet

```
package com.santosh.spring;

import javax.servlet.*;
import javax.servlet.http.*;
import java.util.Map;
import org.springframework.web.servlet.View;

public class MyGifView implements View {

  public String getContentType(){
    return "image/gif";
  }

  public void render(Map model,
      HttpServletRequest request,
      HttpServletResponse response) throws Exception {

    byte[] content=(byte[])model.get("ResponseContent");
    ServletOuputStream sos=response.getOuputStream();
    sos.write(content);
    sos.flush();
    sos.close();
  }
}
```

The code shown in the preceding snippet renders the view as an image, that is, it produces binary content as an output. Here the view implementation is using the response object and directly presenting the output but in some cases the view implementation may simply prepare the model and then dispatch the request to some JSP document using the RequestDispatcher. Spring Web MVC built-in provides various view implementations supporting the most common requirements. Table 14.1 describes the important built-in view implementation.

TABLE 14.1

View implementation class	*Description*
InternalResourceView	The View implementation that wraps the JSP or any other resource in the same web application. This View implementation sets the model objects into request attributes and then forwards the request to the specified URL using the RequestDispatcher. We can use 'url' property to specify the URL of the resource that this view has to wrap.
JstlView	The View implementation that wraps the JSP documents in the application. This View implementation sets the model objects as JSTL-specific request attributes specifying the locale and resource bundle for JSTL's formatting tags, using Spring's locale and message source. We can use 'url' property to specify the URL of the resource that this view has to wrap.
RedirectView	The View implementation that redirects the request to an absolute, context, or request relative URL. This View implementation sets all model objects as HTTP query parameters and then redirects the request to the specified URL.
TilesView	The View implementation that retrieves a tiles definitions. This View implementation depends on a TilesDefinitionsFactory which must be available in the ServletContext. This View considers the 'url' specified as a tiles definition name.
TilesJstlView	A subclass of TilesView implemented to support tiles pages that use JSTL tags. This View implementation sets the model objects as JSTL-specific request attributes specifying locale and resource bundle for JSTL's formatting tags, using Spring's locale and message source and then renders the view using the tiles definition specified using 'url' property.
VelocityView	The View implementation that uses the Velocity templates to render the view.
FreeMarkerView	The View implementation that uses the FreeMarker templates to render the view.
AbstractPdfView	The View implementation that supports to generate PDF documents using Bruno Lowagie's iText API.
AbstractExcelView	The View implementation that supports to generate Excel sheet using Apache POI API.
AbstractJExcelView	The View implementation that supports to generate Excel sheet using JExcel API.

In the various examples demonstrated in the previous chapters explaining the Spring Web MVC we have not concentrated on presenting the response. Rather we were demonstrating the services that takes the input and processes it. Now as we have learnt about the ViewResolver and the various View implementations in this chapter, let us learn how to use some of the View implementations to render the view and present some dynamic content as output to the client.

14.3 WORKING WITH JSTLVIEW

As we know that JSP Standard Tag Library (JSTL) is a collection of custom tag libraries, which provide core functionality used for JSP documents. JSTL reduces the use of scriptlets in a JSP page. The use of JSTL tags allows developers to use predefined tags instead of writing the Java code. JSTL provides four types of tag libraries that can be used with JSP pages as JSTL Core Tags—tags to process core operations in a JSP page; JSTL XML Tags—tags for parsing, selecting, and transforming XML data in a JSP page; JSTL Format Tags—tags for formatting the data used in a JSP page according to locales; JSTL SQL Tags—tags to access the relational database used in a JSP page.

Discussing JSTL in detail is out of the scope of this book . We will limit the JSTL introduction (if you are not aware of JSTL it is strongly recommended that you understand JSTL first before understanding this section – see JDBC, Servlets, and JSP Black Book by author of this book). As discussed in the preceding section, Spring Web MVC includes a built-in view implementation to use JSTL to render the view. The org.springframework.web.servlet.view.JstlView class is a view implementation that supports using JSTL view technology to render the view. The following code snippet shows the bean definition of declaring the JstlView.

Code Snippet

```
<bean name="myview" class=" org.springframework.web.servlet.view.JstlView">
  <property name="url" value="/WEB-INF/jsps/MyResponse.jsp"/>
</bean>
```

The 'url' property of JstlView specifies the location path of the JSP document that it has to use while rendering the view. In general, these type of views are configured by using InternalResource ViewResolver as shown below.

Code Snippet

```
<bean
class="org.springframework.web.servlet.view.InternalResourceViewResolver">
  <property name="prefix" value="/WEB-INF/jsps/"/>
  <property name="suffix" value=".jsp"/>
  <property name="viewClass"
    value="org.springframework.web.servlet.view.JstlView"/>
</bean>
```

Now, as we have learnt about the JstlView and its configurations let us implement a small example that can demonstrate the use of JSTL tags in preparing the view rendering the model created by the Spring Web MVC controller. The example demonstrates the implementation of the employee search usecases. The following diagram shows the usecase diagram that this example implements.

To implement the usecases shown in the preceding figure we can write one controller for each use case. However, it can be identified that all the four usecases depend on the same set of resources and even the model content that they prepare will be the same. Thus it is a better practice to implement all the four use cases into a single controller class using MultiActionController (see Chapter 13, Sec. 13.7

for further details on MultiActionController). List 14.1 shows the controller implementing the request handling logic for all the four usecases described in Fig. 14.1.

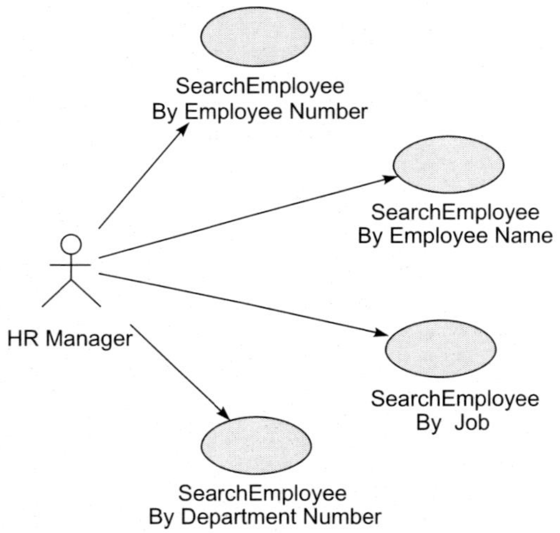

FIGURE 14.1 Usecase diagram of the example

List 14.1: SearchEmployeeController.java

```
package com.santosh.spring;

import java.util.Collection;

import javax.servlet.http.HttpServletRequest;
import javax.servlet.http.HttpServletResponse;

import org.springframework.web.servlet.ModelAndView;

import com.santosh.spring.dao.EmpDAO;

/**
 * @author Santosh
*/
public class SearchEmployeeController {

  private EmpDAO empDAO;

  public SearchEmployeeController(EmpDAO empDAO){
    this.empDAO=empDAO;
  }
  public ModelAndView searchByEmpno(
      HttpServletRequest request,
      HttpServletResponse response)throws Exception {

    int  empno=Integer.parseInt(request.getParameter("searchKey"));
```

```
    EmpDetails empDetails =
              empDAO.getEmployeeDetailsByEmpno(empno);

    return new ModelAndView(
      "successSingleEmp",
      "empdetails", empDetails);
  }
  public ModelAndView searchByEname(
      HttpServletRequest request,
      HttpServletResponse response)throws Exception {

    String ename=request.getParameter("searchKey");
    Collection empDetails =
            empDAO.getEmployeeDetailsByName(ename);

    return new ModelAndView(
      "successMultipleEmps",
      "empdetails", empDetails);
  }
  public ModelAndView searchByJob(
      HttpServletRequest request,
      HttpServletResponse response)throws Exception {

    String job=request.getParameter("searchKey");
    Collection empDetails =
            empDAO.getEmployeeDetailsByJob(job);

    return new ModelAndView(
      "successMultipleEmps",
      "empdetails", empDetails);
  }
  public ModelAndView searchByDeptno(
      HttpServletRequest request,
      HttpServletResponse response)throws Exception {

    int deptno=Integer.parseInt(request.getParameter("searchKey"));
    Collection empDetails =
            empDAO.getEmployeeDetailsByDeptno(deptno);

    return new ModelAndView(
      "successMultipleEmps",
      "empdetails", empDetails);
  }
}
```

List 14.1 shows the implementation of a simple controller encapsulating the handler logic for the four search employee usecases. It can be observed that the controller depends on the EmpDAO (a DAO interface) that represents the employee details. Let us first write the EmpDAO interface followed by its implementation.

List 14.2: EmpDAO.java

```
package  com.santosh.spring.dao;

import  java.util.Collection;
import  com.santosh.spring.EmpDetails;
/**
 * @author Santosh
 */
public interface EmpDAO {

  Collection  getAllEmployeeDetails();
  EmpDetails  getEmployeeDetailsByEmpno(int  empno)  ;
  Collection  getEmployeeDetailsByName(String  name);
  Collection  getEmployeeDetailsByDeptno(int  deptno);
  Collection  getEmployeeDetailsByJob(String  job);
}
```

Now, let us implement the EmpDAO interface that is shown in List 14.2. The EmpDAOImplDB class implements the EmpDAO interface that uses the JdbcTemplate to perform database operations. List 14.3 shows the code for EmpDAOImplDB.

List 14.3: EmpDAOImplDB.java

```
package  com.santosh.spring.dao;

import  java.sql.ResultSet;
import  java.sql.SQLException;
import  java.util.Collection;
import  org.springframework.jdbc.core.JdbcTemplate;
import  org.springframework.jdbc.core.ResultSetExtractor;
import  com.santosh.spring.EmpDetails;
/**
 * @author Santosh
 */
public class  EmpDAOImplDB  implements  EmpDAO  {

  public  EmpDAOImplDB(JdbcTemplate  jdbcTemplate){
    this.jdbcTemplate=jdbcTemplate;
  }

  public  void  setMapper(EmpRowMapper  empRowMapper){
    this.empRowMapper=empRowMapper;
  }

  public  Collection  getAllEmployeeDetails()  {

    String  query="select  *  from  emp";
    return  jdbcTemplate.query(  query,  empRowMapper);
  }
```

```
  public EmpDetails getEmployeeDetailsByEmpno(final int empno) {

    String query= "select * from emp where empno=?";

    return (EmpDetails) jdbcTemplate.query(
        query, new Object[]{new Integer(empno)},
        new ResultSetExtractor(){
          public Object extractData(ResultSet rs)throws SQLException {
            if (rs.next()){
              EmpDetails ed=new EmpDetails();
              ed.empno=empno;
              ed.ename=rs.getString(2);
              ed.job=rs.getString(3);
              ed.mgr=rs.getInt(4);
              ed.hiredate=rs.getDate(5);
              ed.sal=rs.getDouble(6);
              ed.comm=rs.getDouble(7);
              ed.deptno=rs.getInt(8);
              return ed;
            }
            else
              return null;
          }
        });
  }

  public Collection getEmployeeDetailsByName(final String name) {

    String query="select * from emp where ename like ?";

    return jdbcTemplate.query(query, new Object[]{name}, empRowMapper);
  }

  public Collection getEmployeeDetailsByDeptno(final int deptno) {

    String query="select * from emp where DEPTNO=?";

    return jdbcTemplate.query(
        query, new Object[]{new Integer(deptno)}, empRowMapper);
  }

  public Collection getEmployeeDetailsByJob(final String job)  {

    String query="select * from emp where job=?";

    return jdbcTemplate.query(query, new Object[]{job}, empRowMapper);
  }

  private JdbcTemplate jdbcTemplate;
  private EmpRowMapper empRowMapper;
}
```

List 14.3 shows the implementation of EmpDAO for accessing the data employee details in a database. The EmpDAOImplDB class uses JdbcTemplate, a utility class provided under the Spring JDBC abstraction framework (see Chapter 6 for more details) and EmpRowMapper, a RowMapper implementation used by the JdbcTemplate as a call back object to map the results of the domain model object. List 14.4 shows the code for EmpRowMapper.

List 14.4 : EmpRowMapper.java

```
package com.santosh.spring.dao;

import java.sql.ResultSet;
import java.sql.SQLException;
import org.springframework.jdbc.core.RowMapper;
import com.santosh.spring.EmpDetails;
/**
 * @author Santosh
 */
public class EmpRowMapper implements RowMapper {

  public Object mapRow(ResultSet rs, int rowcount) throws SQLException {
    EmpDetails ed=new EmpDetails();
    ed.empno=rs.getInt(1);
    ed.ename=rs.getString(2);
    ed.job=rs.getString(3);
    ed.mgr=rs.getInt(4);
    ed.hiredate=rs.getDate(5);
    ed.sal=rs.getDouble(6);
    ed.comm=rs.getDouble(7);
    ed.deptno=rs.getInt(8);
    return ed;
  }
}
```

List 14.4 shows the EmpRowMapper an implementation of RowMapper used by the EmpDAO ImplDB to map the results to EmpDetails, our domain model object. List 14.5 shows the EmpDetails model class that can encapsulate the employee details.

List 14.5: EmpDetails.java

```
package com.santosh.spring;

import java.io.Serializable;
import java.util.Date;
/**
 * @author Santosh
 */
public class EmpDetails implements Serializable{

  public EmpDetails(){}

  public String ename, job;
```

```
    public int empno, deptno, mgr;
    public double sal, comm;
    public Date hiredate;

    public double getComm() { return comm; }
    public int getDeptno() { return deptno; }
    public int getEmpno() { return empno; }
    public String getEname() { return ename; }
    public Date getHiredate() { return hiredate; }
    public String getJob() { return job; }
    public int getMgr() { return mgr; }
    public double getSal() { return sal; }
}
```

List 14.5 shows code for EmpDetails, which is a Transfer Object designed to transfer the Employee details between the Controller, Model (DAO) and View. Now let us configure the EmpDAO and its dependents in a Spring Beans XML configuration file.

List 14.6: services-context.xml

```
<beans  xmlns="http://www.springframework.org/schema/beans"
xmlns:xsi="http://www.w3.org/2001/XMLSchema-instance"
xsi:schemaLocation="http://www.springframework.org/schema/beans
http://www.springframework.org/schema/beans/spring-beans-2.0.xsd">

  <!--Configuring DataSource-->
  <bean id="datasource" class="org.apache.commons.dbcp.BasicDataSource">
    <property name="driverClassName"
          value="oracle.jdbc.driver.OracleDriver"/>
    <property name="url" value="jdbc:oracle:thin:@localhost:1521:sandb"/>
    <property name="username" value="scott"/>
    <property name="password" value="tiger"/>
  </bean>

  <!--Configuring JdbcTemplate-->
  <bean id="jdbctemp" class="org.springframework.jdbc.core.JdbcTemplate">
    <constructor-arg>
      <ref local="datasource"/>
    </constructor-arg>
  </bean>

  <bean id="empRowMapper"
      class="com.santosh.spring.dao.EmpRowMapper"/>

  <bean id="empDAO" class="com.santosh.spring.dao.EmpDAOImplDB">
    <constructor-arg>
      <ref local="jdbctemp"/>
    </constructor-arg>
    <property name="mapper" ref="empRowMapper"/>
  </bean>
</beans>
```

List 14.6 shows the Spring Beans XML configuration file that defines the EmpDAO and its dependencies as EmpRowMapper, JdbcTemplate, and DataSource. After configuring the services let us configure the controller and the views into a separate Spring Beans XML configuration file (even though this can be done in a single XML document it is a better practice to define the beans into multiple XML documents for better maintenance). List 14.7 shows the bean XML configuration declaring the controller and views.

List 14.7: webConfig-context.xml

```
<beansxmlns="http://www.springframework.org/schema/beans"
xmlns:xsi="http://www.w3.org/2001/XMLSchema-instance"
xsi:schemaLocation="http://www.springframework.org/schema/beans
http://www.springframework.org/schema/beans/spring-beans-2.0.xsd">

  <!--configuring the controller-->
  <bean id="searchController"
      class="com.santosh.spring.SearchEmployeeController">
    <constructor-arg ref="empDAO"/>
  </bean>
  <bean name="/search.spring"
class="org.springframework.web.servlet.mvc.multiaction.MultiActionController">
    <property name="methodNameResolver" ref="methodNameResolver"/>
    <property name="delegate" ref="searchController"/>
  </bean>
  <bean id="methodNameResolver"
class="org.springframework.web.servlet.mvc.multiaction.ParameterMethodNameResolver">
    <property name="paramName" value="searchBy"/>
  </bean>

  <!--configuring BeanNameViewResolver-->
  <bean
  class="org.springframework.web.servlet.view.BeanNameViewResolver"/>

  <!--configuring exception resolver-->
  <bean class=
  "org.springframework.web.servlet.handler.SimpleMappingExceptionResolver">
    <property name="exceptionMappings">
      <props>
        <prop key="org.springframework.dao.DAOException">
          dberrorView
        </prop>
        <prop key="java.lang.NumberFormatException">
          notANumber
        </prop>
      </props>
    </property>
  </bean>
```

```
  <!--configuring Views required to render the view for /search.spring request-->
  <bean name="successSingleEmp"
      class="org.springframework.web.servlet.view.JstlView">
    <property name="url" value="/WEB-INF/jsps/EmployeeDetails.jsp"/>
  </bean>
  <bean name="successMultipleEmps"
      class="org.springframework.web.servlet.view.JstlView">
    <property name="url" value="/WEB-INF/jsps/EmployeeList.jsp"/>
  </bean>
  <bean name="dberrorView"
      class="org.springframework.web.servlet.view.JstlView">
    <property name="url" value="/WEB-INF/jsps/DBError.jsp"/>
  </bean>
  <bean name="notANumber"
      class="org.springframework.web.servlet.view.JstlView">
    <property name="url" value="/WEB-INF/jsps/NotANumberError.jsp"/>
  </bean>
  <!--Configuring the message resources for this application context-->
  <bean id="messageSource"
  class="org.springframework.context.support.ResourceBundleMessageSource">
    <property name="basename" value="ApplicationResources"/>
  </bean>
</beans>
```

List 14.7 shows the Spring Beans XML configuration file (webConfig-context.xml) that defines the SearchEmployeeController, MultiActionController, ParameterMethodNameResolver, and view beans for describing the context to use BeanNameViewResolver. The XML file even defines the bean for HandlerExceptionResolver. Now as we have completed the code for controller and the configurations let us implement the JSP documents that use JSTL tags to render the view helping the JstlView. From the preceding beans configuration we can identify that the example uses four views—EmployeeDetails.jsp, EmployeeList.jsp, DBError.jsp, and NotANumberError.jsp. Apart from these four views we need Search.jsp. First let us start with implementing Search.jsp that allows the user to make an employee search request.

List 14.8: Search.jsp

```
<%@taglib  uri="http://java.sun.com/jstl/core" prefix="c"%>
<%@taglib uri="http://java.sun.com/jstl/fmt" prefix="fmt"%>

<fmt:setBundle basename="ApplicationResources"/>
<html>
  <head><title><fmt:message key="search.title"/></title></head>

  <body>
     <form action="search.spring" method="post">
       <table border="0">
```

```
        <tr>
         <td><fmt:message key="search.label"/></td>
         <td><input  type="text"  name="searchKey"/></td>
        </tr>
        <tr>
         <td><fmt:message key="search.searchby"/></td>
         <td>
           <select  name="searchBy">
             <option value="searchByEmpno">Employee Number</option>
             <option value="searchByEname">Employee Name</option>
             <option value="searchByJob">Job</option>
             <option value="searchByDeptno">Department  Number</option>
           </select>
         </td>
        </tr>
        <tr>
         <td  colspan="2"  align="center">
           <input  type="submit" name="submit"
               value="<fmt:message key="search.submit"/>"/>
         </td>
        </tr>
        </tr>
         <td  colspan="2" align="center"><fmt:message  key="search.desc"/></td>
        </tr>
      </table>
    </form>
  </body>
</html>
```

List 14.8 shows the code for Search.jsp that renders the view to present one text field allowing us to enter the search key, select the box to select the criteria and a submit button to submit the request. List 14.9 shows the EmployeeDetails.jsp.

List 14.9: EmployeeDetails.jsp

```
<%@taglib uri="http://java.sun.com/jstl/core_rt"   prefix="c"%>
<%@taglib uri="http://java.sun.com/jstl/fmt_rt"  prefix="fmt"%>

<html>
  <head>
     <title><fmt:message  key="searchresult.title"/></title>
  </head>
  <body>
    <fmt:message  key="searchResult.header"/>

  <c:choose>
  <c:when  test="${empty  requestScope.empdetails}">
    <fmt:message  key="searchResult.noresult"/>
```

```
  </c:when>
  <c:otherwise>
   <table border="0">
    <tr align="left">
      <th><fmt:message key="empno"/></th>
      <td>: <c:out value="${requestScope.empdetails.empno}"/></td>
    </tr>
    <tr align="left">
      <th><fmt:message key="ename"/></th>
      <td>: <c:out value="${requestScope.empdetails.ename}"/></td>
    </tr>
    <tr align="left">
      <th><fmt:message key="job"/></th>
      <td>: <c:out value="${requestScope.empdetails.job}"/></td>
    </tr>
    <tr align="left">
      <th><fmt:message key="mgr"/></th>
      <td>: <c:out value="${requestScope.empdetails.mgr}"/></td>
    </tr>
    <tr align="left">
      <th><fmt:message key="hiredate"/></th>
      <td>: <c:out value="${requestScope.empdetails.hiredate}"/></td>
    </tr>
    <tr align="left">
      <th><fmt:message key="sal"/></th>
      <td>: <c:out value="${requestScope.empdetails.sal}"/></td>
    </tr>
    <tr align="left">
      <th><fmt:message key="comm"/></th>
      <td>: <c:out value="${requestScope.empdetails.comm}"/></td>
    </tr>
    <tr align="left">
      <th><fmt:message key="deptno"/></th>
      <td>: <c:out value="${requestScope.empdetails.deptno}"/></td>
    </tr>
   </table>
   </c:otherwise>
   </c:choose>
   <br/>
  <fmt:message key="searchResult.searchAgain"/> <a href="Search.jsp">
   <fmt:message key="searchResult.click"/>
  </a>
 </body>
</html>
```

The EmployeeDetails.jsp uses the JSTL core and formatting tags to present the search results that produce only one employee detail. It is observed that unlike in Search.jsp here we have not used the JSTL setBundle formatting element to set the message resource bundle since the EmployeeDetails.jsp is used by the JstlView implementation of view to render the view. As discussed earlier the JstlView object takes the responsibility to prepare the context for the JSTL documents to render the view and one of the operations performed by JstlView is to make the message resource bundle of Spring Web MVC application context available to JSTL tags. The message resource bundle for the Spring Web MVC application context is configured by declaring the ResourceBundleMessageSource bean in webConfig-context.xml (see List 14.7).

> **Note:** In this example we are accessing the Search.jsp directly instead from the context of Spring Web MVC, which is why we have to explicitly use setBundle JSTL formatting tag to set the message resource bundle in Search.jsp. In general we prefer to invoke all the pages of our Spring Web MVC application through the Spring Web MVC workflow using the Spring Views but here intentionally Search.jsp is designed to request directly to practically demonstrate that JstlView takes the responsibility to configure resource bundle for JSTL tags. This can be objected to by removing the setBundle tag from Search.jsp and then accessing the page. You will find that JSTL formatting tags cannot resolve the messages. List 14.10 shows the EmployeeList.jsp.

List 14.10: EmployeeList.jsp

```
<%@taglib uri="http://java.sun.com/jstl/core_rt" prefix="c"%>
<%@taglib uri="http://java.sun.com/jstl/fmt_rt" prefix="fmt"%>

<html>
  <head>
     <title><fmt:message key="searchresult.title"/></title>
  </head>
  <body>
    <fmt:message key="searchResult.header"/><br/>

    <c:choose>
    <c:when test="${empty requestScope.empdetails}">
      <fmt:message key="searchResult.noresult"/>
    </c:when>
    <c:otherwise>
      <table border="1">
      <tr>
        <th><fmt:message key="empno"/></th>
        <th><fmt:message key="ename"/></th>
        <th><fmt:message key="job"/></th>
        <th><fmt:message key="mgr"/></th>
        <th><fmt:message key="hiredate"/></th>
        <th><fmt:message key="sal"/></th>
        <th><fmt:message key="comm"/></th>
        <th><fmt:message key="deptno"/></th>
```

```
      </tr>
        <c:forEach items="${requestScope.empdetails}" var="emp">
        <tr>
          <td><c:out value="${emp.empno}"/></td>
          <td><c:out value="${emp.ename}"/></td>
          <td><c:out value="${emp.job}"/></td>
          <td><c:out value="${emp.mgr}"/></td>
          <td><c:out value="${emp.hiredate}"/></td>
          <td><c:out value="${emp.sal}"/></td>
          <td><c:out value="${emp.comm}"/></td>
          <td><c:out value="${emp.deptno}"/></td>
        </tr>
      </c:forEach>
     </table>
    </c:otherwise>
    </c:choose>
     <br/>
     <fmt:message key="searchResult.searchAgain"/> <a href="Search.jsp">
     <fmt:message key="searchResult.click"/>
    </a>
  </body>
</html>
```

The EmployeeList.jsp presents the search results details that produce multiple records. Now, let us write the JSP documents that can present some view in case of errors in the handler. As per the configurations done in webConfig-context.xml (see List 14.7) for DAOException, the DBError.jsp view and for NumberFormatException the NotANumberError.jsp view is presented. List 14.11 shows DBError.jsp.

List 14.11: DBError.jsp

```
<%@taglib uri="http://java.sun.com/jstl/core_rt" prefix="c"%>
<%@taglib uri="http://java.sun.com/jstl/fmt_rt" prefix="fmt"%>

<html>
  <head>
     <title><fmt:message key="searchresult.title"/></title>
  </head>
  <body>
    <fmt:message key="searchResult.header"/>
    <br/>

    <fmt:message key="search.invalid.dberror"/> <a href="Search.jsp">
    <fmt:message key="searchResult.click"/>
   </a>
  </body>
</html>
```

List 14.12 shows the NotANumberError.jsp that is used to render the view in case the handler throws NumberFormatException.

List 14.12: NotANumberError.jsp

```
<%@taglib uri="http://java.sun.com/jstl/core_rt"   prefix="c"%>
<%@taglib uri="http://java.sun.com/jstl/fmt_rt"  prefix="fmt"%>

<html>
  <head>
   <title><fmt:message key="searchresult.title"/></title>
  </head>
  <body>
    <fmt:message key="searchResult.header"/>
    <br/>

    <fmt:message key="search.invalid.number"/> <a href="Search.jsp">
    <fmt:message key="searchResult.click"/>
   </a>
 </body>
</html>
```

The views shown in the above lists use the JSTL formatting tags to get localized messages from the resource bundle ApplicationResources. List 14.13 shows the ApplicationResources_en.properties, that is, resource properties for the English locale.

List 14.13: ApplicationResources_en.properties

```
#ApplicationResources_en.properties
empno=EmpNo
ename=Employee Name
job=Job
mgr=ManagerID
hiredate=Hiredate
sal=Salary
comm=Commision
deptno=DeptNo

search.title=<b>Employee Search Page</b>
search.label=<b>Search Key :</b>
search.searchby=<b>Search By :</b>
search.submit=Search>

search.desc=<font size=3>For searching the employees by <b>Employee Name</b><br/
>you can use % to match all the records with the given pattern </font><br/><font
size="2"><i>e.g. <b>S%</b> for search by <b>Employee Name</b> matches all the
employees whose name starts with character <b>S</b></i></font>
```

```
searchresult.title=<b>Employee Search Results</b>
searchResult.header=<center><b>Employee Search Results</b></center>

searchResult.noresult=<b><i>There are no records matching your search criteria</
i></b>

searchResult.searchAgain=Want to search again with different condition 
searchResult.click=Click Here

#error keys used in Search Action

search.invalid.dberror=<b><i>An internal problem occurred while processing your
request please try again</i></b>

search.invalid.number=<i>Employee number/Department number entered is not a number,
to try again </i>
```

Similarly, we can write some other property files, each for one locale that our application wants to support. Now, finally after writing all the 13 files shown in the lists so far we want to configure the DispatcherServlet in the web.xml file.

List 14.14: web.xml

```
<web-app xmlns="http://java.sun.com/xml/ns/j2ee"
xmlns:xsi="http://www.w3.org/2001/XMLSchema-instance"
xsi:schemaLocation="http://java.sun.com/xml/ns/j2ee
http://java.sun.com/xml/ns/j2ee/web-app_2_4.xsd"
version="2.4">
  <servlet>
    <servlet-name>ds</servlet-name>
    <servlet-class>
      org.springframework.web.servlet.DispatcherServlet
    </servlet-class>

    <init-param>
      <param-name>contextConfigLocation</param-name>
      <param-value>
        /WEB-INF/services-context.xml
        /WEB-INF/webConfig-context.xml
      </param-value>
    </init-param>

    <load-on-startup>0</load-on-startup>
  </servlet>

  <servlet-mapping>
    <servlet-name>ds</servlet-name>
    <url-pattern>*.spring</url-pattern>
  </servlet-mapping>
</web-app>
```

After writing all the files shown under Lists 14.1 through 14.14 compile the Java files and arrange all the files as shown in Fig. 14.2.

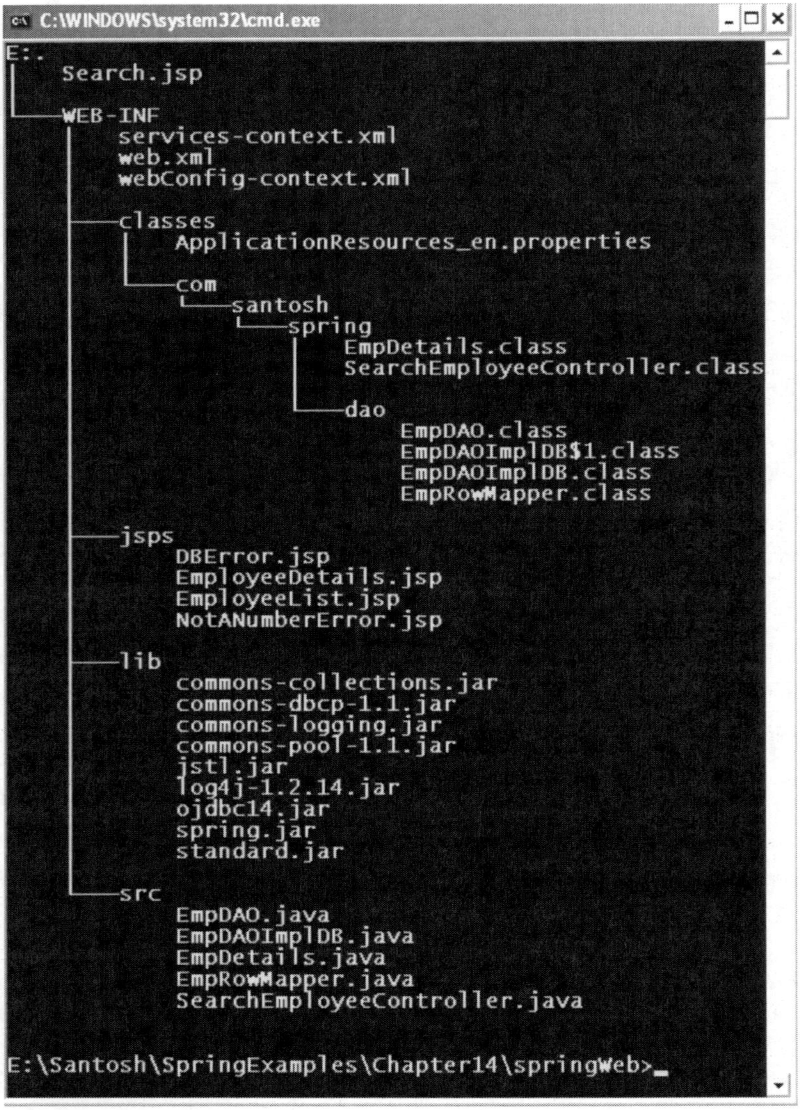

FIGURE 14.2 Tree structure of the searchEmp application files

Now, copy the springWeb folder into <tomcat home>\webapps folder and browse the example using the URL **http://localhost:8080/springWeb/Search.jsp** after the server is started. You will find the search page where you can search for the employee details based on the employee number, name, job, and department number. Enter some employee number in the search key; select the 'Employee Number' option in 'search by' and submit the form as shown in Fig. 14.3.

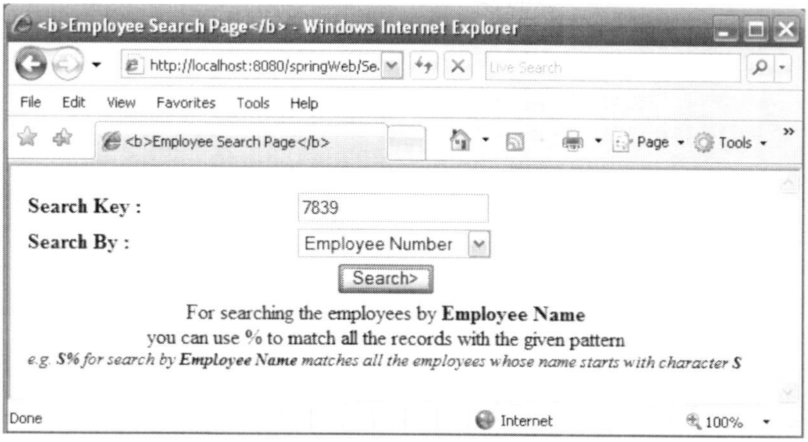

FIGURE 14.3 Search employee home page

If the given employee number is found then the employee details are presented as shown in Fig. 14.4.

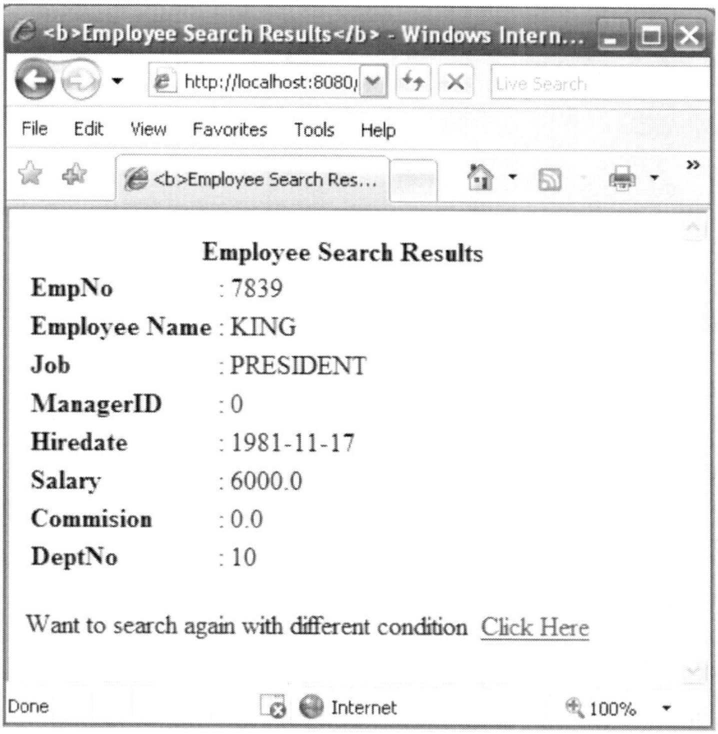

FIGURE 14.4 Employee details

If the employee number is not found then it displays a message describing that the employee is not found as shown in Fig. 14.5.

FIGURE 14.5 Employee search results page when no record is found

In case the search key is not a number and the search by option is selected as 'Employee Number' or 'Department Number' then as per the configurations the NotANumberError.jsp page is used to render the view as shown in Fig. 14.6.

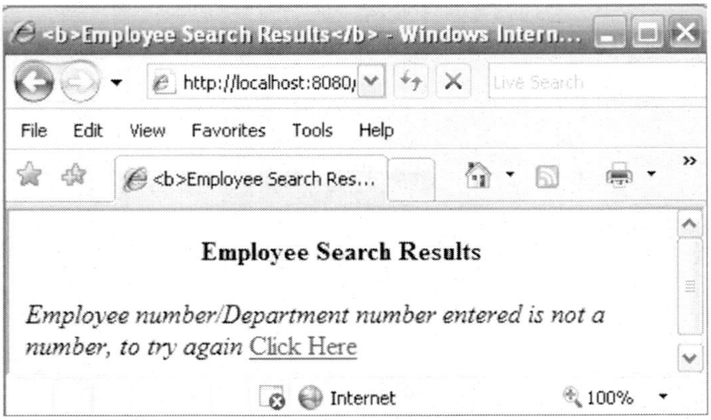

FIGURE 14.6 Error View, when the given employee or department number is not a number.

Similarly, you can search for employees based on the employee name by giving a pattern as shown in Fig. 14.7.

FIGURE 14.7 Search Employee home page

Figure 14.7 illustrates the submission of a request to search for all the employees whose name starts with 'S'. The output of this request is shown in Fig. 14.8.

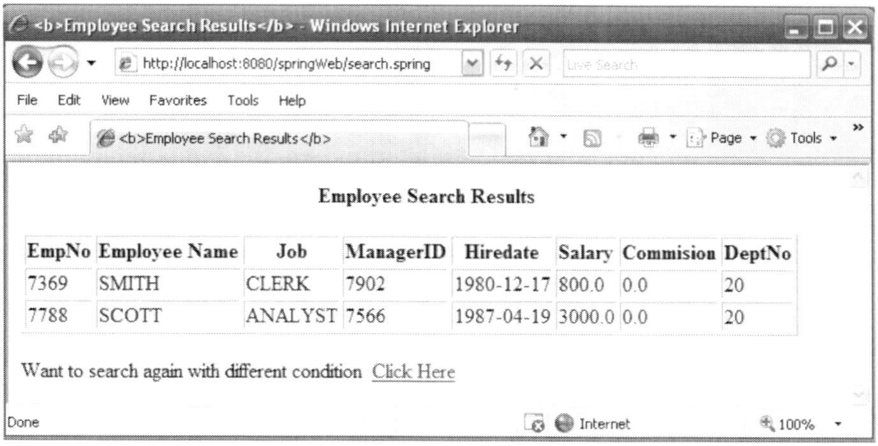

FIGURE 14.8 Employee Search results

Similarly, you can use the other search by options in the application such as search by Job and search by Department Number. In this example, we have used JSTL tags to render the view and we have used JstlView a view implementation to integrate the view pages with the Spring Web MVC application. Even though it was convenient to use JSTL tags in the JSP document to render the view in most applications while implementing complex views designers prefer to use template-based technologies like Velocity as an alternative to JSP. The next section explains you how to use Velocity.

14.4 GENERATING VIEWS USING VELOCITY

Velocity is a template engine that allows web page designers to use a simple template language for accessing Java objects created by controllers implemented in Java. That means the web page creators can easily access Java objects in the view using the simple template language instead of using the Java syntax, which makes non-java developers easily create and maintain web pages. Moreover, Velocity is a project of Apache Software Foundation (ASF) implemented purely in Java which can be easily embedded into our application. Velocity is released under the Apache Software License as an open source freeware for public. Velocity supports MVC-based web application development allowing clear separation between the user interface logic and business logic allowing thecreation of web pages (views) and rest of the application development simultaneously. Velocity provides a proper responsibility division allowing the web page creators to completely concentrate on the user interface design making the view appear with high-quality. The programmers can concentrate on the application code, making it efficient. The Velocity support for separating the Java code from the web pages has made it a significant alternative to Java Server Pages (JSP). Looking at the benefits of Velocity it is a most widely accepted template language for creating web pages with dynamic content after the JSP. Therefore it is obvious that we may have a requirement to implement the views in the Spring Web MVC applications using Velocity. Spring well understands this requirement and thus it has included as built-in support to use Velocity as a template language to create views. Spring includes VelocityView an implementation of View to support Velocity based view development. Let us see how to use Spring Web MVC support in using Velocity as a view technology.

14.4.1 Configuring Spring Web MVC to use Velocity

If we want to use Velocity as a view technology for rendering the model objects created by the Spring handlers and prepare views we can use the VelocityView (similar to the JstlView that we have used in the earlier case) but in addition to this we need to configure the Velocity engine. To configure the Velocity engine we need to declare org.springframework.web.servlet.view.velocity.VelocityConfigurer in the application context as shown in the following code snippet.

Code Snippet

```
<bean id="velocityConfigurer"
    class="org.springframework.web.servlet.view.velocity.VelocityConfigurer">
  <property name="resourceLoaderPath"value="/WEB-INF/velocity/"/>
</bean>
```

The preceding code snippet configures the Velocity engine in the application context that can be used in rendering the views created using the Velocity template language. The 'resourceLoaderPath' property specifies the location where the velocity templates can be located; here we have configured it to locate the velocity templates in/WEB-INF/velocity folder. Apart from this property we can configure 'velocityProperties' to specify the various properties that we would specify in 'velocity.properties' while developing a simple Velocity application (that is, without integrating with Spring Framework). After configuring the VelocityConfigurer we can use the VelocityView to render the view using velocity template. The following code snippet shows the XML configuration to use VelocityView.

Code Snippet

```
<!--configuring BeanNameViewResolver-->
<bean class="org.springframework.web.servlet.view.BeanNameViewResolver"/>

<!--configuring VelocityView-->
<bean name="successSingleEmp"
     class="org.springframework.web.servlet.view.velocity.VelocityView">
  <property name="url" value="EmployeeDetails.vm"/>
</bean>
```

The preceding code snippet shows the VelocityView configuration that is located using the BeanNameViewResolver, that is, if the view name represented by the ModelAndView object returned from the handler is 'successSingleEmp' then as per the ViewResolver configured it is resolved to locate the VelocityView. However, most of the times we use VelocityViewResolver to resolve the view names to be rendered using VelocityView, just like how we prefer to use InternalResourceViewResolver for JSP documents. Let us now look at an example that can demonstrate how to work with Velocity to render the view.

14.4.2 Working with Velocity

As discussed earlier in this chapter Spring Web MVC provides a clear separation between the view and controller of MVC that enables us to implement handlers of Spring Web MVC completely independent of the view technologies used to render the view. Now, as we have to demonstrate the configurations of VelocityView that can use the velocity templates to render the view, we take here an opportunity to show practically that Spring Web MVC handlers are independent of view technology. We do this by modifying the views to use Velocity template language instead of JSTL, without changing the controller of the search employee application implemented earlier in this chapter. Here we need to write the following files:

- Search.html
- EmployeeDetails.vm
- EmployeeList.vm
- NotANumberError.vm
- DBError.vm

Apart from the preceding files we need to modify the 'webConfig-context.xml' file configuring VelocityView instead of JstlView.

Let us implement the files, first starting with Search.html.

List 14.15: Search.html

```
<html>
  <head>
    <title>Employee Search Page</title>
  </head>

  <body>
    <form action="search.spring" method="post">
      <table border="0">
```

```
        <tr>
           <td><b>Search Key :</b></td>
           <td><input type="text" name="searchKey"/></td>
        </tr>
        <tr>
           <td><b>Search By :</b></td>
           <td>
              <select name="searchBy">
                 <option value="searchByEmpno">Employee Number</option>
                 <option value="searchByEname">Employee Name</option>
                 <option value="searchByJob">Job</option>
                 <option value="searchByDeptno">Department Number</option>
              </select>
          </td>
        </tr>
        <tr>
          <td colspan="2" align="center">
           <input type="submit" name="submit" value="Search>"/>
          </td>
        </tr>
        <tr>
          <td colspan="2" align="center">
           <font size=3>For searching the employees by <b>Employee Name</b>
           <br/>you can use % to match all the records with the given pattern </font>
           <br/><font size="2"><i>e.g. <b>S%</b> for search by <b>Employee
           Name</b> matches all the employees whose name starts with character
           <b>S</b></i></font></td>
        </tr>
      </table>
    </form>
  </body>
</html>
```

List 14.15 shows the code for Search.html that renders the view to present one text field allowing us to enter the search key, select a box to select the criteria and a submit button to submit the request. List 14.16 shows the EmployeeDetails.vm.

List 14.16: EmployeeDetails.vm

```
<html>
  <head> <title>Employee Search Result</title> </head>
  <body>
    #if(!$empdetails)
      <b><i>There are no records matching your search criteria</i></b>
    #else
     <table border="0">
```

```
      <tr align="left">
        <th>EmpNo</th> <td>: $empdetails.empno</td>
      </tr>
      <tr align="left">
        <th>Employee Name</th> <td>: $empdetails.ename</td>
      </tr>
      <tr align="left">
        <th>Job</th> <td>: $empdetails.job</td>
      </tr>
      <tr align="left">
        <th>ManagerID</th> <td>: $empdetails.mgr</td>
      </tr>
      <tr align="left">
        <th>Hiredate</th> <td>: $empdetails.hiredate</td>
      </tr>
      <tr align="left">
        <th>Salary</th> <td>: $empdetails.sal</td>
      </tr>
      <tr align="left">
        <th>Commision</th> <td>: $empdetails.comm</td>
      </tr>
      <tr align="left">
        <th>DeptNo</th> <td>: $empdetails.deptno</td>
      </tr>
     </table>
    #end
    <br/>
   Want to search again with different condition   <a href="Search.html">
    Click Here</a>
  </body>
</html>
```

List 14.17 shows the EmployeeDetails.vm, which includes the velocity template code (all the highlighted code). Velocity uses its own language Velocity Template Language (VTL) for control flow and object access. For more details on Velocity and VTL visit http://velocity.apache.org. Let us implement the velocity templates for other views.

List 14.17: EmployeeList.vm

```
<html>
  <head>
    <title>Employee Search Results</title>
  </head>
  <body>
    <center><b>Employee Search Results</b></center><br/>
    #if(!$empdetails)
```

```
    <b><i>There are no records matching your search criteria</i></b>
  #else
   <table border="1">
    <tr>
      <th>EmpNo</th>
      <th>Employee Name</th>
      <th>Job</th>
      <th>ManagerID</th>
      <th>Hiredate</th>
      <th>Salary</th>
      <th>Commision</th>
      <th>DeptNo</th>
    </tr>
      #foreach($emp in $empdetails)
      <tr>
        <td>$emp.empno</td>
        <td>$emp.ename</td>
        <td>$emp.job</td>
        <td>$emp.mgr</td>
        <td>$emp.hiredate</td>
        <td>$emp.sal</td>
        <td>$emp.comm</td>
        <td>$emp.deptno</td>
      </tr>
    #end
   </table>
   #end
    <br/>
   Want to search again with different condition  <a href="Search.html">
    Click Here</a>
  </body>
</html>
```

List 14.18 shows the code for EmployeeList.vm that is used by VelocityView for rendering the view to present the search results that has located multiple employee records, that is, a situation in which the search employee request based on the employee name, job, and department number is successfully executed. Now we will implement the velocity template for the error pages first for DAO errors.

List 14.18: DBError.vm

```
<html>
  <head>
    <title>Employee Search Results</title>
  </head>
  <body>
    <center><b>Employee Search Results</b></center>
```

```
    <br/>
    <b><i>An internal problem occurred while processing your request please try again
</i></b> <a href="Search.html">
    Click Here</a>
  </body>
</html>
```

The last view that we want to implement is a view to present a NumberFormatException, that is, the error page if the search key is not a number while making a request to search by employee or department number.

List 14.19: NotANumberError.vm

```
<html>
  <head>
    <title>Employee Search Results</title>
  </head>
  <body>
    <center><b>Employee Search Results</b></center>
    <br/>
    <i>Employee number/Department number entered is not a number, to try again
</i> <a href="Search.html">
    Click Here</a>
  </body>
</html>
```

Now as we have implemented the view documents let us configure the views in the application context.

List 14.20: webConfig-context.xml

```
<beans xmlns="http://www.springframework.org/schema/beans"
xmlns:xsi="http://www.w3.org/2001/XMLSchema-instance"
xsi:schemaLocation="http://www.springframework.org/schema/beans
http://www.springframework.org/schema/beans/spring-beans-2.0.xsd">

  <!--configuring the controller-->
  <bean id="searchController"
      class="com.santosh.spring.SearchEmployeeController">
    <constructor-arg ref="empDAO"/>
  </bean>
  <bean name="/search.spring"
class="org.springframework.web.servlet.mvc.multiaction.MultiActionController">
    <property name="methodNameResolver" ref="methodNameResolver"/>
    <property name="delegate" ref="searchController"/>
  </bean>
  <bean id="methodNameResolver"
class="org.springframework.web.servlet.mvc.multiaction.ParameterMethodNameResolver">
    <property name="paramName" value="searchBy"/>
```

```
  </bean>

  <!--configuring BeanNameViewResolver-->
  <bean
  class="org.springframework.web.servlet.view.BeanNameViewResolver"/>

  <!--configuring exception resolver-->
  <bean class="
org.springframework.web.servlet.handler.SimpleMappingExceptionResolver">
     <property name="exceptionMappings">
        <props>
           <prop key="org.springframework.dao.DAOException">
              dberrorView
           </prop>
           <prop key="java.lang.NumberFormatException">
              notANumber
           </prop>
        </props>
     </property>
  </bean>

  <!—configuring Views required to render the view for /search.spring request—>
  <bean name="successSingleEmp"
        class="org.springframework.web.servlet.view.velocity.VelocityView">
     <property name="url" value="EmployeeDetails.vm"/>
  </bean>
  <bean name="successMultipleEmps"
        class="org.springframework.web.servlet.view.velocity.VelocityView">
     <property name="url" value="EmployeeList.vm"/>
  </bean>
  <bean name="dberrorView"
        class="org.springframework.web.servlet.view.velocity.VelocityView">
     <property name="url" value="DBError.vm"/>
  </bean>
  <bean name="notANumber"
        class="org.springframework.web.servlet.view.velocity.VelocityView">
     <property name="url" value="NotANumberError.vm"/>
  </bean>
  <!--Configuring the message resources for this application context-->
  <bean id="messageSource"
  class="org.springframework.context.support.ResourceBundleMessageSource">
     <property name="basename" value="ApplicationResources"/>
  </bean>
  <!--Configuring VelocityConfigurer-->
  <bean id="velocityConfigurer"
     class="org.springframework.web.servlet.view.velocity.VelocityConfigurer">
     <property name="resourceLoaderPath" value="/WEB-INF/velocity/"/>
  </bean>
</beans>
```

List 14.20 shows the code for configuring the search controller, view resolver, and VelocityView to use for rendering the response of the/search.spring request. Here we have used BeanNameViewResolver but we can use any other view resolver to resolve the view name in ModelAndView to locate the VelocityView. After writing all these files arrange the files as shown in Fig. 14.9.

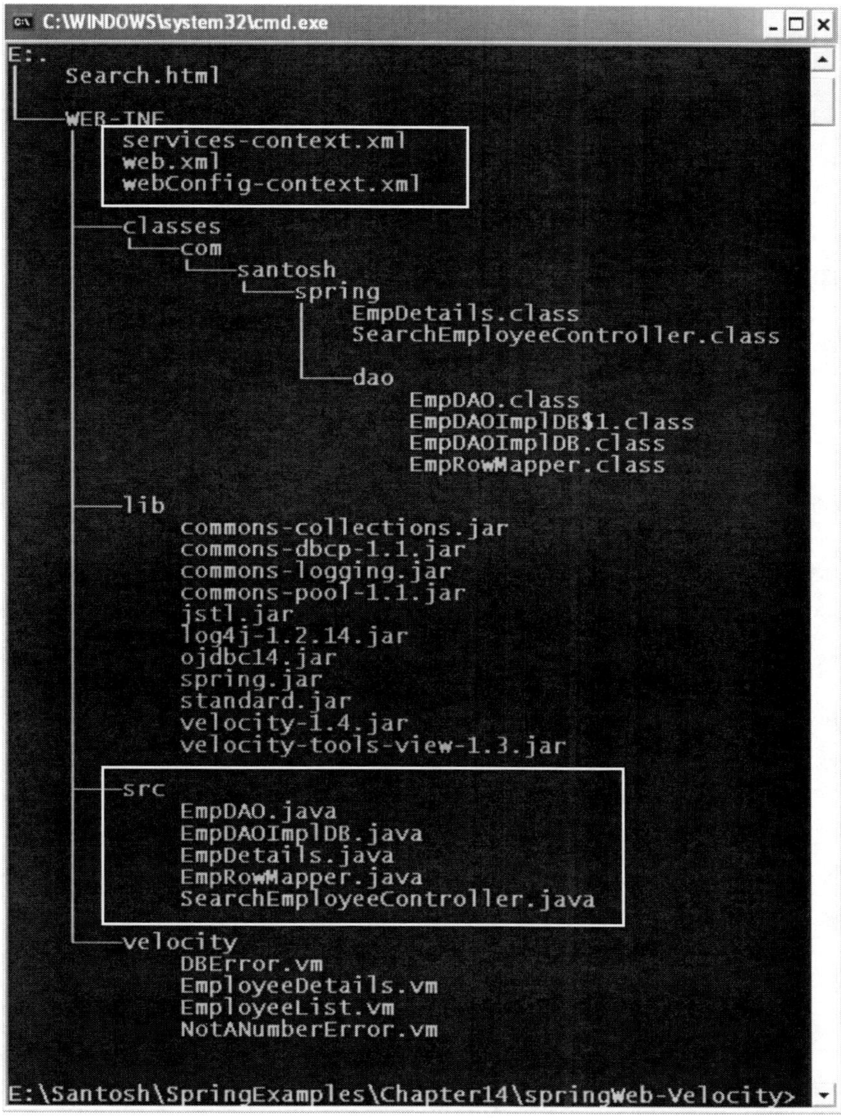

FIGURE 14.9 Directory structure showing all the files of velocity using spring webmvc example

As we are modifying the search employee application that is used earlier to demonstrate that use of JstlView, we need to get the controller and model implementations from the previous example. For convenience, Table 14.2 specifies the file name and the list under which its code is available.

TABLE 14.2 Files for Velocity with Spring WebMVC example

File name	*List*
SearchEmployeeController.java	List 14.1
EmpDAO.java	List 14.2
EmpDAOImplDB.java	List 14.3
EmpRowMapper.java	List 14.4
EmpDetails.java	List 14.5
services-context.xml	List 14.6
web.xml	List 14.14

In addition to all these files we need to copy the velocity distribution jar files into our web application lib folder. We can find these jar files in the spring distribution lib folder. Now, copy the springWeb-Velocity folder into <tomcat home>\webapps folder and browse the example using the URL **http://localhost:8080/springWeb-Velocity/Search.html**. After the server is started you will find the search page where you can search for the employee details based on the employee number, name, job, and department number. Enter some employee number in the search key; select the 'Employee Number' option in 'search by' and submit the form as shown in Fig. 14.10.

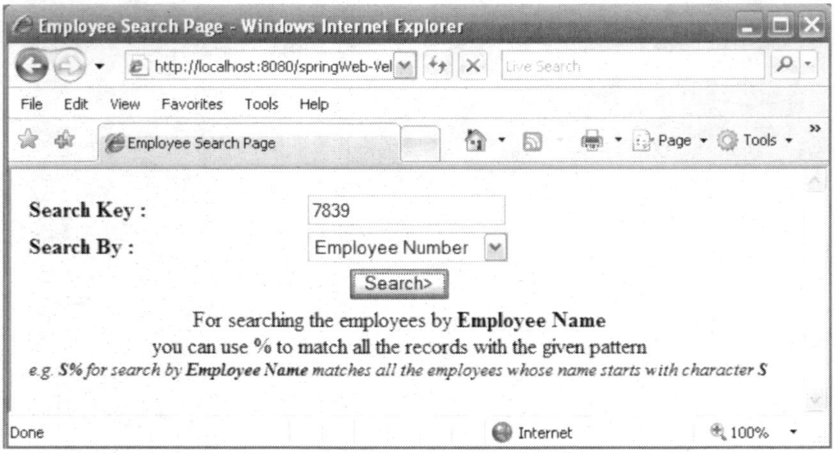

FIGURE 14.10 Search Employee home page

If the given employee number is found then the employee details are presented as shown in Fig. 14.11. If the employee number is not found then it displays a message describing that the employee is not found.

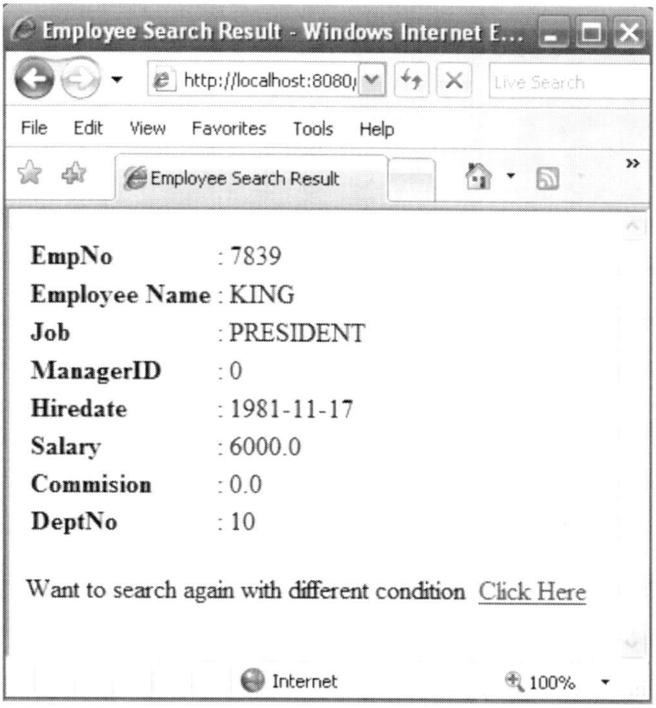

FIGURE 14.11 Employee Search result view

Figure 14.11 shows the view presenting employee details of an employee with the employee number 7839. In case if the search key is not a number and the search by option is selected as 'Employee Number' or 'Department Number' then as per the configurations the NotANumberError.vm page is used to render the view. Similarly, you can search for employees based on the job as shown in Fig. 14.12.

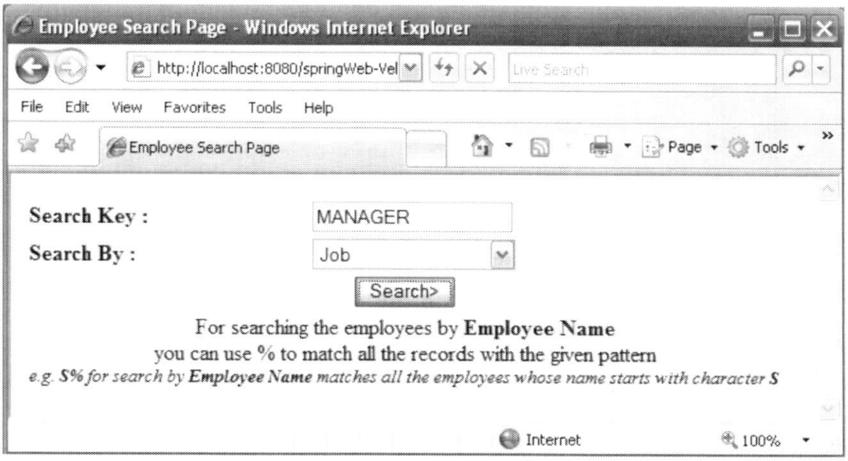

FIGURE 14.12 Employee search form

Figure 14.12 shows the view to submit a request to search for all the managers. The output of this request is shown in Fig. 14.13.

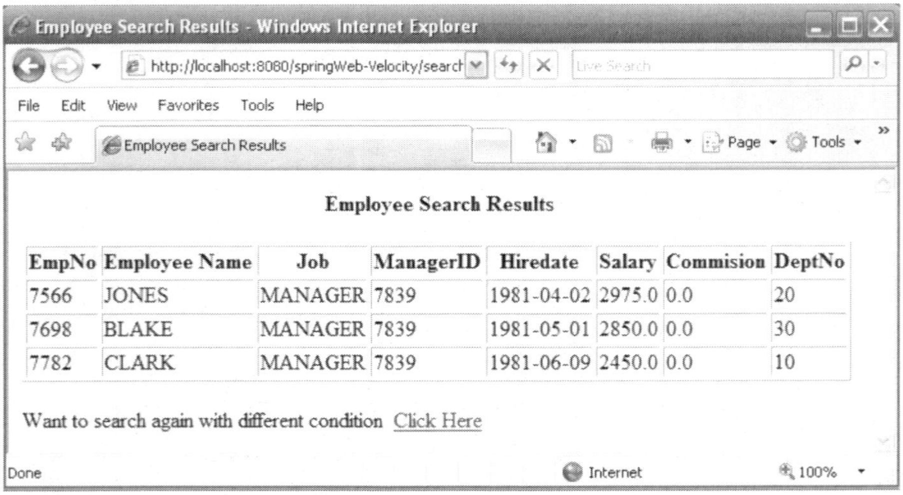

FIGURE 14.13 Employee search results

Similarly, you can use the other search by options in the application such as search by Employee Name and search by Department Number. In this example, we have used Velocity template language to render the view and we have used VelocityView, a View implementation to integrate the view pages with the Spring Web MVC application. So far in this chapter we have learnt how to render html-based views but the modern web applications also have a requirement to render document-based views such as reports in PDF or Excel documents. Let us learn the Spring Web MVC support for rendering document-based views.

14.5 GENERATING EXCEL SPREADSHEET VIEWS

As discussed earlier in this chapter Spring Web MVC provides a clear separation between the view and controller of MVC that enables us to implement handlers of Spring Web MVC completely independent of the view technologies used to render the view. This means, all that we need to do here is to build a view that can produce an Excel spreadsheet and associate it to work with the handlers. Generating the Excel Spreadsheet views is the most common requirement in web applications. Thus Spring Web MVC includes AbstractExcelView and AbstractJExcelView implementation of view providing convenience for rendering a view of Excel documents. The Jakarta POI and JExcel are the two most popular API in Java to prepare excel spreadsheets. The org.springframework.web.servlet.view.document.AbstractExcelView class can be sub-classed to prepare a view of the Excel sheet using Jakarta POI API and org.springframework.web.servlet.view.document.AbstractJExcelView class for using JExcel API to render Excel document views. When using the AbstractExcelView we need to override the buildExcelDocument() method. The method signature of buildExcelDocument is shown in the following code snippet.

Code Snippet

```
protected void buildExcelDocument(
    Map model, HSSFWorkbook workbook,
     HttpServletRequest request, HttpServletResponse response) throws Exception
```

The first argument of the buildExcelDocument() method describes the model data that is prepared by the handler. Moreover, the second argument 'workbook' of HSSFWorkbook type represents the high-level representation of a workbook that provides the methods for creating new sheets and read/write the data into workbook.

To use JExcel API for preparing the documents as discussed we need subclass AbstractJExcelView and override buildExcelDocument() method whose method signature is as shown in the following code snippet.

Code Snippet

```
protected void buildExcelDocument(
     Map model, jxl.write.WritableWorkbook workbook,
     HttpServletRequest request, HttpServletResponse response) throws Exception
```

The first argument of the buildExcelDocument() method describes the model data that is prepared by the handler. Moreover, the second argument 'workbook' of jxl.write.WritableWorkbook type represents the high-level representation of a workbook for completing the workbook using JExcel API.

> **Note:** While deciding between the Jakarta POI and JExcel API for preparing the Excel Spreadsheets, consider the JExcel API support to include images in the excel sheet and Jakarta POI API's most active community that can help in solving the problems in using POI or bugs in POI API.

14.5.1 Modifying the Search Employee Example to Generate Excel View

In the preceding section we have discussed the support from Spring Web MVC to generate Excel spreadsheets. Let us implement one view to demonstrate it practically. To do this we will implement a subclass of AbstractExcelView to generate a view for 'successMultipleEmps' that is presented when the search controller locates multiple employee records based on the given search key. List 14.21 shows the view implementation to render an Excel spreadsheet output.

List 14.21: EmployeeListExcelView.java

```
package com.santosh.spring.view;

import java.util.Collection;
import java.util.Map;

import javax.servlet.http.HttpServletRequest;
import javax.servlet.http.HttpServletResponse;
```

```
import  org.apache.poi.hssf.usermodel.HSSFSheet;
import  org.apache.poi.hssf.usermodel.HSSFWorkbook;
import  org.springframework.web.servlet.view.document.AbstractExcelView;

import  com.santosh.spring.EmpDetails;

/**
 * @author Santosh
 *
 */
public class EmployeeListExcelView extends AbstractExcelView {

  protected void buildExcelDocument(Map model, HSSFWorkbook workbook,
      HttpServletRequest request, HttpServletResponse response)
      throws Exception {

    HSSFSheet sheet = workbook.createSheet("Employees Details");
    sheet.setDefaultColumnWidth((short) 10);
    //Set the header
    getCell(sheet, 0, 0).setCellValue("EmpNo");
    getCell(sheet, 0, 1).setCellValue("Employee Name");
    getCell(sheet, 0, 2).setCellValue("Job");
    getCell(sheet, 0, 3).setCellValue("ManagerID");
    getCell(sheet, 0, 4).setCellValue("Hiredate");
    getCell(sheet, 0, 5).setCellValue("Salary");
    getCell(sheet, 0, 6).setCellValue("Commision");
    getCell(sheet, 0, 7).setCellValue("DeptNo");

    Collection<EmpDetails> empdetails =
      (Collection<EmpDetails>) model.get("empdetails");
    if (empdetails == null || empdetails.isEmpty()) {
      getCell(sheet, 2, 2).setCellValue(
          "There are no records matching your search criteria");
      return;
    }
    int row = 2;
    for (EmpDetails emp : empdetails) {
      getCell(sheet, row, 0).setCellValue(emp.empno);
      getCell(sheet, row, 1).setCellValue(emp.ename);
      getCell(sheet, row, 2).setCellValue(emp.job);
      getCell(sheet, row, 3).setCellValue(emp.mgr);
      getCell(sheet, row, 4).setCellValue(emp.hiredate);
      getCell(sheet, row, 5).setCellValue(emp.sal);
      getCell(sheet, row, 6).setCellValue(emp.comm);
      getCell(sheet, row, 7).setCellValue(emp.deptno);
      row++;
    }
  }
}
```

The getCell() method used in the preceding class is a utility method available in the AbstractExcelView class. This method takes the HSSFSheet object representing the sheet in which lies the cell we want to get, the row number (starting from 0) and then the third argument as column number (starting from 0, that is, the row number and column number are '0' based). And the remaining API used is of Jakarta POI API for preparing the worksheet. For more information on Jakarta POI API visit http://poi.apache.org.

Now, compile the view class whose code is shown in List 14.21. Note that we need to additionally set 'poi-2.5.1.jar' also into the classpath for successfully compiling the EmployeeListExcelView class. After writing the view class and compiling, let us configure it to work with our employee search application. For this change the 'successMultipleEmps' bean definition in 'webConfig-context.xml' file (see List 14.7) with the bean definition is shown in the following code snippet.

Code Snippet

```
<bean  name="successMultipleEmps"
    class="com.santosh.spring.view.EmployeeListExcelView "/>
```

Now, arrange the files as shown in Fig. 14.14.

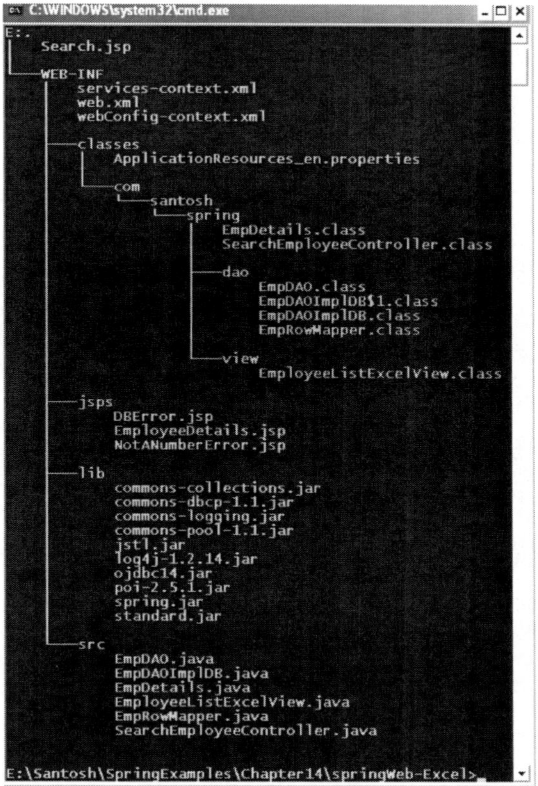

FIGURE 14.14 Directory structure for the files of the example showing the spring webmvc generating excel view

The codes for EmployeeListExcelView.java file is shown in List 14.21. For all the remaining source files see Lists 14.1 through 14.14. Now deploy the application into the server like copy the springWeb-Excel folder into <tomcat home>\webapps folder and browse the example using the URL **http://localhost:8080/springWeb-Excel/Search.jsp.** After the server is started you will find the search page where you can search for the employee details based on the employee number, name, job, and department number. Enter the department number in the Search Key text box, select the 'Department Number' option in 'Search By' select box, and submit the form as shown in Fig. 14.15.

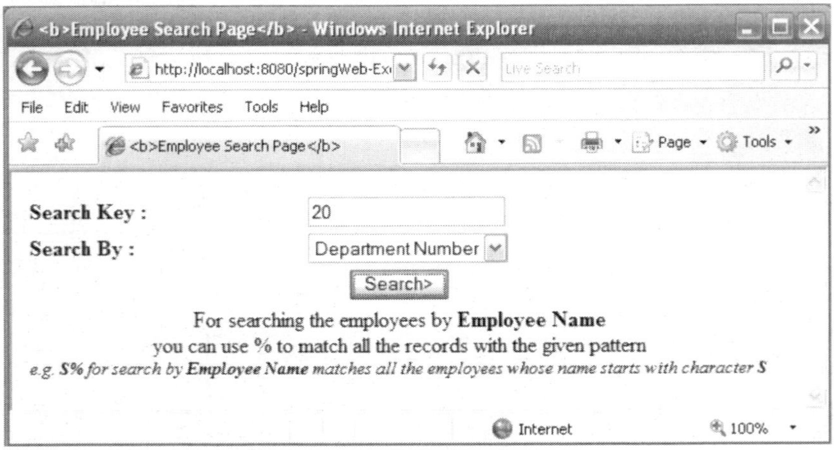

FIGURE 14.15 Employee search form

Figure 14.15 shows the view to submit a request to search for all the employees working under Department 20. The output of this request is shown in Fig. 14.16.

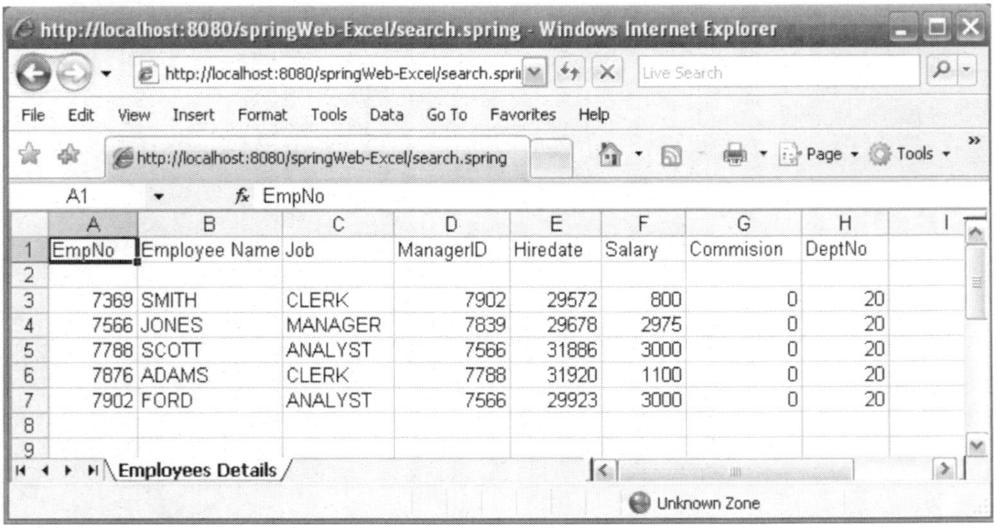

FIGURE 14.16 Employee search results as an excel sheet

When a request is made to search for the employees working under Department 20 since we have some records with deptno 20 in the 'emp' table, it results to prepare a collection of the EmpDetails object. Further, the controller returns a ModelAndView object that represents the view name 'successMultipleEmps' and the collection of EmpDetails as a model object. Again as per the configurations in the 'webConfig-context.xml' file the view name 'successMultipleEmps' will be resolved to locate com.santosh.spring.view.EmployeeListExcelView. The EmployeeListExcelView whose code is shown under List 14.21 renders the view as an Excel spreadsheet as shown in Fig. 14.16. In this section we have learnt how to use the Spring Web MVC infrastructure to generate Excel spreadsheet views. The following section explains how to prepare the PDF document views.

14.6 GENERATING PDF DOCUMENT VIEWS

As discussed earlier, apart from html-based views most web applications require to present document-based views for presenting the reports, the Excel spreadsheet documents are generally convenient to present the tabular content as demonstrated in the preceding section, the view which presents a list of employee details. Moreover, to present content with accurate formatting and making it viewable on many different platforms, save the report and take a printout of the report it is a better practice to present PDF document as a view. Spring Web MVC understands this importance and includes a support for rendering the view as PDF documents. The org.springframework.web.servlet.view.document.AbstractPdfView is an abstract class providing the convenience for preparing the PDF document views using Bruno Lowagie's iText API. The subclass of the AbstractPdfView requires to implement the buildPdfDocument() method to produce the PDF document. The buildPdfDocument() method signature is shown in the following code snippet.

Code Snippet

```
protected abstract void buildPdfDocument(Map model,
                    com.lowagie.text.Document document,
                    com.lowagie.text.pdf.PdfWriter writer,
                    HttpServletRequest request,
                    HttpServletResponse response) throws Exception
```

As mentioned earlier, the AbstractPdfView provides an abstraction to prepare PDF documents using itext PDF API. The buildPdfDocument() method has the Document and PdfWriter arguments (that is, itext PDF API objects) allowing us to complete the document. Apart from these two arguments the model describes the model Map that is created by the handler, and the HttpServletRequest, HttpServletResponse objects of this request. Let us see how this is implemented to generate a PDF view.

14.6.1 Modifying the Search Employee Example to Generate PDF View

In the preceding section we have discussed the support from Spring Web MVC to generate PDF document. Let us implement one view to demonstrate it practically. To do this we will implement a subclass of AbstractPDFView to generate view for 'successSingleEmp' that is presented when the search controller locates a single employee record based on the given search key. List 14.22 shows the view implementation to render a PDF document output.

List 14.22: EmployeeDetailsPDFView.java

```
package com.santosh.spring.view;

import java.util.Map;

import javax.servlet.http.HttpServletRequest;
import javax.servlet.http.HttpServletResponse;

import org.springframework.web.servlet.view.document.AbstractPdfView;

import com.lowagie.text.Document;
import com.lowagie.text.Paragraph;
import com.lowagie.text.Table;
import com.lowagie.text.pdf.PdfWriter;
import com.santosh.spring.EmpDetails;

/**
 * @author Santosh
 *
 */
public class EmployeeDetailsPDFView extends AbstractPdfView {

  protected void buildPdfDocument(
          Map model, Document doc, PdfWriter pdfWriter,
          HttpServletRequest request, HttpServletResponse response)
                                                  throws Exception {

    EmpDetails  empDetails=(EmpDetails)model.get("empdetails");

    if (empDetails==null){
      doc.add(
        new Paragraph("There are no records matching your search criteria"));
      return;
    }
    Paragraph p=new Paragraph("Employee Search Results");
    p.setAlignment("center");
    p.setSpacingAfter(15);

    doc.add(p);
    Table empTable=new Table(2);
    empTable.setWidth(50);
    empTable.setBorder(0);
    empTable.setDefaultCellBorder(0);

    empTable.addCell("EmpNo");
    empTable.addCell(empDetails.empno+"");
    empTable.addCell("Employee Name");
    empTable.addCell(empDetails.ename);
    empTable.addCell("Job");
```

```
        empTable.addCell(empDetails.job);
        empTable.addCell("ManagerID");
        empTable.addCell(empDetails.mgr+"");
        empTable.addCell("Hiredate");
        empTable.addCell(empDetails.hiredate+"");
        empTable.addCell("Salary");
        empTable.addCell(empDetails.sal+"");
        empTable.addCell("Commision");
        empTable.addCell(empDetails.comm+"");
        empTable.addCell("DeptNo");
        empTable.addCell(empDetails.deptno+"");
        doc.add(empTable);
    }
}
```

The com.lowagie.text.Table object is used to create a table in the document. The table constructor takes the number of columns the table needs to be constructed. Here we have used the two describing the table as having two columns. The addCell() method used in the preceding class is a method available in the table class. This method takes the content that should be inserted into the current cell. For more information on Bruno Lowagie's iText API visit http://www.lowagie.com/iText.

Now, compile the view class whose code is shown in List 14.21. Note that we need to additionally set 'itext-1.4.8.jar' also into the classpath for successfully compiling the EmployeeDetailsPDFView class. After writing the view class and compiling, let us configure it to work with our employee search application. For this change the 'successSingleEmp' bean definition in 'webConfig-context.xml' file (see List 14.7) with the bean definition shown in the following code snippet.

Code Snippet

```
<bean  name="successSingleEmp"
    class="com.santosh.spring.view.EmployeeDetailsPDFView "/>
```

After doing the preceding additions for the springWeb application used to demonstrate the JstlView browse the application to search employee by employee number to find the PDF output.

14.7 SPRING FRAMEWORK FORM TAG LIBRARY

In addition to the support for working with the existing view technologies to build the views, Spring Framework provides some tags that can be used in JSP documents to prepare the view. The Spring form tags provides an easier approach of implementing JSP pages that works with the data binding features, which binds the form data to command objects. To use these tags, we need to add the following directive in the JSP document:

```
<%@taglib  prefix="form"  uri="http://www.springframework.org/tags/form"%>
```

The form tag library is described in spring-form.tld file, which is included into spring-webmvc.jar file. Please refer Appendix-A for the description on the various tags defined in spring-form.tld file.

Summary

In this chapter we have learnt about the ViewResolver and View infrastructural elements of Spring Web MVC. In the first part of this chapter we have discussed on the ViewResolver and its importance in the Spring Web MVC request processing workflow, where we have understood that a ViewResolver allows us implement the handler (controller) independent of the view technology used to render the view providing the convenience to freely use any view technology to render the view without changing the handlers. Then we have learnt about the various Spring Web MVC built-in ViewResolver implementation, its uses and how to configure it. With this we have come to the end of the discussion on ViewResolver. The next part of the chapter was dedicated to discuss view and its implementations. Moreover, in this chapter we have learnt how to use the View technologies like JSTL and Velocity to generate tag-based (html-based) responses. We ended the discussion by learning how to render document-based views like Excel spreadsheet and PDF using the Jakarta POI and iText APIs, respectively. In the next chapter we will learn how to integrate Spring Framework with other Web Frameworks to utilize Spring services in other Web Application Frameworks like Struts.

Integrating Spring with other Web Frameworks

15 CHAPTER

Objectives

In Chapter 11 we introduced the Spring Web MVC Framework explaining its importance and architecture overview. Later in Chapter 12 through 14, we learnt the Spring Web MVC Framework in detail and its importance. While going through Chapters 11 through 14 we understood that Spring Web MVC framework is extremely convenient for implementing Model-2 based Web MVC applications in Java by providing the most infrastructural concerns as a built-in service, even allowing for customizations such as customizable navigation and view management, which is not supported with most of the other Web MVC frameworks.

Even though Spring Web MVC Framework provides a complete environment and is an ideal option for implementing Web MVC applications it still does not restrict using other Web frameworks such as Struts in the project. Spring provides support for working with other web frameworks for the following two important reasons:

- To support one of the important benefits that describes to introduce Spring incrementally into existing projects. Like we might choose to use Spring only to simplify the business objects implementation initially leaving the presentation tier to implement using other Web MVC framework.
- We may have resources which are experienced in other Web MVC framework but yet not familiar working with the Spring Web MVC framework. However, we would like to use Spring for implementing other layers/tiers such as business and integration/data access layers, taking its support for AOP, IoC, transactions, security, etc.

In this chapter we will cover:

- How to integrate Spring with Struts Web MVC Framework.

15.1 STRUTS FRAMEWORK

Struts framework is an open-source web application framework implemented by Apache Software Foundation (ASF). Struts framework is one of the efficient and high-performance open source implementation of Model-2 based Model-View-Controller (MVC). Struts framework provides utility classes to handle many of the most common tasks in Web application development. Struts was originally started as a small project by Craig McClanahan in May 2000, but later he donated it to Apache Software Foundation which later added many features to it that are more commonly required for web application development.

15.1.1 Overview of Struts Architecture

Even though this chapter is dedicated to explain how to integrate Spring with Struts framework we want to have a brief discussion on Struts framework architecture so that we can understand at which point of this architecture we need to integrate with Spring framework and for what services it may require this. Let us have a brief look on Struts framework architecture. Figure 15.1 shows the Struts architecture.

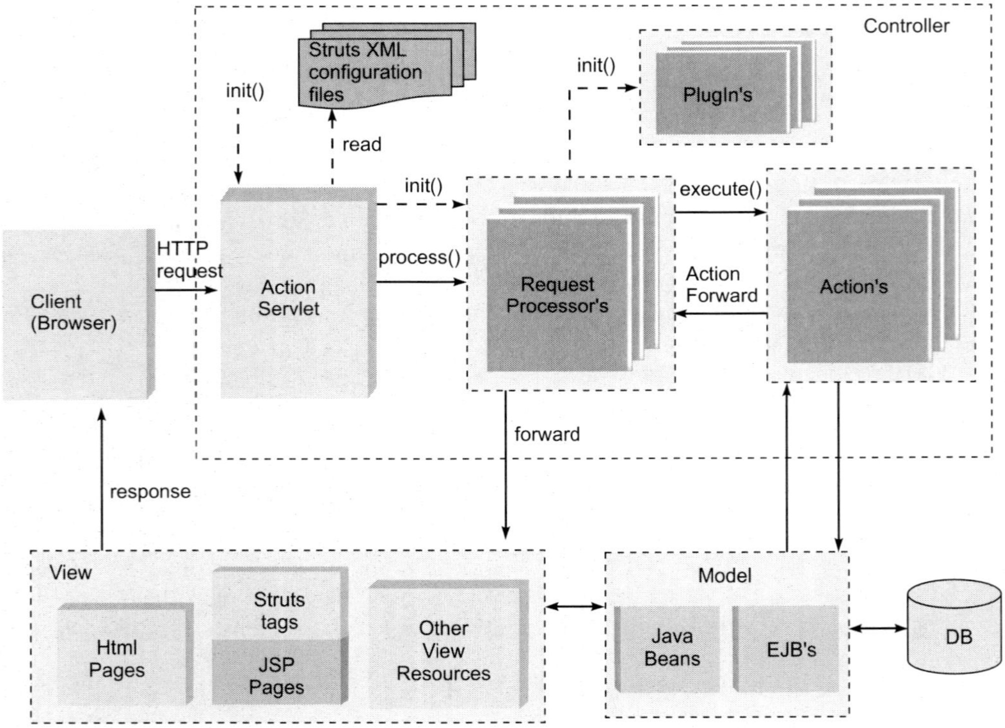

FIGURE 15.1 Struts framework architecture

> **Note:** In the above architecture the dotted arrows shows the initialization process and solid arrows shows the request processing.

Now, let us have a brief discussion on the various elements of Struts framework shown in Fig. 15.1, starting with ActionServlet.

15.1.1.1 The ActionServlet

The ActionServlet of Struts framework is an implementation of Front Controller pattern that provides centralized access point for the Struts application. The ActionServlet is a Java Servlet component, that is, a Servlet Front for Struts application.

15.1.1.1.1 Initialization

The ActionServlet init() method finds the user configured Struts modules and locates the Struts configuration file of each module. Then it reads, validates the configurations, and loads the details into ModuleConfig object. After creating the ModuleConfig object successfully ActionServlet creates a RequestProcessor object and initializes it injecting this ModuleConfig object. Now, the Request Processor uses the ModuleConfig object to get all the module specific details and performs the necessary initializations such as instantiating and initializing all the configured plugins. Once all these initializations are successfully done then the ActionServlet instance is put into service, which provides an entry point to serve the client requests using the configurations loaded.

15.1.1.1.2 Handling the request

The ActionServlet is a Servlet implemented as a subtype of HttpServlet. The ActionServlet accepts HTTP GET and POST method request where the doGet() and doPost() method implementations of ActionServlet just invokes the protected process() method of the same class where all the request handling logic is implemented. The ActionServlet process() method identifies the module that the client has requested for. This is done by matching the first part of the request URL with the configured module paths. Thereafter it gets the RequestProcessor instance of the selected module and delegates the request to that RequestProcessor instance, invoking the process() method.

15.1.1.2 The RequestProcessor

The RequestProcessor of Struts framework is an implementation of Application Controller pattern, implementing many infrastructural concerns such as Action Management and View Management. The RequestProcessor is a plain Java class. This object is created and initialized by ActionServlet, as a part of its initialization process as explained in the preceding section. As described in the preceding section ActionServlet delegates the request to RequestProcessor by invoking process() as a part of handling the request, that is, process() method of RequestProcessor is invoked every time the client requests for this module. The process method is responsible to handle the request where it needs to perform a number of request processing tasks. The RequestProcessor class uses the Chain of Responsibility (COR) pattern to implement these tasks. The RequestProcessor class implements separate methods to process each request-processing task. As shown in the architecture the RequestProcessor delegates the request to Action so that the application provider can add the application-specific code to execute request handling.

15.1.1.3 The Action Class

The action class is a class that is a subtype of org.apache.struts.action.Action. The action class that is a part of controller provides an entry point where we can start with our application code to process the request. As shown in the architecture, RequestProcessor delegates the request to action by invoking the execute() method of the action. The action communicates with the model components and prepares the data for the view that is required to prepare presentation. We need to configure the action in the Struts configuration file using <action> tag and map it to a unique path so that the RequestProcessor can map the incoming request to our action. The following code snippet shows the mapping configuration in Struts configuration file.

Code Snippet

```
<action path="/login"
      type= "com.santosh.struts.LoginAction"/>
```

15.1.1.4 The PlugIn Class

Struts framework implements a number of infrastructural concerns required for web application development in Java. In addition, it allows us to use frameworks or services provided by the other vendors or implemented by us. The plugin feature allows us to configure any external services to start along with the Struts framework. That is, it integrates with the Struts framework.

Now after reviewing the basics of the Struts framework let us end this overview with a sample application.

15.1.2 Working with Struts

To make the example simple we are implementing a login process which is well-known. This example consists of a Login.html which provides an entry point for this application by providing login view allowing the user to make a login action. List 15.1 shows code for Login.html.

List 15.1: Login.html

```
<html> <body>
<form action="login.do"> <pre>
User Name : <input type="text" name="uname"/>

Password  : <input type="password" name="pass"/>

<input type="submit" value="LogIN"/>
</pre></form> </body> </html>
```

The request made using the Login.html is received by the ActionServlet, which then dispatches the request to the RequestProcessor. The RequestProcessor after some request processing tasks invokes the execute method on the action class object. The processing of the login request by the LogicAction class is shown in List 15.2.

List 15.2: LoginAction.java

```
package com.santosh.struts;

import org.apache.struts.action.*;
import javax.servlet.http.*;
/**
 * @author Santosh
 */

public class LoginAction extends Action {

  public ActionForward execute(
```

```
          ActionMapping am,
          ActionForm af,
          HttpServletRequest req,
          HttpServletResponse res) throws Exception {

    String uname= req.getParameter("uname");
    String pass= req.getParameter("pass");

    LoginModel lm=new LoginModel();

    String type=lm.validate(uname, pass);

    if (type==null)
     return am.findForward("notValid");

    return am.findForward(type);

  }//execute
}//class
```

As shown in List 15.2, LoginAction execute() method uses the validate() method of LoginModel to validate the user. The LoginModel is a plain java class designed to perform business logic operations, that is, validate the login details. List 15.3 shows the code for LoginModel.java.

List 15.3: LoginModel.java

```
package com.santosh.struts;

import java.sql.*;
/**
 * @author Santosh
 */
public class LoginModel {

  public String validate(String uname, String pass) {
    Connection con=null;
    try {
      Class.forName("oracle.jdbc.driver.OracleDriver");
      con=DriverManager.getConnection(
            "jdbc:oracle:thin:@localhost:1521:sandb","scott","tiger");

      Statement st=con.createStatement();

      ResultSet rs=st.executeQuery(
        "select type from userdetails where username=\'"+
        uname+"\' and userpass=\'"+pass+"\'");

      if (rs.next()) return rs.getString(1);
    }//try
    catch(Exception e){
      e.printStackTrace();
    }
```

```
    finally{
      try{con.close();}
      catch(Exception e){}
    }//finally
    return null;
  }//validate
}//class
```

As we have discussed in the above sections we need to configure the action into the Struts configuration file. List 15.4 shows the code for struts-config.xml file.

List 15.4: struts-config.xml

```
<!DOCTYPE struts-config PUBLIC
     "-//Apache Software Foundation//DTD Struts Configuration 1.3//EN"
      "http://struts.apache.org/dtds/struts-config_1_3.dtd">

<struts-config>
  <action-mappings>
    <action type="com.santosh.struts.LoginAction" path="/login">
      <forward name="notValid" path="/Login.html"/>
      <forward name="admin" path="/AdminHome.jsp"/>
      <forward name="user" path="/UserHome.jsp"/>
    </action>
  </action-mappings>
</struts-config>
```

List 15.5 shows the AdminHome.jsp, a view that is presented to the client in case the login details submitted are validated as an admin type user.

List 15.5: AdminHome.jsp

```
<html> <body>
  Welcome to the Admin Home page <br/>
  User Name : <%=request.getParameter("uname")%>
</html> </body>
```

List 15.6 shows the UserHome.jsp, a view that is presented to the client in case the login details submitted are validated as a user type.

List 15.6: UserHome.jsp

```
<html> <body>
  Welcome to the Non-Admin User Home page <br/>
  User Name : <%=request.getParameter("uname")%>
</html> </body>
```

Finally, we need to configure ActionServlet in web.xml since it is also a normal servlet as any other servlet. List 15.7 shows the code for web.xml.

List 15.7: web.xml

```
<!DOCTYPE web-app PUBLIC
  "-//Sun Microsystems, Inc.//DTD Web Application 2.3//EN"
  "http://java.sun.com/dtd/web-app_2_3.dtd">

<web-app>
  <servlet>
    <servlet-name>as</servlet-name>
     <servlet-class>org.apache.struts.action.ActionServlet</servlet-class>
    <load-on-startup>0</load-on-startup>
  </servlet>
  <servlet-mapping>
      <servlet-name>as</servlet-name>
      <url-pattern>*.do</url-pattern>
  </servlet-mapping>
</web-app>
```

Now, compile the Java files and arrange the files as shown in Fig. 15.2.

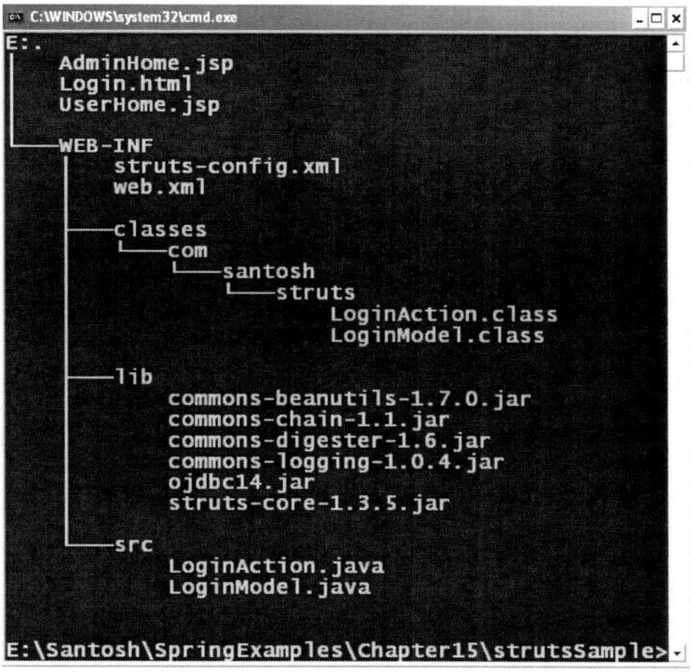

FIGURE 15.2 Directory structure showing files of struts simple example

You can download the Struts binary from **http://struts.apache.org/download.cgi** after preparing the application create database table and some test record using the SQL commands shown in the code snippet below.

Code Snippet

```
drop table userdetails;

create table userdetails(
 username varchar2(20),
 userpass varchar2(20),
 email varchar2(30),
 address varchar2(30),
 mobile number(10),
 type varchar2(5)
);

insert into userdetails values('Santosh', 'kumar', 'to_santoshk@yahoo.com', 'hyd',
9704309999, 'admin');
```

Now, deploy the application into any Web Application server like Tomcat and browse the application. If deployed into Tomcat server running on 8080 port then use http://localhost:8080/strutsSample/Login.html URL to browse the application. After running the example let us have a quick look on the flow of the example.

15.1.2.1 Understanding the Example

Figure 15.3 shows the flow diagram of the preceding example. Observe the diagram and proceed through the brief discussion on the example and diagram.

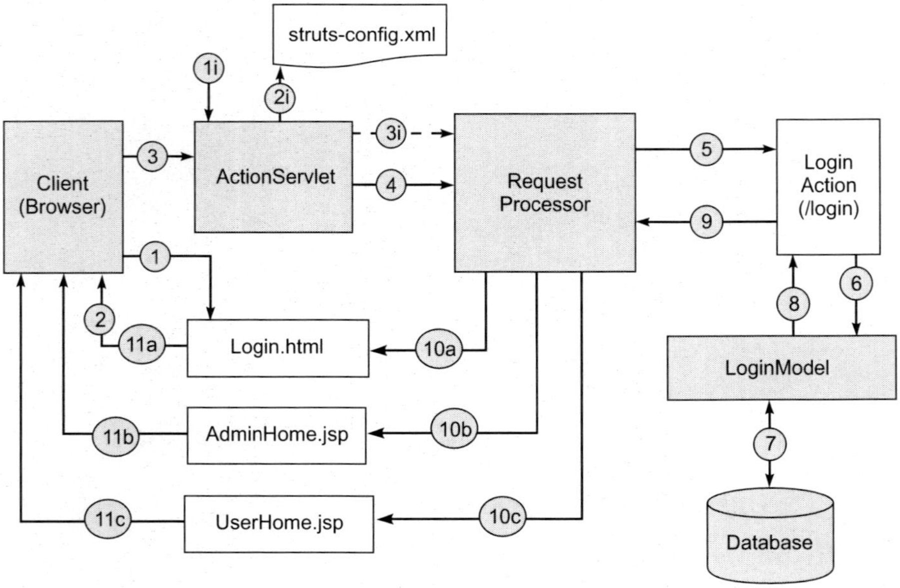

FIGURE 15.3 Flow diagram explaining the preceding example

The following steps are performed in the initialization process of the preceding example:

(i) Container invokes init() method of ActionServlet similar to any other servlet we write (Step **1i** in the diagram).

(ii) ActionServlet reads the init parameters and finds the number of modules configured for this application. In this case it does not find any additional module. Here we have only the default module.

(iii) For each of the module configured it performs the following operations (in this example, only one):

  (a) reads the Struts configuration file and validates it (Step **2i** in diagram)

  (b) prepares a ModuleConfig object that encapsulates all the configuration details described in the modules config file, like action paths, forwards, etc.

  (c) Instantiates and initializes a RequestProcessor object (Step **3i** in diagram).

(iv) Stores some details like ActionServlet instance etc into context scope

The following steps are performed when the client makes a request for action (that is, Step **3** in diagram):

(i) Container delegates the request to ActionServlet, that is, invoking service() method.

(ii) ActionServlet resolves the Request URI to identify the module and the respective RequestProcessor object that can handle this request.

(iii) ActionServlet delegates the request to the RequestProcessor, invoking process() method (Step **4** shown in diagram).

(iv) The process() method of RequestProcessor performs various operations, as a part of these chain of processes the two methods are important to be considered in this flow.

  (a) processActionCreate()—this method locates the action object that has to handle this request, if not found it creates a new one.

  (b) processActionPerform()—this method delegates the request to action, invoking execute() method. In this case it is com.santosh.struts.LoginAction object since /login path is configured to com.santosh.struts.LoginAction in struts-config.xml file shown in List 15.4 (Step **5** shown in diagram).

(v) As we have coded the execute() method of LoginAction to communicates with LoginModel, which uses DB to validate the user details and return the user type (admin or user). Alternatively, if the user details are not valid, it returns null. (Steps **6**, **7**, and **8**)

(vi) The execute() method of LoginAction returns an ActionForward with the user type (admin or user) or fail if LoginModel returns null (Step **9** in diagram).

(vii) Now, based on the ActionForward returned by LoginAction RequestProcessor it dispatches the request to Login.html if 'fail' (Step **10a**), AdminHome.jsp if 'admin' (Step **10b**), and UserHome.jsp if 'user' (Step **10c**). Thereafter the respective page prepares the presentation for the client, that is, Step **11a, 11b,** or **11c.**

In this section we learnt about the request processing workflow of Struts application. Moreover, with this we will conclude the discussion on reviewing the Struts framework. Now, after looking at the architecture of the Struts framework let us find for what Struts wants to integrate with Spring framework and further continue the discussion to understand how it integrates with Spring.

15.2 WHAT FOR STRUTS WANT TO INTEGRATE WITH SPRING?

As discussed in the preceding section Struts framework provides utility classes to handle many of the most common tasks of Web application. However, Struts does not include any support for implementing the business objects, which requires declarative transactions, security, IoC, etc. Moreover, as we know that Spring framework includes an excellent support such as AOP, IoC, declarative transactions, security, etc., for implementing enterprise-level business objects as POJOs. This is an important reason where Struts framework wants to integrate with Spring framework. That means while using Struts framework to implement web application we may want to access the beans configured in Spring application context, that is, access the beans managed by Spring core container. Let us learn how Struts integrates with Spring framework to use its core and other services.

15.3 INTEGRATING SPRING WITH STRUTS

In the preceding section we have understood why Struts integrates with the Spring framework. Now, we will learn how Struts integrates with Spring. As we know that Action class in Struts framework is a handler implemented by the application developer to implement system-specific request handling logic such as communicating with the model components, we want Struts action class to access the beans managed by the Spring container. That means either we want to inject the Spring beans into Struts action class or provide WebApplicationContext for Struts action. The following two steps are involved in integrating Spring with Struts framework.

Step 1: Initialize the Spring application context along with the Struts framework.
Step 2: Make the Spring beans available to Struts Actions.

Let us discuss these two steps in detail.

15.3.1 Initializing Spring Application Context along with Struts Framework

In integrating Spring with Struts framework the first thing that we need to do is to initialize the Spring core container at the time of starting the Struts framework. We know that Struts framework allows executing custom code at the time of initialization, in the form of Struts PlugIn. The configured PlugIn classes are instantiated and initialized as a part of initializing the respective modules RequestProcessor, and further while destroying the RequestProcessor the PlugIns are informed for finalizations. That means Struts framework's PlugIn feature allows us to configure any external services to start along with the Struts framework, that is, integrate with Struts framework, enabling us to use frameworks or services provided by the other vendors or implemented by us. Therefore the Struts PlugIn support can be used to initialize the Spring core container (that is, application context) along with Struts Framework. The ContextLoaderPlugIn is a Struts plugin implemented by Spring Framework, to integrate Spring with Struts Framework. Let us have a closer look on the Context LoaderPlugIn.

15.3.1.1 The ContextLoaderPlugIn

The ContextLoaderPlugIn is a Struts plugin implementation, which loads the Spring application context for Struts application. The ContextLoaderPlugIn is packaged into org.springframework.web.struts package. The following code snippet shows the plugin tag that can be included into the struts configuration file for using ContextLoaderPlugIn.

Code Snippet

```
<plug-in   className="org.springframework.web.struts.ContextLoaderPlugIn">
  <set-property  property="contextConfiLocation"
                 value="/WEB-INF/services-context.xml"/>
</plug-in>
```

The 'contextConfigLocation' property specifies the Spring beans XML configuration files. The 'contextConfigLocation' property allows to specify multiple configuration files using comma (that is, ',') as a separator. If this property is not configured, the ContextLoaderPlugIn takes the default location as */WEB-INF/<namespace>.xml*. To specify the *<namespace>* we can use 'namespace' property. If not configured it defaults to *<servlet name of struts ActionServlet>-servlet.xml*, that is, if ActionServlet is configured with a name 'action', in web.xml file, the default configuration file path is considered as /WEB-INF/action-servlet.xml. The ContextLoaderPlugIn creates an instance of XmlWebApplicationContext class; however, we can configure the web application context class name using 'contextClass' property. After initializing the web application context it is published to the ServletContext. We can use a single ContextLoaderPlugIn for all Struts modules, or define one ContextLoaderPlugIn per Struts module. Now, as the Spring application context is initialized we want to access the application context from Struts action classes so that we can use the Spring beans configured in the Spring XML configuration files. So let us move to second step in integrating Spring with Struts framework, which makes the Spring WebApplicationContext available to Struts Actions.

15.3.2 Making Spring Beans Available to Struts Actions

After configuring the ContextLoaderPlugIn to initialize the Spring application context, we want the Spring context in Struts Actions so that they can access the Spring beans (that is, spring managed beans). Spring provides options to implement Struts actions that can work with Spring beans.

Option 1: Lookup the WebApplicationContext to access Spring beans
Option 2: Configure the Struts Actions as Spring beans

Let us understand both of these options in detail.

15.3.2.1 Looking up the WebApplicationContext to Access Spring Beans

As we have discussed earlier, the ContextLoaderPlugIn initializes the WebApplicationContext and publishes it to ServletContext. That means the Struts Actions can retrieve the WebApplicationContext from the ServletContext. The org.springframework.web.context.support .WebApplicationContext Utils class includes convenience methods for accessing the WebApplicationContext in a given Servlet Context.

Code Snippet

```
public ActionForward execute( … ) throws Exception {
  …
  WebApplicationContext webApplicationContext=
    WebApplicationContextUtils.getWebApplicationContext(
      getServlet().getServletContext());
  …
}
```

The preceding code snippet shows the code in a Struts Action to retrieve WebApplicationContext in the current ServletContext. Alternative to this approach of retrieving the WebApplicationContext, an easier way is to extend Spring's ActionSupport classes for Struts. The ActionSupport class provides a convenience method getWebApplicationContext() for accessing the WebApplicationContext in the current ServletContext. The following code snippet shows the action class defined as a subtype of ActionSupport.

Code Snippet

```
public class MyAction extends ActionSupport {

  public ActionForward execute(ActionMapping am, ActionForm af,
          HttpServletRequest request, HttpServletResponse response)
                 throws Exception {
      ...
      WebApplicationContext webAppCtxt=getWebApplicationContext();
      MyBusinessObject mbi=(MyBusinessObject)
                          webAppCtxt.getBean("mybean");
      ...
  }
}
```

Apart from ActionSupport Spring includes subclasses for the standard Struts actions such as DispatchActionSupport for DispatchAction, LookupDispatchActionSupport for LookupDispatch Action, and MappingDispatchActionSupport for MappingDispatchAction.

15.3.2.2.1 Working with Spring ActionSupport

In the Login process implemented earlier to demonstrate the Struts basic elements, the execute method of LoginAction class creates a new instance of LoginModel for each time it is invoked, which is not suggestible, even observing the implementation of LoginModel we can identify that it is stateless and need not to be used in a threadsafe environment. Thus we can share a single LoginModel instance to service various requests. To implement this strategy we need to implement singleton pattern for LoginModel. Integrating Spring with Struts framework in this case will eliminate the need of implementing the singleton pattern. Apart from this we can use Spring JDBC abstraction framework to simplify the LoginModel implementation. Let us redesign the login process example to work with Spring container. Modifying the login process example to work with spring container requires an additional file application-context.xml to implement and the following files need to be modified.

- LoginAction.java
- LoginModel.java
- struts-config.xml

Let us do the changes and additions, first starting modifying LoginModel to use Spring JDBC abstraction framework for communicating with database. List 15.8 shows the code for LoginModel.java.

List 15.8: LoginModel.java

```
package com.santosh.spring;

import org.springframework.jdbc.core.*;
import org.springframework.dao.*;
/**
 * @author Santosh
 */
public class LoginModel {

  private JdbcTemplate jdbcTemplate;

  public LoginModel(JdbcTemplate jdbcTemplate){
    this.jdbcTemplate=jdbcTemplate;
  }

  public String validate(String uname, String pass) {
    try {
      return (String)jdbcTemplate.queryForObject(
        "select type from userdetails where username=\'"+
                         uname+"\' and userpass=\'"+pass+"\'",
        String.class);
    }//try
    catch(EmptyResultDataAccessException emptyResultException){
        return null;
    }
  }//validate
}//class
```

Now, let us implement a Struts action (LoginAction) with the support to access Spring container services, that is, using Spring Action's (ActionSupport).

List 15.9: LoginAction.java

```
package com.santosh.spring.struts;

import com.santosh.spring.LoginModel;
import org.apache.struts.action.*;
```

```
import javax.servlet.http.*;
import org.springframework.web.struts.*;
import org.springframework.web.context.*;
/**
 * @author Santosh
 */
public class LoginAction extends ActionSupport {

  public ActionForward execute(
                        ActionMapping am,
                        ActionForm af,
                        HttpServletRequest req,
                        HttpServletResponse res) throws Exception {

    String uname= req.getParameter("uname");
    String pass= req.getParameter("pass");

    WebApplicationContext webAppCtxt= getWebApplicationContext();

    LoginModel  lm=(LoginModel)webAppCtxt.getBean("loginModel");

    String type=lm.validate(uname, pass);

    if (type==null)
      return am.findForward("notValid");

    return am.findForward(type);
  }//execute
}//class
```

After implementing the LoginModel and LoginAction we need to configure the LoginModel and its dependencies in a Spring beans XML configuration file application-context.xml. The application-context.xml file declares the LoginModel bean as a Spring bean so that it can be accessed by the LoginAction using the WebApplicationContext.

List 15.10: application-context.xml

```
<beans  xmlns:xsi="http://www.w3.org/2001/XMLSchema-instance"
xsi:schemaLocation="http://www.springframework.org/schema/beans
http://www.springframework.org/schema/beans/spring-beans-2.0.xsd"
xmlns="http://www.springframework.org/schema/beans">

  <!--Configuring DataSource-->
  <bean id="datasource" class="org.apache.commons.dbcp.BasicDataSource">
    <property name="driverClassName"
          value="oracle.jdbc.driver.OracleDriver"/>
```

```
    <property name="url" value="jdbc:oracle:thin:@localhost:1521:sandb"/>
    <property name="username" value="scott"/>
    <property name="password" value="tiger"/>
  </bean>

  <!--Configuring JdbcTemplate-->
  <bean id="jdbctemp" class="org.springframework.jdbc.core.JdbcTemplate">
    <constructor-arg ref="datasource"/>
  </bean>

  <bean id="loginModel" class="com.santosh.spring.LoginModel">
    <constructor-arg ref="jdbctemp"/>
  </bean>
</beans>
```

Now, finally we need to modify the Struts XML configuration file to add Spring plugin that initializes the WebApplicationContext using the specified Spring beans XML configuration files, and publishes it to current ServletContext. List 15.11 shows the code for Struts XML configuration file for this application.

List 15.11: struts-config.xml

```
<!DOCTYPE struts-config PUBLIC
        "-//Apache Software Foundation//DTD Struts Configuration 1.3//EN"
         "http://struts.apache.org/dtds/struts-config_1_3.dtd">

<struts-config>
  <action-mappings>
    <action type="com.santosh.spring.struts.LoginAction" path="/login">
      <forward name="notValid" path="/Login.html"/>
      <forward name="admin" path="/AdminHome.jsp"/>
      <forward name="user" path="/UserHome.jsp"/>
    </action>
  </action-mappings>

  <plug-in  className="org.springframework.web.struts.ContextLoaderPlugIn">
    <set-property property="contextConfigLocation"
          value="/WEB-INF/application-context.xml"/>
  </plug-in>
</struts-config>
```

Now, compile the Java files and arrange all the files as shown in Fig. 15.4.

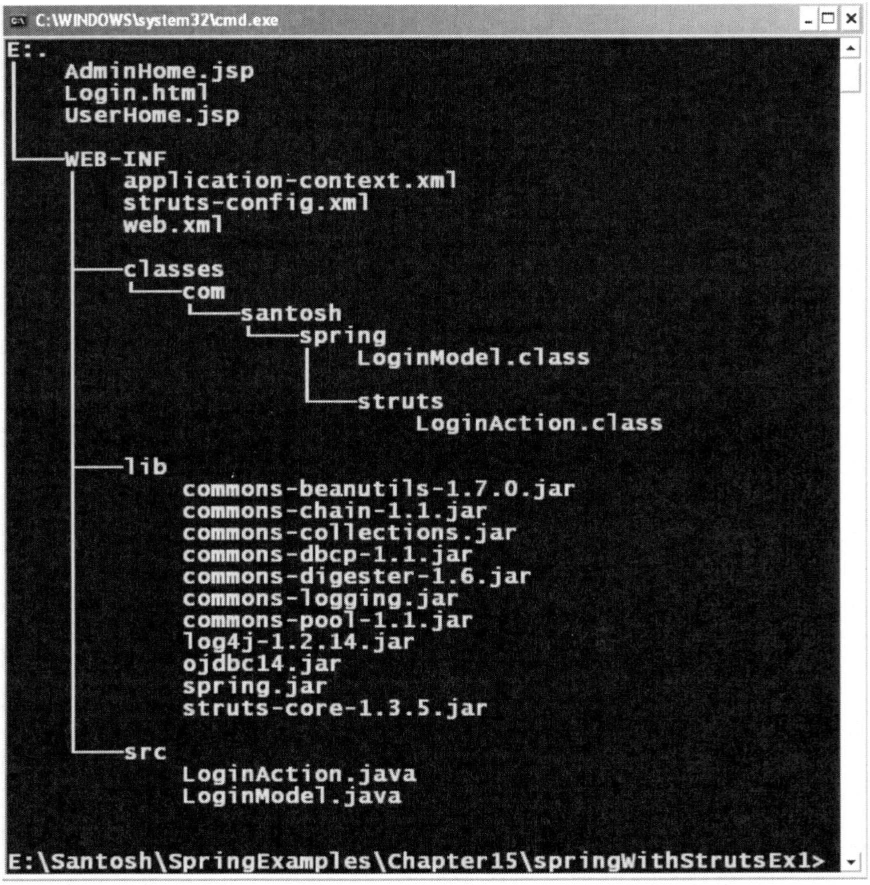

FIGURE 15.4 Directory structure showing all the files of spring with struts example

The Login.html, AdminHome.jsp and UserHome..jsp files code can be found in the Lists 15.1, 15.5, and 15.6, respectively. After preparing the web application deploy it and browse the application using URL http://localhost:8080/springWithStrutsEx1/Login.html.

In this section we have learnt how the Struts action can access the Spring beans from the WebApplicationContext initialized by the ContextLoaderPlugIn. Alternative to this approach we can wire our Struts Actions as Spring beans, passing references to them via IoC rather than looking up references in a programmatic fashion. Let us examine this approach.

15.3.2.2.2 Configuring the Struts Actions as Spring Beans

In the preceding section we learnt how Struts Action can retrieve the WebApplicationContext and use it to get the Spring beans (that is, dependencies) programmatically. Alternatively, Spring allows us to configure the Struts actions as Spring beans so that the dependencies can be pushed into the actions via IoC instead of looking up the objects. Spring provides two approaches to do this:

1. Configure DelegatingRequestProcessor
2. Use DelegatingActionProxy

Let us take a closer look at these two approaches.

15.3.2.2.3 Configuring DelegatingRequestProcessor

The org.springframework.web.struts.DelegatingRequestProcessor class is a subclass of Struts default RequestProcessor. The DelegatingRequestProcessor overrides the processActionCreate() method of Struts default RequestProcessor to locate the Spring bean (that is, Spring managed Struts actions) using the WebApplicationContext loaded by ContextLoaderPlugIn. The following code snippet shows the <controller> tag to use in struts XML configuration file to configure DelegatingRequestProcessor.

Code Snippet

```
<controller processorClass=
  "org.springframework.web.struts.DelegatingRequestProcessor"/>
```

Note that if we are using Tiles in our Struts application then instead of DelegatingRequestProcessor configure DelegatingTilesRequestProcessor. The default implementation of DelegatingRequest Processor/ DelegatingTilesRequestProcessor is to locate a Spring beans mapping the action path to the bean name in the WebApplicationContext. That means if we have an action path '/login' in the struts configuration file then we must define the action bean with '/login' name in the application context. The following code snippet shows both the element in Struts configuration file and Spring beans XML configuration file.

Code Snippet

```
<!--In struts configuration file-->
<action path="/login" type="com.santosh.struts.LoginAction"> ... </action>

<!--In Spring beans XML configuration file-->
<bean name="/login" class="com.santosh.struts.LoginAction"> ... </bean>
```

Note that in this case the 'type' specified in the action declaration of struts configuration file does not have any significance. In fact, we can even avoid configuring the 'type' attribute in the <action> element. One more important point to remember is that if we are using DelegatingRequestProcessor with Struts modules (that is, other than default module) then the Spring bean name should include the module prefix, that is, if '/login' action path is declared in 'admin' module then the bean name in Spring beans XML configuration file should be '/admin/login'.

15.3.2.2.4 Using DelegatingActionProxy

In some cases we may not be able to use DelegatingRequestProcessor since we may have to use a custom RequestProcessor. In such cases we can use DelegatingActionProxy approach. In this case the org.springframework.web.struts.DelegatingActionProxy is configured as type in the struts action mapping, which delegates the request to the Spring managed Struts actions. That means the DelegatingActionProxy is a subtype of Action class. The following code snippet shows the declaration of DelegatingActionProxy in the struts XML configuration file.

Code Snippet

```
<action  path="/login"
  type="org.springframework.web.struts.DelegatingActionProxy">
...
</action>
```

The form bean configurations, forward and exception mappings can be configured as usual. The bean definition in Spring beans XML configuration file remains the same as discussed with DelegatingRequestProcessor. After learning how to integrate Spring with Struts framework let us look at a sample code showing how Spring works with Struts framework.

15.4 USING SPRING WITH STRUTS FRAMEWORK

Earlier, in Chapter 14 we implemented the search employee use cases using the Spring framework completely, that is, the web presentation tier is implemented using Spring's Web MVC framework, data access logic using Spring JDBC abstraction framework, and all the DAOs (POJOs) managed by the Spring WebApplicationContext. Now, in this section we will implement the same use cases to demonstrate the use of Spring framework even if we have decided (due to the reasons explained earlier in this chapter) to use Struts framework for implementing the web presentation tier. Figure 15.5 shows the various elements of the system and its arrangement.

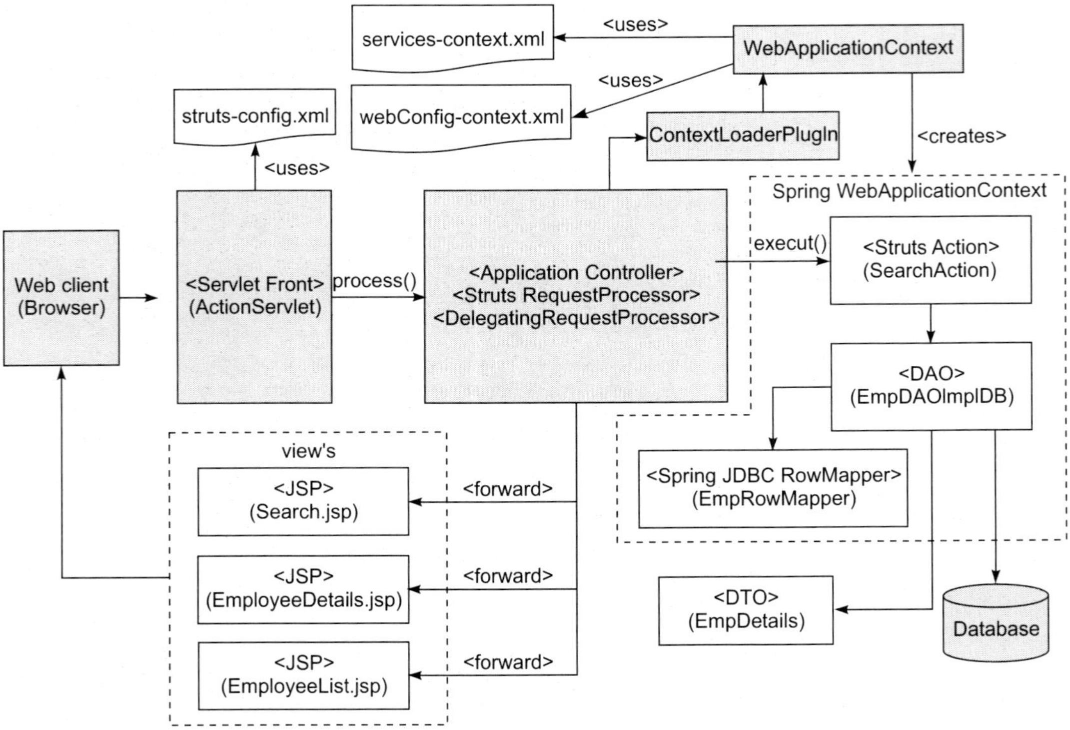

FIGURE 15.5 Architecture of an example to demonstrate Spring working with Struts

The architecture shown in Fig. 15.5 represents the various elements for implementing the search employee module that uses Struts framework for implementing web presentation layer and Spring for managing the POJOs encapsulating the data access logic. All the shaded elements are built-in elements or external entities; let us see the code for the remaining elements. First starting with implementing the SearchAction, that is, Struts action.

List 15.12: SearchAction.java

```
package com.santosh.struts;

import java.util.Collection;
import javax.servlet.http.HttpServletRequest;
import javax.servlet.http.HttpServletResponse;
import org.apache.struts.action.ActionErrors;
import org.apache.struts.action.ActionForm;
import org.apache.struts.action.ActionForward;
import org.apache.struts.action.ActionMapping;
import org.apache.struts.action.ActionMessage;
import org.apache.struts.action.ActionMessages;
import org.apache.struts.action.DynaActionForm;
import org.apache.struts.actions.DispatchAction;
import com.santosh.spring.dao.EmpDAO;
import com.santosh.spring.EmpDetails;
/**
 * @author Santosh
 */
public class SearchAction extends DispatchAction {

  private EmpDAO empDAO;

  public void setEmpDAO(EmpDAO empDAO){
    this.empDAO=empDAO;
  }

  public ActionForward searchByEmpno(
                ActionMapping mapping, ActionForm form,
                HttpServletRequest request, HttpServletResponse response)
                                                throws Exception {

    DynaActionForm searchForm = (DynaActionForm) form;

    Object o = searchForm.get("searchKey");
    if (o == null) {
        ActionErrors am = new ActionErrors();
        am.add("searchForm", new ActionMessage("search.invalid.entry"));
        saveErrors(request, am);
```

```
        return  mapping.findForward("fail");
    }

    int empno;
    try {
        empno = Integer.parseInt((String) o);
    } catch (NumberFormatException e) {
        ActionErrors am = new ActionErrors();
        am.add("searchForm", new ActionMessage("search.invalid.empno"));
        saveErrors(request, am);
        return  mapping.findForward("fail");
    }

    EmpDetails empDetails = empDAO.getEmployeeDetailsByEmpno(empno);
    request.setAttribute("empdetails", empDetails);
    return  mapping.findForward("successSingleEmp");
}

public ActionForward searchByEname(
                ActionMapping mapping, ActionForm form,
                HttpServletRequest request, HttpServletResponse response)
                                                  throws Exception {

    DynaActionForm searchForm = (DynaActionForm) form;

    String ename =(String) searchForm.get("searchKey");
    if (ename == null) {
        ActionErrors am = new ActionErrors();
        am.add("searchForm", new ActionMessage("search.invalid.entry"));
        saveErrors(request, am);
        return  mapping.findForward("fail");
    }

    Collection empDetails = empDAO.getEmployeeDetailsByName(ename);
    request.setAttribute("empdetails", empDetails);
    return  mapping.findForward("success");
}

public ActionForward searchByJob(
                ActionMapping mapping, ActionForm form,
                HttpServletRequest request, HttpServletResponse response)
                                                  throws Exception {

    DynaActionForm searchForm = (DynaActionForm) form;
```

```
    String job =(String) searchForm.get("searchKey");
    if (job == null) {
      ActionErrors am = new ActionErrors();
      am.add("searchForm", new ActionMessage("search.invalid.entry"));
      saveErrors(request, am);
      return mapping.findForward("fail");
    }

    Collection empDetails = empDAO.getEmployeeDetailsByJob(job);
    request.setAttribute("empdetails", empDetails);
    return mapping.findForward("success");
  }

  public ActionForward searchByDeptno(
              ActionMapping mapping, ActionForm form,
              HttpServletRequest request, HttpServletResponse response)
                                               throws Exception {

    DynaActionForm searchForm = (DynaActionForm) form;

    Object o = searchForm.get("searchKey");
    if (o == null) {
      ActionErrors am = new ActionErrors();
      am.add("searchForm", new ActionMessage("search.invalid.entry"));
      saveErrors(request, am);
      return mapping.findForward("fail");
    }

    int deptno;
    try {
        deptno = Integer.parseInt((String) o);
    } catch (NumberFormatException e) {
        ActionErrors am = new ActionErrors();
        am.add("searchForm", new ActionMessage("search.invalid.deptno"));
        saveErrors(request, am);
        return mapping.findForward("fail");
    }

    Collection empDetails = empDAO.getEmployeeDetailsByDeptno(deptno);
    request.setAttribute("empdetails", empDetails);
    return mapping.findForward("success");
  }
}
```

List 15.12 shows the implementation of a Struts action encapsulating the handler logic for the four search employee use cases. It can be observed that the action depends on the EmpDAO (a DAO interface) that represents the employee details; you can find the code for EmpDAO interface, its implementation EmpDAOImplDB and its associated class such as EmpRowMapper and EmpDetails under Lists 14.2, 14.3, 14.4, and 14.5, respectively. The Spring beans XML configuration file that declares the EmpDAO and its dependents, that is, services-context.xml code is shown in List 14.6. Now, let us configure the DelegatingRequestProcessor, form beans and action mappings in Struts XML configuration file. List 15.13 shows the code for struts-config.xml file.

List 15.13: struts-config.xml

```
<?xml version="1.0" encoding="UTF-8"?>
<!DOCTYPE struts-config PUBLIC
    "-//Apache Software Foundation//DTD Struts Configuration 1.3//EN"
    "http://struts.apache.org/dtds/struts-config_1_3.dtd">

<struts-config>
  <form-beans>
    <form-bean name="searchForm"
               type="org.apache.struts.action.DynaActionForm">
      <form-property name="searchBy" type="java.lang.String" />
      <form-property name="searchKey" type="java.lang.String" />
    </form-bean>
  </form-beans>

  <action-mappings>
    <action name="searchForm" parameter="searchBy"
      path="/search" scope="request" validate="false">
     <exception
        key="error.daoexception" path="/Search.jsp"
        type="org.springframework.dao.DAOException" />
      <forward name="success" path="/EmployeeList.jsp" />
      <forward name="successSingleEmp" path="/EmployeeDetails.jsp" />
      <forward name="fail" path="/Search.jsp" />
    </action>
  </action-mappings>

  <controller processorClass=
      "org.springframework.web.struts.DelegatingRequestProcessor"/>

  <message-resources parameter="ApplicationResources"/>

  <plug-in className="org.springframework.web.struts.ContextLoaderPlugIn">
  <set-property property="contextConfigLocation"
                value="/WEB-INF/webConfig-context.xml,
                       /WEB-INF/services-context.xml"/>
 </plug-in>
</struts-config>
```

List 15.13 shows the code for struts-config.xml file that declares one form bean, an action mapping, etc. We have not configured a type for the action mapping configured in this configuration file, since the DelegatingRequestProcessor locates the struts action from the WebApplicationContext instead of creating an instance of the specified type. To return a Struts Action object for handling the request, DelegatingRequestProcessor locates the Spring bean whose name matches with the action path. List 15.14 shows the code for webConfig-context.xml file that defines the Struts actions as Spring beans.

List 15.14: webConfig-context.xml

```
<beans  xmlns="http://www.springframework.org/schema/beans"
xmlns:xsi="http://www.w3.org/2001/XMLSchema-instance"
xsi:schemaLocation="http://www.springframework.org/schema/beans
http://www.springframework.org/schema/beans/spring-beans-2.0.xsd">

  <!--configuring the Spring managed Struts actions-->
  <bean name="/search" class="com.santosh.struts.SearchAction">
        <property name="empDAO" ref="empDAO"/>
  </bean>
</beans>
```

This example requires three views Search.jsp, EmployeeDetails.jsp, and EmployeeList.jsp. Let us look at the code for these views first,

List 15.15: Search.jsp

```
<%@ taglib uri="http://struts.apache.org/tags-bean" prefix="bean" %>
<%@ taglib uri="http://struts.apache.org/tags-html" prefix="html" %>
<%@ taglib uri="http://struts.apache.org/tags-logic" prefix="logic" %>

<html>
  <head>
     <title><bean:message key="search.title"/></title>
  </head>

  <body>
    <html:errors/><br/>

     <html:form action="/search" method="post">
      <table border="0">
       <tr>
          <td><bean:message key="search.label"/></td>
          <td><html:text property="searchKey"/></td>
       </tr>
       <tr>
          <td><bean:message key="search.searchby"/></td>
        <td>
          <html:select property="searchBy">
```

```
            <html:option value="searchByEmpno">
              By Employee Number</html:option>
            <html:option value="searchByEname">
              By Employee Name</html:option>
            <html:option value="searchByJob">By Job</html:option>
            <html:option value="searchByDeptno">
              By Department Number</html:option>
        </html:select>
        </td>
       </tr>
       <tr>
        <td colspan="2" align="center">
        <html:submit>
          <bean:message key="search.submit"/>
        </html:submit>
      </td>
     </tr>
    </table>
   </html:form>
 </body>
</html>
```

List 15.15 shows the code for Search.jsp, which presents a view allowing client to make a search for employee(s) details request. After the search request is processed, if a single employee is selected then the results are presented to the client using EmployeeDetails.jsp whose code is shown in List 15.16.

List 15.16: EmployeeDetails.jsp

```
<%@ taglib uri="http://struts.apache.org/tags-bean" prefix="bean" %>
<%@ taglib uri="http://struts.apache.org/tags-html" prefix="html" %>
<%@ taglib uri="http://struts.apache.org/tags-logic" prefix="logic" %>

<html:html lang="true">
 <head>
   <title><bean:message key="searchresult.title"/></title>
 </head>
 <body>
  <bean:message key="searchResult.header"/>

  <logic:empty name="empdetails" scope="request">
     <bean:message key="searchResult.noresult"/>
  </logic:empty>
  <logic:notEmpty name="empdetails" scope="request">
    <table border="0">
     <tr>
       <th><bean:message key="empno"/></th>
```

```
      <td>: <bean:write name="empdetails" property="empno"/></td>
    </tr>
    <tr>
      <th><bean:message key="ename"/></th>
      <td>: <bean:write name="empdetails" property="ename"/></td>
    </tr>
    <tr>
      <th><bean:message key="job"/></th>
      <td>: <bean:write name="empdetails" property="job"/></td>
    </tr>
    <tr>
      <th><bean:message key="mgr"/></th>
      <td>: <bean:write name="empdetails" property="mgr"/></td>
    </tr>
    <tr>
      <th><bean:message key="hiredate"/></th>
      <td>: <bean:write name="empdetails" property="hiredate"/></td>
    </tr>
    <tr>
      <th><bean:message key="sal"/></th>
      <td>: <bean:write name="empdetails" property="sal"/></td>
    </tr>
    <tr>
      <th><bean:message key="comm"/></th>
      <td>: <bean:write name="empdetails" property="comm"/></td>
    </tr>
    <tr>
      <th><bean:message key="deptno"/></th>
      <td>: <bean:write name="empdetails" property="deptno"/></td>
    </tr>
    </table>
   </logic:notEmpty>
    <br/>
     <bean:message key="searchResult.searchAgain"/> <html:link href="Search.jsp">
    <bean:message key="searchResult.click"/>
   </html:link>
  </body>
</html:html>
```

List 15.16 shows the code for EmployeeDetails.jsp that uses Struts tags for preparing a view presenting the result of the employee search request selecting a single employee. If the search request results to select multiple employees then the details need to be presented in the form of a table. To do this we implement a separate page EmployeeList.jsp. List 15.17 shows the code for EmployeeList.jsp.

List 15.17: EmployeeList.jsp

```
<%@ taglib uri="http://struts.apache.org/tags-bean" prefix="bean" %>
<%@ taglib uri="http://struts.apache.org/tags-html" prefix="html" %>
<%@ taglib uri="http://struts.apache.org/tags-logic" prefix="logic" %>

<html:html lang="true">
  <head>
    <title><bean:message key="searchresult.title"/></title>
  </head>
  <body>
    <bean:message key="searchResult.header"/><br/>

    <logic:empty name="empdetails" scope="request">
      <bean:message key="searchResult.noresult"/>
  </logic:empty>
  <logic:notEmpty name="empdetails" scope="request">
      <table border="1">
      <tr>
       <th><bean:message key="empno"/></th>
       <th><bean:message key="ename"/></th>
       <th><bean:message key="job"/></th>
       <th><bean:message key="mgr"/></th>
       <th><bean:message key="hiredate"/></th>
       <th><bean:message key="sal"/></th>
       <th><bean:message key="comm"/></th>
       <th><bean:message key="deptno"/></th>
    </tr>
    <logic:iterate name="empdetails" id="emp">
      <tr>
          <td><bean:write name="emp" property="empno"/></td>
          <td><bean:write name="emp" property="ename"/></td>
          <td><bean:write name="emp" property="job"/></td>
          <td><bean:write name="emp" property="mgr"/></td>
          <td><bean:write name="emp" property="hiredate"/></td>
          <td><bean:write name="emp" property="sal"/></td>
          <td><bean:write name="emp" property="comm"/></td>
          <td><bean:write name="emp" property="deptno"/></td>
        </tr>
      </logic:iterate>
      </table>
```

```
    </logic:notEmpty>
      <br/>
     <bean:message key="searchResult.searchAgain"/> <html:link href="Search.jsp">
    <bean:message  key="searchResult.click"/>
   </html:link>
 </body>
</html:html>
```

List 15.17 shows the code for EmployeeList.jsp that prepares a view for presenting multiple employee details selected for the search request. Finally we need to configure Struts ActionServlet in the web.xml file so that we can initialize the Struts framework for our application, which further initializes the Spring WebApplicationContext. List 15.18 shows the web.xml for this example.

List 15.18: web.xml

```
<?xml  version="1.0"  encoding="UTF-8"?>
<web-app  xmlns="http://java.sun.com/xml/ns/j2ee"
xmlns:xsi="http://www.w3.org/2001/XMLSchema-instance"  version="2.4"
xsi:schemaLocation="http://java.sun.com/xml/ns/j2ee
http://java.sun.com/xml/ns/j2ee/web-app_2_4.xsd">
  <servlet>
    <servlet-name>action</servlet-name>
    <servlet-class>org.apache.struts.action.ActionServlet</servlet-class>
    <load-on-startup>0</load-on-startup>
  </servlet>
   <servlet-mapping>
      <servlet-name>action</servlet-name>
      <url-pattern>*.do</url-pattern>
   </servlet-mapping>
</web-app>
```

After implementing all the files shown in the preceding listings compile the Java files and arrange them in a directory structure as shown in Figure 15.6.

After preparing the web application deploy the application and browse the example using the URL http://localhost:8080/springWithStrutsEx2/Search.jsp, considering the web server is running in the same machine and it is providing its services on 8080 port. If not then change these elements in the URL to access the services implement in this example.

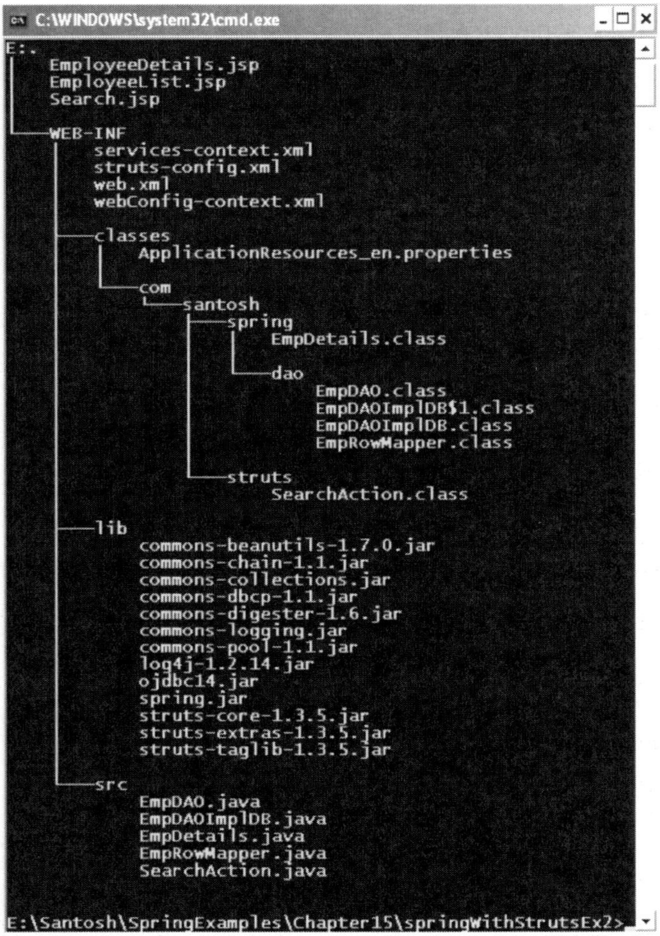

FIGURE 15.6 Figure showing all the files of an employee search example demonstrating Spring with Struts

Summary

In this chapter we learnt about integrating Spring with other Web Frameworks. We started this chapter with the discussion of why Spring needs to integrate with other frameworks when we have an ideal option for implementing Web MVC applications using Spring Web MVC Framework. Here we identified two important reasons—we may have invested a lot on other web frameworks and may not be well familiar to use Spring Web MVC framework and it wants to provide a support for incremental adoption of spring framework into the projects. Later, we had an overview of Struts framework with a working sample. Thereafter we learnt why the Struts framework wanted to integrate with Spring framework, and here we identified that Struts application wants to integrate with Spring for its enterprise-level declarative services like IoC, AOP, transaction, etc. This discussion was followed through understanding the various approaches to integrate Spring with Struts framework.

Implementing Remoting with Spring

16 CHAPTER

Objectives

In this chapter we will cover:

- Spring Framework's support for using the existing Remoting technologies like RMI, Hessian, and Burlap to implement distributed systems in Java
- Spring provided (its own) Remoting service HTTP invoker

16.1 REMOTING WITH RMI

RMI (Remote Method Invocation) provides standards for developing distributed (Remoting) components in Java. RMI is an integral part of Java Platform, Standard Edition. RMI uses Java serialization to marshal the content and its own binary protocol (JRMP) to transfer the content. Since RMI uses Java Serialization it supports full-object serialization. RMI is convenient to use when we want to exchange complex objects with customized serialization. RMI provides all these convenience but to expose and access services as RMI remote object we need to follow RMI rules while implementing the object instead of allowing to expose plain Java objects. The Spring Framework provides a high-level support for implementing Remoting with RMI. The following sections explains you the configurations to use Spring to work with RMI.

16.1.1 UNDERSTANDING RMISERVICEEXPORTER

Spring framework includes *org.springframework.remoting.rmi.RmiServiceExporter* class that provides a high level and convenient approach of exposing POJO as an RMI remote object. The RmiServiceExporter registers a given service POJO with the RMI registry making it available for the remote RMI clients. Alternatively, RmiServiceExporter can be configured with traditional RMI service object, that is, a class implementing an interface that is a subtype of java.rmi.Remote. In case of configuring a plain Java object, the RMI exporter creates an RmiInvokerWrapper that wraps the proxy for the configured service object (plain Java object). That means Spring RMI service exporter creates an RMI invoker only if the configured service is a plain Java object instead of RMI service object. The following code snippet shows configuration of the RmiServiceExporter to expose the POJO (spring-bean) as an RMI remote object.

Code Snippet (Spring beans XML configuration file snippet)

```
<bean id="employeeServices" class="com.santosh.spring.EmployeeServicesImpl"/>

<bean class="org.springframework.remoting.rmi.RmiServiceExporter">
  <property name="serviceName" value="EmployeeServices"/>
  <property name="service" ref="employeeServices"/>
  <property name="serviceInterface"
          value="com.santosh.spring.EmployeeServices"/>
  <property name="registryPort" ref="7483"/>
</bean>
```

Considering com.santosh.spring.EmployeeServices is a plain old Java interface, as per the configurations shown in the preceding code snippet, the RmiServiceExporter creates an RMI invoker object that wraps the proxy of employeeServices spring bean object, which is then exported using java.rmi.server.UnicastRemoteObject. The RmiServiceExporter creates an in-process registry if it fails to locate the registry at the configured port (here in the preceding code snippet it is 7483), that is, there is no registry found at the configured port. We can configure the alwaysCreateRegistry property of RmiServiceExporter to *true*, that describes the exporter to create a new in-process registry without attempting to locate an existing registry.

The various properties RmiServiceExporter can be configured to are described in Table 16.1.

TABLE 16.1 RmiServiceExporter properties

Property Name	*Description*
alwaysCreateRegistry	Specifies whether to always create the registry in-process, not attempting to locate an existing registry at the specified port. Configuring to *true* describes the exporter to create a new in-process registry without attempting to locate an existing registry. This property is optional, if not configured it defaults to "false".
service	Specifies the RMI service or plain Java object to export.
serviceInterface	Specifies the interface of the service object to export.
serviceName	Specifies the name of the exported object, in other words the name with which the RMI service object has to be bound into the registry.
servicePort	Specifies the port on which the exported RMI service should work. Defaults to 0, which describes to use anonymous port.
registry	This property is of type java.rmi.regsitry.Registry. Specifies the registry object to register the exported RMI service object. Optional to configure, if not this property is not set then the exporter locates or creates an RMI registry on the configured registryPort.
registryHost	Specifies the host of the registry for the exported RMI service.
registryPort	Specifies the port number on which the RMI registry should be located or created to bind the RMI object. Defaults to 1099.
clientSocketFactory	Describes the custom RMI client socket factory to use for exporting the RMI service. The object configured to this should be subtype of java.rmi.server.RMIClientSocketFactory. If the object is even implementing java.rmi.server.RMIServerSocketFactory then it will be automatically registered as server socket factory.

(Contd.)

serverSocketFactory	Describes the custom RMI server socket factory to use for exporting the RMI service. This is required to be configured separately only if the client socket factory is not configured and/or the client socket factory object is not implementing java.rmi.server.RMIServerSocketFactory.

Now, after understanding the various properties of RmiServiceExporter let us understand the workflow of RmiServiceExporter to export the RMI service object, that is, the initialization of RmiServiceExporter. Figure 16.1 describes this workflow with the help of a flow diagram.

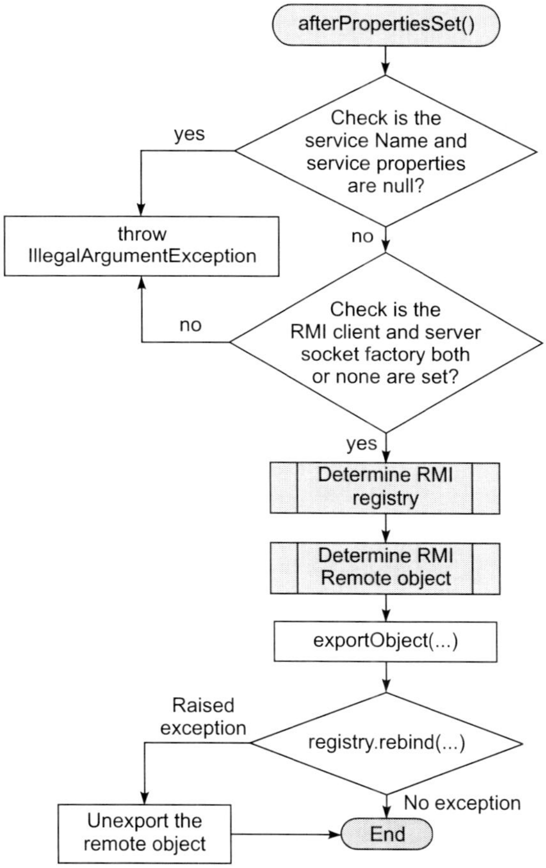

FIGURE 16.1 Flow diagram explaining the workflow of the RmiServiceExporter initialization

The following steps explain the RmiServiceExporter initialization workflow in detail.

Step 1: Check service properties

As shown in the preceding flow diagram the initialization process of RmiServiceExporter starts with checking whether the service and serviceName properties are set. In case if any of these properties are not set, an IllegalArgumentException is thrown and terminates the initialization process.

Step 2: Check RMI client and server socket factories

Once the service properties are found valid then the workflow continues to check whether the clientSocketFactory is configured. If so it determines whether the clientSocketFactory is implementing RMIServerSocketFactory too. Then the client socket factory object is set as a serverSocketFactory. There after, RmiServiceExporter finds whether the client socket and server socket factory are both set. If it finds that either client or server socket any one of them is set, it throws an IllegalArgument Exception describing that both the factories or none of them have to be set.

Step 3: Determine RMI registry

In this step of workflow the RMI exporter finds whether *registry* property is set. If so it uses the configured registry object. If registry property is not set then it executes the following operations to locate or create an RMI registry.

- Checks whether *alwaysCreateRegistry* property is set to true. If so then a new in-process RMI registry is created to register the exported object. Thereafter, it completes this step without executing the remaining operations.
- Locates an RMI registry at the configured host and port (that is, registryHost and registryPort). If found it holds the registry reference and completes this step. If not a new in-process RMI registry is created to register the exported object.

Step 4: Determine the remote object

Once after the preceding three steps of operations are successfully performed the RMI service exporter finds whether the configured service object is an RMI service object or a POJO (Plain Old Java Object). If the service object is plain Java object then an RmiInvocationWrapper object that wraps the proxy of the plain Java object is created. That is, an RMI invoker is created that wraps the configured service object.

Step 5: Export the remote object

After determining the remote object now RMI service exporter exports the remote object using *UnicastRemoteObject* exportObject() method, with the configured servicePort, and RMI client and server socket factories if configured.

Step 6: Bind RMI object

After the remote object is exported successfully the RMI service exporter binds the object into registry determined in Step 3. The remote object is bound into the registry with the configured serviceName. In case this process fails, that is, it is unable to bind the object, the remote object is unexported.

After understanding how to configure an RmiServiceExporter to export RMI service or plain Java object as RMI remote object, it is time to learn Spring frameworks support for accessing the RMI remote object service.

16.1.2 Understanding RmiProxyFactoryBean

Spring framework includes *org.springframework.remoting.rmi.RmiProxyFactoryBean* class that provides a high-level and convenient approach to access RMI remote object services. The RmiProxy FactoryBean uses ProxyFactory to build a dynamic proxy for the specified serviceInterface and exposes to the application for use as a bean reference. The serviceInterface can be conventional RMI service interface or a matching non-RMI business interface. In case if the non-RMI business interface is proxied then the java.rmi.RemoteException thrown by the remote stub will be converted Spring's unchecked RemoteAccessException. The RmiProxyFactoryBean supports both conventional RMI service and RMI invokers. Table 16.2 shows the various properties of RmiProxyFactoryBean.

TABLE 16.2 RmiProxyFactoryBean properties

Property Name	*Description*
serviceUrl	Specifies the URL to locate the RMI remote object service object from the registry. This should be a valid RMI URL like "rmi://localhost:1099/EmployeeServices".
serviceInterface	Specifies the interface of the service object to proxy.
lookupStubOnStartup	Specifies whether the stub object has to lookup while initializing the proxy or wait for the first request to the proxy. Setting this property to *false* enables the lazy lookup of stub object. If not configured it defaults to *true*.
cacheStub	Specifies whether to cache the RMI stub object once it has been located. Setting this property to *false* disables the stub caching, allowing us to use hot restart of the RMI server; in this case the RMI stub object is located for each invocation. If not configured it defaults to *true*.
refreshStubOnConnectFailure	Specifies whether to refresh the RMI stub object on connection failure. Setting this property to *true* enables the stub refresh on connection failure allowing us to use hot restart of the RMI server; in this case, if the cached stub throws RMI exception (which indicates connection failure) for a method invocation, then the RMI stub object is fetched to retry the invocation.

The following code snippet shows the RmiProxyFactoryBean configuration.

Code Snippet

```
<bean id="employeeServices_Remote"
      class="org.springframework.remoting.rmi.RmiProxyFactoryBean">
  <property name="serviceInterface"
          value="com.santosh.spring.EmployeeServices"/>
  <property name="serviceUrl" value="rmi://mysys:7483/EmployeeServices"/>
</bean>
```

In this section we learnt RmiProxyFactoryBean, and in the preceding section we understood how to export a service object as an RMI remote object. To throw more light on this let us work out with a small sample code that can demonstrate the configurations learnt in the preceding sections.

16.1.3 Working with RMI based Remoting using Spring

To demonstrate the Spring Frameworks infrastructures in implementing RMI-based Remoting we will expose employee services to the remote client. Let us start creating the service interface that defines an abstraction to access the employee services.

List 16.1: EmployeeServices.java

```
package com.santosh.spring;

import java.util.Collection;

public interface EmployeeServices {
```

```
  void createEmployee(Employee e);
  Employee getEmployee(int empno);
  Collection<Employee> getAllEmployees();

  boolean incrementSalary(int empno, double amt);
}//class
```

List 16.1 shows the EmployeeServices interface that dealers four methods createEmployee—for creating a new employee, getEmployee()—for getting the employee details selected using the given employee number, getAllEmployees()—for getting all the employee details, and incrementSalary()—increments the salary of the given employee with the given amount. List 16.2 shows the implementation of the EmployeeServices interface.

List 16.2: EmployeeServicesImpl.java

```
package com.santosh.spring;

import com.santosh.spring.dao.EmployeeDAO;
import java.util.Collection;

public class EmployeeServicesImpl implements EmployeeServices {

  public void setEmployeeDAO(EmployeeDAO ed){
    employeeDAO=ed;
  }

  public void createEmployee(Employee e){
    employeeDAO.create(e);
  }
  public Employee getEmployee(int empno){
    return employeeDAO.find(empno);
  }
  public Collection<Employee> getAllEmployees(){
    return employeeDAO.findAll();
  }
  public boolean incrementSalary(int empno, double amt) {
    double sal=employeeDAO.getSal(empno);
    sal+=amt;
    employeeDAO.setSal(empno, sal);
    System.out.println(sal);
    return true;
  }//incrementSal

  private EmployeeDAO employeeDAO;
}//class
```

From List 16.2 we can observe that the EmployeeServicesImpl depends on the EmployeeDAO and Employee types. Let us create these dependent types. List 16.3 shows the Employee class.

List 16.3: Employee.java

```
package com.santosh.spring;

import java.io.Serializable;
public class Employee implements Serializable {
  public int empno, deptno;
  public String ename, job;
  public double sal;
}
```

The Employee class shown in List 16.3 is used to transfer the employee details between the client and server.

> **Note:** Here we are not required to process Employee object using Java Bean API and we don't have any limitations in accessing the fields. Thus we don't required to implement setter and getter methods.

List 16.4 shows the EmployeeDAO interface that declares few methods to access the employee details in database.

List 16.4: EmployeeDAO.java

```
package com.santosh.spring.dao;

import com.santosh.spring.Employee;
import java.util.*;

public interface EmployeeDAO {
  void create(Employee e);
  Employee find(int empno);
  Collection<Employee> findAll();

  double getSal(int eno);
  void setSal(int eno, double sal);
}
```

Now, we will implement the EmployeeDAO that can communicate with database using JdbcTemplate of Spring JDBC Abstraction Framework.

List 16.5: EmployeeDAODBImpl.java

```
package com.santosh.spring.dao;

import com.santosh.spring.Employee;
import org.springframework.jdbc.core.*;
import java.sql.*;
import java.util.*;
```

```
public class EmployeeDAODBImpl implements EmployeeDAO {

  public EmployeeDAODBImpl(JdbcTemplate jdbcTemplate) {
    this.jdbcTemplate=jdbcTemplate;
  }//cons

  public void create(final Employee e){
    jdbcTemplate.update(
      "insert into emp(empno, ename, job, deptno, sal) value(?,?,?,?,?)",
      new PreparedStatementSetter(){
       public void setValues(PreparedStatement ps)throws SQLException{
         ps.setInt(1,e.empno);
         ps.setString(2, e.ename);
         ps.setString(3, e.job);
         ps.setInt(4, e.deptno);
         ps.setDouble(5, e.sal);
       }//setValues
    });
  }
  public Employee find(int empno){
    return  (Employee)jdbcTemplate.queryForObject(
      "select empno, ename, job, deptno, sal from emp where empno="+empno,
      new RowMapper(){
       public Object mapRow(ResultSet rs, int rowNum)throws SQLException{
         Employee employee=new Employee();
         employee.empno=rs.getInt(1);
         employee.ename=rs.getString(2);
         employee.job=rs.getString(3);
         employee.deptno=rs.getInt(4);
         employee.sal=rs.getDouble(5);
         return employee;
       }
    });
  }

  public Collection<Employee> findAll(){
    return  (Collection<Employee>)jdbcTemplate.query(
      "select empno, ename, job, deptno, sal from emp",
      new RowMapper(){
       public Object mapRow(ResultSet rs, int rowNum)throws SQLException{
         Employee employee=new Employee();
         employee.empno=rs.getInt(1);
         employee.ename=rs.getString(2);
         employee.job=rs.getString(3);
         employee.deptno=rs.getInt(4);
```

```
            employee.sal=rs.getDouble(5);
            return employee;
        }
    });
}

public double getSal(int eno) {
    return (Double)jdbcTemplate.queryForObject(
        "select sal emp where empno="+eno, Double.class);
}//getSal

public void setSal(int empno, double sal) {
    jdbcTemplate.update("update emp set sal=? where empno=?",
        new Object[]{sal, empno});
}//setSal

private JdbcTemplate jdbcTemplate;
}//class
```

This completes the domain model implementing the employee services. Now, let us write a Spring Beans XML configuration file that can configure and export EmployeeServicesImpl object as an RMI remote object. List 16.6 shows the server-context.xml file that declares the EmployeeServices bean.

List 16.6: server-context.xml

```
<beans xmlns="http://www.springframework.org/schema/beans"
xmlns:xsi="http://www.w3.org/2001/XMLSchema-instance"
xsi:schemaLocation="http://www.springframework.org/schema/beans
http://www.springframework.org/schema/beans/spring-beans-2.0.xsd">

  <bean id="dataSource" class="org.apache.commons.dbcp.BasicDataSource">
    <property name="driverClassName" value="oracle.jdbc.driver.OracleDriver"/>
    <property name="url" value="jdbc:oracle:thin:@localhost:1521:sandb"/>
    <property name="username" value="scott"/>
    <property name="password" value="tiger"/>
  </bean>
  <bean id="jdbcTemplate" class="org.springframework.jdbc.core.JdbcTemplate">
    <constructor-arg ref="dataSource"/>
  </bean>
  <bean id="empdao" class="com.santosh.spring.dao.EmployeeDAODBImpl">
    <constructor-arg ref="jdbcTemplate"/>
  </bean>

  <bean id="employeeServices" class="com.santosh.spring.EmployeeServicesImpl">
    <property name="employeeDAO" ref="empdao"/>
  </bean>
```

```
  <bean id="employeeServices_Remote"
          class="org.springframework.remoting.rmi.RmiServiceExporter">
    <property name="service" ref="employeeServices"/>
    <property name="serviceName" value="EmployeeServices"/>
    <property name="serviceInterface"
              value="com.santosh.spring.EmployeeServices"/>
    <property name="registryPort" value="7483"/>
  </bean>
</beans>
```

List 16.6 shows the Spring Beans XML configuration file declaring the employee services exposing it to the remote client as an RMI remote object. To test the configuration shown in List 16.6 that can create and activate the RMI service, we will write a simple test case. List 16.7 shows the simple test case that initializes the Spring Core Container using the configurations written in server-context.xml file.

List 16.7: RmiExporterTestCase.java

```
import org.springframework.context.*;
import org.springframework.context.support.*;

public class RmiExporterTestCase {

  public static void main(String s[]) throws Exception {

    ApplicationContext context=new ClassPathXmlApplicationContext(
                                      "server-context.xml");
    /**
     * The preceding statement initializes the Spring Core Container
     * using the 'server-context.xml' file, which includes to instantiate
     * and initialize RmiServiceExporter configured with
     * a bean id 'employeeServices_Remote'
     */
    System.out.println("Server Started");
  }//main
}//class
```

Now, as we have written the domain model and RMI exporter test case compile all the Java files and run RmiExporterTestCase for starting the server. Figure 16.2 shows the directory structure and command to start the server.

Figure 16.2 shows starting of the server. As we have started the server let us configure the RmiProxyFactoryBean to access the employee services remote object using the Spring RMI Remoting infrastructure. List 16.8 shows the Spring Beans XML configuration file for configuring the RmiProxyFactoryBean.

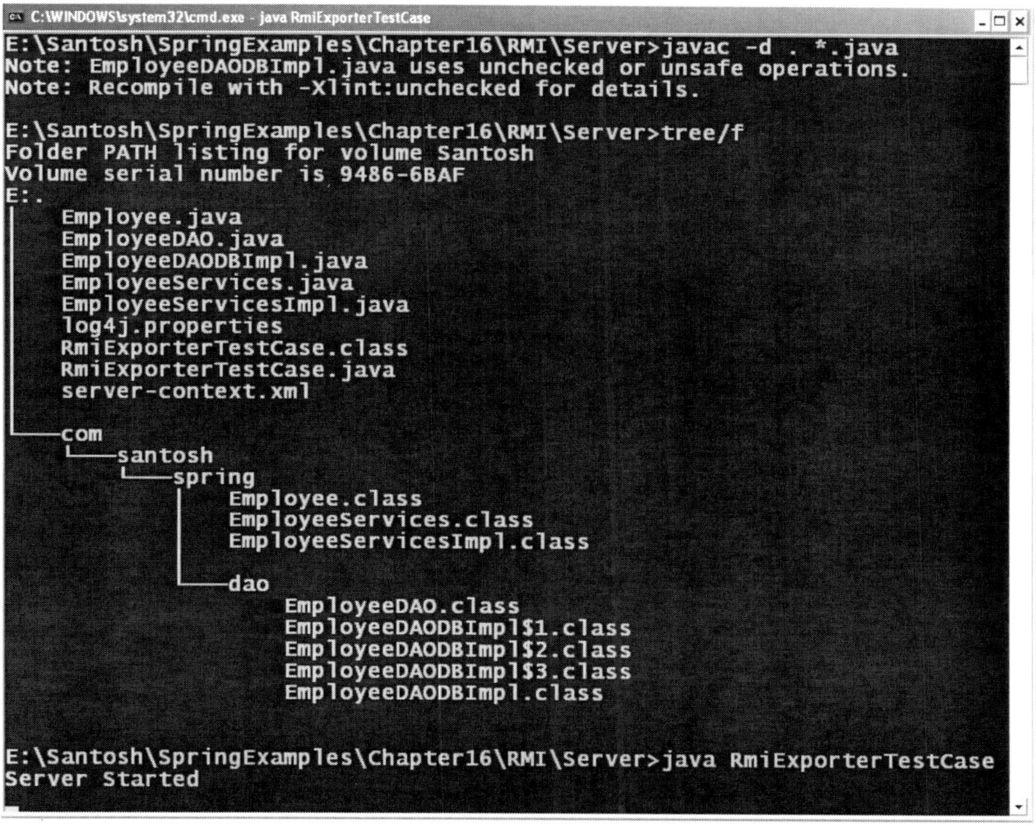

FIGURE 16.2 Starting the server, which initializes the RMI services

List 16.8: client-context.xml

```
<beans  xmlns="http://www.springframework.org/schema/beans"
xmlns:xsi="http://www.w3.org/2001/XMLSchema-instance"
xsi:schemaLocation="http://www.springframework.org/schema/beans
http://www.springframework.org/schema/beans/spring-beans-2.0.xsd">

  <bean id="employeeServices_Remote"
        class="org.springframework.remoting.rmi.RmiProxyFactoryBean">
    <property name="serviceUrl"
            value="rmi://seminal1:7483/EmployeeServices"/>
    <property name="serviceInterface"
            value="com.santosh.spring.EmployeeServices"/>
  </bean>
</beans>
```

Now, List 16.9 shows the test client that uses the configured RmiProxyFactoryBean to access the remote services (employee services).

List 16.9: RmiProxyFactoryTestCase.java

```
import org.springframework.context.*;
import org.springframework.context.support.*;

import com.santosh.spring.EmployeeServices;
import com.santosh.spring.Employee;

public class RmiProxyFactoryTestCase {

  public static void main(String s[]) throws Exception {

    ApplicationContext context=new ClassPathXmlApplicationContext(
                                  "client-context.xml");
    /**
     * The preceding statement initializes the Spring Core Container
     * using the 'client-context.xml' file, which includes to instantiate
     * and initialize RmiProxyFactoryBean configured with
     * a bean id 'employeeServices_Remote'
     */
     //To get RMI Proxy for EmployeeServices
     EmployeeServices employeeService=
       (EmployeeServices)context.getBean("employeeServices_Remote");

     Employee employee=employeeService.getEmployee(Integer.parseInt(s[0]));
     System.out.println("Employee Details:");
     System.out.println("  Empno : "+ employee.empno);
     System.out.println("  Name  : "+ employee.ename);
     System.out.println("  Salary: "+ employee.sal);
     System.out.println("  Job   : "+ employee.job);
  }//main
}//class
```

To run the test case shown in List 16.9 we need EmployeeServices and Employee classes. Figure 16.3 shows the arrangement of the files and the output of the test case shown in List 16.9.

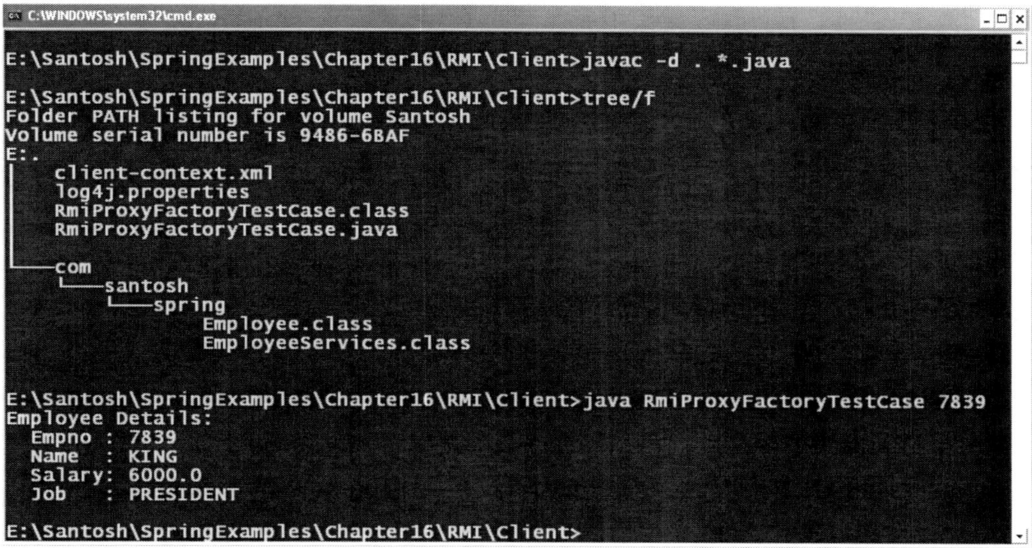

FIGURE 16.3 Output of RmiProxyFactoryTestCase

Figure 16.3 shows the output of the RmiProxyFactoryTestCase that uses RmiProxyFactoryBean of Spring Framework to access the RMI remote object, EmployeeServices, methods.

> **Note:** RMI uses a heavy-weight protocol that supports full-object serialization which is useful when using a complex data models. However, RMI objects can be accessed using HTTP protocol if we use HTTP tunneling.

Now as we have discussed about the infrastructural services provided by Spring framework for exposing and accessing the objects using RMI-based Remoting, let us learn the Spring support for other Remoting technologies.

16.2 REMOTING WITH HESSIAN

Hessian is a simple and compact binary protocol for implementing distributed systems that can communicate via a lightweight HTTP protocol. Hessian protocol is from the Caucho company, the makers of Resin application server. Hessian, a slim binary protocol allows connecting web services without requiring a large framework and without learning the low-level protocol complexity. This uses HTTP as its transport mechanism. Hessian uses its own binary serialization algorithms for primitives (basic) types and collections. The Spring Framework provides a high-level support for implementing Remoting with Hessian. The following sections explain the configurations to use Spring to work with Hessian.

16.2.1 Understanding HessianServiceExporter

Spring framework includes *org.springframework.remoting.caucho.HessianServiceExporter* class that provides a high-level and convenient approach for exposing POJO as a Hessian remote object. The

HessianServiceExporter is implemented as handler of Spring Web MVC framework. The HessianServiceExporter exports a given service (POJO) at a given HTTP URL making it available for the Hessian clients. The following code snippet shows configuring the HessianServiceExporter to expose the POJO (spring-bean) as a Hessian remote object.

Code Snippet (Spring beans XML configuration file snippet)

```
<bean id="employeeServices" class="com.santosh.spring.EmployeeServicesImpl"/>

<bean name="/employeeServices.spring"
class="org.springframework.remoting.caucho.HessianServiceExporter">
    <property name="service" ref="employeeServices"/>
    <property name="serviceInterface"
            value="com.santosh.spring.EmployeeServices"/>
</bean>
```

Considering com.santosh.spring.EmpServices is a plain old Java interface, as per the configurations shown in the preceding code snippet the HessianServiceExporter creates a proxy for the EmpServicesImpl object described by empServices bean and exports it at '/employeeServices.spring' path. Here we are using the default BeanNameUrlHandlerMapping to map the incoming request to the handler. Alternatively, we can configure any of the handler mappings to map the incoming request to the handler (that is, HessianServiceExporter). The handler mappings are discussed in Chapter 12. As we do with the other Spring Web MVC application we need to configure DispatcherServlet to provide an entry point for the http requests. The following code snippet shows the configuration of DispatcherServlet in web.xml.

Code Snippet: web.xml

```
<web-app>
 <servlet>
  <servlet-name>ds</servlet-name>
   <servlet-class>org.springframework.web.servlet.DispatcherServlet</servlet-class>
  <load-on-startup>0</load-on-startup>
 </servlet>
 <servlet-mapping>
  <servlet-name>ds</servlet-name>
  <url-pattern>*.spring</url-pattern>
 </servlet-mapping>
</web-app>
```

As per the preceding configuration of DispatcherServlet the Spring Beans XML configuration file name should be ds-servlet.xml. Now, let us find how to access the Hessian services using spring services.

16.2.2 Understanding HessianProxyFactoryBean

The HessianProxyFactoryBean class packaged into org.springframework.remoting.caucho package provides a high-level and convenient approach to access Hessian remote object services. The

HessianProxyFactoryBean uses ProxyFactory to build a dynamic proxy for the specified serviceInterface and exposes to the application for use as a bean reference to access the hessian remote object services. The following code snippet shows configuring the HessianProxyFactoryBean to access the Hessian service.

Code Snippet

```
<bean id="employeeServices_Remote"
      class="org.springframework.remoting.caucho.HessianProxyFactoryBean">
  <property name="serviceInterface"
          value="com.santosh.spring.EmployeeServices"/>
  <property name="serviceUrl"
          value="http://mysys:8080/myctxt/employeeServices.spring"/>
</bean>
```

As per the configurations shown in the preceding code snippet the HessianProxyFactoryBean builds a proxy for com.santosh.spring.EmployeeServices interface representing the services at http://mysys:8080/myctxt/employeeServices.spring.

In this section we have learnt HessianProxyFactoryBean and in the preceding section we understood how to export a service object as a Hessian remote object. To put more light on this let us work out with a small sample code that can demonstrate the configurations learnt in this and the preceding sections.

16.2.3 Working with Hessian based Remoting using Spring

To demonstrate the Spring Frameworks infrastructures in implementing Hessian-based Remoting services, we will use the employee service domain model designed under the section 'Working with RMI-based Remoting using Spring' that we have used to demonstrate how to expose the services to remote clients using Spring RMI support. List 16.10 shows the Spring Beans XML configuration file that declares the EmployeeServices and its dependencies.

List 16.10: services-context.xml

```
<beans xmlns="http://www.springframework.org/schema/beans"
xmlns:xsi="http://www.w3.org/2001/XMLSchema-instance"
xsi:schemaLocation="http://www.springframework.org/schema/beans
http://www.springframework.org/schema/beans/spring-beans-2.0.xsd">

  <bean id="dataSource" class="org.apache.commons.dbcp.BasicDataSource">
      <property name="driverClassName"
                value="oracle.jdbc.driver.OracleDriver"/>
      <property name="url" value="jdbc:oracle:thin:@localhost:1521:sandb"/>
      <property name="username" value="scott"/>
      <property name="password" value="tiger"/>
  </bean>
  <bean id="jdbcTemplate" class="org.springframework.jdbc.core.JdbcTemplate">
       <constructor-arg ref="dataSource"/>
  </bean>
```

```
  <bean id="empdao" class="com.santosh.spring.dao.EmployeeDAODBImpl">
       <constructor-arg ref="jdbcTemplate"/>
  </bean>

  <bean id="employeeServices"
         class="com.santosh.spring.EmployeeServicesImpl">
         <property name="employeeDAO" ref="empdao"/>
  </bean>
</beans>
```

Now, to export the employeeServices bean declared in the services-context.xml file (shown in List 16.10) to Hessian service we can use HessianServiceExporter, as discussed in the preceding section. List 16.11 shows the Spring Beans XML configuration file that exports the employeeServices using a HessianServiceExporter.

List 16.11: controllers-context.xml

```
<beans xmlns="http://www.springframework.org/schema/beans"
xmlns:xsi="http://www.w3.org/2001/XMLSchema-instance"
xsi:schemaLocation="http://www.springframework.org/schema/beans
http://www.springframework.org/schema/beans/spring-beans-2.0.xsd">

    <bean name="/employeeServices.spring"
        class="org.springframework.remoting.caucho.HessianServiceExporter">
    <property name="service" ref="employeeServices"/>
    <property name="serviceInterface"
             value="com.santosh.spring.EmployeeServices"/>
  </bean>
</beans>
```

As discussed in the preceding section Hessian uses HTTP protocol as a transport protocol for exchanging the messages between the client and server. Thus we need to deploy this service into a web server. Here while working with Spring we need to configure the DispatcherServlet since the HessianServiceExporter is implemented as handler of Spring Web MVC framework. List 16.12 shows the web.xml declaring the DispatcherServlet that is configured to use services-context.xml and controllers-context.xml configuration files.

List 16.12: web.xml

```
<?xml version="1.0" encoding="UTF-8"?>
<web-app version="2.4"
  xmlns="http://java.sun.com/xml/ns/j2ee"
  xmlns:xsi="http://www.w3.org/2001/XMLSchema-instance"
  xsi:schemaLocation="http://java.sun.com/xml/ns/j2ee
  http://java.sun.com/xml/ns/j2ee/web-app_2_4.xsd">
  <servlet>
    <servlet-name>ds</servlet-name>
```

```
    <servlet-class>
        org.springframework.web.servlet.DispatcherServlet
    </servlet-class>
    <init-param>
      <param-name>contextConfigLocation</param-name>
      <param-value>
        /WEB-INF/services-context.xml
        /WEB-INF/controllers-context.xml
      </param-value>
    </init-param>
    <load-on-startup>0</load-on-startup>
  </servlet>
  <servlet-mapping>
    <servlet-name>ds</servlet-name>
    <url-pattern>*.spring</url-pattern>
  </servlet-mapping>
</web-app>
```

Now, compile the java files and arrange all the files as shown in Fig. 16.4.

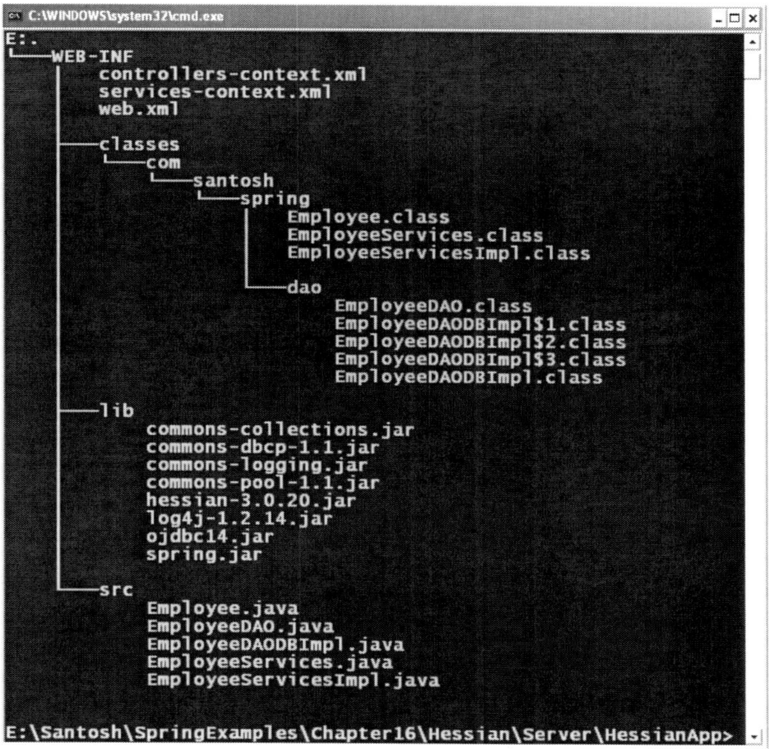

FIGURE 16.4 Directory structure showing the files of Hessian with Spring example

Note that the jar files can be found in the spring downloads. For the EmployeeDAO, Employee DAODBImpl, EmployeeServices, EmployeeServicesImpl, and Employee files see List 16.1 through 16.5. After arranging all the files as shown in Fig. 16.4 deploy the application into any Java Web Application Server. Here we are using Tomcat. Start the server, and now the service is ready to be accessed by the Hessian remote clients. Let us write a simple test case that can demonstrate how to access employeeServices exposed as Hessian service. First declare HessianProxyFactoryBean that can build dynamic proxy for accessing Hessian service (employeeServices). List 16.13 shows the client-context.xml declaring HessianProxyFactoryBean.

List 16.13: client-context.xml

```
<beans xmlns="http://www.springframework.org/schema/beans"
xmlns:xsi="http://www.w3.org/2001/XMLSchema-instance"
xsi:schemaLocation="http://www.springframework.org/schema/beans
http://www.springframework.org/schema/beans/spring-beans-2.0.xsd">

  <bean id="employeeServices_Remote"
       class="org.springframework.remoting.caucho.HessianProxyFactoryBean">
    <property name="serviceUrl"
          value="http://seminal1:8080/HessianApp/employeeServices.spring"/>
    <property name="serviceInterface"
            value="com.santosh.spring.EmployeeServices"/>
  </bean>
</beans>
```

Finally we want to write a simple test case to access employeeServices using the HessianProxy FactoryBean built dynamic proxy as per the configurations in the client-context.xml file. List 16.14 shows the HessianiProxyFactoryTestCase class that initializes the Spring Core container using client-context.xml file.

List 16.14: HessianiProxyFactoryTestCase.java

```
import org.springframework.context.*;
import org.springframework.context.support.*;

import com.santosh.spring.EmployeeServices;
import com.santosh.spring.Employee;

public class HessianiProxyFactoryTestCase {

  public static void main(String s[]) throws Exception {

    ApplicationContext context=new ClassPathXmlApplicationContext(
                                "client-context.xml");
     //To get Hessian Proxy for EmployeeServices
     EmployeeServices employeeService=
```

```
        (EmployeeServices)context.getBean("employeeServices_Remote");
      Employee employee=employeeService.getEmployee(Integer.parseInt(s[0]));
      System.out.println("Employee Details:");
      System.out.println("  Empno : "+ employee.empno);
      System.out.println("  Name  : "+ employee.ename);
      System.out.println("  Salary: "+ employee.sal);
      System.out.println("  Job   : "+ employee.job);
   }//main
}//class
```

After writing the two files shown in the preceding lists compile the test case Java file and execute it as shown in Fig. 16.5.

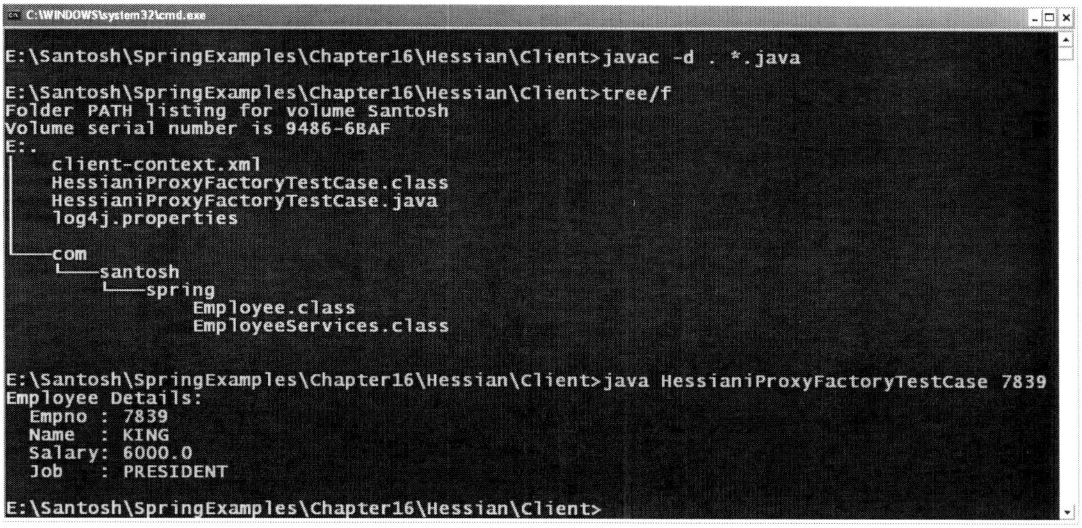

FIGURE 16.5 Output of HessianProxyFactoryTestCase

Figure 16.5 shows the output of the HessianProxyFactoryTestCase implemented to access the employeeServices (Hessian service) using the Spring provided support for Hessian.

> **Note:** To execute this example we need spring.jar, hessian-3.0.20.jar, commons-logging.jar, commons-dbcp.jar, commons-pool.jar, log4j-1.2.14.jar, and ojdbc14.jar in the classpath. Make sure that the Java Web Server (here we have used Tomcat) is started and the web application is successfully started.

In this section we have learnt about Spring Frameworks support for Hessian service, which is implemented by Caucho, the makers of Resin application server. Hessian uses HTTP as its transport mechanism to transfer the messages of its own binary serialization algorithm supporting to implement Remoting in Java. As described in the preceding sections Hessian uses its own binary format to describe the messages. In the next section we will learn about Burlap that uses XML-based protocol.

16.3 REMOTING WITH BURLAP

Burlap is a simple and XML-based protocol for implementing distributed systems that can communicate via a lightweight HTTP protocol. Burlap protocol is from the Caucho company, the same vendor implementing Hessian. This uses HTTP as its transport mechanism. Burlap uses its own XML serialization algorithm for primitives (basic) types and objects. Note that Hessian and Burlap are not able to deserialize a state that is held in final instance fields, as they need to be able to rebuild an object's fields through reflection. Moreover, they are not able to detect objects with customized serialization. For example, Hibernate collections often cause deserialization failures. The Spring Framework provides a high-level support for implementing Remoting with Burlap. The following sections explains you the configurations to use Spring to work with Burlap.

16.3.1 Understanding BurlapServiceExporter

Spring framework includes *org.springframework.remoting.caucho.BurlapServiceExporter* class that provides a high-level and convenient approach for exposing POJO as a Burlap remote object. The BurlapServiceExporter is implemented as handler of Spring Web MVC framework, similar to HessianServiceExporter. The BurlapServiceExporter exports a given service (POJO) at a given HTTP URL making it available for the burlap clients. The following code snippet shows configuring the BurlapServiceExporter to expose the POJO (spring-bean) as a burlap remote object.

Code Snippet (Spring beans XML configuration file snippet)

```
<bean id="employeeServices" class="com.santosh.spring.EmployeeServicesImpl"/>

<bean name="/employeeServices.spring"
class="org.springframework.remoting.caucho.BurlapServiceExporter">
     <property name="service" ref="employeeServices"/>
     <property name="serviceInterface"
               value="com.santosh.spring.EmployeeServices"/>
</bean>
```

Observing the configuration in the preceding code snippet, this is same as configuring HessianServiceExporter. As we do with the other Spring Web MVC applications and even while working with spring Hessian service we need to configure DispatcherServlet to provide an entry point for the http requests. Now, let us find how to access the burlap services using spring services.

16.3.2 Understanding BurlapProxyFactoryBean

The BurlapProxyFactoryBean class packaged into *org.springframework.remoting.caucho* package provides a high-level and convenient approach to access burlap remote object services. The BurlapProxyFactoryBean uses ProxyFactory to build a dynamic proxy for the configured serviceInterface, exposes to the application for use as a bean reference to access the burlap remote object services. The following code snippet shows configuring the BurlapProxyFactoryBean to access the burlap service.

Code Snippet

```
<bean id="employeeServices_Remote"
      class="org.springframework.remoting.caucho.BurlapProxyFactoryBean">
  <property name="serviceInterface"
          value="com.santosh.spring.EmployeeServices"/>
  <property name="serviceUrl"
          value="http://mysys:8080/myctxt/employeeServices.spring"/>
</bean>
```

As per the configurations shown in the preceding code snippet the BurlapProxyFactoryBean builds a proxy for com.santosh.spring.EmployeeServices interface representing the services at *http://mysys:8080/myctxt/employeeServices.spring*.

In this section we learnt about the BurlapProxyFactoryBean, and in the preceding section we understood how to export a service object as a burlap remote object. From the discussion in this and the preceding section it can be understood that the Burlap configurations are the same as Hessian except that we need to use Burlap in the place of Hessian, that is, instead of HessianServiceExporter use BurlapServiceExporter and HessianProxyFactoryBean use BurlapProxyFactoryBean. Thus we do not require to demonstrate burlap service by writing a separate example.

Note: Hessian and/or Burlap technologies are recommended to use when we want to use light-weight protocol to access the services in cross-platform environment,that is, i.e. we want non-Java clients to access the remote services implement in Java since Hessian and Burlap provides a support for non-Java clients.

16.4 SPRING LIGHTWEIGHT REMOTING

Spring HTTP invoker service provides a simple and lightweight protocol to implement Remoting in Java. In the preceding sections of this chapter we have learnt about protocols like RMI, Hessian, and Burlap for implementing Remoting in Java, but all these three protocols have some limitations. RMI uses a complex low-level protocol as its transport protocol, thus it is heavyweight. Hessian and Burlap uses their own serialization mechanisms as opposed to Java Serialization mechanism which has problems in de-serializing a state that is held in final instance fields. Moreover, Hessian and Burlap are not able to detect objects with customized serialization. For example, Hibernate collections often cause de-serialization failures. Because of these reasons Spring Framework apart from providing an infrastructure to simplify implementing Remoting in Java using any of these protocols, has implemented its own Remoting implementation named Spring HTTP Invoker. The 'Spring HTTP Invoker' itself describes that it uses HTTP as its transport protocol. The Spring HTTP Invoker uses the Java serialization mechanism to prepare the messages to be exchanged over HTTP protocol. Using HTTP invoker is an advantage for applications whose arguments and/or return types are complex types that cannot be serialized using the serialization mechanisms used by Hessian and Burlap. Now as we have discussed what Spring HTTP Invoker is, let us understand how to use this service to implement the distributed system. The following sections explain the Spring provided infrastructural elements to use Spring HTTP Invoker for implementing distributed systems in Java.

16.5 UNDERSTANDING HTTPINVOKERSERVICEEXPORTER

The *org.springframework.remoting.httpinvoker.HttpInvokerServiceExporter* class provides a high-level and convenient approach for exposing POJO as a remote object exposing the services using Spring HTTP invoker service. The HttpInvokerServiceExporter is implemented as a handler of Spring Web MVC framework, similar to HessianServiceExporter and BurlapServiceExporter. The configuration of HttpInvokerServiceExporter to export service objects is similar to that of configuring the HessianServiceExporter. The following code snippet shows configuration of the HttpInvoker ServiceExporter to expose the POJO (EmployeeServicesImpl configured as a spring-bean) as a HTTP invoker remote object.

Code Snippet (Spring beans XML configuration file snippet)

```
<bean id="employeeServices" class="com.santosh.spring.EmployeeServicesImpl"/>

<bean name="/employeeServices.spring"
class="org.springframework.remoting.httpinvoker.HttpInvokerServiceExporter">
    <property name="service" ref="employeeServices"/>
    <property name="serviceInterface"
            value="com.santosh.spring.EmployeeServices"/>
</bean>
```

Now, as we have discussed about the configurations to export a spring-bean as a HTTP invoker remote object, let us learn how to access this service as a remote client.

16.5.1 Understanding HttpInvokerProxyFactoryBean

The org.springframework.remoting.httpinvoker.HttpInvokerProxyFactoryBean class provides a high-level and convenient approach to access HTTP invoker remote object services. The HttpInvokerProxy FactoryBean uses ProxyFactory to build a dynamic proxy for the configured serviceInterface, exposes to the application for use as a bean reference to access the HTTP invoker remote object services. The following code snippet shows configuring the HttpInvokerProxyFactoryBean to access the HTTP invoker service.

Code Snippet

```
<bean id="employeeServices_Remoting"
class="org.springframework.remoting.httpinvoker.HttpInvokerProxyFactoryBean">
   <property name="serviceInterface"
           value="com.santosh.spring.EmployeeServices"/>
   <property name="serviceUrl"
           value="http://mysys:8080/myctxt/employeeServices.spring"/>
</bean>
```

As per the configurations shown in the preceding code snippet the HttpInvokerProxyFactoryBean builds a proxy for com.santosh.spring.EmployeeServices interface representing the services at *http://mysys:8080/myctxt/employeeServices.spring*.

In this section we learnt about the HttpInvokerProxyFactoryBean, and in the preceding section we understood how to export a service object as a HTTP invoker remote object. As it can be observed working with HTTP invoker is almost same as the hessian and burlap. Thus we do not find a requirement for demonstrating a separate example. If you want to workout with the HTTP invoker service practically use the example explained under the section 'Working with Hessian based Remoting using Spring' doing the changes with the names of service exporter in controllers-context.xml and proxy factory bean in client-context.xml file.

> **Note:** Spring HTTP invoker is recommended to use when we want to use light-weight protocol HTTP- based Remoting but also use Java Serialization supporting full-object serialization. However, it is important to consider that HTTP invoker is a Java-to-Java Remoting solution and even it also puts a limitation to use Spring on both the client and server side.

Summary

In this chapter we learnt Spring Frameworks support for implementing distributed systems in Java using the existing Remoting technologies like RMI, Hessian, and Burlap. We also learnt Spring HTTP invoker service that is Spring's own Remoting solution. In the next chapter we will learn how to access EJBs using Spring.

Working with EJBs using Spring

17 CHAPTER

Objectives

As we know that the EJB component architecture of J2EE platform also addresses the infrastructural concerns for implementing enterprise-level applications. Moreover, so far in this book we have learnt about the various services provided by the Spring lightweight application framework, addressing most infrastructure concerns for implementing enterprise applications without EJB, providing POJOs with the power of EJB. By this time, after reading this book it can be understood that Spring Framework provides a complete substitution for EJB component architecture by providing the lightweight well-configurable declarative services such as transaction, security, data access, remoting, multi-request handling, etc., that are required in implementing multi-tier enterprise applications. Even though Spring Framework provides a complete environment for enterprise-level applications it still does not restrict the use of EJBs in the project. In fact, Spring provides support to easily access and implement EJBs. Spring provides support for working with EJBs for the following two important reasons:

- To support one of the important benefits that introduces Spring incrementally into existing projects. For example, we might choose to use Spring only to simplify the Web tier implementation, initially leaving the EJBs to take the responsibility of representing the business services.
- We may have a requirement to implement a Business to Business (B2B) application in which we want our enterprise application built by using Spring framework to access the other business application probably implemented using EJB.

In this chapter, we will cover:

- Spring Framework's support that simplifies accessing and implementing the EJB components.
- Traditional approach of accessing EJB and its problems

17.1 TRADITIONAL APPROACH OF ACCESSING EJB

The traditional approach of accessing local or remote EJB involves low-level code with logic to handle various exceptions which makes the client code difficult to implement, understand, and test. The following three steps are generally involved in accessing EJB.

- Obtain EJB Home Object, which is generally done by performing the JNDI lookup.
- Obtain the EJB Object using the lifecycle method like create.
- Invoke the required business logic method on the EJB Object obtained in the preceding step.

Implementing the three steps of operations for accessing EJB involves low-level code, such as code to set up the environment for using JNDI objects and handling system-level exceptions such as naming, EJB, and remote exceptions. The following code snippet shows the sample code that uses traditional approach to access EJB.

Code Snippet

```
try{
  Hashtable ht= new Hashtable();
  ht.put(Context.INITIAL_CONTEXT_FACTORY,
        "weblogic.jndi.WLInitialContext");
  ht.put(Context.PROVIDER_URL, "t3://localhost:7001");

  InitialContext ic=new InitialContext(ht);

  Object obj=ic.lookup( "com.santosh.ejb.AccountsHome");
  obj=PortableRemoteObject.narrow(obj, com.santosh.ejb.AccountsHome.class);
  AccountsHome accountsHome=(AccountsHome)obj;

  AccountsRemote accountsRemote=accountsHome.create();

  boolean flag=accountsRemote.transferAmount(...);
  ...
}//try
catch(NamingException namingException){
    //handle naming exception
}
catch(RemoteException remoteException){
    //handle remote exception
}
catch(CreateException createException){
    //handle create exception
}
```

Observe the preceding code. To invoke the transferAmount() method of EJB we require to implement tedious low-level code—most of which is boilerplate code. In general, to avoid implementing such a low-level code, EJB clients use the Service Locator and Business Delegate design patterns. That is to hide the JNDI lookup operations of accessing EJB, EJB clients can use Service Locator, which locates the EJB Home Object and return to the client. Further, to make the client code more understandable we can use Business Delegate, which uses Service Locator to obtain EJB Home Object and then use it to access EJB on behalf of the client. However, this approach demands the implementation of the Service Locator and Business Delegate which includes code duplication where we need to write many methods in Business Delegate that simple invokes the respective EJB method.

17.2 ACCESSING EJB USING SPRING

The Spring Framework provides simple two ways to access EJB. One is using the

JndiObjectFactoryBean that helps in declaratively lookup the EJB Home Object. The other is using the dynamically generated proxy object that encapsulates the EJB client code, representing the services as a POJO (that is, as a simple Spring Bean). This approach is applicable only for Stateless Session Bean. Let us start understanding the first approach, that is using JndiObjectFactory.

17.2.1 Understanding the JndiObjectFactoryBean

The org.springframework.jndi.JndiObjectFactoryBean, an implementation of FactoryBean, looks up a JNDI object using the JNDI API and exposes it for bean. The 'jndiName' property is used to specify the JNDI name of the object to lookup. The following code snippet shows the configuring JndiObjectFactoryBean to lookup the Accounts EJB Home.

Code Snippet

```
<bean id="accounts" class="org.springframework.jndi.JndiObjectFactoryBean">
  <property name="jndiName" value="com.santosh.ejb.AccountsHome"/>
</bean>

<bean id="accountsDelegate" class="com.santosh.delegates.Accounts">
  <constructor-arg ref="accounts"/>
</bean>
```

As per the configurations shown in the preceding code snippet, the JndiObjectFactoryBean looks up the JNDI object on startup and caches it to avoid multiple lookups for the same object. We can use 'lookupOnStartup' and 'cache' properties of JndiObjectFactoryBean to customize its behavior. The lookupOnStartup property specifies whether the lookup operation needs to be performed at startup or not. If the lookupOnStartup property is set to 'true', then the lookup operation is performed at startup, which is default. Else, it fetches the JNDI object for the first time when the client accesses the object. In this case, it is mandatory to specify the proxy interface. The 'proxyInterface' property is used to specify the JNDI object type to lookup. The cache property specifies a boolean value describes whether to cache the JNDI object once it is fetched; if this property is not configured it default to true that specifies to cache the JNDI object. The following code snippet shows the JndiObjectFactoryBean configuration with lazy lookup.

Code Snippet

```
<bean id="accounts" class="org.springframework.jndi.JndiObjectFactoryBean">
  <property name="jndiName" value="com.santosh.ejb.AccountsHome"/>
  <property name="lookupOnStartup" value="false"/>
  <property name="proxyInterface" value="com.santosh.ejb.AccountsHome"/>
</bean>

<bean id="accountsDelegate" class="com.santosh.delegates.Accounts">
  <constructor-arg ref="accounts"/>
</bean>
```

From the preceding code, since the 'lookupOnStartup' property is set to false the JndiObjectFactory Bean prepares a dynamic proxy implementing the specified proxy interface (AccountsHome), which further looks up the JNDI object on its first access. Apart from this we can use 'defaultObject' property to configure the default object that has to be returned in case if the JNDI lookup fails. The 'deaultObject' property cannot be used if the 'proxyInterface' is configured.

Note that the JndiObjectFactoryBean generated proxy internally uses JNDI API to communicate with the naming service. Moreover, to use JNDI API for accessing the naming service we need to configure naming properties such as 'java.naming.factory.initial', 'java.naming.provider.url', etc. We know that the naming properties can be configured into system properties or alternately into a Hashtable that is injected into an InitialContext in the following code snippet.

Code Snippet

```
System.setProperty("java.naming.factory.initial", "weblogic.jndi.WLInitialContext");
System.setProperty("java.naming.provider.url", "t3://localhost:7001");

InitialContext ic=new InitialContext();
                    (or)
Hashtable ht= new Hashtable();
ht.put("java.naming.factory.initial", "weblogic.jndi.WLInitialContext");
ht.put( "java.naming.provider.url", "t3://localhost:7001");

InitialContext ic=new InitialContext(ht);
```

Therefore, the JndiObjectFactoryBean also needs the naming properties to locate the naming registry for performing the lookup operation. To configure the naming properties we can use 'jndiEnvironment' property. If this property is not set, the naming properties are obtained from the *jndi.properties* file in the classpath. If not found, it locates the local registry finding the properties in the System properties (assuming this code is running inside the server, such as a web application). However, it is a better practice to specify the JNDI properties using the 'jndiEnvironment' property of JndiObjectFactoryBean. The following code snippet shows configuring the JndiObjectFactoryBean with 'jndiEnvironment' property.

Code Snippet

```
<bean id="accounts" class="org.springframework.jndi.JndiObjectFactoryBean">
  <property name="jndiName" value="com.santosh.ejb.AccountsHome"/>
  <property name="lookupOnStartup" value="false"/>
  <property name="proxyInterface" value="com.santosh.ejb.AccountsHome"/>
  <property name=" jndiEnvironment">
    <props>
      <prop key="java.naming.factory.initial">
        weblogic.jndi.WLInitialContextFactory
      </prop>
      <prop key="java.naming.provider.url"> t3://localhost:7001</prop>
    </props>
  </property>
</bean>

<bean id="accountsDelegate" class="com.santosh.delegates.Accounts">
  <constructor-arg ref="accounts"/>
</bean>
```

This shows the JndiObjectFactoryBean configuration using the basic <bean> tag. Alternatively, we can use the jee namespace tag <jee:jndi-lookup> introduced in Spring 2.0. The following code snippet shows the equivalent of the above configuration using <jee:jndi-lookup> tag:

Code Snippet

```
<beans xmlns="http://www.springframework.org/schema/beans"
xmlns:xsi="http://www.w3.org/2001/XMLSchema-instance"
xsi:schemaLocation="http://www.springframework.org/schema/beans
http://www.springframework.org/schema/beans/spring-beans-2.0.xsd
http://www.springframework.org/schema/jee http://www.springframework.org/schema/jee/
spring-jee-2.0.xsd">

  <jee:jndi-lookup id="accounts" jndi-name="com.santosh.ejb.AccountsHome"
    lookup-on-startup="false" proxy-interface="com.santosh.ejb.AccountsHome">
    <jee:environment>
      java.naming.factory.initial=weblogic.jndi.WLInitialContextFactory
      java.naming.provider.url=t3://localhost:7001
    </jee:environment>
  </jee:jndi-lookup>

  <bean id="accountsDelegate" class="com.santosh.delegates.Accounts">
    <constructor-arg ref="accounts"/>
  </bean>
</beans>
```

This declares an object with an id accounts to lookup from the registry using JNDI lookup. This an equivalent for using JndiObjectFactoryBean but more simplified and descriptive to configure. The various attributes used in the <jee:jndi-lookup> tag shown in the preceding code along with the other attributes that it supports are explained in Table 17.1.

TABLE 17.1 Various attributes used in the <jee:jndi-lookup> tag

Attribute name	*Description*
Id	Specifies a bean id that can be used to refer to the definition. In the preceding code snippet we have specified accounts which it referred in the accountsDelegate bean definition.
jndi-name	Specifies the JNDI name to lookup.
lookup-on-startup	Specifies whether the JNDI lookup is to be performed immediately on startup or on the first access, as described for the lookupOnStartup property of JndiObjectFactoryBean. If this is set to true (that is, default) JNDI lookup is performed at startup, otherwise the lookup is performed on the first access.
proxy-interface	Specifies the proxy interface name to use builds proxy for wrapping the JNDI object. Needs to be specified because the actual JNDI object type is not known in advance in case of a lazy lookup.
cache	Specifies a boolean value to describe whether the object returned from the JNDI lookup should be cached after lookup. If true it specifies to cache the object.
environment-ref	Specifies the bean name of the java.util.Properties object that describes the JNDI environment properties.

In addition to the above specified attributes <jee:jndi-lookup> tag allows one optional child element <jee:environment>. The <jee:environment> tag is used to specify the JNDI environment properties as a newline-separated, key-value pairs (as shown in the preceding code snippet).

After understanding the configurations of JndiObjectFactoryBean let us find how to use it in the client (that is, in the Accounts class as per the preceding configuration). The following snippet shows the code for Accounts class (that is, Business Delegate).

Code Snippet

```
package com.santosh.delegates;
import com.santosh.ejb.AccountsHome;
import com.santosh.ejb.AccountsRemote;
import java.rmi.RemoteException;
import javax.ejb.EJBException;

public class Accounts {

  public AccountsHome accountsHome;

  public Accounts(AccountsHome accountsHome){
    this.accountsHome=accountsHome;
  }

  public boolean transferAmount( ... ) {
    try {

      AccountsRemote accountsRemote=accountsHome.create();
      boolean flag=accountsRemote.transferAmount( ... );
      ...
    }//try
    catch(RemoteException remoteException){
      //handle remote exception
    }
    catch(CreateException createException){
      //handle create exception
    }
  }
}
```

As shown in the preceding code snippet, the transferAmount() method of the Accounts (Business Delegate) invokes the create() method to obtain the EJB Object (that is, AccountsRemote). The AccountsHome object is injected into the Accounts as a constructor argument, which is configured to lookup using JndiObjectFactoryBean. Thereafter, the accountsRemote is used to invoke the transferAmount() remote method (EJB Business logic method). Moreover, the delegate is responsible to handle the RemoteException and CreateException.

In this section we have learnt how to use the JndiObjectFactoryBean to lookup the JNDI object, that is, how to use it to fetch the EJB Home Object (local or remote). Even though the JndiObjectFactory Bean provides a convenience to access the EJB Home Object, nevertheless, the client code requires to use create() method for obtaining the EJB Object to invoke the business methods of EJB. Moreover, the client needs to handle the RemoteException. To avoid these problems for the EJB clients in accessing Stateless Session beans the Spring Framework provides a more convenient approach of accessing the Stateless session beans. Let us learn how to use this approach.

17.2.2 Accessing Stateless Session Beans

In the preceding section we have learnt about the JndiObjectFactoryBean that can lookup a JNDI object, which we have used to encapsulate the EJB Home object lookup to simplify the EJB client code. However, the client was still required to invoke the create() method to access the EJB Object and invoke the EJB business logic methods, handling the remote exceptions. The Spring Framework includes org.springframework.ejb.access.SimpleRemoteStatelessSessionProxyFactoryBean class that builds a dynamic proxy for the specified business interface encapsulating the EJB calls to provide a simplest approach of accessing the EJB. This provides the client power of accessing the EJB methods as simple POJO methods, without worrying about the remote exceptions. That means the SimpleRemoteStatelessSessionProxyFactoryBean is a factory class for remote Stateless Session EJB proxies. The following code snippet shows the basic configuration.

Code Snippet

```
<bean id="test" class=
"org.springframework.ejb.access.SimpleRemoteStatelessSessionProxyFactoryBean">
  <property name="jndiName" value=" com.santosh.ejb.SLSBHome"/>
  <property name="businessInterface"
            value="com.santosh.ejbexamples.SLSBRemote"/>
</bean>
```

The 'jndiName' property is used to specify the JNDI name of the EJB Home to lookup from the registry. The 'businessInterface' property is used to specify the proxy interface we are proxying. The business interface can be the EJB components remote interface itself or its super type or a plain Java interface that represents the EJB business methods. In case of specifying the plain Java interface as a business interface, if the methods representing the EJB business methods do not declare RemoteException then the proxy automatically converts the RemoteException thrown by the EJB method and it is automatically converted to Spring's RuntimeException—RemoteAccessException. Apart from the 'jndiName' and 'businessInterface' properties we can use the 'lookupOnHomeStartup' property which is similar to the 'lookupOnStartup' property of JndiObjectFactoryBean discussed in the preceding section. To configure JNDI properties we can use 'jndiEnvironment' property, as done with JndiObjectFactoryBean. The following code snippet shows the configuration of proxy factory with the JNDI properties.

Code Snippet

```
<bean id="test" class=
"org.springframework.ejb.access.SimpleRemoteStatelessSessionProxyFactoryBean">
  <property name="jndiName" value="MyObject"/>
  <property name="businessInterface"
          value="com.santosh.ejbclient.SLSBBusinessInterface"/>
  <property name="jndiEnvironment">
    <props>
      <prop key="java.naming.factory.initial">
        weblogic.jndi.WLInitialContextFactory
      </prop>
      <prop key="java.naming.provider.url">t3://localhost:7001</prop>
    </props>
  </property>
</bean>
```

As per the configuration show in the preceding code snippet the spring bean defined with an id 'test' represents a dynamic proxy built as a subtype of SLSBBusinessInterface (that is, businessInterface). The proxy encapsulates the JNDI object fetched from the JNDI registry. The JNDI object is located in the registry using the specified jndiName (here it is MyObject). The JNDI object located is expected to be a remote EJB Home Object. Now, when a method is invoked on this proxy object, it performs a two-step operation to service the request. First, the proxy obtains EJB Object, the default behavior of proxy is to invoke create() method on the cached EJB Home Object and get the EJB Object. However, this can be customized by overriding the getSessionBeanInstance() method. First, it successfully obtains the EJB Object. Second, it invokes the requested method on the EJB Object (that is, delegates the request to the actual EJB), collects the response, and returns to the client. In case the EJB method throws a RemoteException, proxy throws the same to client if the business interface method is declared with throws RemoteException. If this is not so then the proxy converts the RemoteException to RemoteAccessException and throws it to client.

In this section we have learnt how to use Spring support for accessing remote EJB. Similarly, we can use LocalStatelessSessionProxyFactoryBean instead of SimpleRemoteStatelessSessionProxy FactoryBean for accessing local EJB. The following code snippet shows how to configure the LocalStatelessSessionProxyFactoryBean.

Code Snippet

```
<bean id="test" class=
"org.springframework.ejb.access.LocalStatelessSessionProxyFactoryBean">
  <property name="jndiName" value="MyObject"/>
  <property name="businessInterface"
        value="com.santosh.ejbclient.AccountsInterface"/>
</bean>
```

Alternative to SimpleRemoteStatelessSessionProxyFactoryBean and LocalStatelessSessionProxy FactoryBean we can use jee namespace tags (<jee:remote-slsb> and <jee:local-slsb> respectively) introduced in Spring 2.0. The following code snippet shows the configuration equivalent to the preceding code snippet using <jee:local-slsb> tag.

Code Snippet

```
<jee:local-slsb id="test" jndi-name="MyObject"
                business-interface="com.santosh.ejbclient.AccountsInterface">
```

Now let us look at a sample code that can demonstrate the use of SimpleRemoteStatelessSession ProxyFactoryBean.

17.2.2.1 Working with SimpleRemoteStatelessSessionProxyFactoryBean

To demonstrate the simple approach of accessing Stateless Session bean using the SimpleRemote StatelessSessionProxyFactoryBean, we will design a simple EJB component representing one method that takes an input String and returns a message in the form of String to client (that is, a simple Hello World program that you would have learnt while starting with EJB). Here we are taking up a simple example of EJB as our intention is not to understand how to implement but concentrate on the configurations associated to access it by using Spring support.

Let us start with remote interface for the Stateless Session bean. The following list shows the remote interface for our SLSB.

List 17.1: SLSBRemote.java

```
package com.santosh.ejb;

import javax.ejb.EJBObject;
import java.rmi.RemoteException;

public interface SLSBRemote extends EJBObject {

  String sayHello(String inputMsg) throws RemoteException;
}
```

The EJB remote interface shown in the preceding list extends the javax.ejb.EJBObject interface and declares one method named 'sayHello' with one input String and return of String type. Note that here we have not used a business interface considering that the legacy EJB component that we want to access may not implement the business interface pattern, since using business interface is not mandatory for defining EJB remote interface. Moreover, one should show the importance of Spring Framework that provides a support for accessing the EJB to implement business interface pattern. However, it is a general practice of implementing business interface pattern. Let us now design the home interface for this EJB.

List 17.2: SLSBHome.java

```
package com.santosh.ejb;

import javax.ejb.EJBHome;
import javax.ejb.CreateException;
import java.rmi.RemoteException;

public interface SLSBHome extends EJBHome {

  SLSBRemote create() throws RemoteException, CreateException;
}
```

List 17.2 shows the code for home interface of a Stateless Session bean as we know it can declare only one method named 'create' with no-arguments and return type as our remote interface (in this case, SLSBRemote). After the remote and home interface, now we will implement the bean.

List 17.3: SLSBBean.java

```
package com.santosh.ejb;

import javax.ejb.SessionBean;
import javax.ejb.SessionContext;

public class SLSBBean implements SessionBean{

  public void setSessionContext( SessionContext sessionContext) {
        this.sessionContext=sessionContext;
  }
  public void ejbCreate() {}
  public void ejbRemove() {}
  public void ejbActivate(){}
  public void ejbPassivate(){}

  public String sayHello(String inputMsg) {
        return "Hello from SLSB EJB to "+inputMsg;
  }

  private SessionContext sessionContext;
}
```

The EJB bean class shown in List 17.3 has a simple implementation leaving most of the methods empty, implementing the sayHello() method and returning a String message. Let us design the deployment descriptors for our EJB. List 17.4 shows the ejb-jar.xml.

List 17.4: ejb-jar.xml

```
<!DOCTYPE ejb-jar PUBLIC "-//Sun Microsystems, Inc.//DTD Enterprise JavaBeans 2.0//
EN" "http://java.sun.com/dtd/ejb-jar_2_0.dtd">

<ejb-jar>
  <enterprise-beans>
    <session>
      <ejb-name>myslsb</ejb-name>
      <home>com.santosh.ejb.SLSBHome</home>
      <remote>com.santosh.ejb.SLSBRemote</remote>
      <ejb-class>com.santosh.ejb.SLSBBean</ejb-class>
      <session-type>Stateless</session-type>
      <transaction-type>Bean</transaction-type>
    </session>
  </enterprise-beans>
</ejb-jar>
```

List 17.4 shows the vendor independent deployment descriptor document. Finally, to complete the EJB implementation we need to write a vendor dependent deployment descriptor file that describes vendor-specific configurations like JNDI name to which this EJB Home object is to be bounded. Here List 17.5 shows the vendor-specific deployment descriptor for deploying the application into WebLogic server.

List 17.5: weblogic-ejb-jar.xml

```
<!DOCTYPE weblogic-ejb-jar PUBLIC "-//BEA Systems, Inc.//DTD WebLogic 8.1.0 EJB//EN"
"http://www.bea.com/servers/wls810/dtd/weblogic-ejb-jar.dtd">

<weblogic-ejb-jar>
  <weblogic-enterprise-bean>
    <ejb-name>myslsb</ejb-name>
    <jndi-name>com.santosh.ejb.SLSBHome</jndi-name>
  </weblogic-enterprise-bean>
</weblogic-ejb-jar>
```

As we have completed implementing the EJB component along with the deployment descriptors now we need to compile and prepare the module to deploy into the weblogic server. Figure 17.1 shows the classpath configuration, commands for compiling Java, and preparing ejb jar.

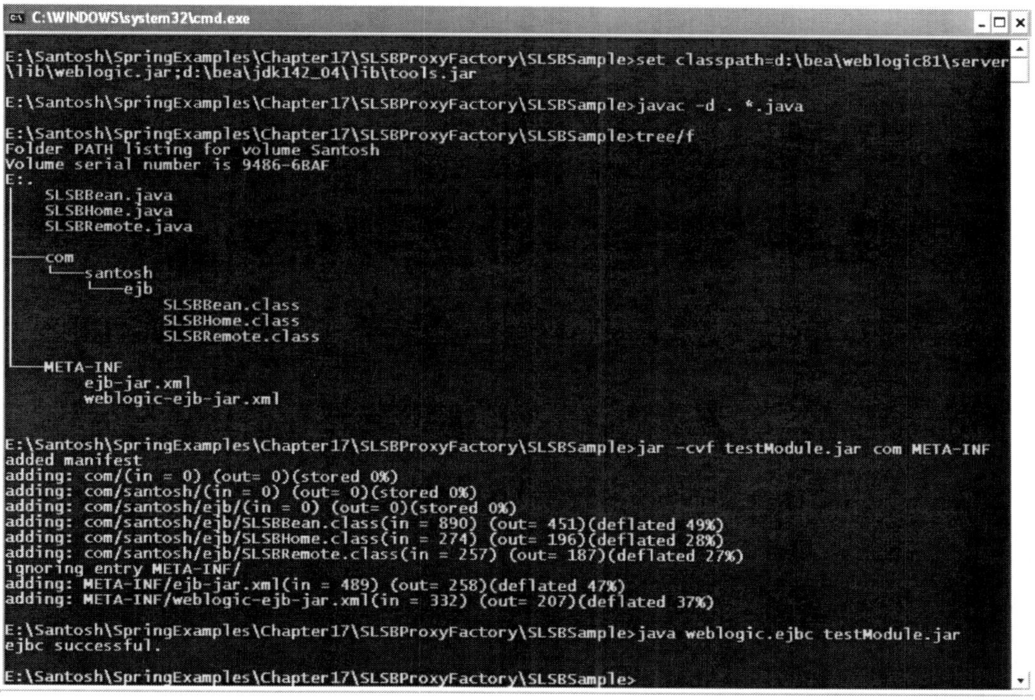

FIGURE 17.1 Steps preparing ejb jar (ejb module)

Now, after preparing the jar file as shown in Fig. 17.2, deploy the module into the weblogic server using any of the deployment options. Once the server is started and our module is deployed then our EJB is ready for access. Let us now see how to access this EJB using Spring. First, let us write a plain Java interface that acts as a business interface

List 17.6: SLSBBusinessInterface.java

```
package com.santosh.ejbclient;

public interface SLSBBusinessInterface {

  String sayHello(String inputMsg);
}
```

The code shown in the List 17.6 is a plain Java interface which does not have any relation with our SLSB remote interface. But here this interface can be used as a business interface and the sayHello() method of this interface represents the SLSBRemote's sayHello() method. To use Spring for accessing EJB it is not mandatory to write a plain Java interface (business interface). Instead we can use the EJB remote interface (in this case SLSBRemote) itself as a business interface. However, designing a plain Java interface as a business interface is a better practice since it can make EJB clients independent of EJB API and makes it more manageable and easy to test. Now after writing the business interface, configure the SimpleRemoteStatelessSessionProxyFactoryBean to access the SLSB implemented above.

List 17.7: application-context.xml

```
<beans xmlns="http://www.springframework.org/schema/beans"
xmlns:xsi="http://www.w3.org/2001/XMLSchema-instance"
xsi:schemaLocation="http://www.springframework.org/schema/beans
http://www.springframework.org/schema/beans/spring-beans-2.0.xsd">

  <bean id="slsbRemote" class=
"org.springframework.ejb.access.SimpleRemoteStatelessSessionProxyFactoryBean">
  <property name="jndiName" value="com.santosh.ejb.SLSBHome"/>
  <property name="businessInterface"
          value="com.santosh.ejbclient.SLSBBusinessInterface"/>
  <property name="jndiEnvironment">
    <props>
      <prop key="java.naming.factory.initial">
         weblogic.jndi.WLInitialContextFactory
      </prop>
      <prop key="java.naming.provider.url">t3://localhost:7001</prop>
    </props>
  </property>
  </bean>
</beans>
```

After configuring the SimpleRemoteStatelessSessionProxyFactoryBean as shown in List 17.7 let us test the configuration. List 17.8 shows the test case code.

List 17.8: SLSBRemoteTestCase.java

```
import com.santosh.ejbclient.SLSBBusinessInterface;
import org.springframework.beans.factory.*;
import org.springframework.beans.factory.xml.*;
import org.springframework.core.io.*;
import org.apache.log4j.*;

public class SLSBRemoteTestCase {

  public static void main(String s[]) throws Exception {

    Logger rootLogger=Logger.getRootLogger();
    rootLogger.setLevel(Level.OFF);

    BeanFactory beans=new XmlBeanFactory(
      new FileSystemResource("application-context.xml"));
    SLSBBusinessInterface slsbObj=

      (SLSBBusinessInterface)beans.getBean("slsbRemote");

    System.out.println(slsbObj.sayHello("Readers"));
  }
}
```

Now, compile and run the test case as shown in Fig. 17.2.

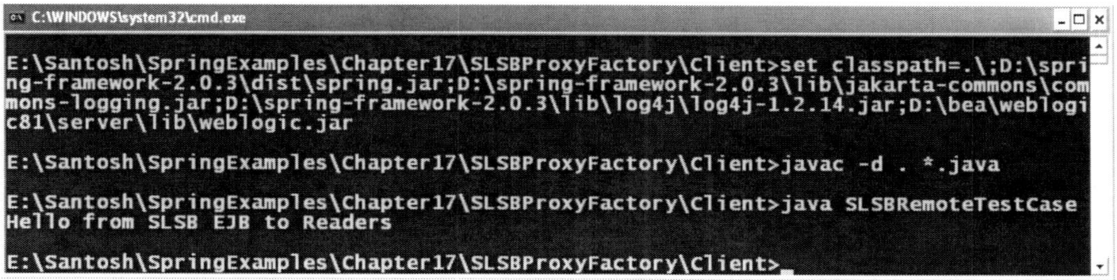

FIGURE 17.2 Output of SLSBRemoteTestCase

In this example we have used SimpleRemoteStatelessSessionProxyFactoryBean to access the remote EJB.

Note that the Spring support for accessing EJB explained in this section is applicable only for Stateless Session bean. If we want to access Stateful Session Beans then we need to use the first approach (that is, use JndiObjectFactoryBean) explained in the earlier section. In this section we have learnt how to use Spring to access EJB (local and remote). The next section explains Spring Framework's support in implementing EJBs.

17.3 IMPLEMENTING EJB USING SPRING

In the preceding sections we have seen Spring assisting in accessing EJBs conveniently for apart from this Spring includes support for simplifying the EJB implementation. The Spring Framework's support for implementing EJBs includes simple adapter classes that are convenient to subclass for implementing EJB bean class for SLSB, SFSB, and Message-driven Bean. Apart from this, the adapter classes provides access for the spring application context that makes the EJB bean use the spring beans configured in the Spring Beans XML configuration file. The convenient adapter classes for simplifying the EJB development are:

- AbstractStatelessSessionBean.
- AbstractStatefulSessionBean.
- AbstractMessageDrivenBean.

Let us understand these adapter classes in detail.

17.3.1 The AbstractStatelessSessionBean

The org.springframework.ejb.support.AbstractStatelessSessionBean is an abstract adapter class, which is a subtype of javax.ejb.SessionBean. This class implements all the Session Bean lifecycle methods such as setSessionContext, ejbCreate, ejbActivate, ejbPassivate and ejbRemove, providing convenience for implementing Stateless Session Bean. The various methods of AbstractStateless SessionBean and their default behavior is explained in the following sections.

The **setSessionContext()** method sets the given SessionContext to the instance variable for further use. This is the general boilerplate code that is implemented in the EJBs bean class. The subclass can override this method to write custom logic but in such a case it is mandatory for us to invoke this method in super class to make this abstract class's instance variable initialize.

The **ejbCreate()** method loads the BeanFactory. The BeanFactory is loaded using the Spring Bean XML configuration file specified by the EJB environment entry named 'ejb/BeanFactoryPath'. This BeanFactory is available for the bean through getBeanFactory() method. After loading the BeanFactory successfully the ejbCreate() method invokes onEjbCreate() method allowing the subclass to include an additional custom initialization code. The following code snippet shows the default implementation of the ejbCreate() method.

Code Snippet

```
public void ejbCreate() throws CreateException {
  loadBeanFactory();
  onEjbCreate();
}
```

> **Note:** Do not override this method, even though this method can not be declared final (as per the EJB specifications), to implement custom initializations use onEjbCreate() method.

The **onEjbCreate()** method is the only abstract method in AbstractStatelessSessionBean class. The subclass must implement this method to add any custom initialization logic that in general we would implement in ejbCreate() method.

The **ejbActivate()** method of this class simply throws an IllegalStateException describing 'ejbActivate must not be invoked on a stateless session bean' message.

The **ejbPassivate()** method of this class simply throws an IllegalStateException describing 'ejbPassivate must not be invoked on a stateless session bean' message.

The **ejbRemove()** method invokes the onEjbRemove() allowing the customized finalization implemented by the subclass to execute. There after it unloads the BeanFactory, the BeanFactory is loaded in ejbCreate() using the Spring Bean XML configuration file specified by the EJB environment entry named 'ejb/BeanFactoryPath'. The following code snippet shows the default implementation of the ejbRemove() method.

Code Snippet

```
public void ejbRemove() {
  onEjbRemove();
  unloadBeanFactory();
}
```

> **Note:** Do not override this method, even though this method can not be declared final (as per the EJB specifications), to implement custom finalizations use onEjbRemove() method.

The **onEjbRemove()** method is a abstract method with an empty implementation. The subclass can implement this method to add any custom finalization logic that in general we would implement in ejbRemove() method.

Now let us look at the complete EJB bean class implemented using the AbstractStatelessSession Bean. The following code snippet shows the SLSBBean class.

Code Snippet

```
package com.santosh.ejb;

import org.springframework.ejb.support.AbstractStatelessSessionBean;

public class SLSBBean extends AbstractStatelessSessionBean {

  public void onEjbCreate() {}

  public String sayHello(String inputMsg) {
    return "Hello from SLSB EJB to "+inputMsg;
  }
}
```

Observe the SLSBBean code shown in the preceding code which is implemented using the Spring support and the SLSBBean code shown under List 17.3 which is implemented using the traditional approach supported by EJB. The bean implemented using Spring support eliminates all the boilerplate code from the bean class making it easy to implement and understand. Now let us look at how to implement Stateful Session Bean using Spring support.

17.3.2 The AbstractStatefulSessionBean

The org.springframework.ejb.support.AbstractStatefulSessionBean is an abstract adapter class, which is a subtype of javax.ejb.SessionBean. This class implements the Session Bean lifecycle methods such as setSessionContext and ejbRemove, providing convenience for implementing Stateful Session Bean. The various methods of AbstractStatefulSessionBean and their default behavior are explained below.

The **setSessionContext()** method sets the given SessionContext to the instance variable for further use. This is the general boilerplate code that is implemented in the EJBs bean class. The subclass can override this method to write custom logic but in such a case it is mandatory for us to invoke this method in super class to make this abstract class's instance variable initialize.

The **ejbRemove()** method invokes the onEjbRemove() allowing the customized finalization implemented by the subclass to execute. Thereafter it unloads the BeanFactory. The following code snippet shows the default implementation of the ejbRemove() method.

Code Snippet

```
public void ejbRemove() {
   onEjbRemove();
   unloadBeanFactory();
}
```

> **Note:** Do not override this method, even though this method can not be declared final (as per the EJB specifications), to implement custom finalizations use onEjbRemove() method.

The **onEjbRemove()** method is a abstract method with an empty implementation. The subclass can implement this method to add any custom finalization logic that in general we would implement in ejbRemove() method.

Apart from these methods the subclass needs to implement the ejbActivate(), ejbPassivate() and ejbRemove() to meet the EJB specifications. The ejbCreate() and ejbActiavte() methods should invoke loadBeanFactory() method to load the BeanFactory using the Spring Bean XML configuration file specified by the EJB environment entry named 'ejb/BeanFactoryPath'.

Now let us look at the complete EJB bean class implemented using the AbstractStatefulSession Bean. The following code snippet shows the SFSBBean class.

Code Snippet

```
package com.santosh.ejb;

import org.springframework.ejb.support.AbstractStatefulSessionBean;

public class SFSBBean extends AbstractStatefulSessionBean {

   public void onEjbRemove() {
       //To Do: finalizations
   }
```

```
    public void ejbCreate(String uid) {
        loadBeanFactory();
        //custom initializations
    }
    public void ejbActivate() {
        loadBeanFactory();
    }
    public void ejbPassivate(String uid) {
        unloadBeanFactory();
        setBeanFactoryLocator(null);
        /*
        Since the default BeanFactoryLocator (i.e. ContextJndiBeanFactoryLocator)
        used by the superclass is not serializable.
        */
    }
}
```

Similarly, the AbstractMessageDrivenBean is a convenient super class for implementing Message Driven Beans (MDB).

Summary

In this chapter we have learnt how to use spring support for accessing and implementing EJBs. However, the various services provided by the Spring lightweight application framework addresses most infrastructure concerns such as transaction, security, data access, remoting, multi-request handling, etc., for implementing multi-tier enterprise applications without EJB, providing POJOs with the power of EJB. We have learnt that Spring provides support to easily access and implement EJBs. We have understood that Spring Framework includes this support for two reasons—support incremental adoption of Spring Framework into our project and support the requirement of implementing B2B applications that want to access EJB components of another business application. In this chapter we have learnt how to use JndiObjectFactoryBean and SimpleRemoteStatelessSession ProxyFactoryBean for accessing EJBs. Further we have learnt the support of AbstractStatelessSession Bean and AbstractStatefulSessionBean for implementing EJBs easily. In the next chapter we will learn how to send or receive asynchronous messages communicating with enterprise messaging systems.

Implementing JMS using Spring

18 CHAPTER

Objectives

In the previous chapter we have learnt how to use Spring Framework for accessing EJBs, and in Chapter 6 we have learnt about the Spring JDBC abstraction framework that helps to eliminate shortcomings found in the use of JDBC API directly to implement DAOs which simplifies the programming model by making the application code free from the boiler plate code. Similarly, Spring Framework provides a JMS integration framework that simplifies the use of the JMS API. In this chapter we will cover:

- How to use Spring utilities for sending/receiving asynchronous messages
- Spring provided utility API for sending and receiving asynchronous messages
- Spring integration framework for using JMS API

18.1 INTRODUCING SPRING JMS INTEGRATION FRAMEWORK

Java Message Service (JMS) API of J2EE provides a standard abstraction for Java applications to communicate with different enterprise messaging systems to create, send, receive, and read messages. JMS defines a common set of enterprise messaging concepts and facilities, to minimize the efforts of a Java language programmer to use enterprise messaging products, and to maximize the portability of messaging applications. It supports point-to-point (PTP) and publish-subscribe (pub/sub) messaging models. JMS API includes a separate class hierarchy for programming PTP and pub/sub models, which is a lengthier process where plenty of boilerplate code is involved. This is changed in JMS 1.1; the JMS 1.1 comes with a simpler programming model by providing domain independent (that is,PTP or pub/sub) approach for client programming, enabling us to include queues and topics into a single transaction. Although JMS 1.1 has simplified the use of client API for accessing messaging systems, there are still some shortcomings in the use of JMS directly to implement JMS clients. Some of these shortcomings are code duplication, resource leakage, and exception handling. To solve these problems Spring Framework provides a thin, robust, and highly extensible JMS integration framework.

The JMS integration framework from Spring is a value-added service that takes care of all the low level details like retrieving connection, preparing the session, releasing the resources, and creating sending and receiving messages. While using the JMS integration framework of Spring for accessing the enterprise messaging systems the application developer needs to specify the message and destination to send for producing the messages, and specify the destination to consume the messages. Since all the low level logic have been written once and correctly into the abstraction layer provided by the Spring JMS integration framework, this helps to eliminate the shortcomings found in using JMS API to implement JMS clients. The JmsTemplate is the core template class simplifying the use of JMS. The following section explains about the JmsTemplate and its use.

18.2 WHAT IS JMSTEMPLATE

The JmsTemplate designed following a core template pattern is the basic element and a central class of the Spring JMS integration framework. It includes the most common logic (that is, the parts of code that remains fixed) in using JMS API to access enterprise messaging systems, such as handling the creation of connection, session, sending messages, and release of resource. This also catches the JMS exceptions and converts them to the standard and more explanatory exceptions defined in the org.springframework.jms package. The JmsTemplate instance can be shared among multiple beans safely since this is thread-safe once it is initialized, which means that we can use a single JmsTemplate instance for the complete application. The org.springframework.jms.core.JmsTemplate class can be instantiated using any one of the following constructors:

- **JmsTemplate():** Constructs a new JmsTemplate instance. This constructor is provided to allow Java Bean style of instantiation. Note that when constructing an object using this constructor we need to use setConnectionFactory() method to set the ConnectionFactory before using this instance.
- **JmsTemplate(ConnectionFactory):** Constructs a new JmsTemplate instance using the given ConnectionFactory.

Note that if we are working with the JMS 1.0.2 version, use org.springframework.jms.core. JmsTemplate102 class instead of JmsTemplate. The JmsTemplate102 is a subtype of JmsTemplate. Now, as we know how to construct the JmsTemplate object it is time to learn how to use JmsTemplate for sending and receiving messages. We will begin by learning how to send messages.

18.3 USING JMSTEMPLATE FOR SENDING MESSAGES

The JmsTemplate provides many convenience methods for sending message such as send() and convertAndSend(). The send() method is overloaded—it has the following three versions:

- **send(javax.jms.Destination destination, MessageCreator message)**: This method sends the message returned by the MessageCreator to the specified JMS Destination.
- **send(String destinationName, MessageCreator message):** This method sends the message returned by the MessageCreator to the JMS Destination located using the specified destination name. If the destination name specifies a JNDI name, we need to set the destinationResolver property of this JmsTemplate to an instance of JndiDestinationResolver.
- **send(MessageCreator message)**: This method sends the message returned by the given MessageCreator to the default JMS Destination. Note that this method works only if the default destination is set to this instance. We use setDefaultDestination(Destination destination) or

setDefaultDestination(String destinationName) methods to set the default destination for this JmsTemplate instance.

The org.springframework.jms.core.MessageCreator is a callback interface used by JmsTemplate's send methods. This interface contains only one method with the signature shown in the following code snippet.

```
public Message createMessage(Session session) throws JMSException
```

The implementation classes of this interface needs to implement the createMessage() method, which takes the responsibility of preparing the JMS Message object to be sent using the given session, but it does not need to worry about handling the JMSException raised while preparing the Message. The JMSException will be caught and handled by the JmsTemplate calling this implementation. Now, let us see the JmsTemplate in action for sending messages. The following list shows the code for sending a message using JmsTemplate.

List 18.1: SendJMSMessage.java

```
package com.santosh.spring.jms;
import javax.jms.*;
import org.springframework.jms.core.*;

public class SendJMSMessage {

  private JmsTemplate jmsTemplate;
  private Destination destination;

  public void setJmsTemplate(JmsTemplate jmsTemplate) {
        this.jmsTemplate = jmsTemplate;
  }

  public void setDestination(Destination destination) {
        this.destination = destination;
  }

  public void sendMessage(String message) {
        jmsTemplate.send(destination, new MessageCreator() {
              public Message createMessage(Session session)
                                        throws JMSException {
                    return  session.createTextMessage(message);
        }});
    }
}
```

The SendJMSMessage object can be configured in the Spring beans XML configuration file as shown in the following list.

List 18.2: spring-beans.xml

```
<beans xmlns="http://www.springframework.org/schema/beans"
xmlns:xsi="http://www.w3.org/2001/XMLSchema-instance"
xsi:schemaLocation="http://www.springframework.org/schema/beans
http://www.springframework.org/schema/beans/spring-beans-2.0.xsd">

  <!--Lookup JMS Destination (Queue)-->
  <bean id="myQueue" class="org.springframework.jndi.JndiObjectFactoryBean">
    <property name="jndiName" value="MyQueue"/>
    <property name="proxyInterface" value="javax.jms.Destination"/>
  </bean>

  <!--Lookup JMS ConnectionFactory-->
  <bean id="connectionFactory"
            class="org.springframework.jndi.JndiObjectFactoryBean">
    <property name="jndiName" value="javax.jms.ConnectionFactory"/>
    <property name="proxyInterface" value="javax.jms.ConnectionFactory"/>
  </bean>

  <!--Configuring JmsTemplate-->
  <bean id="jmsTemplate" class="org.springframework.jms.core.JmsTemplate">
    <constructor-arg ref="connectionFactory"/>
  </bean>

  <!--Configuring SendJMSMessage-->
  <bean id="sendJMSMessage" class="com.santosh.spring.jms.SendJMSMessage">
    <property name="destination" ref="myQueue"/>
    <property name="jmsTemplate" ref="jmsTemplate"/>
  </bean>
</beans>
```

This declares sendJMSMessage bean along with all its dependencies such as JmsTemplate and destination objects. Here we have used JndiObjectFactoryBean for looking up the JMS ConnectionFactory and JMS Destination from the JNDI registry. If we are using this configuration out of box (external to the server) then we would want to set the jndiEnvironment property of JndiObjectFactoryBean (see 'Understanding the JndiObjectFactoryBean' in Chapter 17). Now, as we have understood how to send JMS Message let us learn how to receive the messages.

18.4 USING JMSTEMPLATE TO RECEIVE MESSAGES

The JmsTemplate provides the receive() method to receive messages in synchronous mode. Although JMS is used for asynchronous communication, we can consume the messages (that is, from the messaging system) synchronously. In this case the calling thread is blocked until a message becomes available. JmsTemplate provides the following receive() methods to consume the messages synchronously:

- **receive(Destination destination):** This method receives the message from the specified JMS Destination. It waits for the message until the specified timeout. We use the setReceiveTimeout (long receiveTimeout) method to specify the timeout.
- **receive(String destinationName):** This method receives the message from the specified JMS Destination located using the specified destination name. If the destination name specifies a JNDI name, we need to set the destinationResolver property of this JmsTemplate to an instance of JndiDestinationResolver. Waits for message until the specified timeout, we use setReceive Timeout(long receiveTimeout) method to specify the timeout.
- **receive():** This method receives the message from the default JMS Destination. We use setDefaultDestination(Destination destination) or setDefaultDestination(String destination Name) methods to set the default destination for this JmsTemplate instance. Note that this method works only if the default destination is set to this instance.

All the above three receive() methods wait for messages until the specified timeout using the setReceiveTimeout(long receiveTimeout) method. These methods return javax.jms.Message object or a null value if timeout expires.

18.5 USING MESSAGELISTENER TO RECEIVE MESSAGES

In addition to the receive() methods of JmsTemplate, Spring JMS integration framework provides another approach for receiving JMS messages. In this case we need to implement a message listener and configure it to the MessageListenerContainer. This is similar to EJB's Message Driven Bean (MDB), but here the receiver component is a POJO. Thus it is referred to as message-driven POJO (MDP) allowing us to receive messages asynchronously. The following list shows the code for MDP:

List 18.3: MyMessageListener.java

```
package com.santosh.spring.jms;

import javax.jms.*;

public class MyMessageListener implements MessageListener {

  public void onMessages(Message message) {
        try{
              // understand and process the message
        } catch(JMSException exception){
              //Handle JMSException
        }
  }
}
```

As mentioned earlier, the MessageListener implementation needs to be configured to the MessageListenerContainer as shown in the list below:

List 18.4: beans-context.xml

```
<beans xmlns="http://www.springframework.org/schema/beans"
xmlns:xsi="http://www.w3.org/2001/XMLSchema-instance"
xsi:schemaLocation="http://www.springframework.org/schema/beans
http://www.springframework.org/schema/beans/spring-beans-2.0.xsd">

  <!--Lookup JMS Destination (Queue)-->
  <bean id="myQueue" class="org.springframework.jndi.JndiObjectFactoryBean">
    <property name="jndiName" value="MyQueue"/>
    <property name="proxyInterface" value="javax.jms.Destination"/>
  </bean>

  <!--Lookup JMS ConnectionFactory-->
  <bean id="connectionFactory"
      class="org.springframework.jndi.JndiObjectFactoryBean">
    <property name="jndiName" value="javax.jms.ConnectionFactory"/>
    <property name="proxyInterface" value="javax.jms.ConnectionFactory"/>
  </bean>

  <!--Configuring MyMessageListener-->
  <bean id="myMessageListener"
        class="com.santosh.spring.jms.MyMessageListener"/>

  <!--Configuring MessageListenerContainer-->
  <bean id="JMSMessageListenerContainer"
      class="org.springframework.jms.listener.DefaultMessageListenerContainer">
    <property name="destination" ref="myQueue"/>
    <property name="connectionFactory" ref="connectionFactory"/>
    <property name="messageListener" ref="myMessageListener"/>
  </bean>
</beans>
```

This declares MessageListenerContainer bean along with all its dependencies such as MessageListener, JMS ConnectionFactory and JMS Destination objects. Here we have used JndiObjectFactoryBean for looking up the JMS ConnectionFactory and JMS Destination from the JNDI registry.

> **Note:** If we are working with JMS 1.0.2 then we need to useDefaultMessageListenerContainer102 instead of DefaultMessageListenerContainer class.

The one restriction that we have in this approach of using the Spring JMS abstraction framework is the MDP class must implement javax.jms.MessageListener and override onMessage() method where we need to handle the JMSException (which can be observed from the code shown under List 18.3). However, Spring provides its own listener interface and message adapter to solve these problems. The following sections explain the usage of the Spring specific message listener and how the MessageListenerAdapter is used to receive messages.

18.5.1 Using SessionAwareMessageListener

The org.springframework.jms.listener.SessionAwareMessageListener interface is a spring which specifies the message listener interface and is a direct alternative to the standard JMS MessageListener. The MessageListenerContainer supports the MDPs implementing javax.jms.MessageListener and SessionAwareMessageListener. For maximum compatibility it is recommended to use MessageListener interface instead of the Spring specific message listener. However, using the SessionAwareMessageListener provides us some benefits such as making the underlying JMS Session available, and eliminates the need of handling JMSException. The SessionAwareMessageListener interface declares only one method as shown below:

```
public void onMessage(Message message, Session session) throws JMSException
```

This is a callback method used by the MessageListenerContainer to process the received JMS message. This even provides the underlying JMS session, which can be used to send rely messages without the need to access an external session or ConnectionFactory. Another point to notice from the preceding code snippet is that the onMessage() method includes throws JMSException Thus we do not require to handle the JMSException while processing the message. List 18.5 shows the code implementing SessionAwareMessageListener.

List 18.5: MyMessageListener.java

```
package com.santosh.spring.jms;

import javax.jms.*;
import org.springframework.jms.listener.*;

public class MyMessageListener implements SessionAwareMessageListener {

  public void onMessages(Message message, Session session)
                                             throws JMSException {
        // understand and process the message
  }
}
```

This implements the SessionAwareMessageListener to listen for the messages asynchronously. The MyMessageListener is configured to the MessageListenerContainer in the same way it was done while implementing JMS MessageListener (see List 18.4). In addition to this Spring JMS integration framework provides a MessageListenerAdapter that allows any class as listener. This makes the listener class completely independent of JMS API.

In this section we have learnt about the Spring Framework support in using JMS for communicating with enterprise messaging systems. Spring Framework 2.5 includes some new features for simplifying the JMS configurations which are explained in the following section explains.

18.6 USING JMS NAMESPACE SUPPORT

The Spring Framework support for JMS is simplified in Spring 2.5 by providing a simplified JMS configuration. Spring 2.5 provides a JMS XML namespace which defines the configuration elements in support Spring JMS integration framework. The JMS XML namespace elements allow configuring MessageListenerContainer's in a simplified XML style. To use the new JMS elements we need to reference the JMS schema and import the JMS namespace in the Spring beans XML configuration file as shown below:

```
<beans xmlns:xsi="http://www.w3.org/2001/XMLSchema-instance"
xsi:schemaLocation="http://www.springframework.org/schema/beans
http://www.springframework.org/schema/beans/spring-beans-2.5.xsd
http://www.springframework.org/schema/jms http://www.springframework.org/schema/jms/
spring-jms-2.5.xsd"
xmlns="http://www.springframework.org/schema/beans"
xmlns:jms="http://www.springframework.org/schema/jms">
```

After referencing the JMS schema and importing the JMS namespace we can use the JMS XML namespace tags for configuring the JMS listeners and containers. The JMS namespace contains only two top level elements called <listener-container> and <jca-listener-container>. Both of these tags are used for configuring MessageListenerContainer—the former creates a simple or default message listener container and the later creates a JCA-based message listener container. The <listener-container> element can contain the following attributes:

TABLE 18.1 Attributes of <listener-container> element

Attribute name	*Description*
container-type	Specifies the type of this MessageListenerContainer. Allows any one of the following four values: • **default :** Specifies to use DefaultMessageListenerContainer. • **default102 :** Specifies to create DefaultMessageListenerContainer102 and is used while working with JMS 1.0.2. • **simple :** Specifies to create SimpleMessageListenerContainer. • **simple102 :** Specifies to create SimpleMessageListenerContainer102 and is used while working with JMS 1.0.2. If this attribute is not used it defaults to 'default'.
connection-factory	Specifies the bean name of the JMS ConnectionFactory. If not used it defaults to 'connectionFactory'.
destination-resolver	Specifies the bean name of the DestinationResolver implementation such as JndiDestinationResolver. This is useful when we want to specify the destinationName instead of JMS Destination reference.
message-converter	Specifies the bean name configuring the MessageConverter that should be used to convert the JMS messages to listener method arguments. If not used it defaults to SimpleMessage Converter.
destination-type	Specifies the JMS destination type for this listener. Accepts queue or topic or durableTopic. If not used it defaults to 'queue'.

(Contd.)

client-id	Specifies the client Id for the JMS connection. This is required to specify when the destination type is specified to use durableTopic.
acknowledge	Specifies the acknowledgement mode to use with this MessageListenerContainer. Accepts auto or client or dups-ok or transacted. If not used it defaults to 'auto'.
	cache Specifies the cache level for JMS resources.
concurrency	Specifies the number of concurrent sessions to start for each listener.
transaction-manager	Specifies the bean name configuring the PlatformTransactionManager implementation (see Chapter 17 for more details on PlatformTransactionManager).

The <listener-container> can contain one or more <listener> elements. The <listener> element is used to define a MessageListener. The <listener> element can contain the following attributes:

TABLE 18.2 Attributes of <listener> element

Attribute name	*Description*
id	Specifies a unique identifier for a listener.
destination	Specifies the destination name for this listener, which is resolved using the destination-resolver configured to the parent listener-container. This attribute is mandatory to use, no default is taken.
ref	Specifies the bean name of the listener object, implementing the MessageListener or SessionAwareMessageListener. This attribute is mandatory to use, no default is taken.
subscription	Specifies the subscription name for the durable subscriber. Useful only when the parent <listener-container> element's destination-type attribute specifies durableTopic.
method	Specifies the name of the listener method to invoke when message is received by the listener container. If not specified then the listener class needs to implement MessageListener or SessionAwareMessageListener interface so that onMessage() method will be invoked.
response-destination	Specifies the name of the default response destination to send response messages to.

The following list shows the sample code configuring the JMS listener container using the JMS namespace tags.

List 18.6: beans-context.xml

```
<beans xmlns:xsi="http://www.w3.org/2001/XMLSchema-instance"
xsi:schemaLocation="http://www.springframework.org/schema/beans
http://www.springframework.org/schema/beans/spring-beans-2.5.xsd
http://www.springframework.org/schema/jms
http://www.springframework.org/schema/jms/spring-jms-2.5.xsd"
xmlns="http://www.springframework.org/schema/beans"
xmlns:jms="http://www.springframework.org/schema/jms">

  <!–Lookup JMS ConnectionFactory –>
  <bean id="connectionFactory"
        class="org.springframework.jndi.JndiObjectFactoryBean">
    <property name="jndiName" value="javax.jms.ConnectionFactory"/>
    <property name="proxyInterface" value="javax.jms.ConnectionFactory"/>
  </bean>
```

```
<!--Configuring DestinationResolver-->
<bean id="destinationResolver"
  class="org.springframework.jms.support.destination.JndiDestinationResolver"/>

<!--Configuring MyMessageListener-->
<bean id="myMessageListener"
    class="com.santosh.spring.jms.MyMessageListener"/>

<!--Configuring JMS listener container-->
  <jms:listener-container connection-factory="connectionFactory"
                          destination-type="durableTopic"
                          client-id="client1"
                          destination-resolver="destinationResolver">

    <jms:listener id="MyListener1" ref="myMessageListener"
                  subscription="subscriber1" destination="MyTopic"/>

  </jms:listener-container>
</beans>
```

This configures the JMS listener container with one listener, using the new JMS namespace tags introduced in Spring 2.5. The MyMessageListener is a listener class implementing MessageListener or SessionAwareMessageListener as shown in Lists 18.3 or 18.5, respectively. We can observe that using JMS namespace tags to configuring the listener container is simple and more descriptive compared to the Spring 2.0 style of configuring the listener container (shown under List 18.4). Here we have configured a single listener. However, we can configure multiple listeners under a single listener container. Moreover each of the listeners can be specified with a separate destination to connect. In this section we have learnt how to use the new JMS namespace tags introduced in Spring 2.5 to configure the JMS listener container and listeners.

Summary

In the previous chapter we have learnt how to use Spring JMS integration Framework that simplifies the use of JMS API for communicating with asynchronous messaging systems to send/receive asynchronous messages. The Spring JMS integration framework helps to eliminate the shortcomings such as code duplication and resource handling found in using JMS API directly to communicate with the messaging systems, simplifying the programming model by making the application code free from the boilerplate code. We have learnt that a JmsTemplate provides the convenience send() methods for sending asynchronous messages. Then we have learnt that JmsTemplate even includes receive() methods for receiving messages but synchronously since invoking the receive() method blocks the current thread until the timeout expires. However, Spring JMS integration framework includes a MessageListenerContainer that enables us to receive messages asynchronously. We implement a listener class as a subtype of org.springframework.jms.listener.SessionAwareMessageListener or javax.jms.MessageListener interfaces and configure it to the MessageListenerContainer implementation object such as DefaultMessageListenerContainer or SimpleMessageListener Container. At the end of the chapter we have discussed about the JMS namespace tags newly introduced in Spring 2.5 for configuring the listener and listener container in a simplified manner. Up till now, we have discussed the various services supported by Spring with individual examples to understand the configurations clearly. Now let us apply the Spring concepts to implement a small project. The next chapter shows how to apply the Spring concepts to implement a project.

Spring Framework's Form Tags

A

APPENDIX

Spring Framework 2.0 provides a set of tags for implementing JSP pages managing form elements when using JSP and Spring Web MVC data binding features. The Spring's form tag library includes a set of tags used to create forms that contains input fields like text field, password, radio, checkbox, radio-button etc. Most of the tags in the form tag library correspond to the HTML tags, each tag supports the attributes of its corresponding HTML tag counterpart, making the tags recognizable to use. Instead of using HTML tags to create forms, using their corresponding Spring form tags allows us to present the fields with the values available in the corresponding command bean. These tags are declared in a spring-form.tld packaged into spring-webmvc.jar, we can refer this tld using the URI http://www.springframework.org/tags/form with the recommended prefix is ***form.*** The JSP document can include the taglib directive element as shown in the following code snippet to make the JSP document available with the Spring form tags.

```
<%@taglib prefix="form" uri="http://www.springframework.org/tags/form"%>
```

The Spring's form tag library declares the following 14 tags in which 2 are newly introduced in Spring 2.5.

- <form:form>
- <form:input>
- <form:password>
- <form:hidden>
- <form:textarea>
- <form:label>
- <form:select>
- <form:option>
- <form:options>
- <form:radiobutton>
- <form:radiobuttons>
- <form:checkbox>
- <form:checkboxes>
- <form:errors>

Let's discuss these tags and its attributes

A.1 THE <FORM:FORM> TAG

The <form:form> element finds the form backing object (command object) associated with the specified commandName, and stores it into the PageContext scope, which can be accessed by the inner tags. The *form* tag renders an HTML <form> element. Note that all the other tags in this tag library are nested tags of this tag. The syntax of this element is shown in the following snippet.

Snippet

```
<form:form attributes>
   Body content
 </form:form>
```

The body content of this tag accepts JSP content and the attributes are described in the following table.

Table A.1 The <form:form> attributes

Attribute Name	*Description*
action	This attribute takes the action path to which this form is to be submitted.
commandName (or) modelAttribute	Specifies the name of the attribute to which the form backing object is bounded. If not specified defaults to 'command'
method onsubmit	Takes the HTTP request method that has to be used to submit this form, default is POST. This allows to set the java script function that has to be executed when this form is submitted

Note: The above table describes only some important attributes you can find the other attributes like onclick, onreset, cssClass, cssStyle etc, which has the same meaning as there respective fields in the html <form> element.

The following code snippet shows the form elements use.

Code Snippet

```
<form:form action="login.spring" method="POST">
  ....
 </form:form>
```

A.2 THE <FORM:INPUT> TAG

The <form:input> element renders an HTML <input> element of type text and value as the value bounded to the specified property, we use path attribute to specify the property. This tag is valid only when nested inside a <form:form> tag. The syntax of this element is shown in the following snippet.

Snippet

```
<form:input attributes/>
```

The <form:input> tag is an empty tag, it accepts the various attributes such as cssErrorClass, cssClass, title and etc. Some of the important attributes are described in the following table.

Table A.2 The general attributes of <form:input> tag attributes

Attribute Name	*Description*
path	Specifies the path to the property for data binding. That is this attribute specifies the property name in the form backing object whose value is to be bounded to this field.
id	Specifies a unique identifier that distinguishes this element (component) from all the rest in the document. This identifier can be used to associate the style rule for this element, naming this attribute value as an ID selector. When rendering an HTML equivalent element this value is set to the id attribute of the HTML equivalent.
htmlEscape	Specifies boolean value, enabling or disabling HTML escaping of rendered values.
cssClass	This has the same meaning as the HTML 'class' attribute.
cssStyle	Attribute equivalent to the HTML 'style' attribute.
title	Specifies the value that has to be displayed as a tooltip for this element.
onclick	This allows to set the JavaScript function that has to be executed when an enter button is typed in this text field.
ondblclick	Specifies the JavaScript function name that has to be executed on double click.
onmousedown	Specifies the JavaScript function name that has to be executed on mouse down.
onmouseup	Specifies the JavaScript function name that has to be executed on mouse up.
onmouseover	Specifies the JavaScript function name that has to be executed on mouse over.
onmousemove	Specifies the JavaScript function name that has to be executed on mouse move on this component.
onmouseout	Specifies the JavaScript function name that has to be executed on mouse exit.
onkeypress	Specifies the JavaScript function name that has to be executed on any key press when the cursor is on this element.
onkeydown	Specifies the JavaScript function name that has to be executed on any key down when the cursor is on this element.
onkeyup	Specifies the JavaScript function name that has to be executed on any key up when the cursor is on this element.
onfocus	Specifies the JavaScript function name that has to be executed when this element gets focus.
onblur	Specifies the JavaScript function name that has to be executed when this element loses the focus.
onchange	Specifies the JavaScript function name that has to be executed when a value of this element is changed.
tabindex	Specifies a number that indicates the sequence of this element within the tabbing order of all focusable elements in the document.

In addition to the general attributes described in the above table, the <form:input> tag supports some attributes specific to the input text element. The following table describes the input text specific attributes.

Table A.3 The <form:input> tag specific attributes

Attribute Name	*Description*
size	Specifies the size of the input text field. In practical this describes the character width of the text field. The actual width of the text field is calculated based on the font setting.
maxLength	Specifies the maximum length (i.e. number of characters) accepted by this field.
readonly	Specifies whether this field is readonly. Setting the value of this attribute to *true* will make the HTML element readonly.
alt	Specifies the text message that has to be displayed in case if browser is not capable of displaying component.
autocomplete	Specifies whether the value of the text field should be auto completed based on the values that are buffered.

A.3 THE <FORM:PASSWORD> TAG

The <form:password> element renders an HTML <input> element of type password and value as the value bounded to the specified property, we use path attribute to specify the property. This tag is valid only when nested inside a <form:form> tag. This tag supports all the attributes similar to the <form:input> tag as described under Tables A.1 and A.2, in addition it supports showPassword attribute. The showPassword attribute specifies whether to show the password, defaults to false.

A.4 THE <FORM:HIDDEN> TAG

The <form:hidden> element renders an HTML <input> element of type hidden and value as the value bounded to the specified property. We use the path attribute to specify the bean property. The following table describes the attributes of <form:hidden> tag.

Table A.4 The <form:hidden> tag specific attributes

Attribute Name	*Description*
path	Specifies the path to the property for data binding. That is this attribute specifies the property name in the form backing object whose value is to be bounded to this field.
id	Specifies a unique identifier that distinguishes this element (component) from all the rest in the document. This identifier can be used to associate the style rule for this element, naming this attribute value as an ID selector. When rendering an HTML equivalent element this value is set to the id attribute of the HTML equivalent.
htmlEscape	Specifies boolean value, enabling or disabling HTML escaping of rendered values.

A.5 THE <FORM:TEXTAREA> TAG

The <form:textarea> element renders an HTML <textarea> element. The content of the <textarea> tag is rendered as the value bounded to the specified property, we use path attribute to specify the property. This tag is valid only when nested inside a <form:form> tag. This tag supports all the common attributes similar to the <form:input> tag as described under Table A.1, in addition it supports the following attribute:

Table A.5 The <form:textarea> tag specific attributes

Attribute Name	*Description*
	rows Specifies the height of the text area element based on the number of lines of text that are to be displayed without scrolling.
cols	Specifies the width of the editable space of the text area element.
readonly	Specifies whether this field is readonly. Setting the value of this attribute to *true* will make the HTML element readonly.
onselect	Specifies the JavaScript function that has to be executed when this element is selected.

A.6 THE <FORM:LABEL> TAG

The <form:label> element renders an HTML <label> element. The value of the <label> tag is rendered as the value bounded to the specified property, we use path attribute to specify the property. This tag is valid only when nested inside a <form:form> tag. This tag supports all the common attributes similar to the <form:input> tag as described under Table A.1, in addition it supports 'for' attribute. The 'for' attribute specifies the element ID of the input element to which the label is to be associated. The attribute 'for' is necessary only when we choose not to wrap the input element inside the label element.

A.7 THE <FORM:SELECT> TAG

The <form:select> element renders an HTML <select> element. This supports data binding to the selected options. This tag is valid only when nested inside a <form:form> tag. This tag supports all the common attributes similar to the <form:input> tag as described under Table A.1, in addition it supports the following attributes.

Table A.6 The <form:select> tag specific attributes

Attribute Name	*Description*
Items	Specifies the path of the property describing the inner options. The property specified should be a Collection, Map or array type. The items in the specified Collection or Map or array are used to generate the inner <option> tags.
ItemValue	Specifies name of the property mapped to 'value' attribute of the <option> tag.
ItemLabel	Specifies name of the property mapped to the inner text of the <option> tag.
Size	Specifies the number of rows of option elements should appear in the select element. If the value is 1, the select element displays its content as a pop-up menu. With a value greater than 1 the select element displays as a list box.
Multiple	Specifies whether the user is allowed to make multiple selections from the list of options.

For example:

```
<form:select items="${countries}" path="country"/>
```

Here countries property represents Collection of String objects describing the country name. And country is the property to which the selected value has to be assigned.

```
<form:select items="${countries}" itemValue="code" itemLabel="name" path="country"/>
```

Here countries property represents Collection of Country objects with two properties 'code' and 'name', describing the country name and code. Where the 'code' property of Country object describes the country code and 'name' property describes the country name.

In addition to the attributes for data binding the <form:select> tag supports to use <form:option> or <form:options>. The following sections explain these tags.

A.8 THE <FORM:OPTION> TAG

The <form:option> element renders an HTML <option> element. This tag is valid only when nested inside a <form:select> tag. This tag supports all the common attributes similar to the <form:input> tag as described under Table A.1, in addition it supports 'value' and 'label' attributes. The 'value' attribute specifies the value for the option and the 'label' attribute specifies the inner text for the <option> tag. Example:

```
<form:select path="country">
 <form:option value="INDIA"/>
 <form:option value="Sri Lanka"/>
 <form:option value="Nepal"/>
</form:select>
```

A.9 THE <FORM:OPTIONS> TAG

The <form:options> element renders a list of HTML <option> elements. This tag is valid only when nested inside a <form:select> tag. This tag supports all the common attributes similar to the <form:input> tag as described under Table A.1, in addition it supports 'items', 'itemValue' and 'itemLabel' attributes. The description of these three additional tags is same as described in Table A.6. Example:

```
<form:select path="country">
 <form:options items="${countries}" itemValue="code" itemLabel="name"/>
</form:select>
```

A.10 THE <FORM:RADIOBUTTON> TAG

The <form:radiobutton> element renders an HTML <input> element of type radio. This tag supports all the common attributes similar to the <form:input> tag as described under Table A.1, in addition it supports 'value' and 'label' attributes. The 'value' attribute specifies the value for the radio button and the 'label' attribute specifies the value to be displayed as part of the tag. Example:

```
<form:radiobutton path="smoking" value="Yes"/>
<form:radiobutton path="smoking" value="No"/>
```

A.11 THE <FORM:RADIOBUTTONS> TAG

The <form:radiobuttons> element renders multiple HTML <input> element of type radio. This tag supports all the common attributes similar to the <form:input> tag as described under Table A.1, in addition it supports the following attributes.

Table A.7 The <form:radiobuttons> tag specific attributes

Attribute Name	*Description*
items	Specifies the path of the property describing the input tags of type radio. The property specified should be a Collection, Map or array type. The items in the specified Collection or Map or array are used to generate the <input> tags with type radio.
itemValue	Specifies name of the property mapped to 'value' attribute of the <input> tag with type radio.
itemLabel	Specifies name of the property mapped to the value to be displayed as part of the <input> tag with type radio.
delimiter	Specifies the delimiter to use between each <input> tag with type radio. There is no delimiter by default.
element	Specifies the HTML element that is used to enclose each 'input' tag with type 'radio'. Defaults to 'span'.

For example:

```
<form:radiobuttons items="${smokingOptions}" path="smoking"/>
```

A.12 THE <FORM:CHECKBOX> TAG

The <form:checkbox> element renders an HTML <input> element of type checkbox. This tag supports all the common attributes similar to the <form:input> tag as described under Table A.1, in addition it supports 'value' and 'label' attributes. The 'value' attribute specifies the value for the checkbox and the 'label' attribute specifies the value to be displayed as part of the tag. Example:
<form:checkbox path="certifications" value="SCJP"/>
<form:checkbox path="certifications" value="OCP"/>

Here certifications property is considered to be a Collection or array.

A.13 THE <FORM:CHECKBOXES> TAG

The <form:checkboxes> element renders multiple HTML <input> element of type checkbox. This tag supports all the common attributes similar to the <form:input> tag as described under Table A.1, in addition it supports the following attributes.

Table A.8 The <form:checkboxes> tag specific attributes

Attribute Name	*Description*
items	Specifies the path of the property describing the input tags of type radio. The property specified should be a Collection, Map or array type. The items in the specified Collection or Map or array are used to generate the <input> tags with type checkbox.
itemValue	Specifies name of the property mapped to 'value' attribute of the <input> tag with type checkbox.
itemLabel	Specifies name of the property mapped to the value to be displayed as part of the <input> tag with type checkbox.
delimiter	Specifies the delimiter to use between each <input> tag with type checkbox. There is no delimiter by default.
element	Specifies the HTML element that is used to enclose each <input> tag with type checkbox. Defaults to 'span'.

For example:

```
<form:radiobuttons items="${certificationsList}" path="certifications"/>
```

A.14 THE <FORM:ERRORS> TAG

The <form:errors> element renders field errors in an HTML <span> element. This presents the errors created by the controller or by any validators associated with the controller, see section 'Working with Validators' in Chapter13. Example:

```
<form:errors path="* "/>
```

This displays the entire list of errors for the given page. We can use 'delimiter' attribute to specify the delimiter for displaying multiple error messages. If not specified it defaults to 'br'. We can also specify the name of the property whose errors have to be displayed. We use the 'path' attribute to specify the property name. Example:

```
<form:errors path="uname"/>
```

This displays all the errors associated with 'uname' field. In addition, we can use 'element' attribute to specify the HTML element that is used to render the enclosing errors.

Summary

In this Appendix we have listed all the Spring framework's form tags and understood the various attributes that they support.

Hibernate Configurations

B

APPENDIX

Hibernate allows us to add configuration parameters and mapping files location to the Configuration object using its properties, in a programmatic approach as explained in Chapter 7. Instead of configuring the properties each time in the application code we can use a hibernate.properties file to add configuration parameters. However hibernate.properties file allows us to configure only the configuration parameters thus we need to add the mapping files location using the Configuration properties. Alternatively we can use XML configuration file to specify the configuration parameters and the location of persistent mapping XML documents. In general it is more comfortable to use an XML configuration file rather than properties file or even programmatic property configuration. Since we can prepare different XML configuration files and switch them programmatically to use different configuration parameters and mapping files depending on the database and some times based on working environment such as development or production. Here we will learn the various properties that are supported by Hibernate Configuration. The Hibernate configuration properties can be divided into the following category to understand and remember them easily:

- General configuration properties
- JDBC Connection properties
- Cache properties
- Transaction properties

Now, let's list all the configuration properties along with its use.

B.1 GENERAL CONFIGURATION PROPERTIES

The following table shows the Hibernate general configuration properties that control the behavior of Hibernate at runtime.

Table B.1 Hibernate general configuration properties

Property Name	***Description***
hibernate.dialect	Specify the qualified class name of a Hibernate Dialect which allows Hibernate to generate SQL optimized for a particular relational database. See table xxx for the list of available dialects.
hibernate.show_sql	Specify whether to write the SQL statements to console. If this specifies true, the SQL statements are written to the output console. Defaults to false.

(Contd.)

hibernate.default_schema	Specify the database schema to qualify the unqualified tablenames. This value can be overridden using the schema attribute of the <class> tag in the Hibernate mapping file.
hibernate.default_catalog	Specify the catalog name to qualify the unqualified tablenames in generated SQL.
hibernate.session_factory_name	Specify the JNDI name to which the SessionFactory has to be bound to, after it is created.
hibernate.max_fetch_depth	Set the maximum "depth" for the outer join fetch tree for single-ended associations (one-to-one, many-to-one). Specifying 0 (zero) disables default outer join fetching. It is highly recommended to use values between 0 and 3.
hibernate.default_batch_fetch_size	Set the default size for Hibernate batch fetching of associations. It is highly recommended to use values 4, 8, 16.
hibernate.default_entity_mode	Set a default mode for entity representation for all sessions opened from this SessionFactory.
hibernate.order_updates	Specifies whether to order SQL updates by the primary key value of the items being updated. This will result in fewer transaction deadlocks in highly concurrent systems.
hibernate.generate_statistics	Specifies whether Hibernate should log the statistics. If enabled, Hibernate will collect statistics which is useful for performance tuning.
hibernate.use_identifer_rollback	If enabled, generated identifier properties will be reset to default values when objects are deleted.
hibernate.use_sql_comments	If turned on, Hibernate will generate comments inside the SQL, for easier debugging, defaults to false.

Note: While configuring these properties using XML based Hibernate configuration file avoid specifying 'hibernate' prefix for the property names. For example to specify the 'hibernate.dialect' property, use property name as 'dialect'.

As described in Table B.1 we must specify the qualified class name of a Hibernate Dialect, which allows Hibernate to generate SQL optimized for a particular relational database. To do this we use hibernate.dialect property of Hibernate Configurations. Table B.2 shows the list of built-in dialects.

Table B.2 Hibernate built-in dialects

Database	*Dialect Class Name*
DB2	org.hibernate.dialect.DB2Dialect
DB2 AS/400	org.hibernate.dialect.DB2400Dialect
DB2 OS390	org.hibernate.dialect.DB2390Dialect
PostgreSQL	org.hibernate.dialect.PostgreSQLDialect
MySQL	org.hibernate.dialect.MySQLDialect
MySQL with InnoDB	org.hibernate.dialect.MySQLInnoDBDialect
MySQL with MyISAM	org.hibernate.dialect.MySQLMyISAMDialect
Oracle 8i or lower version	org.hibernate.dialect.OracleDialect
Oracle 9i/10g	org.hibernate.dialect.Oracle9Dialect
Sybase	org.hibernate.dialect.SybaseDialect
Sybase Anywhere	org.hibernate.dialect.SybaseAnywhereDialect
Microsoft SQL Server	org.hibernate.dialect.SQLServerDialect

(*Contd.*)

SAP DB	org.hibernate.dialect.SAPDBDialect
Informix	org.hibernate.dialect.InformixDialect
HypersonicSQL	org.hibernate.dialect.HSQLDialect
Ingres	org.hibernate.dialect.IngresDialect
Progress	org.hibernate.dialect.ProgressDialect
Mckoi SQL	org.hibernate.dialect.MckoiDialect
Interbase	org.hibernate.dialect.InterbaseDialect
Pointbase	org.hibernate.dialect.PointbaseDialect
FrontBase	org.hibernate.dialect.FrontbaseDialect
Firebird	org.hibernate.dialect.FirebirdDialect

B.2 JDBC CONNECTION PROPERTIES

Hibernate needs JDBC connections to perform various persistent operations requested by the user. Hibernate obtains and pool the connections using java.sql.DriverManager if we set the following properties:

Table B.3 JDBC connection properties

Property Name	*Description*
hibernate.connection.driver_class	Specifies the JDBC driver class name, e.g. oracle.jdbc.driver.OracleDriver
hibernate.connection.url	Specifies the JDBC URL, e.g. jdbc:oracle:thin:@mysys1:1521:sandb
hibernate.connection.username	Specifies the database user name.
hibernate.connection.password	Specifies the database user password.
hibernate.connection.pool_size	Specifies the maximum number of pooled connections.

By default Hibernate uses its own connection pooling algorithm. However this quite simple, thus it is not intended for use in a production system or even for performance testing. The default built-in connection pooling algorithm is basically intended to help us get started to work with Hibernate, we are recommended to use a third party pool for best performance and stability. While using the third party connection pooling service the hibernate.connection.pool_size property is not applicable alternatively use connection pool specific settings. For example, if we like to use C3P0 connection pool service, we need to set the *hibernate.c3p0.** properties, which turns off the Hibernate's internal pool. The following table shows some of these properties:

Table B.4 Hibernate.c3p0.* properties

Property Name	*Description*
hibernate.c3p0.min_size	Specifies the minimum (or initial) number of pooled connections.
hibernate.c3p0.max_size	Specifies the maximum number of pooled connections.
hibernate.c3p0.timeout	Specifies the timeout period for the connection.
hibernate.c3p0.max_statements	Specifies the maximum number of statements to cache.

Apart from configuring Hibernate to manage the connection pool, we can configure Hibernate to obtain connections from an application server DataSource registered in JNDI registry. The following properties can be set when we want to use external connection pool:

Table B.5 Hibernate properties to use external connection pool

Property Name	*Description*
hibernate.connection.datasource	Specifies the DataSource JNDI name.
hibernate.jndi.url	Specifies the URL of the JNDI provider.
hibernate.jndi.class	Specifies the JNDI provider given class name implementing the InitialContextFactory interface of JNDI API.
hibernate.connection.username	Specifies the database user name.
hibernate.connection.password	Specifies the database user password.

In addition to the above specified properties Hibernate supports the following properties that affect the behavior of the Connection pool or connection:

Table B.6 Hibernate properties that affect the behaviour of connection pool

Property Name	*Description*
hibernate.jdbc.fetch_size	Specifies the JDBC fetch size. Accepts a positive integer value greater than zero. This calls the setFetchSize() method of Statement object.
hibernate.jdbc.batch_size	Specifies the batch size. Accepts a positive integer value greater than zero. This enables to use JDBC 2.0 batch updates. It is highly recommended to use values between 5 and 30.
hibernate.jdbc.batch_versioned_data	Set this property to true if your JDBC driver returns correct row counts from executeBatch() (it is usually safe to turn this option on). Hibernate will then use batched DML for automatically versioned data. Defaults to false.
hibernate.jdbc.factory_class	Select a custom Batcher. Most applications will not need this configuration property.
hibernate.jdbc.use_scrollable_resultset	Enables use of JDBC 2.0 scrollable ResultSet's by Hibernate. This property is only necessary when using user supplied JDBC connections, Hibernate uses connection metadata otherwise.
hibernate.jdbc.use_streams_for_binary	Use streams when writing/reading binary or serializable types to/from JDBC (system-level property).
hibernate.jdbc.use_get_generated_keys	Enable use of JDBC 3.0 getGeneratedKeys() method of Prepared Statement object to retrieve natively generated keys after insert. Note: This requires JDBC 3.0+ driver and JRE1.4+, set to false if the driver has problems with the Hibernate identifier generators. By default, tries to determine the driver capabilities using DatabaseMetadata.
hibernate.connection.provider_class	Specifies the classname of a custom ConnectionProvider which provides JDBC connections to Hibernate. This is required when we want to define our own plugin strategy for obtaining JDBC connections. This class should implement org.hibernate.connection.ConnectionProvider interface.
hibernate.connection.isolation	Set the JDBC transaction isolation level. Note that most databases do not support all isolation levels.
hibernate.connection.autocommit	Specifies the autocommit mode for JDBC pooled connections. Defaults to false.

(Contd.)

hibernate.connection.release_mode	Specify when Hibernate should release JDBC connections. By default, a JDBC connection is held until the session is explicitly closed or disconnected. For an application server JTA datasource, we should use after_statement to aggressively release connections after every JDBC call. For a non-JTA connection, it often makes sense to release the connection at the end of each transaction, by using after_transaction. auto will choose after_statement for the JTA and CMT transaction strategies and after_transaction for the JDBC transaction strategy.
hibernate.connection.<*propertyName*>	Used to specify the JDBC property propertyName to getConnection() method of DriverManager.
hibernate.jndi.<*propertyName*>	Used to specify the property propertyName to the JNDI InitialContextFactory.

B.3 CACHE PROPERTIES

The cache exits in between of the application and database representing the current database state close to the application, as a local copy either in memory or on disk. Managing the cache avoids database hit when application request for persistent objects. The Hibernate supports two level cache mechanisms, which improves the performance by avoiding repeated request for retrieving the persistent objects. Hibernate caching system supports some configuration properties to tune, and manage the first- and second-level caches. The following table describes the Hibernate configuration properties that affect the behavior of Hibernate cache.

Table B.7 Hibernate cache properties

Property Name	***Purpose***
hibernate.cache.provider_class	Specify the classname the CacheProvider. See table xx for the built-in cache provider classes.
hibernate.cache.use_minimal_puts	Specify whether to optimize the second-level cache operation by minimizing the writes, at the cost of more frequent reads. This setting is most useful for clustered caches. This property is enabled by default for clustered cache implementations.
hibernate.cache.use_query_cache	Specify to enable the query cache, individual queries still have to be set cacheable.
hibernate.cache.use_second_level_cache	Specify to disable the second level cache, which is enabled by default for classes which specify a <cache> mapping.
hibernate.cache.query_cache_factory	Specify the classname of a QueryCache implementation, defaults to the built-in StandardQueryCache.
hibernate.cache.region_prefix	Specify the prefix to use for second-level cache region names.
hibernate.cache.use_structured_entries	Specifies Hibernate to store data in the second-level cache in a more human-friendly format.

The following table lists the Hibernate built-in cache provider classes.

Table B.8 Hibernate built-in cache provider classes

Provider Class	*Description*
org.hibernate.cache.HashtableCacheProvider	The Hashtable based cache provider, this is not intended for production use. This maintains the cached object in memory. Note that this is not cluster safe, but supports query cache.
org.hibernate.cache.EhCacheProvider	This maintains the cached object in memory or disk. Note that this is not cluster safe, but supports query cache.
org.hibernate.cache.OSCacheProvider	This maintains the cached object in memory or disk. Note that this is not cluster safe, but supports query cache.
org.hibernate.cache.SwarmCacheProvider	This type of cache is cluster safe. This type of cache doesn't support query cache.
org.hibernate.cache.TreeCacheProvider	The JBoss tree based cache is cluster safe and even transactional. This type of cache supports query cache also.

B.4 TRANSACTION PROPERTIES

Hibernate supports the following configuration properties related to transaction management.

Table B.9 Hibernate transaction properties

Property Name	*Purpose*
hibernate.transaction.factory_class	Specify the TransactionFactory implementation's classname to use with Hibernate Transaction API. Defaults to JDBCTransactionFactory.
jta.UserTransaction	Specify the JNDI name to be used by the JTATransactionFactory to obtain the JTA UserTransaction from the application server.
hibernate.transaction.manager_lookup_class	Specify the classname of a TransactionManagerLookup. This is required only when JVM-level caching is enabled or when using hilo generator in a JTA environment.
hibernate.transaction.flush_before_completion	Setting this property to true tells Hibernate that the session will be automatically flushed during the before completion phase of the transaction.
hibernate.transaction.auto_close_session	Setting this property to true tells Hibernate that the session will be automatically closed during the after completion phase of the transaction.

Summary

In this appendix we have listed the various Hibernate configuration properties that can be configured to control the behavior of Hibernate at runtime.

Annotation-based Controller Configurations

C APPENDIX

Spring Framework 2.5 includes a support for configuring web MVC framework components using annotations such as @RequestMapping, @RequestParam, @Controller, @ModelAttribute, @SessionAttributes etc. This annotation support allows us to implement the controller without defining it as a subtype of specific base class or interface. This appendix explains how to use annotation-based controller configuration for implementing Spring web MVC application.

C.1 DESCRIBING CONTROLLER

The @Controller annotation acts as a stereotype for the annotated class, indicating is as a controller class. As discussed earlier in Chapter 13 there is no need to implement the controller class as a subtype of any controller base class, however if we need to access servlet specific features we are still able to reference Servlet-specific objects such as ServletRequest and ServletResponse. The annotated controller beans can be defined explicitly, using a standard Spring bean definition in the context. However, the @Controller stereotype also allows for autodetection supported by Spring 2.5, for detecting component classes in the classpath and auto-registering bean definitions.

To enable auto-detection of annotated controllers, we need to add component scanning to our configuration. The following code snippet shows the context XML document configuring the auto-detection:

Code Snippet

```
<?xml version="1.0" encoding="UTF-8"?>
<beans xmlns="http://www.springframework.org/schema/beans"
xmlns:xsi="http://www.w3.org/2001/XMLSchema-instance"
xmlns:context="http://www.springframework.org/schema/context"
xsi:schemaLocation="http://www.springframework.org/schema/beans
http://www.springframework.org/schema/beans/spring-beans-2.5.xsd
http://www.springframework.org/schema/context
http://www.springframework.org/schema/context/spring-context-2.5.xsd">

<context:component-scan base-package="com.santosh.spring"/>
 ...
</beans>
```

The above code snippet shows the XML document declaring the <context:component-scan> tag declaration. This enables the auto-detection for the package com.santosh.spring, recognizing the classes with @Controller stereotype and registers them as a controller bean. Now, as we have understood how to describe a class as a controller using @Controller annotation to the dispatcher, let's discuss how to map the incoming request to the controller.

C.2 MAPPING WEB REQUEST TO HANDLER

The @RequestMapping annotation is used for mapping the incoming request to specific handler class and/or handler method. This uses URL based mapping. The @RequestMapping annotation can be used at type-level and method-level.

The @RequestMapping annotation used at the type-level maps the incoming request to the controller class; in this case the request processing code would be encapsulated into the method with signature similar *handleRequest* method of Controller interface. In addition we can use @RequestMapping annotation to method for narrowing the primary mapping. The following code snippet shows an example declaring the RequestMapping for a controller:

Code Snippet

```
@Controller
@RequestMapping("/login.do")
public class LoginController {

   @RequestMapping(method="GET")
   public String login(…){
   …
   }
}
```

The @RequestMapping annotation can be used at the method-level to map the URLs to methods. This is useful to configure a multi-action controller i.e. the controller that responds to multiple URLs. The following code snippet shows the sample code using @RequestMapping at method-level for describing multi-action controller:

Code Snippet

```
@Controller
public class ArithmeticController {

   @RequestMapping("/add.do")
   public String add(…){
   …
   }
   @RequestMapping("/subtract.do")
   public String subtract(…){
   …
   }
}
```

The above code snippet configures the ArithmeticController class as a controller, which responds to two URLs */add.do* and */subtract.do*. The incoming request with a request URL */add.do* maps to add() method, and request URL */subtract.do* maps to subtract() method.

The *org.springframework.web.servlet.mvc.annotation.DefaultAnnotationHandlerMapping* and *org.springframework.web.servlet.mvc.annotation.AnnotationMethodHandlerAdapter* are the Handler Mapping and HandlerAdapter that can resolve the @RequestMapping annotation based web request mapping. These are by default available to the DispatcherServlet. However we need to configure these beans in the context XML document explicitly in case if we want to configure custom HandlerAdapter's or HandlerMapping's, and use @RequestMapping annotation for mapping the web requests to the respective handlers. The following code snippet shows the XML configuration, explicitly configuring the *DefaultAnnotationHandlerMapping* and *AnnotationMethodHandler Adapter*:

Code Snippet

```
<?xml version="1.0" encoding="UTF-8"?>
<beans xmlns="http://www.springframework.org/schema/beans"
xmlns:xsi="http://www.w3.org/2001/XMLSchema-instance"
xsi:schemaLocation="http://www.springframework.org/schema/beans
http://www.springframework.org/schema/beans/spring-beans-2.5.xsd">
  <bean
class="org.springframework.web.servlet.mvc.annotation.DefaultAnnotationHandlerMapping"/
>
  <bean
class="org.springframework.web.servlet.mvc.annotation.AnnotationMethodHandlerAdapter">
      <property name="synchronizeOnSession" value="true"/>
    </bean>
   ...
</beans>
```

The AnnotationMethodHanlderAdapter supports some properties that allow customizing the handler adapter, for example we can set '*synchronizeOnSession*' property to '*true*' as shown in the preceding code snippet, which makes the session access thread-safe even if multiple requests are allowed to access a session concurrently.

In this section we learnt how to map the incoming client request to the handler method, and configure the application context to support the annotation based mapping. Next section explains you the rules involved in defining the handler method.

C.3 DEFINING HANDLER METHODS

The Spring framework supports to have very flexible signatures for the handler methods which are annotated with @RequestMapping.

The handler methods can have arguments of the following types, in any order:

- Servlet Request and/or Response
- HttpSession
- org.springframework.web.context.request.WebRequest
- java.util.Locale (specifies the current request locale)
- java.io.InputStream / java.io.Reader for access to the request's content.
- java.io.OutputStream / java.io.Writer for generating the response's content.
- @RequestParam annotated parameters for access to specific Servlet request parameters. Parameter values will be converted to the declared method argument type.
- org.springframework.ui.Model /org.springframework.ui.ModelMap / java.util.Map for moving the implicit model objects to the view.
- Command/form objects to bind parameters to
- org.springframework.validation.Errors / BindingResult
- org.springframework.web.bind.support.SessionStatus

> **Note:** As specified, any of the above listed argument types can appear in arbitrarily, however while using validation results, the BindingResult need to follow right after the corresponding command object, if desired.

The following types supported as return type for handler methods defining using the @HandlerMapping annotation:

- org.springframework.web.servlet.ModelAndView
- org.springframework.ui.Model
- java.util.Map
- org.springframework.web.servlet.View
- java.lang.String
- void
- Any other return type will be considered as single model attribute to be exposed to the view, using the attribute name specified through @ModelAttribute at the method level (or the default attribute name based on the return type's class name). The model will be implicitly augmented with command objects and the results of @ModelAttribute annotated reference data getter methods.

C.4 BINDING REQUEST PARAMETERS TO THE HANDLER METHOD ARGUMENTS

We use @RequestParam annotation to bind the request parameters to the handler method arguments. Note that this is supported only for the handler methods mapped using @RequestMapping annotation. The following code snippet shows the usage of @RequestParm annotation:

Code Snippet

```
@Controller
@RequestMapping("/login.spring")
public class LoginController {

@RequestMapping
public String login(@RequestParam("userId") String userId, @RequestParam("pass")
String pass) {
    ...
}
...
```

The @RequestParam annotation supports two optional elements:

- required – is of boolean type, specifies whether the parameter is required. If this is set to true an exception is thrown in case of the parameter missing in the request. If this is set to false a null reference is injected in case of the parameter missing. If not specified the default is true.
- value – if of String type, specifies the request parameter name to bind.

In this section we have seen how to bind the request parameters to the handler method arguments, the next section explains you how to bind the parameters to model object.

C.5 BINDING DATA TO MODEL OBJECTS

We use @ModelAttribute annotation to bind the data to the handler fields. The @ModelAttribute can be used on a method parameter to map a model attribute as shown below:

Code Snippet

```
@Controller
@RequestMapping("/editUser.spring")
public class EditUserDetailsForm {

...
      @ModelAttribute("userDetails")
      public void setUserDetails(UserDetails ud) {userDetails=ud;}

      @RequestMapping public String processRequest(...) {
              ...
      }
}
```

The above code shows how the controller gets a reference to the object holding the data entered in the form. Note that the @ModelAttribute annotated methods will be executed before the chosen @RequestMapping annotated handler method. They effectively pre-populate the implicit model with specific attributes, often loaded from a database. Such an attribute can then already be accessed through @ModelAttribute annotated handler method parameters in the chosen handler method, potentially with binding and validation applied to it.

In addition to this, the parameter can be declared as the specific type of the form backing object rather than as a generic java.lang.Object, thus increasing type safety.

The @ModelAttribute is also used at the method level to provide reference data for the model as shown below.

Code Snippet

```
@Controller
@RequestMapping("/editUser.spring")
public class EditUserDetailsForm {

...
      @RequestMapping public String processRequest(
                @ModelAttribute("userDetails") UserDetails ud,
                BindingResult result, SessionStatus status) {
            ...
      }
}
```

In the preceding code the UserDetails model attribute is set to the 'ud' argument of processRequest() method. Note that for this usage the method signature can contain the same types as documented above for the @RequestMapping annotation.

C.6 DECLARING SESSION ATTRIBUTE

The @SessionAttributes is a type-level annotation used to declare session attributes for a handler. This will typically list the names of model attributes which should be transparently stored in the session or some conversational storage, serving as form-backing beans between subsequent requests.

The following code snippet shows the usage of this annotation:

Code Snippet

```
@Controller
@RequestMapping("/editUser.spring")
@SessionAttributes("userDetails")
public class EditUserDetailsForm {

    ...

    @RequestMapping public String processRequest(
              @ModelAttribute("userDetails") UserDetails ud,
              BindingResult result, SessionStatus status) {
        ...
    }
}
```

The above code shows the declaration of a session attribute named 'userDetails' which is mapped to the 'ud' local variable of processRequest() method.

Summary

In this appendix we have listed out the annotations that are used to implement Spring Web MVC application. These annotations are new in Spring 2.5. The annotation support for implementing Spring Web MVC application simplifies the application development. This annotation support allows us to implement the controller without defining it as a subtype of specific base class or interface.

Index

M

N

O

P

Q

R

S

T

U

V

W

X

Author's Profile

Santosh Kumar K is currently associated with SANTOSH technologies, a prestigious training division at Ameerpet, Hyderabad, imparting specialized training in Java and its related frameworks useful for enterprise application development. He has been associated with training and development on Java and its related technologies since 2001 and was pioneer in introducing full-fledged training on Spring and Hibernate Frameworks at Hyderabad. He has conducted training programs for the corporate sector involved in enterprise application developments on J2EE technologies and other frameworks like Struts, JSF, Spring, and Hibernate. His seminars and workshops are well known for their high-quality content backed by his unique style of delivery. He has also worked as an independent consultant developing critical applications for companies such as InnoMinds, Satyam, and ESoft. He is the author of *JDBC, Servlets and JSP BlackBook*.

He maintains a popular group on J2EE technologies at http://groups.yahoo.com/group/santosh_j2ee.

Santosh is the founder of SANTOSH technologies (http://www.santoshtechnologies.com) started with the motto to provide quality education with a high technical content and deliver technology driven business solutions.

Made in United States
North Haven, CT
05 November 2026

21780736R10298